W9-ADB-445

C++ for Business Programming

John C. Molluzzo
Pace University

Prentice Hall
Upper Saddle River, New Jersey 07458

To Maria, John, and Charles

Library of Congress Cataloging-in-Publication Data

Molluzzo, John C.
   C++ for business programming / John C. Molluzzo.
      p.   cm.
   Includes bibliographical references and index.
   ISBN 0-13-577594-9
   1. C++ (Computer program language) 2. Business—Computer
programs.   I. Title.
HF5548.5.C125M65 1999   99–10476
650'.0285'5133—dc21   CIP

Publisher: Alan Apt
Acquisition Editor: Laura Steele
Editor-in-Chief: Marcia Horton
Managing Editor: Eileen Clark
Assistant Vice President of Production and Manufacturing: David W. Riccardi
Art Director: Gus Vibal
Cover Designer: Jayne Conte
Manufacturing Manager: Trudy Pisciotti
Production Supervision/Composition: WestWords, Inc.
Editorial Assistant: Toni Holm

© 1999 by Prentice-Hall, Inc.

TRADEMARK INFORMATION
ANSI is a registered trademark of American National Standards Institute. Borland C++ and Turbo C++ are registered
trademarks of Borland International, Inc.—now Inprise Corp. Visual C++ and MS-DOS are registered trademarks of
Microsoft Corp. IBM is a registered trademark of International Business Machines Corp. UNIX is a registered trademark of AT&T. AT&T is a registered trademark of AT&T.

All rights reserved. No part of this book may be
reproduced, in any form or by any means,
without permission in writing from the publisher.

The author and publisher of this book have used their best efforts in preparing this book. These efforts include the
development, research, and testing of the theories and programs to determine their effectiveness. The author and publisher make no warranty of any kind, expressed or implied, with regard to these programs or the documentation contained in this book. The author and publisher shall not be liable in any event for incidental or consequential damages
in connection with, or arising out of, the furnishing, performance, or use of these programs.

Printed in the United States of America
10 9 8 7 6 5 4 3 2

ISBN 0-13-577594-9

Prentice-Hall International (UK) Limited, *London*
Prentice-Hall of Australia Pty. Limited, *Sydney*
Prentice-Hall Canada Inc., *Toronto*
Prentice-Hall Hispanoamericana, S.A., *Mexico*
Prentice-Hall of India Private Limited, *New Delhi*
Prentice-Hall of Japan, Inc., *Tokyo*
Prentice-Hall (Singapore) Pte. Ltd., *Singapore*
Editora Prentice-Hall do Brasil, Ltda., *Rio de Janeiro*

Brief Contents

Contents

Preface

C++ for Business Programming is an introduction to C++ programming. The power of C++ lies in its object-oriented extensions of the C language. However, I believe that it is best for beginning students to learn the basics of programming without the extra encumbrance of having to learn object-oriented concepts. Therefore, the book is divided into two sections. Part I, Basic C++, covers the procedural parts of C++. Part II, Object-Oriented Programming, covers all the essential object-oriented ideas through inheritance and polymorphism.

Unlike most books on C++, which emphasize applications to computing or mathematics, this book emphasizes business applications. This book is most appropriate to business and information systems students. The entire book can be covered in one semester if the students have a good background in programming in another language. In such a class, it is possible to quickly cover the essential programming constructs from Part I and then to concentrate on object-oriented programming in Part II. For students who have little programming experience, we suggest covering Part I in one semester and Part II in a second semester. The material in Part I can be supplemented as needed by material from Appendix A (Computers and Data) and Appendix B (Program Control).

We emphasize good pedagogy throughout the book.

- Each chapter begins with a set of learning objectives.
- Each chapter ends with a review section that includes important terms, a chapter summary, and review exercises.
- Concepts are explained in clear, understandable language and are illustrated by many examples.
- Important definitions, concepts, and rules are appropriately highlighted in Notes.
- Programming pointers and pitfalls are noted in the margins of the text.
- One of the best ways to learn a programming language is to read programs in that language. Every important idea is illustrated in an example program and the accompanying output. There are nearly 150 complete programs in the text, each of which is carefully explained.
- The book contains more than 800 exercises of varying types and levels of difficulty. These are placed at the end of each section rather than at the end of each chapter so students can immediately reinforce their new knowledge. These exercises include Exercises, Experiments, and Programming Problems.
  - Almost every section contains Exercises on the syntax and semantics of C++. Most of these are of the paper and pencil type, although some require writing a simple program.
  - The Experiments, which ask the student to investigate various aspects of the C++ language, are a unique feature of the Exercise sections. The Experiments improve the student's understanding of the finer points of C++ and help the student avoid common errors made by beginning programmers.
  - The Programming Problems, which range from 10–20 line programs to full-scale projects that require the use of several user-defined functions and classes, are found in most sections of the book. The chapter illustrative programs and Programming Problems emphasize the business applications of C++.

- The book conforms to the new ANSI C++ standard. All illustrative programs, however, can easily be adapted to older compilers that do not adhere to the standard. This book can be used with any of the popular C++ compilers.

- Topics are introduced on a need-to-know basis to provide motivation for the student. Therefore, the book is not encyclopedic in its coverage of C++. In some cases, all the relevant ideas surrounding a topic are spread throughout several sections or chapters.

- Appendix A (Computers and Data) and Appendix B (Program Control) provide supplementary material for students who have a weak background in computing. Appendices A and B contain exercises.

Chapters 1–9 constitute Part I, C++ Basics. Chapter 1, Introduction to C++, introduces the student to the basic anatomy of a C++ program. It covers the input and output objects `cin` and `cout`, variables, integer data types, and arithmetic. Chapter 2, Real Numbers, introduces the `float` and `double` data types, the compound assignment, and increment and decrement operators.

Chapters 3 and 4 discuss the basic control structures of programming. Chapter 3, Iteration, begins by covering relation conditions. Then it proceeds to discuss indefinite iteration (the `while` and `do` statements), definite iteration (the `for` statement), and nested loops. Chapter 4, Decision Making, covers the `if` statement, the logical operators, nested `if` statements, and the `switch` statement.

Chapter 5 introduces the important concept of functions. Because the function is new to most students, the concept is developed gradually—first functions that do not return a value, then functions that have arguments, and finally, functions that return a value. A discussion of scope and duration is also included. An entire section is devoted to discussing three programs that use functions. Special care is taken to show how the program logic is modularized into functions. The chapter closes with a discussion of macros and inline functions and a comparison of the two.

Chapter 6, Arrays, shows how to properly define an array and reference its elements. Care is taken to show how to use a `for` loop to process the elements of an array. Using the standard bubble sort to sort an array is also covered in some detail. Finally, we show how to declare and process multidimensional arrays.

Chapter 7 introduces pointers. To help the student understand this important topic, we quickly put pointers to work by applying them to strings. Illustrative programs show how to count characters in a string, display a string in reverse, and count words in a string. Arrays of strings and arrays of pointers are also discussed.

Chapter 8, Pointers, Arrays, and Functions, reinforces the student's knowledge of strings and pointers. Call by address using pointers, call by reference, passing arrays as function arguments, and functions that return pointers are discussed in detail. Some useful string library functions and character classification and conversion functions are also covered. The use of dynamic memory allocation using the `new` and `delete` operators are also explored.

Chapter 9, User-Defined Data Types and Tables, discusses `typedef`, enumerated types, and structures. Special attention is given to the use of structures in defining tables. A major application involves sorting and searching a table (an array of structures), including both sequential and binary searches. The chapter also discusses pointers to structures and using them as function arguments.

Chapters 10–14 comprise Part II—Object-Oriented Programming. The material in Chapters 10–12 is unified through the gradual development of an `Account` class. As new OOP concepts are introduced, they are added to the `Account` class. Chapter 10 introduces the reader to classes and objects. We discuss how to declare a class, instantiate objects, and code constructors and destructors. The chapter ends with a thorough discussion of function overloading, default function arguments, and function templates.

Chapter 11, Manipulating Objects, is the longest chapter in the book. Some of the topics, as outlined in the chapter introduction, can be omitted at first reading. The chapter begins by discussing how to include array and pointer data members in a class and how to use dynamic memory allocation in a constructor and destructor. The chapter next discusses the copy constructor and when it is used. The many ways of using the keyword `const` in C++ are then covered in detail. We also discuss functions that return objects as well as how to pass objects to functions by value, pointer, and reference. Several of the issues relating to the dynamic allocation of objects are covered along with the uses of `static` class data members and functions.

Chapter 12 explores the important topics of `friend` functions and operator overloading. We emphasize the extensibility of the C++ operators by showing how to overload the arithmetic operators, assignment, the insertion and extraction operators, the compound assignment operators, the relational operators, and the unary operators.

Chapter 13 covers the important concept of inheritance and related ideas. One major example is used throughout most of the chapter to unify the material. After introducing the basic terminology of inheritance and how to construct a class hierarchy, the chapter discusses the uses of functions in such a hierarchy and the concept of polymorphism. Pure virtual functions and abstract base classes complete the chapter.

Chapter 14 gives a thorough treatment of file processing in C++. The chapter begins with a discussion about Input/Output streams, the standard I/O class hierarchy, and how to process simple text files. It then shows how to process a file a character at a time. Next we discuss binary files and the random access member functions. These ideas are then applied to the problems of processing a binary sequential file of records and to randomly processing a binary file of records. The chapter culminates with a random file access update program.

I would like to thank all the people at Prentice Hall who made this book possible, especially my editor, Laura Steele, and Alan Apt. Thanks to Jennifer Maughan and her staff at WestWords for guiding me through the production process. A special thanks to Dean Susan Merritt of Pace University who gave this project and me her enthusiastic support for the many years it took to complete. Thanks also to Chin-Mei Huang for her helpful comments on an early version of the manuscript, Anna Kristoferitsch for helping to solve some of the chapter exercises, and especially Kenyatta Mulet, who spent many long hours solving the Programming Problems and exercises. I also want to give special thanks to Professor Gerald Wohl of Pace University for having the courage to use the first draft of this book in his C++ courses, for catching many errors and typos, and for providing me with many helpful comments about the book. Finally, I would like to thank my family—my wife, Maria, my sons, John and Charles, and my furry friend, Larrabee—for the help and love they have given me.

A note about the typefaces used in this book: In the program outputs, data that the user inputs in response to program prompts is set in boldface to distinguish it from output produced by the programs.

Part

I

Basic C++

Introduction to C++

Objectives

- To write a simple C++ program.
- To use comments in a program.
- To declare variables of different integer data types and decide when to use them.
- To use the `cout` output stream to display strings and variable values.

- To use the `cin` input stream to input data.
- To use the arithmetic operators.
- To understand and use the operator precedence rules.
- To solve simple problems involving integers.

Why Study C++?

C++, pronounced "C plus plus," is one of the most popular programming languages used to develop applications on PCs and minicomputers. Many corporate computing departments have adopted C++ as the language in which to develop in-house applications. Many software vendors use C++ to write their application software. C++ has become so mainstream that nearly every issue of many popular magazines, such as *PC Magazine* and *PC Computing*, contains listings of programs in C++. Why is C++ so popular and why is it important to learn it?

C++ has become the language of choice for several reasons.

- *C++ is a "middle-level" language.* Programming languages can be categorized as high level or low level. Assembly languages are low-level languages. An assembly language allows the programmer maximum control over the computer system. The programmer can directly interface with and control the computer's hardware and operating system. This control comes at a price, however. Assembly languages are hard to learn because they are highly symbolic and the programmer must take care of all the details of the program. Assembly language programs are also difficult to maintain and debug. Perhaps most important, assembly language programs are not portable. An assembly language program is specific to the hardware and operating system of the computer system on which it is developed. Thus, you cannot directly execute a PC assembly language program on a Macintosh.

  By contrast, high-level languages such as COBOL, Visual Basic, and Pascal are easier to learn, maintain, and debug than assembly languages. The program statements in such languages use English words and familiar mathematical symbols to express instructions to the computer. Each instruction typically replaces several equivalent assembly language instructions. Using a high-level language is much easier than using an assembly language. However, the price for this ease of use is the loss of direct control over the computer system that you have in an assembly language.

  C++, although it is a high-level language (and therefore easier to learn and use than an assembly language), contains many of the low-level capabilities of an assembly language. Thus, C++ is sometimes called a "middle-level" language. It is possible through C++ to attain almost as much control over the computer as you can achieve with an assembly language.

- *C++ is portable.* Most high-level languages are portable in the sense that a program written in a high-level language should execute, with minor modifications, on several different computer systems. C++ is one of the most portable of all the high-level languages. Properly written, a C++ program can run on several computer systems with no modifications. Portability is important because it is now common for a business to have several different types of computer systems (a mainframe, several minicomputers, workstations, PCs, and Macintoshes.) A properly written application in C++ should be portable to most, if not all, these systems. Portability eliminates the cost of developing the application several times for different platforms.

- *C++ is small.* The C++ language does not contain many of the built-in features present in other programming languages, which further enhances its portability. For example, COBOL has nearly 300 reserved words (a reserved word is a word that has special meaning in the language), which attests to the language's complexity. C++, on the other hand, has about 50 reserved words (in C++ they are called keywords). COBOL contains extensive capabilities to do input and output to several types of files. These facilities make writing programs that process such files relatively easy for the COBOL programmer. However, it greatly increases the complexity of the COBOL language. In contrast, input/output facilities are not built into the C++ language. Instead, C++ provides them through input/output objects. (We shall learn about some of these objects later in the chapter.) To keep the language as simple as possible, its designers did not include input/output facilities as part of C++. This simplicity gives the C++ programmer great flexibility and allows the language to be highly portable.

- *C++ is an object-oriented extension of the C programming language.* Dennis Ritchie developed C at Bell Laboratories in 1972 to help write the UNIX operating system for the PDP-11 minicomputer. Today many mainframes and most minicomputers, including RISC workstations, use the UNIX operating system. In addition, there are several versions of UNIX that are designed for the PC. All versions of UNIX contain a version of C as their native language. In other words, UNIX speaks C. Why is this important? Before C, a systems programmer on such a computer system needed to use assembly language to directly communicate with the computer. Now, the applications programmer and the systems programmer can use C. In the early 1980s, Bjarne Stroustrup of AT&T Bell Labs developed C++, which is an object-oriented extension of C.

  C is an example of a procedure-oriented programming language. To develop a C program to accomplish a task, the programmer breaks down the task into a series of steps. On the other hand, to develop an object-oriented C++ program, the programmer views the problem as a set of interacting objects, each with its own properties and behaviors.

This book is divided into two parts. In Part I, Chapters 1 through 9, we concentrate on the non-object-oriented aspects of C++. This will enable you to learn the basic constructs of C++ without the additional burden of learning object-oriented terminology and concepts. In the second part of the book, we cover all the important object-oriented constructs that make C++ one of the most powerful tools for development of object-oriented software.

Finally, it is important for you to learn C++, even if you do not intend to become a professional programmer. As a person who is professionally involved with computers, it is important that you know a little of the language that most programmers speak. Not to do so would be like beginning your professional career in a foreign country without knowing a word of the native language. You would quickly find out that you must learn some of the native tongue to perform efficiently on the job. Similarly, so that you can communicate effectively with your colleagues, you should learn at least some of the "native tongue" of the modern programmer—C++.

1.1 Our First C++ Program

One of the best ways to learn about the basic features of a programming language is to study a small program written in that language. In this section, we discuss a simple C++ program that displays a two-line message on the computer screen. Before we do so, we discuss some general ideas about how to develop a program.

The Program Development Cycle

You must take several steps each time you develop a program. The following five steps are typical when developing a C++ program. See Figure 1.1.

Step 1: Design the Program

There are several ways to describe program design. Two common methods are by flowcharts and pseudocode. A **flowchart** is a graphic description of a program design that uses combinations of various standard flowchart symbols. Figure 1.2 shows some

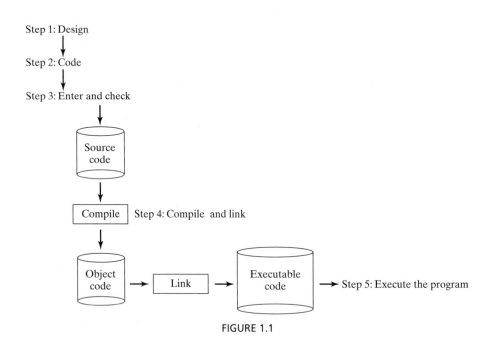

FIGURE 1.1

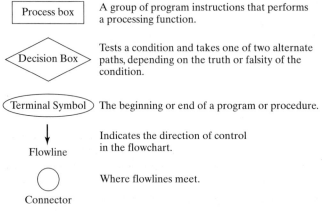

FIGURE 1.2

standard symbols and the operations they represent. We shall use flowcharts to represent only the basic program control structures.

Pseudocode (literally, "false code") describes program design using English. Pseudocode avoids the syntax of a programming language, and instead emphasizes the design of the problem solution. There is no standard form of pseudocode—you make up your own rules. The only guideline is that the meaning of the pseudocode should be clear to anyone reading it. We shall include a description of the pseudocode of each program control structure that we introduce in the text. We shall design most programs using pseudocode.

When you design a program, it is important to check its logic *before* you start to write the program code itself. If possible, have a friend or coworker check your program design. The program designer is frequently too close to his or her design to see errors.

Step 2: Code the Program

After you complete and check the program design, hand code the program with pencil and paper. To **code** a program means to translate the design from Step 1 into a computer programming language (C++, in our case). After completing the code, check it for **syntax errors** (errors in the grammar of the programming language). If possible, have a friend or coworker check your program code for syntax errors to find any that you may have missed.

Step 3: Enter and Check the Program

Write the program onto a disk file using either the text editor provided with your version of C++, your computer system's text editor, or a standard word processing program (saving the file as a plain text file).

After you enter the program, check it at the monitor or print the contents of the file that contains the program code. This printout is the **program listing**. Thoroughly check the program listing for syntax errors and correct the errors immediately. In the next step of the program development cycle you will submit the program code, called the **source program** or the **source code**, to the computer for compilation. It is therefore very important that it is as correct as possible.

Step 4: Compile and Link the Program

The only language a given computer understands is its own **machine language**. A machine language instruction is a binary coded instruction (consisting of zeros and ones) that commands the computer to do one specific task, such as add 1 to a register. Each computer has its own machine language. The machine language for a Sun minicomputer is different from the machine language of a Macintosh, which is different from the machine language of an IBM PC, and so on. Because machine language is in binary, it is difficult to write and find errors in machine language programs.

However, almost all source programs are in **high-level languages** like C++. A high-level language uses English-like statements and mathematical symbolism to express instructions to the computer. Computer scientists designed high-level languages for two reasons. First, because high-level languages use English/mathematical terminology, they are easier for people to understand and use. Second, unlike machine languages, high-level languages are **machine independent**, or **portable**. A C++ program written for an IBM PC should, with some minor modifications, run on a Sun computer.

The portability of C++ across many types of computers is an important reason for the popularity of the language for developing applications. Throughout this book we shall explain how to write portable C++ programs.

Since a computer understands only its own machine language, it cannot execute high-level language instructions directly. The computer uses a program called a **compiler** to translate a high-level language program into an equivalent machine language program. A compiler is a specialist. It translates only one high-level language into a specific machine language. An IBM PC-based C++ compiler translates C++ into IBM PC machine language. The compiler cannot translate a different language (such as Pascal) and cannot be used on a different type of computer (such as a Macintosh.)

A compiler has two main functions. First, it checks the source program for syntax errors. If there are any fatal syntax errors (that is, errors so severe that the compiler does not understand the statement and cannot translate the statement into machine language), the compiler will stop and notify you of the errors it found. If the compiler finds no fatal errors, it translates each high-level language instruction into one or more machine language instructions. This machine language version of the source program is the **object program**.

Although it is in machine language, the object program may not be ready to execute. The program may contain references, called **external references**, to other programs that a user may have written or that the C++ compiler provides for use by all system users. In either case, you must use a program called a **linker** to **resolve** these external references. The linker finds the other programs and makes them part of your program. We call this process **linking**. The linker resolves external references and combines the object code with these other programs to produce the **executable code**. It is the executable code that the computer executes.

The steps necessary to compile and link a program depend on the computer system and compiler on which you develop the program. Some compilers simply require selecting the compile and link options from pull-down menus. Some compilers require you to create a project in which to run your program. Other compilers require executing one or two statements at command level to compile and link a program. Consult your compiler's user's manual or on-line help for instructions on the procedure to follow.

Step 5: Execute the Program

Once you have compiled and linked the program, you are ready to execute the program. Executing the program is usually quite simple. On some systems, all you need to do is select the execute option from a menu. On other systems, you must execute the program at the command level. Consult you compiler's user's guide for the procedure to follow.

Errors in the Cycle   The five steps in developing a program form a cycle—the **program development cycle**. An error at any step can force you to go back to an earlier step and start over. Following are some errors that can occur in the cycle.

Errors in Step 1: After the initial program design, you or a friend might discover a flaw in the design. If this is the case, you have to redesign part or the entire program.

Errors in Step 2: Besides discovering syntax errors, a flaw in design might show up in Step 2. If so, you must go back to Step 1. This might require recoding a good part of the coding.

Errors in Step 3: Part of Step 3 is to check the program that you entered into the computer system. If you find syntax errors, change the saved version of your program by using your text editor. If a design error shows up at this stage, go back to Step 1, redesign the program, recode the changed parts of the program, and use your text editor to make the changes to the saved program.

Errors in Step 4: If the compiler finds any fatal errors in your program, it will not complete the translation of your program into machine language. You will receive a list of error messages detailing the type and location of each error the compiler found. Then you must go back to Step 2, correct your errors, and start the process over. Besides fatal errors, the compiler also may advise you of what it thinks are mistakes. The compiler usually calls these **warnings**. Warnings are not serious enough to stop the translation, but the compiler thinks you should be made aware of them. If the compiler issues warnings, the compilation will take place. However, you should try to correct the source of these warnings before you execute the program unless you coded the source of the warning on purpose. Statements that cause the compiler to issue warnings can cause some very subtle errors in program output when you execute the program. In short, do not execute your program until you have removed all syntax errors.

After a successful compile, there can be an error in the linking process. A linker error is usually caused by the linker's inability to resolve an external reference. The most common cause of this error is misspelling the name of an external program. The linker cannot find the misspelled program because it does not exist. Whatever the cause of the linker error, you must find and correct it.

Errors in Step 5: Assuming the compilation is successful, you can execute your program. Two types of errors can now occur. First, the program may end during execution because it cannot execute a particular instruction. This is a **run-time error**. When a program abnormally ends, the computer displays a message showing the type of error that occurred. You must now locate the cause of the error (which could be in the data processed by your program, not in the program itself!) and make the necessary changes. Many compilers have techniques that you can use to locate run-time errors. These techniques include step-by-step tracing of program instructions and the ability to stop the program at a predetermined place to inspect the values of variables. Consult your compiler's user's guide or on-line help for instructions on how to locate run-time errors.

The second type of error that can occur when you execute your program is more difficult to detect. Although a program executes, produces output, and ends successfully, it is not necessarily correct. Check your output to see if it is unreasonable or if it contains obvious errors. If so, you must find the cause of the error. At this point in the program development cycle, the error must be a **logic error**. The compiler checks the program for syntax errors, but it cannot check for errors in logic. Faulty program design causes most logic errors. If your program contains a logic error, you must find its cause (which is sometimes very difficult), go back to Step 1, redesign, recode, re-enter, recompile, relink, and re-execute the program (and hope that you do not introduce new errors along the way!).

Occasionally, **faulty coding** causes logic errors. Faulty coding is code that is syntactically correct but incorrectly translates the program design into program code. If your program contains faulty coding, locate and correct the faulty code and then re-enter, recompile, relink, and re-execute the program. As we work through this book, we shall point out some common errors caused by faulty coding.

The general rule of program development is *catch errors early*. A mistake in Step 1 might not show until Step 5. If this happens, you must go back to Step 1 and start the cycle again. This wastes your time, computer time, and money. Be cautious and work slowly and deliberately. If you are careful at the beginning of program development, your efforts will pay off in the end.

Displaying a Two-line Message—dem01-1.cpp

Shown below is our first C++ program, dem01-1.cpp, followed by its output. The program contains features of C++ that we will use throughout this book. Read the program carefully. After the program code we explain each line of the program.

```
// dem01-1.cpp

// John C. Molluzzo

#include <iostream.h>

using namespace std;     //Required by the new C++ standard

int main()
{
  cout << "\nThis is our first C++ program.";
  cout << "\nIt works!!!";

  return 0;
}
```

Program Output

```
This is our first C++ program.
It works!!!
```

Comments

Programming
Pointers

The first two nonblank lines of dem01-1.cpp are **comments**. A comment begins with the two characters // and continues to the end of the line. The first comment gives the name of the program and the second gives the author of the program. A comment is not an executable statement. That is, a comment does not cause the computer to take any action. Comments, which can appear anywhere in a C++ program, help to describe parts of the program and are a valuable documentation tool. For example, comments might describe what a program's variables represent or the purpose of a section of the program. Remember that comments are not executable statements and, therefore, the C++ compiler ignores everything from // to the end of the line.

Comment your programs to explain their code. You can follow the style that we use in the programs in this book, although programmers frequently use other commenting styles. Be sure to include at least the name of the program and your name as comments in your own programs.

The first comment shows that the name of this program is dem01-1.cpp. We use the convention that a C++ source-code program name should be eight or fewer characters in length (the characters can be letters, digits, or the hyphen), followed by the .cpp file-name extension. This naming convention conforms to the requirements of most C++ compilers. (Note: Many UNIX C++ compilers require the extension .C on the name of a C++ source code file.)

There is a blank line separating the two comment lines in dem01-1.cpp. You can insert blank lines anywhere in a C++ program. We shall separate the important parts of each program by one or more blank lines to enhance the readability of our program code.

Comments can span several lines, as shown by the following.

```
// This is our first C++ program. This line is a comment line.
// It is common practice to write multiple-line comments
// like this.
```

We will discuss the remainder of the program before explaining the #include and using lines in dem01-1.cpp.

The Function main()

A C++ program is a collection of **functions** that work together to solve a problem. We shall not discuss the exact nature of a C++ function until Chapter 5. For now, think of a function as a part of a program that performs a single task. The collection of functions that make up a C++ program must contain exactly one function called main(). The function main() controls the C++ program by executing C++ statements and executing other functions. A C++ program automatically begins execution at the first executable statement of the function main().

A function in C++ can either produce a value that can be used by the system or it can produce no value at all. The word int that precedes the word main() tells the C++ compiler that main() produces an integer value. In Chapter 5 we will discuss how to write functions that do not produce a value. For now, place the word int before the word main().

The word int is an example of a **keyword** (or **reserved word**), which is a word that has a special meaning in the C++ language. Table 1.1 lists the C++ keywords. Note that there are other keywords that have been proposed for the C++ Standard, so the keywords listed in Table 1.1 may not be all the keywords your compiler recognizes. Check your compiler's documentation for a list of the keywords it recognizes. You will learn the meanings of most of these keywords as you work through this book.

The statements of main() must be enclosed in braces {...}. Thus the name main() is followed by a left brace {, which begins the function main(). The left brace is followed by the program statements. The program ends with the matching right brace }. When program execution reaches this matching right brace, the program stops. Code the left and right braces in main() in column one and indent the program statements two spaces.

TABLE 1.1

auto	double	namespace	switch
asm	else	new	template
break	enum	operator	this
case	extern	private	throw
catch	float	protected	try
char	for	public	typedef
class	friend	register	union
const	goto	return	unsigned
continue	if	short	using
default	inline	signed	virtual
delete	int	sizeof	void
do	long	static	volatile
		struct	while

This indenting convention, which we use throughout the book, makes the program easier to read.

Each `cout` statement in dem01-1.cpp ends in a semicolon. Semicolons are very important in C++, as stated in Note 1.1.

NOTE 1.1—SEMICOLONS

Each statement in a C++ program must end with a semicolon. Omitting a required semicolon will cause a compiler syntax error.

Programming
Pitfalls

A statement in C++, which can span several lines, ends with a semicolon in much the same way as an English sentence ends with a period. Omitting a required semicolon is like omitting a period in English—you are writing the equivalent of a run-on sentence.

Because C++ is statement oriented, we can code the function `main()` of dem01-1.cpp as follows and cause no syntax errors.

```
int main(){cout << "\nThis is our first C++ program."; cout <<
"\nIt works!!!"; return 0;}
```

This code, however, is hard to read. Note 1.2 gives a good rule of thumb to use when coding a C++ program.

NOTE 1.2—CODING STATEMENTS

Code one statement on each line unless

1. The statement is too long to fit on one line, or
2. Writing the statement over several lines clarifies the meaning of the statement.

Programming
Pitfalls

It is very important to keep in mind that C++ is **case sensitive**. That is, when coding C++ statements there is a difference between uppercase and lowercase letters. Coding

```
int Main()
```

is incorrect because we used an uppercase M instead of a lowercase m in the word `main`. When a C++ program begins executing, it looks for a function named `main()`, not a function named `Main()`. Later we shall adopt conventions for naming various C++ program elements. These conventions will allow the use of uppercase letters to help us recognize the type of element each name represents. Until then, use lowercase letters for everything except what appears inside double quotes " ", where you can use whatever combination of letters you require.

The function `main()` can execute any of the following:

1. A built-in C++ statement. The program dem01-1.cpp does not contain any built-in C++ statements. Much of this book is devoted to discussing the built-in C++ statements.

2. A function. The function `main()` can use any function whether it is a **user-defined function** (one that the programmer defines and codes) or a **standard library function** (a precoded function that is part of the C++ system). We shall learn about C++ functions throughout the rest of the book.

3. Operations on C++ streams, which we explain in the next section.

4. Other operations, which we shall encounter in later chapters.

The Output Stream `cout`

In C++, output is written to a **data stream**, which you can think of as a sequence of characters. The stream `cout` (read "see out") represents the standard output stream, which is automatically "attached" to the user's monitor when the C++ program begins. Data can be sent to, or inserted into, the output stream `cout` using the **insertion operator**, <<, which you can read as "inserts" or "gets". Since the stream is attached to the monitor, the data appears on the screen. See Figure 1.3.

To insert a **string** (that is, a set of characters) into the output stream, enclose the string in quotation marks. (Remember that you must end the statement with a semicolon.) Thus,

```
cout << "Hello";
```

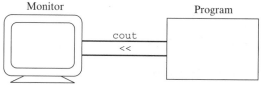

Use the output stream `cout` and the insertion operator << to send data to the output stream.

FIGURE 1.3

inserts the word `Hello` into the output stream, which in turn makes the word appear on the monitor, beginning at where the cursor was when the statement was executed. If we follow the above `cout` by

```
cout << "Goodbye";
```

the following would appear on the monitor

```
HelloGoodbye
```

After `Hello` is printed, the cursor is left following the letter o. Therefore, when the next `cout` is executed, the characters it sends to the output stream appear beginning at the current location of the cursor.

Programming
Pointers

To force the cursor to the first position of a new line, we use a special pair of characters called an **escape sequence**. There are many escape sequences that you can use in a string that you send to `cout`. Each escape sequence begins with the backslash character \ . The escape sequence that causes the cursor to move to the beginning of a new line on the monitor is \n, the **new-line character**. Therefore, the first of the statements

```
cout << "\nThis is our first C++ program.";
cout << "\nIt works!!!";
```

causes the cursor to move to the beginning of a new line and then displays

```
This is our first C++ program.
```

The second of the two statements causes the cursor to move to the beginning of the next line before displaying

```
It works!!!
```

The net effect is the following output.

```
This is our first C++ program.
It works!!!
```

If we omit the \n in the second `cout` statement as follows,

```
cout << "\nThis is our first C++ program.";
cout << "It works!!!";
```

then the program would display the following.

```
This is our first C++ program.It works!!!
```

One `cout` statement can display data on several lines. For example, the following `cout` produces the same output as the two `cout` statements of dem01-1.cpp.

```
cout << "\nThis is our first C++ program.\nIt works!!!";
```

The second `\n` in the string causes the cursor to move to the beginning of the next line before displaying It `works!!!`

To obtain double spacing between the displayed lines, code the following.

```
cout << "\nThis is our first C++ program.";
cout << "\n\nIt works!!!";
```

The two `\n` escape sequences move the cursor down two lines before displaying the second line.

```
This is our first C++ program.

It works!!!
```

The chapter exercises ask you to experiment with some escape sequences. Table 1.2 lists the common escape sequences. To use an escape sequence in a `cout` statement, the escape sequence must be contained in a quoted string.

The `return` Statement

The last statement executed by `main()` should be the `return` statement. We noted previously that we declare the function `main()` to produce an integer value. The `return` statement does two things. First, it ends the execution of `main()`. Second, it sends the integer value `0` back to the operating system to indicate that the program ended normally. In Chapter 5, we shall see how to construct functions that can return other types of values or no value at all.

TABLE 1.2

Escape Sequence	Meaning
\a	Alert (bell)
\b	Backspace
\f	Form feed
\n	New line
\r	Carriage return
\t	Horizontal tab
\v	Vertical tab
\'	Single quotation mark
\"	Double quotation mark
\\	Single back slash
\?	Question mark

The Preprocessor Directive #include

Compiling a C++ program is a two-step procedure. First, a program called the **preprocessor** analyzes the C++ source-code program and carries out all **preprocessor directives**. Each preprocessor directive begins with a # character in the first position of a line. Therefore, in dem01-1.cpp, the line

```
#include <iostream.h>
```

is a preprocessor directive. The preprocessor carries out its directives before the second step in the compilation procedure, which translates your program into machine code. Preprocessor directives usually occur before the main() statement, as in dem01-1.cpp.

Programming
Pointers

Note that in the new C++ standard, you can omit the .h suffix in a #include directive. If your compiler conforms to the new standard, you can code the directive as follows:

```
#include <iostream>
```

The #include directive causes the preprocessor to replace the line containing the #include directive with the text of the named **header file** (so called because it usually appears at the beginning of the program) that appears inside the angle brackets <>. Thus, the text of the named header file effectively becomes part of your program and is subsequently compiled along with your program statements.

Header files usually contain information about constants, functions, and other C++ elements that frequently appear in C++ programs. (We shall learn about these as we proceed through this book.) The header file iostream.h, which stands for "input/output stream header", is one of a standard set of **system header files** that every C++ compiler provides. All system header file names have the file-name extension .h. The header file iostream.h contains information about the standard input/output streams. In particular, it contains information about the object cout, which appears in dem01-1.cpp. We use the header file iostream.h so often that we shall adopt the rule of Note 1.3.

NOTE 1.3—THE iostream.h **HEADER FILE**

Always code

```
#include <iostream.h>
```

in all your programs. Code it before main().

Note that the preprocessor directive

```
#include <iostream.h>
```

Programming
Pitfalls

does not end with a semicolon because a preprocessor directive is not a C++ language statement. A preprocessor directive is an instruction that the preprocessor carries out prior to the compilation of the program.

NOTE 1.4—PREPROCESSOR DIRECTIVES AND SEMICOLONS

Preprocessor directives *do not* end with a semicolon.

As we learn how to use other features of C++, we will introduce other standard header files and learn how to define our own personal header files. We will also learn several other preprocessor directives.

The `using` Directive

The C++ language compiler uses many files to build a C++ executable program. In addition to the source file, that is the C++ program that you code, the compiler uses one or more header files, such as iostream.h, and libraries of standard and user-defined functions to create the executable program. Therefore, many programmers, including you, have been involved in writing the code that goes into making your program work. It is therefore possible that two or more people might have used the same name for two entirely different things. This would lead to a compiler error. To avoid such conflicts, C++ provides the mechanism of the **namespace**, which divides the names that programmers can use into named scopes. The directive

```
using namespace std;
```

allows us to code `cout` (and later `cin`) in our programs without having to qualify these by coding `std::cout` (and `std::cin`.) The `using` directive basically says that we can use all names within the `std` namespace (`cout` and `cin` are two such names) without qualification.

Programming
Pitfalls

Note that the `using` directive is a new requirement of the C++ standard, which was approved in 1998. Older compilers will not recognize the `using` directive. If the `using` directive causes errors when you compile dem01-1.cpp, you probably have an older compiler that does not conform to the new standard. In that case, remove the `using` directive and recompile your program. It will then be necessary to make the same change to all the sample programs in the book.

Execution of dem01-1.cpp

Now enter, compile, and execute the program dem01-1.cpp. How you do this depends on the particular C++ compiler you use. Refer to your C++ language manual, your instructor, or a local expert. Some chapter exercises ask you to make slight changes to dem01-1.cpp or to write your own simple C++ program. To do this, you must be familiar with the editor that accompanies your compiler or a word processor that produces ASCII text files. Again, refer to the appropriate language manual or your instructor.

About the Exercises, Experiments, and Programming Problems

At the end of most sections of this book is some combination of exercises, experiments, and programming problems. You can do most of the exercises with paper and pencil, although some may require you to write a short program. The exercises reinforce the ideas discussed in the chapter. Try to complete as many as possible before going on to the next section.

The experiments usually ask you to modify a program discussed in the text or ask you to code and execute a simple program and interpret the output. Working with computers is an experimental science. You can treat each of your programs as an experiment—will the program work as you expect? To answer this question, carefully examine and interpret the output of the program (the result of the experiment) and decide whether the program (the experiment) worked correctly. Chemists, physicists, and biologists learn from both successful and failed experiments. You can also learn a great deal about programming from programs that work as required and from programs that do not work as required. In addition, the experience gained from doing the experiments will help you to avoid making mistakes when writing your own programs. Try to do as many experiments as possible. The more you do, the more you will learn.

The programming problems range in difficulty from simple, straightforward problems to problems that require a considerable time to design, code, and test. Attempt at least one programming problem in each chapter. In each programming problem, design the program, write the code, compile the program, and then test the program with sample input data.

EXERCISES 1.1

1. What is wrong with the following attempt at a multiline comment?

```
// dem01-1.cpp
// John C. Molluzzo

#include <iostream.h>

using namespace std;

int main()
{                                   // This is the body of the
                         function main()
cout << "\nThis is our first C++ program.";
cout << "\nIt works!!!";

return 0;

}
```

2. What, if anything, is wrong with the following `cout` statement?

```
cout >> "\My name is Maria;
```

"\nMy name is MARIA";

3. What, if anything, is wrong with the following program?

```
#Include <iostream>          main(){          cout << "\nIs there

something wrong "       cout << "\n\nwith this program"?;
```

(handwritten annotations: `.h` above iostream, `7"` above program, `Return 0; }`)

EXPERIMENTS 1.1

For each experiment concerning dem01-1.cpp, start with a fresh copy of dem01-1.cpp and make the indicated changes.

1. Delete the #include <iostream.h> preprocessor directive from dem01-1.cpp. Attempt to compile and execute the resulting program. What message does your compiler issue?

2. As mentioned in this section, C++ is case sensitive. Replace the i in the preprocessor directive #include by I and compile the resulting program. What message does your compiler issue? Now replace the word cout by COUT. What message does the compiler issue?

3. Every C++ statement must end with a semicolon. Intentionally omit the semicolon at the end of the first cout statement in dem01-1.cpp and compile the resulting program. What message does your compiler issue?

4. A preprocessor directive must not end with a semicolon. Put a semicolon at the end of the #include directive in dem01-1.cpp and compile the resulting program. What message does your compiler issue?

5. The body of the function main() must be enclosed in braces { }. Omit either the left brace { or the right brace } in dem01-1.cpp and compile the resulting program. What message does your compiler issue?

6. If you are not sure if your compiler conforms to the new C++ standard, write a program that will find out.

7. If your compiler conforms to the new C++ standard, remove the using statement from dem01-1.cpp and compile the program. What happens?

8. If your compiler conforms to the new C++ standard, remove the using statement from dem01-1.cpp and replace all occurrences of cout by std::cout. Recompile the resulting program. What happens?

9. If your compiler conforms to the new C++ standard, remove the .h from the #include directive. Recompile the resulting program. What happens?

10. A useful escape sequence is the horizontal tab \t. It works like the tab stops on a typewriter. Enter, compile, and execute the following program. What does the tab escape sequence do?

```
// Tabs

#include <iostream.h>

using namespace std;

int main()
```

```
{
    cout << "\nOne\tTwo\tThree\tFour";
    cout << "\n\tFive\tSix\tSeven";
    cout << "\n\t\tEight\tNine";
    cout << "\n\t\t\tTen";

    return 0;
}
```

Based on the output, at what positions are your computer's tabs set?

11. Another useful escape sequence is the alert \a, also called the bell or audible tone. Enter, compile, and execute the following program. What does the alert escape sequence do?

```
// Alert

#include <iostream.h>

using namespace std;

int main()
{
    cout << "\n\a\a\aWake up!";
    cout << "\n\nThe program ran!!";

    return 0;
}
```

12. When outputting a string with the cout statement, the double quote " indicates the beginning or end of a character string and the backslash \ denotes the beginning of an escape sequence. If you want the character string you are displaying to contain either of these characters, you must use a corresponding escape sequence. Enter, compile, and execute the following program. What do the \" and \\ escape sequences do?

```
// Quotes and Backslashes

#include <iostream.h>

using namespace std;

int main()

{
    cout << "\nThe following is enclosed in double quotes: \"Quote\"";
    cout << "\n\nThis is a backslash: \\";

    return 0;
}
```

Why are there two double quotes near the end of the first `cout` statement?

PROGRAMMING PROBLEMS 1.1

1. Write a program that displays the following triple-spaced lines.

```
Hello!


This is your computer.


What is your name?
```

2. Write a program that has the same output as the program of Programming Problem 1, but uses just one `cout` statement.

3. Write a program that displays the following.

```
* * * * * * * * * * *  * Welcome *  * * * * * * * * * *
```

4. Write a program that uses asterisks to display your first initial in block form. For example, the program that John writes would display the following.

```
* * * * * * * * *
        *
        *
        *
        *
* * * * *
```

1.2 Integers and Arithmetic

The simplest type of numeric data that a programmer can define in a C++ program is integer data. This section discusses how to declare and name integer variables, assign values to them, and to do arithmetic with them.

Identifiers

All programming languages, including C++, require that the programmer name various items that a program uses. We refer to the names of these items as **identifiers**. An identifier can be any name you choose as long it conforms to the rules of Note 1.5.

NOTE 1.5—IDENTIFIER NAMING RULES

An identifier consists of up to 31 characters subject to the following rules:

1. The characters can be letters (upper- or lowercase), digits, and underscores (_).
2. An identifier cannot begin with a digit.
3. An identifier cannot have the same spelling as a keyword.

The following identifier names are valid.

```
salary          employee_discount      _name4
x               total_cost             margin
Tax_Rate        VAR                    Margin
```

Programming
Pointers

Good programming practice requires that an identifier name reflect the purpose or meaning of what the identifier represents. For example, do not use the identifier v to represent the value of a property. Instead, use either the identifier `value` or the identifier `property_value`.

An identifier cannot contain a space. Therefore, to improve readability, we shall use the underscore to separate words. The identifier `total_cost` is easier to read than the identifier `totalcost`. Although an underscore can be the first character in an identifier, we suggest that you avoid that use to avoid conflict with identifiers used in system header files. (Some programmers capitalize the first word of multiword identifiers instead of using underscores. For example, they would use `TotalCost` instead of `total_cost`.)

Do not forget that C++ is case sensitive. Therefore, the identifier `profit_margin` is different than the identifier `Profit_Margin`.

Variables

A **variable** is a named location in the computer's main memory that stores a particular type of data. Since it is a location in computer memory, a variable can assume any one of a set of permissible values. This is why we call such a location a variable.

In a C++ program, we define a variable in a **declaration**. A variable declaration begins with the variable's **data type**, which tells the kind of data that a program can store at the location named by the variable. There are many data types in C++, including built-in data types and user-defined data types. The data type is followed by the name of the variable, which is followed by a semicolon .

The name of a variable is an identifier and is subject to Note 1.5. However, we shall adopt the variable naming convention of Note 1.6. Remember that this is just a convention, a rule that is used in this book. It is not a C++ language rule.

NOTE 1.6—VARIABLE NAMES

We use only lowercase letters and the underscore for names of variables.

For example, the following is a variable declaration.

```
int i1;
```

In this declaration, the keyword `int` means that the named variable, `i1`, is of the integer data type. On IBM PCs running under DOS, an integer variable occupies two bytes of storage, that is 16 bits. We can represent $2^{16} = 65,536$ integers (positive, negative, and zero) in an integer variable. Half the integers in this range are negative (that is, less than zero) and half are nonnegative (that is, greater than or equal to zero). Therefore, an integer variable can have a value in the range $-32,768$ to $+32,767$.

(In computers that store `int` type variables in four bytes, the range for an `int` variable is the same as that for a `long` type variable on an IBM PC. We discuss the type `long` later in this chapter.)

It is possible to declare more than one variable in one declaration. For example, the following declares three integer variables `i1`, `i2`, and `sum`.

```
int i1,
    i2,
    sum;
```

Note that there is a comma after each of `i1` and `i2`, and that the declaration ends with a semicolon after the last variable name. You can declare any number of variables of the same type by separating their names by commas and ending the declaration by a semicolon.

Programming
Pointers

A variable can be declared anywhere in a C++ program. Although not required by C++, for now we shall adopt the practice of placing each variable declared at the beginning of `main()` on a separate line. This improves the readability of our programs and allows us to place a comment after a variable's name to explain its function in the program. In later chapters, we will discuss when it is appropriate to declare a variable elsewhere in the program.

Programming
Pointers

The **value** of a variable is the data stored at that location in computer memory. Declaring a variable does not give the variable any specific value. A declaration simply reserves storage for that variable in the computer's memory and associates the declared name with that storage. Before the program places data into a variable, the value of the variable is meaningless to the program. In this case, we say that the variable contains **garbage**. It is up to the programmer to make sure that the program places meaningful data into each variable.

Using Integer Variables—dem01-2.cpp

The second program that we discuss in this chapter asks the user to input values for two integers, does arithmetic on these values, and displays the results. To write this program, you need to learn how to input values into the variables, how to do arithmetic, and how to display the results.

The program dem01-2.cpp has the following four-part structure.

1. Declare the variables.
2. Obtain the data from the user.
3. Do the required calculations with the data.
4. Output the results.

Many programs in the first part of this book have this four-part structure. We discuss the new features of the program after the program code.

```cpp
// dem01-2.cpp

// This program demonstrates the use of integers in C++.
// The user enters two integers. The program adds, subtracts,
// multiplies, and divides the integers and outputs the
// results of the calculations.

#include <iostream.h>

using namespace std;

int main()
{
  // Declare the variables

  int i1,
      i2,
      sum,
      difference,
      product,
      quotient,
      remainder;

  // Obtain the data from the user

  cout << "Input an integer followed by a return: ";
  cin >> i1;

  cout << "Input an integer followed by a return: ";
  cin >> i2;

  // Do the arithmetic

  sum = i1 + i2;
  difference = i1 - i2;
  product = i1 * i2;
  quotient = i1 / i2;
  remainder = i1 % i2;
```

```
// Output the results

cout << "\nThe sum of " << i1 << " and " << i2 << " is " << sum;
cout << "\nThe difference of " << i1 << " and " << i2 << " is "
    << difference;
cout << "\nThe product of " << i1 << " and " << i2 << " is "
    << product;
cout << "\nThe quotient of " << i1 << " and " << i2 << " is "
    << quotient;
cout << "\nThe remainder when " << i1 << " is divided by " << i2
    << " is " << remainder;

return 0;

}
```

Program Output

```
Input an integer followed by a return: 15
Input an integer followed by a return: 6

The sum of 15 and 6 is 21
The difference of 15 and 6 is 9
The product of 15 and 6 is 90
The quotient of 15 and 6 is 2
The remainder when 15 is divided by 6 is 3
```

Variable Declarations

The declaration in dem01-2.cpp reserves storage for seven integer variables but does not place values into the seven storage locations. The program needs the variables `i1` and `i2` to store the integers input by the user. It also needs the variables `sum`, `difference`, `product`, `quotient`, and `remainder` to store the results of each arithmetic calculation. Remember that since each of these variables is an integer, each of their values must be in the range $-32,768$ to $+32,767$. Experiment 4 addresses the question of what happens if one of these numbers is outside the permissible range.

Asking the User for Input—Prompts

Programming
Pointers

The first `cout` statement in dem01-2.cpp, which is called a **prompt**, asks the program user to enter an integer followed by a return. A program should always prompt the user for the data that the program expects the user to enter. The prompt should be short and should clearly specify the kind of data the user is to enter. Since the prompt ends in a colon followed by a space, the `cout` leaves the cursor after this blank space. The prompt looks like the following on the screen.

```
Input an integer followed by a return: _
```

The Input Stream `cin`

Just as output in C++ is done via the output stream, input is done via the input stream. The input stream `cin` is to input what `cout` is to output: `cin` obtains the next data item from the input stream, which is attached to the keyboard, and places it into the variable following the **extraction operator, >>**. When we use the extraction operator on `cin`, `cin` obtains the next data item from the input stream, that is the next data item you type at the keyboard, and places a copy of it into the variable that follows >>. See Figure 1.4. The statement `cin >> i1;` gets the integer that the user enters at the keyboard in response to the prompt and places the integer's value into the variable `i1`.

The second `cout` statement in dem01-1.cpp prompts the user for the second integer. The statement `cin >> i2;` obtains the integer the user enters and places its value into the variable `i2`.

The integer that the user enters can be preceded by a + or − sign, but it cannot contain a comma or decimal point. After retrieving the sign, if present, `cin` retrieves only digits from the input buffer up to but not including the first non-digit it encounters. Thus, if the user enters 13,708 in response to the first prompt, `cin` will retrieve only 13 and assign it to `i1`. See Experiment 2.

As Figure 1.5 shows, we shall diagram a variable by a square. The name of the variable is at the top of the square. The data type of the variable is in parentheses at the bottom of the square, and the value of the variable is in the square.

Assume that the user enters 15 in response to the first prompt and 6 in response to the second. After the program executes the `cin` statements, we have the situation shown in Figure 1.6.

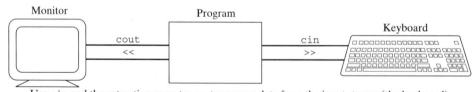

Use `cin` and the extraction operator >> to remove data from the input stream (the keyboard).

FIGURE 1.4

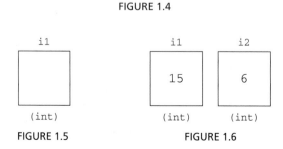

FIGURE 1.5   FIGURE 1.6

The Input Buffer

The integers that the user enters at the keyboard are not immediately sent to the program for processing. Instead, the computer places the characters in a temporary storage location called the **input buffer**. The computer sends these characters to the program when the user presses the return key. We call this action **flushing the input buffer**.

In response to the first prompt of dem01-2.cpp, if the user enters an integer and does not press the return key, the program will do nothing. When the user presses the return key, the computer flushes the buffer and sends its contents to the program for processing.

Programming
Pointers

Remember that a variable does not have a valid value until the program in some way assigns a value to the variable. Using `cin` and the extraction operator is one way to assign a value to a variable. Next we discuss another way to place a value into a variable.

The Assignment Operator and Integer Constants

Recall that until the program assigns a value to a variable, the variable does not have a valid value. That is, the variable contains garbage. After the `cin` statements execute, the variables i1 and i2 have valid values. However, at this point the variables sum, difference, product, quotient, and remainder contain garbage. We give values to these variables by using arithmetic expressions and the assignment operator.

After the program inputs the integers and places their values into the variables i1 and i2, the program can do its calculations. The statements in this part of the program are all similar. Each statement begins with a variable name, followed by the =, followed by an arithmetic expression, followed by a semicolon.

```
sum = i1 + i2;
difference = i1 - i2;
product = i1 * i2;
quotient = i1 / i2;
remainder = i1 % i2;
```

The **assignment operator** = (read "becomes" or "is replaced by") works as follows: The computer evaluates the expression to the right of = (we shall see how very shortly) and assigns the resulting value to the variable on the left of =. A variable name must appear on the left side of the assignment operator. Thus, the following assignment gives the variable sum the value 2345.

```
sum = 2345;
```

The expression on the right of the preceding assignment is an **integer constant**. An integer constant is a whole number (positive, negative, or zero) written as a sequence of digits, the first of which is not zero. (The only exception to this rule is the integer constant 0.) An integer constant cannot contain a space, a comma, or a decimal point. An integer constant may be preceded by a + or a − to show its sign. If you omit a sign, the computer assumes the integer is positive. Thus,

    0 2345 −56 +10782

are valid integer constants. The following are not valid integer constants.

    034 5,678 93.0

The first begins with a 0, the second contains a comma, and the third contains a decimal point.

You can assign an initial value to a variable in its declaration. For example, the declaration

```
int i = 42;
```

defines the integer variable `i` and assigns it the value 42. Program statements can later change the value of `i`.

The Arithmetic Operators

Generally, the expression to the right of the assignment operator involves one or more operators. The program dem01-2.cpp uses the five basic **arithmetic operators**: **addition** (+), **subtraction** (−), **multiplication** (*), **division** (/), and the **remainder** operator (%).

The first assignment statement

```
sum = i1 + i2;
```

executes as follows. The computer's CPU adds the values of the variables `i1` and `i2` and assigns the result to the variable `sum`. If the user enters 15 and 6 for the two integers, the assignment has the result shown in Figure 1.7.

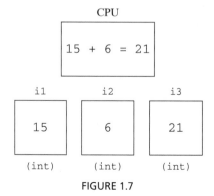

FIGURE 1.7

Programming
Pitfalls

It is important to note that the assignment operator in C++ is different from equality in elementary algebra. In C++ and most other programming languages, an assignment such as the following is legal and makes sense.

```
i1 = i1 + 1;
```

If `i1` has the value 15, this assignment works as follows. The computer evaluates the expression to the right of the =. Since `i1` has the value 15, the expression has the value 16. The computer assigns this result to the variable `i1`, which appears to the left of the operator =. The net effect of the assignment is to increase the value of `i1` by one. Reading the assignment properly helps to understand its meaning—"The value of `i1` becomes the value of `i1` plus 1."

The second and third assignments of dem01-2.cpp behave similarly to the first. The second assignment subtracts the value of `i2` from the value of `i1` and assigns the result (9) to the variable `difference`. The third assignment multiplies the values of `i1` and `i2` and assigns the result (90) to the variable `product`.

Programming
Pitfalls

The fourth assignment, which involves division, might not behave as you expect. Since `i1` and `i2` are integer variables, the division `i1/i2` is an integer division. Therefore, the result of the division must be an integer. The computer discards any remainder resulting from the division. If the user enters the integers 15 and 6, the statement

```
quotient = i1 / i2;
```

assigns the value 2 to `quotient` because 15 divided by 6 gives a quotient of 2 with a remainder of 3. The assignment discards the remainder 3. See Experiment 3 for what happens when you attempt to divide by zero.

You can assign the remainder produced by an integer division to a variable by using the **remainder** operator %. The assignment

```
remainder = i1 % i2;
```

divides the value of `i1` by the value of `i2` and assigns the remainder of the division to the variable `remainder`. If `i1` and `i2` have the values 15 and 6, the statement assigns 3 to the variable `remainder`.

Operator Precedence Rules

You can form more complicated arithmetic expressions by combining two or more arithmetic operators and using parentheses. For example, you could declare

```
int result;
```

and code the following assignment statement:

```
result = i1 * (i1 + i2);
```

As in elementary algebra, when an expression contains parentheses, you evaluate the expression in parentheses first. Thus, if `i1` and `i2` have the values 15 and 6, the computer evaluates the assignment as follows: First evaluate the expression in parentheses—the value of `i1 + i2` is 21. Then multiply the value of `i1`, that is 15, by 21. Finally, assign the answer, 315, to the variable `result`.

Without parentheses, the computer evaluates an expression according to the operator precedence rules of Note 1.7.

NOTE 1.7—ARITHMETIC OPERATOR PRECEDENCE RULES

Without parentheses, the computer evaluates the arithmetic operators in an expression according to the following:

1. Do multiplications, divisions, and remainder operations first. If there is more than one such operation, work in order from left to right.

2. Next, do additions and subtractions. If there is more than one such operation, work in order from left to right.

The operator precedence table, Table 1.3, summarizes the rules of Note 1.7 and includes the unary plus and minus operators.

The higher an operator appears in the table, the higher its precedence. The associativity rule determines how the computer applies operators on the same precedence level—either left to right (as is true for the arithmetic operators) or right to left as is true for the unary plus and minus.

A unary minus might appear in an expression as follows.

```
result = -i1 + i2;
```

Since there is no operand to the left of the minus sign, the minus is a unary minus and not the subtraction operator. Since the unary minus has higher precedence than addition, the computer first applies the unary minus and then does the addition. If `i1` and `i2` have the values 15 and 6, the above assignment gives the value −9 to `result`.

The C++ language has many operators and we will study most of them in this book. As we do so, we will expand the operator precedence table to include the new operators.

TABLE 1.3

Operators	Associativity
( )	Left to right (i.e. from inside out)
+ (unary) − (unary)	Right to left
* / %	Left to right
+ −	Left to right
=	Right to left

To discuss several more examples of the precedence rules, we use the following declaration.

```
int i = 14,
    j = 5,
    k = 3,
    r1,
    r2,
    r3;
```

What value does the following assignment place into r1?

```
r1 = i + j * 2 - i / 3;
```

The expression contains no parentheses. Therefore, the computer first executes the multiplications and divisions, from left to right.

```
i  +  j * 2  -  i / 3;
i  +    10   -    4
```

Next, the computer does additions and subtractions, from left to right.

```
i      +  10   -   4
      24       -   4
              20
```

The statement assigns 20 to the variable r1.
As a second example, what value does the following assignment place into r2?

```
r2 = (i + j) * 2 - i / 3;
```

The computer executes the expression inside parentheses first.

```
(i + j)   *   2  -  i / 3;
    19    *   2  -  i / 3
```

Next, the computer executes multiplications and divisions, from left to right. Finally, the computer does the subtraction.

```
19      *   2   -   i / 3
           38   -   4
              34
```

The statement assigns 34 to the variable r2.

As a final example, what value does the following assignment place into r3?

```
r3 = i % j + k * 5;
```

There are no parentheses in the expression. The computer does multiplications and remainders, from left to right, and then does the addition.

```
i   %   j   +   k   *   5;
    4       +       15
            19
```

The assignment places 19 into the variable r3.

The Object cout Revisited

Besides displaying a character string, as we did in dem01-1.cpp and in the prompt of dem01-2.cpp, cout also can display the values of variables. Consider the first of the last five cout statements of dem01-2.cpp.

```
cout << "\nThe sum of " << i1 << " and " << i2 << " is " << sum;
```

This statement sends a string to the output stream followed by the value of i1, followed by another string, followed by the value of i2, followed by a third string, followed by the value of sum. When several insertion operators are used in the same cout statement, read the first one as "gets" and the subsequent ones as "followed by." The space after the word "of" places a space between that word and the value of the variable i1, and similarly with the other strings. The variable values are not automatically followed by a space. Thus, the output appears as follows.

```
The sum of 15 and 6 is 21
```

Note that a cout statement can span several lines as in the last three cout statements in dem01-2.cpp. In each case, the semicolon at the end of the second line ends the cout statement.

EXERCISES 1.2

In exercises 1–16, find the value assigned to the variable on the left of the assignment operator =. Work each problem independently of the others. Assume the following declarations.

```
int i = 2,
    j = 3,
```

```
k = 4,
result;
```

1. `result = 5 * i - j;`

2. `result = 5 * (i - j);`

3. `result = 33 / i * j;`

4. `result = 33 / (i * j);`

5. `result = 33 % i * j;`

6 `result = i - j + k;`

7. `result = i - (j + k);`

8. `result = 17 % k - i * j + 6;`

9. `result = 17 % (k - i) * j + 6;`

10. `result = i * (7 + (j + 3) / 2) - k;`

11. `j = j + k;`

12. `i = i * 2;`

13. `i = i % 3;`

14. `i = i / j + k;`

15. `k = k - 5;`

16. `k = (i + j) * k / 4;`

EXPERIMENTS 1.2

1. Compile and execute dem01-2.cpp.
2. Execute dem01-2.cpp and enter 13,708 for the first integer (include the comma) and 14.2 for the second integer. What happens and why?
3. Execute dem01-2.cpp and enter 0 for the second integer. What happens and why? Can you suggest a way to help the user avoid this mistake?
4. Execute dem01-2.cpp and enter 20000 and 15000 for the two integers. If the results displayed by the program are incorrect, what does this tell you about the amount of storage required for an `int` type variable?
5. In dem01-2.cpp, one `cin` statement can obtain both integers. Replace the two `cout`/`cin` pairs in dem01-2.cpp by the following.

```
cout << "\nEnter two integers: ";
cin >> i1 >> i2;
```

Note that the input prompt does not specify how to enter the integers. Compile the resulting program and execute it twice as follows.

(a) Enter the integers 19 and 7 separated by a space and then hit return.

(b) Enter the integer 19, hit return, enter the integer 7, and hit return.

Is there any difference in the resulting output? Explain why or why not.

PROGRAMMING PROBLEMS 1.2

1. An arithmetic expression, rather than a variable, can appear in the variable list of a `cout` statement. For example, you can replace the first `cout` statement of dem01-2.cpp by

```
cout << "\nThe sum of " << i1 << " and " << i2 << " is " << i1 + i2;
```

With this change to dem01-2.cpp, you can eliminate the variable `sum` from the program and eliminate the assignment statement that gives `sum` the value of `i1 + i2`.

Recode dem01-2.cpp by (a) eliminating the variables `sum`, `difference`, `product`, `quotient`, and `remainder`, (b) eliminating the associated assignments, and (c) replacing the `cout` statements by statements such as the previous one that contains the required arithmetic operations. Compile and execute the program. Does it work in the same way as dem01-2.cpp?

2. Write a program that asks the user to enter two integers. The program should divide the first integer by the second and then display the resulting quotient and remainder.

1.3 Solving a Problem with Integers

In this section we develop a program to calculate the charge for parts and labor done by mechanics at an automobile service outlet.

Problem 1.1

An automobile service outlet charges its customers for the parts it uses to repair customer vehicles and for the labor required for the repair. The labor charge is $44 per hour. Write a C++ program that prompts the user to enter the total cost of parts for a customer and the number of hours of labor required for the repair. Assume the total cost of parts and the number of hours are integers. The program should display the cost of the parts, the charge for labor, and the total charge for the repair (the sum of the cost of parts and labor).

Discussion of Problem 1.1

To solve this problem, we first design a high-level solution using pseudocode. **Pseudocode** (literally, "false code") describes program design using English. Pseudocode avoids the syntax of a programming language, and instead emphasizes the design of the problem solution. There is no standard form of pseudocode—you make up your own rules. The only guideline is that the meaning of the pseudocode should be clear to anyone reading it.

Pseudocode for Problem 1.1:

Obtain the input data from the user.

Calculate the labor and total charges.

Display the results.

The pseudocode does not specify the variables to use or how to obtain the input data, calculate the charges, or display the results. We will fill in these details when we code the program. At this point in the solution design, the pseudocode just specifies what the program must do and the order in which it the program must do it.

The Program prb01-1.cpp

Before considering the code, we select the variables necessary to solve our problem. The user is to input two numbers—the cost of parts and the number of hours worked. We must declare a variable for each of these quantities. Suppose we call these variables parts and hours. Since the program must calculate the labor charge and the total charge of the repair, we also declare the variables labor and total.

What range of values can these variables assume? The total cost of the repair is the largest number the program will handle. The total cost should not exceed the largest possible value for an integer variable, 32767 (at least not soon!). Therefore, we declare all four of the variables as type int.

Following is the program code that solves our problem.

```cpp
// prb01-1.cpp

// This program calculates the total charge for parts and labor

#include <iostream.h>
#include <iomanip.h>

using namespace std;

int main()
{
  const int HOURLY_RATE = 44;

  int parts,            // Cost of parts
      hours,            // Number of hours worked
      labor,            // Labor charge
      total;            // Total charge to customer

  // Obtain the input data

  cout << "\nEnter the cost of parts: ";
  cin >> parts;
  cout << "\nEnter the number of hours worked: ";
  cin >> hours;
```

```
// Do the calculations

labor = HOURLY_RATE * hours;
total = parts + labor;

// Display the results

cout << "\nCost of parts: " << setw(5) << parts;
cout << "\nLabor charge: " << setw(6) << labor;
cout << "\n-------------------";
cout << "\nTotal charge: " << setw(6) << total;

return 0;
}
```

Program Output

```
Enter the cost of parts: 239

Enter the number of hours worked: 2

Cost of parts:    239
Labor charge:      88
-------------------
Total charge:     327
```

Header Files

We include the `iostream.h` header file as usual. The header `iomanip.h` is included for the `setw()` I/O manipulator, which we shall discuss shortly.

Defined Constants

Programming
Pointers

A variable declaration preceded by the keyword `const` declares a "constant variable." As any other variable, such a variable can be initialized in its declaration. However, once so initialized, no statement in the program can change the value of a `const` variable. The variable thus becomes a constant in the program. Thus, the declaration

```
const int HOURLY_RATE = 44;
```

defines the variable HOURLY_RATE, which represents the hourly labor rate of $44 per hour, as a constant. We will use the convention (this is not a rule of C++, but a convention that we use in this book) that defined constant names are in uppercase letters. This makes it easier to distinguish between defined constants and ordinary variables.

Using defined constants makes program maintenance easier. If the hourly labor rate should change next week, then to update the program all we need to do is change the value assigned to the defined constant HOURLY_RATE in its declaration. It is not necessary to search through the program for the line or lines in which the hourly rate of 44 appears.

Declaration of Variables

As stated earlier, the four variables the program uses are of type int. The comment on each line that declares a variable describes the quantity that the variable stores.

The Prompts and Calculations

The program statements are in three sections—obtain the input data, do the calculations, and display the results. The program obtains input data by prompting the user and retrieving the input by cin statements.

The calculations are straightforward. The cost of labor is HOURLY_RATE (remember, this has a value of 44) multiplied by the number of hours worked.

```
labor = HOURLY_RATE * hours;
```

The total charge to the customer is the sum of the cost of parts and the cost of labor.

```
total = parts + labor;
```

The Output—I/O Manipulators

The cout statements that display the results contain a new feature, the setw() **I/O manipulator**. You can think of an I/O manipulator as a message to the output stream cout to display the output in a particular way. The setw() manipulator sets the width of the display field of the next item output. The item is displayed right justified, that is, it is displayed in the rightmost positions of the field. For example, the cout statement

```
cout << "\nCost of parts: " << setw(5) << parts;
```

first displays the string "Cost of parts: " at the beginning of a new line. Then the setw(5) manipulator tells cout to display the next item in a field of width 5. Thus, the value of the variable parts, 239, is displayed in the rightmost three positions of the five-position field as follows.

| field of width 5

C	o	s	t		o	f		p	a	r	t	s	:				2	3	9

Likewise, the second cout statement

```
cout << "\nLabor charge: " << setw(6) << labor;
```

displays the value of the variable `labor` in a field of width 6. This field is one position larger than the field set by the previous `setw()` because the string "Labor charge: " contains one less character than the string "Cost of parts: ". Thus, the value of the variable `labor`, 88, is displayed as follows.

|field of width 6

L	a	b	o	r		c	h	a	r	g	e	:						8	8

In this way, we can use `setw()` to align the numbers on the right as they usually are when displayed in column form.

To use the manipulator `setw()` you must place the `#include <iomanip.h>` statement at the beginning of your program. In the next chapter we introduce several other I/O manipulators that are of use in displaying numbers that contain decimal points.

NOTE 1.8—THE `iomanip.h` **HEADER FILE**

To use an I/O manipulator, you must place the following preprocessor statement at the beginning of your program.

```
#include <iomanip.h>
```

EXERCISES 1.3

1. Code a defined constant that represents the number of feet in a mile.
2. Code a defined constant that represents the number of people enrolled in your class.

PROGRAMMING PROBLEMS 1.3

1. Write a program that asks the user to enter the dollar amount of the opening balance of an account, the dollar amount of deposits to the account, and the dollar amount of withdrawals from the account during the last month. The program should then display the closing balance (opening balance plus deposits minus withdrawals) in the account.

2. Write a program that asks the user to enter the integer lengths (in centimeters) of the dimensions of a box that will hold gumdrops. The program should then display the volume of the box (the product of the three dimensions) in cubic centimeters.

3. Write a program that asks the user to enter the duration of a baseball game by first asking for the number of hours and then asking for the number of minutes. The program should display the total number of minutes that the game lasted.

1.4 Other Integer Data Types

In this section we introduce the other integer data types and solve a problem that requires these types.

Unsigned, Long, and Short Integers

Recall that on some computer systems a variable of type int can assume any value in the range −32,768 to +32,767. Sometimes this range is inadequate to store the values of the variables a program requires. For example, if the variable nyc_pop is to store the population of New York City, it would have to assume a value of more than 8,000,000.

The C++ programmer can use other kinds of integer variables that have a larger range of values than type int. If a variable can assume only nonnegative values, then you could declare it as type unsigned int, or equivalently unsigned. The declaration

```
unsigned i1;
```

declares i1 to be of type unsigned integer. On IBM PCs, an unsigned integer variable occupies two bytes of storage (just as an int type variable does). However, an unsigned integer variable must be nonnegative. Therefore, its value can be in the range from 0 to +65,535.

If an integer variable requires a wider range of positive and negative values, you can declare the variable to be of type long int, or equivalently long. On IBM PCs, a variable of type long occupies four bytes (that is, 32 bits). Such a variable, therefore, can assume any of 2^{32} = 4,294,967,296 values. Since half these values represent negative numbers and half represent nonnegative numbers, a variable of type long has a range of values from −2,147,483,648 to +2,147,483,647. Therefore, if we declare

```
long nyc_pop;
```

then the variable nyc_pop could store the value of New York City's population.

Finally, if an integer variable, by virtue of what values it represents, cannot assume a negative value, you can declare it as an unsigned long. On an IBM PC, an unsigned long occupies four bytes, but can assume only nonnegative values. Therefore, such a variable can assume a value in the range from 0 to 4,294,967,295. Since the value of New York City's population cannot be negative, it is safe to make the following declaration for the variable nyc_pop.

```
unsigned long nyc_pop;
```

C++ also permits variables of the data type short int, or equivalently short. On an IBM PC, a variable of type short occupies only one byte of storage and therefore has a value range from −128 to +127. Also, an unsigned short int, or equivalently unsigned short has a range from 0 to 255.

The specific data type you choose for an integer variable depends on the kind (nonnegative only or not) and the range of values the variable can assume. Make sure that you choose the correct data type and be consistent in your program.

Mixing Data Types

C++ allows variables of different data types to appear in the same expression. To do arithmetic on the values of such an expression, C++ converts all the data to a common data type. The rules that C++ uses to decide this common data type are complex and we will not discuss them. For now, however, the rule of Note 1.9 will suffice for our work.

NOTE 1.9—EXPRESSIONS WITH MIXED DATA TYPES

If an arithmetic expression contains mixed data types, to do the arithmetic, C++ converts all values to that of the most general type.

For example, suppose the following declarations.

```
short k = 3;
int   i = 8;
long  j = 56;
```

To evaluate the expression, i + j + k, C++ converts the value of i, which is an int, to the equivalent long. Then, C++ converts the value of k, which is a short, to the equivalent long. Finally, C++ adds the resulting values to the value of j.

The variable on the left of an assignment also can be of a different type than the expression on the right. For example, suppose we have the following declarations.

```
int int1,
    int2;
long long1,
     long2;
```

The following assignment is valid.

```
long1 = int1 + int2;
```

Programming
Pointers

C++ automatically attempts to convert the value of the expression on the right to the type of variable on the left of the assignment operator. The conversion is successful if the value of the expression on the right of the assignment is within the range of the variable type on the left of the assignment. The previous assignment is always valid because it is always valid to convert an int to a long.

However, the following assignment is valid only if the value of the expression on the right is within the range of an int variable.

```
int1 = long1 + long2;
```

Programming
Pitfalls

If the value of long1 + long2 is not within the range of an int variable, an invalid result will be assigned to int1. The assignment given will cause some compilers to issue a warning message.

Using the Other Integer Types—Problem 1.2

A taxicab company has awarded a contract to the automobile repair outlet in Problem 1.1 to service its fleet of 103 cabs. The repair company will bill the taxi company once a month for the month's repairs. Change the program prb01-1.cpp so the user can enter the total cost of parts for the taxis and the total number of hours spent repairing the taxis for the entire month

Discussion of Problem 1.2

We can use the same prompts and calculations as those of prb01-1.cpp. However, we need to change the variable declarations. Over the period of one month the cost of parts for a fleet of 103 taxi cabs could exceed $32,767. Therefore, we should declare the variable parts as type long, which can store a value of more than two billion. The other variables in prb01-1.cpp must also be redeclared as type long.

The program prb01-2.cpp also contains the endl I/O manipulator, which sends an end-of-line message to the output stream. Thus, endl serves the same purpose as the \n escape sequence. You can use endl or the \n escape sequence, or both in your programs to place the cursor at the beginning of a new line. Just remember that \n must be contained in a quoted string, but endl is not enclosed in quotes. We will use both methods in the programs in this book.

```cpp
// prb01-2.cpp
// This program calculates the total charge for parts and labor

#include <iostream.h>

using namespace std;

int main()
{
    const int HOURLY_RATE = 44;

    long parts,         // Cost of parts
         hours,         // Number of hours worked
         labor,         // Labor charge
         total;         // Total charge to customer

    // Obtain the input data

    cout << endl;
    cout << "Enter the cost of parts: ";
    cin >> parts;
```

```
cout << endl;
cout << "Enter the number of hours worked: ";
cin >> hours;

// Do the calculations

labor = HOURLY_RATE * hours;
total = parts + labor;

// Display the results

cout << endl;
cout << "Cost of parts: " << setw(9) << parts << endl;
cout << "Labor charge: " << setw(10) << labor << endl;
cout << "----------------------" << endl;
cout << "Total charge: " << setw(10) << total << endl;

return 0;
}
```

Program Output

```
Enter the cost of parts: 52731

Enter the number of hours worked: 97

Cost of parts:      52731
Labor charge:        4268
----------------------
Total charge:       56999
```

EXERCISES 1.4

In Exercises 1–5 state the type (or types) of integer variable that are appropriate for storing the given quantity.

1. The number of cars that pass a given intersection during a 24-hour period.
2. The yearly salary of a major league baseball player.
3. The temperature, to the nearest degree, outside your house at noon on any given day of the year.
4. The enrollment at your school during a typical Fall semester.
5. The balance, to the nearest dollar, in a checking account that has overdraft privileges of up to $2,000 (that is, you can write checks for a total of $2,000 more than your balance).

EXPERIMENTS 1.4

1. Consider the following program.

```
#include <iostream.h>

using namespace std;

int main()
{
    int i1, i2;
    unsigned u1, u2;
    long lg1, lg2;

    lg1 = 20000;
    lg2 = 20000;
    i1 = lg1 + lg2;

    cout << "\n The sum of the longs " << lg1 << " and " << lg2
         << " is the int " << i1;

    return 0;
}
```

(a) Compile and execute the program. Does your compiler issue any warning messages? What does the program display?

(b) Try assigning the sum of two `unsigned` integers to a `long`, two `int`s to an `unsigned`, and so on. Does your compiler issue any warning messages? What does the program display in each case?

PROGRAMMING PROBLEMS 1.4

In each program, be sure to use a type of integer variable that is suitable for the values it can assume. Also, use symbolic constants where appropriate.

1. Write a program that asks the user to enter the integer lengths (in inches) of the dimensions of a refrigerator shipping crate. The program should display the volume of the box in cubic inches.

2. A swimming pool maintenance company resurfaces the inside surfaces of an inground concrete pool for $2 per square foot of surface area. Write a program to calculate what the company should charge to resurface a pool. The program should ask the user to input the length, width, and depth of the pool, each to the nearest foot. The program should display the cost of resurfacing the pool. The following formula gives the inside surface area of a pool.

    surface = 2*depth*(length + width) + length*width

3. Your pulse rate is the number of times your heart beats each minute (usually about 70 per minute for an adult and higher for children.) Write a program that asks the user to enter his or her approximate age—first ask for the number of years, then the number of months. The program should display the approximate number of times the person's heart has beat since their birth. To do this, first calculate the approximate number of minutes the person has lived (2160 times the

number of months entered, plus 525,600 times the number of years entered). Then multiply the result by 80, which is the approximate average number of heartbeats per minute for a person throughout their lifetime. Make sure that the program gives valid results, even for a senior citizen.

4. A cattle feed company has two grades of feed, A and B. Feed A costs $2 per 100 pounds and feed B costs $3 per 100 pounds. Ranchers can order a mixture of feeds A and B. Write a program that calculates the charge for a feed order. The program should ask the user to enter the number of hundreds of pounds of feed A ordered and the number of hundreds of pounds of feed B ordered. The program should display the amount of each type of feed ordered and its cost, and the total cost of the order.

5. A baseball stadium has three types of seats. Bleacher seats cost $3 each, reserved seats cost $8 each, and box seats cost $12 each. Write a program that calculates the total revenue from gate receipts at the ballpark (that is, the total amount received by selling seats). The program should ask the user to enter the number of bleacher seats sold, the number of reserved seats sold, and the number of box seats sold. The program should display the total amount of revenue from the gate receipts.

6. Your city's Parking Violation Bureau wants you to write a program to compute fines for parking violations. There are four types of violations: type A carries a fine of $10, type B carries a fine of $20, type C carries a fine of $30, and type D carries a fine of $50. The program should ask for the number of type A violations, the number of type B violations, and so on. The program should display the total fine for each individual.

Chapter Review

Terminology

Define each of the following terms.

flowchart	program development cycle
pseudocode	run-time error
syntax error	logic error
program listing	faulty coding
source program	comment
machine language	function
high-level language	keyword
machine independence	semicolon
compiler	case sensitive
object program	user-defined function
external reference	standard library function
linker	string
executable code	output stream

```
cout                              prompt
insertion operator ( << )         cin
escape sequence                   extraction operator ( >> )
new-line character                input buffer
preprocessor directive            assignment operator
header file                       integer constant
system header file                arithmetic operator
iostream.h                        const
using namespace std;              setw()
identifier                        iomanip.h
variable                          unsigned
declaration                       short
data type                         long
int                               unsigned short
value of a variable               unsigned long
garbage                           endl
```

Summary

- Every C++ program contains a function `main()` that controls execution of the program.
- Every C++ statement must end in a semicolon (Note 1.1).
- Use the output stream `cout` and the insertion operator `<<` to display strings and variable values.
- Always code the preprocessor directive `#include <iostream.h>` in all your programs (Note 1.3).
- Always code the `using namespace std;` directive if your program conforms to the C++ standard.
- An identifier can consist of up to 31 characters (uppercase and lowercase letters, digits, and the underscore.) An identifier can neither begin with a digit nor can it be a keyword (Note 1.5).
- A variable is a named location in computer memory that stores a particular type of data.
- A variable declaration must begin with the variable's data type.
- The integer types are `int`, `unsigned`, `long`, `unsigned long`, `short`, and `unsigned short`.
- A nonzero integer constant cannot begin with the digit zero or contain a decimal point or a comma.
- Use `cin` and the extraction operator `>>` to obtain a datum from the input stream (the keyboard) and place it into a variable.
- The arithmetic operators are +, −, *, /, and %.
- The arithmetic operators follow the usual precedence rules (Note 1.7).
- Use `const` to declare defined constants.

- The `setw()` I/O manipulator determines the width of the field in which `cout` places the next data item. To use `setw()`, use the preprocessor directive `#include <iomanip.h>` (Note 1.8)

Review Exercises

1. Describe the steps in the program development cycle and the errors that can occur at each step.
2. How can you insert a comment in a C++ program?
3. What is a C++ program?
4. What is a keyword in C++?
5. What is the purpose of the word `int` before `main()`?
6. With what punctuation mark must each C++ statement end?
7. What is meant by saying that C++ is case sensitive?
8. What data stream can you use to output data? What operator should you use with that data stream?
9. What is the preprocessor and what is it used for? What is a preprocessor directive and how do you code one?
10. What is a header file and which one should you include in each of your C++ programs?
11. What is an identifier and what are the rules for naming an identifier?
12. What is a variable and how do you declare one?
13. What data stream can you use to input data? What operator should you use with that data stream?
14. What are the five basic arithmetic operators in C++?
15. What are the arithmetic operator precedence rules?
16. What is pseudocode and how is it useful in program development?
17. What is the purpose of the keyword `const`?
18. What is an I/O manipulator? What header file do you have to include to use one?
19. What are the integer data types and how do they differ?

Chapter

2

Real Numbers

Objectives

- To declare `float` and `double` variables.

- To use `cin` to input and `cout` to display nicely formatted decimal numbers.

- To solve problems involving decimal numbers.

- To use mixed-mode arithmetic expressions and type casts.

- To understand the value of a C++ expression.

- To use the compound assignment, increment, and decrement operators.

Besides integers, C++ also allows variables to store real numbers. Dollar and cents amounts, which are used in most business programs, are examples of real numbers. This chapter shows how to declare and use real numbers in a C++ program.

The C++ programming language has many operators. Chapter 1 discusses the basic arithmetic operators of addition, subtraction, multiplication, and division of integers. In this chapter, we extend the use of these operators to real numbers. We also discuss several additional arithmetic operators that enable the programmer to code some common types of statements more compactly.

2.1 Real Numbers

Real Number Variables and Constants

A **real,** or **floating point,** number is one that has a fractional part. That is, a floating point number is one that has a decimal point. There are two floating point data types in C++—`float` and `double`. The following declarations define the variable `fl` to be of type `float` and the variable `db` to be of type `double`.

```
float  fl;
double db;
```

The two floating point types differ in their **precision** (that is, the number of significant digits that each type stores) and in the amount of storage each type requires. For example, in Turbo C++ on an IBM PC, a variable of type `float` occupies four bytes and has a precision of 7 digits. A variable of type `double` occupies eight bytes and has a precision of 15 digits. On other computers, the precision and storage requirements may differ from those of IBM PCs.

The following are examples of valid **floating point constants.**

8.45

−1298.45678

+0.68

15.

Just as for integer constants, a floating point constant may be preceded by a + or − to show its sign. If you omit the sign, C++ considers the sign to be plus. Also, like integer constants, a floating point constant cannot contain a comma. However, a floating point constant must contain a decimal point, even if the decimal point is not followed by a digit as illustrated in the last constant listed.

The following are examples of invalid floating point constants.

3,620.78

195

The first number contains a comma and is therefore invalid. The second number does not contain a decimal point and so is not a floating point constant. However, the number is a valid integer constant.

The C++ compiler always stores floating point constants as type `double`. Therefore, on an IBM PC, a floating point constant can have up to 15 significant digits.

You can initialize a floating point variable in its declaration with the value of a floating point constant. For example,

```
float  fl =  3.14159;
double db = −0.0023156;
```

Floating point variables can appear in arithmetic statements in the same way as integer variables. For example, consider the following declarations and assignment.

```
double db1 = 3.14159,
       db2 = -83.01267,
       db3;

db3 = 2 * db1 + db2;
```

The assignment gives the value −76.72949 to the variable db3. The expression on the right of the assignment operator contains mixed data types. Before it carries out the arithmetic, the computer automatically converts the integer 2 appearing in the expression on the right of the assignment to a floating point 2.0. Then the computer multiplies the value of db1 by 2.0, which gives 6.28318. Finally, the computer adds this result to the value of db2, which gives −76.72949. The computer then assigns the result to db3. (See the discussions of Problems 2.2 and 2.3 for further information on mixed data types in arithmetic expressions.)

Input and Output of Real Numbers

To input a real number, use cin with a variable of type float or double. The user must enter a number (optionally preceded by a + or −) that can include a decimal point, but cannot include a comma. If the number the user enters does not contain a decimal point, for example 216, cin automatically converts the integer to the equivalent floating point number, 216.0.

Consider the following simple example. Suppose that a program contains the following declaration and code, and that the user enters 356.091 in response to the prompt.

```
double db;
cout << "\nEnter a floating point number: ";
cin >> db;
```

Suppose we now want to display the value of db. The cout statement

```
cout << "\nThe value of db is " << db;
```

displays the following.

```
The value of db is 356.091
```

Three Difficulties When Displaying Decimal Numbers With cout

Programming
Pitfalls

Sometimes cout does not display a number the way you might expect. For example, the cout statement

```
cout << 356.70;
```

displays the number as 356.7, without the trailing zero.

Another problem with `cout` is that it sometimes displays a number in scientific notation rather than decimal notation. For example, the `cout` statement

```
cout << 3456789.70 / 2;
```

Programming
Pitfalls

displays the result of the division as 1.72839e+06. This form of the answer would be inappropriate for the output of a business application. Instead, we would want the answer to display as 1728394.85.

Finally, we would also like to control the number of digits that display to the right of the decimal point. For example, if we calculate sales tax of 8.25% on an amount of 19.95, we would want `cout` to display the product 0.0825 * 19.95 to the nearest penny. However, the following `cout` displays the product as 1.64588.

Programming
Pitfalls

```
cout << 0.0825 * 19.95
```

The problems of loosing trailing zeros, the switch to scientific notation, and the control of the number of digits displayed to the right of the decimal point are interrelated. To solve them, we must use **I/O**(or Input/Output) **manipulators.** Recall from Chapter 1 that you can think of an I/O manipulator as an instruction to the `cout` stream to display numbers in a certain way. The manipulators we shall use are `setprecision()`, which sets the number of digits that display to the right of the decimal, and `setiosflags()`, which controls various settings for `cout`. We shall include the following `cout` statement at the beginning of `main()` in any program that displays dollar and cents amounts. To use the statement, you must include the header file `iomanip.h` using the preprocessor directive `#include <iomanip.h>`.

Programming
Pointers

```
cout << setprecision(2) // number of digits to right of decimal to 2
    << setiosflags(ios::fixed)     // display numbers in fixed form
    << setiosflags(ios::showpoint);        // print trailing zeros
```

The `setiosflags()` manipulator has a complicated syntax. In parentheses after the `setiosflags` manipulator name is the class name `ios`. We shall learn about classes in a later chapter. Right now, just follow the requirements of the syntax. The class name `ios` must be followed by two colons :: followed by what is called a **flag** name. The `fixed` flag tells the `cout` stream that floating point numbers are to be displayed in fixed point format as opposed to scientific format. The `showpoint` flag tells the `cout` stream to print trailing zeros. These settings remain in effect until they are changed by sending a different `setiosflags()` setting to `cout`.

When used in conjunction with `setiosflags(ios::fixed)`, the `setprecision(2)` manipulator sets the number of digits that will display to the right of the decimal point to two. The number is displayed rounded to two places. If we had coded `setprecision(3)`, then three digits would display to the right of the decimal point, appropriately rounded. Thus, the integer in parentheses after the `setprecision` name determines the number of digits that will display to the right of the decimal point. Whatever precision is set, it remains in effect until reset by sending another `setprecision()` message to the `cout` stream. [If you use `setprecision()` without using `setiosflags(ios::fixed)`, then `setprecision()` determines the total number of digits displayed, not just the number of digits to the right of the decimal.]

Now, consider the following code.

```
cout << setprecision(2)
        << setiosflags(ios::fixed)
        << setiosflags(ios::showpoint);

cout << 3456789.70 / 2 << endl;
cout << 0.0825 * 19.95 << endl;
cout << 356.70 << endl;
```

The output is:

```
1728394.85
1.65
356.70
```

Note that displaying the value of `db` to one or two decimal places does not affect the value stored in `db`. The actual value stored in `db` is still 356.091.

NOTE 2.1—DISPLAYING DOLLAR AND CENTS AMOUNTS

Include the following statement at the beginning of any program that displays dollar and cents amounts.

```
cout << setprecision(2)
        << setiosflags(ios::fixed)
        << setiosflags(ios::showpoint);
```

To use this statement, you must also include the header file `iomanip.h` with the following statement at the beginning of your program.

```
#include <iomanip.h>
```

Programming
Pointers

The precision and the `ios` flag settings stay in effect until they are reset. To change the precision, use `setprecision()` again with a different value. To reset either the `ios::fixed` or the `ios::showpoint` flag, you must send `resetios-flags(ios::fixed)` or `resetiosflags(ios::showpoint)` to `cout`.

Calculating Sales Tax—dem02-1.cpp

The following program illustrates the ideas we have discussed so far. A retailer wants to know how much an item's selling price will be after adding the sales tax. Assume that the sales tax rate is 8.25%. The program dem02-1.cpp uses floating point arithmetic to do the necessary calculations.

```
// dem02-1.cpp

// This program calculates the sales tax and price of an item.

#include <iostream.h>
#include <iomanip.h>

main()
{
  const double TAX_RATE = 0.0825;
  double base_price,            // The price of the item
         tax,                   // The tax on the item
         price;                 // The selling price (price + tax)

  //Set up output stream for currency output

  cout << setprecision(2)
       << setiosflags(ios::fixed)
       << setiosflags(ios::showpoint);

  cout << "\nEnter the price of the item: ";
  cin >> base_price;

  tax = base_price * TAX_RATE;
  price = base_price + tax;

  cout << "\nThe base price is" << setw(11) << base_price;
  cout << "\nThe tax is" << setw(18) << tax;
  cout << "\nThe price is" << setw(16) << price << endl;
}
```

Program Output

```
Enter the price of the item: 100.00

The base price is      100.00
The tax is               8.25
The price is           108.25
```

The sales tax rate of 8.25% as a decimal is 0.0825. The program uses const double to declare the defined constant TAX_RATE, whose value equals 0.0825.

The program requires three variables. The variable base_price stores the number input by the user. The variables tax and price store the amount of the sales tax and the total price of the item (base_price + tax).

Programming
Pointers

Since all three variables store dollar and cents amounts (that is, decimal numbers), we declare all three variables as type double. We use type double instead of type float for two reasons. First, a type double has more precision than a type float. Therefore, arithmetic with variables of type double is generally more accurate than

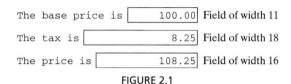

FIGURE 2.1

arithmetic with variables of type `float`. Second, most computers automatically convert floats to doubles, then do the arithmetic, and finally convert the result from type `double` back to type `float`. Using type `double` in the first place avoids these conversions.

Inputting the base price and doing the calculations are straightforward. Note the use of the defined constant `TAX_RATE` in the first assignment statement.

The `setw(11)` in the `cout` that displays the base price creates a field that can hold a number with as many as eight digits to the left of the decimal. (The decimal point and the two digits to the right of the decimal account for the other three positions in the field.) Therefore, a number as large as 99999999.99 can appear in the field. The `setw(18)` and `setw(16)` in the next two `cout` statements force the alignment of the decimal points of the three numbers. See Figure 2.1. Remember that if a number has more digits than the field width allows, `cout` displays the number in its entirety. In this case, the numbers may not align correctly when `cout` displays them. See Experiment 2. In Section 3.4, Definite Iteration, we show how to use `setw()` to arrange output in column form.

EXERCISES 2.1

In Exercises 1–10, find the value that the expression assigns to the variable on the left of the assignment operator. Work each problem independently of the others. Assume the following declarations.

```
double d1 =    3.167,
       d2 = -41.823,
       d3 =    0.2513,
       result;
```

1. result = 2.4 + 3.1 * d1;

2. result = d1 − (d2 − d3);

3. result = d2 / d1 + 4 * d3;

4. result = d1 * d2 * d3;

5. result = d1 * d1 * d1;

6. d1 = d1 + 2.089;

7. d1 = d2 − d3;

8. d2 = d2 * d2;

9. d2 = d1 * 4.53 + 47.1;

10. d3 = d3 − d3;

In Exercises 11–15, find exactly what each `cout` statement displays. Assume the following declarations and `cout` statement.

```
double d1 = 285.3451;
       d2 = -51.768465;
       d3 =   0.0036245;

cout << setprecision(2)
     << setiosflags(ios::fixed)
     << setiosflags(ios::showpoint);
```

11. `cout << d1 << d2;`

12. `cout << d1 << " " << d2;`

13. `cout << setw(10) << d1 << setw(10) << d2;`

14. `cout << setw(11) << d1 << setw(11) << d3;`

15. `cout << setprecision(4) << setw(11) << d1 << setw(11) << d3;`

EXPERIMENTS 2.1

For each experiment concerning dem02-1.cpp, start with a fresh copy and make the indicated changes.

1. Defining the sales tax rate as a defined constant limits the program dem02-1.cpp. Different localities have different sales tax rates even within the same state. Recode dem02-1.cpp so it prompts the user for the sales tax rate. Use this sales tax rate in the calculation of the tax.

2. In dem02-1.cpp, enter 950000000.00 in response to the prompt. What happens to the output? Recode the program so that if the user enters 950000000.00 in response to the prompt, the program vertically aligns the displayed numbers on the right. Compile and execute the resulting program.

3. Algebraically, what should the following program display? Compile and execute the program. What does the program display? Can you explain why?

```
#include <iostream.h>

main()
{
   cout << setprecision(8)
        << setiosflags(ios::fixed)
        << setiosflags(ios::showpoint);

   double db;
   db = 3.0 * (1.0 / 3.0);
   cout << "db = " << setw(10) << db;
}
```

4. Not all real numbers are representable on a computer because of the limited precision of floating point numbers. Compile and execute the following program.

```cpp
#include <iostream.h>

main()
{
   cout << setprecision(12)
        << setiosflags(ios::fixed)
        << setiosflags(ios::showpoint);

   float fl1 = 1.2345678,
         fl2 = 1.2345679;

   cout << "\nfl1 = " << setw(15) << fl1;
   cout << "\nfl2 = " << setw(15) << fl2;
}
```

What numbers are output? Can you explain why? What does the output tell you about the number of digits stored in a float type variable?

5. Code, compile, and execute a program similar to the one in Experiment 4 that will enable you to decide how many digits your computer stores in a variable of type `double`.

6. The following program illustrates many floating point number concepts that we discussed in this section.

```cpp
// This program demonstrates the use of variables of type
// float and of type double.

#include <iostream.h>

main()
{
   // Declaration and initialization of float and double type
   // variables.

   cout << setprecision(2)
        << setiosflags(ios::fixed)
        << setiosflags(ios::showpoint);

   float  fl = 123.4567,
          fl1;
   double db = -.0000000000078945,
          db1;

   cout << "\nfl = " << fl << " db = " << db;
   cout << "\nfl = " << setw(5) << fl << ", db = " << setw(5) << db;
```

```
cout << "\nfl = " << setw(10) << fl << ", db = " << setprecision(20)
     << setw(5) << db;

cout << "\nEnter a float: ";
cin >> fl1;

cout << "\nEnter a double: ";
cin >> db1;

cout << setprecision(5);
cout << "\nThe float you entered was " << fl1;
cout << "\nThe double you entered was " << db1;
}
```

Compile and execute this program on your computer. How do the `cout` statements display the values of `fl` and `db`?

7. By default, `cout` displays output right justified in each output field. You can control the type of justification `cout` uses by coding the `ios::left` and `ios::right` flags with `setioflags()`. Note that either of these flags causes the justification to stay in effect until it is changed by another call to `setiosflags()`. For example, the following code displays 3.14159 left justified in a field of width 10 and then displays 7.890 right justified in a field of width 10.

```
cout << setprecision(2)
     << setiosflags(ios::fixed)
     << setiosflags(ios::showpoint);
cout << setiosflags(ios::left);

cout << setw(10) << 3.14159 << endl;
cout << setiosflags(ios::right);
cout << setw(10) << 7.890;
```

Recode dem02-1.cpp and left justify all displayed output.

8. By default, `cout` does not show the plus sign when it displays positive numbers. Using the `ios::showpos` flag with `setiosflags()` causes `cout` to display positive numbers preceded by a plus sign. For example, the following code displays 3.14159 preceded by a plus sign in a field of width 10.

```
cout << setprecision(2)
     << setiosflags(ios::fixed)
     << setiosflags(ios::showpoint);
cout << setiosflags(ios::showpos);

cout << setw(10) << 3.14159 << endl;
```

Recode dem02-1.cpp with all numbers displayed with a plus sign. Note that to reset the `ios::showpos` flag you must send `resetiosflags(ios::showpos)` to `cout`.

1. Write a program that asks the user to enter the prices of two items. The program should then apply a 7.5% discount to the sum of the prices. The program should display the two prices, the sum of the two prices, the discount (7.5% of the sum of the prices) and the discounted price (the sum of the prices minus the discount).

2. Write a program that asks the user to enter a student's grades on four exams. The program should display the four grades and the average of the four grades, rounded to the nearest tenth.

3. The State Highway Traffic Violations Bureau wants you to write a program to compute the amount of a moving violation. The program should prompt the user to enter the illegal speed in miles per hour at which the person was driving. Calculate the fine as follows: $50 plus $5 for each mile per hour over the legal limit of 55.

4. Write a program that asks the user to enter a student's midterm and final exam scores. The program should display the midterm and final exam scores and the student's final grade. Compute the final grade by taking the sum of 40% of the midterm exam score and 60% of the final exam score.

5. A bank teller needs a program to total the amount of money in his coin tray. Write a program that asks the user to enter the number of each type of U.S. coin (half dollars, quarters, nickels, dimes, and pennies) and that displays the total value of the coins in dollars and cents.

6. An account executive must keep track of her expenses on a business trip. Write a program that totals the executive's expenses. The program should ask the user to enter the number of miles driven (calculate this expense by multiplying the number of miles driven by 0.30, that is 30 cents per mile), the amount spent on highway tolls and parking, the amount spent on meals, the amount spent on lodging, and the amount spent on entertainment.

2.2 Solving Problems With Real Numbers

In this section we state and solve three problems that involve real numbers. In doing so, we discuss how C++ evaluates expressions that contain variables of different data types. We also discuss how to alter the data type of a constant or variable by using a type cast.

Simulating a Cash Register—Problem 2.1

The C++-Side Restaurant wants you to write a program that simulates a simple cash register. The program should ask the user to enter the price of the meal. The program should calculate the sales tax (8.25% of the meal price) and add it to the price to obtain the total price, which it should display for the user. The program is then to ask for the amount tendered, (the amount the customer gives to pay the bill). After the user enters the amount tendered, the program should display the amount tendered, the total price of the meal, and the change due.

Program Design

The program design follows the steps outlined in the statement of the problem. Following is a pseudocode solution to the problem.

Pseudocode for Problem 2.1

> Obtain the meal price.
> Calculate the tax and total price of the meal.
> Display the price, tax, and total.
> Obtain the amount tendered.
> Calculate the change.
> Display the amount tendered, total price, and change due.

This program requires five variables. Since the variables store dollar and cents amounts, they will all be floating point variables. As we did in dem02-1.cpp, all the variables will be declared as type `double`. We need the variable `meal_price` to store the price of the meal. The variables `sales_tax` and `total` store the amount of the sales tax (8.25% of `meal_price`) and the total price of the meal (`meal_price + sales_tax`). Finally, the variable `amt_tendered` stores the amount the customer gives to pay for the meal and the variable `change` stores the change (`amt_tendered − total`) that the customer receives.

The Program prb02-1.cpp

Following is the program solution to Problem 3.1.

```cpp
// prb02-1.cpp
// This program simulates a simple cash register.

#include <iostream.h>
#include <iomanip.h>

using namespace std;

int main()
{
   const double SALES_TAX_RATE = 0.0825;

   double meal_price,     // Price of meal entered by user
         sales_tax,      // Amount of sales tax
         total,          // Total bill: meal_price + sales_tax
         amt_tendered,   // Amount received from customer
         change;         // Change: amt_tendered − total

   // Set up output stream for currency output
   cout << setprecision(2)
        << setiosflags(ios::fixed)
        << setiosflags(ios::showpoint);
```

```cpp
    // Display banner and obtain price
    cout << "\n\n*** C++-Side Restaurant *** \n\n";
    cout << "\nEnter the price of the meal: $";
    cin >> meal_price;
    cout << "\n";

    // Calculate tax and total price
    sales_tax = meal_price * SALES_TAX_RATE;
    total = meal_price + sales_tax;

    // Display price tax and total
    cout << "\nPrice of Meal: " << setw(6) << meal_price;
    cout << "\nSales Tax: " << setw(10) << sales_tax;
    cout << "\n--------------------";
    cout << "\nTotal Amount: " << setw(7) << total;

    // Obtain amount tendered
    cout << "\n\n\nEnter amount tendered: $";
    cin >> amt_tendered;
    cout << "\n";

    // Calculate change
    change = amt_tendered - total;

    // Display amounts and change
    cout << "\nAmount Tendered: $" << setw(7) << amt_tendered;
    cout << "\nTotal Amount:    $" << setw(7) << total;
    cout << "\n---------------------";
    cout << "\nChange:          $" << setw(7) << change;

    // Print closing banner
    cout << "\n\n*** Thank You ***\n\n";

    return 0;
}
```

Program Output

```
*** C++-Side Restaurant ***


Enter the price of the meal: $52.95


Price of Meal:   52.95
Sales Tax:        4.37
--------------------
Total Amount:    57.32
```

```
Enter amount tendered: $70.00



Amount Tendered: $ 70.00
Total Amount:    $ 57.32
- - - - - - - - - - - - - - - - - - - - - -
Change:          $ 12.68

*** Thank You ***
```

Discussion of prb02-1.cpp

The program code closely follows the pseudocode for the problem. First, the program displays an opening banner giving the name of the restaurant. Next, it prompts the user to enter the amount of the meal and then calculates the sales tax and the total amount of the meal. Then, the program prompts the user to enter the amount tendered, calculates the amount of the change due, and displays the results. Finally, the program displays a closing banner. Note that the program uses the `setw()` manipulator to force decimal point alignment.

If prb02-1.cpp were to be used commercially, users would soon notice several serious flaws in the program. First, the program does not check the amounts input by the user to see if they are valid. For example, suppose the user enters 2w.75 for the meal price instead of 23.75. How would the program behave? It certainly would not give the correct total price. See Experiment 1. What would happen if the amount tendered was less than the total cost of the meal? See Experiment 2.

Programming
Pointers

The necessity of validating input data makes even simple problems a good deal more challenging. As we work through the book, we will discuss some data validation techniques. You must program defensively when writing a program that will be used by others. Assume the user will make mistakes at every opportunity. Try to design your program so that it can recover from these mistakes.

Averaging Quiz Grades—Problem 2.2

Your instructor wants you to write a program that calculates the average of three quiz grades you have taken this semester. Write a program that prompts the user for three integer quiz grades, calculates the average of the three grades, and displays the average to the nearest tenth.

Program Design—Mixed Types and Type Casts

At first, calculating an average appears to be a simple problem. Following is a pseudocode solution.

Pseudocode for Problem 2.2

> Obtain the three quiz grades.
> Calculate the quiz average.
> Display the quiz average.

The difficulty in the program lies in the types of variables it uses. The problem statement requires that each quiz grade be an integer and that the program display the average as a real number accurate to the nearest tenth. Therefore, the quiz grades should be of type `int` and the average of type `double`. Suppose we code the following declarations.

```
int    quiz1,       // Quiz 1 grade
       quiz2,       // Quiz 2 grade
       quiz3;       // Quiz 3 grade
double average;     // Average of the three quiz grades
```

After obtaining the values of the quiz grades from the user, suppose the program calculates the average by the following assignment.

```
average = (quiz1 + quiz2 + quiz3) / 3;
```

The parentheses around the sum of the quiz grades are necessary because the program must add the quiz grades before dividing the sum by three. If the parentheses were not present, `quiz1 + quiz2 + quiz3 / 3`, by the precedence rules, `quiz3` would be divided by three and then the values of `quiz1` and `quiz2` would be added to that result.

If the sum of the three quiz grades is not divisible by three, the assignment might not place the correct value into `average`. The three variables `quiz1`, `quiz2`, and `quiz3`, and the constant that the sum is divided by, 3, are of type `int`. Therefore, the computer does integer arithmetic when evaluating the right side of the assignment. The computer discards any fractional part that results from the division before making the assignment to `average`. If the user enters 78, 91, and 82 in response to the prompts, the actual average will be $(78 + 91 + 82) / 3 = 251 / 3 = 83.66666$. However, in integer arithmetic, the result of $251 / 3$ is the quotient 83. The remainder is discarded. Therefore, the computer assigns the result of the integer arithmetic, 83, to `average`. The specifications of the problem, however, require that this average be computed as 83.7, a decimal number rounded to the nearest tenth.

Programming
Pointers

To correct this problem, we must force the computer to do floating point arithmetic when evaluating the expression to the right of the assignment operator. There are two ways to do this. One way is to mix the data types that appear in the expression. We cannot directly change the data types of the quiz grades (we can change the type indirectly, as we shall see shortly.) However, we can change the data type of the constant that appears in the division. Suppose we recode the assignment as follows.

```
average = (quiz1 + quiz2 + quiz3) / 3.0;
```

Now, we have a **mixed-mode expression,** which is an expression containing mixed data types: an integer, namely the sum of the three quiz grades, divided by a floating point constant. The computer now carries out the arithmetic according to the rule in Note 2.2.

NOTE 2.2—DATA TYPE CONVERSIONS IN AN EXPRESSION

When an arithmetic expression contains numbers of type `int` or `long` and numbers of type `float` or `double`, C++ automatically converts all the numbers to type `double` before doing the arithmetic. The result, therefore, is of type `double`.

Because of the floating point constant 3.0 in the new expression, the computer automatically converts the sum of the quiz grades to a `double` before dividing the sum by 3.0. Then the computer assigns the result, which is of type `double`, to `average` with no loss of its fractional part. See Experiment 3.

Programming
Pointers

The second way to force the computer to do floating point arithmetic in the arithmetic expression is to use a **type cast.** A type cast is one of C++'s data types followed by an expression enclosed in parentheses. A type cast changes the data type of the value of the expression in parentheses to the type specified. If we declare

```
int i = 5;
```

then `double(i)` is the value of i converted to the `double` 5.0.

To correct the assignment involving the average, we could code the following.

```
average = double(quiz1 + quiz2 + quiz3) / 3;
```

The cast `double()` converts the value of the sum of the quiz grades to the equivalent floating point number before the computer divides this value by the integer constant 3. We now have an expression that contains mixed types, so Note 2.2 applies. The computer converts the integer constant 3 to the equivalent double 3.0 and then carries out the arithmetic.

We also can type cast a constant. The assignment to average could be coded as follows.

```
average = (quiz1 + quiz2 + quiz3) / double(3);
```

This is equivalent to the first way in which we corrected this problem. See Experiment 4. Type casting has several other important applications, which we shall encounter later.

Another way to solve the truncation problem is to disregard the requirement that the quiz grades be integers. We could declare the three quiz grade variables to be of type `double`. In this way, the `cin` statements would convert the integers entered by the user to the equivalent floating point numbers. According to Note 2.2, the computer would carry out the arithmetic in the following assignment statement in floating point.

```
average = (quiz1 + quiz2 + quiz3) / 3;
```

Although this solution works (see Experiment 5), it is not completely acceptable. The solution does not conform to the specifications of the problem, which require the grades to be integers. It is very important to conform to a problem's specifications unless you have a compelling reason not to do so. Deviating from a problem's specifications often leads programmers to solve a related, but wrong, problem. If you want to change a problem's specifications, get permission to do so from the person who gave you the problem.

The Program prb02-2.cpp

Following is the program code that solves Problem 2.2. We use the method of type casting the sum of the quiz grades to force floating point arithmetic. Note that we include statements at the beginning of main() to cause the average to be displayed to the nearest tenth.

```
// prb02-2.cpp

// This program calculates the average of three quiz grades
// entered by the user.

#include <iostream.h>
#include <iomanip.h>

using namespace std;

int main()
{
   int quiz1,            // Quiz 1 grade
       quiz2,            // Quiz 2 grade
       quiz3;            // Quiz 3 grade
   double average;       // Average of the three quize grades

   // Setup output stream for one decimal place

   cout << setprecision(1)
        << setiosflags(ios::fixed)
        << setiosflags(ios::showpoint);

   cout << "\nEnter the grade for Quiz 1: ";
   cin >> quiz1;
   cout << "\nEnter the grade for Quiz 2: ";
   cin >> quiz2;
   cout << "\nEnter the grade for Quiz 3: ";
   cin >> quiz3;

   // The type cast double() is required to convert the sum of the
   // quiz grades, which is an integer, to a floating point. Failure
```

```
// to convert the expression on the right of the assignment would
// result in the average being truncated to an integer.

average = double (quiz1 + quiz2 + quiz3) / 3;

cout << "\nThe average of the three quizzes is " << average << endl;

return 0;
}
```

Program Output

```
Enter the grade for Quiz 1: 84
Enter the grade for Quiz 2: 78
Enter the grade for Quiz 3: 95
The average of the three quizzes is 85.7
```

Metric Conversion—Problem 2.3

Many people have trouble thinking in terms of metric units. Write a program that converts a distance in miles and feet, entered as integers, to the equivalent distance in kilometers and meters. One mile equals 1.60935 kilometers. One foot equals 0.30480 meters. The program should ask the user to enter the number of miles and the number of feet to convert. The program should display the equivalent number of kilometers and meters as integers.

The solution to the preceding problem involves some complicated arithmetic with integers and floating point numbers. It also illustrates expressions that have mixed data types and data conversions across the assignment operator.

Program Design

The design of this program is simple, as the following pseudocode illustrates.

Pseudocode for Problem 2.3.

> Obtain the number of miles and feet from the user.
> Convert miles and feet to kilometers and meters.
> Display the equivalent number of kilometers and meters.

The difficult part of this problem is the arithmetic it requires. The integer variables `miles`, `feet`, `kilometers`, and `meters` will store the corresponding distances. Two `cin` statements will input values for the variables `miles` and `feet`. The problem is how to convert these to the equivalent number of kilometers and meters.

The strategy is first to convert the total distance to the equivalent number of meters. Then, convert the number of meters to kilometers and meters. To show how to do this, let's consider an example.

Suppose the user enters 2 for the number of miles and 1000 for the number of feet. To convert the number of feet to meters, multiply the value of `feet` (1000) by the number of meters per foot, 0.30480. In our example this gives 304.80. To convert the number of miles to meters, multiply the value of `miles` by the number of meters per mile. (The number of meters per mile is $1.60935 \times 1000 = 1609.35$.) In our example this gives 2 * 1609.35 = 3218.7. Now, add these two results and obtain the total distance in meters. This gives 3218.7 + 304.80 = 3523.50.

We store the answer to the previous calculation in the variable `total_meters`, which is of type `double`. The following assignment statement incorporates the calculations of the previous paragraph.

```
total_meters = miles * 1609.35 + feet * 0.30480;
```

Thus the value of `total_meters` is 3523.50.

Now convert this number of meters to kilometers and meters. To convert from meters to kilometers, divide the number of meters by 1000. In our example, the result is 3523.50/1000 = 3.52350 kilometers. We store this result in the variable `total_kilometers`, which is of type `double`. The following assignment statement does this calculation.

```
total_kilometers = total_meters / 1000;
```

Now convert the distance in kilometers, 3.52350 in our example, to the equivalent number of integer kilometers and meters. To do this, we take advantage of C++'s ability to convert types across the assignment operator.

When the data type of the value of the right side of an assignment differs from the data type of the variable on the left of the assignment, C++ tries to convert the right side's value to the type of the variable on the left. For example, suppose the following declarations.

```
int       i1 = 17,
          i2 = 5,
          i3;
double    d1 = 9.74,
          d2;
```

The assignment,

```
d2 = i1 + i2;
```

results in the `double` 22.0 being assigned to `d2`. The value of the right side is the integer 22. When this is assigned to the `double` `d2`, C++ converts the integer 22 to the equivalent `double` 22.0.

The assignment,

```
i3 = d1;
```

results in the integer 9 being assigned to `i3`. The value of the right side is the `double` 9.74. When this is assigned to the integer `i3`, C++ converts 9.74 into an integer. C++ does this by truncating the `double` to the integer 9.

NOTE 2.3—DATA TYPE CONVERSIONS ACROSS AN ASSIGNMENT

In arithmetic assignments, when the data type of the right side differs from the data type of the left side, C++ converts the value of the right side to the data type of the variable on the left side.

Recall that the variable `kilometers` is of type `int`. By Note 2.3, the assignment

```
kilometers = total_kilometers;
```

causes the computer to truncate the fractional part of `total_kilometers` before it assigns the equivalent integer to the variable `kilometers`. Thus, the assignment gives `kilometers` the value 3.

Now convert the fractional part of `total_kilometers` to the equivalent number of meters. To get rid of the integer part of `total_kilometers`, subtract the value of `kilometers` from `total_kilometers`. This gives 3.52350 − 3 = 0.52350 kilometers. Multiplying this result by 1000 gives the equivalent number of meters: 0.52350 × 1000 = 523.50 meters. To truncate the fractional part of this answer, assign it to a variable of type `int`. Experiment 6 shows how to round this answer to the nearest meter.

The following assignment statement gives the variable `meters` the value 523.

```
meters = (total_kilometers - kilometers) * 1000;
```

Thus, a distance of 2 miles, 1000 feet is equivalent to approximately 3 kilometers, 523 meters.

The Program prb02-3.cpp

Following is the program code that solves Problem 2.3. The program uses the formulas we developed in the previous subsection. Defined constants represent the conversion factors.

```
// prb02-3.cpp

#include <iostream.h>

using namespace std;

int main()
{
  const double M_PER_MILE = 1609.35;
  const double M_PER_FOOT = 0.30480;

  int  miles,
       feet,
       kilometers,
       meters;
  double total_meters,
       total_kilometers;

  // Obtain data from user

  cout << "\nEnter the number of miles: ";
  cin >> miles;
  cout << "\nEnter the number of feet: ";
  cin >> feet;

  // Convert everything to meters
  total_meters = miles * M_PER_MILE + feet * M_PER_FOOT;

  // Calculate the number of kilometers
  total_kilometers = total_meters / 1000;
  kilometers = total_kilometers;             // truncates to intger

  // Convert decimal part of total_kilometers to meters
  meters = (total_kilometers - kilometers) * 1000;

  // Display results
  cout << "\n\nThe distance is " << kilometers << " kilometers, "
       << meters << " meters.";

  return 0;
}
```

Program Output

```
Enter the number of miles: 2

Enter the number of feet: 1000


The distance is 3 kilometers, 523 meters.
```

EXERCISES 2.2

Use the following declarations in Exercises 1–6. Do each exercise independently of the others. In each case, find the value that the expression assigns to the variable on the left of the assignment operator.

```
int    i = 5,
       j = 3,
       k;
double x = 8.95,
       y = 15.4,
       z;
```

1. `k = y * x;`

2. `k = int(y) * int(x);`

3. `k = i * j / 2;`

4. `z = i * j / 2;`

5. `z = double(i * j / 2);`

6. `z = double(i) * j / 2;`

EXPERIMENTS 2.2

1. Compile and execute prb02-1.cpp. Enter 2w.75 in response to the first prompt. What happens?

2. Compile and execute prb02-1.cpp. Enter 23.75 for the price of the meal and 20.00 for the amount tendered. What happens?

3. Change the assignment statement in prb02-2.cpp to the following.

```
average = (quiz1 + quiz2 + quiz3) / 3.0;
```

Compile and execute the resulting program, entering 70, 94, and 87 as the three quiz grades. Does the program run correctly?

4. Change the assignment statement in prb02-2.cpp to the following.

```
average = (quiz1 + quiz2 + quiz3) / double(3);
```

Compile and execute the resulting program, entering 70, 94, and 87 as the three quiz grades. Does the program run correctly?

5. Change prb02-2.cpp by declaring all variables to be of type `double`. Compile and execute the resulting program, entering 70, 94, and 87 as the three quiz grades. Does the program run correctly?

6. The last assignment statement in prb02-3.cpp truncates the number of meters. Recode prb02-3.cpp so that the program rounds rather than truncates the number of meters. To do this, add 0.5 to the value appearing on the right of the assignment. Compile and execute the resulting program, inputting 2 miles and 1000 feet as the distance to convert. Does the program properly round the number of meters to 524? If so, explain why adding 0.5 works.

PROGRAMMING PROBLEMS 2.2

1. Write a program that asks the user to enter the weight of a box of cereal to the nearest tenth of an ounce. The program should then display the equivalent weight of the box measured to the nearest tenth of a gram. One ounce is equivalent to 28.349527 grams.

2. Write a program that asks the user to enter his or her weight in pounds. The program should display the person's weight in kilograms. One pound equals 0.453592 kilograms.

3. If you invest P dollars, the principal, for t years in an account that earns simple interest at the annual interest rate of r, then the formula $I = P*r*t$ gives the total interest I that the investment earns. The total amount A in the account after t years is the principal plus the interest, or $A = P + I = P + P*r*t$. Write a program that asks the user to enter the principal, the interest rate as a percent (for example, 7.5), and the number of years at interest. The program should display the interest and the total amount in the account after the given number of years. Be sure to have the program convert the percent entered to the corresponding decimal before using it in the calculations.

4. Write a program that calculates the miles per gallon that the user gets on her car during a vacation trip. The program should ask the user to enter the number of miles traveled and the number of gallons of fuel consumed. The program should display the number of miles per gallon achieved on the trip.

5. Some self-service gas stations require that you pay for the gas before you pump it. If you want to fill your tank, you must estimate the cost of the amount of gas that you require. Suppose you know how many miles per gallon (mpg) your car gets on average and the number of miles (miles) you have traveled since your last fill-up. Then miles/mpg equals the number of gallons consumed and, therefore, the number of gallons you require for a fill-up. Multiply this number by the price per gallon to obtain the estimate for the cost of filling up your gas tank. Write a program that calculates the cost of the gas required to fill your tank. The program should ask the user to enter the miles per gallon the car gets on average, the number of miles traveled since the last fill-up, and the price per gallon of gasoline. The program should display the cost of filling up the tank.

6. Write a program that converts pounds and ounces to kilograms and grams. One pound is 0.453592 kilograms or 453.592 grams. One ounce is 28.349527 grams. The program should ask the user to enter the number of pounds and ounces. The program should display the equivalent number of kilograms and grams. (Hint: Convert everything to grams first.)

2.3 More On Arithmetic

The Value of an Expression

Note 2.4 states a very important principle of the C++ language.

NOTE 2.4—EVERY EXPRESSION HAS A VALUE

Every expression in C++ has a numeric value.

The most basic application of Note 2.4 is that the expression on the right side of an assignment has a value. For example, suppose we have the following declaration and assignment statements.

```
int i1,
    i2,
    result;

i1 = 3;
i2 = 6;
result = i1 + 2 * i2;
```

The expression to the right of the assignment operator in the third assignment has the value 15, which the statement assigns to the variable `result`.

Note 2.4 also explains why an expression can appear in the argument list of a `cout` statement. For example, using the previous declarations, consider the following `cout` statement, which displays the value of the expression `i1 + 2 * i2`, namely 15.

```
cout << "\nThe value of result is " << i1 + 2 * i2;
```

An entire assignment is also an expression and consequently, by Note 2.4, has a value.

NOTE 2.5—THE VALUE OF AN ASSIGNMENT

The value of an assignment is the value assigned.

Therefore, the entire assignment `i1 = 3;` has the value 3. The assignment `i2 = 6` has the value 6. Note 2.5 allows us to code some odd-looking statements. For example, using the previous declarations, the following is a valid assignment statement.

```
result = (i1 = 9) + (i2 = 7);
```

The parentheses force the computer to make the assignment `i1 = 9` first. The value of this assignment, by Note 2.5, is 9. Then the computer makes the second assignment `i2 = 7`, which itself has a value of 7. Next, the computer adds the values of the two assignments and assigns 16 to the variable `result`.

Just because you can code such assignment statements does not mean that you should! Statements like the previous are not easy to understand so you should avoid coding them.

In the next section and in several other places in this book we will discuss several important applications of Notes 2.4 and 2.5.

Multiple Assignment Statements

It is sometimes necessary to assign the same value to two or more variables. For example, suppose that a program must initialize the variables `sum` and `count` to zero. We could do this in two assignments as follows.

```
sum = 0;
count = 0;
```

Another way to make the assignments is to use a **multiple assignment statement** such as the following, which places the value zero into both variables `sum` and `count`.

```
sum = count = 0;
```

Multiple assignments work because an assignment has a value (see Notes 2.4 and 2.5) and because of the right-to-left associativity of the assignment operator (see Table 1.3). In the multiple assignment statement

```
sum = count = 0;
```

the computer executes the right-most assignment first, which assigns 0 to `count`. By Note 2.5, the value of this assignment is the value assigned, namely 0. Therefore, the left-most assignment is equivalent to `sum = 0`. The net effect is to assign zero to both variables. See Figure 2.2.

You also can assign the same value to more than two variables in a multiple assignment statement. The following initializes the four integer variables `i`, `j`, `k`, and `h` to 3.

```
i = j = k = h = 3;
```

```
sum    =    (count = 0)
             \_______/
                 0        value of right assignment

sum    =         0        which is used in the left
                          assignment
```

FIGURE 2.2

The following program, dem02-2.cpp, illustrates multiple assignment statements.

```cpp
// dem02-2.cpp

// This program illustrates multiple assignment statements

#include <iostream.h>

using namespace std;

int main()
{
  int h = 17,
      i,
      j,
      k;

  i = j = k = h;

  cout << "\nh = " << h;
  cout << " i = " << i;
  cout << " j = " << j;
  cout << " k = " << k;

  return 0;
}
```

Program Output

```
h = 17   i = 17   j = 17   k = 17
```

The Compound Assignment Operators

Besides the basic arithmetic operators introduced in Chapter 1, C++ also has **compound assignment operators** available, which simplify writing some common arithmetic expressions. Table 2.1 lists four of the compound assignment operators and how to read them, which also explains their meanings.

In programming, it is common to increase the value of a variable by the value of another variable. For example, suppose that a problem requires increasing the value of

TABLE 2.1

Operator	Read As
+=	Is increased by
−=	Is decreased by
*=	Is multiplied by
/=	Is divided by

`balance` by the value of `deposit`. One way of coding this in C++, which is how a programmer would code this assignment in many other programming languages, is as follows.

```
balance = balance + deposit;
```

When executing this statement, the computer adds the value of `deposit` (say, 300.00) to the current value of `balance` (say, 545.50) and assigns the result (845.50) to the variable `balance`.

An equivalent way of coding the previous assignment using the compound assignment operator += is as follows.

```
balance += deposit;
```

which we read as "`balance` is increased by `deposit`."

If a problem requires decreasing the `balance` in an account by the value of `withdrawal`, the corresponding assignment in a C++ program could be

```
balance = balance - withdrawal;
```

Equivalently, using the compound assignment operator $-=$, we could code the assignment as

```
balance -= withdrawal;
```

which we read as "`balance` is decreased by `withdrawal`". Thus, if the value of `balance` is 845.50 and the value of `withdrawal` is 200.00, the previous compound assignment gives the value 645.50 to `balance`.

To replace a number by its square, we could code the statement

```
num = num * num;
```

Alternatively, we could use the compound assignment operator *= and code the statement as follows.

```
num *= num;
```

which we read as "num is multiplied by num". If the value of `num` is 7.5 before the assignment, its value is 56.25 after the assignment.

If we must replace the value of `price` by half its original value, we could code

```
price = price / 2.0;
```

Instead, we could use the compound assignment operator /= and code

```
price /= 2.0;
```

which we read as "`price` is divided by 2.0". If the value of `price` is 104.50 before the assignment, then its value is 52.25 after the assignment.

The following program, dem02-3.cpp, illustrates the compound assignment operators.

```cpp
// dem02-3.cpp

// This program illustrates the compound assignment operators

#include <iostream.h>
#include <iomanip.h>

using namespace std;

int main()
{
  double balance    = 545.50,
         deposit    = 300.00,
         withdrawal = 200.00,
         num        =   7.5,
         price      = 104.50;

  cout << setprecision(2)
       << setiosflags(ios::fixed)
       << setiosflags(ios::showpoint);

  balance += deposit;
  cout << "\nThe value of balance is " << balance;

  balance -= withdrawal;
  cout << "\nThe value of balance is " << balance;

  num *= num;
  cout << "\nThe value of num is " << num;
  price /= 2.0;
  cout << "\nThe value of price is " << price;

  return 0;
}
```

Program Output

```
The value of balance is 845.50
The value of balance is 645.50
The value of num is 56.25
The value of price is 52.25
```

Assignment and all the compound assignment operators must take their place in the operator precedence rules. The compound assignment operators have the same

TABLE 2.2

Operators	Associativity
( )	Left to right (insideout)
+ (unary) − (unary) ++ −−	Right to left
* / %	Left to right
+ −	Left to right
= += −= *= /=	Right to left

precedence as the simple assignment operator =, which is lower than that of all the arithmetic operators. In addition, *all assignment operators associate from right to left*. Thus, if there are more than one assignment operators in an expression, the computer executes them from right to left. The operator precedence table, Table 2.2, summarizes these rules. We shall discuss the ++ and −− operators in the next section.

The low precedence of assignment makes an assigment work the way we expect. For example, in the assignment

```
result = i1 + 2 * i2;
```

the computer first evaluates the value of the right side of the assignment before giving this value to the variable `result`. The computer executes the assignment last because assignment has a lower precedence than the arithmetic operators.

Increment and Decrement Operators

Two common assignments in programming increase the value of a variable by one and decrease the value of a variable by one. We can easily write statements to do either of these tasks with the operators we have learned so far. To increase the value of the variable `count` by one, we could code the following.

```
count = count + 1;
```

To decrease the value of the variable `limit` by one we could code the following.

```
limit = limit − 1;
```

We could even use the compound assignment operators for these assignments as follows.

```
count += 1;
limit −= 1;
```

The C++ language, however, has still another way of coding these assignments using the **increment operator (++),** and the **decrement operator (−−),** as follows.

```
++count;
−−limit;
```

Read the statement ++count as "count is increased by one" or "increment count," the amount of the increment is understood to be one. Read the statement −−limit as "limit is decreased by one" or "decrement limit," the amount of the decrement is understood to be one.

The operators ++ and −− are **unary operators** because each operates on only one item. We can code the ++ operator either before the variable name, in which case it is a **preincrement,** or after the variable name, in which case it is a **postincrement.** Similarly, coded before the variable name, −− is a **predecrement.** Coded after the variable name, −− is a **postdecrement.** Thus, we can increase count by one and decrease limit by one by the following statements.

```
count++;
 limit--;
```

Is there a difference between preincrementing and postincrementing a variable, and between predecrementing and postdecrementing a variable? Note 2.6 gives the answer to this question.

NOTE 2.6—RULES FOR EVALUATING ++ AND −−

The following rules apply to pre- and postincrementing and decrementing.

1. If the value produced by ++ or −− is not used in an expression, it *does not matter* whether it is a preincrement (predecrement) or a postincrement (or postdecrement).

2. If the value produced by ++ or −− is used in an expression, it *does matter* whether the ++ or −− is before or after the variable name.

   (a) When ++ (or −−) is used *before* the variable name, the computer first increments (or decrements) the value of the variable and then uses this new value to evaluate the expression.

   (b) When ++ (or −−) is used *after* the variable name, the computer uses the current value of the variable to evaluate the expression and then increments (or decrements) the variable.

When it does not matter whether we use pre- or postincrement or decrement, we shall prefer to preincrement and predecrement. Placing the operator before the variable name, when possible, makes the operator more noticeable.

Rule 2 of Note 2.6 is a consequence of Note 2.4, namely every expression has a value. Assume that j is an int variable. The expressions ++j and j++ have values. The value of the expression ++j is the value of j *after* adding one to the value of j. On the other hand, the value of the expression j++ is the value of j *before* the computer increases it by one. Likewise, the value of the expression −−j is the value of j *after* subtracting one from j. The value of j−− is the value of j *before* subtracting one from j.

The program dem02-4.cpp illustrates the second part of Note 2.6.

```cpp
// dem02-4.cpp

// This program illustrates the difference between predecrement
// and postdecrement.

#include <iostream.h>

using namespace std;

int main()
{
  int i,
      j;

  i = 7;                        // Give i an initial value
  j = 4 + --i;
  cout << "\nPredecrementing i yields i = " << i << " and j = " << j;

  i = 7;                        // Reinitialize i to 7
  j = 4 + i--;
  cout << "\nPostdecrementing i yields i = " << i << " and j = " << j;

  return 0;
}
```

Program Output

```
Predecrementing i yields i = 6 and j = 10
Postdecrementing i yields i = 6 and j = 11
```

To explain the first line of the program's output, consider the statements

```cpp
i = 7;
j = 4 + --i;
```

The value of the expression $--i$ is the value of i after decreasing it by one. Therefore, the program uses 6 in the addition, which results in 10 being assigned to j.

To explain the second line of the program's output, consider the statements

```cpp
i = 7;
j = 4 + i--;
```

The value of the expression $i--$ is the value of i before the computer decreases it by one. Therefore, the program uses 7 in the addition, which results in 11 being assigned to j.

TABLE 2.3

	Expression	
	`j = 4 + --i`	`j = 4 + i--`
Initial value of `i` is 7		
Value of `i` used	6	7
Value assigned to `j`	10	11
Final value of `i`	6	6

Table 2.3 summarizes the assignments of dem02-4.cpp.

The operators ++ and −− are unary operators and have the same precedence as the other unary operators, as shown in Table 2.2. In the chapters that follow, we shall make frequent use of the compound assignment operators and the increment and decrement operators.

EXERCISES 2.3

Use the following declarations in Exercises 1–6. Work each exercise independently of the others. State the values of each variable involved after the computer executes each statement.

```
int i = 6,
    j = 3,
    k = -2,
    h,
    m;
```

1. `i += 3;`

2. `k *= 4;`

3. `k -= i;`

4. `j /= 2;`

5. `i += j + 4;`

6. `i -= j -= 1;`

Use the following declarations in Exercises 7–13. Work each exercise independently of the others. State the values of each variable involved after the computer executes each statement.

```
int i = 6,
    j = 3,
    k = -2,
    h,
    m;
```

7. `++j;`

8. k++;

9. h = j-- + i;

10. h = --j + i;

11. h = --j + ++i;

12. h = j-- + ++i;

13. h = ++i;
  m = i++;

In Exercises 14–17, rewrite the given statement using the increment, decrement, or a compound assignment operator.

14. i = i - 3;

15. j = j * i;

16. k = k + 9;

17. i = i / j;

In Exercises 18–19, replace the given statements by a single assignment that uses the increment, decrement, or a compound assignment operator.

18. i = i + 1;
  h = j + 2 * i;

19. i = j / 3 - k;
  k = k - 1;

EXPERIMENTS 2.3

1. Code, compile, and execute a short program that determines how your compiler interprets the expression i+++j. Initialize i to 2 and j to 3. Does the compiler interpret it as i++ + j or as i + ++j?

2. Code, compile, and execute a short program that determines what value your compiler gives the expression ++i + i++ after executing a statement that initializes i to 1. What value does i have after the computer evaluates the expression?

3. Compile and execute the following program. Try to determine the value that the program will display before you execute the program. The value that the program displays depends on the compiler you use. Why does your compiler give the answer it does?

```
#include <iostream.h>

using namespace std;

int main()
{
  int i = 7;
```

```
i = i++ + 1;

cout << "\ni = " << i;

return 0;
}
```

PROGRAMMING PROBLEMS 2.3

1. Write a program that asks the user to enter the dollar amount of the opening balance of an account. Then the program should ask the user to enter the dollar amount of deposits to the account. Use the += operator to add this amount to the balance. Next, ask the user to enter the dollar amount of withdrawals from the account during the last month. Use the −= operator to subtract this from the balance. The program should then display the closing balance in the account.

2. Write a program that asks the user to enter a student's grades on four exams. The program should display the four grades and the average of the four grades, rounded to the nearest tenth. To add the grades, use a variable called total_grade, which you should initialize to zero. As the program prompts for and obtains each grade, add the grade to total_grade using the += operator.

3. A bank teller needs a program to total the amount of money in his coin tray. Write a program that asks the user to enter the number of each type of U.S. coin (half dollars, quarters, nickels, dimes, and pennies) and that displays the total value of the coins in dollars and cents. Use the variable total_amount, which you should initialize to zero, to total the value of the coins. As the number of each type of coin is input by the user, use the += operator to increase the value of total_amount.

4. Write a program that asks the user to enter the price of an item and the sales tax rate as a percent. The program should display the total price of the item (price plus sales tax.) After obtaining the input from the user, the program should use the *= operator to calculate the total price of the item using the equivalent of the following formula.

```
price = price * (1 + sales_tax_rate)
```

5. An account executive must keep track of her expenses on a business trip. Write a program that totals the executive's expenses. Use the variable total_expenses, which you must initialize to zero, to store the executive's total expenses. The program should ask the user to enter the number of miles driven (calculate this expense by multiplying the number of miles driven by 0.30, that is 30 cents per mile), the amount spent on highway tolls and parking, the amount spent on meals, the amount spent on lodging, and the amount spent on entertainment. The program should use the += operator to add each expense to total_expenses as they are computed.

6. You want to estimate your income over the next three years. Write a program that asks the user to enter his or her annual salary and an estimated yearly rate of

growth for the salary as a percent. For example, the user's present salary might be $30,000 per year and she may estimate a rate of growth of 6% per year for the next three years. The program should display the estimated salary for each of the next three years. Be sure to change the entered rate of growth to the corresponding decimal. Use the += operator to increment the salary.

7. Write a program to compute telephone bills for the local telephone company. Each customer has a base charge of $12.95 per month and gets charged extra for each local call and each long distance call. The program should prompt the user for the number of local calls made during the month. The charge for each local call is $0.10. Use the += operator to add the cost of the local calls to the total bill. Then the program should prompt the user for the total charge for long distance calls made during the month. Use the += operator to add the long distance charges to the total bill. Finally, the program should calculate the tax on the total bill. The tax rate is 8.72%. Use the *= operator to add the tax to the total bill by multiplying the total bill by 1.0872.

Chapter Review

Terminology

Define the following terms.

real number	resetiosflags(ios::showpoint)
floating point number	mixed-mode expression
float	type cast
double	compound assignment operators (+=,
floating point constant	-=, *=, /=)
precision of a floating point number	increment operator (++)
setprecision()	decrement operator (--)
flag	unary operator
setiosflags(ios::fixed)	pre- and postincrement operators
setiosflags(ios::showpoint)	pre- and postdecrement operators
resetiosflags(ios::fixed)	

Summary

- The two floating point number types are float (7-digit precision) and double (15-digit precision.)
- Floating point constants must contain a decimal point but cannot contain a comma.
- Use the I/O manipulators setprecision() and setiosflags() to control the format of decimal numbers displayed using cout (Note 2.1).
- If integer and decimal types appear in the same arithmetic expression, C++ converts all numbers to type double before doing the arithmetic (Note 2.2).

- A type cast (a C++ data type followed by an expression in parentheses) changes the data type of the value of the enclosed expression to the specified type.
- When the data type of the right side of an assignment differs from the data type of the variable on the left side, C++ converts the value of the right side to the data type of the variable on the left side (Note 2.3).
- Every expression in C++ has a numeric value (Note 2.4). The value of an assignment is the value assigned (Note 2.5).
- The compound assignment operators +=, −=, *=, /=, combine assignment with the indicated arithmetic operator.
- The increment operator, ++, increases a variable by one. The decrement operator, −−, decreases a variable by one.
- The increment and decrement operators can be used before or after the variable on which they operate (Note 2.6).

Review Exercises

1. What are the two floating point types in C++ and how do they differ?
2. How can you use the `setprecision()` and `setiosflags()` manipulators to control the output of decimal numbers?
3. Explain how C++ handles an arithmetic expression that contains different numeric data types.
4. What is a type cast and how do you make one? Why is a type cast sometimes necessary?
5. How are data types converted across the assignment operator?
6. What is the value of an assignment expression?
7. Explain how a multiple assignment works.
8. What are the compound assignment operators and how do they work?
9. What are the increment and decrement operators and how do they work?
10. What is the difference between pre- and postincrement?

Chapter

3

Iteration

Objectives

- To write relation conditions using the relational operators.

- To use the `while` statement to code indefinite iteration loops.

- To declare and use `char` type variables.

- To use `cin.get()` to obtain a character from the input buffer.

- To use embedded assignment in the condition of a `while` loop.

- To use the `do` statement to code an indefinite iteration loop.

- To use counters and accumulators.

- To use the `for` statement to code definite iteration loops.

- To code nested `while` and `for` loops.

Most of a computer's power lies in its ability to repeatedly execute the same set of instructions. This process, called iteration or looping, is the subject of this chapter. We assume that you are familiar with the basic iteration control structures, namely the **while** loop, the **do** loop, and the **for** loop. If you are not familiar with this material, refer to Appendix B.

To stop an iteration requires testing a condition. Therefore, before we learn how to code the `while`, `do`, and `for` loops in C++, we must learn how to code simple conditions.

3.1 Relation Conditions

The simplest type of condition is the **relation condition**, which compares the values of two operands. You code relation conditions in C++ by using the **relational operators**. Table 3.1 lists the relational operators and their meanings.

Programming
Pitfalls

Note that the operator that tests for equality is ==, not =, which is the assignment operator. The C++ compiler may not detect the mistake of incorrectly substituting = for ==. (Some compilers will issue a warning message that a conditional expression is expected.) Therefore, it is very important to use = when you want an assignment and == when you want to test for equality. See Experiment 1, Section 3.2.

Each relational operator compares the values of the expressions that appear on either side of the operator for the indicated relation and yields either true or false. Suppose, for example, that we have the following declarations.

```
int i = 10,
    j = 10,
    k = 15;
```

The relation condition i == j is true because the value of the expression to the left of the == operator equals the value of the expression to its right. Similarly, the relation condition i >= 15 is false.

NOTE 3.1—THE VALUE OF A RELATION CONDITION

In C++, if a relation condition is true, the whole condition has the numeric value 1. If a relation condition is false, the whole condition has the numeric value 0. In fact, C++ considers any nonzero value to be true and 0 to be false.

Recall that Note 2.4 stated that every expression in C++ has a value. Thus, the condition i == j has the value 1 because it is true. Table 3.2 shows the precedence of the relational operators relative to the other operators that we have discussed so far.

TABLE 3.1

Relational Operator	Meaning
==	Equal to
!=	Not equal to
<	Less than
<=	Less than or equal to
>	Greater than
>=	Greater than or equal to

TABLE 3.2

Operators	Associativity
( )	Left to right (inside out)
+ (unary) – (unary) ++ – –	Right to left
* / %	Left to right
+ –	Left to right
< <= > >=	Left to right
== !=	Left to right
= += –= *= /=	Right to left

We see from Table 3.2 that the equality operator and the inequality operator (!=) have a lower precedence than the other relational operators. Also, all relational operators have a lower precedence than all arithmetic operators.

Using the previous declarations of j and k, the condition j != k – 5 has the value 0 because it is false. The computer evaluates the expression j != k – 5 as follows. Of the two operators appearing in the expression, subtraction has higher precedence. Therefore, the computer first evaluates k – 5, which gives 10. Then the computer performs the second operation, namely the inequality test, and determines that the condition is false. See Experiments 1 and 2.

EXERCISES 3.1

Translate the statements of Exercises 1–5 into valid C++ relation conditions. Assume the following declarations.

```
int i,
    j,
    k;
```

1. The value of i is greater than the value of j multiplied by the value of k.
2. The value of j is not less than 300.
3. The value of k is less than or equal to the value of i.
4. Twice the value of i is not greater than three less than the value of k.
5. Five more than the value of j is greater than the value of i.

Determine whether the relation conditions in Exercises 6–9 are true or false. Assume the following declarations.

```
int i = 12,
    j = 9,
    k = 21;
```

6. `(i == j + 3)`

7. `(2 * j >= k)`

8. `(j - i != k - 18)`

9. `(k - j + i < 20)`

EXPERIMENTS 3.1

1. Compile and execute the following program. Explain its output.

```
#include <iostream.h>

using namespace std;

int main()
{
    int i = 3,
        j = 8,
        k;

    k = (i >= 0) + (i == j);
    cout << "k = " << k;

    return 0;
}
```

2. Compile and execute the following program. Explain its output.

```
#include <iostream.h>

using namespace std;

int main()
{
    int i = 3,
        j = 8,
        k = 5,
        result;

    result = (i < j < k);
    cout << "result = " << result;

    return 0;
}
```

3.2 Indefinite Iteration: The while and do Statements

The while Statement

Figure 3.1 shows how to express indefinite iteration, or looping, in flowchart and pseudocode forms.

To code the indefinite iteration loop, or while loop, of Figure 3.1 in C++, we use the while statement, which has the following form.

while (control-expression)
    loop body

The control-expression, which must be enclosed in parentheses, can be any valid C++ expression. For now, we assume that the control-expression is a simple relation condition and concentrate on how the while statement works. The loop body can be a single C++ statement ending with a semicolon or it can be a compound statement. We will discuss compound statements shortly.

Programming
Pointers

Consider the following declaration and code.

```
int count = 0;

while (count < 5)
  ++count;

cout << "\nThe value of count is " << count;
```

The code begins by declaring and initializing the integer variable count to zero. Next, the while statement executes. The while statement first tests the loop condition. Since the value of count is 0, the loop condition is true. Therefore, the loop body, which consists of the one statement ++count; executes. This statement increases the

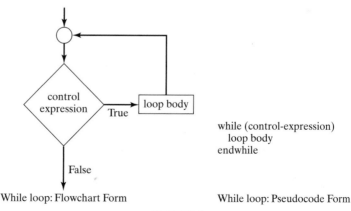

while (control-expression)
   loop body
endwhile

While loop: Flowchart Form   While loop: Pseudocode Form

FIGURE 3.1

TABLE 3.3

Value of `count`	Loop Condition (`count<5`)
0 (initial value)	True
1	True
· 2	True
3	True
4	True
5	False

value of `count` by one, making its value 1. Now the program tests the loop condition again. The condition is still true because the value of `count`, 1, is less than 5. Therefore, the loop body executes again and increases the value of `count` by 1, making it 2. The program continues to execute the loop body as long as the loop condition is true.

Table 3.3 shows a **trace** of the values of `count` and the loop condition. Tracing a section of a program's code or tracing the entire program is one of the simplest techniques for understanding or debugging a program.

Thus the loop condition is false when the value of `count` is 5. At this point the program exits the loop and executes the `cout` statement. The `cout` statement displays the current value of the variable `count` as follows.

```
The value of count is 5
```

We can arrive at this same conclusion without doing the trace by remembering that the loop condition (`count<5`) is false when the program exits the loop. Therefore, the value of `count` must be greater than or equal to 5 when the program executes the `cout` statement. Since the program initializes `count` to zero and increases its value by one each time through the loop, the first value of `count` that makes the loop condition false is 5. Therefore, the `cout` statement displays the value 5.

Programming
Pointers

The body of a `while` loop can be a **compound statement**—a set of statements enclosed in braces {}. We have been using braces since we discussed our first C++ program, dem01-1.cpp. Since braces enclose the statements of the function `main()`, the body of `main()` is a compound statement.

Now consider the following declaration and code.

```
int count = 0;

while (count < 5)
   {
      ++count;
      cout << "\nHello";
   }

cout << "\n\nHello was displayed " << count << " times.";
```

Programming
Pointers

The initial value of `count` and the loop condition are exactly as they were in the previous example. The body of this `while` loop is a compound statement that consists of two simple statements. We indent the braces two places under the reserved word `while` and indent the statements in the compound statement two places beyond the braces. The C++ language does not require this method of indentation. However, the program is easier to read because the indentation emphasizes the body of the `while` loop. Note also that each statement in the compound statement ends in a semicolon, but there is no semicolon after the closing brace of the compound statement.

As in the first example, the loop body executes five times. The program code displays the following.

```
Hello
Hello
Hello
Hello
Hello

Hello was displayed 5 times.
```

An Example of Indefinite Iteration and the `char` data type

Coding an indefinite iteration using the `while` statement is most appropriate when you do not know how many times the loop body will execute. This is why such a loop is called indefinite. Suppose we want to write a program that counts the number of characters the user enters on one line at the computer keyboard. A line is a stream of characters ended by a return. The return is not part of the line and does not count as a character. The program does not know the number of characters that the user will enter. Therefore, an indefinite iteration loop is appropriate.

Programming
Pointers

To write such a program, we need a variable that keeps a tally of the characters as the program counts them. This variable, which we will call `num_chars` for "number of characters," is an example of a **counter variable**, or **counter**. A counter is a variable that counts the number of times an event occurs during program execution. In our program, we wish to count the number of times the user types a character.

Your programs must handle counters correctly. Note 3.2 states how you should use them.

NOTE 3.2—HOW TO USE A COUNTER

To use a counter variable properly, the program must execute the following steps.

1. Initialize the counter, usually to zero.
2. Increment the counter, that is, increase the counter by one, when the event it counts occurs.
3. Use the counter. You are using the counter variable for a purpose. Make sure you use it for that purpose.

The steps outlined in Note 3.2 apply to the counter `num_chars`. Before the program begins, the user has not entered any characters. Therefore, the program should initialize `num_chars` to zero. Whenever the program obtains a character from the user, it will increase `num_chars` by one. Finally, after the user inputs the line, the program displays the value of `num_chars`.

Programming
Pointers

As stated in the previous paragraph, whenever the program obtains a character from the user, it increases `num_chars` by one. This is obviously an iterative process—obtain a character, increment `num_chars`; , obtain a character, increment `num_chars`; and so on, until the user ends the line by entering a return. Since we do not know how many characters the user will enter, this is an indefinite iteration, which calls for the use of a `while` loop.

We also need a variable in which to store a character when the program obtains it. We use the `char` data type to declare a variable that will store a *single* character. You cannot store two or more characters in a variable of type `char`. Thus, the following declares the variable `ch` in which we can store a single character.

```
char ch;
```

A **character constant** is a single character enclosed in apostrophes. Thus, `'A'` and `';'` are character constants. You can assign a character constant to a character variable in the same way that you assign a numeric constant to a numeric variable. The following assigns the character constant `'A'` to the character variable `ch`, which was declared previously.

```
ch = 'A';
```

The Member Function `cin.get()`

Programming
Pointers

Before developing the `while` loop itself, we discuss how the program is to obtain the characters that the user inputs. Recall from Chapters 1 and 2 that you can view an I/O manipulator, such as `setw()` or `setprecision()`, as a message that we send to the output stream `cout` to control the form of our output. Similarly, we can send messages to the input stream `cin` to make it behave in certain ways. Coding `cin.get()` sends a message to `cin` to obtain the next character in the input stream and make it available to the program. You use `cin.get()` as follows. First declare a character variable, say `ch`.

```
char ch;
```

Then, the following statement assigns the next character from the input stream to the variable `ch`.

```
ch = cin.get();
```

If the next available character in the input stream is M, then executing

```
ch = cin.get();
```

assigns the character M to the variable `ch`. Note that you do not use the >> operator when using `cin.get()`.

The Program dem03-1.cpp

The `while` statement's condition determines when the loop stops executing. In our program, we want the loop to stop executing when the character the user enters, which the program stores in the variable `ch`, is equal to the new-line character `'\n'`. Therefore, we want the loop to execute as long as the character that the user enters is *not* equal to the new-line character; that is, the loop condition should be (`ch != '\n'`).

The first time the program tests the loop condition, the variable `ch` must have a valid value. Before it executes the `while` statement, the program must input the first character by executing the assignment

```
ch = cin.get();
```

Following is the code of dem03-1.cpp.

```
// dem03—1.cpp

// This program counts the number of characters input
// by the user on one line. The line is terminated by
// a return. The return is not counted as a character.

#include <iostream.h>

using namespace std;

int main()
{
   char ch;                // Used to store the input character
   int  num_chars = 0;     // Counts the number of characters

   cout << "\nEnter any number of characters terminated by return.\n\n";

   ch = cin.get();         // Obtain the first character

   while (ch != '\n')      // Get characters until the end of the line
      {
      ++num_chars;
      ch = cin.get();
      }
```

```
     cout << "\n\nYou entered " << num_chars << " charcters.\n";

     return 0;
}
```

Program Output

```
Enter any number of characters terminated by return.

aaB1, 34


You entered 8 characters.
```

The program stores each character it obtains in the character variable `ch`. The integer counter `num_chars`, which the program initializes to zero in its declaration, stores the number of characters input by the user.

The program prompts the user to enter characters. When the user hits the return key, the computer transmits the entire line (including the return character) to the input stream. The first execution of `cin.get()` retrieves the first character from the input stream and stores it in `ch`. The `while` statement now tests the condition (`ch != '\n'`). If the user did not enter a return as the first character, this condition is true and the body of the loop executes.

The loop body is a two-statement compound statement. Since program execution is now in the body of the `while` loop, the loop condition is true. This means that the user entered a character. To count this character, the program increases the variable `num_chars` by one. Before ending the body of the loop, the program obtains the next character from the input stream by the assignment statement

```
ch = cin.get();
```

After completing execution of the loop body, the program tests the loop condition again, but now with the new character that it obtained by executing `cin.get()` in the loop body. If this next character is not a new-line character, the loop body executes again. The program counts the new character by increasing `num_chars` by one and it then obtains the next character from the keyboard input buffer by executing `ch = cin.get()`.

This process continues until executing `ch = cin.get()` in the loop body assigns the new-line character, `'\n'`, to `ch`. Now, the loop condition is false. The loop stops executing and control falls through to the following `cout` statement, which displays the value of `num_chars`.

The process used in dem03-1.cpp occurs many times in computing. The program obtains the first character from the user before entering the loop. The body of the `while` loop processes the character. At the end of the loop body, the program obtains the next character from the user. Note 3.3 gives the general outline of this process.

NOTE 3.3—PROCESSING AN UNKNOWN NUMBER OF INPUTS

To process an unknown number of inputs using a `while` loop, structure your program as follows:

```
Obtain input data from the user              // the priming input
while (there is more data to process)
{
        // loop body statements to process current data
        Obtain input data from the user
}
```

How the program obtains input data from the user depends on the particular program. In dem03-1.cpp, the program obtains data from the user one character at a time. Therefore, the program obtains the input by executing `ch = cin.get()`. How you code the condition in the `while` loop of Note 3.3 also depends on how the program obtains the data from the user and in what form it stores the data. In dem03-1.cpp, there is more data to process if the character obtained from the user, which is stored in the variable `ch`, is not equal to `'\n'`. Thus, we coded the loop condition as `(ch != '\n')`. Finally, only after the program fully processes the current character in the body of the `while` loop, does it obtain the next character from the user.

See Experiments 3 and 4 for some variations of the outline of Note 3.3. The program prb03-1.cpp, which we develop in Section 3.3, also follows the outline of Note 3.3.

Embedded Assignment—Recoding dem03-1.cpp

Following is another version of dem03-1.cpp, which counts the number of characters entered by the user on one line at the computer keyboard. It illustrates another application of Note 2.4, which states that each C++ expression has a value.

```
// dem03-2.cpp

// This program counts the number of characters input
// by the user on one line. The line is terminated by
// a return. The return is not counted as a character.
// The program uses embedded assignment to obtain
// and test characters.

#include <iostream.h>

using namespace std;

int main()
{
```

```
char ch;              // Used to store the input character
int  num_chars = 0;   // Counts the number of characters

cout << "\nEnter any number of characters terminated by return.\n\n";

// The loop condition contains an embedded assignment

while ( (ch = cin.get()) != '\n')
  ++num_chars;

cout << "\n\nYou entered " << num_chars << " characters.\n";

return 0;
}
```

Program Output

```
Enter any number of characters terminated by return.

aaB1, 34


You entered 8 characters.
```

The declaration and initial prompt are the same as in dem03-1.cpp. However, there is apparently no priming input and the program apparently does not obtain the next data from the user at the end of the loop body (see Note 3.3). Both of these seemingly missing elements are present in the loop condition in the form of an **embedded assignment**. We already know enough to understand this loop condition, so let's take a careful look at it.

```
while ( (ch = cin.get()) != '\n')
```

The control-expression is a relational condition—it tests to see if something is unequal to '\n'. See Figure 3.2.

The left side of the relation condition is the assignment (ch = cin.get()). The program tests the value of this assignment to see if it is unequal to '\n'. To evaluate the assignment, the program executes ch = cin.get() (which obtains the next character from the input stream) and assigns this character to ch. By Note 2.4, the

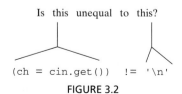

FIGURE 3.2

value of this assignment is the character assigned to `ch`. The computer tests this character against `'\n'` in the relation condition.

Now we explain how the loop works. When the program first encounters the `while` loop, it tests the loop condition. The act of testing the condition causes the statement `ch = cin.get()` to obtain the first character from the input stream and assign it to `ch`. This takes the place of the priming input. The computer then tests the value of this assignment, which is the value of the character obtained from the input stream, against `'\n'`. If they are unequal, that is if the character obtained from the keyboard is not `'\n'`, then the loop body executes. The loop body contains one statement, which increments the counter `num_chars`.

The computer then tests the loop condition again. Doing so obtains the next character from the input stream, (this is equivalent to obtaining the next character at the end of the loop body) assigns it to `ch` and tests it against `'\n'`. The loop continues to execute until the character obtained by `ch = cin.get()` equals `'\n'`.

The `do—while` Loop

A `while` loop tests the loop condition before it executes the loop body. If the loop condition is false the first time it is tested, the program will never execute the loop body. Sometimes we want to guarantee that the program executes the body of a loop at least once. That is, we require the program to execute the loop body before it tests the loop condition. This type of loop is called a `do—while`, or `do`, loop. A flowchart depicting the `do—while` loop and the corresponding pseudocode appears in Figure 3.3.

In C++, you code the `do-while` loop by using the `do` statement, as follows:

```
do
  loop body
while (loop condition);
```

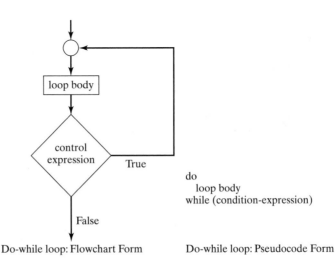

```
do
  loop body
while (condition-expression)
```

Do-while loop: Flowchart Form   Do-while loop: Pseudocode Form

FIGURE 3.3

The loop body can be a single statement or a compound statement. Note that you must code a semicolon after the closing parenthesis of the loop condition. Following is a code fragment that displays the word "Hello" five times by using a do statement.

```
int count = 0;

do
   {
      ++count;
      cout << "\nHello";
   }
while (count < 5);

cout << "\n\nHello was displayed " << count << " times";
```

It is also possible to recode dem03-1.cpp using a do loop as follows.

```
// dem03-3.cpp

// This program counts the number of characters input
// by the user on one line. The line is terminated by
// a return. The return is not counted as a character.
// This program, which uses a do statement, is a version
// of dem03-1.c.

#include <iostream.h>

using namespace std;

int main()
{
   char ch;              // Used to store the input character
   int  num_chars = 0;   // Counts the number of characters

   cout << "\nEnter any number of characters terminated by return.\n\n";

   do
      {
         ch = cin.get();
         ++num_chars;
      }
   while (ch != '\n');

   --num_chars;

   cout << "\n\nYou entered " << num_chars << " characters.\n";

   return 0;
}
```

Program Output

```
Enter any number of characters terminated by return.

aaB1, 34


You entered 8 characters.
```

Since the program does not test the loop condition until after it executes the loop body, it is not necessary to have the priming input as required by dem03-1.cpp. The do—loop body first obtains a character and then counts it by increasing num_chars by one. The loop condition tests this character to see if it is the new-line character. If not, the loop body executes again. The only difficulty with the do loop is that the program counts the new-line character that the user enters (and that ends the loop) as a character. Before displaying the value of num_chars, the program decreases the value of num_chars by one using the statement

```
--num_chars;
```

Programming Pitfalls

Although you must code a semicolon following the while condition in a do—while loop, do not code a semicolon after the while condition in a while loop. See Exercise 4.

EXERCISES 3.2

1. How many times does the following while loop display the word "Hello"?

```
int count = 1;
while (count < 10)
   {
      cout << "\nHello";
      count += 2;
   }
```

2. How many times does the following while loop display the word "Hello"?

```
int count = 1;
while (count > 10)
   {
      cout << "\nHello";
      count += 2;
   }
```

3. How many times does the following while loop display the word "Hello"?

```
int count = 0;

while (count != 10)
```

```
    {
        cout << "\nHello";
        count += 2;
    }
```

4. What is the value of `count` after the following executes?

```
int count = 0;

while (count < 7) ;
    ++count;
```

5. What are the values of `total` and `count` after the following executes?

```
int count = 0,
    total = 0;
while (count < 7)
    {
        total += count;
        ++count;
    }
```

6. Rewrite the `while` loop of Exercise 1 as a `do` loop so that it displays the word "Hello" the same number of times.

7. Rewrite the `while` loop of Exercise 5 as a `do` loop so that `total` and `count` have the same final values as in Exercise 5.

EXPERIMENTS 3.2

1. We mentioned in this chapter that the compiler does not usually detect the mistake of incorrectly replacing the relational operator == by the assignment operator =. This experiment shows what can happen if you make this mistake. The following program asks the user to enter several Xs followed by a return. The program then displays the number of Xs the user entered.

```
#include <iostream.h>

using namespace std;

int main()
{
    char ch;
    int x_count = 0;

    cout << "\nEnter several Xs, followed by a return.\n\n";
    ch = cin.get();
    while (ch == 'X')
```

```
          {
            ++x_count;
            ch = cin.get();
          }
      cout << "\n\nYou entered " << x_count << " Xs.";

      return 0;
}
```

Compile and execute this program to ensure that it works properly. Now replace the == in the loop condition by =. Compile and execute the resulting program. Use the same number of Xs that you used to test the original program. After you enter a return, does the new program print the number of Xs that you entered? (If the program will not stop, hit the Break key while holding down the Ctrl key.)

2. Recode dem03-1.cpp using `cin` and the extraction operator in place of `cin.get()`.

3. See Note 3.3. Omit the priming input from dem03-1.cpp. Compile and execute the resulting program. Explain what happens.

4. A student writes the following program to count the number of characters the user enters on one line. Does the program work properly? Explain why or why not.

```cpp
#include <iostream.h>

using namespace std;

int main()
{
    char ch = 'a'; // initialized to guarantee entry into while loop
    int num_chars = 0;
    cout << "\nEnter any number of characters terminated by return.\n\n";

    while (ch != '\n')
      {
        ch = cin.get();
        ++num_chars;
      }

    cout << "\n\nYou entered " << num_chars << " characters.\n";

    return 0;
}
```

5. Predict the outcome of executing the following program.

```cpp
#include <iostream.h>

using namespace std;
```

```
int main()
{
  int num;
  while (num = 1)
  {
    cout << "\nThe first three positive integers are " << num << ", "
        << num + 1 << ", and " << num + 2;
    num = 0;
  }

  return 0;
}
```

Compile and execute the program. Was your prediction correct? Explain why or why not.

3.3 Solving a Problem With Indefinite Iteration

The program prb02-3.cpp of Chapter 2 simulates a simple cash register, but processes only one customer. In this section we discuss a program that processes many customers and displays summary information at the end of the day's business.

Problem 3.1

The C++-Side Restaurant (see Problem 2.1) wants you to write a program that simulates a simple cash register. The program should ask the user if a customer is to be processed. If the user responds yes, the program prompts the user to enter the price of the meal. Then the program calculates the sales tax and calculates the total price, which it should display to the user. Next, the program asks the user to enter the amount tendered, and displays the amount tendered, the total price, and the customer's change. The program then asks the user if there is another customer to process. If the user responds yes, the program processes the next customer in the same manner. This procedure continues indefinitely until the user responds no to the prompt for another customer. Finally, the program displays the total number of customers it processed and the grand total of all the meal prices.

Program Design

Since the program must process an indefinite number of customers, we use a `while` loop and apply Note 3.3 as shown in the following high-level pseudocode.

Prompt for a customer
while (there is another customer)
  Process the meal
  Prompt for a customer
endwhile
Display totals

Our program first asks the user if there is a customer to process (the priming input). The `while` loop's condition tests the user's response to this question. If the user indicates that there is another customer to process, the `while` loop's body executes, processing one customer's data. At the end of the loop body, the program asks the user if there is another customer to process.

To keep track of the number of customers that the program processes, we use a counter called `num_customers`. In addition, the program must keep a running total of the meal prices. When there are no more customers to process, the program must display the final value of the running total of the meal prices. This requires the use of an **accumulator**, which is a variable that totals the values that another variable assumes.

You use an accumulator to add numbers in much the same way as you use a calculator to add a set of numbers. The calculator's display acts as an accumulator. To use the calculator, you first clear the calculator display—that is, enter zero into the display. Clearing the display ensures that you rid the display of any numbers. Next, you add each number to the number in the display. Finally, after entering the last number, you press the equals key (=), and the final total appears in the calculator display.

An accumulator acts like a special calculator display for adding the values of a particular variable. Therefore, every accumulator must go through the three steps of Note 3.4, which follows. It is good programming practice to check that each accumulator goes through these three steps.

NOTE 3.4—HOW TO USE AN ACCUMULATOR

To use an accumulator properly, the program must execute the following steps.

1. Initialize the accumulator, usually to zero.

2. Increment the accumulator, that is, increase the accumulator by the value of the variable that the accumulator is totaling.

3. Use the accumulator. You are using the accumulator for a purpose. Make sure you use it for that purpose.

In the program we shall develop to solve Problem 3.1, the variable `total` stores the total cost of the meal, including tax. The program adds each meal total to the accumulator variable `grand_total`. This accumulator must go through the steps of Note 3.4. Before the user enters the price of the first meal, the value of `grand_total` should be zero. We need to initialize `grand_total` to zero before using it.

To increase the accumulator, we code the following assignment statement:

```
grand_total += total;
```

This statement is the equivalent of adding a number (`total`) to the number in a calculator's display (`grand_total`). The program increases the value of `grand_total` by the current value of `total`. Following is a detailed pseudocode solution for Problem 3.1.

Initialize the counter and accumulator
Prompt for a customer
while (there is another customer)
  Obtain the meal price
  Calculate the tax and total price of the meal
  Display the price, tax, and total
  Obtain the amount tendered
  Calculate the change
  Display the amount tendered, total price, and change
  Increment the counter and accumulator
  Prompt for a customer
endwhile
Display the counter and accumulator

The Program prb03-1.cpp

Following is the program solution to Problem 3.1.

```cpp
// prb03—1.c

// This program simulates a simple cash register. It processes
// an indefinite number of customers. At the end of the program,
// the program prints the total number of customers processed and
// the grand total of the meal prices.

#include <iostream.h>
#include <iomanip.h>

using namespace std;

int main()
{
  const double SALES_TAX_RATE = 0.0825;
  double meal_price,      // Price of meal entered by user
         sales_tax,       // Amount of sales tax
         total,           // Total bill: meal_price + sales_tax
         amt_tendered,    // Amount received from customer
         change,          // Change: amt_tendered — total
         grand_total;     // Grand total of total meal prices
  int    num_customers,   // Counts number of customers processed
         response;        // yes = 1, no = 0

  //Set up output stream for currency output

  cout << setprecision(2)
       << setiosflags(ios::fixed)
```

```
                    << setiosflags(ios::showpoint);

    // Initialize counter and accumulator
    grand_total = 0.0;
    num_customers = 0;

    // Display banner
    cout << "\n\n*** C++ Side Restaurant ***\n\n";

    // Ask for a customer
    cout << "\n\nDo you want to process a customer?";
    cout << "\nEnter 1 for Yes or 0 for No): ";
    cin >> response;

    // Main processing loop
    while (response == 1)
      {
        cout << "\nEnter the price of the meal: $";
        cin >> meal_price;
        cout << "\n\n";

        // Calculate tax and total price
        sales_tax = meal_price * SALES_TAX_RATE;
        total = meal_price + sales_tax;

        // Display price tax and total
        cout << "\nPrice of Meal: " << setw(6) << meal_price;
        cout << "\nSales Tax: "     << setw(6) << sales_tax;
        cout << "\n----------------------";
        cout << "\nTotal Amount: "  << setw(6) << total << "\n\n";

        // Obtain amount tendered
        cout << "\nEnter amount tendered: $";
        cin >> amt_tendered;
        cout << "\n\n";

        // Calculate change
        change = amt_tendered - total;

        // Display amounts and change
        cout << "\nAmount Tendered: $" << setw(6) << amt_tendered;
        cout << "\nTotal Amount:    $" << setw(6) << total;
        cout << "\n------------------------";
        cout << "\nChange:          $" << setw(6) << change;

        // Increment counter and accumulator
        ++num_customers;
        grand_total += total;

        // Ask for a customer
        cout << "\n\nDo you want to process a customer?";
```

```
       cout << "\nEnter 1 for Yes or 0 for No): ";
       cin >> response;
    }

    // Display total customers and grand total
    cout << "\n\nGrand Totals:";
    cout << "\n\nTotal Customers: " << num_customers;
    cout << "\n\nTotal Receipts: " << grand_total;

   // Print closing banner
   cout << "\n\n*** Thank You ***\n\n";

   return 0;
}
```

Program Output

```
*** C++-Side Restaurant ***



Do you want to process a customer?
Enter 1 for Yes or 0 for No): 1

Enter the price of the meal: $34.50



Price of Meal:    34.50
Sales Tax:         2.85
----------------------
Total Amount:     37.35


Enter amount tendered: $40.00



Amount Tendered: $ 40.00
Total Amount:    $ 37.35
------------------------
Change:          $  2.65


Do you want to process a customer?
Enter 1 for Yes or 0 for No): 1

Enter the price of the meal: $75.23
```

```
Price of Meal:    75.23
Sales Tax:         6.21
---------------------
Total Amount:     81.44


Enter amount tendered: $100.00



Amount Tendered: $100.00
Total Amount:    $ 81.44
-----------------------
Change:          $ 18.56

Do you want to process a customer?
Enter 1 for Yes or 0 for No): 1

Enter the price of the meal: $57.92



Price of Meal:    57.92
Sales Tax:         4.78
---------------------
Total Amount:     62.70


Enter amount tendered: $70.00



Amount Tendered: $ 70.00
Total Amount:    $ 62.70
-----------------------
Change:          $  7.30

Do you want to process a customer?
Enter 1 for Yes or 0 for No): 0


Grand Totals:

Total Customers: 3

Total Receipts: 181.48

*** Thank You ***
```

Discussion of prb03-1.cpp

The program code follows the pseudocode exactly. Because the program declares the counter `num_customers` as an `int` and the accumulator `grand_total` as a `double`, it uses two separate assignment statements for the initializations. (Most compilers will accept the multiple assignment statement

```
num_customers = grand_total = 0;
```

but issue a warning message that the statement involves incompatible data types.)

The prompt that asks the user if there is a customer to process displays a message over two lines.

```
// Ask for a customer
  cout << "\n\nDo you want to process a customer?";
  cout << "\nEnter 1 for Yes or 0 for No): ";
  cin >> response;
```

The second `cout` statement says that the user must enter 1 for a Yes or 0 for a No. The program stores the user's answer in the integer variable `response`. In a later chapter, we will discuss how to allow the user to enter Y or N in response to such a prompt. For now, we ask the user to enter an integer response to yes/no questions. See Experiments 1 and 2 for variations of prb03-1.cpp.

More on Control Expressions

Programming
Pointers

In the programs of this chapter, the `while` loop control-expressions were simple relation conditions. However, a control-expression can be any valid C++ expression. Recall that Note 3.1 stated that C++ considers any nonzero value as true, and 0 as the only false value. Thus, when a program evaluates the control-expression in a `while` statement, if its value is nonzero, the program considers the expression true and the loop body executes once. If the value of the control-expression is 0, the expression is false and the program exits the loop. This is why the C++ compiler never catches when you inadvertently replace == with =.

NOTE 3.5 CONTROL-EXPRESSIONS

The control-expression in a `while` or `do` loop can be any valid C++ expression. If the value of the expression is 0, the expression is considered false. If the value of the expression is nonzero, the expression is considered true.

To illustrate, suppose that in prb03-1.cpp we replace the `while` statement's condition (`response == 1`) with the assignment (`response = 1`). No matter what value the user enters for `response`, the assignment gives the value 1 to `response`.

Therefore, the assignment (which is the control-expression in this case) has the value 1, which is true. This causes the `while` loop to never terminate—a so-called **infinite loop**. See Experiment 1.

Although it may seem strange that any C++ expression can be a control-expression, it does allow the C++ programmer to write more compact code. For example, you can code the `while` loop's condition in prb03-1.cpp as follows.

```
while (response)
```

Remember that when the computer evaluates the control-expression, `response` has the last value the user entered. If the value of `response` is anything other than zero, the control-expression is true and the loop body executes once. If the value of `response` is zero, the control-expression is false and the program exits the loop. See Experiment 2.

To consider another example, in Section 3.2 we wrote the following simple program to display the word "Hello" five times.

```
int count = 0;

while (count < 5)
   {
     ++count;
     cout << "\nHello";
   }

cout << "\n\nHello was displayed " << count << " times.";
```

We can write the `while` loop more compactly as follows.

```
while (count++ < 5)
   cout << "\nHello";
```

In the condition-expression, the variable `count` is postincremented. The condition tests the current value of `count` and then `count` is incremented by one, which is what happens in the original code. However, the value of `count` after the program exits the `while` loop is different. What is the final value of `count`? See Experiment 5.

EXPERIMENTS 3.3

1. In prb03-1.cpp, replace the `while`'s condition by

```
while (response = 1)
```

Compile and execute the resulting program. Explain what happens and why.

2. In prb03-1.cpp, replace the `while`'s condition by

```
while (response)
```

Compile and execute the resulting program. Explain why the program does or does not work.

3. How many times does the following loop display "Hello"? Carefully explain how the loop condition works.

```
int count = 5;
while (--count)
  cout << "\nHello";
```

4. In Experiment 3, what would happen if count were initialized to −1? Try it by incorporating the code in a small program. Considering the range of `int` variables, is the loop really what it seems to be? Compile and execute the resulting program. Explain what happens and why.

5. Write a simple program to determine the final value of `count` upon exit from the two `while` loops discussed at the end of this section.

PROGRAMMING PROBLEMS 3.3

1. A swimming pool maintenance company wants you to write a program to estimate the cost of resurfacing the inside of in-ground pools. The program is to process an indeterminate number of estimates. To make an estimate, the program should ask the user to input the length, width, and depth of the pool, each to the nearest tenth of a foot. The company charges $2.25 per square foot. The following formula gives the inside surface area of a pool.

2 * depth (length + width) + length * width

Include a sales tax of 7.75% in the estimate. The program should display the dimensions of the pool and the estimated cost to the nearest penny for each customer it processes. Write the required program.

2. A cattle feed company needs a program to help process feed orders. The program is to process an indeterminate number of orders. Each customer orders one or both of two types of feed, A and B. Feed A costs $2.50 per 100 pounds and feed B costs $3.15 per 100 pounds. Amounts less than 100 pounds are to be charged proportionally. For each customer, the program should ask the user to enter the actual number of pounds ordered for each of feeds A and B to the nearest tenth of a pound. The program should display the amount and cost of each type of feed and the total cost of the order. When no more customers are to be processed, the program should display the total number of customers processed, the total amounts of feed A and feed B ordered to the nearest tenth of a pound, and the total receipts. Write the required program.

3. A computer science instructor needs a program that averages the grades on a quiz she gives to her class. Each grade is an integer between 0 and 100. She does not know the number of grades at this time. Write a program that asks the user to enter quiz grades one at a time. After the user has completed entering grades, the program should display the number of grades entered and the sum of the grades entered. The program should also display the average of the grades, rounded to the nearest tenth.

4. A computer science instructor wants you to write a program to compute final grades for her introduction to computers course. The program is to process an indeterminate number of students. For each student the program should ask the user to enter the midterm and final exam scores and then display the student's final grade. The final grade is the sum of 45% of the midterm exam score and 55% of the final exam score. After it processes all the students, the program should display the number of students it processed, and the average midterm exam score, average final exam score, and average final grade all to the nearest tenth. Write the required program.

5. A bank wants you to write a program to calculate the amounts in accounts that earn simple interest. The program should process an indeterminate number of accounts. The following formula gives the amount in an account where the principal is the initial investment.

amount = principal + interest

The following formula gives the interest, where the rate is the annual interest rate as a decimal and time is the number of years the principal is at interest.

interest = principal * rate * time

For each account, the program should ask the user to input the principal, the interest rate to the nearest tenth as a percent (for example, 7.7), and the number of years at interest. The program should then display the principal, the interest, and the amount in the account after the given number of years. When there are no more customers to process, the program should display the number of accounts processed and the total principal and total interest paid. Write the required program.

3.4 Definite Iteration

Indefinite iteration is appropriate whenever you do not know how often the program will execute a loop body. For example, in developing a program to count the number of characters input by the user, it is appropriate to use a `while` loop. However, sometimes during program design you know exactly how often the program will execute the loop body. We call such a loop a **definite iteration loop**.

The `for` Statement

The best way to code a definite iteration loop in C++ is by using the `for` statement, which we shall introduce by an example. While a user is interacting with a program, it is sometimes necessary to clear the monitor screen before continuing the exchange between the user and the program. A primitive way to do this (which is not the best way available to the C++ programmer!) is for the program to display as many new-line characters as are necessary to cause the contents of the monitor to "scroll" off the top of the screen. If your monitor displays 25 lines, displaying 25 new-line characters accomplishes this task.

The following `cout` statement, which contains 25 new-line characters enclosed in quotes, is a simple but crude way to scroll the screen. Unfortunately, counting is the only way to ensure that this statement displays exactly 25 new-line characters.

```
cout << "\n\n\n\n\n\n\n\n\n\n\n\n\n\n\n\n\n\n\n\n\n\n\n\n\n";
```

Instead of treating the 25 new-line characters as a unit, as in the previous `cout` statement, we can view this problem as an iteration: Display one new-line character 25 times using a loop. The following `while` loop accomplishes this.

```
int line_count = 1;

while (line_count <= 25)
  {
    cout << "\n";
    ++line_count;
  }
```

The variable `line_count` counts the number of times the program displays a new-line character. The program initializes `line_count` to one in its declaration, uses it in the condition of the `while` loop, and increments it by one in the loop body. When the value of `line_count` exceeds 25, that is when the program has displayed 25 new-line characters, the loop ends.

This loop differs from the loops of dem03-1.cpp and prb03-1.cpp. In dem03-1.cpp, we did not know before running the program how many characters the user would enter. In prb03-1.cpp, we did not know before running the program how many customers the user would process. Therefore, in both cases we used a `while` statement (an indefinite iteration loop) to code the iteration. In our present problem, we know exactly how often the loop is to execute (25) as we are designing the program. This is an example of a **definite iteration loop**. Because a counter variable controls the loop, we also call such a loop a **counter-controlled loop**.

It is always possible to code a definite iteration loop using a `while` statement as we did previously. However, C++'s `for` statement is specifically designed for definite iteration loops. The first line of a `for` statement contains all three things that a program must do to the counter—initialize, test, and increment. For example, the following `for` statement has the same effect as the previous `while` statement.

```
int line_count;

for (line_count = 1; line_count <= 25; ++line_count)
  cout << "\n";
```

This `for` statement works as follows. When program execution first encounters the `for` statement, the computer executes the first statement inside the parentheses (in this case, `line_count = 1`). This is the **loop initialization**, which the program executes only once upon entering the loop. Next, the program evaluates the second statement inside the parentheses (in our case, the condition `line_count <= 25`). This expression is the **loop test**. If the expression evaluates to true (that is, any nonzero value), the loop body executes once. (In our example, executing the loop body displays one new-line character.) Then the program executes the third statement inside the parentheses, the **loop adjustment** (in our case, `++line_count`). Then the program again tests the loop condition, that is it evaluates the second expression inside the parentheses. If the expression evaluates to true, the loop body executes again, and so on. Eventually the loop test expression evaluates to false (in our example, the value of `line_count` will exceed 25) and the loop ends.

It is extremely important to understand the flow of control in a `for` statement. The dashed line in Figure 3.4 traces the flow of control of the previous `for` statement in a flowchart-like diagram, called a **definite iteration box**.

The program executes the loop initialization first and then makes the loop test. If the test is true, the loop body executes once, the computer adjusts the counter, and makes the test again. If the test is false, the loop ends.

Following is the same definite iteration in pseudocode form.

> for (each line_count from 1 to 25)
>   print '\n'
> endfor

The phrase "from 1 to 25" shows that the counter variable is to range from 1 to 25. The word "each" means that `line_count` is incremented by 1 for each loop iteration. The pseudocode word endfor indicates the end of the loop body.

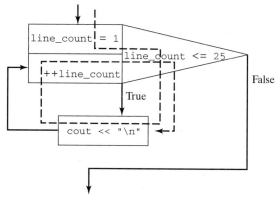

FIGURE 3.4

Following is the general form of the `for` statement in C++. The semicolons are required after both the loop initialization and loop test statements. There must not be a semicolon after the loop adjustment statement.

for (loop initialization; loop test; loop adjustment)
    loop body

Following are five important facts about the `for` statement.

1. When execution exits the loop, the loop condition is false. In the loop that displays 25 new-line characters, the loop condition is (`line_count <= 25`). When the program exits the loop, the value of `line_count` is greater than 25. The program initializes `line_count` at 1 and increments `line_count` by 1 each time through the loop. When control exits the loop, the value of `line_count` must be 26.

Programming
Pointers

2. In a `for` loop, the counter can be initialized to any number, and the counter can be incremented by any number. For example, the following displays all the multiples of 5 from 5 to 95 on one line.

Programming
Pointers

```
int multiple;

cout << "\n";
for (multiple = 5; multiple <= 95; multiple += 5)
   cout << setw(3) << multiple;
cout << "\n";
```

The first `cout` statement causes the cursor to start on a new line. The `for` statement initializes `multiple` to 5. Since this value is less than or equal to 95, the loop body executes once, which displays the value of the variable `multiple` in a three-character field. The loop adjustment statement increases `multiple` by 5, making it 10. In this way, `multiple` takes the values 5, 10, 15, 20, ..., 95. When the loop increases `multiple` to 100, the loop condition is no longer true. The loop ends and the next `cout` statement places the cursor on a new line. Therefore, the loop produces the following output.

```
  5  10  15  20  25  30  35  40  45  50  55  60  65  70  75  80  85  90  95
```

3. The loop counter can be decremented each time through the loop. The following displays the word "Hello" on five separate lines.

Programming
Pointers

```
int count;

for (count = 5; count > 0; --count)
   cout << "\nHello";
```

This loop initializes the counter variable `count` to 5 and decreases it by 1 each time through the loop. The loop condition (`count > 0`) remains true as long as the value of `count` is positive. When `count` has the values 5, 4, 3, 2, 1, the loop body executes. When `count` becomes 0, the loop condition is false and the loop ends. The loop produces the following output.

```
Hello
Hello
Hello
Hello
Hello
```

Programming
Pointers

4. The loop counter can be a non-integer. For example, consider the following code, which displays the tax on amounts ranging from $2.50 to $3.00 in increments of $0.10. (What is the purpose of the `cout` statement that follows the for statement?)

```
double price;
cout << setprecision(2)
     << setiosflags(ios::fixed)
     << setiosflags(ios::showpoint);

for (price = 2.50; price <= 3.00; price += 0.10)
  cout << "\nTax on " << setw(4) << price
       << " is " << setw(4) << price * 0.0825;
cout << "\n";
```

This code fragment initializes the variable `price` to 2.50. Each time through the loop, the statement increases the value of `price` by 0.10. The loop ends when the value of `price` exceeds 3.00. The loop produces the following output. What is the value of `price` when the loop ends?

```
Tax on 2.50 is 0.21.
Tax on 2.60 is 0.21.
Tax on 2.70 is 0.22.
Tax on 2.80 is 0.23.
Tax on 2.90 is 0.24.
Tax on 3.00 is 0.25.
```

Using a non-integer to control a `for` loop can lead to unexpected results. See Experiment 3.

Programming
Pointers

5. The body of a `for` loop can be a compound statement. The following produces the same output as the previous loop.

```
double price,
       tax;

cout << setprecision(2)
     << setiosflags(ios::fixed)
     << setiosflags(ios::showpoint);

for (price = 2.50; price <= 3.00; price += 0.10)
  {
    tax = price * 0.0825;
    cout << "\nTax on " << setw(4) << price
         << " is " << setw(4) << tax;
  }
cout << "\n";
```

The difference between this loop and the previous one is that this loop computes the tax in a separate assignment statement inside the loop body. Therefore, the loop body, which now consists of two statements, must be a compound statement. See Experiment 4 for more variations on the `for` loop.

An Example of Definite Iteration

The program dem03-4.cpp uses `for` loops to display the following banner.

```
* * * * * * * * * * * * * * * * * * * * * * * * * * * * * * * * * * * * * * * * * * * * * * * * * * * * * * *
* *                                                                       * *
* *                        Welcome to C++                                 * *
* *                                                                       * *
* * * * * * * * * * * * * * * * * * * * * * * * * * * * * * * * * * * * * * * * * * * * * * * * * * * * * * *
```

The design of the program is simple, as the following pseudocode shows.

Clear the screen.
Display line 1.
Display line 2.
Display line 3.
Display line 4.
Display line 5.
Move the banner up 10 lines.

To display a line requires use of one or more `for` statements. For example, we can expand the pseudocode statement "Display line 2" by the following pseudocode.

print '**'
for (each position from 3 to 58)
    print ' '
endfor
print '**'

We leave as an exercise how to expand the pseudocode for displaying lines 1 and 3. Following is the program code for dem03-4.cpp.

```cpp
// dem03-4.cpp

// This program prints a welcome banner.

#include <iostream.h>

using namespace std;

int main()
{
  const char SYMBOL = '*';

  int i,
      position;

  for (i = 1; i <= 25; ++i)                           // Clear screen
    cout << "\n";

  for (position = 1; position <= 60; ++position)      // Print line 1
    cout << SYMBOL;

  cout << "\n" << SYMBOL << SYMBOL;                    // Print line 2
  for (position = 3; position <= 58; ++position)
    cout << " ";
  cout << SYMBOL << SYMBOL;

  cout << "\n" << SYMBOL << SYMBOL;                    // Print line 3
  for (position = 3; position <= 24; ++position)
    cout << " ";
  cout << "Welcome to C";
  for (position = 37; position <= 58; ++position)
    cout << " ";
  cout << SYMBOL << SYMBOL;

  cout << "\n" << SYMBOL << SYMBOL;                    // Print line 4
  for (position = 3; position <= 58; ++position)
    cout << " ";
  cout << SYMBOL << SYMBOL;

  cout << "\n";                                        // Print line 5
  for (position = 1; position <= 60; ++position)
    cout << SYMBOL;

  for (i = 1; i <= 10; ++i)                            // Move display up
    cout << "\n";                                      // 10 lines

  return 0;
}
```

Program Output

```
************************************************************
* *                                                    * *
* *                  Welcome to C++                     * *
* *                                                    * *
************************************************************
```

The character that the program uses to make the border (SYMBOL) is a symbolic constant. This allows us to use a different symbol for the banner's border later. A simple for loop clears the screen. Another for loop displays the first line of the banner by printing 60 asterisks. The value of the variable position keeps track of where the cursor is on the line. In the for loop, position ranges from 1 to 60.

The cout statement in the body of this loop

```
cout << SYMBOL;
```

displays one copy of the character represented by SYMBOL.

To display line two, a single cout displays a new-line character and two SYMBOLs to begin the line.

```
cout << "\n" << SYMBOL << SYMBOL;
```

Then, a for loop displays blanks in positions 3 through 58. Finally, a cout displays the last two SYMBOLs.

To display line three, a cout displays a new-line character and two SYMBOLs. Then a for loop displays the blanks (in positions 3 through 24) that appear before the message. A single cout then displays the message. Another for loop displays the blanks (in positions 37 through 58) that appear after the message. Finally, a cout displays the two SYMBOLs that end the line.

Line four is exactly like line two and line five is exactly like line one. Displaying 10 new-line characters moves the banner up 10 lines. See also Experiments 1 and 2.

Calculating Interest on a CD—Problem 3.2

The following problem uses a for loop to construct an interest table for a Certificate of Deposit. A local bank needs a program to calculate the monthly interest on a Certificate of Deposit (CD). The user is to enter the amount of the deposit, the term of the certificate in months, and the annual interest rate as a percent. The interest is to be compounded monthly. The program should display a table that lists the interest for each month, the total interest accumulated up to each month, and the balance in the account at the end of each month. After the program lists the table, it should display summary information listing the amount of the initial deposit, the total interest accumulated, and the final total amount in the CD account.

The interest earned on a CD is **compound interest**. The interest that a compound-interest account earns each month is added to the account balance. The new account balance then earns interest for the next month. In a compound-interest account, the interest earns interest.

The interest rate that the user provides to the program is an annual interest rate in percent form. Before using it in calculations, the program must convert the rate to a percent by dividing it by 100. This gives the annual rate as a decimal number. Then, the program must divide the annual rate by 12 to give the monthly interest rate.

For example, suppose you make a deposit of $10,000 in a CD that earns 9% interest annually. The annual rate as a decimal is $9/100 = 0.09$. The monthly rate is $0.09/12 = 0.0075$. The interest for the first month is $(10000.00)*(0.0075) = 75.00$. The program adds this interest to the balance. Therefore, the opening balance at the beginning of the second month is 10,075.00. The interest for the second month is $(10075.00)*(0.0075) = 75.56$. The program adds this interest to the balance, giving an opening balance of 10,150.56 for the third month. This process continues for the life of the CD.

Following is the pseudocode for Problem 3.2.

Obtain deposit amount, term, and annual rate from user.
Calculate monthly interest rate.
Initialize total interest accumulator to 0.
Initialize account balance to deposit amount.
Display table headings.
for (each month from 1 to term)
  Calculate interest for current month
  Increment account balance
  Increment total interest
  Display data for current month
endfor
Display deposit amount, total interest, final balance

After obtaining the input data from the user, the program converts the annual interest rate to the equivalent decimal monthly interest rate. The program initializes the total interest accumulator to zero and the account balance to the value of the deposit. The `for` loop does its calculations once for each month of the term of the CD. In the `for` loop's body, the program calculates the interest for the current month, increments the account balance and the total interest accumulator, and displays the required information for the current month. When the program exits the `for` loop, it displays the summary data.

Following is the program code for prb03-2.cpp.

```
// prb03-2.cpp

// This program illustrates the use of a for loop to calculate
// the monthly interest on a CD.
```

```
// The user enters the amount deposited, the term, and the
// interest rate. The program outputs a table listing the
// interest, accumulated interest, and account balance for
// each period.

#include <iostream.h>
#include <iomanip.h>

using namespace std;

int main()
{
   double annual_rate,      // Annual interest rate as a percent
          monthly_rate,     // Per period interest rate
          deposit,          // Amount of deposit
          acct_balance,     // Monthly account balance
          interest,         // Monthly interest
          total_interest;   // Total interest
   int    month,            // Counts the periods of the CD
          term;             // Term of the CD in months

   // Set output for currency

   cout << setprecision(2)
        << setiosflags(ios::fixed)
        << setiosflags(ios::showpoint);

   cout << "\n\nEnter amount deposited in CD: ";
   cin >> deposit;
   cout << "\nEnter term of CD in number of months: ";
   cin >> term;
   cout << "\nEnter the annual CD interest rate in %: ";
   cin >> annual_rate;

   monthly_rate = (annual_rate / 100) / 12;
   total_interest = 0.00;
   acct_balance = deposit;

   cout << "\n\nPERIOD    INTEREST  TOTAL INTEREST  NEW BALANCE";
   cout << "\n------------------------------------------------";

   for (month = 1; month <= term; ++month)
     {
       interest = monthly_rate * acct_balance;
       acct_balance += interest;
       total_interest += interest;
       cout << "\n" << setw(4) << month
            << setw(14) << interest
            << setw(13) << total_interest
            << setw(15) << acct_balance;
     }
```

```
cout << "\n-------------------------------------------------";
cout << "\n\n\tSummary";
cout << "\n\nInitial Deposit:" << setw(8) << deposit;
cout << "\nInterest: "        << setw(8) << total_interest;
cout << "\nFinal Total: "     << setw(8) << acct_balance;

return 0;
}
```

Program Output

```
Enter amount deposited in CD: 1000.00

Enter term of CD in number of months: 12

Enter the annual CD interest rate in %: 7.5

PERIOD     INTEREST  TOTAL INTEREST  NEW BALANCE
-------------------------------------------------
  1          6.25          6.25        1006.25
  2          6.29         12.54        1012.54
  3          6.33         18.87        1018.87
  4          6.37         25.24        1025.24
  5          6.41         31.64        1031.64
  6          6.45         38.09        1038.09
  7          6.49         44.58        1044.58
  8          6.53         51.11        1051.11
  9          6.57         57.68        1057.68
 10          6.61         64.29        1064.29
 11          6.65         70.94        1070.94
 12          6.69         77.63        1077.63
-------------------------------------------------

     Summary

Initial Deposit: 1000.00
Interest:          77.63
Final Total:     1077.63
```

The program code closely follows the pseudocode. One assignment calculates the monthly_rate.

```
monthly_rate = (annual_rate / 100) / 12;
```

The parentheses in the expression on the right of the assignment are not necessary, but we include them to clarify the purpose of the expression. After the program initializes acct_balance and total_interest, it displays the heading line of the table.

The counter variable `month` controls the `for` loop and ranges from one to the value of `term`. In the body of the `for` loop, the program calculates the interest as `monthly_rate * acct_balance`. At this point in the loop body, `acct_balance` is the opening balance for the month currently being processed by the loop. After calculating the interest, the program increases `acct_balance` and `total_interest` by the value of `interest`. This new updated value of `acct_balance` is the closing balance at the end of the current month.

Finally, the `cout` statement displays the row of the table that contains the data for the current month. The `setw()` manipulators align the variable values in the columns of the table. Each `setw()` defines a field on the output line into which a value is placed. We selected the field widths so that the values align vertically with the column headings. See Figure 3.5. Recall that the values appear right justified in each field.

EXERCISES 3.4

In Exercises 1–7 assume the following declarations.

```
int i;
double f;
```

For each `for` statement find the number of times the loop body executes and the value of the loop counter when the program exits the loop.

1. `for (i = 1; i <= 27; ++i)`
    `cout << "\n" << i;`

2. `for (i = 0; i < 27; ++i)`
    `cout << "\n" << i;`

3. `for (i = 3; i <= 27; i += 2)`
    `cout << "\n" << i;`

4. `for (i = 25; i > 10; --i)`
    `cout << "\n" << i;`

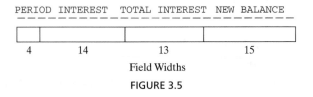

FIGURE 3.5

5. `for (f = 1.05; f <= 2.0; f += 0.10)`
   `cout << "\n" << f;`

6. `for (f = 2.0; f <= 100.0; f *= 2.0)`
   `cout << "\n" << f;`

7. `for (i = 1; i <=10; ++i)`
   `cout << "\n" << i++;`

8. Write a `while` loop and associated statements that are equivalent to the `for` loop in Exercise 1.

9. Write a `while` loop and associated statements that are equivalent to the `for` loop in Exercise 5.

10. Write a `do` loop and associated statements that are equivalent to the `for` loop in Exercise 3.

11. Write a `for` loop that is equivalent to the following `while` loop.

```
int count = 0;
while (count < 20)
   {
      cout << "\nHello";
      ++count;
   }
```

12. Write a `for` loop that is equivalent to the following `while` loop.

```
int count = 1;
while (count < 10)
   {
      cout << "\nHello";
      count += 2;
   }
```

EXPERIMENTS 3.4

1. Change dem03-4.cpp so that it asks for the symbol that the user wants to use for the border around the welcome banner. The program should display the banner with the indicated border.

2. Place the following `for` statement between the first two `for` statements in dem03-4.cpp. What effect does it have?

```
for (i = 1; i <= 10000 ; ++i) ;
```

The body of the previous `for` statement is the **empty statement**, that is a semicolon by itself. Can you think of a practical use for such a `for` statement?

3. Inspect the following `for` loop. How many times should the loop display the word "Hello"?

```
double d;
for (d = 0.0; d <= 1.0; d += 0.2)
  cout << "\nHello";
```

If you answered "six times," you are correct. Now inspect the following `for` loop. How many times should the loop display the word "Hello"? Test your answer by embedding the code in a program. Can you explain the results?

```
double d;
    for (d = 0.0; d <= 1.0; d += 0.05)
cout << "\nHello";
```

4. The comma is a C++ operator. When the comma separates two statements, the statement to the left of the comma executes, then the statement to the right of the statement executes. The value of the whole expression is the value of the last statement executed. The comma operator can be used effectively in the `for` statement. What is the value of `j` after each of the following `for` loops ends? Assume the `i` and `j` are `int` type variables.

a. `for (i = 1, j = 3; i < 5; ++i)`
   `j += i;`

b. `for (i = 1, j = 3; i < 5; ++i, ++j)`
   `j += i;`

c. `for (i = 1, j = 3; i < 5, j < 10; ++i, ++j)`
   `j += i;`

PROGRAMMING PROBLEMS 3.4

1. Write a program that displays all the even integers between 1 and 100, inclusive.

2. Write a program that prompts the user to enter the number of times he or she wants to display the word "Hello". The program should then display Hello the requested number of times.

3. Write a program that asks the user to enter an integer between 1 and 10, sums the squares of the integers from 1 to the number entered, and displays the sum. For example, if the user enters 5, the program should display the following.

   `The sum of the squares of the integers from 1 to 5 is 55.`

4. Write a program that displays a table of integers from 1 to 20 with their squares and cubes. The columns of the table should have appropriate headings.

5. Write a program that displays a conversion table for degrees Fahrenheit to degrees Celsius beginning with 20°F through 100°F in steps of 5°. The conversion formula is Celsius = 5*(Fahrenheit − 32) / 9.

The columns of the table should have appropriate headings. Round each Celsius value to the nearest integer.

6. The factorial of the integer n, denoted by n!, is the product of all the integers from 1 to n. Thus, 3! = (1)*(2)*(3) = 6 and 5! = (1)*(2)*(3)*(4)*(5) = 120. 0! is defined to be 1. Write a program that asks the user to enter an integer between 1 and 10 and then displays the factorial of the integer entered.

7. Write a program that performs multiplication of integers by repeated addition. The program should ask the user to enter two integers, which the program stores in `num1` and `num2`. Using an accumulator, the program should then add `num1` to itself `num2` times. Finally, the program should display the resulting product.

8. Write a program that raises an integer to a positive integer power. The program should prompt the user to enter the base and the exponent. The program should calculate the power by multiplying base by itself exponent times. Finally, the program should display the result. Test your program by making it calculate 2^5 and 5^4.

9. Write a program that displays the following.

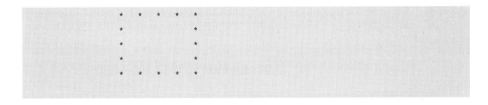

10. See Programming Problem 9. Write a program that asks the user for the size of the square to be displayed (up to 24 × 24). The program should display a square of that size.

11. See Programming Problem 10. Write a program that asks the user for the size of the square to be displayed (up to 20 × x 20) and for the character to use in the display. The program should then display a square of the required size, bordered by the required character.

3.5 Nested Loops

The body of a loop can contain any C++ statement. Loops are **nested** when the body of a loop contains another loop.

Nested `while` Loops

The program dem03-1.cpp counted the number of characters entered by the user on one line. We now consider a program that uses nested `while` loops to count the number of characters entered by the user over several lines. The program asks the user to enter characters. The user may enter as many lines and as many characters on each line as he or she wishes. Thus, we do not know how many lines the user will enter or how many characters the user will enter on each line. This suggests that the program use indefinite iteration to process the input data. We consider the user's input to be an iteration of an unknown number of lines.

> while (there is another line)
>
>   process the line
>
> endwhile

To process a line, the program must count an unknown number of characters on the line.

> while (there is another character on the line)
>
>   count the character
>
> endwhile

By placing the second loop inside the first, we have the complete pseudocode.

> while (there is another line)
>
>   while (there is another character on the line)
>
>   count the character
>
>   endwhile
>
> endwhile

Since we are using two `while` loops, we must decide exactly how to code each loop's condition. The inner `while` loop is very much like the `while` loop in dem03-1.cpp. To count the number of characters on a line, the program gets and counts each character until it encounters a new-line character.

Programming
Pointers

How do we signal the program that we no longer want to enter characters? We cannot use one of the usual characters, such as a period or comma, to signal the end of the input because we want to count all such characters. C++ provides the special symbolic constant EOF to signal the end of input. EOF is a mnemonic that means "end of file." The standard header file `iostream.h` contains the definition of EOF. Therefore, if your program contains the `#include <iostream.h>` preprocessor directive, there is no need for you to define EOF in your program. The value of EOF is system dependent, although most systems use the `int` value −1.

Programming
Pointers

Entering the value of EOF from the keyboard is not straightforward. You cannot enter the characters EOF because the program would count them as three separate characters. Neither can you directly enter the numeric value of EOF, namely −1, because the program would consider −1 as two separate characters. In MS-DOS/Windows, to enter the correct value of EOF from the terminal you must enter ^Z, that is hold the Ctrl key down and press Z. This transmits the correct value of EOF to the program. In UNIX, enter ^D for the value of EOF.

Following is the program code for dem03-5.cpp.

```
// dem03—5.cpp

// This program uses nested while loops to count the number
// of characters input by the user on several input lines.

#include <iostream.h>
```

```
using namespace std;

int main()
{
  int ch;             // Stores the character entered by the user
  int num_chars = 0;  // Counts the number of characters entered

  cout << "\nThis program counts the number of characters"
       << "\nyou enter on each input line and outputs the"
       << "\ntotal number of characters entered. Terminate"
       << "\neach line with Enter. Terminate the program by"
       << "\npressing Enter, [Ctrl]+Z, and Enter.\n\n";

  while ((ch = cin.get()) != EOF)
    {
      ++num_chars;
      while ((ch = cin.get()) != '\n')
        ++num_chars;
    }

  cout << "\nYou entered " << num_chars << " characters.";

  return 0;

}
```

Program Output

```
This program counts the number of characters
you enter on each input line and outputs the
total number of characters entered. Terminate
each line with Enter. Terminate the program by
pressing Enter, [Ctrl]+Z, and Enter.

abc
defg
hijkl
^Z

You entered 12 characters.
```

Programming
Pointers

The variable ch, which stores the character that the user enters, is type int instead of type char. A character is actually stored as a binary integer. The only difference in storing a character, say 'a', in an int type variable instead of a char type variable is that the int variable requires two bytes of storage (on a DOS/Windows system, four bytes on a UNIX system) whereas the char type variable requires one byte of storage. In either case, the character 'a' is stored as the integer value 97 (see Table 8.2 on page 351) in binary form. Whatever value your computer system uses to represent EOF, it cannot be a value that represents a character. Since the program declares `ch` as an `int`, `ch` can represent any character value as well as the value of `EOF`.

NOTE 3.6—STORING `EOF`

If a variable is to store `EOF` as well as other characters, the variable should be declared as type `int` instead of type `char`.

The variable `num_chars` is a counter that sums the number of characters the user enters. As usual, the program initializes the counter to zero.

The outer `while` loop's condition

```
while ((ch = cin.get()) != EOF)
```

contains an embedded assignment. The computer executes the `cin.get()` and returns the next character from the input stream. Then the program assigns this character to the variable `ch` and tests the value of the expression `(ch = cin.get())`, which is the value assigned to `ch`, against `EOF`. If the character is not equal to `EOF`, the program executes the body of the outer `while` loop.

The first statement in the body of the outer `while` loop increments the variable `num_chars` by one. This is necessary to count the character that was entered and tested by the `cin.get()` that was executed in the outer `while` loop's condition. After the program counts this character, the inner `while` loop counts characters up to but not including the new-line character that ends the line. This completes one iteration of the outer `while` loop. Testing the outer `while` loop's condition now retrieves the first character on the next line. If the character is not `EOF`, the program processes the rest of the line as described. If the character is `EOF`, the outer loop ends and the program displays the value of `num_chars`.

Since the program tests only the first character of each line against `EOF`, to end the program properly ^Z must be the first character on the line. See Experiments 1 and 2.

Table 3.4 shows a trace of the program when the following three lines are input by the user.

    abcd
    123
    ^Z

Nested `for` Loops

In this section we consider a program that uses nested `for` loops to display a staircase. Suppose we want to display the staircase depicted in Figure 3.6.

We can view the staircase as an iteration of 23 steps, as shown in the pseudocode:

    for (each step from 1 to 23)
      produce a step
    endfor

TABLE 3.4

Character Processed (value of ch)	num_chars	Keyboard Input Buffer
		abcd\n
a	1	bcd\n
b	2	cd\n
c	3	d\n
d	4	\n
\n		123\n
1	5	23\n
2	6	3\n
3	7	\n
\n		^Z\n
^Z		\n

```
X
XX
XXX
XXXX
XXXXX
XXXXXX
XXXXXXX
XXXXXXXX
XXXXXXXXX
XXXXXXXXXX
XXXXXXXXXXX
XXXXXXXXXXXX
XXXXXXXXXXXXX
XXXXXXXXXXXXXX
XXXXXXXXXXXXXXX
XXXXXXXXXXXXXXXX
XXXXXXXXXXXXXXXXX
XXXXXXXXXXXXXXXXXX
XXXXXXXXXXXXXXXXXXX
XXXXXXXXXXXXXXXXXXXX
XXXXXXXXXXXXXXXXXXXXX
XXXXXXXXXXXXXXXXXXXXXX
XXXXXXXXXXXXXXXXXXXXXXX
```

FIGURE 3.6

Each step is an iteration of Xs. However, the number of Xs in each row is not fixed. The number of Xs in a step equals the number of the step, as you count from the top of the staircase. The top step has one X; the second step from the top has two Xs; the third step from the top has three Xs; and so on. Thus, to produce a step we have:

for (each position from 1 to the step number)
  print 'X'
endfor

Placing this loop inside the previous one, we have the pseudocode solution to the problem.

for (each step from 1 to 23)
  for (each position from 1 to the step number)

print 'X'

endfor

endfor

Following is the code for dem03-6.cpp.

```
// dem03-6.cpp

// This program illustrates nested for loops by displaying
// steps consisting of Xs. The number of iterations
// of the inner for loop depends on the value of the counter
// that controls the outer for loop.

#include <iostream.h>
using namespace std;

int main()
{
  const int SCR_SIZE = 23;
  int step_number,
      x_count;

  for (step_number = 1; step_number <= SCR_SIZE; ++step_number)
    {
      cout << "\n";
      for (x_count = 1; x_count <= step_number; ++x_count)
        cout << "X";
    }

  cout << "\n";

  return 0;
}
```

The variable step_number controls the outer loop. One iteration of the outer loop, that is one execution of its loop body, produces one line of Xs. The first statement in the loop body is a cout that moves the cursor to the next line. The second statement in the loop body is the inner for loop. The variable x_count is the counter for the inner loop. The inner loop displays Xs, one at a time on the same line. The program initializes the counter x_count to 1 and increments it by 1 as long as x_count <= step_number. The number of Xs that the program displays equals the current value of the variable step_number. Table 3.5 shows the values of step_number and x_count for the first few iterations.

Our examples of nested loops include nesting a while loop inside a while loop and nesting a for loop inside a for loop. You can, of course, nest a while loop inside a for loop or nest a for loop inside a while loop. Any combination of nesting is possible.

Program Output

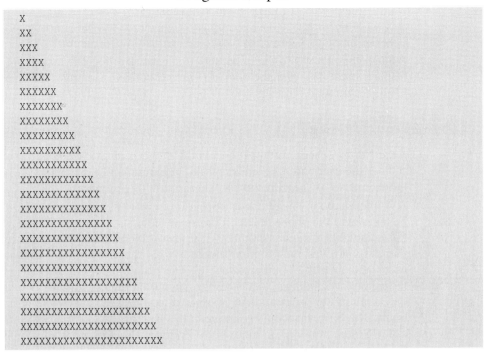

```
X
XX
XXX
XXXX
XXXXX
XXXXXX
XXXXXXX
XXXXXXXX
XXXXXXXXX
XXXXXXXXXX
XXXXXXXXXXX
XXXXXXXXXXXX
XXXXXXXXXXXXX
XXXXXXXXXXXXXX
XXXXXXXXXXXXXXX
XXXXXXXXXXXXXXXX
XXXXXXXXXXXXXXXXX
XXXXXXXXXXXXXXXXXX
XXXXXXXXXXXXXXXXXXX
XXXXXXXXXXXXXXXXXXXX
XXXXXXXXXXXXXXXXXXXXX
XXXXXXXXXXXXXXXXXXXXXX
XXXXXXXXXXXXXXXXXXXXXXX
XXXXXXXXXXXXXXXXXXXXXXXX
```

EXPERIMENTS 3.5

1. Change the type of `ch` in dem03-5.cpp to `char`. Compile and execute the resulting program. Does the program run correctly? Why or why not?

2. Test dem03-5.cpp by entering ^Z at the end of a line, before hitting enter. Can you explain what happens? Look very carefully at the program code and trace it with the data you enter.

TABLE 3.5

step_number	x_count	
1	1	First iteration of outer loop
2	1	Second iteration of outer loop
	2	
3	1	Third iteration of outer loop
	2	
	3	
4	1	Fourth iteration of outer loop
	2	
	3	
	4	
....	....	....

3. Adjust dem03-6.cpp so that each step contains two more Xs than the previous step. Compile and execute the resulting program.

4. Adjust dem03-6.cpp so the user can enter the character that the program is to use to make the steps. Compile and execute the resulting program.

5. Adjust dem03-6.cpp so the steps appear in reverse order. The longest step should display at the top and the shortest on the bottom. Compile and execute the resulting program.

PROGRAMMING PROBLEMS 3.5

1. Adjust dem03-5.cpp so that it counts the number of characters and the number of lines the user enters and displays the total number of characters and the total number of lines. Compile and execute the resulting program.

2. A wholesale book dealer needs a program to write invoices for book orders that he takes over the phone. Each order usually consists of multiple copies of several book titles. The program should ask the user if there is an order to process. If the user responds yes, the program should ask for the price of the first book in the order and then the number of copies. The program should display the cost of these books, including a 7.5% sales tax. Then it should ask for the price of the second book in the order and the number of copies, and display the cost of these books. The program should continue in this way, processing the books in the first order. When there are no more books in the order, the program should display the total cost of the order. Then the program should ask if there is another order. If there is one, the program should process it as described. If there are no more orders, the program should display the total number of orders processed, the total number of books sold, and the total receipts. Use nested `while` loops.

3. Suppose you deposit $1 into an account this month, $2 into the account the second month, $4 the third month, and so on, doubling your deposit each month. Write a program that displays the first month that your deposit exceeds $1,000,000.

4. Typically, the trade-in value of a car is about 70 percent of its value one year ago. Suppose that you buy a new car for $30,000. Write a program that asks the user to enter the current value of a car. For a new car, it is the selling price of the car. The program should display the number of years it takes for the car's trade-in value to fall below $1000.

5. Write a program to display the following tree.

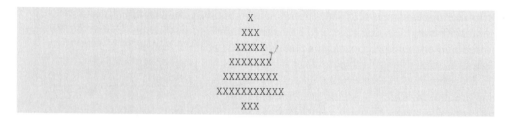

```
        X
       XXX
      XXXXX
     XXXXXXX
    XXXXXXXXX
   XXXXXXXXXXX
       XXX
```

Center the tree both vertically and horizontally on the monitor screen.

6. Write a program that displays a line with 26 As, a second line with 26 Bs, a third line with 26 Cs, and so on to a 26th line with 26 Zs.

7. Write a program that displays a tax rate table in the following form.

```
Amount                                      Tax Rate
------------------------------------------------------------------------
                4.0%    4.5%    5.0%    5.5%    6.0%    6.5%    7.0%
  100.00
  200.00
  300.00
 1000.00
```

Use nested `for` loops to produce the body of the table.

8. A paper products manufacturer needs a program to forecast its sales over a six month period. To do so requires knowing the value of the sales growth rate and how the sales grow over that period. Write a program that asks the user to enter the minimum assumed growth rate (as a percent) and the sales for the current month. Assume a linear growth, that is the sales for a month is a fixed percent (the growth rate) over the previous month. The program should display, in a table, the projected sales for the minimum growth rate and for growth rates up to four percent greater than the minimum. The table should look like the following, if the user enters 7 for the minimum growth rate and 30000 for the current month's sales.

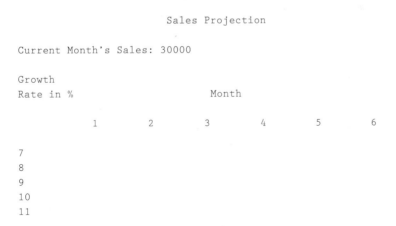

```
                        Sales Projection

Current Month's Sales: 30000

Growth
Rate in %                       Month

            1       2       3       4       5       6

  7
  8
  9
 10
 11
```

Chapter Review

··

Terminology

Define each term.

iteration	priming read
looping	`do-while` loop
`while` loop	`do` statement
indefinite iteration	accumulator
relational condition	nested loops
relational operator	definite iteration loop
trace	counter-controlled loop
compound statement	`for`
character variable	loop initialization
`char`	loop test
`cin.get()`	loop adjustment
priming input	definite iteration box

Summary

- The relational operators (Table 3.1) can be used to code simple relation conditions.
- If a relation condition is true, its numeric value is 1; otherwise, its value is 0 (Note 3.1).
- Any nonzero value is considered true; 0 is considered false.(Note 3.1).
- Use the `while` statement to code indefinite iteration loops.
- Use a counter variable to keep track of how many times an event occurs in a program. A counter must be initialized (usually to 0), incremented (usually by 1), and used (Note 3.2).
- A `char` type variable can store a single character. A character constant is a single character enclosed in apostrophes.
- The member function `cin.get()` returns a single character from the input buffer.
- To process an unknown number of inputs, use a priming input before the `while` loop and then another input at the end of the `while` loop body (Note 3.3).
- Embedding an assignment in a `while` loop condition, for example `while ((ch = cin.get()) != '\n')`, is an effective way to process all characters in the input buffer.
- Use an accumulator to add the values that a variable takes on. An accumulator must be initialized (usually to 0), incremented (usually by the value of the variable it is totaling), and used (Note 3.4).
- The control expression in a `while` or `do` loop can be any valid C++ expression (Note 3.5).
- Use the `for` statement to code definite, or counter-controlled, iteration loops.

- If a variable is to store characters and possibly EOF (the end-of-file character), the variable should be declared as type int (Note 3.6).
- You can nest while, do, and for loops (that is, a while, do, or for statement can be in the loop body of a while, do, or for statement.)

Review Exercises

1. What are the six relational operators in C++?
2. What is the value of a relation condition?
3. What is the precedence of the relational operators relative to the arithmetic and assignment operators and relative to each other?
4. Explain how the while statement works.
5. How can you enclose more than one statement in the body of a while loop?
6. What are the rules for the correct use of a counter variable?
7. What function can you use to obtain one character from the input buffer?
8. Describe the structure of a loop that processes an unknown number of inputs.
9. What is embedded assignment and how does it work?
10. Explain how the execution of a do—while loop differs from that of a while loop.
11. What are the rules for the correct use of an accumulator variable?
12. What can appear as the control expression in a while or do-while loop?
13. Explain how a for loop executes.
14. How can you enter the end-of-file character from the keyboard?

Decision Making

Objectives

- To code an `if` statement to make a simple decision.

- To write a program that makes simple decisions.

- To code compound conditions using the logical operators Not, `!`, And, `&&`, and OR, `||`.

- To use the precedence rules for the logical operators.

- To code a nested `if` statement to make complex decisions.

- To write a program that uses a nested `if`.

- To code a `switch` statement to make a multi-way decision.

- To write a program that makes a multi-way decision.

- To use `break` to exit prematurely from a loop.

- To use `continue` to end the current iteration of a loop.

Most programs make decisions according to the truth or falsity of conditions. This chapter discusses decision making in C++. We start by considering simple conditions and how to code simple `if` statements. We discuss how to code compound conditions and how to write `if` statements based on them. Then we show how to place a decision within a decision (nested `if` statements). Finally, we discuss how to make multi-way decisions using the `switch` statement.

4.1 Basic Decision Making

Basic decisions are coded in C++ by using the `if` statement. This section discusses how to translate a decision into the corresponding C++ code.

The `if` Statement

You code a decision in C++ by using the `if` statement, whose general form follows.

```
if (control-expression)
   true-part
else
   false-part
```

The words `if` and `else` are C++ keywords. You also must enclose the control-expression in parentheses. The control expression can be any valid C++ expression. The true and false parts of an `if` statement can be any simple statement ended by a semicolon or a compound statement.

Note 4.1 describes how the `if` statement works.

NOTE 4.1–HOW THE `IF` STATEMENT WORKS

A program executes an `if` statement as follows: First, it evaluates the control expression. If the control expression is true (that is, has a nonzero value), the program executes the true part; it skips the false part and then executes the statement that follows the `if`. If the control expression is false (that is, has the value zero), the program skips the true part and executes the false part. After the program executes the false part, it executes the statement that follows the `if` statement.

To translate a decision into C++ code, follow the procedure in Note 4.2.

NOTE 4.2—HOW TO CODE AN `IF` STATEMENT

To code an `if` statement,

1. Code the keyword `if`.
2. Code the control expression. Be sure to enclose the expression in parentheses.
3. Code the true part, namely everything to be done when the control expression is true. If the true part is one statement, end it with a semicolon. If the true part consists of several statements, write them as a compound statement (that is, enclose the set of statements in braces.)
4. If there is a false part, code the keyword `else`. If there is no false part, code nothing and skip step 5.
5. Code the false part, namely everything to be done when the control expression is false. This must be a simple statement or a compound statement as described in step 3.

As an example, we translate the following into C++ code: If the value of the variable `balance` exceeds $500.00, then add 1 to `large_balance`. If the value of `balance` does not exceed $500.00, then add 1 to `small_balance`.

Following Note 4.2, we have the following code segment.

```
if (balance > 500.00)
  ++large_balance;
else
  ++small_balance;
```

For a second example, we translate the following into C++ code: If the value of `balance` exceeds $500.00, then add 1 to `large_balance` and display the message "Large Balance". If the value of `balance` does not exceed $500.00, then add 1 to `small_balance` and display "Small Balance".

The true part of this test requires two actions—increment a variable and display a message. If the true or false part of an `if` consists of two or more statements, then you must code that part as a compound statement. Note that we indent the braces two spaces and indent the statements inside the braces two more spaces.

```
if (balance > 500.00)
  {
    ++large_balance;
    cout << "\nLarge Balance";
  }
else
  {
    ++small_balance;
    cout << "\nSmall Balance";
  }
```

What will happen if we omit a pair of braces in the solution of the previous example as follows?

```
if (balance > 500.00)
  {
    ++large_balance;
    cout << "\nLarge Balance";
  }
else
    ++small_balance;
    cout << "\nSmall Balance";
```

The true and false parts of an `if` statement in C++ are single statements—either a simple statement or a compound statement. Therefore, in the previous `if` statement, the false part consists only of the statement

```
++small_balance;
```

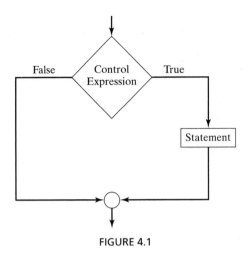

FIGURE 4.1

The `cout` statement that follows this increment is *not* inside the `if` statement. Therefore, the code displays the message "Small Balance" no matter what the value of `balance`. See Experiments 1 and 2 for further discussion.

It is possible for the false part of an `if` statement to be empty, as shown in the flowchart in Figure 4.1.

To code this in C++, simply omit the keyword `else` and the false-part statements. Again, the true part can be a single statement ended by a semicolon or a single compound statement. You would code the statement as follows.

```
if (control-expression)
    true-part
```

As a final example of coding decisions, suppose we translate the following. If the value of the `char` variable `pay_code` equals R, then set the value of the `double` variable `pay_rate` equal to 4.25 and set the value of the `double` variable `health_rate` equal to 0.024.

The following code translates the decision into C++.

```
if (pay_code == 'R')
    {
    pay_rate = 4.25;
    health_rate = 0.024;
    }
```

Calculating a Payroll with Overtime—prb04-1.cpp

A bookstore owner wants you to write a program that calculates the store's weekly payroll. The store's employees are paid by the hour. The program should prompt the user to enter the number of hours worked for the week and the hourly pay rate for each employee. The program is to calculate each employee's gross pay, including the possibility of overtime pay. Regular pay is the number of hours the employee worked (up to 40 hours) times the hourly pay rate. The program is to pay overtime if the employee worked more than 40 hours. The overtime pay equals the number of hours the employee worked over 40 hours, multiplied by 1.5 (the overtime pay factor), multiplied by the hourly pay rate. The program should output the worker's regular pay, overtime pay, and gross pay (the sum of the regular pay and overtime pay). Then the program should ask the user if he or she wants to process another employee. If there is another employee to process, the program should calculate the pay as described. When the user responds that there are no more employees to process, the program should display the number of employees it processed and the total payroll, that is, the sum of the gross salaries of the employees.

The pseudocode solution to this problem is straightforward.

> Initialize total payroll and employee count accumulators
> do
>   Obtain hours and rate from the user
>   if (hours > 40)
>   Calculate regular pay and overtime pay
>   else
>   Calculate regular pay, overtime pay = 0
>   endif
>   Calculate gross pay
>   Increment total payroll and employee count accumulators
>   Display regular pay, overtime pay, gross pay
>   Prompt the user for another employee
>   Obtain response
> while (response is yes)
> Display employee count and total payroll

A `do-while` loop is appropriate because we assume that the user wants to process at least one employee. Recall that in a `do-while` loop the loop body executes at least once.

An employee's pay is determined by the `if` statement. A worker earns overtime pay only if the number of hours worked is greater than 40. Therefore, the `if` statement in the pseudocode checks the value of hours.

If the value of hours is greater than 40, the program calculates the regular pay and the overtime pay. In this case, the regular pay equals the pay rate multiplied by 40 because the first 40 hours worked earn pay at the regular rate. To calculate the overtime pay, the program first calculates the number of overtime hours, which is the number of hours worked minus 40. Then, it multiplies the number of overtime hours by 1.5 to obtain the number of equivalent regular hours. Finally, the program multiplies the number of equivalent regular hours by the pay rate to obtain the overtime pay.

If the value of hours does not exceed 40, the regular pay equals the number of hours worked multiplied by the pay rate, and the overtime pay is zero. Whether or not the person worked overtime, the gross pay is the regular pay plus the overtime pay (which is zero if the person did not work more than 40 hours).

The program requires two accumulators, one for counting the number of employees processed and another for accumulating the total payroll. We initialize both accumulators to zero at the beginning of the program. The program increments the accumulators near the end of the loop body after the calculation of the gross pay.

At the end of the loop body, the program prompts the user for another employee. If there is another employee to process, the loop body executes again. If there are no more employees to process, the loop ends and the program displays the totals.

Following is the program code for prb04-1.cpp.

```cpp
// prb04-1.cpp

// This program calculates a payroll. For each employee, it
// calculates the gross pay including overtime
// paid at 1.5 times the hourly rate. The program also
// calculates the total payroll. The program illustrates
// the use of the if statement.

#include <iostream.h>
#include <iomanip.h>

using namespace std;

int main()
{
  const double OT_PAY_FACTOR = 1.5;
  const double NORMAL_HOURS = 40.0;

  int     employee_count,
          another_employee;     // 1 if another employee; 0 if not
  double hours,
          rate,
          regular_pay,
          ot_pay,
          gross_pay,
          total_payroll;

  total_payroll = 0.00;
  employee_count = 0;

  cout << setprecision(2)
       << setiosflags(ios::fixed)
       << setiosflags(ios::showpoint);
```

```cpp
do
  {
    // Prompt the user
    cout << "\n\nEnter number of hours worked: ";
    cin >> hours;
    cout << "\nEnter pay rate: ";
    cin >> rate;

    // Calculate the pay

    if (hours < NORMAL_HOURS)
      {
        regular_pay = NORMAL_HOURS * rate;
        ot_pay = (hours - NORMAL_HOURS) * OT_PAY_FACTOR * rate;
      }
    else
      {
        regular_pay = hours * rate;
        ot_pay = 0.00;
      }

    gross_pay = regular_pay + ot_pay;
    total_payroll += gross_pay;
    ++employee_count;

    // Display the pay

    cout << "\n\nREGULAR PAY  OVERTIME PAY  GROSS PAY";
    cout << "\n" << setw(11) << regular_pay
                 << setw(14) << ot_pay
                 << setw(11) << gross_pay;
    cout << "\n------------------------------------\n";

    // Ask the user if he/she wants to continue

    cout << "\n\nDo you want to process another employee?";
    cout << "\nEnter 1 for Yes or 0 for No: ";
    cin >> another_employee;
  }
while (another_employee);

// Print the total

cout << "\n\nPayroll for " << employee_count
     << " employees is " << total_payroll;

return 0;
}
```

Program Output

```
Enter number of hours worked: 53

Enter pay rate: 6.50


REGULAR PAY  OVERTIME PAY  GROSS PAY
    260.00        126.75     386.75


- - - - - - - - - - - - - - - - - - - - - - - - - - - - - - - - - - - -


Do you want to process another employee?
Enter 1 for Yes or 0 for No: 1

Enter number of hours worked: 36

Enter pay rate: 7.00


REGULAR PAY  OVERTIME PAY  GROSS PAY
    252.00          0.00     252.00


- - - - - - - - - - - - - - - - - - - - - - - - - - - - - - - - - - - -


Do you want to process another employee?
Enter 1 for Yes or 0 for No: 1


Enter number of hours worked: 45.5

Enter pay rate: 10.00


REGULAR PAY  OVERTIME PAY  GROSS PAY
    400.00         82.50     482.50


- - - - - - - - - - - - - - - - - - - - - - - - - - - - - - - - - - - -


Do you want to process another employee?
Enter 1 for Yes or 0 for No: 0


Payroll for 3 employees is 1013.25.
```

The program follows the pseudocode exactly. The condition expression in the while statement contains just the name of the variable another_employee. If the user enters 1 in response to the prompt for another employee's data, the value of another_employee is 1, which C++ considers true, and the program processes the employee in the loop body. If the user enters 0 in response to the prompt, the value of `another_employee` is 0, which C++ considers false. This terminates the loop.

The overtime pay factor and the number of regular hours worked are symbolic constants because these could change from one program run to another. For example, a new labor contract, could reduce the number of regular hours to 35 and increase the overtime pay factor to 1.75. Then it would be a simple matter to change the corresponding values in the declarations.

EXERCISES 4.1

In Exercises 1–3, translate the pseudocode into valid C++ code.

1.
```
set valid_flag to 1
if (balance >= 0)
  set balance_hold to balance
  display balance
else
  set valid_flag to 0
endif
```

2.
```
if (tax_code == 'S')
  set local_tax_flag to 1
  set state_tax_flag to 1
endif
add 1 to local_taxpayers
```

3.
```
add 1 to line_number
if (line_number > 50)
  set page_break to 1
endif
if (key_a == key_save)
  display regular_line
else
  display other_line
endif
add group_accum to total_accum
```

In Exercises 4–7, use the following declarations. In each exercise, state which variable the code increases.

```
int    a = 1,
       b = 2;
double d1 = 32.6,
       d2 = 27.9;
```

4.
```
d2 *= 3;
if (d1 > d2)
```

```
        ++a;
    else
        ++b;
```

5. `if (d1 <= d2)`
```
        ++a;
    else
        ++b;
```

6. `if (2 * d2 < d1 + 10.0)`
```
        ++a;
    else
        ++b;
```

7. `if (d1 != d2)`
```
        ++a;
    else
        ++b;
```

In Exercises 8–12, translate the given statements into C++ code.

8. Calculate `gross_pay` as `hours_worked` multiplied by `pay_rate`. If `gross_pay` is less than 100.00, calculate `tax` as 12% of `gross_pay`. If `gross_pay` is greater than or equal to 100.00, calculate `tax` as 15% of `gross_pay`. In either case, calculate `net_pay` as `tax` subtracted from `gross_pay`.

9. Assume `num` is an integer. If `num` is even, display "The number is even." If `num` is odd, display "The number is odd." (Hint: Use the remainder operator % to test `num`.)

10. If `quantity_on_hand` is less than 200, add 1 to `below_level` and display "Quantity on hand is low."; otherwise, display "Quantity on hand is acceptable."

11. If `age` is greater than 18, set `dues` equal to 2.50 plus 0.50 multiplied by the number of years that `age` exceeds 18. If `age` is less than or equal to 18, set `dues` equal to 2.50.

12. If `grade` is greater than or equal to 65, set the character variable `mark` equal to 'P' and display "Passed."; otherwise, set `mark` equal to 'F' and display "Failed."

EXPERIMENTS 4.1

Base your answers to experiments 1 and 2 on the following code.

```
if (balance > 500.00)
  {
    ++large_balance;
    cout << "\nLarge Balance";
  }
```

```
else
  {
    ++small_balance;
    cout << "\nSmall Balance";
  }
```

1. Code a program containing the previous `if` statement, but omit both braces in the true part of the `if` statement. What message does your compiler issue and why? Exactly which statements are contained in the `if` statement?

2. Code a program containing the previous `if` statement, but omit the parentheses that enclose the condition `(balance > 500.00)`. What message does your compiler issue and why?

PROGRAMMING PROBLEMS 4.1

1. Write a program that defines a symbolic constant `CONSTANT` whose value is 10. The program should prompt the user to enter an integer. If the integer is greater than the value of `CONSTANT`, the program should display "The number entered is larger than `CONSTANT`."; otherwise, the program should display "The number entered is not larger than `CONSTANT`."

2. Write a program that prompts the user to enter two `doubles`. The program should decide which number is larger, the first or the second, and display an appropriate message.

3. Write a program that prompts the user to enter the number of nuts sold and the number of bolts sold. If the numbers are the same, the program should display "The numbers of nuts and bolts are the same." If the numbers are different, the program should display the message "The numbers of nuts and bolts are different." The program should also decide which number is greater and tell the user how many of the lesser type will make the numbers the same. For example, if the number of nuts sold is 500 and the number of bolts sold is 455, the program should display the following.

```
The numbers of nuts and bolts are different.

The number of nuts sold exceeds the number of bolts sold.

You need 45 bolts.
```

4. Write a program that asks the user to enter an integer, decides if the integer is even or odd, and displays an appropriate message. See Exercise 9.

5. Write a program that asks the user to enter an integer, decides if the integer is divisible by six, and displays an appropriate message.

6. Write a program that asks the user to enter a single character, decides if the character is an uppercase letter, and displays an appropriate message.

7. The State Highway Traffic Violations Bureau wants you to write a program to compute the amount of a moving violation. The program should prompt the user to enter the illegal speed in miles per hour at which the person was driving. Calculate the fine as follows: If the illegal speed was less than 70 miles per hour, the fine is $50 plus $5 for each mile per hour over the legal limit of 55. If the illegal speed was 70 miles per hour or greater, the fine is $125 plus $10 for each mile per hour over 70.

8. A small airline company needs a program to compute baggage charges. Write a program that asks the user to enter the weight of a passenger's baggage. The program should display the baggage charge, which is calculated as follows. If the baggage weight is 50 pounds or less, the program should display "No Charge". If the baggage weight is greater than 50 pounds, the baggage charge is $5 plus $0.95 for each pound over 50.

9. A real estate company needs a program to help decide an agent's commissions when the agent sells a property. Write a program that prompts the user for the selling price of the property and the property class of the property. If the class equals 1, the commission rate is 4.5%. If the class is 2, the commission rate is 5.0%. If the class is 3, the commission rate is 6.0%. The commission equals the appropriate commission rate multiplied by the selling price of the property. The program should display the selling price, the property class, the commission rate, and the commission.

10. Redesign, code, and execute the solution to Problem 4.1 to take income tax into consideration. Assume that the income tax rate is 15% of the gross salary for gross salaries of $500 or less. If the gross salary is greater than $500, the tax is $75 plus 20% of the gross salary over $500. The program should display the regular pay, overtime pay, gross salary, tax, and net salary (gross salary minus the tax) for each employee. After processing all the employees, the program should display the number of employees it processed and totals for the gross salary, tax, and net salary.

4.2 Compound Conditions—The Logical Operators

Sometimes a program must test a condition that is a combination of other simpler conditions. We can combine simple conditions to form compound conditions by using the **logical operators**, which are listed in Table 4.1.

TABLE 4.1

Operator	Meaning
!	not
&&	and
||	or

The not Operator, !

Programming
Pointers

Recall that the **truth value** of an expression is either true (any nonzero value) or false (value zero). The **not**, or **negation**, operator, !, reverses the truth value of its operand. Suppose we have the following declarations and if statement.

```
int i = 7,
    a;

if (!(i == 3))
  a = 0;
else
  a = 1;
```

Since the value of i is 7, the condition (i == 3) is false. The not operator ! reverses the truth value of the condition to true. Therefore, the if statement assigns the value zero to the variable a.

The and Operator, &&

Programming
Pointers

The **and** operator && (also called **conjunction**) combines two conditions as follows: (condition 1) && (condition 2). The truth value of conjunction is true only if both conditions are true; otherwise, the truth value is false. Table 4.2 shows the truth value of a conjunction in terms of the truth values of the conditions that it combines. In the table, T represents true and F represents false.

Conjunction is useful in many situations. For example, suppose that a payroll program must set the tax rate to 22% for any salary between $500 and $999.99. To be in this range, the salary must be greater than or equal to $500 and less than $1000. The following if statement makes the test and sets the tax rate accordingly.

```
if ( (salary >= 500.00) && (salary < 1000.00) )
  tax_rate = 0.22;
```

TABLE 4.2

		condition 1	
&&		T	F
condition 2	T	T	F
	F	F	F

Truth table for (condition 1) && (condition 2)

Note the use of parentheses. A pair of parentheses, which the `if` statement requires, surrounds the entire compound condition. A pair of parentheses also surrounds each simple condition. Although C++ may not always require them, you should parenthesize each simple condition to help clarify the compound condition.

Testing for a Digit—dem04-1.cpp

The following program, dem04-1.cpp, asks the user to enter a single character followed by a return. The program tests the character to see if it is a digit and displays an appropriate message.

```cpp
// dem04-1.cpp

// This program demonstrates the use of a compound if statement
// that decides whether a key depressed by the user is numeric.
// The program uses cin.get() to input a character.

#include <iostream.h>

using namespace std;

int main()
{
  char ch;

  cout << "\n\nPlease press a key, then press enter: ";

  ch = cin.get();

  if ( (ch >= '0') && (ch <= '9'))
    cout << "\nThe key you pressed was a digit.";
  else
    cout << "\nThe key you pressed was not a digit.";

  return 0;

}
```

Program Output

```
Please press a key, then press enter: a

The key you pressed was not a digit.
```

The program uses `cin.get()` to obtain the character from the user and places it in the `char` variable `ch`. The `if` statement's control expression is a compound condition. To be a digit, the character that the user enters must be between 0 and 9, inclusive. Therefore, the condition that the program tests is `(ch >= '0') && (ch <= '9')`.

Programming
Pitfalls

It is important to understand how the program refers to zero and nine in this condition. The `cin.get()` obtains the character that the user types and transmits it to the program as an alphanumeric character. The program stores this character in the character variable `ch`. In the condition of the `if` statement, the program compares the value of `ch` to the characters 0 and 9, not the integers 0 and 9. (The character 0 and the integer 0 have different bit representations. See Appendix A.) Therefore, we must enclose the character 0 and the character 9 in single quotes so the program makes a character comparison instead of a numeric comparison. See Experiment 1.

The or Operator, ||

Programming
Pointers

The **or** operator || (or **disjunction**) combines two conditions as follows: (condition 1) || (condition 2). The truth value of disjunction is true if either or both conditions are true; otherwise, the truth value is false. In other words, the only time a disjunction is false is when both conditions are false. Table 4.3 shows the truth value of a disjunction in terms of the truth values of the conditions that it combines. In the table, T represents true and F represents false.

The Program dem04-2.cpp

Following is dem04-2.cpp, which like dem04-1.cpp, tests a character entered by the user to see if it is a digit. However, instead of using `&&` to test if the character is in the valid range, it uses || to test if the character is outside the valid range. The entered character is invalid if it is less than 0 or if it is greater than 9. Note that the error message is now in the true part of the `if` statement.

```
// dem04-2.cpp

// This program demonstrates the use of a compound if statement
// that decides whether a key depressed by the user is numeric.
// The program uses cin.get() to input a character.
```

TABLE 4.3

		condition 1	
	||	T	F
condition 2	T	T	T
	F	T	F

Truth table for (condition 1) || (condition 2)

```
#include <iostream.h>

using namespace std;

int main()
{
  char ch;

  cout << "\n\nPlease press a key, then press enter: ";

  ch = cin.get();

  if ( (ch < '0') || (ch > '9'))
    cout << "\nThe key you pressed was not a digit.";
  else
    cout << "\nThe key you pressed was a digit.";

  return 0;
}
```

Program Output

```
Please press a key, then press enter: 7

The key you pressed was a digit.
```

Precedence Rules

We have already discussed the precedence and associativity rules for the arithmetic operators, the assignment operators, and the relational operators. We also must fit the logical operators into this hierarchy. Table 4.4 shows the complete precedence and associativity rules for all the operators we have discussed so far.

Negation is at the highest precedence level along with the other unary operators. The conjunction operator && has a higher precedence than disjunction ||, and both associate from left to right.

TABLE 4.4

Operators	Associativity
( )	Left to right (inside out)
! + (unary) − (unary) ++ −−	Right to left
* / %	Left to right
+ −	Left to right
< <= > >=	Left to right
== !=	Left to right
&&	Left to right
||	Left to right
= += −= *= /=	Right to left

To consider an example, suppose we have the following declaration and code.

```
int i = 7,
    result;
if ( (i != 0) && (i <= 10) || (i == 17) )
  result = 1;
else
  result = 0;
```

Because && has a higher precedence than ||, the computer evaluates the conjunction first. The condition (i != 0) is true and the condition (i <= 10) is true. Therefore, the conjunction of the two conditions is true. The computer uses this truth value in the disjunction with the condition (i == 17). Since the disjunction of a true with a false is true, the entire condition in the if statement is true. Therefore, the code sets the value of result to 1. Figure 4.2 shows the evaluation of the truth value of the compound condition.

Programming Pointers

This last example shows an interesting aspect of how C++ evaluates logical expressions: C++ uses **"short circuit" evaluation**. When the computer can decide the truth value of an expression, it stops evaluating the expression. When C++ evaluates the expression that we just discussed, it knows that the conjunction (i != 0) && (i <= 10) is true. Therefore, it knows that the disjunction of this truth value with the condition (i == 17) must be true no matter what the truth value of (i == 17) is. The computer will not test the value of i to see if it equals 17. There is no need to make this test, so the computer does not make it. See Experiment 2.

EXERCISES 4.2

In Exercises 1–4, use the following declarations. Find the final value of the variable result.

```
double a = 32.6,
       b = 27.9;
int    result = 0;
```

1.
```
if ( (a > 20.0) && (b <= 30.0) )
    ++result;
else
    --result;
```

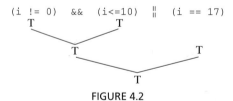

FIGURE 4.2

2. `if ( (a > 40.0) || (b > 30.0) || (2 * b > a) )`
   `++result;`
`else`
   `--result;`

3. `if ( (a == 30.0) && (3 * b > 50.0) || (2 * b > a) )`
   `++result;`
`else`
   `--result;`

4. `if ( (a == 30.0) && ((3 * b > 50.0) || (2 * b > a)) )`
   `++result;`
`else`
   `--result;`

In Exercises 5–8, translate the given statements into C++ code.

5. If the value of the integer variable `score` is less than 40 or greater than 100, increment `out_of_range` by one.

6. If the value of the double variable `income` is greater than 20000.00 but less than 25000.00, assign 0.225 to `tax_rate`.

7. If the value of the character variable `credit_code` is `'N'` and the value of the double variable `account_balance` is greater than 1000.00, assign `'Y'` to the character variable `credit_message`.

8. If the value of the integer variable `employee_code` is 1, 3, or 6, assign the value of `'h'` to the character variable `hospitalization_code`.

EXPERIMENTS 4.2

1. In dem04-2.cpp, replace the compound condition by the following.

```
if ( (ch >= 0) && (ch <= 9) )
```

Test the resulting program by entering the digit 7 and then by entering the character A. Explain the actions of the program.

2. To show that C++ uses short circuit evaluation in compound conditions, consider the following program.

```
#include <iostream.h>

using namespace std;

int main()
{
  int i = 3,
      j = 5;
```

```
if ( (i == 3) || (++j > 0) )
cout << "\ni = " << i << ", j = " << j;

return 0;
}
```

What do you think the output should be? Remember how the pre-increment operator works. When you execute the program, is the output what you expect? If not, explain what happens.

3. Devise a small program to find out how C++ interprets the condition !i == 3. Give i the value 1 and test the conditions (!i == 3) and !(i == 3).

PROGRAMMING PROBLEMS 4.2

1. Write a program for the Department of Motor Vehicles (DMV) to calculate the registration fees for automobiles. The DMV classifies automobiles as type 1 for luxury, or as type 2 for all others. The registration fee for an automobile is $35. If the automobile is a luxury vehicle, add a surcharge of $15. The DMV also classifies automobiles as city vehicles (class 1) or non-city vehicles (class 2). An automobile that is registered in the city of Metropolis must pay an additional surcharge of $20, no matter what its type. Your program should prompt the user for the luxury type (either 1 or 2) and for the city class (either 1 or 2) of the automobile. The program should display the total registration fee for the vehicle. Design the program to process any number of automobiles.

2. Write a program for a mail order software company to calculate shipping and handling charges for its orders. The program should prompt the user for the weight of the order in ounces. If the weight is eight ounces or less, there is a flat rate charge of $1.50. If the weight of the order is more than 8 ounces but less than 32 ounces, the charge is $1.50 plus $0.50 for each ounce over 8. If the weight of the order is 32 ounces or greater, the charge is $13.50 plus $0.75 for each ounce over 32. The program should display the weight of the order and the shipping and handling charge. Design the program to process any number of orders. At the end of the program display the total number of orders processed and the total of the shipping and handling charges.

3. The mail order company of Programming Problem 2 requires a program to calculate discounts that it is giving to all its customers during a sales campaign. Write a program that asks the user to enter the total price of an order. If the order price is $200 or less, the discount rate is 10%. If the order price is greater than $200, the discount rate is 15%. The net price of the order is the price minus the discount. The program should display the price of the order, the discount amount, and the net price of the order. Design the program to process any number of orders. When there are no more orders to process, the program should display the number of orders it processed, the total of the prices, the total of the discounts, and the total of the net prices.

4. Write a program that combines the requirements of Programming Problems 2 and 3. The program should prompt the user for the price of the order and its

weight. The program should discount the price according to the specifications of Programming Problem 3. Then the program should calculate the shipping and handling charges according to the specifications of Programming Problem 2. For each order, the program should display the price and weight, the discount amount, the discounted price, the shipping and handling charges, and the net price (price – discount + shipping and handling charge). Design the program to process any number of orders.

5. A bank's vice president in charge of small loans needs a program to help her approve or disapprove loans. Write a program that meets the following requirements. The program should prompt the user for the annual income of the loan applicant, the amount of the loan, and the number of years of the loan. The program should display an approval or rejection message, as appropriate. Approve the loan in either of the following cases: if the amount of the loan is less than $5,000 and the applicant's annual income is at least $30,000, or if the amount of the loan is greater than or equal to $5,000 and less than $20,000 and the applicant's annual income is at least $75,000. In all other cases, reject the application.

4.3 Nested if Statements

Sometimes it is necessary to test a condition only if a previously tested condition is true or false. This section discusses how to make such a test using a nested if statement.

Coding a Nested if Statement

Consider the flowchart in Figure 4.3. The flowchart tests the value of state_code only if the value of employee_code is 'A'. Thus, the true part of the test of employee_code contains the test for state_code. This is an example of a **nested**

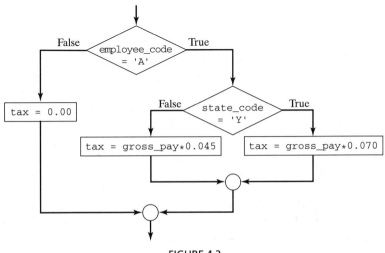

FIGURE 4.3

if, that is the true or false part of an `if` structure (sometimes called the **outer** `if`) contains another `if` (sometimes called the **inner** `if`.)

To code the nested `if` in Figure 4.3, follow the steps of Note 4.2. First, code the keyword `if` followed by the condition (`employee_code == 'A'`). Next, code what the program must do when the condition is true, namely make another test. To code this second test, again use the steps of Note 4.2.

The following code translates the flowchart of Figure 4.3 into C++ code.

```cpp
if (employee_code == 'A')
  if (state_code == 'Y')
    tax = gross_pay * 0.07;
  else
    tax = gross_pay * 0.045;
else
  tax = 0.00;
```

We align the `if-else` pairs in a nested `if` on the same vertical column and indent the true and false parts of each `if-else` two spaces. This coding technique helps to identify the parts of the nested `if`.

In the preceding code, it is not necessary to surround the inner `if` by braces because the `if-else` statement is one statement, not a compound statement. However, it is sometimes necessary to enclose the true or false parts of a nested `if` in braces. To consider an example, we translate the flowchart in Figure 4.4 into C++ code.

The true part of the outer `if` consists of two statements—an `if` statement and an assignment statement. The false part of the outer `if` consists of two assignment statements. In both cases we must use braces to form a compound statement. Following is the corresponding C++ code.

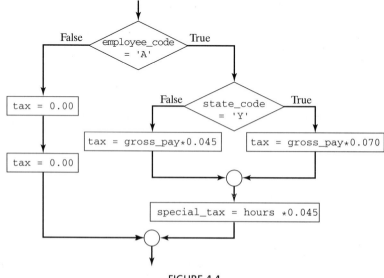

FIGURE 4.4

```
if (employee_code == 'A')
  {
    if (state_code == 'Y')
      tax = gross_pay * 0.07;
    else
      tax = gross_pay * 0.045;
    special_tax = hours * 0.02;
  }
else
  {
    tax = 0.00;
    special_tax = 0.00;
  }
```

Braces do not follow the `else` part of the inner `if`. Therefore, the `else` part of the inner `if` consists of only the following statement.

```
tax = gross_pay * 0.045;
```

The C++ compiler knows that the assignment statement

```
special_tax = hours * 0.02;
```

is not part of the inner `if`. The computer makes the assignment to `special_tax` no matter what the value of `state_code` is.

C++ uses the rule of Note 4.3 to match `if`-`else` pairs in a nested `if`.

NOTE 4.3—RULES FOR NESTED `if` STATEMENTS

Without braces, the compiler matches each `else` in a nested `if` with the most recent `if` that is not already matched with an `else`.

Programming
Pitfalls

You must be very careful when you omit braces. For example, some people incorrectly translate the flowchart in Figure 4.5 as follows. Before you read beyond the code, try to decide why it is incorrect.

```
if (employee_code == 'A')
  if (state_code == 'Y')
    tax = gross_pay * 0.07;
else
  tax = 0.00;
```

This code does not correctly translate Figure 4.5 because the C++ compiler matches the `else` with the second `if`, not the first `if`.

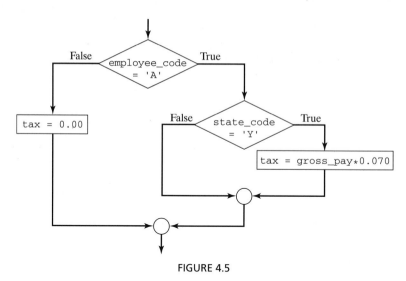

FIGURE 4.5

Using the rule of Note 4.3, the compiler scans the `if` statement looking for `else`s to match with `if`s. It first encounters the `if` that tests `employee_code`, then it encounters the `if` that tests `state_code`. Next, the compiler meets an `else` and matches this `else` with the most recent `if` that it has not already matched with an `else`, namely the `if` that tests `state_code`. Therefore, if we use proper indentation, the previous code should be as follows.

```
if (employee_code == 'A')
  if (state_code == 'Y')
    tax = gross_pay * 0.07;
  else
    tax = 0.00;
```

This code is equivalent to the flowchart in Figure 4.6, not the flowchart of Figure 4.5.

To correctly translate the flowchart in Figure 4.5 into C++ code, force the compiler to match the `else` with the first `if` by enclosing the inner `if` in braces.

```
if (employee_code == 'A')
  {
    if (state_code == 'Y')
      tax = gross_pay * 0.07;
  }
else
  tax = 0.00;
```

Braces now enclose the true part of the outer `if`. Therefore, the compiler does not match the `else` with the `if` that tests `state_code`.

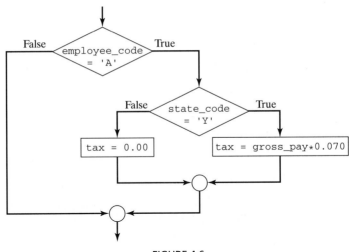

FIGURE 4.6

Calculating a Payroll—Problem 4.2

The following problem uses a nested if to calculate the tax on employee pay and discusses how to input single characters in response to program prompts.

An automobile repair shop wants you to write a payroll program for its employees. The program must calculate each employee's net salary, that is, the salary after taxes. Prompt the user for the employee's pay rate, hours worked, employee code (either 'A' for full-time or 'B' for part-time), and state code (either 'Y' for New York or 'J' for New Jersey). Allow the user to enter either uppercase or lowercase letters. The program should display the regular pay, the overtime pay, the gross pay, the tax, and the net pay.

Calculate the gross pay as follows. If the employee worked 40 hours or less, the regular pay is the pay rate times the hours worked, and overtime pay is zero. If the employee worked over 40 hours, the regular pay is the pay rate times 40 and the overtime pay is 1.5 times the pay rate times the hours worked over 40.

Calculate the tax as follows. If the employee code is 'A', and the state code is 'Y', the tax is 7% of the gross pay. If the employee code is 'A' and the state code is not 'Y', the tax is 4.5% of the gross pay. If the employee code is not 'A', the tax is zero. The net pay is the gross pay minus the tax.

After the program processes the last employee, it should display the total number of employees it processed and the total gross pay, tax, and net pay.

Program Design

A pseudocode solution to Problem 4.2 follows.

Display program banner
Initialize accumulators
do

Obtain pay rate, hours, employee code, and state code
Calculate gross pay
Calculate tax
Calculate net pay
Increment accumulators
Display results
Prompt for another employee
Obtain response
while (response is yes)
Display final totals

We now expand the high-level pseudocode statements "Calculate gross pay" and "Calculate tax". First, to calculate the gross pay we have the following pseudocode.

if (hours > 40)
  calculate regular pay
  calculate overtime pay
else
  calculate regular pay
  overtime pay = zero
endif
gross pay = regular pay + overtime pay

To calculate the tax, we use a nested if structure as follows.

if (employee code = 'A')
  if (state code = 'Y')
    tax = gross pay * 0.07
  else
    tax = gross pay * 0.045
  endif
else
  tax = 0.00
endif

Character Input

Problem 4.2 requires the user to input three characters: A or B in response to the prompt for the employee code; Y or J in response to the prompt for the state code; and Y or N in response to the prompt for another employee. We must be careful about the contents of the keyboard input buffer when a program inputs characters and numbers. According to the pseudocode, the program first obtains the employee's pay rate and number of hours worked. The program obtains these values by executing cin

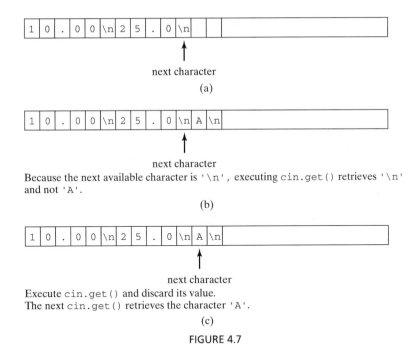

next character

(a)

next character

Because the next available character is `'\n'`, executing `cin.get()` retrieves `'\n'` and not `'A'`.

(b)

next character

Execute `cin.get()` and discard its value.
The next `cin.get()` retrieves the character `'A'`.

(c)

FIGURE 4.7

statements. When retrieving a number from the keyboard input buffer, `cin` skips all white space (new-line characters, tabs, and blanks) and retrieves the next number it encounters. The new-line character that the user enters after entering the number remains in the keyboard input buffer. Figure 4.7a shows the keyboard input buffer after the user enters 10.00 and 25.0 in response to the first two prompts. An arrow shows the next character that is available to the program (a new-line character).

Programming
Pitfalls

According to the pseudocode, the program now prompts for the employee code. Assume the user enters the character 'A' and then a new-line character. Suppose the program obtains the next character from the input buffer by executing `cin.get()`. It would then retrieve the new-line character that it left in the buffer after the user entered the number of hours worked. The program would not retrieve the character 'A'. See Figure 4.7b. To get rid of this new-line character, we make the program execute `cin.get()` and discard the character it returns. The program will execute `cin.get()` again and place the returned character into the variable `employee_code` so the program can test its value later. See Figure 4.7c. Following is the code to accomplish this.

```
cin.get();
employee_code = cin.get();
```

The first `cin.get()` statement obtains the next available character from the input buffer, but does not assign this value to any variable. This, in effect, discards the new-line character that precedes the employee code.

The following program, prb04-2.cpp, uses this technique to obtain values for the other two character variables that the program requires.

The Program prb04-2.cpp

Following is the program code, prb04-2.cpp.

```
// prb04-2.cpp

// This program processes a payroll for a small company. It
// calculates gross pay including the possibility of overtime.
// It also calculates payroll tax depending on the employee
// code and state code. The program displays the gross salary,
// tax, and net salary for each employee. When there are no more
// employees to process, the program displays summary information.

#include <iostream.h>
#include <iomanip.h>

using namespace std;

int main()
{
  const double RESIDENT_RATE = 0.070;
  const double NON_RESIDENT_RATE = 0.045;

  int     employee_count,
          employee_code,
          state_code;
  char    response;
  double  pay_rate,
          hours,
          regular_pay,
          overtime_pay,
          gross_pay,
          tax,
          net_pay,
          total_gross_pay,
          total_tax,
          total_net_pay;

  cout << setprecision(2)
       << setiosflags(ios::fixed)
       << setiosflags(ios::showpoint);

      // Display banner

  cout << "\nThis program calculates the net pay for each employee.";
```

```cpp
cout << "\n\nAt each prompt, enter the requested data.";

    // Initialize accumulators

employee_count = 0;
total_gross_pay = total_tax = total_net_pay = 0.00;

    // Main processing loop

do
  {
            // Obtain input data

    cout << "\n\nEnter the pay rate: ";
    cin >> pay_rate;
    cout << "\nEnter the number of hours worked: ";
    cin >> hours;
    cout << "\nEnter the employee code (A or B): ";
    cin.get();                      // Discard the \n
    employee_code = cin.get();
    cout << "\nEnter the state code (Y or J): ";
    cin.get();                      // Discard the \n
    state_code = cin.get();

            // Calculate the gross pay

    if (hours > 40.0)
      {
        regular_pay = 40.0 * pay_rate;
        overtime_pay = (hours - 40.0) * 1.5 * pay_rate;
      }
    else
      {
        regular_pay = hours * pay_rate;
        overtime_pay = 0.00;
      }
    gross_pay = regular_pay + overtime_pay;

            // Calculate the tax

    if ((employee_code == 'A') || (employee_code == 'a'))
      if ((state_code == 'Y') || (state_code == 'y'))
        tax = gross_pay * RESIDENT_RATE;
      else
        tax = gross_pay * NON_RESIDENT_RATE;
    else
      tax = 0.00;

            // Calculate net pay
```

```
            net_pay = gross_pay − tax;

                    // Display results

        cout << "\n\nRegular Pay: " << setw(7) << regular_pay;
        cout << "\nOvertime Pay: " << setw(7) << overtime_pay;
        cout << "\nTax:          " << setw(7) << tax;
        cout << "\nGross Pay:    " << setw(7) << gross_pay;
        cout << "\n--------------------";
        cout << "\nNet Pay:      " << setw(7) << net_pay;

                    // Increment accumulators

        ++employee_count;
        total_gross_pay += gross_pay;
        total_tax += tax;
        total_net_pay += net_pay;

                    // Prompt for another employee

        cout << "\n\nDo you want to process another employee?(y/n): ";
        cin.get();                // Discard the \n
        response = cin.get();
    }
    while ( (response == 'y') || (response == 'Y') );

        // Display summary information

    cout << "\n\n\nTotal number of employees processed: " << employee_count;
    cout << "\nTotal gross pay:" << setw(9) << total_gross_pay;
    cout << "\nTotal tax:      " << setw(9) << total_tax;
    cout << "\nTotal net pay:  " << setw(9) << total_net_pay;

    return 0;
}
```

Program Output

```
This program calculates the net pay for each employee.

At each prompt, enter the requested data.

Enter the pay rate: 7.25

Enter the number of hours worked: 47

Enter the employee code (A or B): A
```

```
Enter the state code (Y or J): Y

Regular Pay:    290.00
Overtime Pay:    76.12
Tax:             25.63
Gross Pay:      366.12
---------------------
Net Pay:        340.50

Do you want to process another employee?(y/n): y


Enter the pay rate: 8.50

Enter the number of hours worked: 30

Enter the employee code (A or B): A

Enter the state code (Y or J): J

Regular Pay:    255.00
Overtime Pay:     0.00
Tax:             11.47
Gross Pay:      255.00
---------------------
Net Pay:        243.53
Do you want to process another employee?(y/n): y

Enter the pay rate: 6.00

Enter the number of hours worked: 50

Enter the employee code (A or B): B

Enter the state code (Y or J): Y

Regular Pay:    240.00
Overtime Pay:    90.00
Tax:              0.00
Gross Pay:      330.00
---------------------
Net Pay:        330.00

Do you want to process another employee?(y/n): n

Total number of employees processed: 3
Total gross pay: 951.12
Total tax:        37.10
Total net pay:   914.02
```

The program follows the pseudocode very closely. We declare the three variables that store single characters as type `int` according to Note 3.5 of Chapter 3.

The conditions in the nested `if` that decide the tax and the condition in the `do-while` loop test for either a lowercase or an uppercase letter. This is good practice because some users inadvertently enter a lowercase letter when your program expects an uppercase letter, or the other way around.

As a final comment on prb04-2.cpp, note that the body of the `do-while` loop is very long (about 60 lines). Because it is sometimes difficult to understand a long piece of code, we commented each section of the body of the loop and separated the sections by spaces. It would be far better if we could modularize this part of the code so that it looks more like the high-level pseudocode that we developed earlier. This is exactly what we will do in Chapter 5 when we discuss how to write our own functions and how to code modular C++ programs.

EXERCISES 4.3

1. Translate the flowchart in Figure 4.8 into C++ code using a nested `if`.

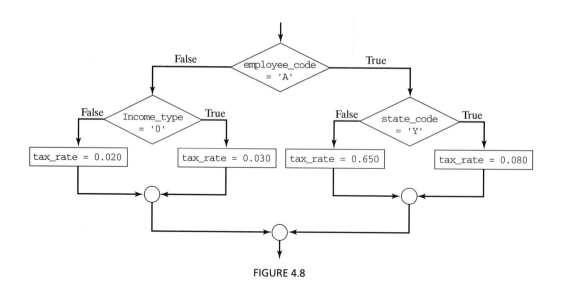

FIGURE 4.8

2. Translate the flowchart in Figure 4.9 into C++ code using a nested `if`.
3. Translate the flowchart in Figure 4.10 into C++ code using a nested `if`.
4. Translate the flowchart in Figure 4.11 in C++ code using a nested `if`.
5. The following nested `if` is correct. Recode the statement using proper indentation.

```
if (a > b) if (c == d) {y = x; s = t;} else u = t; else if (e > f) ++g;
```

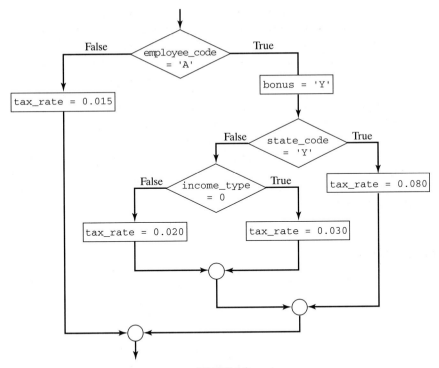

FIGURE 4.9

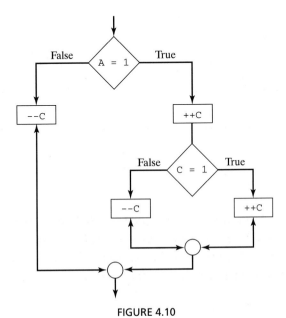

FIGURE 4.10

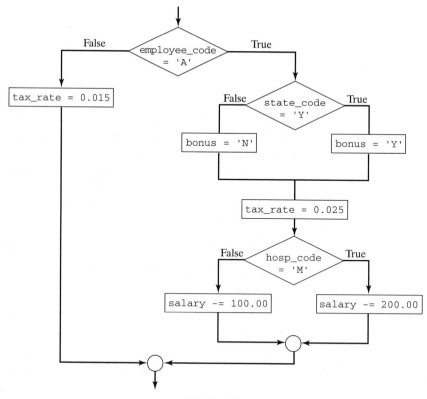

FIGURE 4.11

6. The following is indented correctly but is not coded the way the indentation suggests. Correct the code.

```
if (read_code == 2)
  ++record_count_1;
  ++record_count_2;
else
  ++record_count_3;
```

EXPERIMENTS 4.3

1. The first example in this section contained the following nested if statement.

```
if (employee_code == 'A')
  {
    if (state_code == 'Y')
      tax = gross_pay * 0.07;
    else
      tax = gross_pay * 0.045;
```

```
        special_tax = hours * 0.02;
    }
else
    tax = 0.00;
    special_tax = 0.00;
}
```

Write short programs to see what happens if you omit the first pair of braces. Does the resulting program compile? If the program does compile, what does the nested if assign to tax and special_tax?

2. Using the code segment of Experiment 1, write a short program to see what happens if you omit the second pair of braces. Does the resulting program compile? If the program does compile, what does the nested if assign to tax and special_tax?

3. Using the code segment of Experiment 1, write a short program to see what happens if you omit both pairs of braces. Does the resulting program compile? If the program does compile, what does the nested if assign to tax and special_tax?

PROGRAMMING PROBLEMS 4.3

1. Suppose that the automobile repair shop in Problem 4.2 has a maximum pay rate of $25. Recode prb04-2.cpp so that it issues an error message if the user enters a pay rate greater than $25. The program should prompt the user for a valid pay rate until the user enters a rate of $25 or less.

2. Recode dem04-1.cpp using a nested if to test the character that the user inputs.

3. The loan officer at Humongous National Bank wants you to write a program to help her decide whether to approve small loan applications. The program should prompt the user for the customer's yearly income, the number of years of the loan (the loan period), the amount of the loan (the principal), and the customer status (1 for preferred or 0 for ordinary). To approve a loan, the customer must satisfy one of the following conditions.

   (a) The principal divided by the period must be less than or equal to $\frac{1}{12}$ of the customer's income.

   (b) If the customer is a preferred customer (that is, the customer status is 1), the principal divided by the period must less than or equal to $\frac{1}{10}$ of the customer's income.

   The program should display an appropriate approval or disapproval message for each customer it processes. When there are no more customers to process, the program should display the total number of approvals and disapprovals it processed.

4. At Humongous National Bank, the vice president in charge of credit cards decides to issue a new type of credit card, the Platinum Card. Write a program to help the bank decide which customers to offer a Platinum Card to. The program should

prompt the user for the customer's present credit limit and account balance. If a customer has a credit limit of at least $2000 and an account balance of $500 or less, issue the customer a Platinum card. If a customer has a credit limit of at least $2000 and an account balance of more than $500, send a letter to the customer stating that if their balance falls below $500 he or she will receive a Platinum Card. If a customer does not fall into either of these categories, take no action.

For each customer, the program should display a message that shows the action that the bank should take—issue a Platinum Card, send a letter, or take no action. When there are no more customers to process, the program should display the total number of customers in each category.

5. The Big Racket Tennis Club wants you to write a program to calculate the yearly dues for its members. The program should prompt the user for the membership type (either 'I' for individual, or 'F' for family) and the number of years the person has been a member. Calculate the dues as follows: If the person is a family member and has been a club member for more than three years, the dues are $2400. If the person is a family member and has been a club member for three years or less, the dues are $3000. If the person is an individual member and has been a club member for more than five years, the dues are $1500. If the person is an individual member and has been a club member for five years or less, the dues are $1900.

For each member, the program should display the type of membership, the number of years the person has been a member, and the dues. When there are no more members to process, the program should display the total number of family members and individual members and the total amount of dues.

4.4 The `switch` Statement

The C++ language `switch` statement implements the case structure of structured programming, which effects multi-way branching. Thus, the `switch` statement can be used in certain circumstances in place of a nested `if` statement.

The Case Structure and the `switch` Statement

A real estate broker sets fees for selling properties according to the property type as shown in Table 4.5.

The broker wants you to write a program that prompts the user for the sale price of the property and the property code. The program should then display the dollar

TABLE 4.5

Property Type	`property_code`	Rate
Residential	R	0.060
Multi–dwelling	M	0.050
Commercial	C	0.045

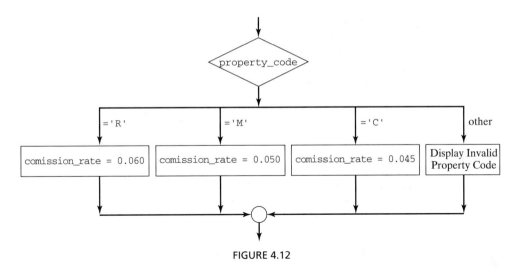

FIGURE 4.12

amount of the broker's commission. If the user enters an invalid property code, the program should display an appropriate error message.

This problem requires the program to take one of four possible paths depending on the value of `property_code`. Thus, the problem requires a multi-way branch, that is a **case structure**, as shown in Figure 4.12.

The C++ programming language implements the case structure with the `switch` statement. The `switch` statement that translates the flowchart in Figure 4.12 follows.

```
switch (property_code)
  {
    case 'R':
      commission_rate = 0.060;
      break;
    case 'M':
      commission_rate = 0.050;
      break;
    case 'C':
      commission_rate = 0.045;
      break;
    default:
       cout << "\nInvalid Property Code! Try Again.";
      break;
  }
```

This `switch` statement works as follows. First, the program evaluates the variable `property_code`. If the value of `property_code` equals R, M, or C, the program branches to the corresponding **case label** and executes the statements that follow the case label. For example, if the value of `catalog_code` is M, the program branches to the label

```
case 'M':
```

and begins to execute the statements that follow the label beginning with

```
commission_rate = 0.050;
```

The program now encounters the statement, break. The break statement causes program control to exit the switch statement. Therefore, after assigning a value to commission_rate, the program exits the switch statement.

If the value of property_code does not equal any of the values in the case labels, the program goes to the default label and executes the statements that follow the label.

To see why the break statement is necessary, consider the following problem. Suppose the program is to allow the user to enter either uppercase or lowercase letters for the property code. Figure 4.13 shows the case structure flowchart to make the assignment to commission_rate.

Following is the switch statement that translates the flowchart in Figure 4.13.

```
switch (property_code)
  {
    case 'R':
    case 'r':
      commission_rate = 0.060;
      break;
    case 'M':
    case 'm':
      commission_rate = 0.050;
      break;
    case 'C':
    case 'c':
      commission_rate = 0.045;
      break;
```

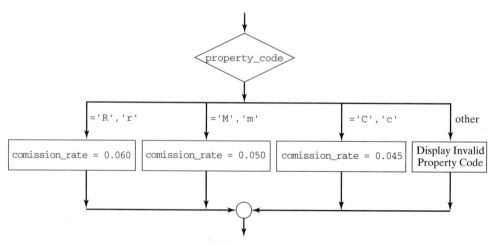

FIGURE 4.13

```
    default:
      cout << "\nInvalid Property Code! Try Again.";
      break;
  }
```

This `switch` statement first evaluates the variable `property_code`. The program branches to the case label that equals the value of `property_code`. If `property_code` is not equal to any case-label value, the program branches to the `default` label. For example, suppose that the value of `property_code` is 'M'. The program branches to the case label

```
case 'M':
```

and executes the statements that follow. The statement that immediately follows this case label (`case: 'M'`) is another case label (`case: 'm'`), which is not an executable statement. Therefore, the program "falls through" the case label and executes the next statement, which is

```
commission_rate = 0.050;
```

followed by the `break` statement. If the `break` statement were not there, the program would fall through the next two case labels and assign 0.045 to `commission_rate`, which would be incorrect.

In some circumstances we want fall through to occur, such as when multiple values lead to the same actions. In other circumstances we do not want fall through to occur, such as when we want to exit the `switch` statement. The `break` statement causes an immediate exit from the body of the `switch` statement.

The `switch` statement has the following general format.

```
switch (integer expression)
  {
    case case-value-1:
       statement-body-1
    case case-value-2:
       statement-body-2
       .
       .
       .
    case    case-statement-n
       statement-body-n
    default:
       default-statement-body
  }
```

Programming
Pointers

The integer expression that follows the keyword `switch` must evaluate to an integer data type. Most often the integer expression is a simple `int` or `char` variable. The body of the `switch` statement must be enclosed in braces as shown.

Programming
Pointers

The body of the `switch` consists of a set of cases. Each case begins with the `case` label. A case label begins with the keyword `case`, followed by a case value, followed by a colon. The case value is a possible value that the integer expression can take on. The case value must be of the same type as the value of the integer expression. The statement body for that case follows the case label. The program executes the statements in the statement body if the integer expression equals the case value that is in the case label. The statement body can consist of no statements.

Programming
Pointers

The `default` label body of the `switch` contains the statements that the program is to execute if the value of the integer expression is not equal to any of the case label values. The `default` case label is optional and need not appear last in the body of the `switch` statement.

The `switch` statement works as follows: The program evaluates the integer expression and compares this value to each case value. If the value of the expression equals a case value, the computer executes all the statements in that case label's statement body. The computer then executes all the following statement bodies, unless otherwise directed (for example, by a `break` statement). We call this behavior **fall through**.

If the value of the integer expression is not equal to any of the case values, the program executes the `default` statement body. If you do not include the `default` case in the `switch` statement and the integer expression is unequal to any case value, then `switch` takes no action. Then, the program executes the statement that follows the `switch`.

Calculating Real Estate Commission—Problem 4.3

A real estate broker sets fees for selling properties according to the property type as shown in Table 4.6.

The broker wants you to write a program that prompts the user for the sale price of the property and the property type code. The program should then display the dollar amount of the broker's commission (the sale price multiplied by the appropriate commission rate). If the user enters an invalid property code, the program should display an appropriate error message and stop. Allow the user to enter uppercase or lowercase letters.

Program Design

The pseudocode solution for Problem 4.3 follows.

Obtain the sale price from the user
Obtain a property code from the user

TABLE 4.6

Property Type	property_code	Rate
Residential	R	0.060
Multi–dwelling	M	0.050
Commercial	C	0.045

Determine the commission rate based on property code

Calculate the commission

Display the commission

The program decides the commission rate using a switch statement similar to the one we developed earlier. The additional feature is that the program must stop if the user enters an invalid property code.

The Program prb04-3.cpp

Here is the program code.

```cpp
// prb04-3.cpp

// This program determines the commission on real estate sales
// depending on the type of property sold.

#include <iostream.h>
#include <iomanip.h>
#include <stdlib.h>

using namespace std;

int main()
{
  const double RESIDENTIAL_RATE = 0.060;
  const double MULTIDWELLING_RATE = 0.050;
  const double COMMERCIAL_RATE = 0.045;

  int    property_code;
  double sale_price,
         commission_rate,
         commission;

  cout << setprecision(2)
       << setiosflags(ios::fixed)
       << setiosflags(ios::showpoint);

  cout << "\nEnter the property's selling price: ";
  cin >> sale_price;

  cout << "\nEnter the property code according to the following.";
  cout << "\n\nResidential,      enter R";
  cout << "\nMultiple Dwelling, enter M";
  cout << "\nCommercial,        enter C";
  cout << "\n\nPlease make your selection: ";
  cin.get();              // Discard the \n
  property_code = cin.get();
```

```
switch (property_code)
  {
    case 'R':
    case 'r':
      commission_rate = RESIDENTIAL_RATE;
      break;
    case 'M':
    case 'm':
      commission_rate = MULTIDWELLING_RATE;
      break;
    case 'C':
    case 'c':
      commission_rate = COMMERCIAL_RATE;
      break;
    default:
      cout << "\n\nInvalid Property Code! Try Again";
      exit(1);
      break;
  }

commission = sale_price * commission_rate;

cout << "\n\nThe commission is " << commission;

return 0;
}
```

Program Output

```
Enter the property's selling price: 270000

Enter the property code according to the following.

Residential,        enter R
Multiple Dwelling,  enter M
Commercial,         enter C

Please make your selection: R


The commission is 16200.00
```

After obtaining the sale price of the property, the program displays a menu of property codes and asks the user to enter a menu option. A `cin.get()` statement skips the new-line character that is in the keyboard input buffer because the user is entering the sale price. The next `cin.get()` places the code into the variable `property_code`.

The `switch` statement decides the value of `commission_rate` depending on the value of `property_code`. If the user enters an invalid code, the program displays an error message and then executes the standard library function exit(). When a program executes the exit() function, the program ends and returns control of the computer to the operating system. The exit() function takes a single argument of type int. Therefore, a call to exit() can take the form exit(0); or exit(1); or exit(2);, and so on. By convention, an argument value of 0 means that the program ended normally; a nonzero argument value means that the program ended abnormally. The programmer can use a nonzero value for the argument to indicate the reason the program did not end successfully. An operating system program can then use this value to act appropriately.

To use the function exit(), the program must include a second header file, stdlib.h, which stands for the "standard library" header file.

More on break

Programming
Pointers

In addition to its use in the switch statement, the break statement can alter the flow of control in a C++ program when used inside the body of a loop. Execution of the break statement causes the program to end the smallest enclosing while, do, or for statement. The program then transfers control to the point just beyond the completed while, do, or for statement. Thus, the break statement causes a premature exit from a loop.

The program dem04-3.cpp illustrates the break statement used in a loop. The program counts the number of characters the user enters before the first @ character.

```
// dem04-3.cpp

// This program counts the number of characters that the user
// enters on a line to the left of the first @ character.

#include <iostream.h>

using namespace std;

int main()
{
   int ch,              // The input character
       count = 0;       // Count of the characters before @

   cout << "\nEnter a line containing @\n";

   while ( (ch = cin.get()) != '\n')
     {
       if (ch == '@')
         break;
       ++count;
     }

   if (ch == '\n')
     {
```

```
        cout << "\nYou did not enter a @ character.";
        cout << "\nYou entered " << count << " characters.";
    }
  else
        cout << "\nYou entered " << count << " characters before the first @";

  return 0;
}
```

Program Output

```
Enter a line containing @
asd,1@34


You entered 5 characters before the first @
```

The program prompts the user to enter a line that contains the character @. The while loop's condition, which we have seen several times before, obtains a character from the keyboard input buffer and tests to see if it is not the new-line character. If the character is not the new-line character, the program enters the loop body. The if statement in the loop body checks to see if the character that the user entered equals the @ character. If it is, the break statement executes. This causes the program to exit the while loop and execute the if statement that follows the while. If the character that the user entered is not the @ character, the program increments the variable count and the next iteration of the while loop obtains the next character from the keyboard input buffer.

When the program reaches the if statement that follows the while, we know that the loop ended for one of two reasons—either an @ character was met and the break statement caused the loop to end, or the user did not enter a @ character and the loop ended by encountering the new-line character. In either case, the character that caused the loop to end is stored in the variable ch. The if statement tests the value of ch to determine why the loop ended.

The continue Statement

Programming
Pointers

The continue statement is another way to alter the flow of control within a while, do-while, or for loop, and may appear only inside such loops. However, instead of ending the enclosing loop as break does, execution of continue ends only the current iteration. The next loop iteration begins immediately.

The program dem04-4.cpp counts the number of uppercase characters that the user enters on one line.

```
// dem04-4.cpp

// This program counts the number of uppercase characters that
// the user enters on one line.
```

```
#include <iostream.h>

using namespace std;
int main()
{
   int ch,           // The character entered
       count = 0;    // The number of uppercase characters

   cout << "\nEnter a line of characters:\n";

   while ( (ch = cin.get()) != '\n')
     {
       if ( (ch < 'A') || (ch > 'Z') )
         continue;
       ++count;
     }

   cout << "\nYou entered " << count << " uppercase characters.";

   return 0;
}
```

Program Output

```
Enter a line of characters:
asDvFF,a12BBa


You entered 5 uppercase characters.
```

The while loop's condition obtains a character from the input buffer and places it into the variable ch. If the value of ch is not '\n', the loop body executes. The if statement in the loop body tests whether the value of ch is not an uppercase letter. If the value of ch is not an uppercase letter, the continue statement executes. This causes the current loop iteration to end. The ++count statement does not execute, and the program executes the next loop iteration. Therefore, the while loop's condition obtains the next character from the keyboard input buffer and the process repeats. If the value of ch is an uppercase letter, the continue statement does not execute and count is incremented by one. The while loop's condition then obtains the next character from the keyboard input buffer.

EXERCISES 4.4

1. A program is to use the integer variable years_employed to define three groups of employees. The groups and the required processing follow in Table 4.7.

   (a) Write a nested if statement that tests years_employed and does the appropriate processing.

TABLE 4.7

years_employed	Processing
0–3	Add 1 to j_count
4–10	Add 1 to r_count
11 or more	Add 1 to s_count

(b) Write a `switch` statement that tests `years_employed` and does the appropriate processing.

2. Recode dem04-3.cpp without using the `break` statement.

3. Recode dem04-4.cpp without using the `continue` statement.

EXPERIMENTS 4.4

1. Place the `default` case in the `switch` statement of prb04-3.cpp before all the case labels. Compile and test the resulting program. Does placing the default label first have any effect on the program?

2. Omit the `default` case in the `switch` statement of prb04-3.cpp. Compile and execute the resulting program. When prompted by the program, enter the value A for the property code. What does the program do?

PROGRAMMING PROBLEMS 4.4

1. The Easy Living resort hotel wants you to write a program to calculate the base charge for its guests. The program should prompt the user for the room type ('G' for garden view, 'P' for pool view, or 'L' for lake view) and the number of days the guest will stay. The program also should prompt for whether the guest will have a refrigerator in the room and whether there will be an extra bed in the room.

   The daily room rates are as follows. A garden-view room is $125 per day; a pool-view room is $145 per day; a lake-view room is $180 per day. A refrigerator costs $2.50 extra per day. An extra bed costs $15 extra each day for either a garden-view room or a pool-view room, but costs $20 extra each day for a lake-view room. Calculate the total bill by multiplying the room rate (adjusted for a refrigerator and extra bed, if necessary) by the number of days the guest will stay.

   The program should display the room type, the number of days of the stay, the basic daily room rate, the daily charge for the refrigerator and bed (only if the guest requests these), and the total charge for the stay.

2. The PCs-R-US computer rental company wants you to write a program to calculate the charge for renting a computer. The program should prompt the user for the type of computer ('F' for a Pentium or 'P' for a Pentium II), whether the customer rented a monitor, whether the customer rented a printer, and the number of days the customer rented the computer system. Table 4.8 gives the daily rate for renting a computer system, depending on the configuration. An X in a box

TABLE 4.8

Pentium	Pentium II	Monitor	Printer	Rate
X				10.50
X		X		12.50
X			X	13.50
X		X	X	15.00
	X			15.50
	X	X		18.50
	X		X	19.00
	X	X	X	21.00

means that the customer selected that option. For example, the daily rate for renting a Pentium with a monitor and no printer is $12.50.

The charge to the customer is the appropriate rate multiplied by the number of days the customer rented the computer. For each customer, the program should display the daily rental charge, the number of days of the rental, and the total rental charge.

When there are no more customers to process, the program should display the total number of customers processed, the number of Pentium systems rented, the number of Pentium II systems rented, and the total of all rental charges.

3. Write a program that asks the user to enter the number of a month of the year and the year. For example, if the user wants to enter June, 1992, he or she would enter 6 and then enter 1992. The program should then display the number of days in that month. Be sure to take leap years into account.

4. After many years of being frustrated by a checkbook that will not balance, you decide to write a program to help balance your money market checking account. The program should begin by asking the user for the month's opening account balance. Then the program should display a menu that lists the following choices: D for a deposit, C for a check, W for a withdrawal, and Q for quit. If the user selects D, ask the user to enter the amount of the deposit, and add the amount to the account balance. If the user enters C, ask the user for the amount of the check, and subtract the check amount from the balance. If the user enters W, ask the user for the amount of the withdrawal, and subtract the amount from the balance. When the user enters Q, the program should display the opening balance, the total amount deposited, the total amount withdrawn, the total amount of the checks, and the final balance. If the user enters something other than D, W, C, or Q, the program should issue an error message and redisplay the menu. Allow the user to enter either uppercase or lowercase letters.

5. Redo Programming Problem 4 with the following change. If at any time during the program a withdrawal or a check results in a negative balance, warn the user that the account is overdrawn. Display the amount by which the account is overdrawn, and end the program as described in Programming Problem 4.

6. Redesign and recode prb04-3.cpp so that it processes any number of real estate transactions. In addition, after the program finishes processing all transactions, the

program should display the total amount of sales, the total commissions for each property type, the grand total of all sales, and the grand total of all commissions.

7. A commodities broker requires a program to calculate brokerage commissions. Write a program that asks the user if the transaction was a sale or a purchase and then asks for the amount of the transaction. The program should then ask the user where the transaction was made. The user should enter E for the Commodity Exchange, C for the New York Cotton Exchange, or M for the Mercantile Exchange. If the amount was a sale, and was made at the Commodity Exchange, the commission rate is 5.0% of the amount. If a sale is made at the New York Cotton Exchange, the commission rate is 3.7% of the amount. If a sale is made at the Mercantile Exchange, the commission rate is 4.2% of the amount. If the transaction was a purchase at the Commodity Exchange, the rate commission is 6.3% of the amount. If a purchase is made at the Cotton Exchange, the commission rate is 4.3% of the amount. If a purchase is made at the Mercantile Exchange, the commission rate is 5.7% of the amount. The program should process any number of transactions.

8. Your city's Parking Violation Bureau wants you to write a program to compute fines for parking violations. There are four types of violations: type A carries a fine of $10, type B carries a fine of $20, type C carries a fine of $30, and type D carries a fine of $50. The program should ask for the number of type A violations, the number of type B violations, and so on. If the number of type A, B, or C violations exceeds 10, impose an additional $50 fine for each category that exceeds 10. If the total number of type A, B, or C exceeds 20 but none of types A, B, or C individually exceeds 10, impose an additional fine of $75. If the number of type D violations exceeds 3, impose an additional fine of $20 for each type D violation over three. The program should display the total fine for the person. The program should process any number of persons.

Chapter Review

· ·

Terminology

Define the following terms.

if

else

logical operators

truth value

negation (!)

conjunction (&&)

disjunction (||)

"short circuit" evaluation

nested if

outer if

inner if

case structure

switch

case label

break

default

fall through

exit ( )

stdlib.h

continue

Chapter Summary

- Use the `if` statement to code a simple decision (Note 4.1 and Note 4.2).
- Use the Not, And, and Or operators, `!`, `&&`, `||`, to code compound conditions.
- The `&&` operator has higher precedence than the `||` operator (Table 4.4).
- The `if` statement can contain other `if` statements, that is you can code nested `if`s (Note 4.3).
- Use `cin.get()` to remove an unwanted new-line character from the input buffer.
- The `switch` statement implements the case structure for multi-way decisions.
- The `break` statement causes exit from the `switch` statement. If a `case` does not contain a `break` statement, fall through occurs to the next `case`.
- The `break` statement causes a premature exit from the smallest enclosing `while`, `do`, or `for` statement.
- The `continue` statement ends the current iteration of the smallest enclosing `while`, `do`, or `for` statement.

Review Exercises

1. Explain how the `if` statement works.
2. How do you code an `if` statement?
3. How can you enclose more than one statement in the true or false part of an `if` statement?
4. What are the logical operators and how do they work?
5. How does the precedence of the logical operators compare to that of the other operators we have covered to this point? Which has higher precedence—`&&` or `||`?
6. How can short circuit evaluation affect the results of a logical expression?
7. What are the rules for coding a nested `if` statement?
8. What must you be careful of when mixing character input with the input of numbers?
9. Explain how the `switch` statement works. What is the function of the `break` statement in a switch statement?
10. What is the difference between a `break` statement and a `continue` statement in the body of a loop?

Chapter

5

Functions

Objectives

- To understand how functions work in C++.

- To declare a function using a prototype.

- To code and use a function that has no arguments and no return value.

- To code and use a function that has arguments and no return value.

- To understand how arguments are passed by value.

- To code and use a function that returns a value.

- To understand and use local and global variables.

- To understand and use static variables.

- To design and code a program that uses functions.

- To define and use a macro.

- To use the conditional operator.

- To define and use inline functions.

Large programs are often divided into a set of modules. A **program module** is a part of a program that performs a single, well-defined task. One of the modules is the main, or control, module. The main module calls, or executes, the other modules of which the program is composed. So far our programs have consisted of only the main module, coded as the function `main()`. In C++, a module is usually coded as a function. In this chapter we shall learn how to define and use our own functions and how to use them to help write programs.

5.1 The Function Concept

Functions are central to all the work that we shall do in the rest of this book. In this section we discuss the nature of a function and learn how to declare, define, and use simple functions.

How Functions Work

To construct a building, a general contractor calls upon the services of subcontractors who specialize in certain areas. For example, to lay the foundation of the building, the contractor hires a company that specializes in laying foundations. The contractor has only to give the foundation company the information (size, shape, and so on) necessary to do its work. The foundation company already knows how to build the foundation, so the contractor need not be concerned with how to perform this task. All the contractor needs to do is tell the foundation company to start. In turn, the foundation company must tell the contractor when it has completed its task and how long the contractor must wait to begin the next phase of construction. (The foundation must harden properly, so a certain time must pass before any work can be resumed on the building.) To complete the rest of the building, the contractor will hire other subcontractors in much the same way. Electrical, plumbing, carpentry, and more will be done by appropriate subcontractors. It is even possible that one of the subcontractors will hire another subcontractor. For example, the carpentry subcontractor might hire a subcontractor to install the interior walls of the building.

Many programming problems can be approached in much the same way as a contractor approaches constructing a building. The function `main()` can act as the contractor. When it is necessary to perform a task, `main()` can call upon the services of another function (subcontractor) that performs that task. Such a function may require some information to perform its task, just as the foundation company needs to know the size and shape of the foundation it is to build. The function, also like the foundation company, has to notify `main()` when it is done and might have to pass back some data for `main()` to use in its processing. Continuing the analogy with the carpentry subcontractor, it is possible for a function to call upon still another function to perform an even more specialized task.

A function that executes another function is generally known as the **calling function**. The function that the calling function executes is known as the **called function**. Thus, if `main()` executes a function named `Func1()`, `main()` is the calling function and `Func1()` is the called function. Note that if `Func1()` then executes a function named `Func2()`, `Func1()` is then the calling function and `Func2()` is the called function. Figure 5.1 shows a diagram of a generalized function.

A function should perform a single, well-defined task. To accomplish this task, the function might require zero or more values, called **arguments**, that are passed to it

A Generalized Function

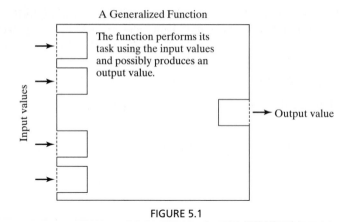

FIGURE 5.1

by the calling function. When the function has completed its task, it can return no or one value, called the **return value**, to the calling function. The calling function can then use the return value in any of its statements.

For example, suppose that in a purchase order processing program we need to calculate the sales tax on the amount of the purchase. Figure 5.2 shows a diagram of a function Calc_Sales_Tax() that could perform this task.

The function Calc_Sales_Tax() requires two arguments because the function must be given the value of the purchase and the applicable sales tax rate. The function main(), which is the calling function in this case, passes the values of purchase_amount and sales_tax_rate to the function. The function uses these values, namely 100.00 and 0.0825, to calculate the sales tax. The function then passes the value of the sales tax back to main(), which assigns it to the variable sales_tax. Exactly how the function computes the sales tax and returns its value is not important right now. We will learn how to do these things later in this chapter.

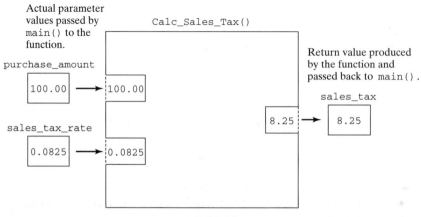

FIGURE 5.2

It is also possible to construct a function to either require no arguments and/or return no value. Since this is the easiest type of function to write, we begin our examples with a function that requires no arguments and returns no value.

A Function With No Arguments and No Return Value

We want to write a program that displays the following pattern on the monitor screen.

```
XXXXXXXXXX
XXXXXXXXXX
XXXXXXXXXX
XXXXXXXXXX
XXXXXXXXXX
```

The pattern consists of five rows of 10 Xs. Since the rows are identical, a `for` loop that executes its loop body five times, each iteration producing a row of 10 Xs, is the appropriate control structure. Following is the pseudocode solution for the problem.

```
main()
        Display new-line
        for (i = 1; i <= 5; ++i)
         Print_10_Xs()
         Display new-line
        endfor
return

Print_10_Xs()
        for (i = 1; i <= 10; ++i)
         Display 'X'
        endfor
return
```

The solution consists of two functions that work together. The body of `main()`'s `for` loop executes five times. On each iteration, when `main()` executes the function `Print_10_Xs()`, `main()` passes control to the function, which carries out its task of displaying 10 Xs. When the function finishes this task, it passes control back to `main()`. Then, `main()` continues execution at the statement that follows the statement `Print_10_Xs()`, which is the statement that displays a new-line character. This ensures that on the next iteration, the 10 Xs begin on a new line. Since this is the end of the loop body, `main()` increments the loop counter, tests the loop counter, and executes the loop body again. This calls the function `Print_10_Xs()` a second time, and so on.

To translate the pseudocode into C++ code requires several new features of C++.

The Function Prototype and Definition

Just as we must declare a variable before using it in a program, we also must declare a function before using it in a program. In C++, we declare a function in a **function prototype**. Note 5.1 shows the format of a function prototype.

NOTE 5.1—DECLARING A FUNCTION

To declare a function, use a function prototype. A prototype has the following format.

    return type function-name(argument type, argument type, ...);

The return type is the data type of the value that the function returns. In parentheses after the function name is a list of the data types of the arguments that are passed to the function.

For example, the function `Calc_Sales_Tax()` that we considered earlier accepts two decimal numbers as its arguments (the purchase amount and the sales tax rate) and returns a decimal number (the sales tax) to `main()`. The prototype for this function is as follows.

```
double Calc_Sales_Tax(double, double);
```

Programming
Pointers

This prototype tells the C++ compiler that the function `Calc_Sales_Tax()` requires two arguments, each of which is a `double`, and returns a value that is a `double`. The prototype does not say what the function does or how it accomplishes its task. The prototype gives the compiler information about the function so the compiler can verify that the program uses the function correctly. For example, each time the function appears in the program, the compiler checks that there are exactly two arguments and that they are both of type `double`.

Note that we capitalize the first letter of each word in the function name. This is another naming convention that we shall use in this book. This convention is not a rule of the C++ language. The convention makes it easier to pick out user-defined function names when reading a program. The only functions whose names *cannot* be capitalized are `main()` and the standard library functions (like `exit()`), which you must spell exactly as C++ expects.

As another example, consider the following prototype.

```
int Func(char, double, int);
```

This prototype tells the C++ compiler the following. The function `Func()` returns a value of type `int`. The function has three arguments. The first argument must be of type `char`, the second must be of type `double`, and the third must be of type `int`.

The function `Print_10_Xs()`, whose pseudocode we developed earlier, has no return value and does not require any arguments. Note 5.2 shows what to do in this case.

NOTE 5.2—USING VOID IN A DECLARATION

If a function does not return a value, use the keyword `void` as the return type in its prototype. If a function has no arguments, either use the keyword `void` for its argument type list or omit the argument type list.

Thus, the prototype for the function `Print_10_Xs()` can be either of the following. The second of these prototypes is the most used style in C++ and is the one that we use in this book.

```
void Print_10_Xs(void);
```

or

```
void Print_10_Xs();     //The style we shall use in this book
```

Note that in C, to specify that a function takes no arguments, you *must* use `void` for the argument type list. If you omit the argument list in C, it gives the computer no information about the number or types of arguments.

As we proceed in this chapter, we will discuss more examples of function prototypes. We can now write the code for `main()`. We will write the code for the function shortly.

```
// dem05—1.cpp

#include <iostream.h>

using namespace std;

void Print_10_Xs();

int main()
{
   int i;

   cout << '\n';
   for (i = 1; i <= 5; ++i)
     {
        Print_10_Xs();
        cout << '\n';
     }

   return 0;
}
```

Programming
Pointers

Note that we code the prototype for `Print_10_Xs()` before the code for `main()` because the compiler must be aware of the function before it sees it in `main()`. Since `Print_10_Xs()` has return type `void`, to cause `main()` to execute the function, all we need to do is code the function's name. Since there is no argument type list, we follow the function's name by an empty set of parentheses (). Thus, when `main()` encounters the statement

```
Print_10_Xs();
```

it passes control to the function. When the function finishes its task, it passes control back to `main()`, which resumes by executing the statement that follows the function call.

We now consider how to write the code for the function `Print_10_Xs()`. The code for a function is separate from the code of `main()`. Some programmers prefer to place the code of their functions before `main()` and some prefer to place the code of their functions after `main()`. We shall place the code of all our functions after `main()` to emphasize that `main()` controls all the other functions in our program.

Note 5.3 gives an outline of how to write the code of a function.

NOTE 5.3—FORMAT OF A FUNCTION DEFINITION

A function definition has the following format.

return-type function-name(type parameter, type parameter, ...)
{
function body
}

Programming
Pointers

The first line of the function definition is the **function definition header**, which looks very much like the function prototype. Note that the header does not end in a semicolon. The difference between the header and the prototype is in the parameter list. The function definition header specifies the name that the function uses for each parameter in addition to the parameter type. In the next section we will explain exactly what a parameter is and see examples of the use of parameters and the parameter list.

The **function body** contains the statements that enable the function to perform its task. You code the function body in the same way that you code the body of the function `main()`. If necessary, you can declare variables and use any C++ language statement or library function that you wish.

The function `Print_10_Xs()` does not return a value and has no arguments. Therefore, just as in its prototype, its definition header specifies the return type as `void` and has no parameter list.

Following is the definition of the function `Print_10_Xs()`.

```
void Print_10_Xs()
{
  int j;

  for (j = 1; j <= 10; ++j)
    cout << 'X';

  return;
}
```

The function displays 10 Xs using a `for` loop. Each iteration of the `for` loop displays one X. The last statement in the function body is the C++ language statement return. The return statement passes control of the computer back to the function that executed Print_10_Xs(), namely the calling function, which is the function main().

If you omit the return statement, the function will automatically return to the calling function when execution reaches the closing brace of the function. Our program dem05-1.cpp is the function main() together with the function Print_10_Xs().

```cpp
// dem05—1.cpp

#include <iostream.h>

using namespace std;

void Print_10_Xs();

int main()
{
   int i;

   cout << '\n';
   for (i = 1; i <= 5; ++i)
     {
        Print_10_Xs();
        cout << endl;
     }

   return 0;
}

void Print_10_Xs()
{
   int j;

   for (j = 1; j <= 10; ++j)
     cout << 'X';

   return;
}
```

Program Output

```
XXXXXXXXXX
XXXXXXXXXX
XXXXXXXXXX
XXXXXXXXXX
XXXXXXXXXX
```

It is important to know how `main()` and `Print_10_Xs()` work together. After displaying a new-line character, `main()` begins executing its `for` loop. When the loop body executes, `main()` executes the function `Print_10_Xs()`.

Control of the computer now passes to the function `Print_10_Xs()`. The function's `for` loop then displays 10 Xs. When the loop finishes, the function executes the `return` statement, which passes control of the computer back to `main()`.

The function `main()` resumes execution at the statement following the function call, which is the `cout << endl;` statement. This ends one iteration of the `for` loop's body in `main()`. The next four iterations behave in a similar fashion.

A Function With Arguments and No Return Value

The function `Print_10_Xs()` is not very versatile because it displays a fixed character, X, exactly 10 times. In this section, we develop a function `Print_Char()`, which can display any character any number of times. We shall pass as argument values to `Print_Char()` the character to display and the number of times to display the character.

We want to write a program that will first ask the user to enter a character. Suppose the user enters Z. Then the program should ask the user in how many rows to display the character. Suppose the user enters 5. The program should display the following on the monitor screen.

```
Z
ZZ
ZZZ
ZZZZ
ZZZZZ
```

We can easily solve this problem using nested `for` loops. However, instead we will use functions to solve the problem. The program must display five lines. Each line has one more character than the preceding line. We shall use one function, `Print_Char()`, to produce each of these lines. Thus, we need to pass information to the function, namely the character the user wants to display and the number of times to display the character.

Programming
Pointers

We pass information to a function that requires data by means of the function's **arguments**. Each data item we pass to a function requires its own argument. The function `Print_Char()` needs to know the character to display and the number of times to display it. Therefore, `main()` must pass two arguments to `Print_Char()` — one of type `char` and one of type `int`. `Print_Char()`, on the other hand, needs to store the argument values it receives. The values that a function receives from the calling function are stored in the function's **parameters**, which are variables declared in the function's definition header. When the function is called, the function initializes its parameters to the arguments that the calling function passed. The parameters, therefore, must be of the same data type as the arguments that are passed.

The pseudocode solution for our problem is as follows.

```
main()
        Prompt for and obtain character ch.
        Prompt for and obtain the number of rows.
        Display newline
        for (i = 1; i <= number_of_rows; ++i)
          Print_Char(ch, i)
          Display newline
        endfor


Print_Char(display_char, count)
        for (j = 1; j <= count; ++j)
          Display display_char
        endfor
```

After obtaining a character from the user and storing it in `ch` and obtaining an integer and storing it in `number_of_rows`, `main()` displays a new-line character. This ensures that the first line of characters that the program displays begins a new-line. The `for` loop in `main()` executes five times. The first statement in the loop body executes the function `Print_Char()`. This function needs two arguments to accomplish its task. The first argument is the value of the character to display, which is stored in the variable `ch`. The second argument is the number of times to display the character, which is stored in the variable `i`. In the first execution of the `for` loop the value of `i` is one. Therefore, on the first iteration, the value of the character that the user entered and the value of `i`, namely one, are passed to `Print_Char()`. `Print_Char()` then displays the character once, and returns control of the computer to `main()`.

The next statement that `main()` executes displays a new-line character so the next displayed line begins on a new line. This ends the `for` loop body in `main()`, which causes the `for` statement to increment `i`. Since the new value of `i` is two, which is less than or equal to `number_of_rows`, the loop body executes again.

On the second iteration, the value of `i` is two. When the program executes `Print_Char()`, it passes the value of the character that the user entered and the value of `i`, namely two, to the function. `Print_Char()` then displays the character twice and returns control of the computer to `main()`.

Similarly, on the third iteration, `Print_Char()` displays the character three times, on the fourth iteration it displays the character four times, and so on until it displays the character `number_of_row` times.

Programming
Pointers

The arguments `main()` uses in the function call to `Print_Char()`, namely `ch` and `i`, contain the actual values that `main()` passes to the function. The pseudocode for `Print_Char()` names the two parameters it uses. The first parameter, `display_char`, is the character the function must display. The second parameter, `count`, is the number of times the function displays the character. A parameter is like a variable in the sense that it is declared in the function header. However, a parameter is unlike a variable because it receives its value from outside the function. The value that a parameter receives is the value of the corresponding argument that `main()` passes to

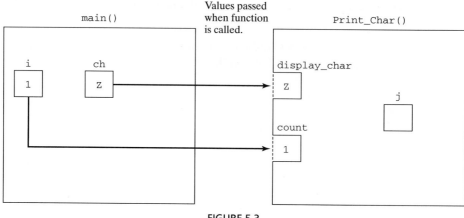

FIGURE 5.3

the function. Thus, inside the function, the parameters represent the values that `main()` passed to the function. The parameter `display_char` receives the value of `ch` passed by `main()`. The parameter `count` receives the value of `i` passed by `main()`.

As this example shows, the names that `Print_Char()` uses for its parameters are not necessarily the same as the names `main()` uses for the arguments. The function `main()` passes the values of `ch` and `i` to `Print_Char()`. These values are assigned to the corresponding parameters in `Print_Char()`. Therefore, in `Print_Char()`, we use the parameters `display_char` and `count` as ordinary variables whose values are assigned when `main()` calls the function.

In Figure 5.3, we represent ordinary variables such as `ch`, `i`, and `j` by closed squares. We represent parameters by squares with one side open to the outside of the function box. This suggests that parameters receive their values from outside the function.

The number of times the loop body executes in `Print_Char()` depends on the value of `count`. The loop body displays the value of `display_char`.

Defining and Using a Function That Has Arguments

Following is the prototype for the function `Print_Char()`.

```
void Print_Char(char, int);
```

The function does not return a value, so the return type is `void`. The function requires two arguments. The first argument is of type `char` and the second is of type `int`. This reflects the use of the function in the pseudocode. The first argument that we will pass to the function will be the character that we want the function to print. The second argument will be the number of times we want the function to display the character.

The code for dem05-2.cpp closely follows the pseudocode.

```cpp
// dem05-2.cpp

#include <iostream.h>

using namespace std;

void Print_Char(char, int);

int main()
{
  int i,
      number_of_rows;
  char ch;

  cout << "\nEnter the character you want to display: ";
  cin >> ch;

  cout << "\nEnter the number of rows you want displayed: ";
  cin >> number_of_rows;

  cout << '\n';
  for (i = 1; i <= number_of_rows; ++i)
    {
      Print_Char(ch, i);
      cout << '\n';
    }

  return 0;
}

void Print_Char(char display_char, int count)
{
  int j;

  for (j = 1; j <= count; ++j)
    cout << display_char;

  return;
}
```

Program Output

```
Enter the character you want to display: Z

Enter the number of rows you want displayed: 5

Z
ZZ
ZZZ
ZZZZ
ZZZZZ
```

We use `Print_Char()` in `main()` in much the same way as we used `Print_10_Xs()` in dem05-1.cpp. Since the function does not return a value, to execute the function we simply code the function name. However, we must pass two arguments to `Print_Char()`, namely the character to display and the number of times to display it. These are the values of `ch` and `i`. Note that we enclose the arguments in parentheses after the function name and separate them by a comma.

Programming Pitfalls

You must be careful to pass the arguments in the correct order. The function expects the first argument to be the value of the character to display and the second to be the number of times to display it. If you mistakenly reverse the order of the arguments and code

```
Print_Char(i, ch);
```

either the compiler will catch the error or the program will produce incorrect results. See Experiment 2.

The function `Print_Char()` has two parameters. The parameter `display_char` holds the value of the character that the function is to display. The parameter `count` holds the number of times that the function is to display the character. The variable `j` declared in the function serves as the loop counter. The `for` loop in the function displays the character stored in `display_char` exactly `count` times. Then the function returns control back to `main()`.

Passing Arguments by Value

Programming Pointers

In dem05-2, `main()` communicated with `Print_Char()` by passing argument values to the function. It is important to understand that these arguments were **passed by value**. Passing by value means that the argument's value is passed to a function, and not the argument itself. In dem05-2.cpp, `main()` passes the value of `ch` to `Print_Char()`. This value is assigned to `Print_Char()`'s parameter `display_char`. Since only the value of `ch` was passed, `Print_Char()` can alter the value of `display_char` with no effect on the value of `ch`.

The following program, dem05-3.cpp, illustrates passing arguments by value. In this program the increment of `parm` in the function `PreInc()` has no effect on the value of `i` in `main()`.

```
// dem05-3.cpp

// This program demonstrates how an argument
// is passed by value in C++.

#include <iostream.h>

using namespace std;

void PreInc(int);
```

```
int main()
{
  int i;

// The variable i is initialized to 5.

  i = 5;

  cout << "\nBefore calling PreInc(), i = " << i;

// The value of i is passed to the function PreInc(), where
// the value is assigned to the parameter parm (see the definition
// of PreInc() below). The function increases the value of its
// parameter by one and returns to main().
// The value of the variable i is not affected by the function
// call to PreInc().


  PreInc(i);

  cout << "\n\nAfter calling PreInc(), i = " << i;

  return 0;
}

void PreInc(int parm)
{

// The value passed to the function is assigned
// to the parameter parm. The function increases the value
// of parm and returns control to main().

  ++parm;
  return;
}
```

Program Output

```
Before calling PreInc, i = 5
After calling PreInc, i = 5
```

C++ also allows **passing arguments by reference**. When an argument is passed by reference, the argument's address in main memory is passed to the function. This way the function can change the value of the argument in the calling program. We shall discuss the use of passing arguments by reference and the use of pointers as arguments in Chapter 8.

In the next section we discuss functions that return a value to the calling program and several concepts that relate to where a variable is declared in a program that contains several functions.

EXERCISES 5.1

In Exercises 1–6 code the appropriate function prototype.

1. A function called `Func1()` that does not return a value and that has two arguments. The first argument is a `double` and the second is an `int`.
2. A function called `Func2()` that returns an `int` and that has one argument, which is of type `double`.
3. A function called `Func3()` that returns a `double` and that has no arguments.
4. A function called `Func4()` that returns a `char` and that has one argument that is also of type `char`.
5. A function called `Func5()` that returns a `double` and that has three arguments, all of which are of type `double`.
6. A function called `Func6()` that returns an `int` and that has three arguments. The first and third arguments are of type `double`. The second argument is of type `int`.
7. Given the following function prototype, is there anything invalid about the use of the function in `main()`? If there is anything invalid, correct it.

```
int Func8(int, double);

int main()
{
   int i = 5,
       j;
   double db = 8.70;

   j = Func8(db, i);

   return 0;

}
```

8. Given the following function prototype, is there anything invalid about the use of the function in `main()`? If there is anything invalid, correct it.

```
void Func9(int, int);

int main()
{
   int i = 4,
       j = 9,
       k;

   k = Func9(j, i);
```

```
return 0;

}
```

9. Code a function `Stars()` that displays a line of 26 asterisks at the beginning of a line.

10. Code a function `Num_Stars()` that takes one integer argument. The function should display as many asterisks as indicated by the value of its argument beginning on a new-line. Therefore, `Num_Stars(14)` displays 14 asterisks at the beginning of a new line.

11. Code a function `Rectangle_Area()` that takes two `double` arguments representing the length and width of a rectangle. The function should display the area (length * width) of the rectangle.

12. Code a function `Rectangle_Perim()` that takes two double arguments representing the length and width of a rectangle. The function should display the perimeter (2*length + 2*width) of the rectangle.

13. Code a function `Circle_Area()` that takes one double argument that represents the radius of a circle. The function should display the area (3.14159 * radius * radius) of the circle.

14. Code a function `Circle_Circum()` that takes one double argument that represents the radius of a circle. The function should display the circumference (3.14159 * 2 * radius) of the circle.

EXPERIMENTS 5.1

1. Recode dem05-2.cpp so that the program prompts the user for the number of steps to display in addition to the character to display.

2. In dem05-2.cpp, intentionally reverse the order of the arguments. Code `Print_Char(i, ch)` in `main()`'s `for` loop. Explain what happens.

3. Write a program that displays the following.

```
a
bb
ccc
dddd
 .
 .
 .
zzzzzzzzzzzzzzzzzzzzzzzzzz
```

Use the function `Print_Char()` in the program.

4. Use the function `Print_Char()` to recode dem05-1.cpp.

5. Recode dem05-2.cpp using nested `for` loops instead of a function.

PROGRAMMING PROBLEMS 5.1

1. Write a program that displays the following.

```
CCCCCCCCCCCC
CC
CC
CC
CC
CC
CC
CCCCCCCCCCCC
```

   Use a function `Cee()` to display the letter.

2. Write a program that displays the following on the screen.

```
* * * * * * * * * * * * * * * * * * * * * * * * * *
*                                                 *
*  I can write functions!  *
*                                                 *
* * * * * * * * * * * * * * * * * * * * * * * * * *
```

   The program should use three functions to accomplish its task. The function `Stars()` should display a line of 26 asterisks. The function `Bar()` should display an asterisk, 24 blanks, and an asterisk. The function `Message()` should display the middle line. None of the functions should return a value.

3. Write a program that draws a rectangle of Xs. Ask the user to enter the dimensions of the rectangle. Then use the function `Rectangle()` to draw a rectangle of the requested size consisting of Xs. `Rectangle()` should have two arguments—the length and width of the rectangle, which must be integers. The function should not return a value.

4. A manufacturer needs a program to display a table of costs of manufacturing certain numbers of her product. She wants to input the cost of producing one unit, the smallest number of products produced, and the largest number of products produced, each in hundreds. For example, she might input 3.46 for the unit cost, and 300 and 700 as the range of numbers. The resulting table should look like the following.

```
                Product Cost Table

    ----------------------------------------------------

    Number Produced                        Cost
    ----------------------------------------------------
    ----------------------------------------------------
         300                              1038.00
         400                              1384.00
         500                              1730.00
         600                              2076.00
         700                              2422.00
```

Use a function `Heading()` to display the table heading lines. `Heading()` should receive no arguments and return no value. Use another function `Table()` to produce the table. `Table()` should have three arguments—the unit cost, the smallest number produced, and the largest number produced. `Table()` should not return a value.

5.2 User-Defined Functions That Return a Value

We now discuss functions that return a value to the calling program, and the concepts of scope and duration. The scope of a variable determines which functions in a program can use the variable. The duration of a variable determines when the variable comes into and passes out of existence.

Using a Function To Calculate Grades

Suppose an English teacher wants you to write a program that calculates her students' final grades. The program should prompt the user for the midterm exam grade and the final exam grade. The final grade is 40 percent of the midterm exam grade plus 60 percent of the final exam grade. The teacher wants the final grade correctly rounded to the nearest integer. For now, write the program to process one student's grade.

Following is the pseudocode solution for this problem.

```
main()
        Prompt for and obtain midterm_exam and final_exam grades
        final_grade = Calc_Grade(midterm_exam, final_exam)
        Display the final_grade

Calc_Grade(midterm_exam, final_exam)
        Calculate the rounded_grade
        Return rounded_grade
```

We use a function, `Calc_Grade()`, to calculate the final grade. This function requires two arguments to accomplish its task—the value of `midterm_exam` and the value of `final_exam`. The function returns the value of `final_grade` to `main()`.

To evaluate the right side of the assignment statement, `main()` calls the function `Calc_Grade()` and passes to the function the values of the midterm exam and the final exam. The function then uses these values to calculate the rounded grade and returns the value of the rounded grade to `main()`. When the program resumes executing in `main()`, `main()` uses the value returned by the function in place of the function call. The rounded grade is assigned to `final_grade`.

Exactly how the function `Calc_Grade()` computes the rounded final grade will be discussed in the next section.

Calculating Grades—The Program dem05-4.cpp

Programming Pointers

Using a function that returns a value is different from using a function that does not return a value. If a function does not return a value, encountering the function's name causes `main()` to execute the function. The called function performs its task and returns control to `main()`. If, however, a function returns a value, `main()` uses the returned value in place of the function call in any expression containing the function's name.

Translating the pseudocode of `main()` into C++ code is straightforward. The return type in the function prototype for `Calc_Grade()` is `int` because the final grade is to be an integer. Since the midterm and final grades are also integers, we declare the two arguments as type `int`. We also declare two symbolic constants representing the weights given to the midterm and final exam grades in the body of the function `Calc_Grade()`. This allows us to change these values easily later. Following is the code for dem05-4.cpp, which closely follows the pseudocode of the previous subsection.

```cpp
// dem05-4.cpp

// This program calculates a final grade based on the midterm and
// final exam scores. It uses a function Calc_Grade() to calculate
// the final grade. The function returns a value to main().

#include <iostream.h>

using namespace std;

int Calc_Grade(int, int);

int main()
{
   int midterm_exam,
       final_exam,
       final_grade;

   cout << "\nEnter the Midterm Exam score: ";
   cin >> midterm_exam;
   cout << "\nEnter the Final Exam score: ";
   cin >> final_exam;

   final_grade = Calc_Grade(midterm_exam, final_exam);

   cout << "\nThe Final Grade is " << final_grade;

   return 0;
}

int Calc_Grade(int midterm, int final)
{
   const double MIDTERM_WEIGHT = 0.40;
   const double FINAL_WEIGHT   = 0.60;

   double grade;
   int rounded_grade;
```

```
grade = MIDTERM_WEIGHT * midterm + FINAL_WEIGHT * final;
rounded_grade = grade + 0.5;

return rounded_grade;
}
```

Program Output

```
Enter the Midterm Exam score: 77

Enter the Final Exam score: 80

The Final Grade is 79
```

To execute the assignment statement in main(), the program first executes the function Calc_Grade(). Then, main() passes the values of midterm_exam and final_exam to the function. The function calculates the grade and returns this value to main(). The returned value is the value of the function call, which main() then assigns to final_grade.

We must explain how Calc_Grade() calculates the final grade. The function receives the midterm and final exam scores as parameter values. The midterm exam is 40 percent of the final grade and the final exam is 60 percent of the final grade. The function should use the following assignment to calculate the grade.

```
grade = 0.40 * midterm + 0.60 * final;
```

By using the symbolic constants declared at the beginning of the function, the assignment becomes the following.

```
grade = MIDTERM_WEIGHT * midterm + FINAL_WEIGHT * final;
```

The problem with this assignment is that the expression on the right is of type double with a fractional part that could be greater than or equal to 0.5. The fractional part would then be truncated when the number is converted to an integer by the assignment. For example, if the value of midterm is 77 and the value of final is 80, the value of the right side of the assignment is 78.8. If we declare grade as type int, the assignment will truncate the fractional part of the answer. This would place 78 into grade, not the correctly rounded answer of 79. Therefore, we declare grade to be of type double so that the assignment places 78.8 into grade. To round the value of grade to the nearest integer, we add 0.5 to the value of grade and assign the result to the integer variable, rounded_grade. If the value of grade is 78.8, adding 0.5 results in 79.3. Assigning this value to rounded_grade truncates the fractional part and stores 79 in rounded_grade.

Note again that the names of the parameters in Calc_Grade() are different from the names of the arguments used in main(). The parameter names and the argument names need not be the same. However, remember that the names you use should be meaningful and reflect their use in the program.

The return statement in `Calc_Grade()` contains an identifier, `rounded_grade`. The `return` statement has the following general form.

```
return expression;
```

The expression in the `return` statement, which is optional (there should be no expression in the `return` statement if the return type of the function is `void`), can be any legal C++ expression. Execution of the `return` statement causes the function to stop and return control to the calling program. If the `return` statement contains an expression, the `return` statement passes the value of the expression back to the calling program for use in place of the function call. The data type of the expression should be the same as the return type declared in the function prototype. In dem05-4.cpp, the return type of `Calc_Grade()` is `int`. Thus, the expression in the return statement of `Calc_Grade()` is also of type `int`.

Programming
Pointers

Variable Attributes

In this section we consider some technical aspects of functions and where and how we declare variables. In C++, each variable has two attributes that determine the variable's scope and duration. The **scope** of a variable is the part of the program that has access to the variable. The **duration** of a variable is the period of time during which the variable exists.

Scope   A variable declared inside a function has **local scope**—the variable is known only inside the function. No statement outside the function in which it is declared can change the value of a variable with local scope. A variable declared outside a function body has **global scope**—the variable is known to all functions *defined* after the point of the variable's declaration. Thus, any function whose definition comes after the declaration of a global variable can change the value of that global variable.

Programming
Pointers

Program dem05-5.cpp illustrates the ideas of local and global scope.

```
// dem05-5.cpp

// This program demonstrates local and global variables.

#include <iostream.h>

using namespace std;

int global01,     // Global variable declarations
    global02;

void Func();
```

```cpp
int main()
{
  // The following assignments are valid because
  // the variables global01 and global02 are global and were
  // declared before main().

  global01 = 88;
  global02 = 99;

  // Display the values of the global variables global01 and global02

  cout << "\nInitial values of the global variables:";

  cout << "\nglobal01 = " << global01
       << " global02 = " << global02;

  // Call the function Func()

  Func();

  // Display the values of the global variables
  // global01 and global02. Either of these variables could
  // have been changed when the function Func() was executed.

  cout <<"\n\nAfter the call to Func(), the global variables are:";
  cout << "\nglobal01 = " << global01
       << " global02 = " << global02;

  return 0;

}


int global03;       // A global variable accessible to Func()

void Func()
{
  int global01,    // Variables local to Func().
      local01;     // The local variable global01 is different than
                   // global variable global01 declared before main().

  global03 = 1;    // Give a value to the global variable global03

  local01 = 2;     // Initialize the local variable local01

  global01 = 3;    // Does not change the value of global global01.

  global02 = 4;     // Since global02 was not declared in this function,
                   // this is the global variable declared before
                   // main(). Therefore, this assignment changes
                   // the value of global02.
```

```
//Display the values of the local variables global01 and local01
// and the global variables global02 and global03.

cout << "\n\nIn Func(), the global variables are:";
cout << "\nglobal02 = " << global02
     << " global03 = " << global03;

cout << "\n\nIn Func(), the local variables are:";
cout << "\nglobal01 = " << global01
     << " local01 = " << local01;
}
```

Program Output

```
Initial values of the global variables:
global01 = 88 global02 = 99

In Func(), the global variables are:
global02 = 4 global03 = 1

In Func(), the local variables are:
global011 = 3 local01 = 2

After the call to Func(), the global variables are:
global01 = 88 global02 = 4
```

The variables global01 and global02 are declared before main(). Therefore, global01 and global02 are global variables whose values are accessible to all the functions defined in the program. The program initializes these variables in main() to 88 and 99 and displays their values.

The variable global03 is declared outside main() and before the function Func(). The variable global3 is a global variable, but is accessible only to the function Func(). Therefore, it is valid for Func() to reference global03, which it does by assigning it the value 1.

The variables global01 and local01 are declared inside the function Func(). Although the local variable global01 has the same name as the global variable global01, it is a different variable. Whenever Func() refers to the variable global01, it references the local variable global01 and not the global variable global01. Later in the function, when global01 is given the value 3, the assignment has no effect on the value of the global variable global01.

The function Func() assigns the value 4 to global02. This assignment is valid because global02 is global and known to all the functions in the program. When control returns from Func() to main(), the value of global02 is 4, not the original value of 88.

Figure 5.4 illustrates the use of variables in dem05-5.cpp. Squares that lie outside the function boxes represent global variables. Squares inside function boxes represent local variables.

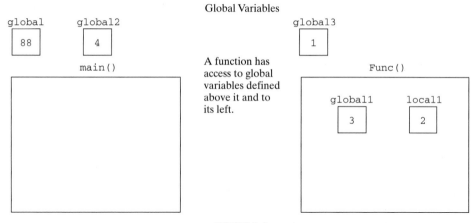

FIGURE 5.4

Programming
Pointers

Any function whose *definition* comes after the declaration of a global variable can access that variable. This makes using global variables dangerous. A function can change the value of a global variable that another function assumes will not change. You should always try to avoid using global variables unless it is absolutely necessary to do so. When data must be shared among functions, do so by means of arguments and return values.

NOTE 5.4—AVOID USING GLOBAL VARIABLES

Avoid using global variables. Share data among functions by means of arguments and return values.

Because local variables are known only to the functions in which they are declared, in a program we can declare variables with the same name in different functions. For example, we can code dem05-1.cpp as follows.

```cpp
// dem05—1A.cpp

#include <iostream.h>

using namespace std;

void Print_10_Xs();

int main()
{
    int i;
```

```
    cout << endl;
    for (i = 1; i <= 5; ++i)
      {
        Print_10_Xs();
        cout << endl;
      }

    return 0;
}

void Print_10_Xs()
{
  int i;

  for (i = 1; i <= 10; ++i)
    cout << 'X';

  return;
}
```

The variable i declared in main() is known only to main(). The variable i declared in Print_10_Xs() is known only to Print_10_Xs(). Each variable i is a different memory location in the computer. When main() changes the value of its variable i, it has no effect on the value of the variable i in Print_10_Xs(). When Print_10_Xs() changes its variable i it has no effect on the value of the variable i in main().

Figure 5.5 illustrates the use of variables in dem05-1A.cpp.

We represent a local variable by a square that lies completely inside the function box in which it is declared. A function knows only the variables inside its own function box. Print_10_Xs() is unaware of the existence of the local variables in main(), as main() is unaware of the local variables in Print_10_Xs(). Thus, main() cannot change the value of a local variable in Print_10_Xs() and Print_10_Xs() cannot (at least directly) change the values of the local variables in main().

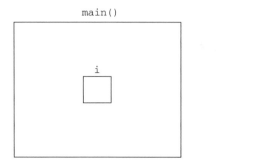
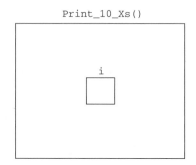

FIGURE 5.5

Duration—Storage Class

The **storage class** of a variable determines its duration. The storage class of a variable can be either `auto` or `static`. (The words `auto` and `static` are C++ language keywords.) A local variable, which by default has storage class `auto`, (and is sometimes called an **automatic variable**) is allocated storage when the function in which it is declared begins executing. When a variable is allocated storage, the computer sets aside a certain amount of storage (depending on the variable type) for that variable and binds the variable name to that location. This enables us to use the name of the variable to represent the storage location. When the function stops executing, the storage set aside for an automatic variable is de-allocated—the storage space can be reused by the computer and the variable name no longer is bound to that location in computer memory. The variable in effect ceases to exist. If `main()` calls the function again, the variable is re-created, possibly in a different location in computer memory.

Programming
Pointers

A `static` **variable** is allocated storage when the program begins. A `static` variable stays in existence as long as the program is executing, independent of which function happens to be active. A global variable has `static` storage class by default. It is possible to create a local `static` variable by beginning the variable's declaration with the keyword `static`. Such a variable is accessible only in the function in which it is declared. However, because its storage class is `static`, the variable stays in existence and retains its value after the function in which it is declared stops executing.

As an example, consider the program dem05-6.cpp.

```cpp
// dem05-6.cpp

#include <iostream.h>

using namespace std;

void Loop_Count();

int main()
{
    int i;

    for (i = 1; i <= 5; ++i)
        Loop_Count();

    return 0;
}

void Loop_Count()
{
    static int count = 0;

    ++count;
```

```
cout << "\nIteration " << count;

    return;
}
```

Program Output

```
Iteration 1
Iteration 2
Iteration 3
Iteration 4
Iteration 5
```

The function `main()` consists of a `for` loop that executes the function `Loop_Count()` five times. In the function `Loop_Count()`, the variable `count` is declared as `static` and is given an initial value of 0. The first time `main()` calls `Loop_Count()`, `count` is initialized to zero and incremented by one. Then the `cout` statement displays the value of `count`, which is 1, and returns control to `main()`. Since `count` is a `static` variable, it remains in existence and retains its value when control resumes in `main()`. The second time `main()` executes `Loop_Count()`, the variable `count` is not re-initialized. Instead, the current value of `count` is incremented by one, giving `count` the value 2. The `cout` statement then displays the value of `count`, namely 2, and returns control to `main()`. This process repeats a total of five times, resulting in the output shown.

EXERCISES 5.2

For Exercises 1–4 assume the following program outline.

```
int i1 = 9;

int main()
{
    int i2 = 5,
        i3;

    i3 = i1 + 7;
    i1 = Func12a(i1,i2);
    Func12b(i2,i3);

    return 0;
}

int i3 = 2;

int Func12a(int i1, int i3)
```

```
{
   static int i2 = 4;

   return i1 + i2 + i3;
}

void Func12b(int j, int k)
{
   int i3 = 1;

   j = i3 + i2 + k;
}
```

1. Identify those variables that are local and those that are global.
2. State which functions have access to each global variable.
3. State which variables are of storage class `auto` and which are of storage class `static`.
4. State which assignment statements are valid and which are invalid.
5. Code a function `Rectangle_Area()` that takes two `double` arguments representing the length and width of a rectangle. The function should return the area (length * width) of the rectangle.
6. Code a function `Rectangle_Perim()` that takes two `double` arguments representing the length and width of a rectangle. The function should return the perimeter (2*length + 2*width) of the rectangle.
7. Code a function `Circle_Area()` that takes one `double` argument that represents the radius of a circle. The function should return the area (3.14159 * radius * radius) of the circle.
8. Code a function `Circle_Circum()` that takes one `double` argument that represents the radius of a circle. The function should return the circumference (3.14159 * 2 * radius) of the circle.
9. Code a function `Min()` that takes two `double` arguments and that returns the value of the smaller of the two arguments.
10. Code a function `Sgn()` that takes one `double` argument and returns +1 if the argument is positive, returns –1 if the argument is negative, and returns 0 if the argument is zero.
11. Code a function `Calc_Discount()` that has two `double` arguments representing the price of an item and a discount amount as a percent. The function should apply the discount to the price and return the discount amount.

EXPERIMENTS 5.2

1. Remove the declaration of the variable `global01` from the function `Func()` in dem05-5.cpp. Compile and execute the resulting program. In what way does this affect the output of the program?

2. Remove the qualifier `static` from the declaration of the variable `count` in the function `Loop_Count()` in the program dem05-6.cpp. Compile and execute the resulting program. In what way does this affect the output of the program?

PROGRAMMING PROBLEMS 5.2

1. Write a program that asks the user to enter two decimal numbers. The program should calculate and display the product and quotient of the two numbers. Use a function `Product()` to calculate the product. The function should have two arguments, which are the two numbers the user inputs. The function should return the product of the numbers. Use a function `Quotient()` that has two arguments, which are the numbers input by the user. The function should return the quotient of the first number divided by the second. If the second number is zero (recall that division by zero is not allowed), display an error message and exit the program.

2. Write a program that asks the user to enter two decimal numbers. The program should display the larger of the two numbers. Use a function `Max()` to find the larger number. `Max()` should have two arguments, which are the numbers that the user input. `Max()` should return the larger of the two numbers.

3. Write a program that raises an integer to a positive integer power. The program should prompt the user to enter the base and the exponent and the program should display the corresponding power. Use a function `Power()` to calculate the power. Pass the base and the exponent to the function. `Power()` should calculate the power by multiplying base by itself exponent times. The function should return the value of the power.

4. Write a program that calculates the mileage you get on your car. The program should ask the user for the number of miles traveled and the number of gallons consumed. Use the function `Mileage()` to calculate the mileage. `Mileage()` should take two arguments—the number of miles traveled and the number of gallons consumed. The function should return the mileage. The program should then display the mileage.

5. Write a program that computes the cost of a taxicab ride. A taxi charges a fixed charge of $2.50 plus an additional charge of $5.50 per mile. The program should ask the user to enter the length of the trip in miles. The program should use the function `Taxi_Charge()` to calculate the fare. `Taxi_Charge()` should have one argument, the length of the trip, and should return the total fare for the ride. The program should display the total fare.

6. Write a program that asks the user to input a grade that he or she received on an exam. The grade is an integer between 0 and 100 inclusive. The program should convert the numeric grade into the equivalent letter grade. Do the conversion by using a function `Letter_Grade()` that converts a numeric grade in the range 0–100 to the equivalent letter grade. The function should have one parameter, the integer grade. The return value of the function should be A if the grade is 90 to 100, B if the grade is 80 to 89, C if the grade is 70 to 79, D if the grade is 65 to 69,

and F if the grade is 64 or lower. After converting the grade, the program should display the numeric grade and the equivalent letter grade.

7. Write a program to compute a person's weekly wage. The program should ask the user to enter the person's pay rate and the number of hours worked. The program should display the person's gross pay, income tax, and net pay. Use a function `Gross_Pay()` to calculate the gross pay. Pass two arguments to the function—the pay rate and the hours worked. The function should return the gross pay, including overtime. Overtime is paid at 1.5 times the regular rate for hours worked over 40. Use a function `Tax()` to calculate the person's tax. Pass one argument to the function—the person's gross pay. `Tax()` should calculate the tax as 15% of the gross pay. The function should return the tax. Use a function `Net_Pay()` to calculate the net pay. Pass two parameters to the function—the gross pay and the tax. The function should return the net pay. The net pay is the gross pay minus the tax. Use a function `Display_Results()` to display the gross pay, tax, and net pay, which you should pass to the function as arguments. `Display_Results()` should not return a value.

8. Write a program that validates a date input by the user. The program should ask for the year, the month number (1 for January, 2 for February, and so on), and the day of the month. Use a function `Valid_Date()` that takes three arguments— the year, the month number, and the day—to validate the date. The function should validate the date as follows. The day must be greater than 0 and must not exceed the correct number of days in the month (remember to check for leap year—a year that is divisible by four—in which February has 29 days). The month number must be between 1 and 12. The year must not be less than 1900 nor greater than 2100. If the date is valid, `Valid_Date()` should return 1, otherwise it should return 0.

5.3 Programs That Use Functions

In this section we discuss three problems whose solutions involve the use of functions. The problems are longer than those we have considered so far. However, by dividing each problem into a set of modules, we can design reasonably simple solutions.

Problem 5.1—Moving Costs

A moving contractor wants you to write a program that he can use to estimate the cost of moving a residential customer. The charge for moving is based on two factors. First, the labor cost is estimated by charging $4 for every 100 pounds of furniture to be moved. Second, the travel charge is $50 plus $1.75 for each mile the furniture is to be moved. The program should prompt the user for the estimated weight of the furniture and the distance the furniture is to be moved. Finally, the program should display the labor charge, the travel charge, and the total charge.

Program Design

The program design is straightforward. The pseudocode solution for the problem is as follows.

Prompt for and obtain the weight and distance.
Calculate the labor charge.
Calculate the travel charge.
Calculate the total charge.
Display the results.

The program shall obtain the input data in the usual way. To calculate the labor charge and the travel charge, the program will use the functions `Calc_Labor()` and `Calc_Travel()`. Similarly, the program will use the function `Display_Charges()` to display the results of the program.

The Program prb05-1.cpp

Following is the code for prb05-1.cpp, the solution to Problem 5.1.

```cpp
// prb05-1.cpp

// This program estimates the charge for moving furniture. It
// uses functions to do calculations and output the results.

#include <iostream.h>
#include <iomanip.h>

using namespace std;

double Calc_Labor(int);
double Calc_Travel(int);
void    Display_Charges(double, double, double);

int main()
{
  int    weight,            // Estimated weight
         distance;          // Estimated distance
  double labor_charge,      // Estimated labor charge
         travel_charge,     // Estimated travel charge
         total_charge;      // Estimated total charge

  cout << setprecision(2)
       << setiosflags(ios::fixed)
       << setiosflags(ios::showpoint);

  cout << "\nEnter the weight in pounds: ";
```

```
  cin >> weight;
  cout << "\nEnter the distance in miles: ";
  cin >> distance;

  labor_charge  = Calc_Labor(weight);
  travel_charge = Calc_Travel(distance);
  total_charge  = labor_charge + travel_charge;

  Display_Charges(labor_charge, travel_charge, total_charge);

  return 0;

} // End of main()

double Calc_Labor(int weight)
{
  const double LABOR_RATE = 4.00;

  double labor_charge;

  labor_charge = (weight / 100) * LABOR_RATE;

  return labor_charge;

} // End of Calc_Labor()

double Calc_Travel(int distance)
{
  const double MILEAGE_RATE     = 1.75;
  const double FLAT_TRAVEL_COST = 50.00;

  double travel_charge;

  travel_charge = FLAT_TRAVEL_COST + distance * MILEAGE_RATE;

  return travel_charge;

} // End of Calc_Travel()

void Display_Charges(double labor_charge, double travel_charge,
                     double total_charge)
{
  cout << "\nThe estimated charges are as follows:\n";
  cout << "\nEstimated Labor:  " << setw(9) << labor_charge;
  cout << "\nEstimated Travel: " << setw(9) << travel_charge;
  cout << "\n--------------------------";
  cout << "\nTotal Estimate:   " << setw(9) << total_charge;

} // End of Display_Charges()
```

Program Output

```
Enter the weight in pounds: 7400

Enter the distance in miles: 230

The estimated charges are as follows:

Estimated Labor:     296.00
Estimated Travel:    452.50
------------------------------
Total Estimate:      748.50
```

The program begins by declaring the three functions that it uses. `Calc_Labor()` returns the labor cost, so we declare the function as returning a `double`. Its only argument is of type `int` because the weight is entered in pounds. `Calc_Travel()`'s prototype also declares it to return a `double`. The only argument that `Calc_Travel` uses, the distance the contractor is to move the furniture, is of type `int`. Finally, `Display_Charges()` takes three arguments: the labor cost, the travel cost, and the total cost. Since `Display_Charges()` does not return a value, its return type is `void`.

The program begins by prompting for and obtaining the weight of the furniture and the distance it is to be moved. The assignment statement

```
labor_charge = Calc_Labor(weight);
```

causes execution of the function `Calc_Labor()`. The function calculates the labor charge based on the weight of the furniture, which is passed as an argument value, and returns the labor charge to `main()`. The program then assigns the returned value to `labor_charge`.

The next assignment statement works similarly, assigning the travel charge returned by `Calc_Travel()` to the variable `travel_charge`. Finally, the `total_charge` is calculated as the sum of the labor and travel charges.

The program then passes the values of `labor_charge`, `travel_charge`, and `total_charge` to `Display_Charges()`, which displays the program's output.

The code for each of the functions that `main()` uses is simple. Note that in `Calc_Labor()` the labor rate, `LABOR_RATE`, is defined as a symbolic constant as are `MILEAGE_RATE` and `FLAT_TRAVEL_COST` in the function `Calc_Travel()`.

Problem 5.2—Calculating Simple Interest

The BigDeal Finance Company wants you to write a program that will help to service its customers who use their Automatic Teller Machines (ATMs). The program is to allow the user to determine the monthly payments, total interest, and total amount on a personal loan.

The program should display a greeting that announces the name of the program and what the program does. The greeting should be as follows.

```
************************************************************************

                    Welcome to the Personal Loan Program

    This program will determine the interest, total amount,
    and monthly payment of your loan.

    Please follow the instructions carefully.

************************************************************************
```

After displaying the greeting, the program is to ask the user for the amount of the loan (the `principal`), the annual interest rate of the loan as a percent (the `rate`), and the number of years of the loan (the `term`). Because the program is to handle only personal loans, the loan amount cannot be smaller than $1,000 and cannot be greater than $20,000. If the loan amount is outside this range, the program should display an appropriate message and terminate. The annual interest rate of the loan cannot be greater than 18.7% as mandated by state law. If the entered interest rate is greater than 18.7%, the program should display an appropriate message and terminate. The longest term possible is five years. If the entered term is greater than five years, the program should display an appropriate message and terminate.

If all the input data is valid, the program should calculate the interest for the full term of the loan, the total amount of the loan, and the monthly payment by using the following formulas.

```
interest = principal * (rate/100) * term
total = principal + interest
monthly payment = total / (12 * term)
```

It is necessary to divide the value of `rate` by 100 in the first formula because the user enters the rate as a percent. If the user enters 10.7 as the rate, the rate we use in the formula must be 10.7/100 = 0.107.

In the third formula, the expression (12 * `term`) is the number of months of the loan. Dividing this into the total amount of the loan gives the monthly payment.

Finally, the program should output the data that the user entered, the interest on the loan, the total amount of the loan, and the amount of the monthly payment.

Program Design

The top-level design of this program is presented in the hierarchy chart of Figure 5.6.

We shall implement the module `Display_Greeting` as a function because the greeting involves displaying many lines. We divide the module `Obtain_Data` into three submodules, each of which we will implement as a function. It is common programming practice to obtain each input value by using a separate function. This enables you to localize in the corresponding function any input data verification that the program must do.

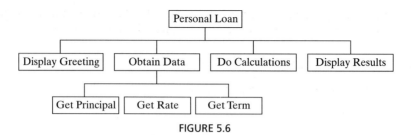

FIGURE 5.6

Since the interest calculations involve three simple formulas, we will not implement the `Do_Calculations` module as a function. Instead, the three formulas will appear in `main()`. Also, the `cout` statements necessary to implement the `Display_Results` module will appear in `main()` and not as a separate function.

The pseudocode for the program based on the hierarchy chart is as follows.
Pseudocode for Problem 5.2

    Display_Greeting
    Obtain_Data:
            Get_Principal
            Get_Rate
            Get_Term
    Do_Calculations
    Display_Results

The three modules that obtain the input from the user are similar in structure. We will develop the pseudocode for `Get_Principal` and leave the pseudocode for the other two as exercises.

The principal cannot be less than 1000.00 nor greater than 20000.00. To test that the principal is in this range, we use a nested `if` statement.
Pseudocode for `Get_Principal`

    Prompt for and get principal
    if (principal < 1000.00)
       Display error message
       Exit program
    else
       if (principal > 20000.00)
         Display error message
         Exit program
       else
         return principal
       endif
    endif

After obtaining the principal, the pseudocode tests to see if the value of `principal` is less than 1000.00. If it is, the program displays an error message and exits the program as required. If `principal` is not less than 1000.00, the pseudocode tests to see if it is greater than 20000.00. If it is, the program displays an error message and exits the program. If the `principal` is not greater than 20000.00, it must be in the range 1000.00 to 20000.00. In this case, the pseudocode returns the value of the `principal` to `main()`.

The Program prb05-2.cpp:

Following is the code for prb05-2.cpp, our solution to Problem 5.2.

```cpp
// prb05-2.cpp

// Simple Interest Program

#include <iostream.h>
#include <iomanip.h>
#include <stdlib.h>

using namespace std;

void   Display_Greeting();
double Get_Principal();
double Get_Rate();
int    Get_Term();

int main()
{
  double interest,
         principal,
         rate,
         total,
         monthly_payment;
  int    term;

  cout << setprecision(2)
       << setiosflags(ios::fixed)
       << setiosflags(ios::showpoint);

// Display Greeting

  Display_Greeting();

// Obtain Data

  principal = Get_Principal();
  rate      = Get_Rate();
  term      = Get_Term();

// Do Calculations

  interest        = principal * (rate/100) * term;
  total           = principal + interest;
  monthly_payment = total / (12 * term);
```

```
    // Display Results

    cout << "\n\nInterest Rate:      " << setw(5) << rate << "%";
    cout << "\nTerm of Loan:       " << term << " Years";
    cout << "\n\nAmount Borrowed:  $" << setw(9) << principal;
    cout << "\nInterest on Loan:  $" << setw(9) << interest;
    cout << "\n----------------------------";
    cout << "\nAmount of Loan:     $" << setw(9) << total;
    cout << "\nMonthly Payment:    $" << setw(9) << monthly_payment;

    return 0;

}  // End of main()

void Display_Greeting()
{
    int position;

    cout << "\n\n";
    for (position = 1; position <= 70; ++position)
        cout << "*";

    cout << "\n\n\t\tWelcome to the Personal Loan Program";
    cout << "\n\nThis program will determine the interest, total amount,";
    cout << "\nand monthly payment of your loan.";
    cout << "\n\nPlease follow the instructions carefully.";
    cout << "\n\n";

    for (position = 1; position <= 70; ++position)
        cout << "*";
    cout << "\n\n\n";

}  // End of Display_Greeting

double Get_Principal()
{
    const double MIN_PRINCIPAL = 1000.00;
    const double MAX_PRINCIPAL = 20000.00;

    double principal;

    cout << "\nEnter amount of the loan: $";
    cin >> principal;

    if (principal < MIN_PRINCIPAL)
        {
            cout << "\nSorry, we do not make loans for under $1,000.00.";
            exit(1);
        }
    else
        if (principal > MAX_PRINCIPAL)
```

```
      {
        cout << "\nSorry, we do not make personal loans";
        cout << " in excess of $20,000.00.";
        cout << "\n\nPlease try our Home Equity Loan\n.";
        exit(1);
      }
    else
      return principal;

} // End of Get_Principal()

double Get_Rate()
{
  const double MAX_RATE = 18.70;

  double rate;

  cout << "\nEnter current annual interest rate (in %): ";
  cin >> rate;

  if (rate > MAX_RATE)
    {
      cout << "\nSorry, the rate exceeds the legal maximum of "
           << MAX_RATE << "%.\n";
      exit(1);
    }
  else
    return rate;

} // End of Get_Rate()

int Get_Term()
{
  const int MAX_TERM = 5;

  int term;

  cout <<"\nEnter the number of years of the loan: ";
  cin >> term;

  if (term > MAX_TERM)
    {
      cout << "\nSorry, the term of your loan cannot exceed "
           << MAX_TERM << " years.\n";
      exit(1);
    }
  else
    return term;

} // End of Get_Term()
```

Program Output

```
*************************************************************************


               Welcome to the Personal Loan Program

This program will determine the interest, total amount,
and monthly payment of your loan.

Please follow the instructions carefully.


*************************************************************************



Enter amount of the loan: $10000.00
Enter current annual interest rate (in %): 10.7
Enter the number of years of the loan: 4

Interest Rate:      10.70%
Term of Loan:       4 Years

Amount Borrowed:    $ 10000.00
Interest on Loan:   $  4280.00
----------------------------------
Amount of Loan:     $ 14280.00
Monthly Payment:    $   297.50
```

Discussion of the Program

The program begins with the function prototypes for the four functions that main() uses. Since Display_Greeting() only displays information on the screen, it does not require any arguments and does not return a value to main(). None of the three functions that obtain the input data require an argument to do its work. If the data that the user enters is acceptable, each of these functions returns that data to main(). The return type of each function corresponds to the type of data the user enters. Since the principal and rate are decimal numbers, the functions Get_Principal() and Get_Rate() return a double. Since the term is an integer, Get_Term() returns an integer.

To display the greeting, main() executes the function Display_Greeting(). The next three assignments execute the functions that obtain the input data and place the appropriate values into the variables principal, rate, and term. Remember that the user enters the rate as a percent.

Next, three assignments place the appropriate values into interest, total, and monthly_payment using the formulas described in the previous section. Finally, a series of seven cout statements displays the results.

The code for Get_Principal() closely follows the pseudocode we developed earlier. The values of the minimum and maximum principals are defined as symbolic constants. The function prompts for and obtains the input value for the principal.

Then it uses a nested `if` to decide if the value is in the valid range for the principal (between `MIN_PRINCIPAL` (1000.00) and `MAX_PRINCIPAL` (20000.00)). If not, a `cout` statement displays an appropriate message and the `exit(1)` function ends the program. If the value is in the valid range, the function returns the value of `princi-pal`. See the exercises for some extensions of the program.

The code for `Get_Rate()` and `Get_Term()` work similarly to that of `Get_Principal()`.

Testing the Program

Whenever you design a program to catch input errors, you should test for each of those input errors. The program output that accompanied the program in the previous section was produced by valid input values. Following are four program runs that test each input error that the program checks for.

Test 1: Principal Too Small

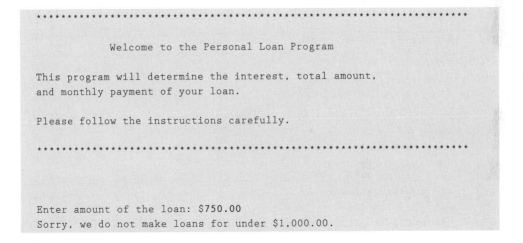

```
***************************************************************

              Welcome to the Personal Loan Program

This program will determine the interest, total amount,
and monthly payment of your loan.

Please follow the instructions carefully.

***************************************************************




Enter amount of the loan: $750.00
Sorry, we do not make loans for under $1,000.00.
```

Test 2: Principal Too Large

```
***************************************************************

              Welcome to the Personal Loan Program

This program will determine the interest, total amount,
and monthly payment of your loan.

Please follow the instructions carefully.

***************************************************************
```

```
Enter amount of the loan: $30000.00
Sorry, we do not make personal loans in excess of $20,000.00

Please try our Home Equity Loan
```

Test 3: Rate Too Large

```
*************************************************************************

                Welcome to the Personal Loan Program

This program will determine the interest, total amount,
and monthly payment of your loan.

Please follow the instructions carefully.

*************************************************************************



Enter amount of the loan: $10000.00
Enter current annual interest rate (in %): 20.0
Sorry, the rate exceeds the legal maximum of 18.70%
```

Test 4: Term Too Large

```
*************************************************************************

                Welcome to the Personal Loan Program

This program will determine the interest, total amount,
and monthly payment of your loan.

Please follow the instructions carefully.

*************************************************************************



Enter amount of the loan: $10000.00
Enter current annual interest rate (in %): 10.7
Enter the number of years of the loan: 7
Sorry, the term of your loan cannot exceed 5 years.
```

Problem 5.3—Calculating Commissions

This program demonstrates the use of a prompting function whose return value controls the main processing loop and how to construct a data validation function that continually prompts the user for valid data.

The Pickering Paper Products Company wants you to write a program to calculate the total income of its sales personnel. The program should prompt the user for the following data: the salesperson number, which must be between 000 and 999; the salesperson salary, which must be between 0.00 and 200.00; and the amount of the salesperson's sales, which must be between 0.00 and 10,000.00. If the user enters invalid data, the program should display an error message and prompt the user to enter correct data. The program should continue to prompt until the user enters valid data.

The salesperson's income is the sum of the salary, the straight commission, and the bonus commission. The straight commission is the sales multiplied by the commission rate of 5.0%. If the sales exceeds the sales quota for the salesperson, the bonus commission is the amount by which the sales exceeds the quota multiplied by the bonus commission rate of 8.5%. The sales quota for a salesperson is five times the salary of the salesperson.

For each salesperson that the program processes, display the salesperson number, salary, sales, and income. After the program processes the last salesperson, it should display the total number of salespersons that it processed.

Program Design

The pseudocode for the main module of the program is as follows. The discussion of the program code in the next section describes exactly how to make the test for another salesperson.

Pseudocode for Problem 5.3

```
while (another salesperson)
  Process_Salesperson
  ++salesperson_count
endwhile
Display salesperson_count
```

The module `Process_Salesperson` requires obtaining valid data from the user, calculating the salesperson income, and displaying the salesperson data.

```
Process_Salesperson
       Get_Valid Sales_No
       Get_Valid_Salary
       Get_Valid_Sales
       Calculate_Income
       Display_Salesperson_Data
```

The three modules that obtain valid data from the user have essentially the same design. Following is a generalized pseudocode that we shall use to develop the data validation modules.

Data Validation Module

```
do
  Get data from user
  If (data is invalid)
   invalid_data = TRUE
  else
   invalid_data = FALSE
  endif
while (invalid_data is TRUE)
return data
```

Programming
Pointers

The pseudocode uses the variable `invalid_data` as a flag. A **flag** is a variable whose value signals the occurrence of an event in a program. If the user enters invalid data, the `if` statement sets the flag `invalid_data` to `TRUE`; otherwise (that is, the user enters valid data) the `if` statement sets `invalid_data` to `FALSE`. The value of `invalid_data` tells the program whether the user entered invalid data. The `do` loop's condition shows that the program will stay in the loop as long as the user enters invalid data. When the program exits the loop, the data that the user entered was valid. Therefore, the module returns the valid data to the program.

The pseudocode for the `Calculate_Income` module is straightforward.

```
Calculate_Income
      quota = salary * 5
      straight_commission = sales * 0.05
      if (sales > quota)
        bonus_commission = (sales − quota) * 0.085
      else
        bonus_commission = 0.00
      endif
      income = salary + straight_commission + bonus_commission
      return income
```

The pseudocode for `Display_Salesperson_Data` is:

```
Display_Salesperson_Data
      Display salesperson_number
      Display salary
      Display sales
      Display income
```

We can now discuss the actual program code.

The Program prb05-3.cpp

Following is the code for the program prb05-3.cpp.

```cpp
// prb05-3.cpp

// This program calculates commissions based on salary and
// sales quota. It validates input data before doing the
// calculations.

#include <iostream.h>
#include <iomanip.h>

using namespace std;

int    Another_Salesperson();
void   Process_Salesperson();
void   Display_Salesperson_Data(int, double, double, double);
int    Get_Valid_Sales_No();
double Get_Valid_Sales();
double Get_Valid_Salary();
double Calculate_Income(double, double);

int main()
{
  int salesperson_count = 0;

  cout << setprecision(2)
       << setiosflags(ios::fixed)
       << setiosflags(ios::showpoint);

  while (Another_Salesperson())
    {
      Process_Salesperson();
      ++salesperson_count;
    }

  cout << "\n\nNumber of Salespersons Processed: " << salesperson_count;

  return 0;

} // End of main()

int Another_Salesperson()
{
  int response;

  cout << "\n\nDo you want to process a salesperson income?";
  cout << "\nEnter 1 for Yes, 0 for No: ";
  cin >> response;

  return response;

} // End of Another_Salesperson()
```

```
void Process_Salesperson()
{
  int    salesperson_number;
  double sales,
         salary,
         income;

  salesperson_number = Get_Valid_Sales_No();
  salary             = Get_Valid_Salary();
  sales              = Get_Valid_Sales();
  income             = Calculate_Income(sales, salary);

  Display_Salesperson_Data(salesperson_number, salary, sales, income);

} // End of Process_Salesperson()

int Get_Valid_Sales_No()
{
  const int TRUE  = 1;
  const int FALSE = 0;

  int salesperson_number,
      invalid_data;

  do
    {
      cout << "\nEnter the Salesperson Number (000-999): ";
      cin >> salesperson_number;

      if ((salesperson_number < 0) || (salesperson_number > 999))
        {
          cout << "\nSalesperson Number must be between 000 and 999.";
          invalid_data = TRUE;
        }
      else
        invalid_data = FALSE;
    }
  while (invalid_data);

  return salesperson_number;

} // End Get_Valid_Sales_No()


double Get_Valid_Salary()
{
  const int TRUE  = 1;
  const int FALSE = 0;

  int    invalid_data;
  double salary;
```

```
      do
        {
          cout << "\nEnter salary (0 - 200): ";
          cin >> salary;

          if ( (salary < 0.00) || (salary > 200.00) )
            {
              cout << "\nSalary is invalid - Please re-enter";
              invalid_data = TRUE;
            }
          else
            invalid_data = FALSE;
        }
      while (invalid_data);

      return salary;

    } // End Get_Valid_Salary()


    double Get_Valid_Sales()
    {
      const int TRUE  = 1;
      const int FALSE = 0;

      int    invalid_data;
      double sales;

      do
        {
          cout << "\nEnter sales (0 - 10,000): ";
          cin >> sales;

          if ( (sales < 0.00) || (sales > 10000.00) )
            {
              cout << "\nSales is invalid - Please reenter";
              invalid_data = TRUE;
            }
          else
            invalid_data = FALSE;
        }
      while (invalid_data);

      return sales;

    } // End Get_Valid_Sales()


    double Calculate_Income(double sales, double salary)
    {
      const double COMMISSION_RATE = 0.050;
```

```
   const double BONUS_RATE      = 0.085;
   const int    QUOTA_FACTOR    = 5;

   double quota,
          income,
          straight_commission,
          bonus_commission;

   quota = salary * QUOTA_FACTOR;

   straight_commission = sales * COMMISSION_RATE;

   if (sales > quota)
     bonus_commission = (sales - quota) * BONUS_RATE;
   else
     bonus_commission = 0.00;

   income = salary + straight_commission + bonus_commission;

   return income;

} // End Calculate_Income()

void Display_Salesperson_Data(int sp_no, double salary, double sales,
                              double income)
{
   cout << "\nData - Salesperson #" << sp_no;
   cout << "\n\nSalary: " << setw(10) << salary;
   cout << "\nSales:  " << setw(10) << sales;
   cout << "\nIncome: " << setw(10) << income;

} // End Display_Salesperson_Data()
```

Program Output

```
Do you want to process a salesperson income?
Enter 1 for Yes, 0 for No: 1

Enter the Salesperson Number (000-999): 123

Enter salary (0 - 200): 150.00

Enter sales (0 - 10,000): 3500.00

Data - Salesperson #123

Salary:     150.00
Sales:      3500.00
Income:      558.75
```

```
Do you want to process a salesperson income?
Enter 1 for Yes, 0 for No: 1

Enter the Salesperson Number (000-999): 826

Enter salary (0 - 200): 375.00

Salary is invalid - Please re-enter
Enter salary (0 - 200): 75.00

Enter sales (0 - 10,000): 2700.00

Data - Salesperson #826
Salary:     175.00
Sales:     2700.00
Income:     465.12

Do you want to process a salesperson income?
Enter 1 for Yes, 0 for No: 1

Enter the Salesperson Number (000-999): 373

Enter salary (0 - 200): 75.00

Enter sales (0 - 10,000): 12000.00

Sales is invalid - Please re-enter
Enter sales (0 - 10,000): 2000.00

Data - Salesperson #373

Salary:      75.00
Sales:     2000.00
Income:     313.12

Do you want to process a salesperson income?
Enter 1 for Yes, 0 for No: 1

Enter the Salesperson Number (000-999): 6789

Salesperson Number must be between 000 and 999.
Enter the Salesperson Number (000-999): 678

Enter salary (0 - 200): 90.00

Enter sales (0 - 10,000): 1500.00

Data - Salesperson #678

Salary:      90.00
```

```
Sales:       1500.00
Income:       254.25

Do you want to process a salesperson income?
Enter 1 for Yes, 0 for No: 0


Number of Salespersons Processed: 4
```

Discussion of the Program

Note that the user made several input-data errors in the program run that follows the listing.

All the functions closely follow the pseudocode that we developed in the previous section. The only function that we did not discuss is `Another_Salesperson()`. When the `while` statement executes, it evaluates its control expression, which causes the function `Another_Salesperson()` to execute. The function prompts the user for a 1 or 0 answer to the prompt for another salesperson. It then places the user's answer into the variable `response` and returns this value to `main()`. Evaluating the `while` loop's condition causes the program to prompt the user and obtain the response. If the user responded by entering 1, which C++ considers true, the `while` statement's condition expression is true and the loop body executes.

EXPERIMENTS 5.3

1. Add a function `Display_Greeting()` to prb05-1.cpp that displays the purpose of the program. After displaying the greeting, the function should pause and display

   ```
   Press any key to continue
   ```

   (Hint: Use `cin.get()`.) The program should then proceed as in the text. Use the function in the program. Recompile, execute, and test the resulting program.

2. Add the function `Calc_Total_Charge()` to prb05-1.cpp. The function should take two arguments representing the labor charge and the total charge. The function should return the sum of its arguments. Use the function in the program. Recompile, execute, and test the resulting program.

3. Add the function `Calc_Payment()` to prb05-2.cpp. The function should calculate the monthly payment as done in the original program. Replace the Do Calculation section of the program by a call to the `Calc_Payment()` function. Recompile, execute, and test the resulting program.

4. In prb05-2.cpp, the principal, rate, and term must all be positive. Include a test in the functions `Get_Principal()`, `Get_Rate()`, and `Get_Term()` to see if the data entered is positive. If the data is not positive, display an error message and exit the program. Use the new functions in the program. Recompile, execute, and test the resulting program.

5. In prb05-3.cpp, validate the response obtained by the function `Another-Salesperson()`. If the response is not 0 or 1, continually prompt until the person enters either 0 or 1. Use the new function in the program. Recompile, execute, and test the resulting program.

6. In prb05-3.cpp, if the user enters invalid data, the program continually prompts for another value until the user enters a valid value. Change all the data validation functions so they prompt the user for valid data a maximum of three times. If the user enters invalid data three times the program should issue a polite message and end.

7. In prb05-3.cpp, why is `salesperson_count` declared in `main()` and incremented in `main()`'s `while` loop and not declared and incremented in `Process_Salesperson()`?

8. In prb05-3.cpp, would it be a good idea to declare the global constants

```
const int TRUE = 1;
const int FALSE = 0;
```

instead of making three pairs of such declarations (one for each validation function) as is done in the text?

PROGRAMMING PROBLEMS 5.3

1. The Big Racket Tennis Club wants you to write a program to calculate the yearly dues for its members. The program should prompt the user for the membership type (either 'I' for individual or 'F' for family) and the number of years the person has been a member. Use a function `Get_Member_Type()` that prompts the user for the membership type, obtains the type from the user, and returns the type to `main()`. Use a function `Years()` that prompts the user for the number of years they have been a member and returns that number to `main()`.

   Use a function `Dues()` to calculate the member's dues. Pass the member type and number of years to the function. Calculate the dues as follows: If the person is a family member and has been a club member for more than three years, the dues are $2400. If the person is a family member and has been a club member for three years or less, the dues are $3000. If the person is an individual member and has been a club member for more than five years, the dues are $1500. If the person is an individual member and has been a club member for five years or less, the dues are $1900. The function `Dues()` should return the dues to `main()`.

   Use a function `Display_Member_Info()` to display the type of membership, the number of years the person has been a member, and the dues, all of which should be passed to the function as arguments.

2. At Humongous National Bank, the vice president in charge of credit cards decides to issue a new type of credit card, the Platinum Card. Write a program to help the bank decide which customers will be offered a Platinum Card. Use a function `Get_Credit_Limit()` to prompt the user for the customer's present credit limit. The function should return the credit limit. Use a function

`Get_Acc_Bal()` to prompt the user for the customer's account balance. The function should return the account balance.

Use a function `Determine_Action()` whose arguments are the customer's credit limit and account balance. `Determine_Action()` should return 0, 1, or 2 according to the following. If a customer has a credit limit of at least $2000 and an account balance of $500 or less, the bank will issue the customer a Platinum Card. In this case, the function should return 2. If a customer has a credit limit of at least $2000 and an account balance of more than $500, the bank will send a letter to the customer. This letter will state that if the customer's balance falls below $500, he or she will receive a Platinum Card. In this case, the function should return 1. If a customer does not fall into either of these categories, the bank will take no action. In this case, the function should return 0.

Use a function `Display_Action()` to display the action that the bank will take for the customer. Pass the value that `Determine_Action()` returned to `Display_Action()`. Based on this value, `Display_Action()` should display a message that shows the action that the bank should take: issue a Platinum Card, send a letter, or take no action.

3. After many years of being frustrated by a checkbook that will not balance, you decide to write a program to help balance your money market checking account. The program should begin by asking the user for the month's opening account balance. Use a function to obtain and validate the input data. The balance cannot be negative.

The program should use a function to display a menu that lists the following choices: D for a deposit, C for a check, W for a withdrawal, and Q for quit. Use a function to obtain and validate the user's choice. If the user enters something other than D, W, C, or Q, the program should issue an error message and redisplay the menu. Allow the user to enter either uppercase or lowercase letters. If the user selects D, use a function to ask the user to enter the amount of the deposit and add the amount to the account balance.

If the user enters C, use a function to ask the user for the amount of the check and subtract the check amount from the balance. However, if the amount of the check exceeds the balance, issue a warning message and exit the program. If the user enters W, use a function to ask the user for the amount of the withdrawal and subtract the amount from the balance. However, if the amount of the withdrawal exceeds the balance, issue a warning message and exit the program. When the user enters Q, the program should use a function to display the opening balance, the total amount deposited, the total amount withdrawn, the total amount of the checks, and the final balance.

4. Generalize the program in Programming Problem 1 as follows. The function `Get_Member_Type()` should validate the membership type. Anything other than 'I' or 'F' is an invalid membership type. Continually prompt the user to enter a valid membership type until he or she does so. The function `Years()` should validate the number of years that the user enters. The number of years should be nonnegative and less than 37, which is the age of the tennis club. Continually prompt the user to enter a valid number of years until he or she does so. The program should also process any number of members.

5. Generalize the program in Programming Problem 2 as follows. Write the program so that it will process any number of customers. The function `Get_Credit_Limit()` should validate the credit card limit that the user entered. The credit card limit must be between 500.00 and 20,000, inclusive. If the user enters an invalid credit card limit, prompt the user again. If the user enters an invalid limit again, the program should stop processing that customer and go on to the next customer. The function `Get_Acc_Bal()` should validate the account balance. The balance must be nonnegative and less than the validated credit limit. If the user enters a negative account balance, prompt the user again for an account balance. If the user enters an invalid account balance again, the program should stop processing that customer and go on to the next customer. If the user enters an account balance that is greater than the validated credit limit, the program should display a message to that effect and go on to the next customer.

6. A piece of equipment, such as a computer, loses value over time. The amount of this lost value is called **depreciation**. The simplest way to determine depreciation is by the **straight-line** method. If the asset has a useful life of n years, the straight-line method of depreciation assumes a depreciation of $1/n$ of the item's value each year. Assume a particular $3,000 computer has a useful life of five years. At the end of the five years, assume it has a **scrap value** of $500. Thus, the net cost of the computer is $3000 - 500 = \$2500$. Using the straight-line method, the computer depreciates $500 (=2500 \times 1/5)$ each of the five years of its useful life. After two years, the computer depreciates $1,000. The **book value** of the computer after two years (the difference between the cost of the item and the depreciation to date) is $2,000 (= 3000 - 1000)$.

   Write a program that calculates the depreciation of an asset using the straight-line method. The program should ask the user for the initial cost of the item, the scrap value of the item, and the item's useful life in years. Use a function `Depreciation()` that calculates and displays a table that shows the book value of the item after each year of its useful life. The function should have three arguments—the initial cost, the scrap value, and the life of the item. The function should not return a value.

7. An automobile part supplier decides to give discounts to this week's customers to help improve customer relations. Write a program to calculate a customer's discount. The discount is based on the value of the customer's order (the invoice amount) and the customer code, which is a single character. If the customer code is A, the discount rate is 5%. If the customer code is B, the discount rate is 8%. If the customer code is C, the discount rate is 12%. A customer code other than A, a, B, b, C, or c is invalid. The discount amount is the amount multiplied by the discount rate. The net invoice amount is the amount minus the discount amount. The program should display the invoice amount, the discount amount, and the net invoice amount.

8. An IRA (Individual Retirement Account) is an example of an annuity. The holder of an IRA can deposit money into the account each year. The amount is usually withdrawn when the depositor is age 65. However, it can be withdrawn without incurring a penalty when the depositor is age 59.5. A bank wants to show its customers the difference between what they will have in their accounts at age

65 and what they will have in their accounts at age 59.5, if equal annual payments are made to the account. Write a program to do this.

The program should prompt for the annual deposit (which should not exceed $2,000), the annual interest rate, and the customer's age when the account was opened. Use a function to obtain each input datum. The function that obtains the interest rate should allow the user to enter the interest rate as a percent (for example, 4.7) but should return the decimal equivalent of the entered percent (for example, 0.047.)

The amount in an IRA after n years of equal annual deposits of R dollars at an annual interest rate of r is given by the following formula.

$$A = R\big(((1 + r)^n - 1)/r\big)$$

To calculate the value of an IRA when the customer is 65, first subtract the customer's age at the time the account was opened from 65. This gives the value of n to use in the formula. The values of R and r are obtained from the user. To calculate the value of an IRA when the customer is 59.5, proceed in the same manner but subtract the customer's age from 59.5 to obtain the value of n.

The program should output the value of the IRA at age 65, the value of the IRA at age 59.5 and the difference between these values. The library function `pow()` should prove useful in this problem. You must include the header file `math.h` to use this function.

9. A bank wants to calculate the monthly payment required to pay off (or amortize) personal loans that it will make to customers. Write a program to do this. The program should prompt the user for the amount of the loan (the principal), the annual interest rate, and the length of the loan in years. The principal cannot exceed $100,000 and the length of the loan cannot exceed five years. Allow the user to enter the interest rate as a percent. Use a function to obtain each input value.

The monthly payment M on an N-year loan with a principal of P at a monthly interest rate of r is given by the following formula.

$$M = Pr/(1 - (1 + r)^{-12N})$$

Calculate the monthly interest rate by dividing the yearly interest rate by 12. The program should output the amount of the loan, the annual interest rate, the length of the loan in years, and the monthly payment.

The library function `pow()` should prove useful in this problem. You must include the header file `math.h` to use this function.

10. A credit card company wants a program to calculate updates on its customer's accounts. The program should prompt for the previous month's balance, the amount of the new purchases, and the amount of the payments received. The program should use a function to calculate the customer's finance charge by first subtracting the payments received from the previous month's balance. Then multiply the result by 1/12 the annual interest rate of 16% to get the finance charge. Next, use a function to calculate the late charge, if any. If the payments received amount is less than 12% of the previous month's balance, the late charge is 0.5% of the difference between the previous month's balance and the payments

received. The minimum late charge is $3. If the payments received amount is 12% or more of the previous month's balance, there is no late charge.

The program should use a function to calculate the new balance. To calculate the new balance, first subtract the payments received from the previous month's balance. From the result, add the finance charge, the late charge, and the new purchases amount to give the new balance.

Finally, use a function to calculate the minimum payment. If the new balance is less than or equal to $100, the minimum payment is the new balance. If the new balance is greater than $100, the minimum payment is 20% of the new balance.

11. Your local county government wants you to write a program that computes the property tax on commercial and residential properties. The program should prompt the user for the type of property (1 for a home, 2 for a commercial property). If the property is a home, the program should ask if the property is a residence (1 for primary residence, 2 for non-primary residence). If the property is commercial, the program should ask if the property contains a building (1 for building, 2 for land only.) Finally, the program should ask for the property tract number and for the assessed value of the property. Use functions to obtain all input values. Invalid input values should be rejected.

The property tax should be calculated according to the following. If the property is a home used for a primary residence, the tax rate is 3.2% of the assessed value. If the property is a home that is a non-primary residence, the tax rate is 4.1% of the assessed value. If the property is commercial and is land only, the tax rate is 5.3% of the assessed value. If the property is a commercial building, the tax rate is 6.2% of the assessed value. Use a function to decide the tax rate. The program should output the property tract number, the type of property, the assessed value of the property, the tax rate, and the amount of the property tax.

12. A garment manufacturer requires a program to calculate the payroll of his piece-work employees. A piece-work employee receives a guaranteed wage, which is based on the seniority of the person. However, a worker can receive incentive pay instead of the guaranteed wage. Incentive pay is determined by the number of units the worker produces. For all units produced up to and including 100, the incentive pay is $3.50 per unit. For all units produced in excess of 100, the incentive pay is $4.50 per unit. An employee cannot receive both a guaranteed wage and incentive pay. Instead, an employee receives the greater of the two. Write a program to compute the payroll.

The program should use a function to obtain the employee's guaranteed wage and a function to obtain the number of units produced. Use a function to calculate the pay based on the guaranteed wage and the number of units produced. Finally, use a function to display the employee's wage and whether it is the guaranteed wage or the incentive pay.

The program should process any number of employees.

13. Your city's Parking Violation Bureau wants you to write a program to compute fines for parking violations. There are four types of violations: type A carries a fine of $10, type B carries a fine of $20, type C carries a fine of $30, and type D carries a fine of $50. The program should ask for the number of type A violations, the number of type B violations, and so on. Use four separate functions to obtain

the number of violations of each type. If the number of type A, B, or C violations exceeds 10, impose an additional fine of $50 for each category that exceeds 10. If the total number of type A, B, or C exceeds 20 but none of types A, B, or C individually exceeds 10, impose an additional fine of $75. If the number of type D violations exceeds 3, impose an additional fine of $20 for each type D violation over 3. Use a function to calculate the total fine. Pass the number of each type of fines to this function. The function should return the total fine. Use a function to display the total fine for the person. The program should process any number of persons.

5.4 Macros and Inline Functions

So far we have defined symbolic constants by declaring them as `const` variables, which is the preferred way in C++. It is also possible to define symbolic constants by using the `#define` preprocessor directive. In fact, you can use the `#define` preprocessor directive to define macros, which can sometimes replace functions.

Symbolic Constants Using `#define`

Recall that the C++ preprocessor is a text replacement mechanism. The `#define` preprocessor directive allows us to replace any expression with a defined name. For example, in prb05-3.cpp, we could replace the declaration

```
const double COMMISSION_RATE = 0.050;
```

by the definition

```
#define COMMISSION_RATE 0.050
```

This directive defines the symbolic constant `COMMISSION_RATE` as the value 0.05. When the preprocessor scans the program code, it replaces every occurrence of the symbol `COMMISSION_RATE` by the value 0.050. When the preprocessor scans the line

```
straight_commission = sales * COMMISSION_RATE;
```

it replaces the symbol `COMMISSION_RATE` by its defined value of 0.050.

Note that the preprocessor directive does not end in a semicolon. Doing so would cause the semicolon to be part of the definition, which could cause a syntax or logic error in your program.

Macro Definitions

Programming
Pointers

The `#define` directive can also be used to define macros with parameters. A **macro** is a name that stands for a statement or expression. For example, consider the following definition.

```
#define SQ(x) x * x
```

When the C++ preprocessor sees this definition, it searches the program for all occurrences of the macro name SQ. The character string that is in parentheses after the macro name replaces the parameter x. The preprocessor then replaces the macro by the expression obtained by replacing the parameter in the macro definition by the character string that is in parentheses after the macro name. For example, the preprocessor would replace the expression

```
s = SQ(count);
```

by

```
s = count * count;
```

Programming
Pitfalls

Since the preprocessor is a text replacement mechanism, it does not check for correctness in syntax or meaning. For example, you cannot put a space after the macro name and before the left parenthesis. Doing so causes the preprocessor to interpret everything that follows the macro name as part of the definition, even the parentheses. Thus, incorrectly defining SQ as

```
#define SQ (x) x * x
```

results in the preprocessor expanding the assignment

```
s = SQ(count);
```

to the following meaningless expression

```
s = (x) x * x(count);
```

Programming
Pitfalls

Also, do not put a semicolon at the end of a macro. Doing so makes the semicolon part of the definition, which could cause a syntax error. For example, incorrectly defining SQ as

```
#define SQ(x) x * x;
```

causes the preprocessor to expand the macro in the following if statement

```
if (count > 3)
   count = SQ(count);
else
   count = 1;
```

as follows

```
if (count > 3)
  count = count * count;;
else
  count = 1;
```

The extra semicolon in the first assignment is a null statement and causes a syntax error.

The given definition of SQ can also cause side effects that result in a change in meaning. Suppose we have the following definitions and assignment.

Programming
Pitfalls

```
int i = 2,
    j = 4,
    k;

k = SQ(i + j);
```

The assignment does not assign the value 36 to k as you might first think. The preprocessor expands the macro in the assignment as follows, replacing each occurrence of the parameter x by the string i + j.

```
k = i + j * i + j;
```

Because the computer evaluates multiplication before addition, the right side of the assignment evaluates to 14.

To avoid this **side effect** of macro expansion, enclose each occurrence of the parameter in the macro definition by parentheses.

Programming
Pointers

```
#define SQ(x) (x) * (x)
```

With this definition, in the assignment to k, the preprocessor would replace each occurrence of x in the definition of SQ with the string i + j. This time, however, the parentheses are part of the macro. The macro expands as follows, which correctly evaluates to 36.

```
k = (i + j) * (i + j);
```

There is still another side effect that can occur with this new macro definition. Using the same definitions of i, j, and k as before, consider the following assignment.

```
k = j / SQ(i);
```

The assignment does not assign 1 to k. Instead, the preprocessor replaces the macro in the assignment by (i) * (i), which results in the following assignment.

```
k = j / (i) * (i);
```

Because multiplication and division are on the same precedence level and they associate from left to right, the computer does the division first. This results in the computer assigning 4 to k.

To avoid this side effect, enclose the entire macro definition in parentheses as follows.

```
#define SQ(x) ((x) * (x))
```

With this new definition, the preprocessor would expand the macro as ((i) * (i)) and the assignment to k would be the following.

```
k = j / ( (i) * (i) );
```

Now the computer evaluates the multiplication first and then the division. This results in the computer assigning 1 to k.

Note 5.5 summarizes the rules for writing macros.

NOTE 5.5—RULES FOR WRITING MACROS

1. Do not code a space between the macro name and the left parenthesis that follows the name.
2. Do not end the macro definition with a semicolon.
3. Enclose each occurrence of each parameter in the macro definition in parentheses.
4. Enclose the entire macro definition in parentheses.

Macros can have more than one parameter. For example, the following macro squares the sum of its two parameters.

```
#define SUM_SQ(x, y) ( ((x) + (y)) * ((x) + (y)) )
```

You also can use a macro in the definition of another macro that has already been defined in the program. For example, the following is legal.

```
#define SQ(x) ( (x) * (x) )
#define SUM_SQ(x, y) ( SQ((x) + (y)) )
```

In the next section we put macros to work in a program and discuss the relative merits of macros and functions.

An Example Using Macros—The Conditional Operator

The following program, dem05-7.cpp, asks the user to enter several numbers. When the user stops entering the numbers, the program displays the smallest and the largest numbers that the user entered. The program uses two macros `MAX(x, y)` and `MIN(x, y)` that find the larger and smaller of the two parameters. The macro definitions use the **conditional operator ?:**, which is the only operator in C++ that has tree operands. The conditional operator has the following form.

conditional-expression ? expression1 : expression2

If the conditional expression is true, the value of the entire operator is expression1. If the conditional expression is false, the value of the entire operator is expression2. Thus, the conditional operator is similar to an `if-else` statement. If the conditional expression is true, the value of the operator is expression1; otherwise, the value of the operator is expression2. For example, suppose we have the following declarations and assignment.

```
int i = 3,
    j = 4,
    k;
```

```
k = (i ==j)? i: j;
```

It helps to read the operator as follows: "`i, if i equals j; else j.`" The statement assigns the value of `i` to `k` if `i` equals `j`; otherwise, it assigns the value of `j` to `k`. Using the initial values of `i` and `j`, the statement assigns 4 to `k`.

A common use of the conditional operator is in macro definitions. For example, the following macro results in the larger of its two parameters.

```
#define MAX(x, y) ( ((x) > (y))? (x): (y) )
```

Thus, `MAX(x, y)` is x if x is greater than y; otherwise, `MAX(x, y)` is y. The following program, dem05-7.cpp, uses this macro and a similar one `MIN(x, y)` that finds the smaller of its two parameters.

```
// dem05—7.c
```

```
// This program uses macros to find the largest and
// smallest of a set of numbers input by the user.
// The macros make use of the conditional operator.
```

```
#include <iostream.h>
#include <iomanip.h>
```

```
using namespace std;
```

```
#define MAX(x, y) ( ((x) > (y))? (x): (y) )
```

```
#define MIN(x, y) ( ((x) < (y))? (x): (y) )

int main()
{
  int     number_count,
          i;
  double number,
          minimum,
          maximum;

  cout << setprecision(6)
       << setiosflags(ios::fixed)
       << setiosflags(ios::showpoint);

  cout << "\nThis program will find the largest and smallest of ";
  cout << "\nthe numbers you enter.";
  cout << "\n\nEnter the number of numbers that you will enter: ";
  cin >> number_count;

  cout << "\n\nNow you will be asked to enter the numbers.";
  cout << "\n\nEnter number 1: ";
  cin >> number;

  minimum = maximum = number;

  for (i = 2; i <= number_count; ++i)
    {
      cout << "\nEnter number " << i << ": ";
      cin >> number;
      minimum = MIN(minimum, number);
      maximum = MAX(maximum, number);
    }

  cout << "\n\nSmallest number: " << minimum;
  cout << "\n\nLargest number: " << maximum;

  return 0;
}
```

Program Output

```
This program will find the largest and smallest of
the numbers you enter.

Enter the number of numbers that you will enter: 10

Now you will be asked to enter the numbers.

Enter number 1: 3.6
```

```
Enter number 2: -5.0

Enter number 3: 6.3

Enter number 4: 9.9

Enter number 5: 2.1

Enter number 6: 12.3

Enter number 7: -7.8

Enter number 8: 10.6

Enter number 9: -3.4

Enter number 10: 5.2


Smallest number: -7.800000

Largest number: 12.300000
```

The program begins by asking the user for the number of numbers that will be entered. After placing that value into `number_count`, the program prompts for the first number. The program places the number that the user enters into the variable `number`. A multiple assignment then places the value of `number` into the variables `minimum` and `maximum`. The variable `minimum` holds the value of the smallest number that the user has entered so far. The variable `maximum` holds the value of the largest number that the user has entered so far. When the user enters the first number, that number is both the smallest and largest number entered so far.

The program then enters a `for` loop that processes the rest of the numbers that the user enters. Each iteration prompts the user for a number. Then, the first assignment replaces `minimum` by the smaller of `minimum` and the number that the user entered. The second assignment replaces `maximum` by the larger of `maximum` and the number that the user entered. Therefore, when the program exits the loop, `maximum` contains the largest number the user entered, and `minimum` contains the smallest number the user entered.

Functions versus Macros

Programming
Pointers

There are several advantages to using macros instead of functions. First, because using a macro does not involve a function call or passing parameters, a macro executes faster than a function. Second, the parameters in a macro do not have a type. For example, the MAX macro of dem05-7.cpp will find the larger of two `int` variables, two `long` variables, or two `double` variables. If you use a function to find the larger of two numbers, you must specify the data type of the numbers. For example, you would need different functions to find the larger of two integers and the larger of two doubles.

Programming Pitfalls

There are also disadvantages to using macros instead of functions. First, as we noted, macros can have side effects that lead to incorrect results. Functions are not subject to these side effects. Second, although there is overhead in calling a function and passing parameters, the function mechanism is safer to use. Remember that the compiler uses the function prototype to ensure that you use the function's parameters and return type correctly. The compiler does no such checking for macros.

Inline Functions

Programming Pointers

In C++ there is a way to combine the efficiency of a macro with the safety of a function by using an **inline function**. If a function is inline, the compiler places a copy of the code of that function at each point where the function is called. Short functions (one or two lines of code) are ideal candidates for inlining. Because the compiler replaces an inline function's call by the code of the function, it follows that the compiler must know the definition of the funciton before any calls to the function are made in the program code. To inline a function, place the keyword `inline` before the function name and define the function before any calls are made to the function. This means that you place the function's definition where you usually place the function prototype. In our programs, this means that inline function definitions are placed before `main()`.

For example, in dem05-7.cpp we used the following macro

```
#define MAX(x, y) ( ((x) > (y))? (x): (y) )
```

An inline function that is equivalent to this macro is the following.

```
inline double Max(double x, double y) {return (x > y)? x : y;}
```

Note that we do not need to use excessive parentheses as was necessary in the macro definition to avoid side effects. Suppose `main()` contains the following declarations and function call.

```
double d1 = 4.8,
       d2 = 9.6,
       d;

d = Max(d1, d2);
```

When the compiler encounters the function call to `Max()`, it replaces the function call with the code of the inline function by using the values of the arguments as the values of the parameters. The assignment is equivalent to the following.

```
d = (d1 > d2)? d1 : d2;
```

We illustrate inline functions by recoding dem05-7.cpp with inline functions in place of macros.

```c
// dem05-8.c

// This program uses inline functions to find the largest and
// smallest of a set of numbers input by the user.
// The macros make use of the conditional operator.

#include <iostream.h>
#include <iomanip.h>

using namespace std;

inline double Max(double x, double y) {return (x > y)? x : y;}
inline double Min(double x, double y) {return (x < y)? x : y;}

int main()
{
  int    number_count,
         i;
  double number,
         minimum,
         maximum;

  cout << setprecision(6)
       << setiosflags(ios::fixed)
       << setiosflags(ios::showpoint);

  cout << "\nThis program will find the largest and smallest of ";
  cout << "\nthe numbers you enter.";
  cout << "\n\nEnter the number of numbers that you will enter: ";
  cin >> number_count;

  cout << "\n\nNow you will be asked to enter the numbers.";
  cout << "\n\nEnter number 1: ";
  cin >> number;

  minimum = maximum = number;

  for (i = 2; i <= number_count; ++i)
    {
      cout << "\nEnter number " << i << ": ";
      cin >> number;
      minimum = Min(minimum, number);
      maximum = Max(maximum, number);
    }

  cout << "\n\nSmallest number: " << minimum;
```

```
    cout << "\n\nLargest number: " << maximum;

    return 0;
}
```

Program Output

```
This program will find the largest and smallest of
the numbers you enter.

Enter the number of numbers that you will enter: 3

Now you will be asked to enter the numbers.

Enter number 1: 3.4

Enter number 2: 6.8

Enter number 3: 4.1


Smallest number: 3.400000

Largest number: 6.800000
```

NOTE 5.6—WHEN AND HOW TO USE INLINE FUNCTIONS

- Consider inlining a function if the function has one or two lines of code.
- To inline a function, place the keyword `inline` before the return type in the function definition. The function's definition must precede any call to the function in the program code.

EXERCISES 5.4

1. Recode prb05-3.cpp replacing all the symbolic constants by their equivalents using #define. Compile and execute the resulting program.
2. Write a macro AREA that finds the area of a rectangle in terms of its length and width.
3. Write an inline function Area() that finds the area of a rectangle in terms of its length and width.
4. Write a macro CELSIUS that converts a Fahrenheit temperature to the equivalent Celsius temperature.

5. Write an inline function `Celsius()` that converts a Fahrenheit temperature to the equivalent Celsius temperature.

6. Write a macro `SALE_PRICE` that computes the sale price of an item given the item's list price. The macro should apply a 25 percent discount on the list price and then add 8.25% sales tax.

7. Write an inline function `Sale_Price()` that computes the sale price of an item given the item's list price. The function should apply a 25 percent discount on the list price and then add 8.25% sales tax.

8. Use the macro `SQ` that we developed in the text to define macros `THR` and `FOR` that compute the third and fourth powers of their parameters.

9. Write a macro that finds the largest among three parameters. Feel free to use the macro `MAX` that we used in dem05-7.cpp.

EXPERIMENTS 5.4

1. Redo dem05-7.cpp using functions instead of macros to find the minimum and maximum between two numbers.

Chapter Review

. . . .

Terminology

Define the following terms.

`return`	duration
user-defined function	local scope
return value	global scope
argument	storage class
function prototype	`auto`
`void`	`static`
function definition header	flag
calling function	macro
called function	side effect
parameter	conditional operator
arguments passed by value	`inline`
arguments passed by reference	
scope	

Summary

- A function is a program module that performs a specific, well-defined task.
- A function can have zero or more arguments (inputs), and zero or one return value.

- A function must be defined in a prototype, which specifies the function name, return type (`void` if none), and the argument types (Notes 5.1 and 5.2).
- Specify what the function does in the function definition (Note 5.3).
- The function parameters, which are initialized to the values of the arguments passed to the function, are declared in the function definition header.
- By default, arguments are passed by value.
- A variable declared inside a function has local scope, that is, it is known only inside that function.
- A variable declared outside a function definition has global scope, that is, it is known to all functions whose definitions follow that of the variable. Avoid using global variables (Note 5.4).
- An automatic variable (local variables are automatic by default) ceases to exist when the function in which it is declared ends.
- A static variable (global variables are static by default; a local variable can be declared static by using the keyword `static` in its declaration) is allocated storage when the program begins executing and remains in existence as long as the program is running.
- Define a symbolic constant or a macro having parameters by using the #`define` preprocesor directive.
- Use parentheses in a macro definition to avoid side effects (Note 5.5).
- The conditional operator can replace a simple condition.
- Macros are often more efficient than functions, but functions do not have side effects.
- An inline function, defined with the keyword `inline`, can combine the efficiency of a macro with the safety of a function (Note 5.6).

Review Exercises

1. What is a function? What is the difference between the calling function and the called function?
2. How many arguments can a function have and how many return values?
3. What is the purpose of a function prototype and how do you code one?
4. How do you code the fact that a function has no arguments? How do you code the fact that a function has no return value?
5. How does a function pass control back to the calling function?
6. What is the purpose of a parameter in a function definition?
7. What is the default method that C++ uses to pass arguments to a function?
8. What is the scope of a variable?
9. What is the difference between local and global scope?
10. What kind of variable has local scope by default?
11. What kind of variable has global scope by default?
12. Why should you avoid using global variables?

13. What is the difference between the `auto` and `static` storage classes?

14. What kind of variable is `auto` by default?

15. What kind if variable is `static` by default?

16. How can you declare a local variable to be `static`? Why can such a variable be useful?

17. What is the purpose of a program flag?

18. How do you define a symbolic constant using #`define`?

19. How do you define a macro with parameters?

20. What are side effects in a macro and how can you avoid them?

21. Discuss the relative merits of using macros versus using functions?

22. Explain when and how to use an `inline` function.

Chapter

6

Arrays

Objectives

- To properly declare an array.
- To use subscripts to access array elements.
- To initialize an array.
- To use a `for` loop to process an array.
- To code an array search.

- To code a bubble sort on an array.
- To properly declare a two-dimensional array.
- To initialize a two-dimensional array.
- To use nested `for` loops to process a two-dimensional array.

Sometimes it is convenient to store related data together as an array. This chapter begins by showing how to declare, initialize, and process the elements in an array. Then we discuss several applications of arrays, including searching an array. We cover how to pass an array as a function argument, and we also use functions in several applications, including sorting an array by using the bubble sort. Finally, we close the chapter by discussing multidimensional arrays.

6.1 Basic Concepts

Sometimes it is advantageous to store a collection of data together as a unit. For example, in a program to compute shipping charges on mail orders, you might want to store the shipping rates for the five shipping regions that your company uses. You could use five different variables to store the rates—rate1, rate2, rate3, rate4, rate5. However, because the five numbers represent shipping rates, it makes more sense to store all five rates in one "variable" called rate. This object called rate is not a variable in the sense that we have used the term so far. It is what we call an **array**. An array stores values similarly to the way a one-row egg carton holds eggs. We can view the egg carton in Figure 6.1a as a single object. We can also consider the array in Figure 6.1b as a single object. The egg carton in Figure 6.1a stores five individual items that you can process (fry, boil, scramble, poach) individually. Likewise, the array in Figure 6.1b stores five shipping rates that a program can individually process.

Definition of an Array. An **array** is a collection of a <u>fixed number</u> of objects all of the <u>same type</u>, which are <u>stored sequentially</u> in computer memory. The objects in an array are the array's **elements**.

The three underlined parts of the definition are important. First, once you decide on the number of elements in an array, that number (the **array size**) stays fixed during the program. However, the values of the individual elements in the array can change as much the program demands.

Second, the elements in an array must all be the same type. They must all be of type int, or all of type char, or all of type double, and so on. The common type of the array's elements is the **array type**. This property of an array ensures that each element in a given array requires the same amount of storage.

Finally, the computer stores the elements in an array sequentially, one after the other in memory. Therefore, if the computer knows the location of the first element of an array, it knows that the second element immediately follows the first, the third

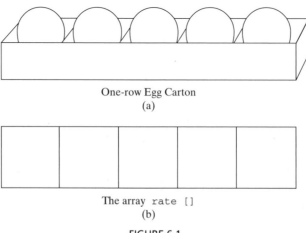

One-row Egg Carton
(a)

The array rate []
(b)

FIGURE 6.1

immediately follows the second, and so on. Figure 6.1b illustrates how array elements are stored. This property of an array is why some refer to an array as a **linear data structure** or **one-dimensional data structure**—the computer stores the elements of an array in the same way as points appear on a line.

Declaring an Array

Programming
Pointers

To use an array in a program, you first must declare the array. The declaration specifies the name of the array, the array type, and the size of the array. Following is the format of an array declaration.

   array-type array-name [array-size];

Thus, the following declares an array of type `double` called `rate` that can store five shipping rates.

```
double rate[5];
```

To read the declaration of an array, follow the rule in Note 6.1.

NOTE 6.1—READING AN ARRAY DECLARATION

Begin reading an array declaration at the array name and proceed clockwise through the declaration to the array type. Read the left bracket [as "is an array of."

Using Note 6.1, we read the previous declaration as "`rate` is an array of five doubles." Also, read the declaration

```
int grade[10];
```

as "`grade` is an array of 10 integers."

Referencing and Initializing Array Elements

Programming
Pointers

Each element in an array is numbered by its **offset**, or **displacement**, from the beginning of the array. Thus, the first element of an array is numbered 0 because it is zero elements from the beginning of the array. The second element of an array is numbered 1 because it is one element from the beginning of the array, and so on. Some people call the offset of an element the element's **subscript** or **index**.

In a program, to refer to a particular element of an array, code the array name and enclose the offset of the element in brackets. Thus, the elements of the array `rate[]` that we declared earlier are `rate[0]`, `rate[1]`, `rate[2]`, `rate[3]`, and `rate[4]` as shown in Figure 6.2. Note that the largest valid offset is one less than the size of the

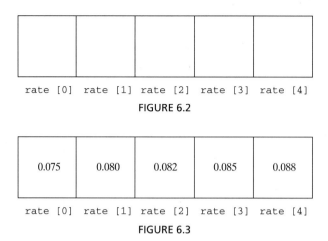

FIGURE 6.2

| 0.075 | 0.080 | 0.082 | 0.085 | 0.088 |

rate [0]   rate [1]   rate [2]   rate [3]   rate [4]

FIGURE 6.3

array. The array name and the left bracket can be separated by one or more spaces, although we shall not generally do so.

NOTE 6.2—SUBSCRIPT RANGE

In an array of size N, the valid offset range (subscript values) is from 0 to N - 1.

It is easy to code assignment statements to initialize the elements of an array. For example, to initialize the five elements of the array `rate[]` to 0.075, 0.080, 0.082, 0.085, and 0.088, we could code the following. See Figure 6.3.

```
rate[0] = 0.075;
rate[1] = 0.080;
rate[2] = 0.082;
rate[3] = 0.085;
rate[4] = 0.088;
```

However, instead of coding five separate lines to initialize the array, we can place initial values into the array in the array's declaration.

NOTE 6.3—INITIALIZING AN ARRAY

- To initialize an array in its declaration, list the elements' initial values in braces. Follow each listed value, except the last value, with a comma.
- If you do not list enough values the compiler will fill the remaining elements with zeros.
- If you list too many elements when initializing an array, the compiler will ignore the extra elements.
- If you initialize an array in its declaration, you can omit the size of the array.

To declare and initialize the array `rate[]` with the values we gave, code the following.

```
double rate[5] = {0.075, 0.080, 0.082, 0.085, 0.088};
```

For example, consider the following declaration.

```
double rate[5] = {0.075, 0.080, 0.082};
```

The C++ compiler creates the array `rate[]` and allocates enough storage for exactly five doubles. The compiler then initializes the first three elements to 0.075, 0.080, and 0.082, and places the double 0.0 into the remaining array elements. See Figure 6.4.

You can initialize an array by setting it equal to the initialization list only in the declaration, not later in an assignment. Thus, the following assignment is illegal.

```
double rate[5];
rate[] = {0.075, 0.080, 0.082, 0.085, 0.088}; // Illegal assignment
```

Programming
Pointers

As a second example, the following declaration initializes all the elements of the array grade to zero. We list one grade in the initialization. The compiler places zero in the other nine array elements.

```
int grade[10] = {0};
```

In the following declaration seven values are listed in the initialization list, but the array is of size five. Thus, the compiler places only the first five numbers in the array `customer_count`.

```
int customer_count[5] = {3, 4, 5, 6, 7, 8, 9};
```

If you initialize an array in the array declaration and omit the size of the array, the compiler will infer the size from the list of elements. For example, the following declaration declares the array `customer_count[]` of size five because we list five elements.

```
int customer_count[] = {3, 4, 5, 6, 7};
```

Programming
Pitfalls

If you omit the size of the array, you must initialize the array. The following declaration is illegal because the compiler cannot determine how much memory to allocate for the array.

```
int customer_count[]; /* Illegal array declaration */
```

0.075	0.080	0.082	0.0	0.0
rate [0]	rate [1]	rate [2]	rate [3]	rate [4]

FIGURE 6.4

Accessing Array Elements by Subscript

The primary advantage of using an array to store data is the ability to refer to the array's elements by number. This allows us to use a variable, usually called a **subscript**, to reference the elements in an array. For example, consider the following declarations.

```
double rate[5] = {0.075, 0.080, 0.082, 0.085, 0.088};
int    i;
```

If we execute the assignment,

```
i = 3;
```

then `rate[i]` refers to the element `rate[3]`, which has the value 0.085. If we now execute the assignment

```
i = 1;
```

then `rate[i]` refers to the element `rate[1]`, which has the value 0.080.

The following program, dem06-1.cpp, shows how to initialize an array and how to use a subscript to access the elements in an array. The program calculates shipping charges based on the price of an item and the shipping region, and calculates the total price of the item. The total price is the sum of the item's price and the item's shipping charge. The program asks the user to enter the price of an item and the shipping region. If the user enters a valid region number (1 to 5), the program calculates the shipping charge by multiplying the price of the item by the shipping rate for the region. If the shipping region that the user enters is invalid, the program issues an error message and stops.

```
// dem06-1.cpp

// This program calculates shipping charges for mail orders
// based on price and sales region. This program
// uses the region number to access the array elements.

#include <iostream.h>
#include <iomanip.h>

using namespace std;

int main()
{
  // The following declaration defines the integer array rate[] as
  // having 5 elements.

  double rate[5] = {0.075, 0.080, 0.082, 0.085, 0.088};
```

```
int     region;
double  price,
        charge,
        total_price;

cout << setprecision(2)
     << setiosflags(ios::fixed)
     << setiosflags(ios::showpoint);

cout << "\n\nEnter the price of the item: $";
cin >> price;
cout << "\nEnter shipping region (1-5): ";
cin >> region;

if ( (region < 1) || (region > 5) )
    cout >> "\n\nInvalid region number entered. Try again.";
else
   {
      charge = price * rate[region - 1];
      total_price = price + charge;
      cout << "\n\nItem Price:      " << setw(9) << price;
      cout << "\nShipping Charge: " << setw(9) << charge;
      cout << "\nTotal Price:     " << setw(9) << total_price;
   }

   return 0;
}
```

Program Output

```
Enter the price of the item: $100

Enter shipping region (1-5): 4



Item Price:        100.00
Shipping Charge:     8.50
Total Price:       108.50
```

The program begins with the declaration and initialization of the array rate[]. The program prompts the user for the price of the item and the shipping region. The if statement checks the validity of the shipping region. If the region is invalid, that is, less than one or greater than five, the program displays an error message, the if statement completes, and the program ends.

If the region is valid, the program calculates the shipping charge. The shipping charge is the item price multiplied by the shipping rate for the entered shipping region. The region number is an integer in the range 1–5. However, the offset that accesses the array elements must be in the range 0–4. The shipping rate for region one is located in rate[0]. The shipping rate for region two is located in rate[1], and so on. To access the proper array element, we must subtract one from the region number. Therefore, we access the shipping rate by the expression `rate[region - 1]`. Note that we can use an expression such as `region - 1` as the subscript in an array reference.

NOTE 6.4—EXPRESSIONS AS SUBSCRIPTS

In C++, it is valid to use an expression as an array subscript if the expression evaluates to an integer type.

Finally, the total charge for the item is the price plus the shipping charge. The `cout` statements display the item's price, shipping charge, and total price.

As a final comment, keep Note 6.5 in mind when using arrays.

NOTE 6.5—VALIDATING SUBSCRIPTS

The C++ compiler does not check that subscripts are in the valid range of offsets for the array. You must write code to check for valid subscript values.

For example, suppose that we incorrectly code the following in dem06-1.cpp.

```
charge = price * rate[region];
```

If the user enters 3 for the region, this assignment would incorrectly access `rate[3]`, which is the rate for region four. As if this isn't bad enough, suppose the user enters 5 for the region. Then the assignment would access `rate[5]`, which is not an element in the array! Instead, `rate[5]` would access a garbage value and the program would produce incorrect results.

In the next section, we show how to use a subscript to apply the same processing to all the elements in an array.

EXERCISES 6.1

1. Declare an array that will store the annual salaries of a typical 25-member major league baseball team. (Most teams have players that earn more than $1,000,000 each year.)

2. Declare an array that will store the attendance at each major league baseball park on July 4th. There are 28 such parks and many of them can seat more than 50,000 people.

3. Declare an array that will store the prices of the 50 stocks of the Dow-Jones Industrial Averages Stock Index.

4. The manager of an automobile dealership wants to store the number of cars each of her 14 sales people sell in one month. Declare an array that will store the data.

5. Declare an array `subscr[]` and initialize each of its 10 elements to the value of its subscript.

Use the following declarations in Exercises 6–8.

```
int arr_1[7] = {3, 4, 6, 12};
int arr_2[] = {9, 6, 7, 3, 5, 2};
int arr_3[7];
int i;
```

6. What are the values of `arr_1[4]`, `arr_2[6]`, `arr_1[0]`, and `arr_2[5]`?

7. If we execute `i = 3;`, what is the value of the expression `arr_1[i] * arr_2[i + 2]`?

8. If we execute `i = 0;`, what is the value of the expression `arr_1[i] * arr_2[i + 2]`?

6.2 Processing an Array: `for` Loops

In this section we discuss how to use a `for` loop to apply the same processing to the elements of an array.

Using `for` Loops

A `for` loop is the ideal control structure to use to process an array. The array subscript acts as the loop counter. Each time through the loop, the loop body processes the array element that the subscript specifies. Let's consider a simple example to clarify the procedure.

In a program she is writing to process student grades, a teacher wants to enter the 10 quiz grades that a student receives during the semester. The program is to display the student's average to the nearest tenth. The teacher decides to store the grades in the 10-element array `grade[]`. To verify that she entered the grades correctly, the teacher wants to display the 10 grades on one line before the program displays the average grade.

We shall first discuss the `for` loop that displays the grades because it is simpler than the `for` loop that inputs the grades. Suppose the 10 grades have already been loaded into the array `grade[]`. The following loop displays the elements of the array on one line.

```
for (quiz = 0; quiz < 10; ++quiz)
    cout << setw(6) << grade[quiz];
```

Programming
Pointers

There are several things to note about this `for` statement. First, the beginning value for `quiz` is zero because the first element in the array is element number zero. Second, the loop test is `quiz < 10`. Thus the program stays in the loop for the following values of `quiz`: 0, 1, 2, 3, 4, 5, 6, 7, 8, and 9, which are the valid offsets for the array. We use the test `quiz < 10` instead of `quiz <= 9` because 10 is the size of the array. Third, the subscript `quiz` is incremented by one each time through the loop so the loop processes every array element. Finally, the loop body processes the element determined by the value of `quiz`. In the loop body we refer to the array element as `grade[quiz]`.

To input the array elements into the array `grade[]`, we can use the following `for` loop.

```
for (quiz = 0; quiz < 10; ++quiz)
  {
    cout << "\nEnter grade for quiz " << quiz + 1 << ": ";
    cin << grade[quiz];
  }
```

The `for` loop prompts the user for the 10 quiz values and enters the values into the array `grade[]`. In the `cout` statement we have the opposite problem to that of dem06-1.cpp. The value of the subscript `quiz` is one less than the number of the quiz grade for which we prompt. When `quiz` is zero, we want to prompt for the grade on quiz one. When `quiz` is one, we want to prompt for the grade on quiz two, and so on. Therefore, the number that we want to display in the prompt is the value of `quiz + 1`. The `cin` statement places the value that the user enters into the array element `grade[quiz]`.

The second `for` loop displays the contents of the array `grade[]`, one element on each line. The `cout` statement also displays the quiz number as the value of `quiz + 1`.

```
// dem06-2.cpp

// This program shows how to find the average of the elements
// in an array.

#include <iostream.h>
#include <iomanip.h>

using namespace std;

#define NUM_QUIZZES 10

int main()
{
  int grade[NUM_QUIZZES];  // The array to store the quiz grades
  int quiz,                // The array subscript
      grade_sum = 0;
```

```
    double grade_avg;

    cout << setprecision(1)
         << setiosflags(ios::fixed)
         << setiosflags(ios::showpoint);

    cout << "\nPlease enter " << NUM_QUIZZES
         << " integer quiz grades.\n\n";
    for (quiz = 0; quiz < NUM_QUIZZES; ++quiz)
      {
        cout << "\nEnter grade for quiz " << quiz + 1 << ": ";
        cin >> grade[quiz];
      }

    for (quiz = 0; quiz < NUM_QUIZZES; ++quiz)
      grade_sum += grade[quiz];

    grade_avg = double(grade_sum) / NUM_QUIZZES;

    cout << "\nThe average quiz grade is " << grade_avg;

    return 0;
}
```

Program Output

```
Please enter 10 integer quiz grades.


Enter grade for quiz 1: 55

Enter grade for quiz 2: 66

Enter grade for quiz 3: 77

Enter grade for quiz 4: 88

Enter grade for quiz 5: 99

Enter grade for quiz 6: 100

Enter grade for quiz 7: 100

Enter grade for quiz 8: 99

Enter grade for quiz 9: 88

Enter grade for quiz 10: 77

The average quiz grade is 84.9
```

First, we define the number of quizzes as a symbolic constant, NUM_QUIZZES. It is good programming practice to do so. It makes changing the program easier. We use NUM_QUIZZES in the cout that labels the output to reflect the number of quizzes that the program processes. We will follow the advice of Note 6.6 in all our programs.

NOTE 6.6—DEFINING THE SIZE OF AN ARRAY

It is good programming practice to define the size of an array as a symbolic constant.

The program declares the accumulator grade_sum, which is initialized to zero, to hold the sum of the grades that the user enters into the array grade[]. The double variable grade_avg will store the average of the 10 grades.

First, the program inputs the 10 quiz grades. The second for loop adds each grade in the array to the accumulator grade_sum. The assignment statement then computes the grade average. A type cast converts the value of the integer variable grade_sum to the equivalent double. Finally, the cout statement displays the value of grade_avg.

Searching an Array

Suppose that our teacher wants to display the quiz number and corresponding grade of the first quiz, if any, on which the student achieved a grade of 85 or better. This is an example of an **array search**—we want our program to find a particular array element. To do this, the program will test each array element beginning with the first. If the grade that the program is testing satisfies the condition (the grade is 85 or greater), it displays the grade and the quiz number and ends the program. If there is no grade equal to or greater than 85, the program should display a message to that effect. This method of searching, namely beginning at the first array element and proceeding through the entire array one element at a time, testing as we go along, is called a **linear** or **sequential search**.

To keep the program as simple as possible, dem06-3.cpp prompts the user for the grades and then displays the first grade of 85 or greater, if there are any.

```
// dem06-3.cpp

// This program shows how find the first element in an array
// that satisfies a condition. The condition tested in this
// program is that the quiz grade is greater than or equal to 85.

#include <iostream.h>
#include <iomanip.h>

using namespace std;

#define NUM_QUIZZES 10
#define MIN_GRADE 85    // The grade cutoff value

int main()
```

```
{
    int grade[NUM_QUIZZES];      // The array to store the quiz grades
    int quiz;                    // The array subscript

    cout << "\nPlease enter " << NUM_QUIZZES
         << " integer quiz grades.\n\n";

    for (quiz = 0; quiz < NUM_QUIZZES; ++quiz)
      {
        cout << "\nEnter grade for quiz " << quiz + 1 << ": ";
        cin >> grade[quiz];
      }

    for (quiz = 0; quiz <NUM_QUIZZES; ++quiz)
      if (grade[quiz] >= MIN_GRADE)
        {
          cout << "\nThe first grade of at least " << MIN_GRADE
               << " is:";
          cout << "\n\nQuiz #" << quiz + 1 << " Grade: "
               << setw(3) << grade[quiz];
          break;
        }

    if (quiz >= NUM_QUIZZES)
      cout << "\nNo grade greater than " << MIN_GRADE
           << " was found.";

    return 0;
}
```

Program Output

Test Run 1

```
Please enter 10 integer quiz grades.


Enter grade for quiz 1: 40

Enter grade for quiz 2: 50

Enter grade for quiz 3: 80

Enter grade for quiz 4: 70

Enter grade for quiz 5: 80

Enter grade for quiz 6: 94
```

```
Enter grade for quiz 7: 85

Enter grade for quiz 8: 68

Enter grade for quiz 9: 73

Enter grade for quiz 10: 90

The first grade of at least 85 is:

Quiz #6 Grade: 94
```

Test Run 2

```
Please enter 10 integer quiz grades.

Enter grade for quiz 1: 40

Enter grade for quiz 2: 50

Enter grade for quiz 3: 60

Enter grade for quiz 4: 70

Enter grade for quiz 5: 80

Enter grade for quiz 6: 70

Enter grade for quiz 7: 60

Enter grade for quiz 8: 70

Enter grade for quiz 9: 80

Enter grade for quiz 10: 84

No grade greater than 85 was found.
```

First note that we define a symbolic constant MIN_GRADE with a value of 85. This makes it easier to change the minimum grade later.

A for loop prompts the user to enter the 10 quiz grades. The for loop that does the linear search is next. The body of this loop consists of a single if statement. If the grade on the quiz being processed is greater than or equal to MIN_GRADE, the search is successful. The program then displays a message that shows the quiz number and the grade on that quiz. In this case, the break statement executes, which causes the program to exit the loop.

When the program exits the second for loop, it does so for one of two reasons. If the search is successful, as described in the previous paragraph, the break statement causes the program to exit the loop before the loop condition (quiz < 10) is false. If the search is unsuccessful, the program exits the loop because the loop condition is false, not because of the break statement. The if statement that follows the second for loop decides which condition caused the program to exit the loop. If the search was unsuccessful, the value of quiz must be greater than or equal to 10 because the loop condition must be false. Therefore, if quiz >= 10, the program displays a message that no grade was found that satisfies the condition. If quiz is not greater than or equal to 10, it must be less than 10. In this case, the program exited the loop because the search was successful. If the condition in the if statement is false, the program does nothing.

EXERCISES 6.2

1. Is there anything wrong with the following for loop that attempts to add each element of arr_1[] to the corresponding element of arr_2[] and place the result in the corresponding element of arr_3[]?

```
for (i = 0; i < 7; ++i)
    arr_3[i] = arr_1[i] + arr_2[i];
```

2. What does the following code display?

```
int arr[9];
int i;

for (i = 0; i < 9; ++i)
    arr[i] = i + 3;

cout << "\n";
for (i = 0; i < 9; ++i)
    cout << setw(4) << a[i];

cout << "\n\n";
for (i = 8; i >= 0; --i)
    cout << setw(4) << a[i];
```

Use the following declarations in Exercises 3–8.

```
double d_array[10] = {3.4, 12.8, 9.5, 2.0, 1.7, 3.8};
char letters[26];
int i;
```

3. Write a for loop to display only the elements of d_array[] that have an even subscript.

4. Write a for loop to display only the elements of d_array[] that have an odd subscript.

5. Write a for loop to display only the first element of d_array[] that is less than 3.0.

6. Write a for loop to display all the elements of d_array[] that are greater than 5.0.

7. Write a `for` loop that sets each element of `letters[]` to a blank.
8. Write a `for` loop that places the lowercase letters of the alphabet into the array `letters[]`.

EXPERIMENTS 6.2

1. What does the following program display?

```
#include <iostream.h>

main()
{
  int arr[] = {3, 4, 5, 6, 7};
  int i;

  for (i = 0; i < 6; ++i)
    cout << "\n" << arr[i];
}
```

2. Recode dem06-3.cpp so that it finds the last element in the array that is at least 85.
3. Suppose the teacher of dem06-2.cpp does not know how many grades she will have at the end of the semester. However, she knows that she will not give more than 12 quizzes. Recode dem06-2.cpp so that it inputs up to 12 quiz grades. To do this you need a counter that counts each grade as it is entered. After the user finishes entering the grades, sum the grades that were entered and calculate the average grade by dividing the grade sum by the number of grades.

PROGRAMMING PROBLEMS 6.2

Be sure to use modular design and functions where appropriate.

1. Bluebird Airlines has flights from Phoenix to six other cities in Arizona. The cities are referred to by number, 1 to 6. The price for a round trip ticket to each of the cities is shown here.

City	1	2	3	4	5	6
Price	56.79	105.69	93.49	155.99	87.49	73.99

Write a program that computes the total price of tickets that a customer orders. The program should prompt the user for the number of the destination city and the number of tickets desired. If the user enters an invalid city number, the program should display an error message and terminate. The program should display the total price of the ticket order. Use an array to store the ticket price table.

2. Rewrite the program of Programming Problem 1 so that it processes any number of ticket orders. The program should also continually prompt the user for a valid city number. When the user indicates that there are no more customers to process, the program should display the total number of tickets sold to each of

the six cities, the total price of the tickets sold to each city, and the grand total of all the ticket prices. Use an array of accumulators to store the number of tickets sold to each city.

3. A bookstore owner wants you to write a program to calculate the store's weekly payroll. The store's employees are paid hourly. Overtime is to be paid at the rate of 1.5 times the normal rate for hours an employee worked over 40. The program should prompt the user to enter the number of hours the employee worked and the pay rate for the employee. The program should display the regular pay, overtime pay, and gross pay for that employee. Then the program should prompt the user to enter the data for another employee. When the user responds that there are no more employees to process, the program should display the number of employees it processed and the total payroll, that is, the sum of the gross salaries of the employees.

   The program should validate the pay rate as it is entered. The only valid hourly pay rates are the following: 3.50, 4.00, 4.50, 4.75, 5.00, 5.25, 5.50, 5.75, 6.00. Store the rates in an array. When a pay rate is entered, search the array for a match. If there is a match, continue the rest of the calculations. If there is no match, display an error message, a list of the valid pay rates, and prompt for another pay rate.

4. Bluebird Airlines needs a program to assign boarding passes on its only plane, which has a seating capacity of 30. The seats in the plane are numbered from 1 to 30. The first 10 seats are first class and the remaining 20 are business class. The program should prompt the user to enter the class of the ticket (1 for first class, 2 for business class). Store the seating information in an array. If a seat is empty, the corresponding array element is zero. If a seat is reserved, the corresponding array element is one. Assign the seats numerically on a first-come-first-served basis. If a passenger requests a seat and there are no more seats of that class, the program should check to see if there are any seats available in the other class. If other seats are available, ask the user if he or she wants a seat in the other class and proceed appropriately. If no other seats are available, display an appropriate message. When there are no more passengers to process (the plane may not be full when it takes off), display the total number of passengers in each class.

5. Write a program that prompts the user to enter text at the terminal. When the user finishes entering text, he or she should enter the appropriate end of file character to terminate input. The program should count the frequency of each letter of the alphabet. The program should not distinguish an uppercase letter from a lowercase letter. When the user finishes inputting text, the program should display each letter and its count.

   Hint: Declare an array of counters, one for each letter. Use the letter itself as the subscript that determines which array element to increment. To do this, the program must convert the letter to the corresponding subscript. Remember that the decimal ASCII values of the lowercase letters are 97-122 and the uppercase letters are 65-90.

6. The marketing department of a large book club wants to analyze the geographical distribution of its customers by categorizing customers by zip code. Write a

program that prompts the user to enter the five digit zip code of a customer. Store the zip codes in an array of integers, and store the counts of the customers in a corresponding array of integers. Assume a maximum of 100 zip codes. When a zip code is entered, search the zip code array for the zip code. If it is not in the array, add it to the end of the array and set the corresponding element of the count array to one. If the entered zip code is in the zip code array, increment the corresponding element of the count array.

When the user completes entering zip codes, the program should display a table that lists the zip codes with their corresponding counts and the percent that count is of the total number of customers. The total number of customers should display at the bottom of the table.

6.3 Sorting an Array

This section introduces array sorting. To sort an array means to arrange the elements of the array in either increasing or decreasing order.

Sorting

Suppose that after inputting the 10 grades for a student, our teacher wants to display the grades in increasing order. To do this, the program must arrange the numbers that it stores in the array grade[] in increasing order. We call this process **sorting** the array. Among the techniques for sorting an array is the **bubble sort**, which programmers frequently use for sorting small arrays. There are several variations of the bubble sort. The one that we describe here is not the most efficient bubble sort, but it works and illustrates the basic technique.

The key idea of the bubble sort is to compare adjacent elements in the array. Begin by comparing the first two array elements. We assume that we want the array in non-decreasing order. If the elements are in order (that is, the first element is less than or equal to the second), leave them alone. If the elements are not in order (that is, the first is greater than the second), interchange them in the array. Then, compare the second and third array elements. Again, if they are out of order, interchange them; otherwise, leave them alone. Continue this process until you compare the last pair of array elements. This completes the first pass over the array.

To illustrate, suppose we start with the following array of five integers.

          7   3   4   8   6

The first pass does the following. Since 7 and 3 are not in order, interchange them.

          3   7   4   8   6

Compare 7 and 4. They are not in order, so interchange them.

          3   4   7   8   6

Compare 7 and 8. They are in order, so leave them alone and go on to the next pair.

Compare 8 and 6. They are not in order, so interchange them.

$$3 \quad\quad 4 \quad\quad 7 \quad\quad 6 \quad\quad 8$$

This completes the first pass. What does the first pass accomplish? The first pass moves the largest number in the array into the rightmost position, which is where we want it when the array is completely sorted. This is why we call this sort the bubble sort. The largest array element "bubbles" up to the top of the array.

Now we make a second pass over the array. This time, however, we do not have to go to the end of the array because the first pass moved the largest array element into the rightmost position. The second pass moves the second largest array element into the next to last position. Following is a trace of Pass Two.

Start with:	3	4	7	6	8	
Begin:	3	4	7	6	8	Leave 3 and 4 alone
	3	4	7	6	8	Leave 4 and 7 alone
	3	4	6	7	8	Interchange 7 and 6

Likewise for Pass Three and Pass Four.

Trace of Pass Three:

Start with:	3	4	6	7	8	
Begin:	3	4	6	7	8	Leave 3 and 4 alone
	3	4	6	7	8	Leave 4 and 6 alone

End of Pass Three.

Trace of Pass Four:

Start with:	3	4	6	7	8	
Begin:	3	4	6	7	8	Leave 3 and 4 alone

End of Pass Four. The array is sorted.

After the fourth pass the array is sorted. Note that the array is sorted at the end of pass two, but the procedure keeps going. It would be more efficient if the procedure recognizes at some point that the array is sorted and ends. See Programming Problem 2.

An important part of the bubble sort is interchanging two array elements. To interchange the values of two variables requires the use of a third variable. For example, consider the following declarations.

```
int i = 5,
    j = 7,
    temp;
```

The following assignments interchange the values of i and j.

```
temp = i;      /* Places 5 into temp */
i = j;         /* Places 7 into i, destroying its contents */
j = temp;      /* Places 5 into j */
```

A Sort Program—dem06-4.cpp

The following program, dem06-4.cpp, prompts the user to enter a 10 element array and displays the array. Then, the program uses the bubble sort to sort the array in increasing order. Finally, the program displays the sorted array.

```cpp
// dem06—4.cpp

// This program shows how to sort the elements
// in an array using the bubble sort.

#include <iostream.h>
#include <iomanip.h>

using namespace std;

#define NUM_QUIZZES 10
int main()
{
  int grade[NUM_QUIZZES];     //The array to store the quiz grades

  int quiz,             // Subscript for the array grade[]
      temp,             // For swapping array elements
      pass,             // The number of the pass
      limit;            // Keeps track of how far to go on a pass

  // Get the grades

  cout << "\nPlease enter " << NUM_QUIZZES
       << " integer quiz grades.\n\n";

  for (quiz = 0; quiz < NUM_QUIZZES; ++quiz)
    {
      cout << "\nEnter grade for quiz " << quiz + 1 << ": ";
      cin >> grade[quiz];
    }

  // Display the quiz grades

  cout << "\n\nThe grades you entered are as follows:\n";
  for (quiz = 0; quiz < NUM_QUIZZES; ++quiz)
    cout << setw(6) << grade[quiz];
  cout << "\n";

  // Do the bubble sort

  limit = NUM_QUIZZES - 2;

for (pass = 1; pass <= NUM_QUIZZES - 1; ++pass)
  {
```

```
        for (quiz = 0; quiz <= limit; ++quiz)
        if (grade[quiz] > grade[quiz + 1])
          {
            temp = grade[quiz];
            grade[quiz] = grade[quiz + 1];
            grade[quiz + 1] = temp;
          }
        --limit;
    }
    // Display the sorted quiz grades

    cout << "\n\nThe grades in increasing order are as follows:\n";

    for (quiz = 0; quiz < NUM_QUIZZES; ++quiz)
      cout << setw(6) << grade[quiz];
    cout << "\n";

    return 0;
}
```

Program Output

```
Please enter 10 integer quiz grades.


Enter grade for quiz 1: 40

Enter grade for quiz 2: 50

Enter grade for quiz 3: 80

Enter grade for quiz 4: 70

Enter grade for quiz 5: 80

Enter grade for quiz 6: 94

Enter grade for quiz 7: 85

Enter grade for quiz 8: 68

Enter grade for quiz 9: 73

Enter grade for quiz 10: 90


The grades you entered are as follows:
    40    50    80    70    80    94    85    68    73    90
```

```
The grades in increasing order are as follows:
    40     50     68     70     73     80     80     85     90     94
```

The program needs the integer array `grade[]` to store the student grades. The variable `quiz` is the array subscript. The program uses the variable `temp` for swapping array elements, the variable `pass` to count the number of passes that the bubble sort makes, and the variable `limit` to keep track of how far to go on a pass.

The program obtains the 10 quiz grades from the user in a `for` loop and stores them in the array `grade[]`. Then, a `for` loop displays the grades in the order in which the user entered them. Now the program uses the bubble sort to arrange the elements of the array into increasing order.

The variable `limit` keeps track of how far to go on a pass. Recall from our discussion that the first pass of the bubble sort compares pairs of adjacent elements up to the last pair. Therefore, in an array with `NUM_QUIZZES` elements, it compares elements 0 and 1, elements 1 and 2, elements 2 and 3, ..., elements `NUM_QUIZZES` − 2 and `NUM_QUIZZES` − 1. Therefore, since the sort always compares an element to the next element, we initialize limit to `NUM_QUIZZES` − 2. At the end of a pass, `limit` is decreased by one so that the next pass considers one less element. Remember that a pass places the next highest element at the right of the array so the sort does not have to consider this element again.

The bubble sort is done in a nested `for` loop. The outer `for` loop initializes the value of `pass` to one. The sort makes a total of `NUM_QUIZZES` − 1 passes over the array, which is reflected in the loop test. The `if` statement in the inner loop's body tests to see if the pair of adjacent array elements is out of order. If they are out of order, the elements are interchanged. If they are in order, nothing is done to the pair.

When the bubble sort finishes sorting the array, the elements of `grade[]` are in increasing order. The program then uses a `for` loop to display the elements of the array `grade[]`, which are now in increasing order.

EXERCISES 6.3

1. Trace the bubble sort using the following integers, which represent the elements in an array.

   5, 7, 3, 8, 6, 7, 3

2. Trace the bubble sort using the following integers, which represent the elements in an array.

   98, 76, 54, 34, 22, 50

EXPERIMENTS 6.3

1. Recode dem06-4.cpp to sort the array in decreasing order.

1. A survey organization telephones 20 homes and records the household income of each family surveyed. Write a program that inputs the 20 incomes into an array and then sorts the array into decreasing order. The program should display the following statistics: the maximum income, the minimum income, the average income, and the median income. The median of a set of sorted numbers is the middle number, if there is an odd number of numbers. If there is an even number of numbers, the median is the average of the two middle numbers.

2. The bubble sort of dem06-4.cpp is inefficient for sorting large arrays because it does not recognize when the array is sorted. The function makes `size−1` passes on an array with `size` elements even if the array is already sorted. The function will be more efficient if, when making a pass over the array, it recognizes if the array is sorted and stops. Recode dem06-4.cpp to do this.

   Hint: Use a flag called `sorted`. Set `sorted` equal to zero immediately before making a pass over the array. If the flag equals one, the array is sorted. In this case, exit the loop and return to the calling function. If the flag equals zero, the array is not sorted. In this case, the program must make a pass over the array. When the function swaps two array elements in the inner loop of the nested for loop, set the flag to one.

6.4 Multidimensional Arrays

Multidimensional arrays are a way of organizing data that you can classify according to two or more categories. This section shows how to define and use multidimensional arrays in C++. We concentrate on two-dimensional arrays because they are the most widely used by programmers and are easy to describe.

Declaring Multidimensional Arrays

As we mentioned in Section 6.1, you can use an array to store a collection of related data. Data are related if you categorize them into a common class. For example, the grades that a student receives on a set of 10 quizzes forms a category. You can consider the 10 grades as belonging to a common class of data.

Sometimes you can classify data according to two or more categories. For example, suppose that our teacher now wants to find the average quiz grade of the five students in her class. We now have 10 quiz grades for five students; a total of 50 integers. We can classify each grade according to two categories—the student that the grade belongs to and the quiz on which the grade was achieved. You can arrange such data in a **two-dimensional array**, or **matrix**. Figure 6.5 shows the class grades stored in the two-dimensional array `class_grades`.

The data are arranged into rows and columns. The five rows represent the five students in the class. The 10 columns represent the 10 quiz grades. The **array size** is 5 × 10, meaning that the array has five rows and 10 columns. In keeping with the way in which C++ refers to array elements, we number the rows from 0 to 4 and the columns from 0 to 9.

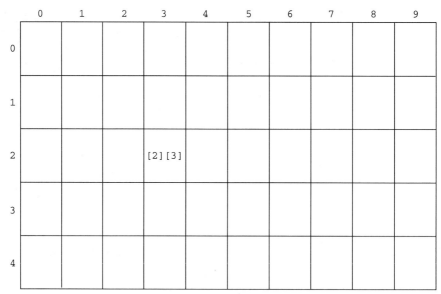

The 5 x 10 Two-Dimentional Array `class_grades [] []`

FIGURE 6.5

Programming
Pointers

Referring to a specific element in the two-dimensional array requires two subscripts. The first subscript specifies the row (that is, the student). The second subscript specifies the column (that is, the quiz). We enclose each subscript in brackets. Thus, `class_grades[2][3]` refers to the grade of student 2 (the third student) on quiz 3 (the fourth quiz).

To declare a two-dimensional array, specify the array type and the size of the array. Place the number of rows and the number of columns each in its own brackets. For example, the following declares a two-dimensional array of integers of size 5 × 10.

```
int class_grades[5][10];
```

To read this declaration, use the rule in Note 6.1. Remember to read a left bracket as "is an array of." Therefore, read the declaration as follows: "`class_grades` is an array of five elements each of which is an array of 10 integers." The two-dimensional array `class_grades` is an array each of whose elements is an array of integers. This fact has implications in the way C++ stores the elements of the array and the way in which you can reference parts of the array.

Figure 6.6 shows how C++ stores the 50 grades. All 10 grades of student 0 are followed by the 10 grades of student 1, and so on. We call this way of storing the grades **row major order**.

It is possible to initialize a two-dimensional array in the array declaration. The following initializes the elements of `class_grades[][]`.

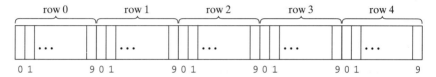

Storage Layout of a Two-Dimensional Array

FIGURE 6.6

```
int class_grades[5][10] = { {50, 56, 87, 67, 98, 90, 68, 54, 67, 30},
                            {70, 68, 64, 78, 97, 57, 68, 90, 67, 74},
                            {64, 76, 87, 67, 95, 67, 56, 83, 60, 78},
                            {76, 65, 84, 47, 86, 65, 46, 66, 87, 65},
                            {76, 57, 65, 45, 90, 76, 76, 44, 67, 82}};
```

Programming
Pointers

We enclose the entire set of values in braces. We also enclose the values in each row in another set of braces. Note the comma after each set of inner braces. The final set of inner braces is not followed by a comma. This technique of organizing the initial values in a two-dimensional array mirrors the logical row-by-column structure of the array. The inner braces help to distinguish one row from the next row. In addition, if too few numbers are enclosed in the inner braces, the compiler automatically sets the remaining row elements to zero. If there are too many elements in the inner braces, the compiler ignores the extra elements in the row. See Experiment 2.

The C++ language does not require this bracing technique to initialize a two-dimensional array. The important thing is that the elements appear in the initialization in the order in which C++ stores them, that is in row major order. See Experiment 3.

Note 6.7 summarizes the rules for initializing a two-dimensional array.

NOTE 6.7—INITIALIZING A TWO-DIMENSIONAL ARRAY

- To initialize a two-dimensional array, enclose the elements of each row in braces. Separate each row's elements by commas. Follow each set of row braces by a comma, except the last row.

- Enclose the entire set of row initializers with braces.

- If a row initializer contains too few elements, the remaining elements of the row are automatically initialized to zero.

- If a row initializer contains too many elements, the compiler ignores the extra elements.

Although we shall not have much use for higher-dimensional arrays, you can define them in C++ in much the same way as two-dimensional arrays. For example, suppose our teacher wants to store the 10 quiz grades for the five students in each of her four classes. We can classify the data into three categories—class, student, and quiz number. We can store all 200 grades in a three-dimensional array `student_grades` of size 4 × 5 × 10. The following declaration defines the storage for the array.

```
int student_grades[4][5][10];
```

The first subscript, which refers to the class, ranges from 0 to 3. The second subscript, which refers to the student, ranges from 0 to 4. The third subscript, which ranges from 0 to 9, refers to the quiz. Thus the element `student_grades[2][3][4]` contains the grade on quiz 4 (that is, the fifth quiz) of student 3 (that is, the fourth student) in class 2 (that is, the third class). See Programming Problem 2.

Processing a Two-Dimensional Array

The major tool for processing a two-dimensional array is the nested `for` loop. Assume the following declaration.

```
int array[NUMBER_ROWS][NUMBER_COLUMNS];
```

Programming
Pointers

We use a nested `for` loop structured as follows to process each element in this two-dimensional array.

```
for (row = 0; row < NUMBER_ROWS; ++row)
    for (column = 0; column < NUMBER_COLUMNS; ++column)
        {process the array element array[row][column]}
```

The outer `for` loop steps through the rows of the array one at a time. When the subscript `row` equals zero, the nested loop processes row number zero; when the subscript `row` equals one, the nested loop processes row number one, and so on. The inner loop processes each element in the row determined by the subscript `row`. The nested loop processes the elements of the array in row-major order. For example, when `row` equals zero, the `for` loop runs the subscript `column` from zero to one less than NUMBER_COLUMNS. Table 6.1 shows how the nested loop varies the subscripts and to which element `array[row][column]` refers in the body of the loop.

The following displays all the grades in the 5 × 10 array `class_grades[][]` that we declared and initialized earlier.

```
int student,
    quiz;

for (student = 0; student < 5; ++student)
    for (quiz = 0; quiz < 10; ++quiz)
        cout << "\nThe grade of student " << student + 1
             << " on quiz " << quiz + 1
             << " is " << class_grades[student][quiz];
```

TABLE 6.1

row	column	Element Process in Loop Body
0	0	`array[0][0]`
	1	`array[0][1]`
	2	`array[0][2]`
	·	
	·	
	·	
	NUMBER_COLUMNS − 1	`array[0][NUMBER_COLUMNS − 1]`
1	0	`array[1][0]`
	1	`array[1][1]`
	2	`array[1][2]`
	·	
	·	
	·	
	NUMBER_COLUMNS − 1	`array[1][NUMBER-COLUMNS − 1]`
	·	
	·	
	·	
NUMBER_ROWS − 1	0	`array[NUMBER_ROWS − 1][0]`
	1	`array[NUMBER_ROWS − 1][1]`
	2	`array[NUMBER_ROWS − 1][2]`
	·	
	·	
	·	
NUMBER_ROWS − 1	NUMBER_COLUMNS − 1	`array[NUMBER_ROWS − 1][NUMBER_COLUMNS − 1]`

Finding Student Averages—dem06-5.cpp

We now write a program to find the average grade of each student in the five classes. The program will prompt the user for the 10 grades of each student, one student at a time. The program will store the grades in a two-dimensional array. It will then calculate and display the average quiz grade for each student, rounded to the nearest tenth.

Following is the pseudocode solution for the problem.

```
for (each student in the class)
  for (each quiz for a student)
    prompt for and get a quiz grade
  endfor
endfor
for (each student in the class)
  calculate the average quiz grade
  display the quiz grade
endfor
```

Following is the code for dem06-5.cpp, our solution to the averaging problem.

```cpp
// dem06-5.cpp

// This program uses a two-dimensional array to store the
// quiz grades of students in several classes. The program
// then calculates the average quiz grade of each student.

#include <iostream.h>
#include <iomanip.h>

using namespace std;

#define NUM_QUIZZES 10
#define NUM_STUDENTS 5

int main()
{
  int class_grades[NUM_STUDENTS][NUM_QUIZZES];
  int student,
      quiz,
      quiz_sum;
  double quiz_average;

  cout << setprecision(1)
       << setiosflags(ios::fixed)
       << setiosflags(ios::showpoint);

  // Obtain and store the quiz grades for each student

   cout << "\nEnter exactly " << NUM_QUIZZES
        << " quiz grades for each student.";
  cout << "\nSeparate the grades by one or more spaces.";

   for (student = 0; student < NUM_STUDENTS; ++student)
    {
      cout << "\n\nGrades for Student " << student + 1 << ": ";
      for (quiz = 0; quiz < NUM_QUIZZES; ++quiz)
        cin >> class_grades[student][quiz];
    }

   // Calculate and display the average quiz grade for each student

   for (student = 0; student < NUM_STUDENTS; ++student)
    {
      quiz_sum = 0;
      for (quiz = 0; quiz < NUM_QUIZZES; ++quiz)
        quiz_sum += class_grades[student][quiz];
        quiz_average = (double) quiz_sum / NUM_QUIZZES;
        cout << "\n\nStudent: " << setw(3) << student + 1
             << "   Quiz Average: " << setw(5) << quiz_average;
```

```
        }

      return 0;
}
```

Program Output

```
Enter exactly 10 quiz grades for each student.
Separate the grades by one or more spaces.

Grades for Student 1: 50 56 87 67 98 90 68 54 67 30


Grades for Student 2: 70 68 64 78 97 57 68 90 67 74


Grades for Student 3: 64 76 87 67 95 67 56 83 60 78


Grades for Student 4: 76 65 84 47 86 65 46 66 87 65


Grades for Student 5: 76 57 65 45 90 76 76 44 67 82


Student: 1 Quiz Average: 66.7

Student: 2 Quiz Average: 73.3

Student: 3 Quiz Average: 73.3

Student: 4 Quiz Average: 68.7

Student: 5 Quiz Average: 67.8
```

The program defines the number of quizzes and the number of students as symbolic constants. In main(), we declare the two-dimensional array class_grades[][] as described earlier, the subscripts student and quiz, the accumulator quiz_sum, and the double variable quiz_average.

Because this program must obtain 50 grades, it does not prompt for each grade individually. Instead, the program asks the user to enter all 10 grades for each student at once. First, the program tells the user how many grades to enter for each student and how to separate the grades. Then, the outer for loop prompts for the 10 grades of one student. The inner for loop obtains the 10 grades for the student and stores them in the array.

The next for loop calculates and displays the average of each student. To calculate the average of the student currently being processed, the body of the loop first initializes the accumulator `quiz_sum` to zero. Next, a `for` loop sums the quiz grades for the student being processed. After exiting the `for` loop, an assignment statement calculates the quiz average. To obtain the quiz average to the nearest tenth, it is necessary to type cast the variable `quiz_sum` to the type `double`. Failure to do so would cause the computer to do integer arithmetic when evaluating the right side of the assignment, which would result in the loss of the decimal part of the division. The last statement in the loop body displays the student number and the student's quiz average.

EXERCISES 6.4

1. Declare a two-dimensional array that contains 15 rows, each of which will store 12 integers.

2. Declare a two-dimensional array that contains 10 rows, each of which will store four doubles.

Use the following declarations in Exercises 3–4.

```
int arr_2d[3][4] = {{4, 5, 6, 7},
                    {2, 6, 1},
                    {8, 7, 2, 1}};
int row, col;
```

3. What are the values of `arr_2d[2][2]`, `arr_2d[0][0]`, `arr_2d[3][4]`, and `arr_2d[1][3]`.

4. What does the following code display?

```
for (row = 1; row < 3; ++row)
  {
    cout << "\n";
    for (col = 0; col < 4; ++col)
      cout << setw(6) << arr_2d[row][col];
  }
```

5. The commissioner of major league baseball wants you to write a program to analyze the salaries of all major league baseball players. As part of the program you decide to store all the salaries in a two-dimensional array. Each row represents one of baseball's 28 teams. In each row are the salaries of the team's 25 players. Write the declaration of such an array.

6. Write a nested `for` loop to enter the salaries of all the players in major league baseball into the array declared in Exercise 5. The loop should prompt the user for each salary.

7. Write code that displays the total salary for each of the 28 major league baseball teams whose player salaries are stored in the array of Exercise 5.

8. Write code to do the following. Declare a three dimensional array arr_3d [] [] [] of size 3 × 4 × 5 and initialize each array element to the sum of its subscripts.

EXPERIMENTS 6.4

1. Dem06-5.cpp displays the average of each student on the 10 quizzes. Recode that program so it displays the average grade on each of the 10 quizzes.

2. Execute the following program and explain what is it displays.

```
#include <iostream.h>
using namespace std;
int main()
{
   int arr_3d[4][3] = {{1},
                       {1, 2},
                       {1, 2, 3},
                       {1, 2, 3, 4}};

   int row, col;

   for (row = 0; row < 4; ++row)
     {
        cout << "\n";
        for (col = 0; row < 3; ++col)
          cout << setw(3) << arr_3d[row][col];
     }
   return 0;
}
```

3. Write a program to see if there is any difference between the following array declarations.

```
int arr1[2][3] = { {1, 2, 3},
                   {4, 5, 6}};

int arr2[2][3] = {1, 2, 3, 4, 5, 6};
```

PROGRAMMING PROBLEMS 6.4

1. A sweatshirt manufacturer wants to take inventory of the college logo sweatshirts that it has in stock. The company makes sweatshirts for seven colleges.

Refer to the colleges by number, 1–7. Sweatshirts come in four sizes—small, medium, large, and x-large. An employee gathers the inventory information by hand. Write a program that prompts the employee to enter the number of sweatshirts in stock for each of the seven colleges in each of the four sizes. Store the inventory information in a two-dimensional array. After inputting the inventory data, the program should display an inventory report in the following format.

```
                              Inventory Report
                                   College
                    1    2    3    4    5    6    7    Size Total

          Small

          Medium
Size
          Large

          XLarge

  College Total

Total Quantity On Hand
```

At the end of each row should be the total inventory for that size. At the bottom of each column should be total inventory of each college. The Total Quantity On Hand should be the total inventory of all sweatshirts.

2. Our teacher wants a program to store the 10 quiz grades of each of the five students in her four classes in a 4 × 5 × 10 three-dimensional array. Write a program that prompts the user to enter the grades on a class-by-class basis. Within each class, the program should prompt the user for the grades of each student. After all the grades are entered, the program should display the following: the average grade of each student on a class-by-class basis and the average grade of the entire class on the 10 quizzes.

3. Recode Programming Problem 2 so it displays the average grade on each of the 10 quizzes.

Chapter Review

Terminology

Define the following terms

array   array type
array element   linear data structure
array size   one-dimensional data structure

offset	sorting
displacement	bubble sort
subscript	two-dimensional array
index	matrix
array search	array size of a two-dimensional array
linear search	row-major order

Summary

- An array is a collection of a fixed number of objects of the same type, which are stored sequentially in computer memory. The number of elements in an array is the array size.

- To read an array declaration, start at the name and proceed clockwise through the declaration to the array type (Note 6.1).

- Each element in an array is numbered (beginning at zero) by its offset from the first element in the array. The largest valid offset is one less than the array size (Note 6.2).

- You can initialize an array in its declaration by setting the array equal to a comma-separated list of initial values enclosed in braces (Note 6.3).

- Any expression that evaluates to an integer can be used as an array subscript (Note 6.4).

- C++ does not check a subscript for validity (Note 6.5).

- Use a `for` loop to process array elements. Use a subscript as the `for`-loop counter.

- In a program, define the size of an array as a symbolic constant (Note 6.6).

- The bubble sort works by comparing pairs of adjacent elements. If the elements are out of order, they are interchanged.

- Use a two-dimensional array to store elements that can be classified according to two categories. Two subscripts are required to reference an element in a two-dimensional array. The first subscript references the row and the second subscript references the column.

- A two-dimensional array can be initialized (Note 6.7).

- Use nested `for` loops to process a two-dimensional array.

Review Exercises

1. What is an array and how do you declare one?
2. What is the valid subscript range in an array of N elements? What happens if you use a subscript outside this range?
3. How do you initialize an array? What happens if you do not list enough elements? What happens if you list too few elements?
4. What C++ statement is best used to process an array?

5. Why should you define the size of an array as a symbolic constant?

6. Explain how a sequential search works.

7. Explain how a bubble sort works.

8. How do you code the declaration for a multidimensional array?

9. Some people say that in C++ there is no such thing as a true multidimensional array. Why do they have this opinion?

10. How do you initialize a two-dimensional array?

11. What C++ statement is best used to process a two-dimensional array?

Chapter

7

Pointers and Strings

Objectives

- To declare a pointer.
- To properly read a pointer declaration.
- To use the address operator to initialize a pointer in a declaration.
- To use the indirection operator to dereference a pointer.
- To use the name of an array as a constant pointer.
- To perform pointer arithmetic.

- To declare and use strings.
- To code string input and output.
- To design and code programs that use pointers and strings.
- To store strings using a two-dimensional character array.
- To store strings using an array of character pointers.
- To design and code programs that use arrays of strings.

Pointers are central to understanding the C++ language. In this chapter we introduce pointers and use pointers to manipulate strings, which are sequences of characters. We discuss how to process strings and how to use the C++ string manipulation library functions. Finally, we show how an array of strings can store a table of names.

7.1 Pointers

This section introduces the idea of pointers and how to declare and initialize them. We also discuss how to use a pointer to change the value of a variable.

Declaring and Initializing Pointers

Every variable has an **address**, which is a number that specifies the location of the variable in the computer's main memory. A variable's address functions like the address of your house. The post office uses your house address to locate your house to deliver your mail. In much the same way, the computer uses the address of a variable to locate the variable so that it can place a value in that location or copy the value that is already stored in that location. A **pointer** is a variable whose value is the address of another variable. In Figure 7.1a, i is an integer variable with a value of 5. We assume that the address of i is 004800. The variable i_ptr is a pointer whose value is the address of i, namely 004800. Since i_ptr contains the location of the variable i, i_ptr in effect points to the variable i. Therefore, we say that i_ptr **points to** i.

Normally, we do not know the actual numeric address of a variable. Therefore, to show that a pointer points to a variable, we draw an arrow from the pointer to the variable it points to, as in Figure 7.1b.

The pointers in Figure 7.1 are depicted as circles rather than squares, which we have been using to symbolize ordinary variables throughout the book. A circle emphasizes that the value of a pointer is an address.

A memory address is not the same as the value of an ordinary variable. Normally we can think of the address of a byte as a number that uniquely identifies the location of that byte in computer storage. See Figure 7.1. Bytes are numbered with addresses from zero to one less than the number of bytes in the computer's memory. This simple concept of computer storage is useful in understanding most of what goes on inside a computer. In some computers, however, the address of a byte consists of several numbers that identify the location of the byte. A good analogy is the address of a typical house, which is not a simple number like 2345. A house address has several parts—

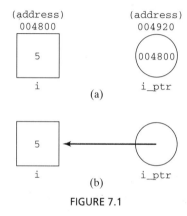

FIGURE 7.1

house number, street, city, state—that together identify the location of the house. Similarly, the address of a byte may have several parts.

Recall that variables of different types can occupy different amounts of storage. Thus, when declaring a pointer we must specify the type of the variable whose address the pointer contains. A pointer has a type just as an ordinary variable has a type. There are pointers to variables of type `int`, pointers to variables of type `double`, and so on.

Because an address might not be a simple integer, we cannot declare a pointer as an ordinary integer. To declare a pointer, we begin with the data type of a variable to which it will point, followed by an asterisk, `*`, followed by the name of the pointer. The following declares two pointers—one of type `int` and one of type `double`.

```
int* i_ptr;
double* d_ptr;
```

To read these declarations, use Note 7.1, which is similar to Note 6.1 for reading array declarations.

NOTE 7.1—READING A POINTER DECLARATION

Begin reading a pointer declaration at the pointer name and proceed clockwise through the declaration. Read the `*` as "pointer."

Read the first pointer declaration as "`i_ptr` is an `int` pointer" and read the second as "`d_ptr` is a `double` pointer." We use the suffix `_ptr` on pointer names to remind us that these variables are pointers.

Programming
Pointers

We append the asterisk in a pointer declaration immediately after the data type to emphasize that the pointer is a data type. The data type `int*`, that is the integer pointer data type, is a different type of object than an integer. Placing the asterisk in the declaration does not modify the data `int` data type, but instead actually refers to a completely different type. Note, however, that it is not required to append the asterisk immediately after the data type. The following declarations are equivalent to that of `i_ptr`. Some programmers use these styles of declaring pointers.

```
int * i_ptr;    //Declares i_ptr as an integer pointer
int *i_ptr;     //Declares i_ptr as an integer pointer
```

Programming
Pointers

Declaring a pointer, like declaring an ordinary variable, does not give the pointer a valid value. Referring to the previous declarations, `i_ptr` and `d_ptr`, although valid pointers, do not yet have valid values. Before using a pointer, make sure you give it a valid value by assigning the address of a variable to the pointer. The unary **address of** operator, **&**, returns the address of the variable to which it is applied. For example, if `i` is an integer variable, then `&i` is its address.

NOTE 7.2—THE ADDRESS OF OPERATOR, &

- The address of operator & is a unary operator. It has the same precedence and right-to-left associativity as the other unary operators.
- Read the address of operator as "the address of."

The following declarations and assignments declare and initialize the pointers `i_ptr` and `d_ptr` to point to the variables `i` and `d`.

```
int      i = 5;
double   d = 3.14;
int*     i_ptr;
double*  d_ptr;

i_ptr = &i;
d_ptr = &d;
```

The value of the right side of the assignment `i_ptr = &i` is the address of `i`. Therefore, the assignment places the address of the variable `i` into the pointer `i_ptr`. Similarly, the assignment `d_ptr = &d` places the address of the variable `d` into the pointer `d_ptr`. See Figure 7.2.

You can also assign a value to a pointer in the pointer's declaration. The following is equivalent to the previous declarations and assignments.

```
int      i = 5;
double   d = 3.14;
int*     i_ptr = &i;
double*  d_ptr = &d;
```

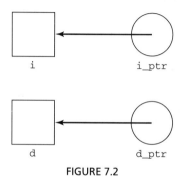

FIGURE 7.2

When assigning the address of a variable to a pointer in the pointer's declaration, you must observe the rule in Note 7.3.

NOTE 7.3—INITIALIZING A POINTER IN ITS DECLARATION

When assigning the address of a variable in a pointer's declaration, the variable must have been previously declared.

Programming
Pitfalls

The following is illegal because i is declared after the declaration and initialization of i_ptr. At the time i_ptr is declared and initialized, the variable i is not known to the compiler.

```
int* i_ptr = &i;       // invalid initialization
int i;
```

No matter how you initialize a pointer, you must initialize it before you use it.

NOTE 7.4—INITIALIZING A POINTER

Make sure that you initialize a pointer to a valid address before using the pointer. Failure to do so will not be caught by the compiler and can lead to unpredictable results.

Be sure that the address type matches the pointer type. For example, the following pointer initialization is illegal.

```
int      i;
double* d_ptr = &i;       // illegal pointer initialization
```

Programming
Pitfalls

You cannot assign the address of an integer variable to a pointer to a double. The compiler will usually detect all such type mismatches. However, do not rely on the compiler. Do not make the mistake in the first place.

Assigning a pointer the address of a variable using the & operator is one way to give a pointer a valid value. With one exception, you cannot directly assign an integer value to a pointer. The following declaration is illegal.

Programming
Pitfalls

```
int* i_ptr = 004600;       // illegal pointer assignment
```

Programming
Pointers

The one exception is the value 0, which is called the **null pointer**. You can also use the predefined constant NULL in place of zero. NULL is defined in several header files including iostream.h. The following are legal.

```
int* i_ptr = 0;          // Legal pointer assignment
int* j_ptr = NULL;       // Legal pointer assignment
```

Initializing a pointer to zero, although giving it a valid value, in effect makes the pointer point to nothing. You can assign the value 0 to a pointer of any type. The following declarations are legal.

```
double* d_ptr = NULL;
char*   c_ptr = NULL;
```

The Indirection Operator

A pointer allows you to indirectly access the value of the variable to which it points. To begin explaining how, we again use the house address analogy. Suppose that you want to give a letter to the President of the United States. One way to do so is to hand deliver the letter and give it to the President directly (if you could get that close!). Another is to give the President the letter by mailing the letter to President, 1600 Pennsylvania Ave., Washington, D.C. This second way gives the letter to the President, but gives it indirectly through the President's address.

The following declarations set up memory as shown in Figure 7.3.

```
int  i;
int* i_ptr = &i;
```

We could place the value 17 into the integer variable i by the following direct assignment.

```
i = 17;
```

Another way to place a value into i is indirectly through the pointer i_ptr using the **indirection operator** *. The following assignment also places the value 17 into the variable i but does so indirectly through the pointer i_ptr.

```
*i_ptr = 17;
```

Read the left side of this assignment as "the value of the target of i_ptr", or simply "the target of i_ptr." The target of i_ptr is the variable to which i_ptr points, namely i. Therefore, the assignment places 17 into the variable i.

i   i_ptr

FIGURE 7.3

Note 7.5 states two important rules about the indirection operator.

NOTE 7.5—THE INDIRECTION OPERATOR

1. The indirection operator * is a unary operator. It has the same precedence and right-to-left associativity as the other unary operators.

2. Read the indirection operator as "the target of." The target of a pointer is the variable to which it points.

Program dem07-1.cpp illustrates the ideas we have discussed so far.

```
// dem07-1.c

// This program illustrates the use of pointers and the indirection
// operator.

#include <iostream.h>

using namespace std;

int main()
{
  int  i;
  int* i_ptr = &i;

  cout << "\nThe address of i is   " << &i;
  cout << "\nThe value of i_ptr is " << i_ptr;

  // Place a value into i using indirection

  *i_ptr = 17;

  cout << "\n\nThe value of i is    " << i;
  cout << "\nThe value of *i_ptr is " << *i_ptr;

  return 0;
}
```

Program Output

```
The address of i is   0x4F6F244C
The value of i_ptr is 0x4F6F244C

The value of i is     17
The value of *i_ptr is 17
```

The values that the first two `cout` statements display depend on the particular system on which you run the program. We ran dem07-1.cpp on a PC running under Windows 95. The address is displayed in hexadecimal format. See Appendix A if you are unfamiliar with the hexadecimal numeration system. If you run dem07-1.cpp under another operating system, you will probably receive different results for the address of `i`. The important thing is that the address of `i` and the value of `i_ptr` are the same. Thus, `i_ptr` is pointing to `i`. Also, the program shows that you can reference the value of `i` either directly through `i` or indirectly through the pointer `i_ptr`.

Pointers and Arrays

We begin with a very important fact about arrays.

NOTE 7.6—THE NAME OF AN ARRAY IS A POINTER

The name of an array is a pointer to the first element in the array and has the same type as the type of the array.

Consider, for example, the following declarations.

```
int nums[5] = {3, 4, 5, 6, 7};
int* nums_ptr;
```

Programming
Pointers

The identifier `nums`, which is the name of the array, is an integer pointer to the first element of the array. Thus, `*nums`, the target of the pointer, is the array element `nums[0]`, which has the value 3. Since `nums` is a pointer to an integer, the following assignment is legal.

```
nums_ptr = nums;       // A legal pointer assignment
```

Programming
Pitfalls

After making this assignment, `*nums_ptr` also refers to the first element of the array `nums[]`, namely `nums[0]`. See Figure 7.4.

However, you must be careful not to make an assignment like the following.

```
nums_ptr = nums[2];    // Illegal pointer assignment
```

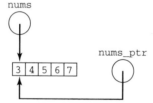

FIGURE 7.4

The left side of this assignment is an integer pointer. The right side is an integer. Therefore, the assignment is invalid.

Programming
Pitfalls

Although we now have two pointers to the first element of the array `nums[]`, there is an important difference between how we can use `nums` and `nums_ptr`. The name of an array is a **constant pointer** in the sense that no C++ statement can change its value. Therefore, the following assignment is illegal.

```
nums = nums_ptr;      // Illegal assignment
```

NOTE 7.7—THE NAME OF AN ARRAY IS A CONSTANT POINTER

The name of an array is a constant pointer. It is, therefore, illegal to try to change the value of the name of an array.

You can do simple integer arithmetic on pointers. For example, assume the following assignment.

```
nums_ptr = nums;
```

We can now execute `++nums_ptr`. This causes the value of `nums_ptr` to point to the next integer value, namely `nums[1]`, or 4. See Figure 7.5. Note, however, that `++nums` is illegal because it is an attempt to change the value of the name of an array, which is a constant pointer.

Programming
Pointers

It is important to note that pointer arithmetic within an array is scaled to the type of the array. For example, suppose the following declaration.

```
double d_array[4] = {3.2, 4.3, 5.4, 6.5};
double* d_ptr = d_array;
```

Thus, `d_ptr` points to the first element of `d_array`, namely 3.2. The statement `++d_ptr` causes `d_ptr` to point to the next `double` in the array, namely 4.3. If we again execute `++d_ptr`, `d_ptr` will point to the next `double` in the array, namely 5.4.

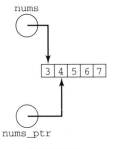

FIGURE 7.5

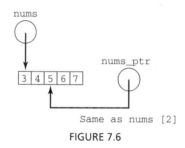

Same as nums [2]

FIGURE 7.6

You can use pointer arithmetic on an array name if it does not result in changing the value of the array name. The following is a valid assignment.

```
nums_ptr = nums + 2;   // Valid pointer assignment
```

Programming
Pointers

This assignment causes the pointer `nums_ptr` to point to the array element `nums[2]`. See Figure 7.6. In general, the expression `nums + i` is a pointer to the array element `nums[i]`. Therefore, `*(nums + i)` is the same element as `nums[i]`. Anywhere that you can use `nums[i]` in a program it is legal to use `*(nums + i)` in its place. (To what does `*nums + i` refer?)

Programming
Pitfalls

When using a pointer and pointer arithmetic to access array elements, you must take care that you do not cause the pointer to increase beyond the limits of the array. For example, in the previous example of Figure 7.6, if we execute `nums_ptr += 3`, the pointer will be pointing to the next integer location after the array. There is no way to tell what is stored in that location. The C++ compiler will not warn you if you make this mistake. The program will simply access the memory locations after the end of the array, whether they have been allocated or not. Accessing such locations could cause a run-time error in the program or could cause the program to produce incorrect results. See Experiment 2.

To understand pointers, you must see them in action and use them in programs. Section 7.2 introduces the idea of strings, which are sequences of characters. Section 7.3 shows how strings, arrays, and pointers are related and discusses several programs that use pointers to manipulate strings.

EXERCISES 7.1

1. Code declarations for the following.
   a. A pointer to a `float` variable. *float *ptr*
   b. A pointer to a `long` integer variable. *long *ptr*
   c. A pointer to the `unsigned` integer variable u and initialize the pointer to the address of u. *unsigned long *u = &u*
   d. A pointer to the `unsigned long` integer variable ul and initialize the pointer to the address of ul. *unsigned long int *ul = &ul*

   Use the following declarations for Exercises 2–5.

```
int i = 9,
    j = 4,
    k,
    1;
int* i_ptr = &i;
int* j_ptr = &j;
int* k_ptr = &k;
int* l_ptr = &l;
```

2. What are the values of the following?

    a. `*j_ptr` 4

    b. `i_ptr` 9

    c. `*(&i)` 9

3. Give the values of i, j, k, and 1 after execution of the following assignments.

```
          13            8        4
    *k_ptr = *i_ptr + *j_ptr;
   17 1 = k¹³ + *j_ptr;
    (*l_ptr)++;
          18
```

4. Is the following assignment legal?

```
i_ptr = 9;  yes
```

5. Is the following assignment legal?

```
*j_ptr = &j;  yes
```

In Exercises 6–11 use the following declarations. In each exercise state the value of the given expression.

```
int arr[] = {1, 2, 3, 4, 5, 6, 7, 8, 9};
int* arr_ptr = arr;
```

6. `*(arr_ptr + 4)` 5

7. `*arr_ptr + 4` 5

8. `arr_ptr[4]` 5

9. `(*arr_ptr)++` 2

10. `*(arr_ptr++)` 2

11. `*arr_ptr++`

EXPERIMENTS 7.1

1. In dem07-1.cpp, remove the initialization of i_ptr to the address of i. Execute the resulting program. Explain what happens.

2. Compile and execute the following program. Explain the output.

```
#include <iostream.h>

void main()
{
    int arr[] = {1, 2, 3, 4, 5, 6, 7, 8, 9};
    int* arr_ptr = arr;

    arr_ptr += 9;   OUT OF RANGE

    cout << *arr_ptr;
}
```

7.2 Strings

This section introduces strings, that is, sequences of characters. We begin with basic ideas and techniques for manipulating strings.

Defining and Initializing a String

Colloquially, a string is a sequence of characters. For example, the previous sentence is a string. In C++, a **string** is an array of characters that ends with the **null character**. The null character is a byte all of whose bits are zero. We denote the null byte in C++ by the escape sequence `'\0'`. The null byte is the way C++ finds the end of the string. If a character array does not end in a null character, the array does not contain a string.

The following declaration and initialization create a string consisting of the word "Hello". To hold the null character at the end of the array, the size of the character array containing the string is one more than the number of characters in the word "Hello".

```
char greeting[6] = {'H', 'e', 'l', 'l', 'o', '\0'};
```

This method of declaring and initializing a string is tedious because we must enclose each character in apostrophes and separate the characters by commas. The C++ language gives another way to initialize a string by using a **string constant**, which is a sequence of characters enclosed in quotation marks. The following declaration and initialization are equivalent to the previous one.

```
char greeting[6] = "Hello";
```

You do not place the null character at the end of a string constant. The C++ compiler automatically places the `'\0'` at the end of the string when it initializes the array. Therefore, this declaration causes the compiler to initialize storage as shown in Figure 7.7.

greeting

H	e	l	l	o	\0

FIGURE 7.7

Also, recall that if you initialize an array in its declaration, you do not have to state the size of the array. The C++ compiler will infer the array size from the initialization value. The following is equivalent to the previous declaration.

```
char greeting[] = "Hello";
```

String Input and Output

So far in this book we have not input strings into our programs. Suppose we wish to write a simple program that asks the user for the name of an item and its price. The program will then display the item name, the tax on the price, and its final cost (the price plus the tax). The only new feature of this program is obtaining the name of the item and displaying the name.

Programming
Pointers

Recall from Chapter 3 that to obtain a single character from the keyboard input buffer, we use `cin.get()`. Similarly, to obtain a string from the keyboard input buffer, we code `cin.getline()`. The `getline()` member function requires two arguments. The first argument must be the name of the array in which to store the string. The second argument should be the size of the array that is the first argument. The `getline()` member function extracts all characters available in the keyboard input buffer up to and including the new-line character, or to one less than the number of characters specified as the second argument, whichever comes first. The extra position is left for the terminating null character. The function places the characters, terminated by the null character, into the array named as its first argument. The result of executing `cin.getline()`, therefore, is to place the line that the user enters into a character array with the null character appended to the end.

For example, suppose the following declaration and statement.

```
char buffer[6];
cin.getline(buffer, 6);
```

The `cin.getline()` statement reads all the characters the user types up to and including the new-line character or up to five characters, whichever comes first. The function places the string, with a null character appended, into the array buffer[]. If the '\n' is read by `cin.getline()`, it is not placed into the buffer.

The program dem07-2.cpp shows how to use `cin.getline()`.

```
// dem07-2.c

// This program demonstrates the use of cin.getline() to input a string
// and cout to display strings in several ways.
```

```cpp
#include <iostream.h>
#include <iomanip.h>

using namespace std;

#define TAX_RATE 0.0825

int main()
{
  char item_name[51];
  double price,
         tax,
         total;

  cout << setprecision(2)
       << setiosflags(ios::fixed)
       << setiosflags(ios::showpoint);

  cout << "\nEnter the name of the item: ";
  cin.getline(item_name, 51);
  cout << "\nEnter the item price: ";
  cin >> price;

  tax = price * TAX_RATE;
  total = price + tax;

  cout << "\nItem: " << item_name << "\n";
  cout << "\nPrice: " << setw(9) << price;
  cout << "\nTax:   " << setw(9) << tax;
  cout << "\n" << "-----------------";
  cout << "\n" << "Total: " << setw(9) << total;

  return 0;
}
```

Program Output

```
Enter the name of the item: System Unit

Enter the item price: 1459.95

Item: System Unit

Price:   1459.95
Tax:      120.45
-----------------
Total:   1580.40
```

We assume that the item name is at most 50 characters. Therefore, the size of the array item_name[] is 51 (remember, we must have room for the null character).

item_name

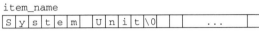

item_name

| S | y | s | t | e | m | | U | n | i | t | \0 | | | ... | |

FIGURE 7.8

After prompting for the name, the program obtains the name from the keyboard input buffer by executing `cin.getline(item_name, 51)`. Figure 7.8 shows the contents of the array `item_name[]` after `cin.getline()` executes.

Next, the program prompts for the item price and calculates the tax and total price. The program uses `cout` to display the item name. When the program sends a character string to `cout`, `cout` recognizes it as a string and outputs it accordingly.

Programming
Pitfalls

A problem that can happen with the `getline()` member function occurs in the following case: If the user enters the maximum number of allowable characters, that is one less than the buffer size, `getline()` does not extract the new-line character from the buffer. Therefore, if the user enters another string, which is to be extracted by `getline()`, the function will retrieve only the new-line character and not the next string the user enters. The following program illustrates the point.

```
//dem07-2a.cpp

#include <iostream.h>

using namespace std;

int main()
{
  char buffer[6];

  cout << "\nEnter five character string: ";
  cin.getline(buffer, 6);

  cout << "\n\nThe string you entered was " << buffer;

  cout << "\nEnter another five character string: ";
  cin.getline(buffer, 6);

  cout << "\n\nThe string you entered was " << buffer;

  return 0;
}
```

Program Output

```
Enter five character string: abcde

The string you entered was abcde
Enter another five character string:

The string you entered was
```

Note that the program did not wait for the user to enter the second string. The first execution of `getline()` leaves the new-line character in the buffer. Therefore, the second `getline()` immediately retrieves that new-line character and stops.

Programming
Pointers

To avoid this problem, we need to clear the input buffer of any extra characters that may remain after executing the first `getline()`. The member function `ignore()`, which removes and discards characters from the input buffer, enables us to do this. The member function `ignore()` requires two arguments. The first argument is an integer, which specifies the maximum number of characters to extract and ignore. The second argument is the delimiter character. The `ignore()` member function extracts and discards characters from the input buffer up to and including the delimiter character, or until it has extracted the number of characters specified in the first argument. Therefore, to solve the problem that occurred in the program dem07-2a.cpp, we place the following statement somewhere between the two calls to `getline()`.

```
cin.ignore(80, '\n');
```

This statement causes all characters in the buffer to be discarded, up to and including the new-line character or until 80 characters have been ignored, whichever comes first. We choose 80 as the first argument to make sure that all extraneous characters are discarded. Following is a corrected version of dem07.2a.cpp.

```
//dem07-2b.cpp

#include <iostream.h>

using namespace std;

int main()
{
  char buffer[6];

  cout << "\nEnter five character string: ";
  cin.getline(buffer, 6);

  cin.ignore(80, '\n'); //Clear the input buffer

  cout << "\n\nThe string you entered was " << buffer;

  cout << "\nEnter another five character string: ";
  cin.getline(buffer, 6);

  cout << "\n\nThe string you entered was " << buffer;

  return 0;
}
```

Program Output

```
Enter five character string: abcde

The string you entered was abcde
Enter another five character string: fghij

The string you entered was fghij
```

We therefore have the following.

> **NOTE 7.8 USING** `cin.getline()`
>
> To ensure that `cin.getline()` retrieves all characters from the input buffer up to and including the new-line character, follow the call to `cin.getline()` with a call to `cin.ignore()`.

String Constants as Pointers

Programming
Pointers

An important relationship between pointers and strings (remember that a string is an array of characters terminated by a null byte) is that a string constant, such as "Hello," is actually a pointer to a character array. When the C++ compiler encounters a string constant in a program, it stores the string (with the null character appended) somewhere in memory. Whenever the compiler encounters the string constant, it treats the string constant as a pointer to the base of the string. Therefore, the following declaration and initialization are legal.

```
char* greeting_ptr = "Hello";
```

The C++ compiler treats the string constant "Hello" as a character pointer to the base of the string "Hello". Hence, the assignment gives the character pointer `greeting_ptr` the value of another character pointer. The expression `*(greeting_ptr + 4)` references the character `'o'` in the string. See Figure 7.9.

In the following sections we discuss several programs that use pointers and pointer arithmetic to manipulate strings.

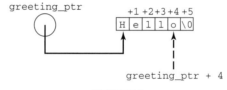

FIGURE 7.9

Counting Characters in a String

It is sometimes important to know how many characters are in a string. The program dem07-3.cpp counts the number of characters in a string entered by the user by using a while loop and a pointer to move through the array and to count the characters in the string.

```c
// dem07-3.c

// This program counts the number of characters input by the
// user on one line. It uses a pointer to move through the string
// and uses a while loop to count the characters.

#include <iostream.h>

using namespace std;

int main()
{
  char line[81];
  char* ch_ptr = line;
  int count = 0;

  cout << "\nEnter a line of characters:\n\n";
  cin.getline(line, 81);

  while ( *ch_ptr != '\0' )
    {
      ++count;
      ++ch_ptr;
    }

  cout << "\nThe string you entered has " << count << " characters.";

  return 0;
}
```

Program Output

```
Enter a line of characters:

Now is the time for good people to come to the aid of their country.

The string you entered has 68 characters
```

Since the normal width of a monitor screen is 80 characters, we declare the array line[] to be of size 81. We declare a character pointer ch_ptr, which we initialize to point to the base of the array `line[]`, and initialize `count` to zero in its declaration. After prompting for and obtaining the string from the user, the `while` loop counts the characters in the string. The loop condition tests the target of `ch_ptr` against the null character. Initially, `ch_ptr` points to the first character in the string that is stored in the array `line[]`. If this is not the null character, the program executes the loop body. The first statement in the loop body increments the variable `count` to count the character. The next statement increments the pointer `ch_ptr` so that it points to the next character in the string. The next time the program tests the loop condition, it tests the next character. The loop executes until the target of `ch_ptr` is the null character. At this point, the counter `count` equals the number of characters in the string.

Displaying a String in Reverse

The following program asks the user to enter a string and then displays the string in reverse.

```
// dem07-4.c

// This program asks the user to enter a string and then displays
// the string in reverse.

#include <iostream.h>

using namespace std;

int main()
{
   char line[81];
   char* ch_ptr = line;

   cout << "\nEnter a line of characters:\n\n";
   cin.getline(line, 81);

   // Find the end of the string

   while ( *ch_ptr != '\0' )
     ++ch_ptr;

   // ch_ptr now points to the null character

   --ch_ptr;

   // ch_ptr now points to the last character in the string

   cout << "\nThe line in reverse is:\n\n";

   // The while loop displays all but the first character
```

```
while ( ch_ptr != line )
  {
    cout << *ch_ptr;
    --ch_ptr;
  }

// Display the first character

cout << *ch_ptr;

return 0;
}
```

Program Output

```
Enter a line of characters:

abcd efgh ijkl

The line in reverse is:

lkji hgfe dcba
```

The program uses the array `line[]` to store the string that the user enters. The pointer `ch_ptr` keeps track of where the program is in the string. Therefore, the declaration of `ch_ptr` initializes it to point to the first character of `line[]`. See Figure 7.10a. Next, the program prompts for and obtains a string from the user. The first `while` loop "slides" the pointer to the end of the string. By this we mean that the loop increments the pointer until the target of the pointer is the null character. When the loop ends, `ch_ptr` is pointing to the null character that ends the string. See Figure 7.10b. Therefore, before displaying a character, the program backs up the pointer to the last character in the string by executing `--ch_ptr`. See Figure 7.10c.

The second `while` loop backs up the pointer to the beginning of the string and displays each character as it does so. Since `ch_ptr` is not equal to `line` (remember that `line` is a pointer to the first character in the string) the loop body displays the target of the pointer and then decrements the pointer. This `while` loop ends when `ch_ptr` equals `line`. Therefore, the loop does not display the first character in the string. See Figure 7.10d. The last `cout` statement displays the first character in the string.

Counting Words in a String

Counting the number of words in a string is a little more difficult than counting the number of characters in a string. We shall consider a word to be any sequence of non-blank characters. Thus, one or more blanks separate words. The only exception is that the null character, which is the end of the string, also signifies the end of a word.

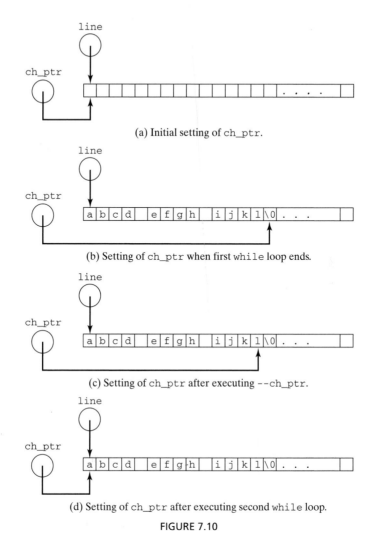

(a) Initial setting of `ch_ptr`.

(b) Setting of `ch_ptr` when first `while` loop ends.

(c) Setting of `ch_ptr` after executing `--ch_ptr`.

(d) Setting of `ch_ptr` after executing second `while` loop.

FIGURE 7.10

Following is the pseudocode for the program.

prompt for and obtain the string
skip leading blanks
while (there is a character)
  count the word
  skip the word
  skip the blanks after the word
endwhile
display the word count

For the program to count words, it must count the number of sequences of nonblank characters (words). Since blanks separate words, whenever the program encounters blanks it skips them. When the program hits a nonblank character, that character is either the beginning of a word or the end of the string (the null character.) If the nonblank character is not the null character, the program increments the word counter and then skips all the characters in the word. It comes to the end of a word when it encounters either a blank or the end of the string. This process continues until the program hits the null character.

The program dem07-5.cpp counts the number of words in a string entered by the user.

```
// dem07—5.cpp

// This program counts the number of words in a string entered
// by the user.

#include <iostream.h>

using namespace std;

int main()
{
  char line[81];
  char* ch_ptr;
  int word_count = 0;

  cout << "\nEnter a line of words:\n\n";
  cin.getline(line, 81);

  // Skip any blanks at the beginning of the line

  for (ch_ptr = line; *ch_ptr == ' '; ++ch_ptr)
    ;

  while (*ch_ptr != '\0')            // Process rest of line
    {
      ++word_count;                  // Count the word

                                     // Skip the word
      for ( ; (*ch_ptr != ' ') && (*ch_ptr != '\0'); ++ch_ptr)
        ;

      for ( ; *ch_ptr == ' '; ++ch_ptr) // Skip blanks after the word
        ;
    }

  cout << "\nThe line you entered has " << word_count << " words.";

  return 0;
}
```

Program Output

```
Enter a line of words:

  Now is the time for good people to come to the aid of their country.


The line you entered has 15 words.
```

It is important to keep in mind throughout this discussion that the pointer ch_ptr keeps track of which character in the string the program is processing. After prompting for and obtaining the line from the user, the program executes the first for loop. (This program shows that you can use for loops just as effectively as while loops to process strings. See Experiment 3.) This first loop skips any blanks that may be at the beginning of the line. The loop initializes ch_ptr to point to the beginning of the string. As long as the target of ch_ptr equals a blank, the loop increments the pointer. The body of this loop is empty because the for statement does all the work that we need.

At the end of this loop, therefore, ch_ptr points to the position of the first non-blank character in the string. See Figure 7.11a.

The while loop processes the rest of the line. As long as the character that the program is processing, namely the target of ch_ptr, is not the null character, the while loop keeps processing characters. The first statement in the loop body increments word_count because the program is at the beginning of a word. The first for loop in the while loop body skips the word. Note that the initialization part of the for statement is empty. The program does not re-initialize ch_ptr because we want ch_ptr to retain the value it had when the program exited the previous for loop. Remember that ch_ptr keeps track of the program's position in the string.

The for loop skips all the characters in the word by incrementing ch_ptr as long as the character being processed, namely *ch_ptr, is nonblank and not the null character. Therefore, when the program exits this loop, the character being processed is either a blank or the null character. See Figure 7.11b. If the character being processed is a blank, the second for loop in the while loop body skips that blank and any others that immediately follow. Thus, when the program exits the second for loop, the character being processed is nonblank. See Figure 7.11c.

The program then tests the condition in the while loop. If the character being processed is not the null character, the program has encountered another word and it executes the while loop body again. If the character being processed is the null character, the program has reached the end of the string. Then, the while loop stops and the program displays the number of words in the string.

EXERCISES 7.2

char my_name[] = "ABIGAIL";

1. Declare a string called my_name and initialize it with your name.
2. Declare a string called my_state and initialize it with the name of the state in which you live. char my_state[] = "ILLINOIS";

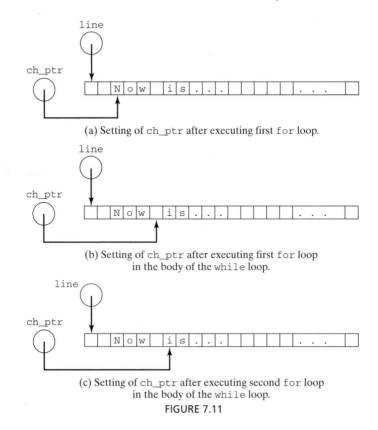

(a) Setting of ch_ptr after executing first `for` loop.

(b) Setting of ch_ptr after executing first `for` loop
in the body of the `while` loop.

(c) Setting of ch_ptr after executing second `for` loop
in the body of the `while` loop.

FIGURE 7.11

3. Declare a string called `birthday_month` and initialize it with the name of the month in which you were born. *Char birthmonth[] = "AUGUST";*

4. Declare a string called `your_city`. Code statements that prompt the user to enter the name of the city in which he or she lives and place the city name into the string `your_city`. *Char your_city [20]; cin.getline (yourccity,20);*

5. Declare a string called `birth_date` that is to hold a date in the form xx/xx/xx. Code statements that prompt the user to enter his or her birth date in the form xx/xx/xx and place the birth date into the string `birth_date`.

EXPERIMENTS 7.2

1. In dem07-2a.cpp, in response to the first prompt, enter a string that contains nine characters. Then enter a second string that contains nine characters. Explain how the program produces the output.

2. In dem07-2b.cpp, remove the `cin.ignore()` statement. Compile and execute the resulting program. In response to the first prompt, enter a string that contains nine characters. Explain what happens.

3. In dem07-5.cpp, replace the two `for` loops in the body of the `while` loop by equivalent `while` loops. Compile, execute, and test the resulting program.

PROGRAMMING PROBLEMS 7.2

1. Write a program that prompts the user to enter a string of up to 80 characters. The program should display the middle character in the string if there is an odd number of characters in the string. If there is an even number of characters in the string, the program should display the middle two characters.

2. Write a program that prompts the user to enter a string and then prompts the user to enter a character. The program should display the number of times the character occurs in the string.

3. Write a program that prompts the user to enter a string and then prompts the user to enter a character. The program should display the location of the first occurrence of the character in the string. For example, if the user enters the string "asfrdbrt" and the character d, the program should say that the character d is character number 5 in the string. If the character does not occur in the string, the program should display an appropriate message.

4. Write a program that prompts the user to enter two strings. The program should display "The strings are identical" if the strings are exactly the same and "The strings are not identical" if the strings are not exactly the same.

5. Write a program that prompts the user to enter a string. The program should output the number of vowels (a, e, i, o, u) contained in the string. For example, the previous sentence contains 26 vowels.

6. Modify the program of Programming Problem 5 to display the number of times each vowel appears in the string input by the user.

7. Write a program that prompts the user to enter a string and then copies the string into another array. The program should display the array in which the string was originally stored and the array in which the copy was placed.

8. Write a program that prompts the user to enter a string. The program should display the string one word per line. Hint: See dem07-5.cpp.

9. Write a program that inserts one string into another. The program should prompt the user for a string. Then the program should prompt the user to enter another string that is to be inserted into the first string. Finally, the program should prompt the user for the position at which to insert the second string. The program should then do the insertion and display the new string. For example, suppose the user enters for the first string "I left my heart in Francisco", for the second string "San " and for the position 19. Then, the program should output "I left my heart in San Francisco".

10. In many industries encoding messages is important to keep important information out of the hands of "industrial spies." Write a program that prompts the user to enter a line of text and then displays the line in code. The program should use the following simple coding scheme. Store the alphabet in two different orderings in two different arrays. For example,

```
char source[] = "qazwsxedcrfvtgbyhnujmikolp";
char target[] = "lkjhgfdsaqwertyuiopmnbvcxz";
```

For each character input by the user, search the `source[]` array for that character and note its subscript. Then encode that character by the character with the corresponding subscript in the `target[]` array. For example, suppose the user enters v. The letter v has subscript 11 in the `source[]` array. Therefore, the letter v gets encoded as the letter e because e has subscript 11 in the `target[]` array. The word "computer" would get encoded as "acnzprdq". Treat uppercase characters the same as lowercase characters. Characters that are not letters of the alphabet should be unchanged.

11. An International Standard Book Number (ISBN) is a code of 10 characters that uniquely identifies a book. The rightmost digit of such a number is a check digit, which helps detect errors in case the number is copied incorrectly. For example, in the ISBN 0132261197, the check digit is 7. The check digit is computed from the other nine digits as follows: First compute the sum of the first digit plus two times the second digit, plus three times the third digit, ..., plus nine times the ninth digit. The check digit is the remainder when this sum is divided by 11. If the remainder is 10, the check digit is X.

For example, the sum for the ISBN 0132261197 is

$1*0 + 2*1 + 3*3 + 4*2 + 5*2 + 6*6 + 7*1 + 8*1 + 9*9 = 161$

The remainder when 161 is divided by 11 is 7, which is the last character of the ISBN. When copying an ISBN, if a digit is copied incorrectly, or the order of two digits is reversed, the check digit can be used to detect the error. For example, suppose that the ISBN is incorrectly written as 0132621197. If you attempt to calculate the check digit from the first nine digits, you obtain the following: The sum is

$1*0 + 2*1 + 3*3 + 4*2 + 5*6 + 6*2 + 7*1 + 8*1 + 9*9 = 157$

The remainder when you divide 157 by 11 is 3. Since this does not agree with the check digit of 7, we know that the ISBN has been incorrectly transcribed.

Write a program that asks the user to enter the name of a book and its ISBN. The program should validate the ISBN and print a message that states that the ISBN is correct or incorrect. Store the ISBN in a character array. To do the summation with the ISBN characters, use the fact that the numeric value of a digit character can be had by subtracting the character '0' from the character. For example, the value of '4' - '0' is 4.

12. See Programming Problem 11. The ISBN is usually written with dashes as follows: 0-13-226119-7. Redo Programming Problem 11 to take the dashes into account. In other words, let the user enter the ISBN with the dashes. The program should validate the number as in Programming Problem 11.

7.3 Arrays of Strings and Pointers

In C++, the elements in an array can be any data type. In this section we consider arrays of strings and arrays of pointers and several applications.

Defining an Array of Strings

Recall that a two-dimensional array is actually an array, each of whose elements is an array. For example, the array

```
char day_names[7][10];
```

is an array of seven elements, each of which is an array of 10 characters. An array of characters can store a string. Therefore, a two-dimensional array of characters, such as day_names[][], is capable of storing strings. Consider, for example, the following declaration and initialization.

```
char day_names[7][10] = {"Monday", "Tuesday", "Wednesday",
                         "Thursday", "Friday", "Saturday", "Sunday"};
```

The 7 × 10 character array day_names[][] can hold seven strings each up to nine characters long. The longest name of the days of the week is Wednesday, which has nine characters. The tenth position is for the null character. Figure 7.12 shows what the declaration places into storage.

Now that we have placed the names of the days of the week into storage, how can we refer to them in a program? Each element of the array day_names[][] is an array of characters. Therefore, the reference day_names[3] accesses element number three of the array, which is the array of characters containing the string "Thursday." Thus, to refer to a particular string in the array, use the array name followed by a single subscript.

NOTE 7.9—STRING REFERENCES IN A TWO-DIMENSIONAL ARRAY

When strings are stored in a two-dimensional array, use the array name followed by one subscript to refer to the individual strings.

day_names

0	M	o	n	d	a	y	\0		
1	T	u	e	s	d	a	y	\0	
2	W	e	d	n	e	s	d	a	y	\0
3	T	h	u	r	s	d	a	y	\0	
4	F	r	i	d	a	y	\0		
5	S	a	t	u	r	d	a	y	\0	
6	S	u	n	d	a	y	\0		

FIGURE 7.12

Using an Array of Strings

A sales manager wants to total the sales for each salesperson in her department and find the day of the week on which the salesperson had the highest sales. Write a program to perform this task. The program should ask the user for the sales of the salesperson for each day of the week. The prompt should include the name of the day of the week. The program should then total the weekly sales. Finally, the program should display the total weekly sales, the name of the day of the week that the salesperson had the highest sales, and what the highest sales amount was.

Following is a pseudocode solution to the problem.

Prompt for and get the name of the salesperson
Prompt for and get the sales amounts for each day
Calculate the total sales
Find the highest sales amount
Display the total sales, name of the day of the highest
    sales, and the highest sales amount

Following is the program prb07-1.cpp which is the solution to the problem.

```
// prb07-1.c

// This program totals weekly sales amounts and finds the highest
// sales for the week. It uses an array of strings to store the
// names of the days of the week.

#include <iostream.h>
#include <iomanip.h>

using namespace std;

int main()
{
   char day_names[7][10] = {"Monday", "Tuesday", "Wednesday",
                            "Thursday", "Friday", "Saturday", "Sunday"};

   double sales[7];
   char   salesperson[41];
   double max_sales,
          total_sales;
   int    day,
          max_day;

   cout << setprecision(2)
        << setiosflags(ios::fixed)
        << setiosflags(ios::showpoint);

   cout << "\nEnter the name of the salesperson: ";
   cin.getline(salesperson, 41);
```

```
for (day = 0; day < 7; ++day)
  {
     cout << "\n\nEnter the sales for "<< day_names[day]<< ": ";
     cin >> sales[day];
  }

total_sales = 0;
max_day = 0;
max_sales = sales[0];

for (day = 0; day < 7; ++day)
  {
     if (sales[day] > max_sales)
       {
          max_sales = sales[day];
          max_day = day;
       }
     total_sales += sales[day];
  }

cout << "\n\nThe total sales for " << salesperson
     << " is " << total_sales << ".";
cout << "\n\nThe highest sales was " << max_sales << ".";
cout << "\n\nThe highest sales occurred on "
     << day_names[max_day]<< ".";

return 0;
}
```

Program Output

```
Enter the name of the salesperson: Joseph Haris


Enter the sales for Monday: 379.90


Enter the sales for Tuesday: 2877.95


Enter the sales for Wednesday: 2661.90


Enter the sales for Thursday: 178.45


Enter the sales for Friday: 3066.20
```

```
Enter the sales for Saturday: 0.00


Enter the sales for Sunday: 2904.77


The total sales for Joseph Harris is 12069.17.

The highest sales was 3066.20.

The highest sales occurred on Friday.
```

The declarations begin with the two-dimensional array `day_names[][]`, which is initialized to the names of the days of the week. The array `sales[]` stores the seven sales amounts. The character array `salesperson[]` stores the name of the salesperson. The double variable `max_sales` stores the highest sales and the variable `total_sales` is the accumulator for totaling the sales amounts. The integer variable `day` acts as the subscript for both the `day_names[][]` array and the `sales[]` array.

The program begins by prompting for and obtaining the name of the salesperson. Next, a `for` loop prompts for and obtains the seven sales amounts and stores them in the array `sales[]`. The `cout` statement displays the name of the day of the week by displaying `day_names[day]`, which is the name of the day corresponding to the day number.

The program prepares to total the sales amounts and find the day of the highest sales by initializing three variables. The accumulator `total_sales` is initialized to zero. To begin the process of finding the highest sales amount, we assume that the highest sale occurs on day zero. Therefore, the program initializes `max_day` to zero and `max_sales` to the sales on the first day, namely `sales[0]`.

The next `for` loop totals the sales and finds the highest sales amount. For each of the seven days, the loop tests the sales of the day being processed, `sales[day]`, against `max_sales`, the highest sales found so far. If `sales[day]` is greater than `max_sales`, the current day's sales is greater than the highest sales seen so far. Therefore, the program replaces the value of `max_sales` by the value of `sales[day]` and replaces the value of `max_day` by the value of the current day, namely `day`. If the value of `sales[day]` is not greater than `max_sales`, no adjustment needs to be made to either `max_sales` or `max_day`. In either case, the value of `total_sales` is increased by the value of `sales[day]`. When the program exits the `for` loop, `total_sales` contains the sum of the seven day's sales, `max_sales` contains the highest sales amount, and `max_day` contains the number of the day on which the highest sales occurred.

The `cout` statements display the results of the program. The first `cout` displays the salesperson's name and the total sales for the week. The second `cout` displays the value of the highest sales. The third `cout` displays the name of the day on which the highest sales occurred. The name of the day is accessed by `day_names[max_day]` because `max_day` is the number of the day of the highest sales.

Using an Array of Pointers To Store Strings

The method we used in the previous section to store strings in a two-dimensional array can be very inefficient. The 7 × 10 array `day_names[][]` occupies 70 bytes of storage. Each row of the array had to be 10 characters long to accommodate the longest name. However, most of the rows are not completely filled. See Figure 7.12. Only 57 of the 70 bytes are actually occupied by the names. Thus, approximately 19% of the array is wasted. In other situations this waste of storage space can be even greater. If you use a two-dimensional array to store the last names of people, the number of columns in the array must be large enough to store the longest last name. If the longest last name is Dimitripopadopolous, each row would have to contain 20 characters. If the average last name is only eight characters long, this means that on average you waste 12 characters per row. If you must store 1000 names, this means wasting about 12,000 bytes of storage.

Programming
Pointers

A more memory-efficient way of storing the names of the days of the week is to define the array of names as an array of character pointers. Consider the following declaration.

```
char* day_names [7] = {"Monday", "Tuesday", "Wednesday",
                       "Thursday", "Friday", "Saturday", "Sunday"};
```

First, be sure to read the declaration correctly. Remember the rule in Note 6.1 for reading array declarations. Begin reading the declaration at the array name and proceed clockwise through the declaration. Thus, `day_names` is an array of seven character pointers. Each element of the array is a pointer to a character. The initialization list contains seven character strings. Recall that a character string is really a pointer to the first character of the string. Figure 7.13 shows what the declaration does.

This declaration of `day_names[]` as an array of pointers saves storage because each string takes up only as much memory as needed. This declaration requires 57 bytes to store the names of the days of the week, not 70 as in the two-dimensional declaration.

To illustrate the use of an array of pointers, consider prb07-2.cpp, which is another version of prb07-1.cpp.

```
// prb07-2.c

// This program totals weekly sales amounts and finds the highest
```

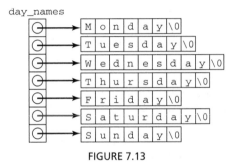

FIGURE 7.13

```cpp
// sales for the week. It uses an array of pointers to store the
// names of the days of the week.

#include <iostream.h>
#include <iomanip.h>

using namespace std;

int main()
{
   char* day_names[7] = {"Monday", "Tuesday", "Wednesday",
                         "Thursday", "Friday", "Saturday", "Sunday"};

   double sales[7];
   char   salesperson[41];
   double max_sales,
          total_sales;
   int    day,
          max_day;

   cout << setprecision(2)
        << setiosflags(ios::fixed)
        << setiosflags(ios::showpoint);

   cout << "\nEnter the name of the salesperson: ";
   cin.getline(salesperson, 41);

   for (day = 0; day < 7; ++day)
     {
       cout << "\n\nEnter the sales for " << day_names[day] << ": ";
       cin >> sales[day];
     }

   total_sales = 0;
   max_day = 0;
   max_sales = sales[0];

   for (day = 0; day < 7; ++day)
     {
       if (sales[day] > max_sales)
         {
           max_sales = sales[day];
           max_day = day;
         }
       total_sales += sales[day];
     }

   cout << "\n\nThe total sales for " << salesperson
        << " is " << total_sales << ".";
   cout << "\n\nThe highest sales was " << max_sales << ".";
```

```
cout << "\n\nThe highest sales occurred on "
     << day_names[max_day] << ".";

return 0;
}
```

Program Output

```
Enter the name of the salesperson: Joseph Harris


Enter the sales for Monday: 379.90


Enter the sales for Tuesday: 2877.95


Enter the sales for Wednesday: 2661.90


Enter the sales for Thursday: 178.45


Enter the sales for Friday: 3066.20


Enter the sales for Saturday: 0.00


Enter the sales for Sunday: 2904.77

The total sales for Joseph Harris is 12069.17.

The highest sales was 3066.20.

The highest sales occurred on Friday.
```

The difference between prb07-2.cpp and prb07-1.cpp is the declaration of the array of names as an array of pointers. The references to day_names are the same as in prb07-1.cpp because only one subscript was used in prb07-1.cpp to access a day name.

EXERCISES 7.3

1. Declare a two-dimensional array of characters that is initialized to the names of the months of the year.
2. Declare an array of character pointers that is initialized to point to the names of the months of the year.

3. Declare a two-dimensional array of characters that is initialized to the names of the Presidents who were elected to office after 1950.

4. Declare an array of character pointers that is initialized to point to the names of the Presidents who were elected to office after 1950.

EXPERIMENTS 7.3

1. Execute dem07-2.cpp and enter an item name that is longer than 50 characters. What happens?

2. Recode dem07-5.cpp by replacing all the `for` loops by equivalent `while` loops. Execute and test the resulting program.

PROGRAMMING PROBLEMS 7.3

1. Write a program that asks the user to enter his or her birthday as three integers in the form month, day, year, for example 7 10 81. The program should output the date in the form month name day, year. Using the previous example input, the program would output July 10, 1981. Use an array of character pointers to store the month name.

2. A software company has seven service representatives who are identified in the payroll system by the ID numbers 1 through 7. Write a program that prompts the user to enter the representative ID number, hours worked, and pay rate. The program should display the representative's name and gross pay (hours * rate.) Store the representatives' names in an array of character pointers.

Chapter Review

Terminology

Define the following terms.

pointer
points to
NULL pointer
address of operator
indirection operator

string
null character
`'\0'`
string constant
`cin.getline()`
constant pointer
`cin.ignore()`

Summary

- A pointer is a variable whose value is the address of another variable.
- Use the asterisk, *, to declare a pointer. For example, `int*  i_ptr;` declares `i_ptr` as an integer pointer (Note 7.1).
- Use the address operator, &, to initialize a pointer. For example, `i_ptr = &i;` initializes the integer pointer `i_ptr` to the address of the integer variable `i` (Note 7.2, Note 7.3, and Note 7.4).

- Use the indirection operator, *, to dereference a pointer. Thus, `*i_ptr` is the value of the target of the pointer `i_ptr` (Note 7.5).
- The name of an array is a constant pointer to the first element of the array (Note 7.6 and Note 7.7).
- You can do simple integer arithmetic on pointers. This arithmetic is scaled to the size of the pointer type.
- A string is a character array that ends in the null character, `'\0'`.
- You can initialize a character array to a character string in its initialization.
- The member function `cin.getline()` returns an entire line from the input buffer.
- The `cin.ignore()` member function removes and discards all characters from the input buffer (Note 7.8).
- A string constant is a character pointer to the string's first character.
- You can store strings in a two-dimensional character array. In this case, the array name followed by one subscript refers to an individual string (Note 7.9). This way of storing strings can waste memory.
- A more efficient way of storing strings is to use an array of character pointers.

Review Exercises

1. What is a pointer and how do you declare one?
2. If all pointers occupy the same amount of storage, why do you have to include a data type in a pointer declaration?
3. Why must you make sure that a pointer is initialized to point to a valid address?
4. What is the null pointer?
5. How do you use the indirection operator?
6. How must you treat the name of an array?
7. What is a string?
8. What function should you use to obtain a string from the input buffer?
9. What function can you use to discard unwanted characters from the input buffer?
10. What is the data type of a string constant?
11. Describe two ways to declare an array of strings. What are the advantages and disadvantages of each?

Chapter

8

Pointers, Arrays, and Functions

Objectives

- To code a function whose argument is passed by address.

- To code a function whose argument is passed by reference.

- To code a function that has an array as an argument.

- To code the bubble sort using a function.

- To code a function whose argument is a string.

- To code a function that returns a pointer.

- To use the standard string library functions, including `strlen()`, `strcpy()`,

- `strcmp()`, and `strcat()`, to manipulate strings.

- To use the character classification and conversion functions to manipulate characters.

- To use the functions `atoi()`, `atol()`, and `atof()` to convert numeric strings to their numeric equivalent.

- To use the `new` operator to dynamically allocate memory on the heap.

- To use the `delete` operator to de-allocate memory on the heap.

In this chapter we discuss how to use functions that have pointers and arrays as arguments and functions that return pointers. We also discuss several string and character functions in the C++ standard library.

8.1 Pointers, Reference Variables, and Functions

A function can have a pointer as an argument and can return a pointer to the calling function. This section discusses how to use these functions.

Call by Address—Pointers as Function Arguments

All arguments to C++ functions are passed by value. This means that the value of the argument, not the argument itself, is passed to the function. Consider the following program.

```
// dem08-1.cpp

// This program demonstrates passing an argument by value.

#include <iostream.h>

using namespace std;

int Neg_By_Value(int);

int main()
{
   int i = 4;

   i = Neg_By_Value(i);

   cout << "\ni = " << i;

   return 0;
}

int Neg_By_Value(int a)
{
   return -a;
}
```

Program Output

```
i = -4
```

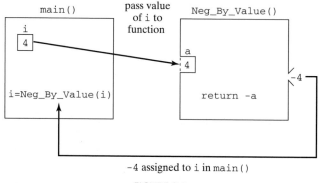

FIGURE 8.1

When `main()` executes the assignment statement, it calls the function `Neg_By_Value()` and passes the value of the variable `i`, namely 4, to the function. The function returns the negative of the value of its argument. Thus, `Neg_By_Value()` has not changed the value of its argument. The function returns the value -4. The assignment statement in `main()` then assigns -4 to the variable `i`. Thus, the assignment statement in `main()` places a new value into the variable `i`. See Figure 8.1.

In C++, anything can be passed as a function argument, even a pointer. When a pointer to a variable is passed as a function argument, the function receives the address of the variable. Using the indirection operator, the function can manipulate the value of the variable as though the variable were local to the function. The program dem08-2.cpp also negates the value of an integer, but uses a function that has a pointer argument.

```cpp
// dem08-2.cpp

// This program demonstrates passing an argument by address

#include <iostream.h>

using namespace std;

void Neg_By_Address(int*);

int main()
{
    int i = 4;

    Neg_By_Address(&i);

    cout << "\ni = " << i;

    return 0;
}

void Neg_By_Address(int* a_ptr)
```

```
{
  *a_ptr = -(*a_ptr);
}
```

Program Output

```
i = -4
```

The function `Neg_By_Address()` negates its integer argument. The type (`int*`) in the function prototype tells the compiler that the argument is an integer pointer. When we use the function, the argument must be the address of an integer. Note that the function does not return a value.

To negate the value of `i`, `main()` executes the following statement.

```
Neg_By_Address(&i);
```

This function call passes the *address* of the variable `i`, not the *value* of `i`, to the function `Neg_By_Address()`. In the function `Neg_By_Address()`, the parameter `a_ptr` is declared as an integer pointer. When `main()` calls the function, the function places the address that `main()` passed into the pointer `a_ptr`. Figure 8.2 shows the parameter `a_ptr` as a circle to show that it is a pointer.

The pointer `a_ptr` now points to the variable `i`. Therefore, the function can use the indirection operator to manipulate the target of `a_ptr`, namely `i`. The body of the function contains only the following statement.

```
*a_ptr = -(*a_ptr);
```

This statement replaces the value of the target of `a_ptr`, namely the value of `i`, by the negative of the target of `a_ptr`. The function `Neg_By_Address()` changes the value of `i` in `main()`.

Passing the address of a variable to a function is referred to as **call by address**.

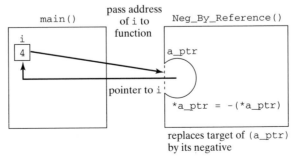

FIGURE 8.2

Swapping Variable Values—An Example of Call by Address

A function can return at most one value to the calling function. However, using call by address, it is possible to make a function change two or more variables in the calling function. Recall that an important part of the bubble sort, which we discussed in Chapter 6, is swapping the values of two integer variables. The program dem08-3.cpp uses the function `Swap_Int()` to interchange the values of two integer variables. Later in this chapter we use `Swap_Int()` in another version of the bubble sort program that uses functions for all major operations.

```cpp
// dem08-3.cpp

#include <iostream.h>

using namespace std;

void Swap_Int(int*, int*);

int main()
{
   int i = 3,
       j = 5;

   cout << "\nBefore swapping: i = " << i<< " j = " << j;

   Swap_Int(&i, &j);

   cout << "\nAfter swapping: i = " << i<< " j = " << j;

   return 0;
}

void Swap_Int(int* a_ptr, int* b_ptr)
{
   int temp;

   temp = *a_ptr;
   *a_ptr = *b_ptr;
   *b_ptr = temp;
}
```

Program Output

```
Before swapping: i = 3, j = 5
After swapping: i = 5, j = 3
```

The function prototype for `Swap_Int()` declares its return value to be `void` because the function does not return a value. Instead, `Swap_Int()` uses pointers to exchange the values of two integer variables in the calling function. The function's arguments are both declared as integer pointers. Thus, we must pass the addresses of two integers to the function.

The declaration of the variables i and j in `main()` initialize the variables to 3 and 5, respectively. A `cout` statement displays the initial values of i and j. Then, `main()` executes the `Swap_Int()` function by executing the following statement, which passes the addresses of i and j to `Swap_Int()`. See Figure 8.3.

```
Swap_Int(&i, &j);
```

The function `Swap_Int()` assigns these addresses to the parameters a_ptr and b_ptr. `Swap_Int()` uses the indirection operator to interchange the values of the targets of a_ptr and b_ptr, namely i and j. The function changes the values of two variables in `main()`.

Reference Variables and Call by Reference

Reference variables and arguments are sometimes an alternative to pointers. A **reference variable** is an alias for an already existing variable. For example, suppose we have the following declarations.

```
int    i = 7;
double d = 1.2;
```

We can declare reference variables for i and d as follows.

```
int&    r = i;
double& s = d;
```

Programming
Pointers

Read the & in these declarations as "reference." Thus, read the first declaration as "r is an integer reference initialized to i," and read the second declaration as "s is a double reference initialized to d."

Think of a variable name as a label attached to the variable's location in memory. You can then think of a reference as a second label attached to that memory location. Therefore, you can access the contents of the variable through either the original variable name or the reference. See Figure 8.4.

We can change the contents of the variable i by using the identifier i or the reference r. For example, either of the following assignments will change the value of i to 9.

```
i = 9;
r = 9;
```

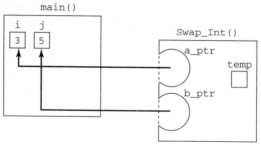

When main() calls Swap_Int()

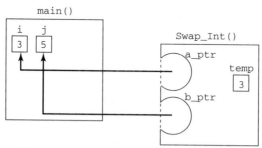

After executing temp = *a_ptr in Swap_Int()

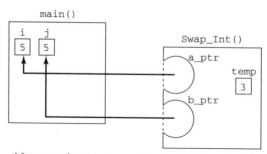

After executing *a_ptr = *b_ptr in Swap_Int()

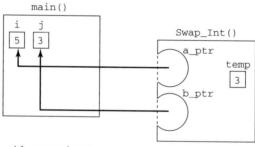

After executing *b_ptr = temp in Swap_Int()

FIGURE 8.3

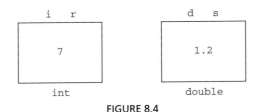

FIGURE 8.4

Just as for pointers, we append the & in a reference declaration to the end of the data type to emphasize that the reference is another type. However, the ampersand can be placed anywhere between the data type and the name of the reference variable. The following are legal declarations.

```
double  & s = d;      //Legal reference declaration
int  &r = i;          //Legal reference declaration
```

Programming
Pointers

In many cases it is easier to use references rather than pointers as function arguments. In this case we are passing arguments by reference or using **call by reference**. As an example of call by reference, consider the following variation of the program dem08-2.cpp.

```
// dem08-2R.cpp

// This program demonstrates passing an argument by reference

#include <iostream.h>

using namespace std;

void Neg_By_Reference(int&);

int main()
{
   int i = 4;

   Neg_By_Reference(i);

   cout << "\ni = " << i;

   return 0;
}

void Neg_By_Reference(int& a)
{
   a = -a;
}
```

Program Output

```
i = -4
```

The function `Neg_By_Reference()`, has an integer reference as an argument and does not return a value. When the function calls `Neg_By_Reference()`, it passes `i` to the function. Then `i` is assigned to the reference parameter `a` in the function. This is equivalent to the declaration and assignment

```
int& a = i;
```

Programming
Pointers

In the function `Neg_By_Reference()`, `a` is an alias for `i`. Any change to `a` is, therefore, a change to `i`. We do not need the dereference operator * as we did in dem08-2.cpp. The function `Neg_By_Reference()` replaces `a` by the negative of `a`. Therefore, the function replaces `i`, which is a variable declared in `main()`, by the negative of `i`.

As another example of call by reference, consider the following variation of dem08-3.cpp

```
// dem08-3R.cpp

//This program illustrates passing arguments by reference

#include <iostream.h>

using namespace std;

void Swap_Int(int&, int&);

int main()
{
  int i = 3,
  j = 5;

  cout << "\nBefore swapping: i = " << i << " j = " << j;

  Swap_Int(i, j);

  cout << "\nAfter swapping: i = " << i << " j = " << j;

  return 0;
}

void Swap_Int(int& a, int& b)
{
  int temp;
```

```
    temp = a;
    a    = b;
    b    = temp;
}
```

Program Output

```
Before swapping: i = 3, j = 5
After swapping: i = 5, j = 3
```

The prototype for the `Swap_Int()` function specifies that the two arguments are integer references. When the function is called, `Swap_Int(i, j)`, the arguments are simply `i` and `j`. (We do not pass the addresses as we did in dem08-3.cpp.) Recall that when a function is called, the arguments are, in effect, assigned to the function's parameters. Within the function, therefore, we have the equivalent of the following declarations and initializations.

```
int& a = i;
int& b = j;
```

Within the body of the function, the parameters `a` and `b` are aliases for `i` and `j`. See Figure 8.5. Therefore, we do not need the dereference operator, *, as we did in the `Swap_Int()` function of dem08-3.

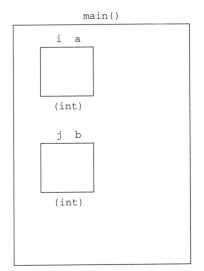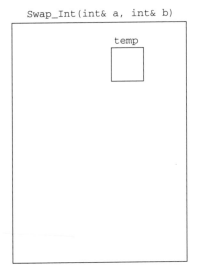

a and b are aliases for i and j

FIGURE 8.5

EXERCISES 8.1

In Exercises 1–5 code the prototype for the given function.

1. A function `Swap_Char()` that interchanges the values of two characters. The function has two arguments, both of which are addresses of characters. The function does not return a value.

2. A function `Sort_Int()` that takes three arguments. Each argument is the address of an integer. The function does not return a value.

3. A function `Calc_Fed_Tax()` that takes four arguments. The first two arguments are the addresses of doubles, the third is the address of an integer, and the fourth is the address of a `double`. The function does not return a value.

4. A function `Calc_Weight()` that takes two arguments and returns a `double`. The two arguments are references to doubles.

5. A function `Total_Price()` that takes two arguments and returns a `double`. The first argument is a reference to an integer. The second argument is a reference to a double.

EXPERIMENTS 8.1

1. Rewrite dem08-3.cpp so that it swaps two doubles.

2. Write and compile a short program in which you declare but do not initialize a reference variable. Does the compiler issue any error messages?

PROGRAMMING PROBLEMS 8.1

1. Write a program to calculate a person's net pay after subtracting federal income tax. The program should ask the user to enter the person's name, social security number, gross pay, and the number of dependents. The program should first determine the tax rate according to the following schedule.

Weekly Income	Tax Rate
0.00–300.00	0.085
300.01–500.00	0.120
500.01–1000.00	0.185
1000.01 and over	0.220

Use a function `Tax_Rate()` to determine the schedule. Pass the gross pay to `Tax_Rate()` and have the function return the rate.

Next, use the function `Calc_Fed_Tax()`, see Exercise 3, to calculate the federal tax. The first argument should be the address of the gross income. The second argument should be the address of the tax rate (as returned by `Tax_Rate()`). The third argument should be the address of the number of dependents. The amount of the federal tax should be returned in the target of the fourth argument.

Finally, the program should calculate the net pay by subtracting the federal tax from the gross income. The program should display the person's name, social security number, gross pay, number of dependents, federal tax, and net pay.

2. Code a solution to Programming Problem 1 in which the arguments to the function `Calc_Fed_Tax()` are passed by reference.

8.2 Arrays and Functions

An array name is a pointer to the base of the array. A string is a character pointer. Thus, passing an array or a string to a function is equivalent to passing a pointer. This section and the next discuss how to pass arrays and strings to functions.

Since an array name is a pointer to the base of the array, you can use an array name in the same way that you use a pointer as an argument in a function. However, since an array has a fixed number of elements, we must take a few special steps when using an array as a function argument. This section discusses how to pass an array to a function and applies this to array sorting.

Passing an Array to a Function

To pass an array to a function, you must make two changes to your function—one in the function prototype and one in the function definition header.

Suppose that the function `Avg()` is to find the average of the integers in an array. We pass the array to the function as one of the function's two arguments. The second argument is the size of the array that we pass as the first argument. The following would be the function's prototype.

```
double Avg(int [], int);
```

`Avg()` returns a value of type `double` and has two arguments. The first argument is an array of type `int`. The brackets [] in the type list tell the compiler that the first argument is an array. The data type preceding the [] determines the array type. `Avg()`'s second argument, which is the array size, is of type `int`.

The function definition header corresponding to the previous prototype is as follows.

```
double Avg(int arr[], int size)
```

Programming
Pointers

`Avg()` returns a value of type `double` and has two parameters. The first parameter, `arr`, is an array of type `int`. The brackets [] after the formal parameter name tell the compiler that the parameter is an array. You do not specify the size of the array in this parameter declaration. The second parameter, `size`, is of type `int`. This second parameter is the size of the array.

The following program, dem08-4.cpp, does the same thing as dem06-2.cpp,—it finds the average of a set of 10 grades input by the user. However, it uses the function `Avg()` to calculate the average of the grades.

```cpp
// dem08-4.cpp

// This program shows how find the average of the elements
// in an array. It finds the average by passing the array
// to a function that computes the average.

#include <iostream.h>
#include <iomanip.h>

using namespace std;

#define NUM_QUIZZES 10

double Avg(int [], int);

int main()
{
  int    grade[NUM_QUIZZES];   // The array to store the quiz grades
  int    quiz;                 // The array subscript
  double grade_avg;

  cout << setiosflags(ios::fixed)
       << setiosflags(ios::showpoint)
       << setprecision(1);

  cout << "\nPlease enter " << NUM_QUIZZES << " integer quiz grades.\n\n";

  for (quiz = 0; quiz < NUM_QUIZZES; ++quiz)
    {
      cout << "\nEnter grade for quiz " << quiz + 1 << ": ";
      cin >> grade[quiz];
    }
  grade_avg = Avg(grade, NUM_QUIZZES);

  cout << "\nThe average quiz grade is " << grade_avg;

  return 0;

} // End of main()

double Avg(int arr[], int size)
{
  int    i,              // The array subscript
         sum = 0;        // The accumulator
  double avg;            // The array average

  for (i = 0; i < size; ++i)
    sum += arr[i];

avg = double(sum) / size;
```

```
    return avg;
}    // End of Avg()
```

Program Output

```
Please enter 10 integer quiz grades.

Enter grade for quiz 1: 67

Enter grade for quiz 2: 55

Enter grade for quiz 3: 83

Enter grade for quiz 4: 75

Enter grade for quiz 5: 57

Enter grade for quiz 6: 86

Enter grade for quiz 7: 58

Enter grade for quiz 8: 100

Enter grade for quiz 9: 86

Enter grade for quiz 10: 96

The average quiz grade is 76.3
```

Programming
Pointers

The program begins with the prototype declaration of the function Avg(), as we described previously. The function's first argument is an array of integers. The second argument is an integer that holds the size of the array. You may wonder why we pass the size of the array as an argument since we know that the array has 10 elements. Passing the array size to a function that manipulates an array makes the function more versatile. You can use the same function for finding the average of any array of integers, no matter how many elements are in the array.

NOTE 8.1—PASS THE SIZE OF AN ARRAY TO A FUNCTION

When you pass an array to a function, also pass the size of the array to the function. Doing so makes the function more useful because it will be able to handle arrays of any size.

The only variables that main() needs are the array grade[], the subscript variable quiz, and the variable grade_avg. It does not need an accumulator, as in dem06-2.cpp, because the function Avg() sums the array elements.

When the program begins, it prompts the user for the 10 quiz grades, which it places into the array `grade[]`. To calculate the average of the numbers in the array `grade[]`, `main()` calls the function `Avg()` by executing the following assignment.

```
grade_avg = Avg(grade, NUM_QUIZZES);
```

Programming
Pointers

`Avg()`'s first argument is the name of the array of integers that we want to pass. Note that you should use only the name of the array because we are passing a pointer to the function `Avg()`. Do not put brackets after the name. The second argument is the number of elements in the array, namely `NUM_QUIZZES`. `Avg()` returns the average of the numbers in the array `grade[]`. The assignment statement places the return value into the variable `grade_avg`. Finally, `main()` displays the value of `grade_avg`.

`Avg()`'s parameters, which are declared in the function header, are `arr` for the array and `size` for the array size. Therefore, in the function body we refer to the array by the name `arr` and the size of the array as `size`. `Avg()` uses three local variables. The variable `i` is the array subscript. The variable `sum` is the accumulator that the program uses to add the array elements. The `double` variable `avg` stores the average of the array elements.

`Avg()` begins by summing the elements in the array by using essentially the same loop as the one used in dem06-2.cpp. The only difference is that the loop test is `i < size` because the number of elements in the array is stored in the parameter `size`.

Next, the function computes the average of the array elements. The type cast `double(sum)` converts the value of `sum` to the equivalent `double` for use in the calculation. Finally, the function returns the value of `avg` to the calling program.

When we pass an array name to a function, we pass the address of the array, which is a pointer to the base of the array. We do not pass the value of an array element or a copy of the entire array. When dem08-4.cpp calls the function `Avg(grade, NUM_QUIZZES)`, it passes the address of the array `grade[]` and the value of `NUM_QUIZZES` to `Avg()`. In the function `Avg()`, the formal parameter `arr` takes on the value of the address of the array `grade[]` in the function `main()`. Thus, in `Avg()`, using `arr[]` is equivalent to using `grade[]` in `main()`. See Figure 8.6.

Sorting an Array

The function `Avg()` in dem08-4.cpp does not change any value in the array. However, if it did change a value in the array `arr[]`, it would change the corresponding value in the array `grade[]` back in the function `main()`.

NOTE 8.2—PASSING AN ARRAY TO A FUNCTION

Pass an array to a function by using the array name as an argument. Doing so passes the address of the array to the function. Therefore, any change that the function makes to the parameter array changes the array in the calling function.

The following program, dem08-5.cpp, does the same thing as dem06-4.cpp. It prompts the user to enter a 10-element array and displays the array. The program then uses the bubble sort to sort the array in increasing order. Finally, the program displays

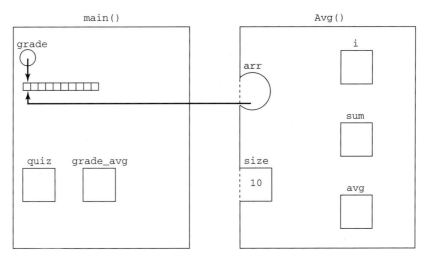

FIGURE 8.6

the sorted array. However, dem08-5.cpp uses functions to obtain the grades from the user, display the grades, and do the bubble sort.

```cpp
// dem08-5.cpp

// This program shows how to sort the elements
// in an array. It uses functions to do all array processing.
// The Swap_Int() function uses call by reference.

#include <iostream.h>
#include <iomanip.h>

using namespace std;

#define NUM_QUIZZES 10

void Get_Grades(int [], int);
void Display_Array(int [], int);
void Bubble_Sort(int [], int);
void Swap_Int(int&, int&);

int main()
{

    int grade[NUM_QUIZZES];              // The array to store the quiz grades

    Get_Grades(grade, NUM_QUIZZES);

    cout << "\n\nThe grades are as follows:";
    Display_Array(grade, NUM_QUIZZES);
```

```cpp
    Bubble_Sort(grade, NUM_QUIZZES);

    cout << "\n\nThe grades in increasing order are as follows:";
    Display_Array(grade, NUM_QUIZZES);

    return 0;

}   // End of main()

void Get_Grades(int arr[], int size)
{
  int quiz;

  cout << "\nPlease enter " << NUM_QUIZZES << " integer quiz grades.\n\n";

  for (quiz = 0; quiz < size; ++quiz)
    {
      cout << "\nEnter grade for quiz :" << quiz + 1 << ": ";
      cin >> arr[quiz];
    }

  return;

} // End of Get_Grades()

void Display_Array(int arr[], int size)
{
  int i;

  cout << endl;
  for (i = 0; i < size; ++i)
    cout << setw(6) << arr[i];
  cout << endl;
  return;

}   // End of Display_Array()

void Bubble_Sort(int arr[], int size)
{
  int i,                    // The array subscript
      pass,                 // The number of the pass
      limit = size - 2;     // Keeps track of how far to go on a pass

  for (pass = 1; pass <= size - 1; ++pass)
    {
      for (i = 0; i <= limit; ++i)
      if (arr[i] > arr[i + 1])
        Swap_Int(arr[i], arr[i + 1]);
      --limit;
```

```
    }

    return;

}    // End of Bubble_Sort()

void Swap_Int(int& a, int& b)
{
    int temp;               // Used for swapping integers

    temp = a;
    a = b;
    b = temp;

    return;
}    // End of Swap_Int()
```

Program Output

```
Please enter 10 integer quiz grades.


Enter grade for quiz 1: 40

Enter grade for quiz 2: 50

Enter grade for quiz 3: 80

Enter grade for quiz 4: 70

Enter grade for quiz 5: 80

Enter grade for quiz 6: 94

Enter grade for quiz 7: 85

Enter grade for quiz 8: 68

Enter grade for quiz 9: 73

Enter grade for quiz 10: 90

The grades are as follows:
    40    50    80    70    80    94    85    68    73    90

The grades in increasing order are as follows:
    40    50    68    70    73    80    80    85    90    94
```

The program uses four functions to do its work. The first argument in the first three functions is the name of the array that the function manipulates. Following the advice of Note 8.1 and how we defined the function `Avg()` in dem08-4.cpp, the second argument of these functions represents the size of the array. Remember that we do this to make the functions more useful. We can use these functions again should the need arise. The function `Get_Grades()` prompts for and obtains the grades from the user. `Display_Array()` displays the contents of an array. The function `Bubble_Sort()` sorts the array named as its first parameter. Finally, the fourth function, `Swap_Int()`, is the same function we used in dem08-3R.cpp. It interchanges the values of two integer variables by using call by reference.

The only variable that `main()` needs is the integer array `grade[]`. Functions accomplish the program's processing. The first function call is to `Get_Grades()`. We pass the name of the array and the size of the array to this function. `Get_Grades()` prompts the user for 10 quiz grades and uses a `for` loop to obtain the grades. Recall from the previous section that when this function refers to the formal parameter `arr[]`, it references the array `grade[]` in the function `main()`. Thus, the `cout` in the body of the `for` loop places the integer it obtains into the array `grade[]` in the function `main()`. See Figure 8.7.

Next, `main()` displays a message and calls the function `Display_Array()`. This function displays the elements in the array `grade[]`, all on one line, in the order in which the user entered them.

Now `main()` calls `Bubble_Sort()`, which sorts the elements in the array `grade[]` into ascending order. `Bubble_Sort()` uses the variable `i` as the array subscript. The variable `pass` is a counter that keeps track of the number of passes that the sort makes over the array. The `for` loop initializes the value of `pass` to one. The sort makes a total of `size` − 1 passes over an array having `size` elements. Therefore, the final value of `pass` is `size` − 1, which is reflected in the loop test condition.

The variable `limit` keeps track of how far to go on a pass. Recall from our discussion in Chapter 6 that the first pass of the bubble sort compares pairs of adjacent elements up to the last pair. Therefore, in an array with `size` elements, it compares elements 0 and 1,

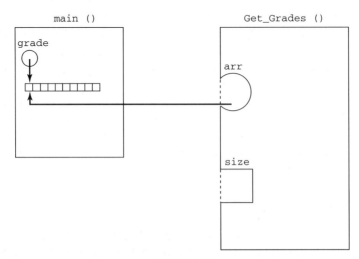

FIGURE 8.7

elements 1 and 2, elements 2 and 3, ..., elements `size − 2` and `size − 1`. Since the sort always compares an array element to the next array element, we initialize `limit` to `size − 2`. At the end of a pass, `limit` is decreased by one so that the next pass considers one less element. Remember that a pass places the next highest element at the right of the array so the sort does not have to consider this element again.

The `if` statement in the inner loop's body tests to see if the pair of adjacent array elements is out of order. If they are out of order, `Swap_Int()` interchanges the elements. If they are in order, the function does nothing to the pair.

When `main()` calls `Bubble_Sort()`, it passes the address of the array `grade[]`. `Bubble_Sort()` manipulates the elements of the array `grade[]`. When `Bubble_Sort()` finishes sorting the array, the elements of `grade[]` are in ascending order. Then, `main()` displays a message and uses `Display_Array()` to display the elements of the array `grade[]`, which are now in ascending order.

EXERCISE 8.2

In Exercises 1–3 code the prototype for the given function.

1. A function `Avg()` that has two arguments. The first argument is an array of doubles. The second argument is the size of the array. The function returns a `double`.

2. A function `Max()` that has two arguments. The first argument is an integer array and the second argument is the size of the array. The function returns an integer.

3. A function `Find_It()` that has three arguments. The first argument is an array of longs and the second argument is the size of the array. The third argument is the address of a `long`. The function returns an integer.

EXPERIMENTS 8.2

1. Rewrite dem08-4.cpp so that it finds the average of the elements in an array of longs.

2. Rewrite the `Swap_Int()` function of dem08-5.cpp so that it uses call by address rather than call by reference. Compile, execute, and test the resulting program.

3. Rewrite dem08-5.cpp so that it sorts an array of doubles.

4. Rewrite dem08-5.cpp so that it sorts the array of integers into decreasing order instead of increasing order.

5. Rewrite dem08-5.cpp so that after it asks the user to enter the integers it then asks in which order the program is to display the array. The program should then sort the array in the given order. Recode the `Bubble_Sort()` function so that it takes a third parameter, which tells it the sort order (for example, 1 for increasing, 0 for decreasing).

PROGRAMMING PROBLEMS 8.2

1. Write a program that asks the user to enter three integers. The program should use the function `Sort_Int()` to sort the three integers into increasing order. Then the program should display the three integers in increasing order.

2. Write a program that asks the user to enter up to 20 integers. Store the integers in an array. Then the program should use the function `Max()` to find the largest integer in the array. Finally, the program should display the largest integer in the array.

3. Write a program that asks the user to enter up to 20 integers. Store the integers in an array of longs. The program should then ask the user to enter an integer. The program should use the function `Find_It()` to locate the integer in the array. The third argument in `Find_It()` is the address of the found integer. The function should return 1 if the integer is found and 0 otherwise. If the integer is found, the program should replace the integer by its negative and display the elements in the array. If the integer is not found, display an appropriate message.

8.3 Strings and Functions

Since a string is equivalent to a character pointer, passing a string to a function is equivalent to passing a pointer to a function. This section discusses how to pass strings to functions. We also discuss how to define and use a function that returns a pointer.

Using a Function To Count the Characters in a String

In this section we discuss a program that asks the user to enter a string and then displays the number of characters in the string. The program uses a function `Len_String()` to count the number of characters in the string. `Len_String()` takes a string as its only argument and returns an integer equal to the number of characters in the string. The following is the prototype for the function.

```
int Len_String(char*);
```

Following is the code for dem08-6.cpp.

```
// dem08-6.cpp

// This program calculates the number of characters input by the
// user on one line. It uses the function Len_String() to count
// the characters.

#include <iostream.h>

using namespace std;

int Len_String(char*);

int main()
{
   char line[81];
```

```
cout << "\nEnter a line of characters:\n";
cin.getline(line,81);

cout << "\nThe string you entered has " << Len_String(line)
     << " characters";

return 0;

}      // End of main()

int Len_String(char* ch_ptr)
{
  int length = 0;

  while ( *ch_ptr != '\0')
    {
      ++length;
      ++ch_ptr;
    }

  return length;
}      // End of Len_String()
```

Program Output

```
Enter a line of characters:
This is a test line.

The string you entered has 20 characters
```

The only variable main() requires is the array line[], which it uses to store the string entered by the user. The program prompts the user to enter a line of characters and obtains the line using cin.getline(). Finally, the program displays the length of the string by displaying the value returned by the function call Len_String(line).

The parameter declared in the function header for Len_String() is the character pointer ch_ptr. When main() executes the call Len_String(line), it passes the value of line (which is a pointer to the first element in the array line[]) to Len_String(). The value of line is assigned to ch_ptr. In Len_String(), ch_ptr initially points to the first character in the string that is stored in line[]. See Figure 8.8. The local variable length, which represents the length of the string, is initialized to zero.

The while loop in Len_String() tests the target of ch_ptr. If the target is not the null character, which is the end of the string, then the body of the loop counts that character by incrementing the variable length. The loop then increases the pointer by one. Thus, on the next iteration of the loop, ch_ptr points to the next character in the string. When the function exits the while loop, ch_ptr points to the null

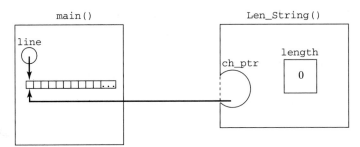

FIGURE 8.8

character and `length` equals the number of characters in the string. Therefore, the
function returns the value of `length`.

Using a Function To Reverse a String in Place

In this section we use a function to reverse a string in place, which means that the string
is reversed in the array in which it is stored. The program does not make a copy of the
string or merely display the string in reverse. Following is the code for dem08-7.cpp.

```cpp
// dem08-7.cpp

// This program uses a function to reverse a string in place

#include <iostream.h>

using namespace std;

void Reverse_String(char*);

int main()
{
   char line[81];

   cout << "\nEnter a string:\n";
   cin.getline(line, 81);
   Reverse_String(line);

   cout << "\nThe string in reverse is as follows:" << endl;
   cout << line;

   return 0;
}

void Reverse_String(char* ch_ptr)
{
   char* front;  // Points to the front of the string
```

```
   char* end;     // Points to the end of the string
   char temp;      // Required to exchange characters

// Initialize pointers

   front = end = ch_ptr;

// Find the end of the string

   while ( *end != '\0' )
     ++end;
   --end;

// Exchange characters until pointers cross

   while ( front < end )
     {
       temp   = *front;
       *front = *end;
       *end   = temp;
       ++front;
       --end;
     }

   return;
}
```

Program Output

```
Enter a string:
abcdefgh


The string in reverse is as follows:
hgfedcba
```

After obtaining the string from the user, the program makes the following function call.

```
Reverse_String(line);
```

The function `Reverse_String()` reverses the string in place. To do this, the function declares two character pointers, `front` and `end`. The function works as follows. The pointers `front` and `end` are initialized to point to the beginning of the string, which is pointed to by the parameter `ch_ptr`. Next, the function uses a `while` loop to set the pointer `end` to the end of the string. When the function exits the `while` loop, `end` points to the null character. The pointer `end` is decreased by one to make it point to the last character in the string. See Figure 8.9a.

The second `while` loop reverses the string by exchanging the characters pointed to by `front` and `end`. If the pointer `front` is less than the pointer `end`, `front` points

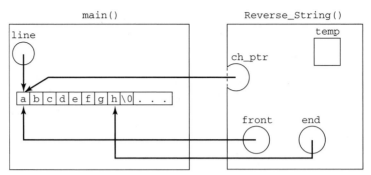

After finding the last character in the string.

(a)

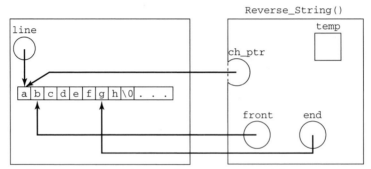

If `font` < `end`, swap characters, increment `front` and decrement `end`.

(b)

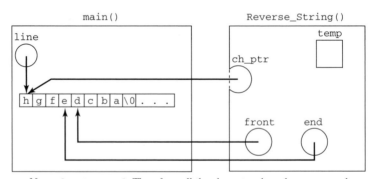

Now, `front` > `end`. Therefore, all the characters have been swapped.

(c)

FIGURE 8.9

to a character to the left of the character pointed to by end. The loop body then exchanges the characters. Next, front is incremented and end is decremented. This readies front and end for the next exchange. See Figure 8.9b.

The loop terminates when front >= end. If front > end, the string has an even number of characters. Then all the string's characters are reversed. See Figure 8.9c. If front = end, the string has an odd number of characters. Both front and end point to the middle character, which does not have to be moved. See Exercise 3.

A Function That Returns a Pointer

A function can return a pointer. Such functions are useful when processing strings. The next program, dem08-8.cpp, asks the user to enter a string. The function Locate_Blank() then attempts to find the first blank in the string. If it finds a blank, the function returns a pointer to the blank. If the function does not find a blank in the string, it returns the NULL pointer.

The prototype for Locate_Blank() shows that the return type is a pointer to a char. The only parameter is a pointer to a char, which is a string.

```
char* Locate_Blank(char*);
```

Following is the code for dem08-8.cpp

```
// dem08—8.cpp

// This program obtains a string from the user and replaces the first
// blank, if any, with a character obtained from the user. It uses a
// function that returns a pointer to the first blank, or the NULL
// pointer if the string does not contain a blank.

#include <iostream.h>

using namespace std;

char* Locate_Blank (char*);

int main()
{
  char line[81];
  char* blank_ptr;
  char ch;

  cout << "\nEnter a string:\n";
  cin.getline(line, 81);

  blank_ptr = Locate_Blank(line);
```

```
   if (blank_ptr == NULL)
      cout << "\nThe string you entered does not contain a blank.";
   else
      {
         cout << "\nEnter a character to replace the blank: ";
         ch = cin.get();
         *blank_ptr = ch;
         cout << "\nThe new string is as follows" << endl;
         cout << line;
      }

   return 0;
}

char* Locate_Blank(char* ch_ptr)
{
   while (*ch_ptr != '\0')
      {
         if (*ch_ptr == ' ')
            return ch_ptr;
         ++ch_ptr;
      }

   return NULL;
}
```

Program Output

Test Run 1

```
Enter a string:
asda sdvfsdv dffa

Enter a character to replace the blank: *

The new string is as follows
asda*sdvfsdv dffa
```

Test Run 2

```
Enter a string:
fsddfahfahfba

The string you entered does not contain a blank.
```

The function `main()` requires three variables. The character array `line[]` stores the string entered by the user. The character pointer `ch_ptr` will point to the first blank character in the string that is stored in `line[]`. The character variable `ch` stores the character that the user enters and that will be inserted in place of the first blank.

The program begins by prompting the user to enter a string and placing the string in the array `line[]`. The program then executes the following assignment.

```
blank_ptr = Locate_Blank(line);
```

`Locate_Blank()` returns a pointer to the first blank in the string, if the string contains a blank. If the string does not contain a blank, the function returns the NULL pointer. In either case, the assignment places the returned value into the pointer `blank_ptr`.

The `if` statement in `main()` tests the value of `blank_ptr`. If `blank_ptr` is NULL, the function did not find a blank in the string contained in `line[]`. Therefore, the program displays the appropriate message. If `blank_ptr` is not the NULL pointer, it points to the position of the first blank in the string that is stored in `line[]`. The program then prompts the user to enter a character. The `cin.get()` statement obtains the character, which is assigned to the variable `ch`. Then, the character in `ch` is assigned to the target of `blank_ptr`, which is the location of the first blank in the string. The program then displays the new string.

The function `Locate_Blank()` works as follows. When `main()` calls the function, the formal parameter `ch_ptr` points to the first character in the array `line[]`. See Figure 8.10a. The `while` loop tests the characters in the string. If the target of `ch_ptr` is not the null character, the loop body tests the character. If the character is a blank, the function returns the value of `ch_ptr`, which points to the first blank in the string. See Figure 8.10b. If the target of `ch_ptr` is not a blank, the `if` statement does nothing, and `ch_ptr` is incremented to point to the next character. If the `while` encounters the null character, the string does not contain a blank. Therefore, the function returns the NULL pointer.

EXERCISES 8.3

In Exercises 1–2 code the prototype for the given function.

1. A function `Count_Char()` that has two arguments. The first argument is a string and the second argument is a character. The function returns an integer.

2. A function `Find_Char()` that has two arguments. The first argument is a string and the second argument is a character pointer. The function returns a character pointer.

3. Trace the values of the pointers `front` and `end` in dem08-7.cpp when the user enters a string with an odd number of characters such as "abcdefg".

PROGRAMMING PROBLEMS 8.3

1. Write a program that first asks the user to enter a string and then asks the user to enter a character. The program should display the number of times the character appears in the string. Use the function `Count_Char()` in Exercise 1.

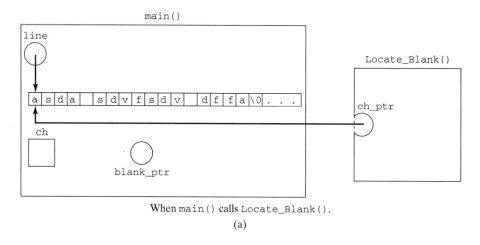

When main() calls Locate_Blank().

(a)

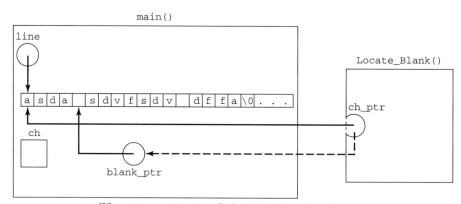

When Locate_Blank() finds a blank, the value of ch_ptr is
returned to main() and assigned to blank_ptr.

(b)

FIGURE 8.10

2. Write a program that first asks the user to enter a string and then asks the user to
   enter a character. The program should use the function Find_Char(), see
   Exercise 2, to determine the location of the first occurrence of the character in
   the string. The program should then ask the user for a replacement character.
   Then the program should replace the original character by the replacement character and display the new string.

8.4 The Standard Library String Functions

The C++ language contains about 20 library functions that manipulate strings. These
functions allow us to perform some common string operations such as finding the
length of a string, assigning one string to another, or testing the equality of two strings.
This section discusses some of the standard string functions.

The prototypes of all the string manipulation functions are in the header file **string.h**. When writing a program that uses any of the functions introduced in this section, you must follow Note 8.3.

NOTE 8.3—THE `string.h` **HEADER FILE**

A program that uses any of the string manipulation functions should contain the following preprocessor directive.

```
#include <string.h>
```

The Length of a String—The Function `strlen()`

The program dem08-6.cpp calculated the length of a string entered by the user by using the function `Len_String()`. We can also use the library function `strlen()` to find the length of a string. The function `strlen()` takes one argument, which must be a string (a character pointer), and returns the number of characters in the string. For example, consider the following declarations and assignment.

```
int length;
char greeting[6] = "Hello";
length = strlen(greeting);
```

The assignment places 5, the number of characters in the string, into the variable `length`. See Experiment 3, which asks you to rewrite dem08-6.cpp using `strlen()`.

String Assignment—The Function `strcpy()`

Using the following declarations, suppose we want to place a copy of the string `greeting1` into the string `greeting2`.

```
char greeting1[6] = "Hello";
char greeting2[10];
```

It is very tempting to code the following invalid assignment.

```
greeting2 = greeting1;  //Invalid Assignment
```

Programming
Pitfalls

However, this assignment causes a compiler error. Recall that the name of an array is a constant pointer whose value cannot change. This assignment tries to assign a new value to the array name `greeting2`, which is invalid. See Experiment 1.

To assign one string to another in C++ requires the use of a function. The library function `strcpy()` assigns one string to another by copying the source string, character by character, to the target string. The `strcpy()` function has the following format.

```
strcpy(target-string-name, source-string-name)
```

The target string must be the first argument and the source string must be the second argument. When using `strcpy()` it is very important to keep Note 8.4 in mind.

NOTE 8.4—MAKE THE TARGET OF `strcpy()` LARGE ENOUGH

When using `strcpy()`, it is the programmer's responsibility to make sure that the target string is large enough to accommodate a copy of the source string. Failure to do so could cause `strcpy()` to overwrite other variables in the program.

To copy the string `greeting1` into the string `greeting2`, we can write the following statement.

```
strcpy(greeting2, greeting1);
```

The function `strcpy()` returns a pointer to the first character in the target string. Assuming the following declaration at the beginning of the program,

```
char* ch_ptr;
```

the following assignment is valid.

```
ch_ptr = strcpy(greeting2, greeting1);
```

Thus, `ch_ptr` points to the first character of `greeting2[]`.
    You could also code the following `cout` statement.

```
cout << strcpy(greeting2, greeting1));
```

This will display the string contained in `greeting2[]`.
    We can use the fact that `greeting1` is a pointer to copy only a part of the string `greeting1` to `greeting2`. For example, the following statement copies the string "llo" to `greeting2`. See Figure 8.11a.

```
strcpy(greeting2, greeting1 + 2);
```

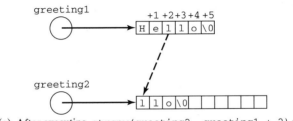

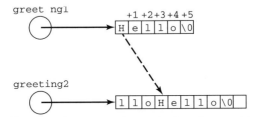

(a) After executing `strcpy(greeting2, greeting1 + 2);`

(b) After executing `strcpy(greeting2 + 3, greeting1);`

FIGURE 8.11

The `strcpy()` function begins copying characters at the address specified in its second argument and places the characters beginning at the address specified in its first argument. The following statements place the string "lloHello" into `greeting2[]`. See Figure 8.11b

```
strcpy(greeting2, greeting1 + 2);
strcpy(greeting2 + 3, greeting1);
```

Comparing Strings—The Function `strcmp()`

After copying the string `greeting1` into the string `greeting2`, suppose that we want to verify that the strings are identical. Again, it is tempting to test for equality by using the equality operator as follows.

```
greeting1 == greeting2
```

Programming
Pitfalls

However, this expression tests the array names, which are pointers, for equality. An array name is a pointer to the address of the first element of the array. Since the arrays we are comparing are different, the comparison always yields false. See Experiment 1.

To compare two strings, we can use the library function `strcmp()`, which has the following format.

```
strcmp(string1, string2)
```

TABLE 8.1

Result of the Compare	Value Returned by `strcmp()`
`string1` is identical to `string2`	0
`string1` precedes `string2`	Negative integer
`string1` follows `string2`	Positive integer

The arguments `string1` and `string2` must be strings, which are character pointers. The function `strcmp()` returns an integer based on the comparison of `string1` to `string2` according to Table 8.1.

The words "precedes" and "follows" in the previous table need some clarification. C++ stores a character as an integer (see Appendix A). The natural order of the integers gives an order to all the characters in the ASCII character set. One character precedes another if the decimal value of the first character is less than the decimal value of the second. Similarly, if the decimal value of one character is greater than the decimal value of a second character, the first character follows the second. We refer to this ordering of the characters in the ASCII character set as the **ASCII collating sequence**.

Referring to Table 8.2, we see that the character $ (decimal value 36) precedes the character + (decimal value 43). The character r (decimal value 114) follows the character R (decimal value 52).

Table 8.2 shows that all the digits precede the uppercase letters, which precede the lowercase letters. Also the digits and the uppercase and lowercase letters retain their usual order—for the digits numeric order and for the letters alphabetic order.

When `strcmp()` compares two strings, it begins comparing the first characters of each string. If the characters are equal, it compares the next pair of characters, and so on. The character-by-character comparison continues until either the end of one or both strings is encountered or until an unequal pair of characters is encountered. If an unequal pair of characters is encountered, the function returns a positive or negative number depending on how the unequal characters compare in the ASCII collating sequence. If each pair of characters is the same and the end of both strings has been encountered, the strings are identical. If each pair of characters is the same and only the end of one string has been encountered, the string with more characters follows the other string. In this case, the function returns the appropriate value. Several examples should help to clarify how `strcmp()` compares strings.

Suppose the following declarations and initializations.

```
char string1[5] = "abcd";
char string2[5] = "abCd";
char string3[7] = "abcd  ";
char string4[5] = "abCd";
```

`strcmp(string1, string2)` returns a positive integer because the character c follows the character C in the ASCII collating sequence. Note that the order in which you compare strings affects the return value. For example, `strcmp(string2, string1)` returns a negative integer because C precedes c.

TABLE 8.2

Decimal	Hex	Symbol	Decimal	Hex	Symbol	Decimal	Hex	Symbol
32	20	(blank)	64	40	@	96	60	`
33	21	!	65	41	A	97	61	a
34	22	"	66	42	B	98	62	b
35	23	#	67	43	C	99	63	c
36	24	$	68	44	D	100	64	d
37	25	%	69	45	E	101	65	e
38	26	&	70	46	F	102	66	f
39	27	'	71	47	G	103	67	g
40	28	(	72	48	H	104	68	h
41	29	)	73	49	I	105	69	i
42	2A	*	74	4A	J	106	6A	j
43	2B	+	75	4B	K	107	6B	k
44	2C	,	76	4C	L	108	6C	l
45	2D	-	77	4D	M	109	6D	m
46	2E	.	78	4E	N	110	6E	n
47	2F	/	79	4F	O	111	6F	o
48	30	0	80	50	P	112	70	p
49	31	1	81	51	Q	113	71	q
50	32	2	82	52	R	114	72	r
51	33	3	83	53	S	115	73	s
52	34	4	84	54	T	116	74	t
53	35	5	85	55	U	117	75	u
54	36	6	86	56	V	118	76	v
55	37	7	87	57	W	119	77	w
56	38	8	88	58	X	120	78	x
57	39	9	89	59	Y	121	79	y
58	3A	:	90	5A	Z	122	7A	z
59	3B	;	91	5B	[	123	7B	{
60	3C	<	92	5C	\	124	7C		
61	3D	=	93	5D	]	125	7D	}
62	3E	>	94	5E	^	126	7E	~
63	3F	?	95	5F	_			

`strcmp(string1, string3)` returns a negative integer. Although the strings are identical up to the character d, `string3` has more characters. Therefore, `string1` precedes `string3`.

`strcmp(string2, string4)` returns zero because the strings are identical.

See Experiment 2 for some hints on the exact value that `strcmp()` returns when the strings it compares are unequal.

Pasting Strings Together—The Function `strcat()`

Sometimes it is necessary to paste one string onto the end of another—a process that we call **concatenation**. For example, suppose the following declarations and initializations.

```
char string1[27] = "abcdef";
char string2[27] = "ghij";
```

Now suppose that we want to paste the contents of `string2` onto the end of the contents of `string1`. After the pasting, `string1` should contain the string "abcde-fghij". The library function `strcat()` concatenates two strings. It has the following format.

```
strcat(target-string, source-string)
```

**Programming
Pitfalls**

The function pastes the source string onto the end of the target string. It is the programmer's responsibility to ensure that the array that holds the target string is large enough to contain the result of the concatenation.

NOTE 8.5—MAKE THE TARGET OF `strcat()` LARGE ENOUGH

When using `strcat()`, it is the programmer's responsibility to make sure that the target string is large enough to accommodate a copy of the source string. Failure to do so could cause `strcat()` to overwrite other variables in the program.

Thus, to paste `string2` onto the end of `string1`, we can execute the following.

```
strcat(string1, string2);
```

See Figure 8.12. The function `strcat()` places the first character of `string2` where the null character in `string1` was located and copies the null character of `string2` into `string1`. The result is a valid string. Note also that `strcat()` does not place blanks after the original contents of `string1`. The function `strcat()` returns a pointer to the first character of the target string.

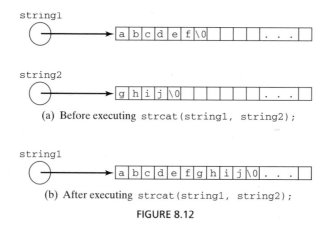

(a) Before executing strcat(string1, string2);

(b) After executing strcat(string1, string2);

FIGURE 8.12

Using the String Functions—dem08-9.cpp

The following program, dem08-9.cpp, uses the string functions that we introduced in this section. The program asks the user to enter his or her first name and last name. Then the program concatenates the first and last names to form the full name. Finally, the program asks the user to enter his or her full name. If the full name that the user enters equals the full name that the program constructed, the program displays a congratulatory message. Otherwise, the program asks the user to execute the program again.

```cpp
// dem08-9.cpp

// This program uses several string library functions

#include <iostream.h>
#include <string.h>

using namespace std;

int main()
{
   char first_name[21];
   char last_name[31];
   char full_name[51];
   char full_name_chk[51];

   cout << "\nPlease enter your first name: ";
   cin.getline(first_name, 81);

   cin.ignore(80, '\n\'); //Clear the input buffer

   cout << "\nPlease enter your last name: ";
   cin.getline(last_name, 81);

   cin.ignore(80, '\n');      //Clear the input buffer

   strcpy(full_name, first_name);
   strcat(full_name, " ");
   strcat(full_name, last_name);

   cout << "\n\nHello " << full_name << " Welcome to the program.";
   cout << "\n\nYour first name has " << strlen(first_name)
        << " characters in it.";
   cout << "\n\nYour last name has " << strlen(last_name)
        << " characters in it.";

   cout << "\n\nNow please enter your first and last names";
   cout << "\nseparated by one space: ";

   cin.getline(full_name_chk, 81);
```

```
if (strcmp(full_name, full_name_chk) == 0)
  cout << "\n\nCongratulations! You followed the instructions.";
else
{
  cout << "\nYou did not follow the instructions!";
  cout << "\nPlease try the program again.";
}

return 0;
}
```

Program Output

```
Please enter your first name: Adam

Please enter you last name: Zapple



Hello Adam Zapple. Welcome to the program.

Your first name has 4 characters in it.

Your last name has 6 characters in it.

Now please enter your first and last names
separated by one space: Adam Zapple


Congratulations! You followed the instructions.
```

The program begins with the declarations of four character arrays—one to contain the first name, one to contain the last name, one to contain the full name that the program constructs, and one to contain the full name that the user will enter.

The program begins by prompting for and obtaining the first and last names of the user. After using `cin.getline()` to obtain the user's first name and the user's last name, the program executes `cin.ignore()` to ensure that the input buffer is clear for the next execution of `cin.getline()`. See Note 7.8. Then the program constructs the user's full name. First, `strcpy()` copies `first_name` into `full_name` (Figure 8.13a). Then `strcat()` pastes a blank onto the end of the contents of `full_name` (Figure 8.13b). Finally, `strcat()` pastes `last_name` onto the end of `full_name` (Figure 8.13c).

Next, the program uses `full_name` to greet the user and displays the number of characters in the user's first and last names. The program asks the user to enter his or her first and last names separated by a space and places the name into `full_name_chk[]`. Then, `strcmp()` decides whether the contents of `full_name_chk` are the same as the contents of `full_name`, which the program constructed earlier. The program issues an appropriate message depending on the outcome of this test.

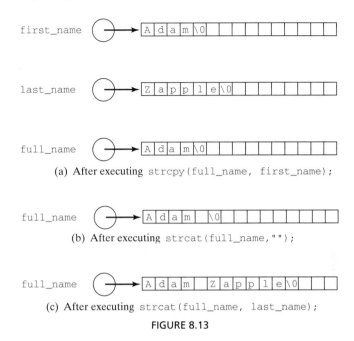

(a) After executing `strcpy(full_name, first_name);`

(b) After executing `strcat(full_name,"");`

(c) After executing `strcat(full_name, last_name);`

FIGURE 8.13

EXPERIMENTS 8.4

1. Write a short program that declares the following strings

```
char string1[] = "Hello";
char string2[] = "Hello";
```

and attempts to test the strings for equality by testing the following condition.

```
if (string1 == string2)
```

Attempt to compile the program. If it compiles successfully, try to execute the program. What are the results?

2. In this chapter you learned that `strcmp()` returns a negative integer if its first argument precedes its second, and a positive integer if its first argument follows its second. Try to discover exactly what integer is returned by `strcmp()` when its arguments are not equal. As a hint, display the values `strcmp()` returns for the following pairs of strings.

       "abcde"   "abdde"

       "abcde"   "abede"

"abcde"   "abbde"

"abcde"   "abade"

3. Rewrite dem08-6.cpp using the library function `strlen()` instead of the user-defined function `Len_String()`.

PROGRAMMING PROBLEMS 8.4

1. Write your own string assignment function `Copy_String()`. The function should copy the string that is its second argument to the string that is its first argument. The function should return a pointer to the first character of the first argument. Test your function by calling it from a simple program.

2. Write your own string compare function `Comp_String()`. The function should take two string arguments and return an integer. The function should return 0 if the strings that are its arguments are equal. If the first string follows the second, the function should return a positive number. If the first string precedes the second, the function should return a negative integer. (To help decide which number to return, see Experiment 2.) Write a program that thoroughly tests your function.

3. Write your own string concatenation function `Cat_String()`. The function should have two string arguments and should paste the second argument onto the end of the first. The function should return a pointer to the first character of the first argument. Write a program that thoroughly tests your function.

4. Write a program that constructs a user ID number from the user's first name, last name, and social security number. The program should prompt the user to enter his or her first name, last name, and social security number. Construct the ID number by taking the first two letters of the last name, followed by the second letter of the first name, followed by the middle three digits of the social security number. All characters are to be converted to uppercase. (For example, the ID number of Ron Zoni who has social security number 123456789 is ZOO456.) The program should then display the newly constructed ID number. Finally, the program should prompt the user to enter the ID number. If the user correctly enters the number, congratulate the user and end the program. If the user does not enter the correct ID number, display it again and ask the user to memorize the ID number. Then end the program.

5. Write a program that asks the user to enter a list of words, one at a time. Store the words in a two-dimensional character array, one word in each row. Assume that no word is more than 20 characters long and that there are at most 100 words. The program should then sort the array of words into increasing alphabetical order. Once the array is sorted, the program should display the alphabetized list.

6. Write a program that validates a date entered by the user. The program should ask the user to enter the month, day, and year. The month is to be entered by name and the day and year as integers. For example, the user might enter March, 30, and 1999 for the month, day, and year. The function `Validate_Date()` should determine if the entered date is valid by returning 1 if the date is valid and 0 otherwise.

For example, the date March 30, 1999 is valid, but the date February 29, 1998 is not. The program should display an appropriate message. Recall that a leap year is a year that is divisible by four. Remember to validate the month name.

8.5 Character Classification and Conversion Functions

The standard C++ library contains several functions that are useful in string manipulation programs. In this section we consider two groups of such functions—the character classification functions and the character conversion functions.

The Character Classification Functions

It is sometimes necessary to classify characters according to common categories. For example, it may be necessary to decide whether a character is a punctuation character. Table 8.3 lists some C++ standard library character classification functions. All the functions names begin with "is" and take a single argument of type `int`. Remember that you can store a character in a variable of type `int`. These functions also work properly if passed an argument of type `char`. Each function returns a nonzero (that is, true) value if the tested character is in the specified category, and returns zero (that is, false) if the character is not in the specified category. The prototypes of the functions are in the header file `ctype.h`.

The following program, dem08-10.cpp, illustrates some character classification functions. It asks the user to enter a string and counts the number of characters in several categories.

```
// dem08—10.cpp

// This program asks the user to enter a string. It uses the
// character classification functions to count the number of
// characters in several categories and displays the results.
```

TABLE 8.3 Character Classification Functions

Prototypes in `ctype.h`	
Function name	Category
`isalnum(ch)`	A digit or letter (either case)
`isalpha(ch)`	A letter (either case)
`isdigit(ch)`	The digits 0 through 9
`islower(ch)`	A lowercase letter
`ispunct(ch)`	A punctuation character (that is, a character that is not a space, digit, or letter)
`isspace(ch)`	A white space character (blank, new-line, carriage return, vertical tab, or form feed)
`isupper(ch)`	An uppercase letter

```cpp
#include <iostream.h>
#include <ctype.h>
#include <iomanip.h>

using namespace std;

int main()
{
  char line[81];
  char* ch_ptr;
  int digit_count = 0,
      lower_count = 0,
      punct_count = 0,
      space_count = 0,
      upper_count = 0,
      total_chars;

  cout << "\nEnter a line of characters:\n";
  cin.getline(line, 81);

  ch_ptr = line;

  while (*ch_ptr != '\0')
    {
      if (isdigit(*ch_ptr))
      ++digit_count;
      else if (islower(*ch_ptr))
      ++lower_count;
      else if (ispunct(*ch_ptr))
      ++punct_count;
      else if (isspace(*ch_ptr))
      ++space_count;
      else if (isupper(*ch_ptr))
      ++upper_count;
      ++ch_ptr;
    }

  total_chars = digit_count + lower_count + punct_count
                + space_count + upper_count;

  cout <<"\nThe string contains the following:";
  cout <<"\n\nDigits:                  " << digit_count;
  cout <<"\nLowercase Letters:       " << setw(2) << lower_count;
  cout <<"\nPunctuation Characters:  " << setw(2) << punct_count;
  cout <<"\nWhite Space Characters:  " << setw(2) << space_count;
  cout <<"\nUppercase Letters:       " << setw(2) << upper_count;
  cout <<"\n--------------------------";
  cout <<"\nTotal Characters:        " << setw(2) << total_chars;

  return 0;
}
```

Program Output

```
Enter a line of characters:
ahlAd,,.>  B33@?,a  ;jjccMM.

The string contains the following:

Digits:               3
Lowercase Letters:    8
Punctuation Characters:  9
White Space Characters:  3
Uppercase Letters:    4
------------------------
Total Characters:     27
```

The program counts only three white space characters. There are two blanks after the > character and there is a tab character after the ,a characters. Note also that the >, @, and ? are counted as punctuation characters.

The program itself is simple. After obtaining the string from the user, a while loop tests each character in the string. A nested if statement tests the character to see in which of the five categories the character belongs and then increments the appropriate accumulator. When the loop ends, the program displays the results.

The Character Conversion Functions

The standard C++ library also contains several functions that are useful for converting individual characters.

If the int variable ch contains a lowercase letter, the function toupper(ch) returns the corresponding uppercase letter as an integer. If the int variable ch contains an uppercase letter, the function tolower(ch) returns the corresponding lowercase letter as an integer. In all other cases, the functions return the argument unchanged. Both function prototypes are contained in ctype.h.

The program dem08-11.cpp asks the user to enter a string and then displays the string first in all uppercase and then in all lowercase.

```cpp
// dem08—11.cpp

// This program asks the user to enter a string and then uses the
// functions toupper() and tolower() to display the strings in all
// uppercase and all lowercase.

#include <iostream.h>
#include <ctype.h>

using namespace std;

int main()
{
    char line[81];
```

```
    char* ch_ptr;

    cout <<"\nEnter a line of characters:\n";
    cin.getline(line, 81);

    cout <<"\nThe line in all uppercase is:\n";
    ch_ptr = line;
    while (*ch_ptr != '\0')
      {
         cout << char(toupper(*ch_ptr));
         ++ch_ptr;
      }

    cout <<"\nThe line in all lowercase is:\n";
    ch_ptr = line;
    while (*ch_ptr != '\0')
      {
         cout << char(tolower(*ch_ptr));
         ++ch_ptr;
      }

    return 0;
}
```

Program Output

```
Enter a line of characters:
abc123.;]XYZ

The line in all uppercase is:
ABC123.;]XYZ
The line in all lowercase is:
abc123.;]xyz
```

Both parts of the program work in essentially the same way, so we will explain how the program displays the line in all uppercase. After obtaining the string from the user, the program initializes the pointer ch_ptr to the first character in the array line[]. The while loop then converts and displays each character in the string.

The function toupper() returns in integer form the uppercase version of the target of ch_ptr if the target is a lowercase letter. Otherwise, it returns the target of ch_ptr unchanged. Since the return value of toupper() is an integer, we must type cast the return value so that cout displays the value in character form rather than in integer form. See Experiment 2. After cout displays the returned character, the pointer ch_ptr is incremented so it points to the next character on the next loop iteration.

Putting the Functions to Work—Testing for a Palindrome

The words "otto" and "mom" are **palindromes**—they read the same forward and backward. A string can also be a palindrome if we ignore spacing, case, and punctuation. For example, the string "Madam, I'm Adam" is a palindrome. In this subsection we develop program prb08-1.cpp, which asks the user to enter a string (up to 80 characters) and decides whether the string is a palindrome.

In principle it is simple to decide if a word is a palindrome. Check to see if the first and last characters are the same. If they are not equal, the string is not a palindrome. If they are equal, check the second and next to last characters. If they are unequal, the string is not a palindrome. If they are equal, move to the next pair of characters and continue checking. See Figure 8.14a. If you arrive at the middle of the word and all pairs of characters are equal, the word is a palindrome. See Figure 8.14b.

When checking a string to see if it is a palindrome, we must be aware that the string can contain blanks, mixed case letters, and punctuation characters. Therefore, to test a string we must first rid the string of all blanks and punctuation characters, and then change all the characters to a common case. The pseudocode for the palindrome problem follows.

> Prompt for and obtain a string.
>
> Copy only the alphabetic characters to form a new string.
>
> Convert the new string, which is a single word, to lowercase.
>
> Test the resulting word for a palindrome.

Suppose that the user enters the string "Madam, I'm Adam!" and the program stores the string in the array line[]. See Figure 8.15a. To clear the string of blanks and punctuation characters, the program copies the string into another array, buffer[]. If the character to be copied is an alphabetic character, the program copies it. Otherwise, the program does not copy it and skips to the next character. See Figure 8.15b. Next, the program changes all the characters in buffer[] to lowercase. See Figure 8.15c. Finally, the program checks to see if the resulting word is a palindrome. See Figure 8.15d.

Following is the code and a sample program run for prb08-1.cpp.

```
// prb08—1.cpp

// This program uses the string and character library functions to
// decide whether a string entered by the user is a palindrome.
// A palindrome is a string that, disregarding case and punctuation,
// reads the same backward and forward.

#include <iostream.h>
#include <ctype.h>

using namespace std;
```

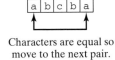

Characters are equal so
move to the next pair.

FIGURE 8.14a

All pairs are equal so
word is a palindrome.

FIGURE 8.14b

line

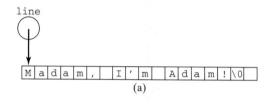

(a)

line

buffer

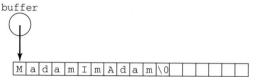

(b) Copy only alphabetic characters into buffer.
Do not copy nonalphabetic characters.

buffer

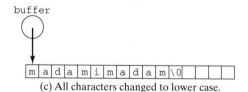

(c) All characters changed to lower case.

buffer

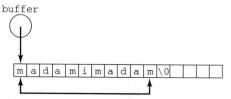

(d) Check all pairs of characters to test for palindrome.

FIGURE 8.15

```
void Copy_Alpha(char*, char*);
void Convert_To_Lower(char*);
int  Palindrome(char *);

int main()
{
  char line[81];
  char buffer[81];

  // Prompt for and obtain a string
```

```cpp
    cout <<"\nEnter a string: \n";
    cin.getline(line, 81);

    // Copy only the alphabetic characters

    Copy_Alpha(buffer, line);

    // Convert the string to all lowercase

    Convert_To_Lower(buffer);

    // Test the result for a palindrome

    if ( Palindrome(buffer) )
      cout <<"\nThe string you entered is a palindrome.";
    else
      cout <<"\nThe string you entered is not a palindrome.";

    return 0;

} // End of main()


void Copy_Alpha(char* target, char* source)
{
  while (*source != '\0')
    {
      if (isalpha(*source))
        {
          *target = *source;
          ++target;
        }
        ++source;
    }
  *target = '\0';

  return;

} // End of Copy_Alpha()

void Convert_To_Lower(char* source)
{
  while (*source != '\0')
    {
      *source = tolower(*source);
      ++source;
    }

  return;

} // End of Convert_To_Lower()
```

```
int Palindrome (char* source)
{
  char* start;
  char* end;

  start = end = source;

  while (*end != '\0')
    ++end;

  --end;

  while (start < end)
    if (*start != *end)
      return 0;
    else
      {
        ++start;
        --end;
      }

  return 1;

} // End of Palindrome()
```

Program Output

```
Enter a string:
Madam, I'm Adam!

The string you entered is a palindrome.
```

The header file `ctype.h` is included at the beginning of the program because the program's functions use several standard library character classification and conversion functions. The program handles each of the major steps in the pseudocode by executing a function. `Copy_Alpha()` takes the string that is its second argument and copies only the alphabetic characters into the string that is its first argument. The prototype for the function declares it as a `void` function with two arguments that are character pointers.

The function `Convert_To_Lower()` converts the string that is its argument to all lowercase. Thus, we declare it as a `void` function with a single argument that is a character pointer.

Finally, the function `Palindrome()` tests the string that is its only argument. It assumes that the string is a single word. If the string is a palindrome, the function returns 1. If the string is not a palindrome, the function returns 0. The function's return type is `int`.

The program begins by prompting the user for a string and placing it in the array `line[]`. The program then executes the function `Copy_Alpha()`, which copies only the alphabetic characters from `line[]` into the array `buffer[]`. To do this, the function tests each character in the string pointed to by `source`, which is the string stored in `line[]`. If the character is an alphabetic character, the target of `source` is assigned to the target of the pointer `target` and the pointer `target` is incremented. The pointer `source` is then incremented to point to the next character. Thus, if the character that was tested is not alphabetic, it is not copied. When the function exits the `while` loop, the "cleaned" string has been copied to the target string except for the null character. Therefore, the function assigns the null character to the target of the pointer `target`.

Next, `main()` executes the function `Convert_To_Lower()`, which converts all the characters in the array `buffer[]` to lowercase. The function does this by replacing each character in the string by its lowercase equivalent.

Finally, `main()` tests the returned value of the function `Palindrome()`. If the value is 1 (remember that C++ considers a nonzero value true), the string stored in `buffer[]` is a palindrome and the program displays an appropriate message. If the value is 0 (that is, false), the string stored in `buffer[]` is not a palindrome and the program displays an appropriate message.

The `Palindrome()` function begins by initializing the character pointers `start` and `end` to point to the beginning of the string being tested. The first `while` loop slides the pointer `end` to the null character at the end of the string. Then `end` is decremented so that it points to the last character in the string. Now, `start` points to the first character in the string and `end` points to the last character in the string. See Figure 8.16a. The `if` statement in the body of the next `while` loop tests the characters pointed to by `start` and `end`. If they are unequal, the string is not a palindrome and the function returns 0. Otherwise, `start` is incremented and `end` is decremented. Thus, `start` and `end` point to the next pair of characters to be tested. See Figure 8.16b. The `while` loop continues as long as `start` is less than `end`. If at some point `start` equals `end`, there is an odd number of characters in the string. The middle character equals itself and all pairs of characters tested are equal. See Figure 8.16c. If at some point `start` exceeds `end`, there is an even number of characters in the string. In either case, all pairs of characters tested are equal and, therefore, the string is a palindrome. The function then returns 1.

Numeric Conversion Functions and Numeric Validation

Suppose the following declaration and statements.

```
int i;

cout << "\nEnter an integer: ";

cin >> i;
```

Consider what happens when the user enters an integer, for example 173. The entered "integer" is actually a three-character string, which is stored in the input buffer. The `cin` statement converts the three-character string into the equivalent binary integer (10101101) and then stores the binary in the integer variable `i`. The conversion is completely automatic and transparent to the programmer and user.

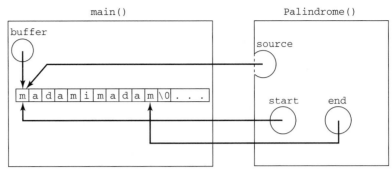

Initially, start points to the first character and end points to the last character.

(a)

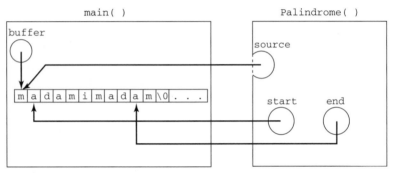

If first pair are equal, increment start and decrement end to point to the next pair.

(b)

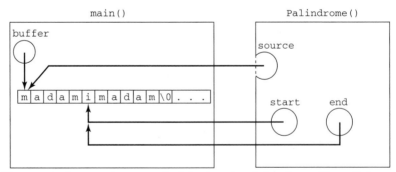

If start equals end and no unequal pair has been found, then the word is a palindrome.

(c)

FIGURE 8.16

Although using cin is very easy and intuitive, it is not very safe. If the user enters a non-integer in response to the prompt, the result is unpredictable as shown in the output to dem08-12.cpp. You will probably obtain different output on your computer.

```
//dem08-12.cpp

#include <iostream.h>

using namespace std;

int main()
{
    int i;

    cout << "\nEnter an integer: ";

    cin >> i;

    cout << "\nThe value of i is " << i;

    return 0;
}
```

Program Output

```
Enter an integer: ASD

The value of i is 18169
```

If the user makes this type of mistake in a program in which arithmetic is done on the entered value, the results of the program will be in error. To avoid this, the program can place the user's response into a character array, using for example `cin.getline()`, and then test the string to see if it represents an integer (or other type of data that the program requires). If the program determines that the entered data is a valid integer, the program must convert the string into the equivalent number. There are three standard library functions that can make the conversion from a string into a number—`atoi()`, which converts a string into an integer; `atol()`, which converts a string into a `long`; and `atof()`, which converts a string into a `double`. To use these functions, you must place `#include <stdlib.h>` in your program.

NOTE 8.6—NUMERIC CONVERSION FUNCTIONS

The following functions convert a numeric string into a number. In each case, the function returns the number that the numeric string represents. Each function stops converting the string when it encounters a non-numeric character. If the function cannot convert the string into a number, the function returns zero. You must code `#include <stdlib.h>` to use the functions.

`atoi()`–converts a numeric string into an integer.

`atol()`–converts a numeric string into a long.

`atof()`–converts a numeric string into a double.

For example, consider the following declarations and assignment.

```
char char_int[] = "123";
char char_long[] = "50000";
char char_double[] = "67.89";

int i;
long long_i;
double db;

i = atoi(char_int);
long_i = atol(char_long);
db = atof(char_double);
```

In the first assignment, `atoi(char_int)` converts the character string "123" into the equivalent integer and stores it in the `int` variable i. The second assignment works in a similar way, converting the string "50000" into the equivalent `long` and storing it in `long_i`. The third assignment converts the string "67.89", which is stored in `char_double[]`, into the equivalent `double` and stores the `double` in the variable db.

The following program illustrates the use of `atoi()`. Using `atoi()` and `atof()` are similar.

```
//dem08-13.cpp

#include <iostream.h>
#include <stdlib.h>

using namespace std;

int main()
{
   char buffer[51];

   int i;

   cout << "\nEnter an integer: ";
   cin.getline(buffer, 51);

   i = atoi(buffer);

   cout << "\nThe value of i is " << i;

   return 0;
}
```

Program Output—Valid Data

```
Enter an integer: 173

The value of i is 173
```

Program Output—Invalid Data

```
Enter an integer: ASD

The value of i is 0
```

In the program, the input data is placed into the character array `buffer[]` using `cin.getline()`. Then the function `atoi()` converts the input string into the equivalent integer. Note how this works with valid input data and with invalid input data. With valid data, this program behaves like dem08-12.cpp. However, with invalid input data, the program places 0 into `i` because the `atoi()` function cannot convert the string into an integer.

The real power of this technique for inputting numeric data as a character string and then converting it into a number lies in the ability to validate the string as an integer (or decimal number) and then, if it is valid, to convert the string into an integer (or `double`.) Program dem08-14.cpp illustrates the technique.

```cpp
//dem08-14.cpp

#include <iostream.h>
#include <stdlib.h>
#include <ctype.h>

using namespace std;

int Validate_Integer(char*);

int main()
{
  char buffer[51];

  int i;

  cout << "\nEnter an integer: ";

  cin.getline(buffer, 51);

  if (Validate_Integer(buffer))
    {
      i = atoi(buffer);
      cout << "\nThe value of i is " << i;
    }
  else
    cout << "\nYou did not enter a valid integer.";

  return 0;
}

int Validate_Integer(char* ch_ptr)
{
```

```
//Skip initial white space

while ( isspace(*ch_ptr) && *ch_ptr != '\0')
  ++ch_ptr;

//If an empty line was input, return 0

if (*ch_ptr == '\0')
  return 0;

//Skip a leading plus or minus

if (*ch_ptr == '-' || *ch_ptr == '+')
  ++ch_ptr;

//Traverse string until a non-digit or end of the string

while (isdigit(*ch_ptr) && *ch_ptr != '\0')
  ++ch_ptr;

//If the end of the string was reached, the string is an integer
if (*ch_ptr == '\0')
  return 1;
else
  return 0;
}
```

Program Output—Valid Data

```
Enter an integer:    -1234

The value of i is -1234
```

Program Output—Invalid Data—Run 1

```
Enter an integer: ASD

You did not enter a valid integer.
```

Program Output—Invalid Data—Run 2

```
Enter an integer: 123A

You did not enter a valid integer.
```

The program uses the function `Validate_Integer()` to validate user input. The function's argument is the character array in which the string to be tested is stored. The function returns 1 if the string represents a valid integer, and returns 0 otherwise. In `main()`, the user is prompted for an integer. The input data is stored as a string in the array `buffer[]` using `cin.getline()`. The `if` statement tests the value returned by `Validate_Integer()`. If the integer string is valid, the string is converted into an integer and stored in the variable `i`. If the integer string is not valid, an error message is displayed.

The function `Validate_Integer()` works by testing the string one character at a time. First, a `while` loop skips all white space. It is possible that the user entered an empty line (that is, responded to the prompt by hitting the enter key). The `if` statement tests to see if the target of `ch_ptr` is the null byte. If it is, then the user did not enter any non-white space characters and the function returns zero. Assuming the function did not return to the calling program, the target of the pointer `ch_ptr` must be a non-white space character. The next `if` statement skips a leading + or – sign. If no sign is present, the `if` statement does nothing. The next `while` loop moves through the string one character at a time until it reaches a non-digit or the end of the string. Recall that when a `while` loop ends, the loop condition is false. Either the target of `ch_ptr` is not a digit or the target of `ch_ptr` is the null character. The last `if` statement decides why the previous `while` loop stopped. If the target of `ch_ptr` is the null character, the pointer went through the entire string without encountering a non-digit. Therefore, the user entered an integer and the function returns 1. Otherwise, the string contains a non-digit and the function returns 0.

EXERCISES 8.5

1. Write a function that returns 1 if its character argument is a digit, a letter, or a space, and returns 0 otherwise. Use as many library functions as you can.

2. Write a function `Invert_Case()` that has one argument, which is a string. The function should not return a value. The function should reverse the case of the characters in the string. Thus, a lowercase letter should get converted to uppercase and vice versa. A non-letter should not be changed.

3. Write a function `Validate_Double()` that validates a numeric string to see if it represents a valid decimal number. Remember that a decimal number can begin with a leading sign and can contain only one decimal point. There can be any number of digits to the left and right of the decimal point. The function should return 1 if the sting is valid; otherwise it should return 0.

EXPERIMENTS 8.5

1. Replace the nested `if` statement in dem08-10 by an equivalent `switch` statement. Compile, execute, and test the resulting program.

2. Remove the type casts from the `cout` statements in dem08-11.cpp. Compile and execute the resulting program. Explain the program's output.

3. Enter 17A in response to the prompt in dem08-13.cpp. What happens? Explain.

4. Recode dem08-13.cpp so that it asks for and validates a double.

5. Write a program that asks the user to enter a decimal number. Use the function `Validate_Double()` in Exercise 3 to validate the user's response.

1. Recode Programming Problem 1, Section 5.3, to include validation of the number of years entered by the user. The entered value must be a valid integer.
2. Recode Programming Problem 2, Section 5.3, to include validation of the credit limit and account balance. Both must be valid decimal numbers. Use the function `Validate_Double()` from Exercise 3.
3. Take any program that you previously wrote and include validation of any integer and decimal input data.

8.6 Dynamic Memory Allocation

The Heap

In program prb07-1.cpp of Chapter 7, we stored the names of the days of the week using a two-dimensional array. However, we saw in the program prb07-2.cpp that we could use memory more efficiently by using an array of pointers to store these names. This was possible because we knew the values of the strings that we wanted to store, namely the names of the days of the week.

Now, suppose that we want to write a program that needs to store the names of five clients, which are to be entered into the program by the user. You could store the names in a two-dimensional array, one name in each row. The problem with this method is that all the rows must be the same size. Therefore, you must ensure that the rows are large enough to store the longest name. Suppose that the longest name that you can imagine is 80 characters long. You must declare the array as follows.

```
char client[5][81];
```

Programming
Pitfalls

The array `client[][]` requires 5 × 81 = 405 bytes of storage. However, the average name may have only 15 to 20 characters. You probably will waste about 300 or more of the 405 bytes allocated to the array `client[][]`. By emulating what we did in Chapter 7, can we save memory by using an array of pointers instead of a two-dimensional array? The problem we have if we try using an array of pointers is that we do not know in advance the values of the strings we need to store as we did in Chapter 7 for the names of the days of the week. Somehow we must have the user enter a name and then store this name in the computer's memory using an appropriate amount of storage.

Programming
Pointers

In C++ it is possible to allocate memory for variables, arrays, and so on from a special area of memory called the **heap**, whenever the memory is needed by the program. Heap memory is completely under your control in the sense that you can allocate and de-allocate the memory when you deem it necessary. The process of allocating and de-allocating memory as a program is executing is called **dynamic memory allocation**.

The C++ operator `new` allocates heap memory, and the operator `delete` de-allocates heap memory. The operator `new` takes one argument, the data type of the storage we want to allocate, and returns a pointer to the allocated space. For example, assume the following.

```
int* i_ptr;
i_ptr = new int;
```

The operator `new` allocates enough heap storage to store an integer and returns a pointer to that storage. The assignment statement then assigns that pointer to `i_ptr`. See Figure 8.17. If there is not enough free heap storage to satisfy the allocation request, `new` returns the null pointer.

As another example, the following assigns the pointer `arr_ptr` to point to enough heap space to store an array of 20 integers.

```
int* arr_ptr;
arr_ptr = new int [20];
```

To properly code a `new` statement, follow Note 8.7.

NOTE 8.7—HOW TO CODE THE `new` STATEMENT

To code a `new` statement,

1. Write an equivalent variable declaration.
2. Remove the variable name from the declaration.
3. Place the keyword `new` in front.
4. Assign the result to a pointer of the appropriate type.

To allocate space for an array of 20 integers:

1. Write an equivalent variable declaration for an array of 20 integers.

```
int arr[20];
```

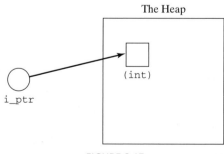

The Heap

(int)

i_ptr

FIGURE 8.17

2. Remove the variable name from the declaration.

```
int [20];
```

3. Place the keyword `new` in front.

```
new int [20];
```

4. Assign the result to a pointer of the appropriate type.

```
arr_ptr = new int [20];
```

To de-allocate space that has been previously allocated using `new`, use the operator `delete`. The operator `delete` takes one argument, namely a pointer to the space on the heap that is to be de-allocated. Thus, the following de-allocates the heap space that was previously allocated by `new`.

```
delete i_ptr;
```

Programming
Pointers

Take care to understand what `delete` does not do—`delete` does not delete the pointer that is its argument. It de-allocates the space pointed to by the pointer so the space can be reused by the system. The pointer itself is still available for use in the program.

Programming
Pointers

Note how to use `delete` to de-allocate space for an array. Assuming that `arr_ptr` points to an array of 20 integers as shown previously, the following de-allocates that space.

```
delete [] arr_ptr;
```

Static, Automatic, and Heap Memory

Heap memory is different from the other areas of memory that your C++ program uses, namely static and automatic memory. If you declare a variable as static by using the `static` keyword or by declaring the variable outside a function, the space for the variable is allocated in static storage before the program begins. The computer de-allocates space for static variables only when `main()` ends. An automatic variable, that is a variable declared inside a block, is created in an area called the stack when the program enters the block. See Variable Attributes in Section 5.2. Such variables are de-allocated when the program exits the block. Space for automatic variables is allocated and de-allocated as the program is running. However, the allocation and de-allocation are done automatically by C++. The programmer has no control over when to allocate and de-allocate automatic variables. Heap storage, on the other hand, is completely under your control. You decide when to allocate and de-allocate heap storage.

Programming
Pointers

Note also that storage allocated on the heap is independent of the block in which the storage is allocated. Thus, if a program allocates heap storage in a function, be sure to de-allocate that storage before the function ends. Failure to do so will result in the system being unable to reuse that storage later in the program. For example, consider the following program outline.

```
int main()
{
  void Func();

  Func();

  return 0;
}

void Func()
{
  int* i_ptr;

  i_ptr = new int;

  *i_ptr = 17;
}
```

The variable `i_ptr`, which points to space for an integer on the heap, is a local automatic variable. Therefore, `i_ptr` ceases to exist when the function `Func()` ends. Thus, the only way we had to access the heap storage in which we stored 17 is now lost. There is no way for `main()` to access or de-allocate the heap storage that was allocated in `Func()`.

NOTE 8.8—DE-ALLOCATE HEAP STORAGE

Before exiting a function, be sure to use the operator `delete` to de-allocate any heap storage that was allocated with the operator `new`.

The Program dem08-15.cpp

Suppose a program requires that you store the names of five clients. The program dem08-15.cpp shows how to dynamically allocate heap space to store the five names in such a way that no storage is wasted.

```
// dem08-15.cpp

// This program illustrates the use of new and delete to dynamically
// allocate storage for an array.

#include <iostream.h>
#include <stdlib.h>
```

```
#include <string.h>

using namespace std;

#define SIZE 5

int main()
{
  char  buffer[81];
  char* client[SIZE];
  int   i;

  cout << "\nEnter " << SIZE << " names.\n";

  for (i = 0; i < SIZE; ++i)
    {
      cout << "\nName: ";
      cin.getline(buffer, 81);

      cin.ignore(80, '\n'); //Clear the input buffer

      client[i] = new char [strlen(buffer) + 1];
      strcpy(client[i], buffer);
    }

  cout << "\nFollowing are the names you entered.\n\n";

  for (i = 0; i < SIZE; ++i)
    cout << endl << client[i];

  for (i = 0; i < SIZE; ++i)
    delete [] client[i];

  return 0;
}
```

Program Output

```
Enter 5 names.

Name: Maria Anne

Name: Charles Anthony Thomas

Name: John Charles

Name: Larrabee

Name: Socrates
```

```
Following are the names you entered.

Maria Ann
Charles Anthony Thomas
John Charles
Larrabee
Socrates
```

In the first `for` loop, the program asks for and stores five names. When the user enters a name, the program places it into the character array `buffer[]`, which is large enough to hold the largest name. (Note that we call the member function `cin.ignore()` after calling `cin.getline()`. This ensures that the input buffer is clear when `cin.getline()` executes on the next iteration of the `for` loop.) The pointer `client[i]` is then assigned the value returned by `new`, which allocates `strlen(buffer) + 1` bytes on the heap for a character array. This is just enough heap space to store the string that is in `buffer[]`. Finally, the function `strcpy()` copies the string from `buffer[]` to the space pointed to by `client[i]`.

To verify that the names are actually saved, the second `for` loop displays the five names in the order in which they are stored. The last `for` loop de-allocates the space previously allocated by `new`.

A Second Example

Suppose that we must write a program that enters an unspecified number of doubles into an array. We could allocate space for a large number of doubles, say 100, and store the numbers in this array. If, however, we only enter a few numbers, the bulk of the space taken by the array is wasted. The following program, dem08-16.cpp, shows how to initially create the array of size 100, and then after the numbers are entered, replace the array with a smaller one that contains the same numbers.

```
// dem08-16.cpp

// This program demonstrates the use of new and delete to
// dynamically allocate heap storage.

#include <iostream.h>
#include <stdlib.h>
#include <ctype.h>

using namespace std;

int main()
{
    double* numbers;      // pointer to an array of doubles
    double* temp_nums;    // pointer to a temporary array
    int     count,        // number of doubles entered
            i;
```

```cpp
char     response;

// Allocate space for an array of 100 doubles

numbers = new double [100];

// Obtain doubles from the user

cout << "\nDo you want to enter a number(Y/N): ";
response = cin.get();

i = 0;
while (toupper(response) == 'Y')
  {
    cout << "\nEnter a number: ";
    cin >> numbers[i];
    ++i;
    cin.get();      //To remove the newline character from the buffer
    cout << "\nDo you want to enter a number(Y/N): ";
    response = cin.get();
  }
// Save the number of numbers in count

count = i;

// Allocate just enough space for the numbers entered

temp_nums = new double [count];

// Copy the numbers from the original array to the new array

for (i = 0; i < count; ++i)
  temp_nums[i] = numbers[i];

// Deallocate the old space

delete [] numbers;

// Set numbers to point to the smaller array

numbers = temp_nums;

// Display the numbers in the array

for (i = 0; i < count; ++i)
  cout << "\nnumbers[" << i << "] = " << numbers[i];

return 0;
}
```

Program Output

```
Do you want to enter a number(Y/N): y

Enter a number: 12.3

Do you want to enter a number(Y/N): y

Enter a number: 35.6

Do you want to enter a number(Y/N): y

Enter a number: 55.789

Do you want to enter a number(Y/N): y

Enter a number: 4

Do you want to enter a number(Y/N): n

numbers[0] = 12.3
numbers[1] = 35.6
numbers[2] = 55.789
numbers[3] = 4
```

The program begins by allocating enough space for an array of 100 doubles. See Figure 8.18a. The program then uses a loop to ask the user to enter numbers. The variable i counts the numbers as they are entered. When the program exits the loop, the value of i is stored in count. See Figure 8.18b. Next, the program allocates just enough heap storage to store an array of count doubles. The for loop then copies the numbers from the original array to the newly allocated array. See Figure 8.18c. The delete [] numbers statement de-allocates the storage that numbers pointed to—the original array in which the numbers were stored. Then, the pointer numbers is set to point to the newly allocated space. See Figure 8.18d. Finally, the last for loop displays the numbers in the array. See Programming Problem 1 for another approach to this problem.

EXERCISES 8.6

1. Write C++ statements that declare a double pointer d_ptr and assign to that pointer space on the heap for storing an array of 100 doubles.

2. Write C++ statements that declare an integer pointer i_ptr and assign to i_ptr space on the heap for storing an array of 50 integers.

In Exercises 3–6, locate and correct any syntax errors.

3. ```
int* i_ptr;
i_ptr = new;
```
```

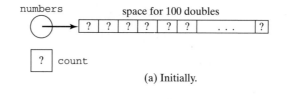

(a) Initially.

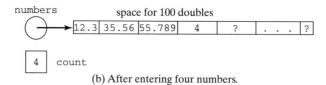

(b) After entering four numbers.

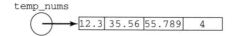

(c) After allocating for temp_nums and copying each element.

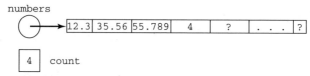

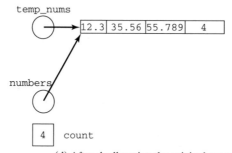

(d) After deallocating the original space and resetting
the pointer numbers.

FIGURE 8.18

4.
```
double db;
db = new double;
```

5.
```
int* i_ptr;
i_ptr = new [] int;
```

6.
```
int* i_ptr, i;
i_ptr = new int;
delete i;
```

EXPERIMENTS 8.6

1. Consider the following program segment.

```
char* ch_ptr;
ch_ptr = new char;

*ch_ptr = 'A';

ch_ptr = new char;

*ch_ptr = 'B';

cout << *ch_ptr;
```

What does the `cout` statement display? What happens to the character 'A'?

2. Recode dem08-12.cpp to include a check for `new` that returns a null pointer.

PROGRAMMING PROBLEMS 8.6

1. In dem08-16.cpp, we initially allocated space for 100 doubles, then allocated space just large enough to hold the numbers that the user entered, and finally deallocated the original space. Another approach to this problem is to initially allocate very little space, say enough for only five doubles. If the user enters a sixth number, then allocate space for a larger array (say an array of twice the size of the present one), copy the original array elements to the new array, and then deallocate the space for the original array. Rewrite dem08-16.cpp using this suggestion.

Chapter Review

Terminology

Define the following terms.

	`isdigit()`
call by reference	`islower()`
`string.h`	`ispunct()`
`strlen()`	`isspace()`
`strcpy()`	`isupper()`
`strcmp()`	`toupper()`
ASCII collating sequence	`tolower()`
concatenation	palindrome
`strcat()`	heap
`ctype.h`	dynamic memory allocation
`isalnum()`	`new`
`isalpha()`	`delete`

Summary

- The address of a variable can be a function argument. In that case, use the indirection operator, `*`, in the function body to refer to the target of the pointer.
- A reference variable, declared by appending `&` to a data type, is another name for an already existing variable.
- Reference variables can be used as function arguments.
- An array can be a function argument. Always pass the array size as an additional argument (Notes 8.1 and 8.2).
- A string, that is, a character pointer, can be a function argument.
- A function can return a pointer.
- To use a function in the standard string library, you must code `#include <string.h>` (Note 8.3).
- Use `strlen()` to find the length of a string.
- Use `strcpy()` to copy a string (Note 8.4).
- Use `strcmp()` to compare two strings. Strings are compared according to the ASCII collating sequence (Table 8.2).
- Use `strcat()` to append one string to the end of another (Note 8.5).
- To use the character classification functions, see Table 8.3. You must code `#include <ctype.h>`.
- To use the character conversion functions `toupper()` and `tolower()`, you must code `#include <ctype.h>`.
- To convert a numeric string to an integer, use `atoi()`; to a `long`, use `atol()`; to a `double`, use `atof()`. To use these functions, you must code `#include <stdlib.h>`.
- Use the `new` operator to dynamically allocate heap space (Note 8.6).
- Use the `delete` operator to de-allocate heap space previously allocated by `new` (Note 8.7).

Review Exercises

1. Explain the differences between passing an argument to a function by value, passing it by address, and passing it by reference.
2. What is a reference variable?
3. How can you pass an array to a function?
4. When you pass an array to a function, why should you also pass the size of the array to the function?
5. What do you have to do in a function prototype and the function definition so that one of the function's arguments is a pointer?
6. How do you code a function that returns a pointer?
7. Which header file must you include to use the string library functions?
8. What standard C++ library function returns the length of a string?

9. Which standard C++ library function allows you to copy a string? What must you be careful of when using this function?

10. Which standard C++ library function allows you to compare two strings?

11. What is the ASCII collating sequence and how does it affect the function of Exercise 10?

12. Which standard C++ library function allows you to paste one string onto the end of another? What must you be careful of when using this function?

13. What header file must you include to use the standard library character classification functions?

14. Name as many of the character classification functions as you can and what they are used for.

15. What are the character conversion functions?

16. What are the numeric conversion functions and what does each do? Which header file must you include to use them?

17. What is meant by dynamic memory allocation?

18. What is the heap? How does heap storage differ from static and automatic storage?

19. How can you allocate memory from the heap? How can you de-allocate memory from the heap?

Chapter

9

User-Defined Data Types and Tables

Objectives

- To use `typedef` to declare new data types.

- To use `enum` to declare an enumerated type.

- To use `struct` to declare a structure, and to declare a structure variable.

- To use the member operator, `.`, to access a structure member.

- To initialize a structure variable.

- To assign one structure variable to another.

- To use an array of structures to define a table.

- To code a program that loads and sorts a table.

- To use a sequential search to do a table lookup.

- To use a binary search to do a table lookup.

- To code a function that has a structure as an argument.

- To code a function that returns a structure.

- To use the $\rightarrow$ operator to access a structure variable member through a pointer.

- To code a function that has a structure pointer as an argument.

- To code a function that has a structure reference as an argument.

This chapter shows how to build other data types from the ones we already know. We start by discussing the `typedef` statement, which enables the programmer to define new data types from an existing data type. Next we discuss the `enum` statement, which enables the programmer to define a data type with a small number of integer values. The remainder of the chapter discusses the `struct` statement, which allows the programmer to define structures—compound data types created from pre-existing data types. We show how to use structures to define and manipulate tables and how to use structures with pointers and functions.

9.1 The `typedef` and `enum` Statements

There are several ways to define new data types in C++. In this section we discuss `typedef`, which can be used to define a new data type from an existing type, and `enum`, which can be used to define a new type whose variables can assume a small number of integer values.

The `typedef` Statement

So far we have discussed the built-in data types (`char`, `int`, `long`, `float`, `double`, etc.), pointers, and arrays of these types. The `typedef` statement allows you to define your own data type from an existing data type.

The `typedef` statement has the following format.

NOTE 9.1—FORMAT OF `typedef`

```
typedef old_type new_type;
```

To understand how to use `typedef`, it is best to consider some examples. The simplest use of `typedef` is to rename an existing data type. For example, a program that manipulates money amounts would use variables of type `double` to represent these amounts. Such a program might contain the following declarations.

```
double value,
       amount;
```

A person reading this program might not know that the variables `value` and `amount` represent money amounts. If these values were output as negative numbers with six digits to the right of the decimal, the person might not suspect that something is wrong with the program.

Suppose instead that we declare the variables as follows.

```
typedef double MONEY_AMOUNT;

MONEY_AMOUNT value,
             amount;
```

The `typedef` statement makes the identifier `MONEY_AMOUNT` equivalent to the type `double`. Therefore, you are allowed to declare variables of type `MONEY_AMOUNT`. The C++ compiler translates a declaration of type `MONEY_AMOUNT` as though it is a declaration of type `double`. By using the type `MONEY_AMOUNT`, the variable declarations give information about the kind of number that the variables represent. Now, if the values of these variables are output incorrectly, a person reading the code is more likely to suspect that the program is in error.

You must first define a new type with a `typedef` statement before declaring a variable of that type. Exactly where you code the `typedef` is up to you. However, the scope rules that apply to variables also apply to types defined by `typedef`. Thus, a type defined by `typedef` within a function is accessible only within that function. A type defined by a `typedef` outside a function is accessible to all functions whose definitions occur after that `typedef`. Programmers usually place all `typedef` statements before `main()`. This makes the types available to all functions in the program.

Another example of the use of `typedef` is in the declaration of character arrays that will store strings. If a program is to store a person's first and last names in arrays, we could code the following.

```
typedef char NAME[51];
```

Here, the new data type is `NAME`. The statement defines `NAME` as an array of 51 characters (to allow for a name of up to 50 characters—remember the `'\0'`). Now, in the program we can code the following, which declares `first` and `last` to be arrays of 51 characters.

```
NAME first,
     last;
```

Another example of the use of `typedef` is to define a string data type. Suppose we code the following `typedef` statement.

```
typedef char* STRING;
```

`STRING` is equivalent to the type character pointer, which is analogous to a string. We can then make the following declaration in a program.

```
STRING street_names [4] = {"Wall", "Spruce", "Cedar", "Pine"};
```

The data item `street_names` is an array of four `STRINGS` (that is, character pointers).

If you use a data type such as `STRING`, be sure not to use an uninitialized pointer. For example, suppose we declare the following string.

```
STRING emp_name;
```

It is dangerous to now execute the following statement.

```
cin.getline(emp_name, 51);
```

The variable `emp_name` is a character pointer and does not yet have an initial value. It points to some unprotected location in memory. The call to `cin.getline()` will place the string entered by the user at that unprotected location. This could cause the `cin.getline()` to overwrite important program data or part of the operating system, which could cause a system crash.

The `enum` Statement

An **enumerated type**, introduced by the keyword `enum`, defines a set of integer constants that are represented by identifiers.

NOTE 9.2—FORMAT OF `enum`

```
enum enumerated-type-name {identifier list}
```

For example, the following declares the enumerated type `BOOLEAN`.

```
enum BOOLEAN {false, true};
```

The identifiers listed in braces have integer values beginning at 0 and are incremented by 1, unless otherwise specified. The identifiers `false` and `true` in the declaration have the values 0 and 1. Once you declare an enumerated type, you can declare variables of that type. For example, we can code the following declaration.

```
BOOLEAN result;
```

This declares the variable `result` as type `BOOLEAN`, which is an enumerated type. Thus, `result` can be assigned the value `true` or `false`.

```
result = true;
```

We can also code the following `while` statement.

```
while (result == true)
  {
   ...
  }
```

An enumerated type is considered a new type by the C++ compiler. For example, the compiler considers the previously declared BOOLEAN to be a data type in the same way as int or double are types. This has implications in terms of the operations that you can perform on an enumerated type. For example, although the arithmetic operator ++ and the cin object are defined for variables of type int, they are not defined for enumerated types. Using ++ or cin on an enumerated type variable can lead to unpredictable results. If you want to treat an enumerated type variable as an integer, you should type cast it as such. We shall see an example of this in dem09-1.cpp.

An enumerated type's values are integers (for example, in the BOOLEAN type, true has a value of 1). However, the C++ compiler will issue a warning message for the following statement.

```
result = 1;
```

The variable result is of type BOOLEAN and the constant 1 is an integer. Although the assignment will assign the correct value to the variable result, the compiler issues a warning message that the types may not be compatible.

In the declaration of an enumerated type, you need not give the listed identifiers consecutive values from 0 on up. Consider the following declaration.

```
enum COLOR {red = 3, green, blue, white = 8, black};
```

Here red is given the value 3. Because green is listed immediately after red and is not given a value, it is automatically given the next integer value, namely 4. Similarly, blue is given the value 5. The identifier white is explicitly given the value 8. Because black is listed immediately after white with no explicit initial value, it is automatically given the value 9.

An Example Using typedef and enum

The program dem09-1.cpp illustrates the uses of typedef and enum that we have discussed. It is based on the program prb07-2.cpp, which totals weekly sales amounts for a salesperson and finds the highest sales for the week. Note how this version of the program is more self-documenting than the original.

```
// dem09-1.cpp

// This program totals weekly sales amounts and finds the highest
// sales for the week. It uses an array of pointers to store the
// names of the days of the week.
// The program makes use of typedef and enum to define several
// data types.


#include <iostream.h>
```

```cpp
#include <iomanip.h>

using namespace std;

typedef char* STRING;
typedef char NAME [41];
typedef double AMOUNT;
enum DAY {mon, tue, wed, thu, fri, sat, sun};

int main()
{
  STRING day_names[7] = {"Monday", "Tuesday", "Wednesday",
                         "Thursday", "Friday", "Saturday", "Sunday"};
  AMOUNT sales[7];
  NAME   salesperson;
  AMOUNT max_sales,
         total_sales;
  DAY    day,
         max_day;

  cout << setprecision(2)
       << setiosflags(ios::fixed)
       << setiosflags(ios::showpoint);

  cout << "\nEnter the name of the salesperson: ";
  cin.getline(salesperson, 41);

  for (day = mon; day <= sun; ++int(day))
    {
      cout << "\n\nEnter the sales for " << day_names[day] << ": ";
      cin >> sales[day];
    }

  total_sales = 0;
  max_day = mon;
  max_sales = sales[mon];

  for (day = mon; day <= sun; ++int(day))
    {
      if (sales[day] > max_sales)
      {
        max_sales = sales[day];
        max_day = day;
      }
      total_sales += sales[day];
    }

  cout << "\n\nThe total sales for " << salesperson
       << " is " << total_sales << ".";
```

```
cout << "\n\nThe highest sales was " << max_sales << ".";

cout << "\n\nThe highest sales occurred on "
     << day_names[max_day] << ".";

return 0;
}
```

Program Output

```
Enter the name of the salesperson: Mack Adamia

Enter the sales for Monday: 345.76

Enter the sales for Tuesday: 239.89

Enter the sales for Wednesday: 100.00

Enter the sales for Thursday: 563.99

Enter the sales for Friday: 0.0

Enter the sales for Saturday: 789.99

Enter the sales for Sunday: 533.90

The total sales for Mack Adamia is 2573.53.

The highest sales was 789.99.

The highest sales occurred on Saturday.
```

The program begins with several `typedef` statements. The first `typedef` defines the `STRING` data type as a character pointer. The program uses `STRING` to define an array of seven strings, which it initializes to the names of the days of the week. The second `typedef` defines the `NAME` data type as an array of 41 characters. The program uses `NAME` to store a salesperson's name. The third `typedef` defines the `AMOUNT` data type as a double. The program uses `AMOUNT` to declare the variables `max_sales` and `total_sales`, which store money amounts. Finally, the fourth declaration defines the `DAY` data type as an enumerated type that gives values to the abbreviations of the names of the days of the week. The program uses `DAY` to declare the variables `day` and `max_day`, which store values corresponding to the days of the week.

The code of `main()` also takes advantage of the enumerated type values. The two `for` loops use the enumerated type values `mon` and `sun` to initialize and test the value of the `DAY` enumerated type variable `day`. Note that in both `for` loops, the variable `day` is incremented by the statement `++int(day)`. Remember that the variable `day` is of type `DAY`. The arithmetic operators are not necessarily defined for variables of this type. Therefore, we type cast the variable to an integer and then do the increment. Type casts are not necessary in the loop initializations or the loop tests. In the initializations we assign a DAY value to a variable of type DAY and in the tests we compare a DAY variable to a DAY value. The same is true in the assignment statements that initialize max_day and max_sales to Monday and Monday's sales.

EXERCISES 9.1

In Exercises 1–6, use `typedef` and `enum` as appropriate.

1. Define a data type to store social security numbers.
2. Define a data type to store a table of 50 names, each of which contains at most 30 characters.
3. Define a data type to store an array of integer pointers.
4. Define an enumerated data type for the sizes small, medium, large, and x-large.
5. Define an enumerated type for months of the year. Use the first three letters of each month as the value of the month name.
6. Define an enumerated type for the seating classes on an airplane. Use first, business, coach, and standby as the values.
7. Assume the following declaration.

```
enum VEGIES {beans, carrots = 6, onions, tomatoes};
```

   What are the numeric values of `beans`, `onions`, and `tomatoes`?

8. **(a)** A corporation's human resources department rates applicants as Superior, Average, and SubAverage. Define an enumerated type that reflects this classification. Be sure to make the numeric values of the categories correspond to their relative standing. For example, Superior should be greater than Average and SubAverage.

   (b) Using the data type defined in part (a), declare a variable called `rating` in which to store an interviewer's rating of an applicant.

   (c) Using parts (a) and (b), write a statement that places the number 1 into the variable `decision` if the value of the rating is Superior or Average.

9. **(a)** The finance department of a corporation is preparing an annual report. The company's revenues will be classified according to quarters. Define an enumerated type with values QTR1, QTR2, QTR3, and QTR4.

   (b) Declare an array of `doubles` in which to store the company's revenues for the four quarters.

   (c) Using the enumerated type defined in part (a), declare a variable `quarter` that will be used as a subscript for the array declared in part (b).

   (d) Write a `for` loop that prompts the user to enter each of the four quarters' revenues and stores them in the array declared in part (b). Use the variable declared in part (c) as the loop counter. Be sure to use the values defined in the enumerated type.

EXPERIMENTS 9.1

1. Compile the following program. What does your compiler do?

```
#include <iostream.h>

using namespace std;

void Func(void);

int main()
{
   typedef int NEW_TYPE;

   NEW_TYPE i = 0;

   Func();

   return 0;
}

void FUNC(void)
{
   NEW_TYPE j = 3;
}
```

2. In some C++ compilers, the values specified in an enumerated type are legal to use in place of the integer values they represent. By using the DAY enumerated type of dem09-1.cpp, we could code the expression wed + thu. This expression has a value of 2 + 3, or 5. A variable of type DAY, for example day, can be assigned values such as mon and tue or numeric values such as 5 or 6. However, C++ does not check that the values you give to day are within the range 0–6. In dem09-1, replace the conditions in each of the for loops by day <= 6. Compile and run the resulting program. Describe what happens and try to explain the results.

9.2 Structures

Arrays allow the programmer to define variables that combine several data items of the same kind. For example, an array of five integers combines five integer values that can be treated as a unit. In this section we introduce the structure, which allows you to combine data items of different kinds. A structure in C++ is similar to a record in languages like Pascal and COBOL.

Defining a Structure

Suppose we want to process inventory information on parts that are stored in a warehouse. For each part, we would like to store the part number (a seven-character code), the quantity on hand (an integer), and the unit price (a double). We could declare a variable for each of these quantities. However, doing so does not reflect that the three variables contain values that are associated with a particular part. We need a single variable in which we can store all three quantities. Most programming languages use a variable called a record for this purpose. In C++, the **structure** can provide this capability. In the next chapter we shall discuss classes, which is another way to accomplish the same thing.

The following defines a structure that we can use to solve our inventory problem.

```
struct PART_STRUCT
  {
    char    part_no[8];
    int     quantity_on_hand;
    double  unit_price;
  };
```

Programming
Pointers

The definition begins with the keyword `struct`. The identifier PART_STRUCT gives a name to the structure. (We place the suffix `_struct` at the end of a structure name to remind us that the identifier is a structure. This is not required by C++, but is a useful programming practice.) The **structure members** are enclosed in braces and follow the structure name. The structure members (analogous to fields in a record) are the parts of the structure and they are declared in the same way as ordinary variables. The PART_STRUCT structure has three members. The first member, `part_no`, is a character array. The second member, `quantity_on_hand`, is an integer. The third member, `unit_price`, is a `double`. Note that the definition of the structure ends in a semicolon.

Programming
Pitfalls

It is important to realize that the definition of the PART_STRUCT structure does not declare a variable. It therefore does not reserve any space in computer storage. A structure definition defines a pattern for the compiler to use when we declare PART_STRUCT variables. As with `enum`, the `struct` statement actually defines another data type. By itself it does not declare a variable. Also, the `part_no`, `quantity_on_hand`, and `unit_price` members of the structure are merely names for the members of the structure and are not variables.

Figure 9.1 shows how we can think of the PART_STRUCT structure data type. The PART_STRUCT structure is divided into three pieces consisting of the three members `part_no`, `quantity_on_hand`, and `unit_price` in that order.

To declare a variable that is of the PART_STRUCT type, we can code the following.

```
PART_STRUCT part;
```

This declaration defines a variable, `part`, that is of the data type PART_STRUCT. Internally, the variable has the structure that we defined in the `struct` statement for PART_STRUCT. Figure 9.2 shows the variable `part`.

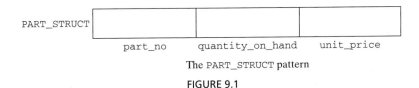

The PART_STRUCT pattern

FIGURE 9.1

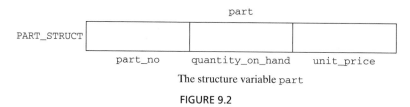

The structure variable part

FIGURE 9.2

Although the PART_STRUCT data type does not reserve computer storage, the variable part does. The variable part requires whatever amount of storage is necessary to store an eight-character array, an integer, and a double. (On a DOS/WINDOWS-based computer, this would most likely be 18 bytes.)

Accessing Structure Members

Programming
Pointers

Now that we have declared a structure variable, how can we access the members of that variable? For example, how can we assign the value 62 to the quantity_on_hand member of part? To access a member of a structure, we must use the **member operator**. The member operator is coded as a period between the structure variable name and the structure member that we wish to access. Thus, we refer to the quantity_on_hand member of part as part.quantity_on_hand. Read this reference either from right to left as "the quantity_on_hand member of part" or as the possessive "part's quantity_on_hand". To assign 62 to this member, we would code the following.

```
part.quantity_on_hand = 62;
```

Again, read this assignment from right to left as "62 is assigned to the quantity_on_hand member of part" or as "part's quantity_on_hand becomes 62".

NOTE 9.3—READING A STRUCTURE REFERENCE

Read an expression that contains a structure member reference either from right to left (reading the member operator as "member of"), or as a possessive.

The following program, dem09-2.cpp, shows how to access the members of a structure.

```
// dem09—2.cpp

// This program illustrates the declaration and use of structure
// variables and the member operator to access structure
// variable members.
```

```cpp
#include <iostream.h>
#include <iomanip.h>

using namespace std;

struct PART_STRUCT
  {
    char   part_no[8];
    int    quantity_on_hand;
    double unit_price;
  };

int main()
{
  PART_STRUCT part;

  cout << setprecision(2)
       << setiosflags(ios::fixed)
       << setiosflags(ios::showpoint);

  cout << "\nEnter the seven-character part number: ";
  cin.getline(part.part_no, 8);

  cout << "\nEnter the quantity on hand: ";
  cin >> part.quantity_on_hand;

  cout << "\nEnter the unit price: ";
  cin >> part.unit_price;

  cout << "\nYou entered the following information:";
  cout << "\n\nPart Number:      " << part.part_no;
  cout << "\nQuantity On Hand: " << setw(7) << part.quantity_on_hand;
  cout << "\nUnit Price:       " << setw(7) << part.unit_price;

  return 0;
}
```

Program Output

```
Enter the seven-character part number: AB12345

Enter the quantity on hand: 62

Enter the unit price: 34.95

You entered the following information:

Part Number:      AB12345
Quantity On Hand:      62
Unit Price:         34.95
```

The program begins with the definition of the structure type that we discussed earlier. In `main()`, we declare the structure variable `part`. The program asks the user for a part number, quantity on hand, and unit price. When working with structures, it is important to keep Note 9.4 in mind.

NOTE 9.4—DATA TYPE OF A STRUCTURE REFERENCE

The data type of a structure member reference is the same as the data type of the right-most element of that reference.

Thus, `part.part_no` has the same data type as `part_no`, which is the name of a character array, that is, a character pointer. Any reference to `part.part_no` should be as the name of a character array, or character pointer. Also, `part.quantity_on_hand` is an integer because `quantity_on_hand` is an integer.

Because the seven-character part number is a string, the program obtains it by a call to `cin.getline()`. The `cin.getline()` function requires the name of a character array as its first argument. The required statement is

```
cin.getline(part.part_no, 8);
```

After prompting for and obtaining the data entered by the user, we can depict the contents of the structure variable `part` as shown in Figure 9.3.

Initializing a Structure Variable

Programming
Pointers

You can initialize a structure variable similarly to the way in which you initialize an array. For example, using the `PART_STRUCT` data type defined earlier, we can declare and initialize the variable `old_part` as follows.

```
PART_STRUCT old_part = {"XY98765", 17, 99.99};
```

To initialize a structure variable, enclose in braces a list of the structure member values. Separate the values by commas. You must take care that the types of the values in the list correspond to the data types of the members of the structure. In our example, the first listed value is a string, the second value is an integer, and the third value is a `double`.

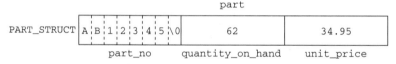

The structure variable `part` with initial values

FIGURE 9.3

More Complicated Structures

A structure can be as simple or as complex as you like. For example, we could use the following simple structure to store the value of a standard playing card.

```
struct CARD_STRUCT
  {
    int value;
    char suit;
  };

CARD_STRUCT card;
```

The structure variable `card` has two members, an `int` representing the face value of the card and a `char` representing the suit (S, H, D, C for spade, heart, diamond, and club.) We can store the 7 of Diamonds in the variable card as follows.

```
card.value = 7;
card.suit = 'D';
```

Figure 9.4 shows the contents of the variable `card` after these assignments.

A structure can also be complex, as was the PART_STRUCT structure of dem09-2.cpp. A structure can even contain other structures. For example, suppose that we want to store the following information on a company's employees: name, address, social security number, and hourly pay rate. The name is to consist of a first name, a middle initial, and a last name. The address is to consist of the street address, the city, the two-character state code, and the five-digit zip code. The social security number is to be stored as a character string. The hourly pay rate is a `double`. Since the name and address are subdivided into parts, it is logical to define structures for the name and the address. Then we will define a structure consisting of the name and address structures and the social security number. Following are such definitions.

```
struct NAME_STRUCT
  {
    char first_name[31];
    char mid_initial;
    char last_name[31];
  };
```

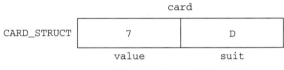

The structure variable `card`

FIGURE 9.4

```
struct ADDRESS_STRUCT
  {
    char st_adress[31];
    char city[31];
    char state[3];
    char zip[6];
  };

struct EMPLOYEE_STRUCT
  {
    NAME_STRUCT    name;
    ADDRESS_STRUCT address;
    char           soc_sec_no[10];
    double         pay_rate;
  };


EMPLOYEE_STRUCT employee;
```

The structure variable `employee` has four members (see Figure 9.5.) The first member, `name`, is a structure of type `NAME_STRUCT`. The second member, `address`, is a structure of type `ADDRESS_STRUCT`. The third member, `soc_sec_no`, is a character array. The fourth member is a `double`.

Be very careful when using the members of such a complicated structure variable. For example, suppose we want to initialize the two-character state code of `employee` to `"NY"`. The member `state` is a member of a member of the variable `employee`. Thus, we need to use the member operator twice. This is how to make the reference:

```
employee.address.state
```

Following Note 9.3, we read the reference from right to left as "the `state` member of the `address` member of `employee`", or as "employee's address' state". Recall that the data type of this reference is the type of the right-most member. The reference is to the name of a character array, or a character pointer. To copy the string `"NY"` into the array, we would use the `strcpy()` function as follows.

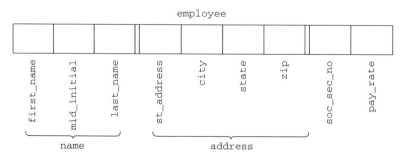

The EMPLOYEE_STRUCT variable employee

FIGURE 9.5

```
strcpy(employee.address.state, "NY");
```

If we want to access the first letter of the state code, we would use the following reference.

```
employee.address.state[0]
```

Again using Note 9.3, you would read this reference from right to left as "element 0 of the `state` member of the `address` member of `employee`", or "`employee`'s `address`' `state` element 0".

Assigning One Structure Variable to Another

Programming
Pointers

A structure variable can be assigned to another structure variable of the same type. For example, consider the `CARD_STRUCT` structure defined in the previous subsection.

```
struct CARD_STRUCT
  {
    int  value;
    char suit;
  };
```

Suppose that we code the following declarations.

```
CARD_STRUCT card1 = {7, 'D'},
            card2;
```

The assignment `card2 = card1` is valid. It is accomplished by a member-by-member copy. The assignment results in the structure variable `card2` having the same value as `card1`, namely the 7 of Diamonds.

Programming
Pitfalls

It is not valid to assign a structure variable of one type to a structure variable of a different type. This is true even if the number and data types of the members are the same. For example, suppose the following declarations and assignment.

```
struct NEW_CARD_STRUCT
{
  int value;
  char suit;
};

NEW_CARD_STRUCT new-card;
new_card = card;        //illegal assignment
```

The assignment is illegal because `card` is of type `CARD_STRUCT` and `new_card` is of type `NEW_CARD_STRUCT`.

EXERCISES 9.2

1. Define a structure type STUDENT_STRUCT described as follows: A 30-character name, a nine-digit student ID number, a three-character student class, a two-character grade, a five-character course code, a 16-character course name.

2. Define a structure type JUROR_STRUCT described as follows. The first member is a structure containing the juror's name, street address, city, and zip code. The second member of JUROR_STRUCT is also a structure, which contains a five-character court code followed by a six-character date.

3. Define a structure type EMPLOYEE_STRUCT described as follows. The first member is a structure containing the employee's name, social security number, street address, city, and zip code. The second member of EMPLOYEE_STRUCT is also a structure. This structure contains the employee's initial date of employment in mm/yy/dd form, the employee's hourly pay rate, and the employee's number of dependents.

EXPERIMENTS 9.2

1. Consider the following structures and variable declarations.

```
struct STRUCT1
  {
    int i;
    double d;
  };

struct STRUCT2
  {
    float f;
    long l;
  };

STRUCT1 struct1_var = {3, 7.5};
STRUCT2 struct2_var;
```

Write a program containing these declarations and make the assignment struct2_var = struct1_var. What happens? Does the program compile? If it compiles, what gets assigned to struct2_var?

9.3 Arrays of Structures: Tables

A **table** is data organized into rows and columns. For example, Table 9.1 shows a list of parts. Each row of the table represents a part. The first column contains the part number, the second column contains the quantity on hand for the part, and the third column contains the unit price for the part. We can use this table to look up a part number and find either the quantity on hand or the unit price. We might also want to update the information on a part. For example, it might be necessary to change the quantity on hand or the unit price.

TABLE 9.1

Part Number	Quantity on Hand	Unit Price
A123456	123	12.99
A987654	53	52.95
D001234	93	22.95
B109897	44	13.95
A035467	15	59.95
C837289	0	57.99
D346246	35	25.99
C253146	104	110.99
B194791	33	14.95
A826749	56	41.95

We use data tables almost every day of our lives. When we look up a word in a dictionary, we use a table. You can think of the dictionary as a two-column table in which the first column contains the word and the second column contains the corresponding definition. The telephone book is also a table. It has three columns containing the name, address, and telephone number.

To look up a part in Table 9.1, find a word in a dictionary, or look up a person's telephone number all require locating a particular row in a table. The column that you use to locate a table entry is the **table key**. In Table 9.1, the table key is the part number column. In a dictionary, the table key is the word column. The table key of a telephone book is the name column.

Sometimes the table rows are in order based on the table key. For example, the dictionary and the telephone book are in order based on their table key. Such a table is **sorted**. On the other hand, some tables, like Table 9.1, are not sorted on the table key. In this case you might want to sort the table before using it to look up the information on a part.

The most frequent operation performed on a table is to look up something in the table. For example, we use the dictionary to look up the definition of words. We use the telephone book to look up telephone numbers. The **search key** is the key value that you are looking for (for example, a particular word in a dictionary or a particular person in the telephone book). The process of finding a match to the search key in the table key column is **table searching**.

This section shows how to use structures to define tables, how to sort a table, and how to do a table search.

Using Structures to Define a Table

Programming
Pointers

A table in C++ is an array of structures. For example, consider the PART_STRUCT structure data type defined in Section 9.2.

```
struct PART_STRUCT
  {
    char    part_no[8];
    int     quantity_on_hand;
    double  unit_price;
  };
```

We can define a table to store data on 10 parts as follows.

```
PART_STRUCT part_table[10];
```

Thus, `part_table` is an array of 10 elements, each of which is of type `PART_STRUCT`. Figure 9.6 shows how to view this table.

Each row of the table is a structure of type `PART_STRUCT`. To access a particular entry in a particular row, you must use the member operator. For example, to assign 102 to the `quantity_on_hand` member of the fifth row of the table (remember, this is subscript 4) you would use the following.

```
part_table[4].quantity_on_hand = 102;
```

Using Note 9.3, read this assignment from right to left as "102 is assigned to the `quantity_on_hand` member of row 4 of `part_table`". Alternatively, read the assignment using a possessive as "`part_table` row 4's `quantity_on_hand` becomes 102".

Loading Table Values

Programming
Pointers

To load a table means to store values in the table. It is possible to load a table with values when the table is declared. This technique is called **"hard coding"** a table. You can usually hard code a table in two circumstances. First, the table should be short. If the table has many rows, it would take too long to enter the table values by hand in the program code. Second, the table values should be stable in the sense that they should not be subject to frequent change. Every time a value in a hard coded table changes, you must edit and recompile the program. If this happens frequently, for example four or five times daily, it can waste a great deal of time. Also, frequent changes to the program code increase the likelihood of introducing errors into the code.

Following is a hard coded table containing the first four parts from Table 9.1.

	part_no	quantity_on_hand	unit_price
0	A123456	123	12.99
1	A987654	53	52.96
2	D001234	93	22.95
3	B109897	44	13.95
4	A035467	15	59.95
5	C837289	0	57.99
6	D346246	35	25.99
7	C253146	104	110.99
8	B194791	33	14.95
9	A826749	56	41.95

A table consisting of an array of structures
of type PART_STRUCT.

FIGURE 9.6

```
PART_STRUCT partial_part_table[4] = { {"A123456", 123, 12.99},
                                      {"A987654", 53, 52.95},
                                      {"D001234", 93, 22.95},
                                      {"B109897", 44, 13.95}
                                    };
```

A program can also load a table interactively. The following program, dem09-3.cpp, shows how to interactively load part_table. After the program loads the table, it displays the table in table form with column headings and the total quantity on hand.

```cpp
// dem09-3.cpp

// This program shows how to define a table and how to interactively
// load the table with values. To verify that the table is loaded
// correctly, the program also displays the table in table form
// with appropriate headings.

#include <iostream.h>
#include <iomanip.h>

using namespace std;

#define TABLE_SIZE 10

struct PART_STRUCT
  {
    char    part_no[8];
    int     quantity_on_hand;
    double  unit_price;
  };

void Load_Part_Table(PART_STRUCT [], int);
void Display_Part_Table(PART_STRUCT [], int);

int main()
{
  PART_STRUCT part_table[TABLE_SIZE];
  int row,
      total_on_hand = 0;

  cout << setprecision(2)
       << setiosflags(ios::fixed)
       << setiosflags(ios::showpoint);

  // Load the table

  Load_Part_Table(part_table, TABLE_SIZE);

  // Calculate the total on hand
```

```
    for (row = 0; row < TABLE_SIZE; ++row)
      total_on_hand += part_table[row].quantity_on_hand;

    // Display the table

    cout << "\nThis is the table you entered.";

    Display_Part_Table(part_table, TABLE_SIZE);

    cout << "\n\n" << setw(20) << "Total On Hand:"
                   << setw(20) << total_on_hand;

    return 0;

}

void Load_Part_Table(PART_STRUCT part_table[], int size)
{
  int row;

  cout << "\nEnter the table values as you are prompted:\n\n";

  for (row = 0; row < size ; ++row)
    {
      cout << "\nFor row #" << row + 1 << " enter:";
      cout << "\nPart Number (7 Characters): ";
      cin.getline(part_table[row].part_no, 8);

      cin.ignore(80, '\n');    //Clear the input buffer

      cout << "\nQuantity On Hand: ";
      cin >> part_table[row].quantity_on_hand;
      cout << "\nUnit Price: ";
      cin >> part_table[row].unit_price;

      cin.ignore(80, '\n');    //Clear the input buffer
}

} //End of Load_Part_Table()

void Display_Part_Table(PART_STRUCT part_table[], int size)
{
  int row;

  cout << "\n\n" << setw(20) << "Part Number"
                 << setw(20) << "Quantity On Hand"
                 << setw(20) << "Unit Price"
                 << endl;

  for (row = 0; row < TABLE_SIZE; ++row)
```

```
            cout << "\n" << setw(20) << part_table[row].part_no
                         << setw(20) << part_table[row].quantity_on_hand
                         << setw(20) << part_table[row].unit_price;

} //End of Display_Part_Table()
```

Program Output

```
Enter the table values as you are prompted:

For row #1 enter:
Part Number (7 Characters): 73456

Quantity On Hand: 123

Unit Price: 12.99

For row #2 enter:
Part Number (7 Characters): A987654

Quantity On Hand: 53

Unit Price: 52.95

For row #3 enter:
Part Number (7 Characters): D001234

Quantity On Hand: 93

Unit Price: 22.95

For row #4 enter:
Part Number (7 Characters): B109897

Quantity On Hand: 44

Unit Price: 13.95

For row #5 enter:
Part Number (7 Characters): A035467

Quantity On Hand: 15

Unit Price: 59.95

For row #6 enter:
Part Number (7 Characters): C837289

Quantity On Hand: 0
```

```
Unit Price: 57.99

For row #7 enter:
Part Number (7 Characters): D346246

Quantity On Hand: 35

Unit Price: 25.99

For row #8 enter:
Part Number (7 Characters): C235146

Quantity On Hand: 104

Unit Price: 110.99

For row #9 enter:
Part Number (7 Characters): B194791

Quantity On Hand: 33

Unit Price: 14.95

For row #10 enter:
Part Number (7 Characters): A826749

Quantity On Hand: 56
Unit Price: 41.95

This is the table you entered.

            Part Number      Quantity On Hand            Unit Price

              A123456              123                     12.99
              A987654               53                     52.95
              D001234               93                     22.95
              B109897               44                     13.95
              A035467               15                     59.95
              C837289                0                     57.99
              D346246               35                     25.99
              C253146              104                    110.99
              B194791               33                     14.95
              A826749               56                     41.95

        Total On Hand:             556
```

The program begins by defining the symbolic constant TABLE_SIZE, which represents the number of rows in the table, and the structure data type PART_STRUCT as we described earlier. The program uses the function `Load_Part_Table()` to load the table, and the function `Display_Part_Table()` to display the table. Both functions return `void` and have two arguments. In both functions, the first argument is a `PART_STRUCT` array, that is, a table. The part table is an array of structures. An array of structures can be passed as an argument in exactly the same way as an array of integers or an array of doubles can be passed as an argument. The second argument for both functions is an integer, which will be the size of the array (that is, the number of rows in the table). Note also that the prototypes for these functions must be placed after the declaration of `PART_STRUCT` because we refer to this structure in the prototypes.

In `main()`, we require three variables: the array `part_table`, and the integer variables `row`, which we use for the table subscript, and `total_on_hand`, which we use to accumulate the quantities on hand for the 10 parts.

The program loads the part table by executing `Load_Part_Table()`. The `for` loop in the function prompts the user for the table data. One iteration of this loop fills a single table row by prompting for and obtaining the part number, the quantity on hand, and the unit price. The `cin.ignore()` at the end of the loop body clears the keyboard input buffer of the new-line character that the user entered after the unit price. Without this call to `cin.ignore()`, on the next loop iteration `cin.getline()` would obtain only the new-line character that was in the keyboard input buffer. Recall that `cin.getline()` obtains all characters up to and including the next new-line character. If the very first character in the keyboard input buffer is a new-line character, the new-line character is all that `cin.getline()` will retrieve.

Next, the `for` loop in `main()` accumulates the `quantity_on_hand` members of each row of the table. The program then displays a message that the table is about to print and executes `Display_Part_Table()`. The `for` loop in this function displays the contents of the table. One iteration of the loop displays one row of the table. Finally, the last `cout` in `main()` displays the value of the total quantity on hand.

In addition to hard coding a table and interactively loading a table, table values can be loaded from a file. We shall see how to do this in Chapter 14.

Sorting a Table

There are many techniques for sorting a table. We shall employ the bubble sort, which we used in Chapter 6 to sort an array of numbers. It might be a good idea at this point to review Section 6.3. Let's assume that we want to sort our tables in **ascending order**. Ascending order means that the row with the lowest table key value is in row 0, the row with the next higher table key value is in row 1, and so on. In the experiments at the end of this section, we ask you to adjust the programs in this section to sort the tables into descending order.

Programming Pointers

There are several differences between sorting an array of numbers and sorting a table. First, we have to know which column of the table is to serve as the table key. When the sort procedure decides if two rows are out of order, it must compare the values in the table key columns. Second, if the table key is a string, as is the part number column of the table we built in dem09-3.cpp, we must use `strcmp()` to do the comparisons. Third, when two rows are out of order, we must swap the entire rows.

Following is dem09-4.cpp, which loads and displays a part table exactly as dem09-3.cpp. The program uses the bubble sort to sort the table in ascending order on the part number and then displays the sorted table.

```cpp
// dem09-4.cpp

// This program interactively loads and displays a table (see
// dem09-3.cpp) and then uses the bubble sort to sort the table
// on the part number. Finally, the program displays the sorted
// table.

#include <iostream.h>
#include <iomanip.h>
#include <string.h>

using namespace std;

#define TABLE_SIZE 10

struct PART_STRUCT
  {
    char    part_no[8];
    int     quantity_on_hand;
    double  unit_price;
  };

void Load_Part_Table(PART_STRUCT [], int);
void Display_Part_Table(PART_STRUCT [], int);

int main()
{
  PART_STRUCT part_table[TABLE_SIZE],
              temp_part;

  int row,
      pass,
      limit,
      total_on_hand = 0;

  cout << setprecision(2)
       << setiosflags(ios::fixed)
       << setiosflags(ios::showpoint);


  // Load the table

  Load_Part_Table(part_table, TABLE_SIZE);

  // Calculate the total on hand
```

```
      for (row = 0; row < TABLE_SIZE; ++row)
        total_on_hand += part_table[row].quantity_on_hand;

      // Display the table

      cout << "\n\nThis is the table you entered.";

      Display_Part_Table(part_table, TABLE_SIZE);

      cout << "\n\n" << setw(20) << "Total On Hand:"
                     << setw(20) << total_on_hand;

   // Sort the table using the bubble sort

      limit = TABLE_SIZE - 2;

      for (pass = 1; pass <= TABLE_SIZE - 1; ++pass)
        {
          for (row = 0; row <= limit; ++row)
            if (strcmp(part_table[row].part_no,
                              part_table[row + 1].part_no) > 0)
              {
                temp_part = part_table[row];
                part_table[row] = part_table[row + 1];
                part_table[row + 1] = temp_part;
              }

          --limit;
        }

      // Display the sorted table

      cout << "\n\nThe table sorted on Part Number is:";

      Display_Part_Table(part_table, TABLE_SIZE);

      cout << "\n\n" << setw(20) << "Total On Hand:"
                     << setw(20) << total_on_hand;

      return 0;

} //End of main()

void Load_Part_Table(PART_STRUCT part_table[], int size)
{
   int row;

   cout << "\nEnter the table values as you are prompted:\n\n";

   for (row = 0; row < size ; ++row)
```

```
      {
        cout << "\nFor row #" << row + 1 << " enter:";
        cout << "\nPart Number (7 Characters): ";
        cin.getline(part_table[row].part_no, 8);

        cin.ignore(80, '\n'); //Clear the input buffer

        cout << "\nQuantity On Hand: ";
        cin >> part_table[row].quantity_on_hand;
        cout << "\nUnit Price: ";
        cin >> part_table[row].unit_price;

        cin.ignore(80, '\n'); //Clear the input buffer
      }

} //End of Load_Part_Table()

void Display_Part_Table(PART_STRUCT part_table[], int size)
{
  int row;

  cout << "\n\n" << setw(20) << "Part Number"
               << setw(20) << "Quantity On Hand"
               << setw(20) << "Unit Price"
               << endl;

  for (row = 0; row < TABLE_SIZE; ++row)
    cout << "\n" << setw(20) << part_table[row].part_no
               << setw(20) << part_table[row].quantity_on_hand
               << setw(20) << part_table[row].unit_price;

} //End of Display_Part_Table()
```

Program Output

```
Enter the table values as you are prompted:

For row #1 enter:
Part Number (7 Characters): A123456

Quantity On Hand: 123

Unit Price: 12.99

For row #2 enter:
Part Number (7 Characters): A987654

Quantity On Hand: 53
```

```
Unit Price: 52.95

For row #3 enter:
Part Number (7 Characters): D001234

Quantity On Hand: 93

Unit Price: 22.95

For row #4 enter:
Part Number (7 Characters): B109897

Quantity On Hand: 44

Unit Price: 13.95

For row #5 enter:
Part Number (7 Characters): A035467

Quantity On Hand: 15

Unit Price: 59.95

For row #6 enter:
Part Number (7 Characters): C837289

Quantity On Hand: 0

Unit Price: 57.99

For row #7 enter:
Part Number (7 Characters): D346246

Quantity On Hand: 35

Unit Price: 25.99

For row #8 enter:
Part Number (7 Characters): C235146

Quantity On Hand: 104

Unit Price: 110.99

For row #9 enter:
Part Number (7 Characters): B194791

Quantity On Hand: 33
```

```
Unit Price: 14.95

For row #10 enter:
Part Number (7 Characters): A826749

Quantity On Hand: 56

Unit Price: 41.95


This is the table you entered.


        Part Number     Quantity On Hand          Unit Price

            A123456            123                   12.99
            A987654             53                   52.95
            D001234             93                   22.95
            B109897             44                   13.95
            A035467             15                   59.95
            C837289              0                   57.99
            D346246             35                   25.99
            C253146            104                  110.99
            B194791             33                   14.95
            A826749             56                   41.95

        Total On Hand:         556

The table sorted on Part Number is:

        Part Number     Quantity On Hand          Unit Price

            A035467             15                   59.95
            A123456            123                   12.99
            A826749             56                   41.95
            A987654             53                   52.95
            B109897             44                   13.95
            B194791             33                   14.95
            C253146            104                  110.99
            C837289              0                   57.99
            D001234             93                   22.95
            D346246             35                   25.99

        Total On Hand:         556
```

This program uses the same PART_STRUCT structure that we used in dem09-3.cpp. In main(), we declare the part_table array of structures that stores the part table. The variable temp_part is of type PART_STRUCT also. We use this variable to swap rows of the table when they are not in order. As in dem09-3.cpp, the variable row serves as the table subscript and `total_on_hand` is the accumulator that totals the quantity on hand amounts in each row of the table. The variables `pass` and `limit` have the same function as they had in dem06-4.cpp—`pass` keeps track of the number of passes over the table and `limit` keeps track of how far down the table to go on the current pass. Recall that on each pass over the table the bubble sort moves the row with the greatest key value to the upper part of the table.

The functions that load and display the table are exactly as they were in dem09-3.cpp. The next section of the program does the bubble sort. First, the variable `limit` is initialized to two less than the size of the table, which is 8. This allows the table subscript to range from 0 to 8 in the first pass over the table.

The nested `for` loops do the actual sorting. The outer `for` loop counts the number of passes over the table, which is one less than the table size. On each pass, the inner `for` loop compares the keys of pairs of adjacent table rows. The `if` statement compares the `part_no` member of adjacent table rows using the `strcmp()` library function. If the part number of a row follows the part number of the next row, the rows are out of order. See Figure 9.7. In this case, the program interchanges the rows. To interchange the rows requires that one row be stored temporarily in the structure variable `temp_part`. Then the second row is assigned to the first. Finally, the row stored in `temp_part` is placed into the second row. See Figure 9.8. These assignments are valid because the rows and `temp_part` are all of type `PART_STRUCT`. In the case that the table rows are not out of order, the sort does nothing to the rows. After comparing all pairs of adjacent rows, the row with the greatest part number has "bubbled" to the top of the table. The variable `limit` is decreased by one in preparation for the next inner loop pass. The last part of dem09-4.cpp redisplays the table, which is now sorted on the part number.

Searching a Table

There are two very common ways to search a table: the sequential search and the binary search. The sequential search is simpler and easier to code. To do a **sequential search** on a dictionary for the word rodomontade (remember that a dictionary is a table), begin at the first dictionary entry and compare it to rodomontade. If the first entry is rodomontade, stop. If it is not, go to the second entry. Continue in this manner

	part_no	quantity_on_hand	unit_price
0	A123456	123	12.99
1	A987654	53	52.96
2	D001234	93	22.95
3	B109897	44	13.95
4	A035467	15	59.95
5	C837289	0	57.99
6	D346246	35	25.99
7	C253146	104	110.99
8	B194791	33	14.95
9	A826749	56	41.95

rows 2 and 3 are out of order (2, 3)

Comparing adjacent rows in the bubble sort.

FIGURE 9.7

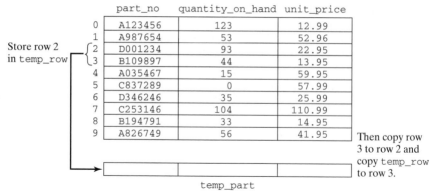

		part_no	quantity_on_hand	unit_price
	0	A123456	123	12.99
	1	A987654	53	52.96
Store row 2	2	D001234	93	22.95
in temp_row	3	B109897	44	13.95
	4	A035467	15	59.95
	5	C837289	0	57.99
	6	D346246	35	25.99
	7	C253146	104	110.99
	8	B194791	33	14.95
	9	A826749	56	41.95

Then copy row 3 to row 2 and copy temp_row to row 3.

temp_part

Swapping two rows in the bubble sort.

FIGURE 9.8

until you find the word rodomontade or come to the end of the dictionary (at which point you would have looked at every word in the dictionary!).

A **binary search** of the dictionary takes advantage of the alphabetical order of the entries in the dictionary—the dictionary is sorted on the word member. To do a binary search, first go to the middle word (approximately) of the dictionary and compare it to rodomontade. If this middle word is rodomontade, stop. If it is not, you can tell which half of the dictionary contains rodomontade by determining whether rodomontade comes alphabetically before or after the middle word. Once this is decided, you take the half of the dictionary that contains rodomontade, divide it in half, and proceed as before. Each step of the search divides the part of the dictionary still under consideration into two equal parts (see Figure 9.9)—hence the name "binary search." Eventually you either find the entry for rodomontade or the search fails.

Programming
Pointers

As a rule, a binary search is much faster than a sequential search. This is especially true when the table has 50 or more rows or when the table must be searched frequently. However, to do a binary search, the table must be sorted on its table key. We will show how to do both a sequential and a binary search.

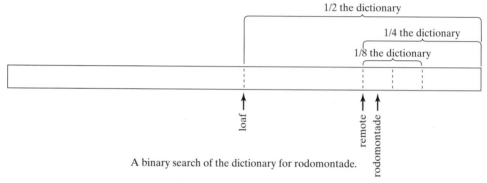

A binary search of the dictionary for rodomontade.

FIGURE 9.9

Sequential Search

The following pseudocode describes the heart of the sequential search. It assumes that the user has input a value for the search key.

```
for (each table row)
    if  (the table key for the row equals the search key)
        break
    endif
endfor

if (search was not successful)
    display search not successful
else
    extract data from table row
    process the extracted data
endif
```

The pseudocode is in two sections. The first section contains a `for` loop that tests each table row. If the table key of the tested row equals the value of the search key, the search is successful. Then, a `break` statement takes control out of the loop because there is no need to test the rest of the table. If the table key of the tested row never equals the value of the search key, the search is not successful.

The `for` loop in the first section of pseudocode can end in one of two ways—the search can be successful or not. The second part of the pseudocode tests why the `for` loop stopped. If the search was not successful, an appropriate message is displayed. If the search was successful, the row number of the row being tested at the time the break statement in the `for` loop was executed is the row number that contains the search key. We then extract and process the appropriate data from that row.

The program dem09-5.cpp shows how to do a sequential search of an unsorted table.

```cpp
// dem09—5.cpp

// This program shows how to do a sequential search of a table.

#include <iostream.h>
#include <iomanip.h>
#include <ctype.h>
#include <string.h>

using namespace std;

#define TABLE_SIZE 10

struct PART_STRUCT
{
  char    part_no[8];
```

```
  int     quantity_on_hand;
  double unit_price;
};


void Load_Part_Table(PART_STRUCT [], int);
void Display_Part_Table(PART_STRUCT [], int);

int main()
{
  PART_STRUCT part_table[TABLE_SIZE];
  int         row;
  char        part_key[8];      // The table search key
  char        response[11];

  cout << setprecision(2)
       << setiosflags(ios::fixed)
       << setiosflags(ios::showpoint);

  // Load the table

  Load_Part_Table(part_table, TABLE_SIZE);

  // Display the table

  cout << "\n\nThis is the table you entered.";

  Display_Part_Table(part_table, TABLE_SIZE);

// Do the table search

  cout << "\n\nDo you want to search the table?(Y/N): ";
  cin.getline(response, 11);

  cin.ignore(80, '\n'); //Clear the input buffer

  while (toupper(*response) == 'Y')
    {
      cout << "\nEnter the part number: ";
      cin.getline(part_key, 8);

      cin.ignore(80, '\n');      //Clear the input buffer

      for (row = 0; row < TABLE_SIZE; ++row)
      if (strcmp(part_table[row].part_no, part_key) == 0)
        break;

      if (row == TABLE_SIZE)
        cout << "\nThe search for " << part_key
             << " was not successful.";
      else
        {
```

```
                  cout << "\nData for " << part_key << ":";
                  cout << "\n\nQuantity On Hand: " << setw(10)
                          << part_table[row].quantity_on_hand;
                  cout << "\nUnit Price: " << setw(10)
                          << part_table[row].unit_price;
             }

          cout << "\n\nDo you want to search the table?(Y/N): ";
          cin.getline(response, 11);

          cin.ignore(80, '\n');    //Clear the input buffer
        }

     return 0;

} //End of main()

void Load_Part_Table(PART_STRUCT part_table[], int size)
{
   int row;

   cout << "\nEnter the table values as you are prompted:\n\n";

   for (row = 0; row < size ; ++row)
     {
        cout << "\nFor row #" << row + 1 << " enter:";
        cout << "\nPart Number (7 Characters): ";
        cin.getline(part_table[row].part_no, 8);

        cin.ignore(80, '\n');    //Clear the input buffer

        cout << "\nQuantity On Hand: ";
        cin >> part_table[row].quantity_on_hand;
        cout << "\nUnit Price: ";
        cin >> part_table[row].unit_price;

        cin.ignore(80, '\n');    //Clear the input buffer
     }
} //End of Load_Part_Table()

void Display_Part_Table(PART_STRUCT part_table[], int size)
{
   int row;

   cout << "\n\n" << setw(20) << "Part Number"
                  << setw(20) << "Quantity On Hand"
                  << setw(20) << "Unit Price"
                  << endl;

   for (row = 0; row < TABLE_SIZE; ++row)
        cout << "\n" << setw(20) << part_table[row].part_no
```

```
                    << setw(20) << part_table[row].quantity_on_hand
                    << setw(20) << part_table[row].unit_price;

} //End of Display_Part_Table()
```

Program Output

```
Enter the table values as you are prompted:

For row #1 enter:
Part Number (7 Characters): A123456

Quantity On Hand: 123

Unit Price: 12.99

For row #2 enter:
Part Number (7 Characters): A987654

Quantity On Hand: 53

Unit Price: 52.95

For row #3 enter:
Part Number (7 Characters): D001234

Quantity On Hand: 93

Unit Price: 22.95

For row #4 enter:
Part Number (7 Characters): B109897

Quantity On Hand: 44

Unit Price: 13.95

For row #5 enter:
Part Number (7 Characters): A035467

Quantity On Hand: 15

Unit Price: 59.95

For row #6 enter:
Part Number (7 Characters): C837289

Quantity On Hand: 0

Unit Price: 57.99
```

```
For row #7 enter:
Part Number (7 Characters): D346246

Quantity On Hand: 35

Unit Price: 25.99

For row #8 enter:
Part Number (7 Characters): C235146

Quantity On Hand: 104

Unit Price: 110.99

For row #9 enter:
Part Number (7 Characters): B194791

Quantity On Hand: 33

Unit Price: 14.95

For row #10 enter:
Part Number (7 Characters): A826749

Quantity On Hand: 56

Unit Price: 41.95

This is the table you entered.


        Part Number     Quantity On Hand          Unit Price

           A123456              123                  12.99
           A987654               53                  52.95
           D001234               93                  22.95
           B109897               44                  13.95
           A035467               15                  59.95
           C837289                0                  57.99
           D346246               35                  25.99
           C253146              104                 110.99
           B194791               33                  14.95
           A826749               56                  41.95

Do you want to search the table?(Y/N): Y

Enter the part number: D001234
```

```
Data for D001234:

Quantity On Hand:         93
Unit Price:            22.95

Do you want to search the table?(Y/N): y

Enter the part number: C012345

The search for C012345 was not successful.

Do you want to search the table?(Y/N): Y

Enter the part number: A826749

Data for A826749:

Quantity On Hand:         56
Unit Price:            41.95

Do you want to search the table?(Y/N): N
```

We declare the table in the usual way using the structure data type `PART_STRUCT`. The variable `row` is the table subscript. The program uses the character array `part_key[]` to hold the value of the search key, which the user inputs. The character array `response[]` holds the user's response to the question about whether he or she wishes to make a search of the table.

The program begins in the same way as dem09-3.cpp by inputting the table values and displaying the table. Next, the program asks the user if he or she wants to search the table. The `while` loop does the search for as long as the user responds 'Y' to the prompt. The condition in the `while` statement converts the first character of the user's answer to the prompt to uppercase. (Recall that the identifier `response` is a pointer to the first character in the array.) If the resulting character equals 'Y', the search begins.

In the `while` loop's body, the user is prompted to enter a part number. This is the value of the search key—the part number whose value we wish to locate in the table. The `for` loop then proceeds to locate the row containing a match to the search key. For each row of the table, the `for` loop's `if` statement compares the `part_no` member to the value in `part_key` using the `strcmp()` library function. Recall that `strcmp()` returns 0 if the two strings that it compares are equal. If the search key matches the part number of the current row, the appropriate row has been found and the `break` statement ends the `for` loop. If the search key is not in the table, the `for` loop ends because `row` becomes equal to `TABLE_SIZE`.

The next `if` statement tests why the `for` loop ended. If the value of `row` equals `TABLE_SIZE`, the search was not successful and the program displays an appropriate message. If `row` is not equal to `TABLE_SIZE`, the `for` loop ended because of the `break` statement, which means that the search was successful. The value of `row` is then the row number of the matching part number. Thus, the program displays the data corresponding to the search key.

Finally, the program asks the user if he or she wants to do another search. If the user responds 'Y', the program proceeds to do another search. If not, the program ends.

Binary Search

The logic of a binary search is more complex than that of a sequential search. To explain the binary search, we first assume that the search key value is in the table. That is, we first assume that the search will be successful.

As we mentioned previously, the binary search successively divides the table in half, zeroing in on the row that contains the search key. The search must have a way of keeping track of which part of the table it is currently searching. We do this by using the variables `lower` and `upper`, which always contain the row numbers of the first and last rows of the part of the table currently being searched. Initially, the value of `lower` is 0 and the value of `upper` is one less than the table size. See Figure 9.10. The value of `lower` should never be greater than the value of `upper`.

The basic idea of the binary search is the following: Compare the search key to the table key of the middle row of the part of the table currently being searched. The variable `middle`, which equals the average of `lower` and `upper`, gives the row number of the middle of the part of the table currently being searched. If the search key equals the table key of row `middle`, the search is successful and the search can stop.

If the search key is less than the table key of row `middle`, the row we want is between row `lower` and row `middle` − 1. See Figure 9.11. On the next pass of the search, we want the new value of `upper` to be `middle` − 1. If the search key is greater than the table key of row `middle`, the row we want is between row `middle` + 1 and row `upper`. On the next pass of the search, we want the new value of `lower` to be `middle` + 1. In either case, the new values of `lower` and `upper` will be closer.

Since we are assuming that the search will be successful, this process must eventually stop. At that point, row `middle` is the row we want. We can then process the data contained in that row.

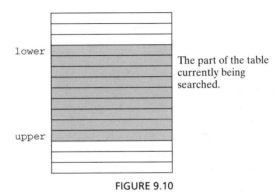

FIGURE 9.10

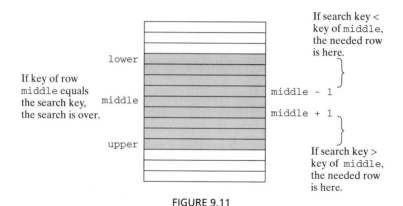

FIGURE 9.11

Now, suppose that the search key value is not in the table. How can we decide that the search is not successful? The search would still proceed as we described. At each pass of the search, we increase `lower` and decrease `upper`. If the search key is not in the table, the procedure eventually will make the value of `lower` greater than the value of `upper`. This contradiction signals an unsuccessful search.

The following pseudocode summarizes the essential parts of a binary search.

```
lower = 0, upper = tablesize - 1, middle = (lower + upper)/2
while (lower <= upper and search key unequal to table key)
  if (search key < table key)
    upper = middle - 1
  else
    lower = middle + 1
  endif
  middle = (lower + upper) / 2;
endwhile

if (lower > upper)
    display unsuccessful search
else
    extract table data from row middle
    process table data from row middle
endif
```

The `while` loop is the heart of the binary search. Its condition says to continue the search as long as the search is not unsuccessful (`lower <= upper`) and as long as we have not yet found the search key (search key unequal to table key). The loop body tests the part of the table that contains the search key and adjusts either `upper` or `lower`. In either case, it calculates the new value for `middle` for the next loop pass.

The second part of the pseudocode decides why the `while` loop ended. The `while` loop ended because a condition in its compound condition was false. If `lower > upper`, the search was not successful. Otherwise, the other condition was false and so the search key must be equal to the table key of row `middle`.

The program dem09-6.cpp shows how to do a binary search of a table. The program is based on dem09-4.cpp, which sorts the table that the user inputs.

```cpp
// dem09-6.cpp

// This program loads a table, sorts it using the bubble sort and
// then uses a binary search to search the table.

#include <iostream.h>
#include <iomanip.h>
#include <string.h>
#include <ctype.h>

using namespace std;

#define TABLE_SIZE 10

struct PART_STRUCT
  {
    char    part_no[8];
    int     quantity_on_hand;
    double  unit_price;
  };

void Load_Part_Table(PART_STRUCT [], int);
void Display_Part_Table(PART_STRUCT [], int);

int main()
  {
    PART_STRUCT part_table[TABLE_SIZE],
                temp_part;

    int row,
        pass,
        limit,
        middle,
        lower,
        upper;
    char part_key[8];      // The table search key
    char response[11];

    cout << setprecision(2)
         << setiosflags(ios::fixed)
         << setiosflags(ios::showpoint);

    // Load the table

    Load_Part_Table(part_table, TABLE_SIZE);

    // Sort the table using the bubble sort
```

```
limit = TABLE_SIZE - 2;

for (pass = 1; pass <= TABLE_SIZE - 1; ++pass)
  {
    for (row = 0; row <= limit; ++row)
    if (strcmp(part_table[row].part_no, part_table[row + 1].part_no) > 0)
      {
        temp_part = part_table[row];
        part_table[row] = part_table[row + 1];
        part_table[row + 1] = temp_part;
      }
    --limit;
    }

// Display the sorted table

cout << "\n\nThe table sorted on Part Number is:";

Display_Part_Table(part_table, TABLE_SIZE);

// Do the table search

cout << "\n\nDo you want to search the table?(Y/N): ";
cin.getline(response, 11);

cin.ignore(80, '\n'); //Clear the input buffer

while (toupper(*response) == 'Y')
  {
    cout << "\nEnter the part number: ";
    cin.getline(part_key, 8);

    cin.ignore(80, '\n'); //Clear the input buffer

    // Do the binary search

    lower = 0;
    upper = TABLE_SIZE - 1;
    middle = (lower + upper) / 2;

    while ( (strcmp(part_table[middle].part_no,part_key))
        && (lower <= upper) )
    {
      if (strcmp(part_key,part_table[middle].part_no) < 0)
        upper = middle - 1;
      else
        lower = middle + 1;
      middle = (lower + upper) / 2;
    }
    if (lower > upper)
      cout << "\nThe search for " << part_key
```

```
                      << " was not successful.";
          else
          {
            cout << "\nData for " << part_key << ":";
            cout << "\n\nQuantity On Hand: " << setw(10)
                    << part_table[middle].quantity_on_hand;
            cout << "\nUnit Price: " << setw(10)
                    << part_table[middle].unit_price;
          }

          cout << "\n\nDo you want to search the table?(Y/N): ";
          cin.getline(response, 11);

          cin.ignore(80, '\n');     //Clear the input buffer
        }

     return 0;

} //End of main()

void Load_Part_Table(PART_STRUCT part_table[], int size)
{
   int row;

   cout << "\nEnter the table values as you are prompted:\n\n";

   for (row = 0; row < size ; ++row)
     {
       cout << "\nFor row #" << row + 1 << " enter:";
       cout << "\nPart Number (7 Characters): ";
       cin.getline(part_table[row].part_no, 8);
       cout << "\nQuantity On Hand: ";
       cin >> part_table[row].quantity_on_hand;

       cin.ignore(80, '\n'); //Clear the input buffer

       cout << "\nUnit Price: ";
       cin >> part_table[row].unit_price;

       cin.ignore(80, '\n'); //Clear the input buffer
     }

} //End of Load_Part_Table()

void Display_Part_Table(PART_STRUCT part_table[], int size)
{
   int row;

   cout << "\n\n" << setw(20) << "Part Number"
                  << setw(20) << "Quantity On Hand"
                  << setw(20) << "Unit Price"
```

```
                        << endl;

    for (row = 0; row < TABLE_SIZE; ++row)
        cout << "\n" << setw(20) << part_table[row].part_no
                     << setw(20) << part_table[row].quantity_on_hand
                     << setw(20) << part_table[row].unit_price;



} //End of Display_Part_Table()
```

Program Output

```
Enter the table values as you are prompted:

For row #1 enter:
Part Number (7 Characters): A123456

Quantity On Hand: 123

Unit Price: 12.99

For row #2 enter:
Part Number (7 Characters): A987654

Quantity On Hand: 53

Unit Price: 52.95

For row #3 enter:
Part Number (7 Characters): D001234

Quantity On Hand: 93

Unit Price: 22.95

For row #4 enter:
Part Number (7 Characters): B109897

Quantity On Hand: 44

Unit Price: 13.95

For row #5 enter:
Part Number (7 Characters): A035467

Quantity On Hand: 15

Unit Price: 59.95
```

```
For row #6 enter:
Part Number (7 Characters): C837289

Quantity On Hand: 0

Unit Price: 57.99

For row #7 enter:
Part Number (7 Characters): D346246

Quantity On Hand: 35

Unit Price: 25.99

For row #8 enter:
Part Number (7 Characters): C235146

Quantity On Hand: 104

Unit Price: 110.99

For row #9 enter:
Part Number (7 Characters): B194791

Quantity On Hand: 33

Unit Price: 14.95

For row #10 enter:
Part Number (7 Characters): A826749

Quantity On Hand: 56

Unit Price: 41.95

The table sorted on Part Number is:

        Part Number    Quantity On Hand        Unit Price

          A035467                   15              59.95
          A123456                  123              12.99
          A826749                   56              41.95
          A987654                   53              52.95
          B109897                   44              13.95
          B194791                   33              14.95
          C253146                  104             110.99
          C837289                    0              57.99
          D001234                   93              22.95
          D346246                   35              25.99
```

```
Do you want to search the table?(Y/N): Y

Enter the part number: D001234

Data for D001234:

Quantity On Hand: 93
Unit Price: 22.95

Do you want to search the table?(Y/N): y

Enter the part number: C012345

The search for C012345 was not successful.

Do you want to search the table?(Y/N): Y

Enter the part number: A826749

Data for A826749:

Quantity On Hand: 56
Unit Price: 41.95

Do you want to search the table?(Y/N): N
```

The first part of the program closely follows dem09-4.cpp—it loads the table and sorts it on the part number. The next part of the program follows the pseudocode for the binary search. Note that the `while` loop's condition contains the following.

```
strcmp(part_table[middle].part_no, part_key)
```

Recall that `strcmp()` returns a nonzero number, which C++ considers true, if the result of the comparison is that the strings are not equal. Thus, the `while` loop's condition tests that the table key is unequal to the search key.

Similarly, in the `while` loop's body, the `if` statement tests the following.

```
strcmp(part_key,part_table[middle].part_no) < 0
```

If this condition is true, `part_key` precedes the value of `part_table[middle].part_no`. Thus, the search key is in the lower part of the table and an adjustment is made to the value of `upper`. If the condition is false, the search key is in the upper part of the table and an adjustment is made to the value of `lower`.

EXERCISES 9.3

Use the following declarations in Exercises 1–6.

```
struct ITEM_STRUCT
  {
     char name[21];
     double quantity,
            price;
  };

ITEM_STRUCT item = {"Hard Disk", 17, 345.99};
ITEM_STRUCT* item_ptr = &item;

ITEM_STRUCT inventory[100];
```

1. What is the value of `item.name[3]`?
2. What is the value of `item.name + 2`?
3. Is the reference `inventory[14].name` legal? If so, to what does it refer?
4. Is the reference `inventory.name` legal? If so, to what does it refer?
5. How would you refer to the `quantity` member of row 37 of the inventory table?
6. **(a)** Use the `STUDENT_STRUCT` structure type defined in Exercise 1, Section 9.2, to declare a table that will store the information on 100 students.
   (b) Write a `for` loop that prompts the user to enter the data necessary to load the table declared in part (a).
7. **(a)** Use the `JUROR_STRUCT` structure type defined in Exercise 2, Section 9.2, to declare a table that will store the information on 30 jurors.
   (b) Write a `for` loop that prompts the user to enter the data necessary to load the table declared in part (a).
8. **(a)** Use the `EMPLOYEE_STRUCT` structure type defined in Exercise 3, Section 9.2, to declare a table that will store the data on 20 employees.
   (b) Write a `for` loop that prompts the user to enter the data necessary to load the table declared in part (a).

EXPERIMENTS 9.3

1. Omit the call to `cin.get()` at the end of the first `for` loop in dem09-3.cpp.
2. Recode dem09-3.cpp by hard coding the parts table. Explain what happens.
3. Change dem09-4.cpp so that it sorts the table in descending order.
4. Recode dem09-6.cpp so that it sorts the parts table in descending order and does a binary search to search the table.

PROGRAMMING PROBLEMS 9.3

1. The following table contains the post office abbreviations and names of five states in the Northeast.

State Name	State Code
New York	NY
New Jersey	NJ
Pennsylvania	PA
Connecticut	CT
Rhode Island	RI

Write a program in which you hard code a similar table that contains the state names and abbreviations of all 50 states. (You can find this table in an encyclopedia or almanac.) The program should prompt the user to enter a state name. Let the program do a sequential search to find the corresponding state postal code. The program should display the postal code.

2. Redo Programming Problem 1 but let the program do a binary search of the table.

3. See Programming Problems 1 and 2. We mentioned in the text that the binary search is faster than the sequential search when the table is about size 50. This programming problem shows how to test this statement. We can measure the efficiency of a search technique by how many table key comparisons the technique makes. In your solutions to Programming Problems 1 and 2, declare a counter variable, which you should initialize to zero in its declaration. Increment the counter for each execution of the `strcmp()` function in the search part of the program. Have each program display the value of this counter before the program ends. Run the sequential search program 10 times and total the number of key compares that the sequential search makes. Now do the same for the binary search program using the same input data that you used for the sequential search program. How do the total number of key comparisons compare? Is the binary search more efficient than the sequential search?

4. A car rental company uses the following table to help compute rental fees.

Car Type	Rate Per Day	Rate Per Mile
Chevrolet	50.00	0.27
Corvette	85.00	0.45
Pontiac	53.00	0.32
Buick	60.00	0.32
Oldsmobile	60.00	0.35
Cadillac	70.00	0.40

Write a program to calculate car rental fees based on this table. The program should prompt the user to enter the name of the type of car that was rented, the number of days the car was rented, and the number of miles the car was driven. The program should search the table for a match on the car type. If there is a match, the rental fee is the number of days rented times the rate per day plus the number of miles traveled times the rate per mile. The program should display the type of car, the number of days rented, the number of miles driven, and the rental fee. If the table search cannot find the car type in the table, display an appropriate error message. Write the program to process any number of rentals.

5. The marketing department of a large book club wants to analyze the geographical distribution of its customers by categorizing customers by zip code. Write a program that prompts the user to enter the five-digit zip code of a customer. Store the customer information in an array of structures that have two integer members—the first member stores a zip code and the second stores the count of the customers that have that zip code. Assume a maximum of 100 different zip codes. When a zip code is entered, search the zip code table for the zip code. If it is not in the table, add it to the end of the table and set the corresponding count to one. If the entered zip code is in the zip code table, increment the corresponding count. When the user completes entering zip codes, the program should display a table that lists the zip codes with their corresponding counts and the percent that count is of the total number of customers. The total number of customers should display at the bottom of the table.

6. Write a program that creates a telephone book. Each telephone book entry is to consist of a name and a 10-digit telephone number. Implement a table entry by a structure with two members—a character pointer called `name` and an array of 11 characters called `tel_no` that stores the telephone number as a string. The program should allow for at most 100 names. The program should ask the user to enter the letter 'I' to insert a name in the directory, 'R' to retrieve a telephone number from the directory, 'P' to display the contents of the directory, or 'Q' to exit the program. If the user enters 'I', the program should prompt the user for a last name and store the name in a character array buffer. Then the program should dynamically allocate enough space for the name and assign the name member of the next available row to the allocated space. Next the program should copy the name, which is stored in the buffer, to the allocated space. The program should then prompt for the corresponding telephone number. If the user enters 'R', the program should search the directory for the corresponding name. If the name is found, display the corresponding telephone number. If the name is not found, display an error message. If the user enters 'P', display the contents of the directory in tabular form with appropriate column headings. If the user enters 'Q', display an ending message and end the program.

9.4 Structures, Functions, and Pointers

Since a structure is a data type, a function can return a structure to a calling function. We can also pass a structure to a function as a function argument. However, a structure is usually a large aggregate of data. Pointers, therefore, can make manipulating structures more efficient. This section discusses how to use structures with functions and how to use pointers to structures.

Functions and Structures

A structure can be a function argument and a function can return a structure. For example, suppose that we need a function to convert a character string that represents a date of the form mm/dd/yy into three integers. The first integer represents the month, the second integer represents the day, and the third integer represents the year. The function will return the three integers in a variable of the following structure type.

```
struct DATE_STRUCT
  {
    int month,
        day,
        year;
  };
```

Once this function converts the date, we want to verify that the date is valid. For example, the date 7/53/95 is invalid. We will verify the date using a function whose argument is a date of type DATE_STRUCT. For a date to be valid, the day number must be within the valid range of days for the associated month, taking leap years into account. Also, to be valid the year must be 80 or greater. The program dem09-7.cpp converts and validates a date and illustrates how to use structures with functions. The program uses the function atoi(), which we discussed in Section 8.5.

```
// dem09-7.cpp

// This program demonstrates the use of structures as function
//arguments and function return values.

#include <iostream.h>
#include <iomanip.h>
#include <stdlib.h>
#include <ctype.h>

using namespace std;
struct DATE_STRUCT
  {
    int month,
        day,
        year;
  };

DATE_STRUCT String_To_MDY(char*);
int         Validate_Date(DATE_STRUCT);
char*       Strchcpy(char*, char*, int);

int main()
{
  char date_string [9];
```

```cpp
    DATE_STRUCT mdy_date;
    char response[8];

    cout << "\n\nDo you want to convert and validate a date?(Y/N): ";
    cin.getline(response, 8);

    cin.ignore(80, '\n'); //Clear the input buffer

    while (toupper(*response) == 'Y')
      {
        cout << "\nEnter the date in mm/dd/yy form: ";
        cin.getline(date_string, 9);

        cin.ignore(80, '\n'); //Clear the input buffer

        mdy_date = String_To_MDY (date_string);

        cout << "\nThe converted date is the following:";
        cout << "\n\nMonth: " << setw(3) << mdy_date.month;
        cout << "\nDay:   " << setw(3) << mdy_date.day;
        cout << "\nYear:  " << setw(3) << mdy_date.year << endl;

        if ( Validate_Date(mdy_date) )
          cout << "\nThe date is valid.";
        else
          cout << "\nThe date is invalid.";

        cout << "\n\nDo you want to convert and validate a date?(Y/N): ";
        cin.getline(response, 8);

        cin.ignore(80, '\n');    //Clear the input buffer
      }

    return 0;
} // End of main()

DATE_STRUCT String_To_MDY(char* date_ptr)
{
    DATE_STRUCT mdy_date;
    char month[3],
         day[3],
         year[3];
    char* ch_ptr;

    ch_ptr = date_ptr;

    ch_ptr = Strchcpy(month, ch_ptr, '/');
    ++ch_ptr;
    ch_ptr = Strchcpy(day, ch_ptr, '/');
    ++ch_ptr;
```

```
    Strchcpy(year, ch_ptr, '\0');

  mdy_date.month = atoi(month);
  mdy_date.day   = atoi(day);
  mdy_date.year  = atoi(year);

  return mdy_date;

} // End of String_To_MDY()

char* Strchcpy(char* target, char* source, int ch)
{
  while (*source != ch && *source != '\0')
    {
      *target = *source;
      ++target;
      ++source;
    }
  *target = '\0';

  return source;

} // End of Strchcpy()

int Validate_Date(DATE_STRUCT date)
{
  int ny_days [13] = {0, 31, 28, 31, 30, 31, 30, 31, 31, 30, 31, 30, 31};
  int ly_days [13] = {0, 31, 29, 31, 30, 31, 30, 31, 31, 30, 31, 30, 31};

  if (date.month < 1 || date.month > 12)
    return 0;

  if (date.day < 1)
    return 0;
  if (date.year % 4 == 0)
    {
      if (date.day > ly_days[date.month])
        return 0;
    }
  else
    if (date.day > ny_days[date.month])
      return 0;

  if (date.year < 80)
    return 0;

  return 1;

} // End of Validate_Date()
```

Program Output

```
Do you want to convert and validate a date?(Y/N): y

Enter the date in mm/dd/yy form: 6/9/93

The converted date is the following:

Month: 6
Day:   9
Year: 93
The date is valid.

Do you want to convert and validate a date?(Y/N): Yes

Enter the date in mm/dd/yy form: 2/29/96

The converted date is the following:

Month: 2
Day: 29
Year: 96

The date is valid.

Do you want to convert and validate a date?(Y/N): Y

Enter the date in mm/dd/yy form: 13/14/83

The converted date is the following:

Month: 13
Day:   14
Year:  83

The date is invalid.

Do you want to convert and validate a date?(Y/N): y

Enter the date in mm/dd/yy form: 3/33/95

The converted date is the following:

Month: 3
Day:  33
Year: 95

The date is invalid.
```

```
Do you want to convert and validate a date?(Y/N): y

Enter the date in mm/dd/yy form: 9/23/76

The converted date is the following:

Month: 9
Day:   23
Year:  76

The date is invalid.

Do you want to convert and validate a date?(Y/N): n
```

The program begins with the definition of the DATE_STRUCT structure type, which the program uses to store the date as a set of three integers. The program uses three user-defined functions. String_To_MDY() converts the date, which the user enters as a string of the form mm/dd/yy, into a date of type DATE_STRUCT. Thus, the return type of String_To_MDY() is DATE_STRUCT. Validate_Date() validates the date passed to it as an argument of type DATE_STRUCT. It returns 1 if the date is valid and returns 0 if the date is invalid. We shall explain the purpose of the third function, Strchcpy(), when we discuss the String_To_MDY() function.

The logic of the main processing loop of dem09-7.cpp should be familiar by now. It asks the user if he or she wants to convert and validate a date. If the response is yes, the program enters the loop. Inside the loop, the program asks the user to enter a date in the form mm/dd/yy. First, cin.getline() retrieves the string and stores it in the character array date_string[]. Next, the program passes date_string to the function String_To_MDY(), which converts it into a date stored as a structure of type DATE_STRUCT. The assignment statement stores the returned structure in the structure variable mdy_date. The cout statements display the converted date.

The condition in the if statement calls the function Validate_Date(). Then an appropriate message is displayed depending on whether the date is valid or invalid. Finally, the program prompts the user again to see if he or she wants to process another date.

The heart of dem09-7.cpp is the function String_To_MDY(), which converts the date as a string into a date as a DATE_STRUCT structure. The function first separates the month, day, and year digits from the string. The month digits are the first digits in the string up to but not including the slash. The day digits are the digits from the digit after the first slash up to but not including the second slash. The year digits are the digits from the digit after the second slash to the end of the string. In all three cases, we must obtain characters in the date string from a certain position up to a specific character (the slash in the first two cases, the '\0' in the third case). Because this is essentially the same operation in all three cases, it is appropriate to use a function, which we call Strchcpy(), to do the job.

The function Strchcpy() has three arguments. The first argument is the target string, which is the string into which the function places the result. The second argument is a character pointer, which points to the character in the source string where the copying begins. The third argument is the character that determines when the copying is to stop. The function returns a pointer to the character that makes the copying stop. Thus, the function copies characters from the position determined by its second argument to the string that is its first argument. The copying stops when the function encounters the character that is the function's third argument. To see how the function works, we explain its uses in `String_To_MDY()`.

The parameter `date_ptr` points to the first character of the string that contains the date in mm/dd/yy form. The first assignment statement in `String_To_MDY()` initializes the character pointer to the value of `date_ptr`. The right side of the next assignment calls the function `Strchcpy()`. We want to copy the digits that specify the month into the character array `month`. Thus, we want to copy the digits up to the first `'/'` from the string pointed to by `ch_ptr` into the array `month`. This is exactly what `Strchcpy(month, ch_ptr, '/')` does. See Figure 9.12. The function returns a pointer to the `'/'` character. To make the next call to `Strchcpy()` work correctly, we increment the pointer `ch_ptr` so that it points to the first character after the `'/'`.

The next assignment statement is similar to the previous one. It copies the day digits into the array `day`. Finally, the third call to `Strchcpy()` copies the year digits into the array `year`. The delimiting character is now the null character `'\0'`.

The digits representing the month, day, and year are separately stored in three character arrays. Now we must convert the three character strings into the corresponding integer values. The next three assignments use the standard library function `atoi()` to convert the numeric character strings into the corresponding integers. Finally, `String_To_MDY()` returns the structure in which the numeric date is stored. (The operation of `String_To_MDY()` depends on the character string that the user enters being in the mm/dd/yy form. What if the user incorrectly enters the date? See Programming Problem 1.)

The function `Strchcpy()` copies characters as follows. The `while` loop in `Strchcpy()` copies one character at a time from the source string to the target string. `Strchcpy()` continues copying until it either finds the delimiter character, which is stored in `ch`, or the end of the source string. Once the `while` loop ends, the function places the null character at the end of the target string. Finally, the function returns the value of the pointer `source`, which points to the character that caused the copying to stop.

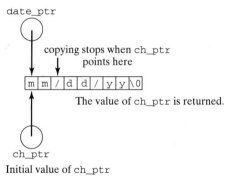

FIGURE 9.12

Once `main()` obtains the date in numeric form in the structure `mdy_date`, it displays the resulting date. Then `main()` executes an `if` statement. The `if`'s condition tests the value returned from the function `Validate_Date()` and displays an appropriate message.

`Validate_Date()` validates the date. The only part of the function that we shall explain is the test to see if the day is too large. The day must be checked against the number of days in the month. The number of days in February depends on whether the year is a leap year—29 days for a leap year, 28 days otherwise. We begin by testing the year. The expression `date.year % 4` is the remainder when the year is divided by four. If the remainder is zero, the year is divisible by four and is, therefore, a leap year. (This test will be valid until the year 2100. See Programming Problem 2.) We then check the value of `date.day` against `ly_days[date_month]`. The integer array `ly_days` holds the number of days in each month in a leap year. We place zero in the first element of this array so that the month number corresponds to the correct subscript value. If `date.day` is greater than `ly_days[date.month]`, the date is invalid and the function returns 0. Note that the inner `if` is enclosed in braces. Without these braces, the compiler would pair the following `else` with the second `if` and not the first `if`, which is what we want.

If the year is not a leap year, the value of `day` is compared to the number of days in the corresponding month for a normal year. This number is stored in the integer array `ny_days[]`. Finally, if the date passes all the tests, it is valid and the function returns the value 1.

Pointers to Structures

Recall that by default, C++ passes the arguments to a function by value. When dem09-7.cpp calls the function `Validate_Date()`, it passes a copy of the structure variable `mdy_date`. Similarly, when `String_To_MDY()` converts the date into three integers, it passes a copy of a `DATE_STRUCT` variable back to `main()`. A variable of type `DATE_STRUCT` is not very large. However, if we were to pass a much larger structure back and forth between functions, it could become very inefficient. It is usually more efficient to pass a structure pointer to a function instead of passing a copy of the structure itself. All pointers are the same size and small (usually four bytes). Therefore, using pointers minimizes the cost of processing structures in functions.

> **NOTE 9.5—USING STRUCTURE POINTERS IN FUNCTIONS**
>
> Use structure pointers to pass structures between functions if the structure contains eight or more bytes.

In C++, pointers are very versatile. A pointer can point to virtually anything, including a structure variable. For example, if `mdy_date` is a variable of type `DATE_STRUCT` as it was in dem09-7.cpp, we can declare the pointer `date_struct_ptr` and initialize it to point to `mdy_date` as follows.

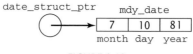

FIGURE 9.13

```
DATE_STRUCT* date_struct_ptr = &mdy_date;
```

Figure 9.13 shows the pointer and its target.

To access the entire structure through the pointer, we can use the indirection operator: `*date_struct_ptr`. To access a particular structure member through the pointer, we can use an expression such as the following.

```
(*date_struct_ptr).day
```

Using Note 9.3, read this reference from right to left as "the day member of the target of `date_struct_ptr`" or "`date_struct_ptr's target's day`." In Figure 9.13, this would have the value 10.

Programming
Pointers

Referencing a structure member through a pointer is so common that C++ has a special operator for this purpose. The "to" operator, $->$, which is a minus followed by a greater than symbol, can be used to reference a structure member through a pointer. To reference the day member of the structure `mdy_date` through the pointer `date_struct_ptr`, we can use the following.

```
date_struct_ptr -> date
```

NOTE 9.6—READING THE "to" OPERATOR

Read the to operator, $->$, as "the member of the target of" or as a possessive of the target.

Read the previous reference from right to left as "the `day` member of the target of `date_struct_ptr`" or "`date_struct_ptr`'s target's `day`".

The program dem09-8.cpp is a second version of dem09-7.cpp. Its functions use structure pointers to access the DATE_STRUCT variables.

```
// dem09-8.cpp

// This program demonstrates the use of structure pointers
// in functions.

#include <iostream.h>
#include <iomanip.h>
#include <stdlib.h>
#include <ctype.h>
```

```cpp
using namespace std;

struct DATE_STRUCT
  {
    int month,
        day,
        year;
  };

void    String_To_MDY(char*, DATE_STRUCT*);
int     Validate_Date(DATE_STRUCT*);
char*   Strchcpy(char*, char*, int);

int main()
{
  char date_string [9];
  DATE_STRUCT mdy_date;
  char response[8];

  cout << "\n\nDo you want to convert and validate a date?(Y/N): ";
  cin.getline(response, 8);

  cin.ignore(80, '\n');     //Clear the input buffer

  while (toupper(*response) == 'Y')
    {
      cout << "\nEnter the date in mm/dd/yy form: ";
      cin.getline(date_string, 9);

      cin.ignore(80, '\n');    //Clear the input buffer

      String_To_MDY (date_string, &mdy_date);

      cout << "\nThe converted date is the following:";
      cout << "\n\nMonth: " << setw(3) << mdy_date.month;
      cout << "\nDay:   " << setw(3) << mdy_date.day;
      cout << "\nYear:  " << setw(3) << mdy_date.year << endl;

      if ( Validate_Date(&mdy_date) )
        cout << "\nThe date is valid.";
      else
        cout << "\nThe date is invalid.";

      cout << "\n\nDo you want to convert and validate a date?(Y/N): ";
      cin.getline(response, 9);

      cin.ignore(80, '\n');    //Clear the input buffer
    }

  return 0;
```

```
} // End of main()

void String_To_MDY(char* date_ptr, DATE_STRUCT* date_struct_ptr)
{
  char month[3],
       day[3],
       year[3];
  char* ch_ptr;

  ch_ptr = date_ptr;

  ch_ptr = Strchcpy(month, ch_ptr, '/');
  ++ch_ptr;
  ch_ptr = Strchcpy(day, ch_ptr, '/');
  ++ch_ptr;
  Strchcpy(year, ch_ptr, '\0');

  date_struct_ptr -> month = atoi(month);
  date_struct_ptr -> day   = atoi(day);
  date_struct_ptr -> year  = atoi(year);

  return;

} // End of String_To_MDY()

char* Strchcpy(char* target, char* source, int ch)
{
  while (*source != ch && *source != '\0')
    {
      *target = *source;
      ++target;
      ++source;
    }

  *target = '\0';
  return source;

} // End of Strchcpy()

int Validate_Date(DATE_STRUCT* date_struct_ptr)
{
  int ny_days [13] = {0, 31, 28, 31, 30, 31, 30, 31, 31, 30, 31, 30, 31};
  int ly_days [13] = {0, 31, 29, 31, 30, 31, 30, 31, 31, 30, 31, 30, 31};

  if (date_struct_ptr -> month < 1 || date_struct_ptr -> month > 12)
    return 0;

  if (date_struct_ptr -> day < 1)
    return 0;
  if (date_struct_ptr -> year % 4 == 0)
```

```
    {
      if (date_struct_ptr -> day > ly_days[date_struct_ptr -> month])
        return 0;
    }
  else
    if (date_struct_ptr -> day > ny_days[date_struct_ptr -> month])
      return 0;

  if (date_struct_ptr -> year < 80)
    return 0;

  return 1;
} // End of Validate_Date()
```

The logic and output of dem09-8.cpp are exactly those of dem09-7.cpp. Therefore, we shall discuss only the uses the program makes of structure pointers. In dem09-8.cpp, `String_To_MDY()` is a `void` function because its second argument is a pointer to a variable of type `DATE_STRUCT`. Instead of returning a copy of the date in a structure, we pass a pointer to such a structure to the function. The function then manipulates the structure variable in `main()`. Similarly, we pass a `DATE_STRUCT` pointer to the function `Validate_Date()` instead of passing a copy of the structure.

After obtaining the date and placing it into the array `date_string`, `main()` calls the function `String_To_MDY()`. `Main()` passes two pointers to `String_To_MDY()` — `date_string`, which points to the beginning of the array containing the date in mm/dd/yy form, and `&mdy_date`, which is the address of the structure variable `mdy_date`. In the function `String_To_MDY()`, the parameter `date_struct_ptr` points to the structure `mdy_date` in `main()`. See Figure 9.14.

Most of the function `String_To_MDY()` is the same as it was in dem09-7.cpp except the last three assignments. In this version of the function, we use the member operator to refer to the members of the target of `date_struct_ptr`. For example, the following assignment places the integer form of the month into the `month` member of the target of `date_struct_ptr`, which is the `month` member of `mdy_date` in `main()`. See Figure 9.14.

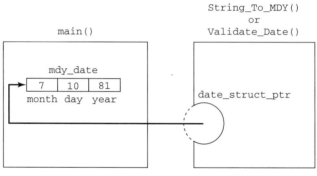

FIGURE 9.14

```
date_struct_ptr -> month = atoi(month);
```

The parameter `date_struct_ptr` in `Validate_Date()` also points to the structure variable `mdy_date` in `main()`. All references to the members of the structure must use the member operator. For example, in the first `if` statement, we refer to the `month` member of date as follows.

```
date_struct_ptr -> month
```

As before, this refers to the `month` member of the structure `mdy_date` in `main()`.

Structure References

Programming
Pointers

You can also pass a structure reference to a function. Using structure references combines the ease of passing a structure by value with the efficiency of using references, which are essentially the same as pointers. Following is dem09-9.cpp, which is still another version of dem09-7.cpp.

```
// dem09-9.cpp

// This program demonstrates the use of structure references
// in functions.

#include <iostream.h>
#include <iomanip.h>
#include <stdlib.h>
#include <ctype.h>

using namespace std;

struct DATE_STRUCT
    {
        int month,
            day,
            year;
    };

void    String_To_MDY(char*, DATE_STRUCT&);
int     Validate_Date(DATE_STRUCT&);
char*   Strchcpy(char*, char*, int);

int main()
{
  char date_string [9];
  DATE_STRUCT mdy_date;
  char response[8];
```

```
   cout << "\n\nDo you want to convert and validate a date?(Y/N): ";
   cin.getline(response, 8);

   cin.ignore(80, '\n');    //Clear the input buffer

   while (toupper(*response) == 'Y')
     {
       cout << "\nEnter the date in mm/dd/yy form: ";
       cin.getline(date_string, 9);

       cin.ignore(80, '\n'); //Clear the input buffer

       String_To_MDY (date_string, mdy_date);

       cout << "\nThe converted date is the following:";
       cout << "\n\nMonth: " << setw(3) << mdy_date.month;
       cout << "\nDay:   " << setw(3) << mdy_date.day;
       cout << "\nYear:  " << setw(3) << mdy_date.year << endl;

       if ( Validate_Date(mdy_date) )
         cout << "\nThe date is valid.";
       else
         cout << "\nThe date is invalid.";
       cout << "\n\nDo you want to convert and validate a date?(Y/N): ";
       cin.getline(response, 9);

       cin.ignore(80, '\n');    //Clear the input buffer
     }

   return 0;
} // End of main()

void String_To_MDY(char* date_ptr, DATE_STRUCT& date_struct)
{
   char month[3],
        day[3],
        year[3];
   char* ch_ptr;

   ch_ptr = date_ptr;

   ch_ptr = Strchcpy(month, ch_ptr, '/');
   ++ch_ptr;
   ch_ptr = Strchcpy(day, ch_ptr, '/');
   ++ch_ptr;
   Strchcpy(year, ch_ptr, '\0');

   date_struct.month = atoi(month);
   date_struct.day   = atoi(day);
   date_struct.year  = atoi(year);
```

```
      return;

} // End of String_To_MDY()

char* Strchcpy(char* target, char* source, int ch)
{
  while (*source != ch && *source != '\0')
  {
    *target = *source;
    ++target;
    ++source;
  }

  *target = '\0';

  return source;

} // End of Strchcpy()

int Validate_Date(DATE_STRUCT& date_struct)
{
  int ny_days [13] = {0, 31, 28, 31, 30, 31, 30, 31, 31, 30, 31, 30, 31};
  int ly_days [13] = {0, 31, 29, 31, 30, 31, 30, 31, 31, 30, 31, 30, 31};

  if (date_struct.month < 1 || date_struct.month > 12)
      return 0;

  if (date_struct.day < 1)
      return 0;
  if (date_struct.year % 4 == 0)
      {
        if (date_struct.day > ly_days[date_struct.month])
          return 0;
      }
  else
        if (date_struct.day > ny_days[date_struct.month])
          return 0;




  if (date_struct.year < 80)
      return 0;

  return 1;

} // End of Validate_Date()
```

The only differences between this program and dem09-8.cpp are that the structure arguments in the functions `String_to_MDY()` and `Validate_Date()` are references instead of pointers. In the code of these funcitons, this allows us to use the member operator on the structure parameters instead of the to operator on the structure pointers. This makes coding the functions a little easier.

EXERCISES 9.4

Use the following declarations in Exercises 1–4.

```
struct ITEM_STRUCT
  {
    char name[21];
    double quantity,
           price;
  };

ITEM_STRUCT item = {"Hard Disk", 17, 345.99};
ITEM_STRUCT* item_ptr = &item;

ITEM_STRUCT inventory[100];
```

1. What is the value of `item_ptr -> price`?
2. What is the value of `item_ptr -> name + 2`?
3. What is the value of `*(item_ptr -> name +2)`?
4. Write a statement that makes `item_ptr` point to the 54th row of the inventory table.
5. **(a)** Refer to Exercise 6, Section 9.3. Write a function `Get_Student_Data_1()` that prompts for and obtains the data for one student. The function should not have any arguments and should pass a copy of the filled student structure back to the calling program. Rewrite the `for` loop of Exercise 6 to use `Get_Student_Data_1()`.
   (b) Write another version of the function of part (a), `Get_Student_Data_2()`, that uses pointers. The function should not return a value and should have one argument, which is a pointer to a variable of type `STUDENT_STRUCT`. Rewrite the `for` loop of Exercise 6 to use `Get_Student_Data_2()`.
6. Repeat Exercise 5 for the structure defined in Exercise 7, Section 9.3.
7. Repeat Exercise 5 for the structure defined in Exercise 8, Section 9.3.

EXPERIMENTS 9.4

1. The standard library function `strchr()` is a string handling function. It takes two arguments. The first argument is a character pointer and the second is a character. The function returns the address of the first occurrence of the character that is its second argument in the string that is its first argument. If the character does not occur in the string, the function returns the NULL pointer. Recode dem09-7 using the function `strchr()` instead of the user-defined function `Strchcpy()`.

2. In dem09-7.cpp, we made the first element of the day number arrays zero so that the month number equaled the subscript number of the number of days in the month. Recode dem09-7.cpp so that the first element of both day number arrays is 31, the number of days in January.

PROGRAMMING PROBLEMS 9.4

In the following programming problems, use `typedef`, enumerated types, structures, and structure pointers where appropriate.

1. The function `String_To_MDY()` assumes that the user correctly enters the date in the form mm/dd/yy. Recode this function to include the following test. Test the string that the user enters to see if it consists of two digits, followed by a slash, followed by two more digits and a slash, followed by two digits. If the string is invalid, issue an error message and exit the program.

2. The test for a leap year that we used in dem09-7.cpp is not quite correct. A year is a leap year if the year number is divisible by four, except if the year number is divisible by 100. Of the years that are divisible by 100, the only ones that are leap years are those divisible by 400. Thus, the year 1900 was not a leap year, but the year 2000 is a leap year. Recode the function `Validate_Date()` to incorporate the correct test for a leap year.

3. Dates are sometimes provided in the conventional form of month name, day of the month, and year (in the form 19yy). Some applications use such dates in computations (for example, calculating how many days a bill is past due). In these cases it is convenient to convert the dates from conventional form to Julian form before the computations that use the dates. (A date's Julian date is the number of days the date is from January 1. Thus, January 1 is day 1, January 2 is day 2, and so on. Write a function that has one argument—a pointer to a structure that contains the date in conventional form. (You must define this structure.) The function should return the Julian date equivalent of the conventional date that is passed to it. Be sure to take leap year into account. The function should use the following table.

Month	Number of First Day (non-leap year)
January	1
February	32
March	60
April	91
May	121
June	152
July	182
August	213
September	244
October	274
November	305
December	335

Write a short program that tests this function.

4. A professor of marketing keeps the following information on each student in her Marketing 101 class: student last name, student first name, social security number, telephone number, grades for five quizzes, grade for the final exam, and the final grade average.

  (a) Design a structure that will store the information on a student.

  (b) Write a function that prompts the user for all the information for one student except the final grade. The function's only argument should be a pointer to a structure of the type defined in part (a).

  (c) Write a function whose only argument is a pointer to a structure of the type defined in part (a) and which computes the final grade of the student as follows: the final grade is 75 percent of the quiz average plus 25 percent of the final exam.

  (d) Write a program that prompts the user to input data on as many as 25 students, which should be stored in a table. The program should use the function of part (b) to input the data. Once the table is loaded, the program should use the function of part (c) to compute the final grade average of each student. Finally, the program should display a report that lists the students in alphabetical order. For each student, display the quiz average, the final exam grade, and the final quiz average.

5. (a) A small airline company needs a program to keep track of the seat availability of its flights. Design the structure type FLIGHT to store a four-digit flight number, the departure date in mmddyy form, the three-character departure airport code, the three-character arrival airport code, and an array SEATS of row structures to store the seating data. The array of row structures is to have 20 elements, one for each row in the airplane. The row structure ROW is to have four integer members called a, b, c, and d, corresponding to the four seats in the row. If a seat is occupied, the corresponding member in the seating array should be 1. Otherwise, the member should be 0.

  (b) Declare an array of five elements of type FLIGHT. Write a function that initializes the array. The function should prompt the user to enter the flight information (flight number, departure date, departure city code, and arrival city code) for all five flights. The function should initialize all the members of the SEATS arrays to 0. Pass the address of the flight array to the function.

  (c) Write a function that displays a list of all the empty seats on a flight. Pass the flight number to the function and a pointer to the flight array. The display should be in tabular form for easy reading. The function should indicate when a flight has no available seats.

  (d) Write a seat reservation program. The program should use the function of part (b) to initialize the array of flights. The program should do the following in a loop: Display a list of the flight numbers, ask the user to enter a flight number, and display a list of all the empty seats on that flight by using the function in part (c). Ask the user to pick an available seat(s) from the list of seats. Mark the seat(s) as occupied.

Chapter Review

Terminology

Define the following terms.

typedef	structure tag
enum	structure members
enumerated type	member operator
structure	hard coding a table
struct	

Summary

- The statement `typedef old-type new-type` defines a new data type (Note 9.1). You can declare variables of this new type.
- The `enum` statement defines a set of integer constants that are represented by identifiers. The `enum` statement defines a data type. You can declare variables of this new type (Note 9.2).
- A structure, declared with the keyword `struct`, defines a data type consisting of data items of different types. A structure is a new data type. You can declare variables of this new type.
- Use the member operator, `.`, to access a member of a structure (Note 9.3).
- The data type of a structure member reference is the same as the type of the rightmost element of that reference (Note 9.4).
- A structure can have a member that is a structure.
- You can assign a structure variable to a structure variable of the same type. The assignment is done on a member by member basis.
- You can define a table as an array of structures.
- A sequential table search tests each row, in sequence, until there is a match to the search key or until the search fails.
- A binary search repeatedly divides that table in half until there is a match to the search key or until the search fails.
- If a table has 50 or more rows, a binary search is more efficient than a sequential search.
- A function can have a structure as an argument.
- A function can return a structure.
- Instead of passing a structure as an argument by value, it is usually more efficient to pass a pointer to the structure (Note 9.5).
- Use the `->` operator to access a structure member through a pointer (Note 9.6). The expression `str_ptr -> member` is equivalent to `(*str_ptr).member`.
- You can use a reference to a structure as a function argument.

Review Exercises

1. Which C++ statement allows you to define a data type in terms of existing data types? Give an example of how you might use this statement.

2. What is an enumerated type? Which C++ statement can you use to declare an enumerated type?

3. What is a structure and how do you declare one?

4. Does a structure declaration reserve computer storage?

5. Which operator can you use to access a structure member?

6. How can you initialize a structure variable?

7. How is one structure variable assigned to another of the same type?

8. How can you declare a table?

9. What is meant by a table key?

10. Describe how a binary search works.

11. How can you declare and define a function that returns a structure?

12. How can you declare and define a function that has a structure as an argument?

13. How can you declare and define a function that has a structure pointer as an argument?

14. What operator can you use to access a structure member through a pointer? Give an example of its use.

Object-Oriented Programming

Chapter

10

Classes and Objects

Objectives

- To define a class and instantiate objects in a program.
- To code class member functions
- To use the scope resolution operator to define a class member function outside the class declaration.
- To access a class member using the "dot" notation.
- To differentiate between accessor and mutator functions.

- To code a class constructor.
- To code a class destructor.
- To assign one object to another.
- To overload class constructors.
- To use default arguments in a function.
- To code and use function templates.

Introduction

In the first nine chapters we used structured techniques to solve programming problems. We developed a procedural solution to each problem by dividing the problem into a series of steps. Beginning in Chapter 5, we used a top-down approach to solve more complicated problems. Some steps in the problem solutions were handled by functions. The functions completed their steps procedurally. In this and the following chapters we discuss a different way of approaching problems: object-oriented programming.

Objects, and the related concept of classes, are central to all object-oriented programming languages, including C++. An **object** consists of one or more data values, which define the state or properties of the object, and a set of functions that can be applied to that object. The functions (also called procedures or methods) associated with an object represent what can be done to the object, how the object can behave, or how the object responds to external influences. An object can be a thing, a person, or even an intangible such as a bank savings account. A **class**, on the other hand, is a general category that defines (1) the characteristics of the data (the data members of the class) that an object of that category contains and (2) the functions (the class member functions) that can be applied to objects of that class. Several examples will help clarify these ideas.

A Book Class: Book is an example of a class. The class Book is an abstraction. Some of the defining characteristics or properties of a Book (and, therefore, the data members of the class) are the title, author, number of pages, and ISBN number. Some of the functions (and, therefore, the member functions of the class) that you can perform on a book are Open_Book(), which opens the book to the first page, and Turn_To_Page(n), which turns to page *n* in the book. Note that we are not discussing any particular book. We are describing the general characteristics of the Book class and operations that we can apply to any book.

A specific book, for example the one you are reading now, is an example of a Book object. It has a specific title, author, number of pages, and ISBN that are unique. You can apply any one of the operations mentioned previously to this book. You can use Open_Book() to open the book and then use Turn_To_Page(n) to open to the page you are reading now. An object is a particular, concrete instance of a class. A class, on the other hand, is an abstraction.

A Student Class: In a college registration system, you might define the class Student. Some of the defining characteristics of the class Student (the class data members) are the name, ID number, completed credits, and current credits. Some operations associated with the class Student (the class member functions) might be Assign_ID(n), which assigns the ID number *n* to a student, and Change_Completed_Credits(c), which increases by *c* the number of credits completed by a student. Suppose Maxwell Larrabee is a student at your school, has completed 52 credits, and is currently taking 15 credits. You would then create the Student object Larrabee that represents this student. When the semester ends, the system would apply Change_Completed_Credits(15) to the object Larrabee to add the 15 credits to his total credits.

A Savings Account Class: In a banking system, you might define a SavingsAccount class. A savings account has an ID number, an owner, and a balance. The operations you might associate with the SavingsAccount class are Deposit(d), which makes a deposit of *d* dollars into a savings account, and Withdraw(w), which withdraws *w* dollars from a savings account (assuming, of course, that there is enough money in the account to cover the withdrawal). If you have a savings account in this bank, you are the owner, the ID number of the account might be 1234, and the balance in the account might be $347.28. The banking system would create a SavingsAccount object, say Jones, which represents your account. If you want to deposit $50 into your account, the banking system would apply Deposit(50.00) to the account object Jones. Once again, the class SavingsAccount is an abstraction and describes the general characteristics of any savings account in this particular banking system. The savings account object Jones that represents your account is a SavingsAccount object. It is a specific account with an owner, an ID number, and a specific balance. Your bank account is a particular instance of the SavingsAccount class.

The Object-Oriented View of a System

In object-oriented programming, we view an application as a system of interacting objects. The objects interact by sending messages to one another and behaving in certain ways in response to the messages. To illustrate, suppose you are asked to construct an automatic teller machine (ATM) system for a small bank. We can think of the ATM system in terms of a set of interacting objects, one type of which are SavingsAccount objects. In addition, you might consider the following objects and how they interact. We can view a customer who uses an ATM as an object of the class Customer. (For simplicity, assume that the customer has signed onto the ATM machine and has provided a password that the system validated.) Suppose the Customer object sends messages to the ATM object (by using a touch screen) to perform a transaction, say a withdrawal of $100. The ATM object then sends a message to that customer's account object (which resides on the bank's central computer) to make a withdrawal of $100. The ATM object might do this by applying Withdraw(100.00) to the customer's SavingsAccount object. The SavingsAccount object then determines if its balance is greater than or equal to $100. If so, the SavingsAccount object decreases its balance by $100 and sends a message to the ATM object to dispense $100 to the person. (It is important to realize that the account object decides if it can make a withdrawal, not the ATM. Also, the account object decreases its own balance. The ATM cannot directly decrease the balance in the account.) If the SavingsAccount object determines that its balance is less than $100, it sends a message to the ATM object that there are insufficient funds in the account to make the withdrawal. That message causes the ATM object to display a message to the Customer object that the withdrawal request must be denied because of insufficient funds.

Familiar Classes and Objects

We have been working with several classes since the first chapter. In Chapter 1, we introduced the standard input and output streams `cin` and `cout`. The C++ language comes with several predefined classes. Two of these are the input class `istream` and the output class `ostream`. The standard input stream `cin` is an `istream` class object. The definition of the `istream` and `ostream` classes and the definitions of `cin` and `cout` are contained in the header file `iostream.h`.

In a program, we can obtain data from the keyboard by applying the extraction operator >> to the `cin` object. We can view the statement

```
cin >> price;
```

as follows: The statement tells the `cin` object to extract a number from the input stream and place the number's value into the variable `price`. We send a message to the `cin` object and it responds in a certain way to that message.

Likewise, we can display data on the monitor by applying the insertion operator `<<` to the `cout` object. We can view the statement

```
cout << "The value is " << price;
```

as sending a message to the `cout` object to display on the monitor screen the string "The value is " followed by the value of the variable `price`.

We have used the function `get()` with `cin` as follows, where `ch` is a variable of type `char`.

```
ch = cin.get();
```

The function `get()` is a member function of the `istream` class. When we code `cin.get()`, we are applying the `get()` member function to the `cin` object. This sends the object the message to return the value of the next character in the input buffer to the program. Note that we use the same dot operator that we use with structures. (More on the relation between structures and classes is found in Section 10.1.)

We can also think of each of the built-in data types in C++ as a class. For example, there is the class `int` of integers. An `int` object, that is an integer constant or `int` type variable, has certain properties. For example, an integer is a whole number whose value can range, on some computers, from $-32,768$ to $+32,767$. Among the operations that we can perform on an integer object are the arithmetic operations of addition, subtraction, multiplication, division, remainder, increment, decrement, the relational operations (for example, greater and less), and assignment. The `int` class is built into C++ so there is no need to define the class. However, to use integers in our programs, we must create `int` objects. To create an `int` object, we declare an integer variable. The following declares an `int` object `i`, which has the value 3, and an `int` object `j`, which has the value 5.

```
int i = 3,
    j = 5;
```

The variables `i` and `j` are, therefore, `int` objects to which we can apply any of the operations mentioned in the previous paragraph. For example, we can apply the increment operator to `i`, `++i`; to increase its value to 4.

10.1 Objects and Classes

Object orientation is powerful because it allows the programmer to define his or her own classes. In this section we discuss how to define a class and how to create objects belonging to that class.

Defining a Class

To show how to declare a class, we discuss an example that contains some of the alternatives you have when writing a program.

```
class Account
{
  private:
    int    id_no;
    double balance;
    double rate;

  public:
    int pub_data_mem;

  public:
    void   Open(int, double, double);
    double Calc_Interest() { return balance * rate; }
};

void Account::Open(int id, double bal, double rt)
{
  id_no = id;
  balance = bal;
  rate = rt;
}
```

The class declaration begins with the keyword `class` followed by the name of the class. As you see, we capitalize the first letter of the name of a class. Following the name of the class is the definition of the class enclosed in braces. Note that the closing brace must be followed by a semicolon. See Experiment 1.

The items declared in the class are the **class members**. The class has four data members, `id_no`, `balance`, `rate`, and `pub_data_mem`, and two member functions, `Open()` and `Calc_Interest()`. There are two new keywords in the class definition: the access specifiers `private` and `public`, which specify the visibility of the class members. The class members defined after the `private` label can be accessed only by functions that are members of the class itself. Thus, `id_no`, `balance`, and `rate`, being private data members, are accessible only to the member functions `Open()` and `Calc_Interest()`. No other function has access to `id_no`, `balance`, or `rate`. If we declare an `Account` object in `main()`, we cannot directly refer to that object's private data members in `main()` because `main()` is not a member function of `Account`. The following statement in `main()` is illegal. See Experiment 2.

```
cout << acc1.rate;
```

Programming
Pointers

Private class members are C++'s way to enforce the principle of "data hiding" or **encapsulation**. This means that the important things that make an object what it is, the object's properties, are kept hidden from the outside world. The only way to change a private data member of an object is through the use of member functions. Encapsulation tightly controls how we may use objects—we can only use them through the member functions.

All class members that follow the label `public` are accessible to all functions. The data member `pub_data_mem`, as well as the two member functions `Calc_Interest()` and `Open()`, are accessible to all functions including `main()`.

Why do we need two types of access? We do not want just anyone to be able to change the ID number, balance, or interest rate of an account. Therefore, it makes sense to make these items `private`. Similarly, we want others (perhaps a bank teller) to be able to open an account and to calculate interest due, so we make the member functions `public`. We included the `public` data member `pub_data_mem` as an example to show that it is possible to have a `public` data member in a class. Later in the chapter we will remove `pub_data_mem` from the class declaration. We shall see in later examples that it is also sometimes desirable to have a `private` member function in a class.

Programming
Pointers

There are no restrictions in C++ on what can be `public` and what can be `private`. (Although good object-oriented design dictates what should be `public` and `private`.) Note also that `private` is the default access specifier. The following declaration is equivalent to the first.

```
class Account
{
    int    id_no;    //These are private by default
    double balance;
    double rate;

  public:
    int pub_data_mem;

  public:
    void Open(int, double, double);
    double Calc_Interest() {return balance * rate;}
};
```

It is common practice, and we shall do so, to keep all the `public` items together and all the `private` items together. However, it is not necessary. The following is legal, but not desirable.

```
class Account
{
  private:
    int id_no;
  public:
    void Open(int, double, double);
  private:
    double balance;
  public:
    int Calc_Interest() {return balance * rate;}
```

```
    private:
      double rate;
    public:
      int pub_data_mem;
};
```

As you can see, we defined the member function `Calc_Interest()` within the class declaration, but defined the other member function, `Open()`, outside the class declaration. You can define a member function inside or outside the class declaration. However, in either case, the member function must be *declared* inside the class declaration.

NOTE 10.1—DECLARING CLASS MEMBER FUNCTIONS

All class member functions must be declared inside the class declaration, including those member functions that are defined outside the class declaration.

Programming
Pointers

The difference between defining a member function inside and outside a class declaration is that a class member function that is defined inside the class declaration is, by default, `inline`. See Chapter 5. Therefore, the declaration of `Calc_Interest()` in the declaration of `Account` is equivalent to the following.

```
inline double Calc_Interest() { return balance * rate; }
```

Programming
Pointers

A common practice is to define short functions (one or two statements) within the class definition (thereby making them `inline`) and longer functions outside the class declaration. You are free, of course, to `inline` any class member function that is defined outside the class by using the `inline` keyword in the function's definition header, as described in Chapter 5.

It is very important to note that the class member functions `Calc_Interest()` and `Open()` have access to all the data members of the class. There is no need to declare class data members inside a class member function—just use the data members in the function.

NOTE 10.2—DATA MEMBERS INSIDE MEMBER FUNCTIONS

All data members of a class are accessible inside all member functions. Therefore, you can code a class member function as though the class data members have been declared inside the function definition.

The `Calc_Interest()` member function computes the interest earned by the account, that is the balance multiplied by the interest rate. The statement in the function body returns the product of the data members `balance` and `rate`.

The `Open()` member function is defined outside the class declaration. Any member function that is defined outside the class declaration must use the **scope resolution operator**, `::`, in its definition header. Note 10.3 describes how to use the scope resolution operator.

NOTE 10.3—THE SCOPE RESOLUTION OPERATOR

If you define a class member function outside the class declaration, you must use the scope resolution operator, `::`, in the function definition header as follows:

```
return-type ClassName::FunctionName(parameter-list)
```

Read the operator `::` as the possessive " 's ".

Read the definition header of `Open()` as "Account's `Open()`." Why is the scope resolution operator necessary? There are situations in which it is necessary to declare several classes. In this case it is possible that two or more of the classes will have member functions with the same name. Suppose, for example, that we also declare a `Checking_Account` class, which also has an `Open()` function. If the `Open()` functions of the two classes are defined inside their respective class declarations, there will be no confusion about which function is being defined. However, if the functions are defined outside the class declarations as we did for the `Open()` function of `Account`, it is necessary to specify to which class each function belongs. The definition `Account::Open()` would be for `Account`'s `Open()` function, and the definition `Checking_Account::Open()` would be for `Checking_Account`'s `Open()` function. See Experiment 3.

Again, inside the definition of `Open()` we can refer to the data members of the class as though they were declared inside the function itself. The purpose of this function is to assign an account its basic data—an ID number, balance, and interest rate. Thus, the function assigns the value of the `id` parameter to `id_no`, the value of the `bal` parameter to `balance`, and the value of `rt` to `rate`. We shall see how to use the `Open()` function shortly.

Using a Class

Having declared `Account`, we can now use it by declaring one or more objects from the class. The act of declaring an object is sometimes called **instantiation**. Declaring, or instantiating, an object is as simple as declaring a variable. For example, to declare the `Account` object `acc1` in `main()`, we would code the following.

```
Account acc1;
```

This declaration creates, or instantiates, the `Account` object `acc1`. The memory this declaration allocates is similar to what the declaration of a structure variable allocates. The object `acc1` consists of four data members `id_no`, `balance`, `rate`, and `pub_data_mem` as shown in Figure 10.1.

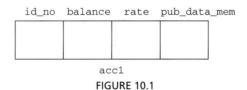

id_no balance rate pub_data_mem

acc1
FIGURE 10.1

Programming
Pointers

The member functions of a class do not take up computer memory in the same sense that the object acc1 does. The member functions of a class are the functions that you can apply to the objects of that class. The member functions are the interface between the outside world and the objects of the class. They allow you to use and manipulate the objects of the class.

We use the same "dot" notation to refer to the public data member of acc1 as we did to refer to the members of a structure. Thus, acc1.pub_data_mem refers to the pub_data_mem member of the object acc1. After the declaration of acc1, the data members of the object contain garbage—we have yet to give them meaningful values. We can give the pub_data_mem member of acc1 a valid value, say 5, by the following statement.

```
acc1.pub_data_mem = 5; //Legal - pub_data_mem is a public member of the class
```

We are allowed to access pub_data_mem in any function, including main(), because it is a public data member of the class. Thus, the preceding assignment is legal. However, as mentioned previously, the private members of the class (id_no, balance, and rate) can only be accessed by the member functions of the class. It is as though id_no, balance, and rate are locked boxes and the class member functions are the only functions with the keys to unlock them. In main() the following statement (or any statement that references the private members of the class) is illegal. See Experiment 2.

```
void main()
{
   .
   .
   .
   cout << acc1.rate;    //Illegal - rate is a private
                         //member of Account
   .
   .
   .
}
```

In earlier chapters, without saying as much, we saw how to apply member functions to objects. As mentioned in the introduction to this chapter, cin is an object in the istream class. The functions get() and getline() are public member functions of the istream class. When we code cin.get() or cin.getline() we are applying these member functions to the cin object. We again use the dot notation to apply a member function to an object. This technique also applies to classes that we declare in our programs. Once we have declared an `Account` object, we can use the dot operator with the class's member functions to manipulate the object. For example, we could code the following statements.

```
acc1.Open(1234, 100.00, 0.06);
cout << "\nThe interest on the account is " << acc1.Calc_Interest();
```

The first statement applies the `Open()` function to the object `acc1`. In this execution of `Open()`, the function uses the `id_no`, `balance`, and `rate` members of the object to which it is applied, namely `acc1`. When `Open()` is applied to `acc1`, the values of the arguments (1234, 100.00, and 0.06) are assigned to the function's parameters (`id`, `bal`, and `rt`). The function's statements then assign the values of the parameters to the data members of `acc1` according to the definition of `Open()`. Figure 10.2 shows what `acc1` now looks like in main memory, assuming that 5 was assigned to the `pub_data_mem` member as we described previously.

Note that in the definition of `Open()`, we do not refer to a specific object. When the function is applied to an object, the function uses the data members of that object.

NOTE 10.4—HOW A MEMBER FUNCTION WORKS

When a member function is applied to an object, all class data member references in the function definition are to the data members of the object to which the function is applied.

In the statement

```
cout << "\nThe interest on the account is " << acc1.Calc_Interest();
```

we apply the member function `Calc_Interest()` to the `acc1` object. Recall that the definition of the `Calc_Interest()` function contained just one statement, namely

```
return balance * rate;
```

When applied to `acc1`, `Calc_Interest()` takes the values of the `balance` and `rate` members of `acc1`, multiplies those values, and returns that value (the interest on the account) to `main()`. It is this value that is output by the `cout` statement.

We now put the pieces together to form a complete program.

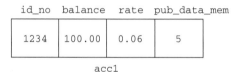

FIGURE 10.2

The Program `dem10-1.cpp`

```
//dem10-1.cpp

//This program illustrates the use of a simple class and member functions

#include <iostream.h>
#include <iomanip.h>

using namespace std;

class Account
{
  private:
    int    id_no;
    double balance;
    double rate;

  public:
    int pub_data_mem;

  public:
    void   Open(int, double, double);
    double Calc_Interest() { return balance * rate; }
};

void Account::Open(int id, double bal, double rt)
{
  id_no   = id;
  balance = bal;
  rate    = rt;
}

int main()
{
  cout << setprecision(2)
       << setiosflags(ios::fixed)
       << setiosflags(ios::showpoint);

  int    id;      //Variables to store input data
  double bal;
  double rt;

  //Obtain Account information from the user

  cout << "\nEnter Account ID: ";
  cin >> id;

  cout << "\nEnter Balance: ";
  cin >> bal;
```

```
        cout << "\nEnter Interest Rate: ";
        cin >> rt;

        Account acc1;           //Create an Account object

        acc1.pub_data_mem = 5;

        acc1.Open(id, bal, rt);    //Initialize the object

        cout << "\nThe interest on the account is " << acc1.Calc_Interest();
        cout << "\n\nThe value of the public data member is " << acc1.pub_data_mem;

    return 0;
}
```

Program Output

```
Enter Account ID: 1234

Enter Balance: 100.00

Enter Interest Rate: 0.06

The interest on the account is 6.00

The value of the public data member is 5
```

The order in which we place the parts of the program can be important. Remember that to use something in a program, it must have been previously declared. In `main()`, we declare an object, `acc1`, which is a member of `Account`. Therefore, we must place the declaration of `Account` before `main()`. In general, we will use the following outline for all our simple programs that use classes.

NOTE 10.5—THE STRUCTURE OF A PROGRAM THAT USES CLASSES

For simple programs that uses classes, we shall use the following program structure:

```
//Preprocessor directives


//Class declarations


//Member function definitions


//Definition of main()
```

(We emphasize that Note 10.5 applies to simple programs. We can divide the program code into several files for more complicated programs. After compiling the source files, the linker combines the object files into one executable program. For now, however, we shall stay with the simple program structure described in Note 10.5.)

Discussion of `dem10-1.cpp`

Within `main()`, we declare the variables `id`, `bal`, and `rt` to use as storage locations for the data input by the user. After prompting for and obtaining the input values from the user, we declare the `acc1` object. (Recall that in C++, you can declare a variable or object anywhere in the program.) Then, we apply the `Open()` function to the object, passing the values of the input data as arguments. The `Open()` function assigns these values to the data members of `acc1`. We assign a value directly to the `pub_data_mem` member of `acc1`. This is legal in `main()` because `pub_data_mem` is a `public` member of the class.

The next to last `cout` statement in `main()` contains the reference `acc1.Calc_Interest()`. The `Calc_Interest()` function returns a value. Just as in ordinary functions, the name of the function represents the value returned by the function. In the case of class member functions that return a value, the function name must be prefixed by the dot operator and the name of the object to which the function is being applied, in our case `acc1.Calc_Interest()`. The value of this expression is, therefore, the value returned by the function when it is applied to `acc1`. The `cout` statement displays the value of the interest, 6.00.

Finally, the last `cout` statement displays the value of the `public` data member of `acc1` to verify that the assignment to `acc1.pub_data_mem` was valid.

The Relation Between `class` and `struct`

Programming
Pointers

A class, like a structure, is an aggregate data type in the sense that its data members can be of different types. See Chapter 9. In C++ there is little difference between a class and a structure. Although we did not do so in Chapter 9, C++ structures can have member functions, just as a class does. What is the difference between a class and a structure? As mentioned previously, the default access in a class is `private`. The default access in a structure, on the other hand, is `public`. Therefore, dem10-1.cpp can be written using a structure instead of a class. See Experiment 8. However, in keeping with common practice, we shall use a class when we want to define a class, that is, when we need to use objects in our program. We shall use structures for aggregate data structures, like a three-part address, which we would not consider as separate objects.

Note that in C, unlike C++, a structure cannot have member functions and there are no such things as the access specifiers `public` and `private`. Also, the keyword `class` is not available in C because there are no such things as classes in the C language.

A More Useful Class—Accessor and Mutator Functions

The `Account` class in the previous section is not very useful for several reasons. First, the `Cal_Interest()` member function only calculates the interest. The function does not apply the interest to the account balance, which is what we would want it to do in an actual application. Also, there is no way of adding or subtracting money from an account after the account is opened. Finally, there is no way to find out how much money is in an account. We now redefine the member function `Calc_Interest()` and add member functions `Get_Balance()`, `Deposit()`, and `Withdraw()`. We will also discard the member `pub_data_mem` because it was included only to illustrate the use of a `public` data member. The new class declaration follows.

```
class Account
{
  private:
    int    id_no;
    double balance;
    double rate;

  public:
    void   Open(int, double, double);
    double Calc_Interest();
    double Get_Balance();
    void Deposit(double);
    int Withdraw(double);
};
```

The new version of `Calc_Interest()` will not only calculate the interest due the account, but will also apply the interest to the account's balance. Since the new version of this function is more complicated than the original, we will define the function outside the class declaration. Recall from Note 10.1, however, that we must still declare the function in the class declaration. Similarly, we declare the new member functions `Deposit()` and `Withdraw()`. Each of these functions has one argument, which is a `double`. We pass to the `Deposit()` function the amount of money that we want to deposit. We pass to the `Withdraw()` function the amount of money we want to withdraw.

The new definition of `Calc_Interest()` follows.

```
double Account::Calc_Interest()
{
  double interest;

  interest = balance * rate;
  balance += interest;

  return interest;
}
```

The definition of `Calc_Interest()` contains the declaration of the local variable `interest`. Local variables that are declared inside class member functions obey the same scope and duration rules as all other local variables. A local variable is known only inside the member function in which it is declared. A local variable comes into existence at the point of declaration in the function and goes out of existence when the function ends. The variable `interest` is given a value by the first assignment statement in the function. The second assignment statement increases the class member `balance` by the value of `interest`. As in the original version of the function, the function returns the value of the `interest`.

The function `Get_Balance()` is very simple.

```
inline double Account::Get_Balance()
{
  return balance;
}
```

This function could be defined within the class declaration, which by default would make it `inline`. However, in this version of `Account`, we decide to define all member functions outside the class declaration. To make the function `inline`, we code the keyword `inline` before the return type in the function definition.

Suppose that `acc1` is an `Account` object that has a `balance` member whose value is 100.00. Then the following statement will display the value of the `balance` member of `acc1`.

```
cout << "\nThe balance in the account is " << acc1.Get_Balance();
```

Programming
Pointers

A member function whose only purpose is to access the value of a private data member of the class is sometimes called an **accessor function**. `Get_Balance()` is an example of an accessor function whose purpose is to access the `balance` member of an `Account` object. It is good programming practice to inline accessor functions because they are usually one-line functions. Accessor functions are necessary because private class members are hidden from all functions except that class's own member functions.

We now define the `Deposit()` function.

```
void Account::Deposit(double amount)
{
  balance += amount;
}
```

Again we emphasize that all class members are accessible to a class member function, without the need for redeclaration. Therefore, `Deposit()` has access to the class member `balance`. The statement in the function definition increases the `balance` by the `amount` of the deposit. To apply a deposit of $55.42 to an account, say `acc1`, we would code the following.

```
acc1.Deposit(55.42);
```

When this statement executes, the function's `amount` parameter is assigned the value 55.42. Then the `balance` member of `acc1` (which we will assume has the value

100.00) is increased by the value of `amount` (55.42), making the new `balance` member's value 155.42. `Deposit()` is an example of a function that changes the value of a class data member. Such a function is sometimes called a **mutator** function.

The definition of `Withdraw()` must take into account that a withdrawal cannot be made on an account if the amount of the withdrawal exceeds the balance in the account. If the withdrawal can be made, the function will make the withdrawal and return +1. If the withdrawal cannot be made, the function will leave the balance as it is and return 0. Following is the definition of `Withdraw()`.

```cpp
int Account::Withdraw(double amount)
{
  int result;

  if (amount <= balance)
    {
      balance -= amount;
      result = 1;
    }
  else
    result = 0;

  return result;
}
```

The function tests the value of `amount`, which is the amount that we want to withdraw from the account. If the value of `amount` is less than or equal to the `balance` in the account, the withdrawal is made and the value of `result` is set to 1. Otherwise, that is if the `amount` to withdraw is greater than the `balance`, `result` is set to 0. In either case, the function returns the value of `result`.

You may wonder why we did not have `Withdraw()` display an error message to the user in the case where `amount` is greater than `balance`. The decision not to do so is essentially a design decision that was made for the following reason. The `Withdraw()` function should just be concerned with making a withdrawal and should not be concerned with interfacing with the user. That responsibility should be the province of the function that uses `Withdraw()`. The `Withdraw()` function should signal only the action it takes—that is the purpose of returning either +1 or 0.

We now use our new class definition in a program.

```cpp
//dem10-2.cpp

//This program uses an expanded version of the Account class
//introduced in dem10-1.cpp.

#include <iostream.h>
#include <iomanip.h>

using namespace std:
```

```
class Account
{
  private:
    int    id_no;
    double balance;
    double rate;

  public:
    void   Open(int, double, double);
    double Calc_Interest();
    double Get_Balance();
    void Deposit(double);
    int Withdraw(double);
};

void Account::Open(int id, double bal, double rt)
{
  id_no   = id;
  balance = bal;
  rate    = rt;
}

inline double Account::Get_Balance()
{
  return balance;
}

double Account::Calc_Interest()
{
  double interest;

  interest = balance * rate;
  balance += interest;

  return interest;
}

void Account::Deposit(double amount)
{
  balance += amount;
}
int Account::Withdraw(double amount)
{
  int result;

  if (amount <= balance)
    {
      balance -= amount;
      result = 1;
    }
```

```
      else
        result = 0;

      return result;
    }


    int main()
    {
      cout << setprecision(2)
           << setiosflags(ios::fixed)
           << setiosflags(ios::showpoint);

      int id;
      double bal;
      double rt;
      double amount;

      cout << "\nEnter Account ID: ";
      cin >> id;

      cout << "\nEnter Balance: ";
      cin >> bal;

      cout << "\nEnter Interest Rate: ";
      cin >> rt;

      Account acc1;

      acc1.Open(id, bal, rt);

      cout << "\nThe balance in the account is now " << acc1.Get_Balance();

      cout << "\n\nEnter an amount to deposit: ";
      cin >> amount;

      acc1.Deposit(amount);

      cout << "\n\nA deposit of " << amount << " was made.";
      cout << "\nThe balance in the account is now " << acc1.Get_Balance();

      acc1.Calc_Interest();

      cout << "\n\nInterest was applied to the account.";
      cout << "\nThe balance in the account is now " << acc1.Get_Balance();

      cout << "\n\nEnter an amount to withdraw: ";
      cin >> amount;

      if (acc1.Withdraw(amount))
          cout << "\n\nA withdrawal of " << amount << " was made.";
```

```
    else
        cout << "\n\nWITHDRAWAL NOT MADE: Insufficient funds.";

    cout << "\nThe balance in the account is now " << acc1.Get_Balance();

    return 0;
}
```

Program Output

```
Enter Account ID: 1234

Enter Balance: 100.00

Enter Interest Rate: 0.06

The balance in the account is now 100.00

Enter an amount to deposit: 55.42


A deposit of 55.42 was made.
The balance in the account is now 155.42

Interest was applied to the account.
The balance in the account is now 164.75

Enter an amount to withdraw: 120.00


A withdrawal of 120.00 was made.
The balance in the account is now 44.75
```

EXERCISES 10.1

Design a class for the objects in Exercises 1–5. In each case, state possible data members and useful member functions. Think about what data items characterize each object. Think about what you would want to do to each object and what behavior you would expect from each object. Do not worry at this point about how to represent the data members, how many data members you think of, or how to code the member functions.

1. A stock on the New York Stock Exchange.
2. A customer for a roofing contractor.
3. A supplier for an office equipment store.
4. A building in a data base of buildings to be used by a local real estate company.
5. A class in a data base of classes used by the registrar at a university.

6. (a) Code a declaration for the class `Rectangle`. The class has two private double data members: `length` and `width`. The class has two functions, which you should declare but not define. The first member function, `CreateRectangle()`, has two arguments that represent the length and width of a rectangle. The second member function, `Area()`, has no arguments, but returns the area of the rectangle.

   (b) Define the `CreateRectangle()` member function. The function assigns its first argument to the `length` class member and its second argument to the `width` class member.

   (c) Define the `Area()` member function. The function returns the area of the rectangle.

7. (a) Code a declaration for the class `DigitalClock`. The class has three private integer data members: `hours`, `minutes`, and `ampm`. The class has three functions, which you should declare but not define. The first member function, `SetTime()`, has three arguments. The first argument represents the hour (an integer between 1 and 12), the second argument represents the minutes (an integer between 0 and 59), and the third argument represents either AM or PM (0 for AM, 1 for PM.) The class also has a function `ShowTime()` that displays the time in an appropriate format. The third member function `Tick()` advances the time by one minute.

   (b) Define the `SetTime()` member function. The function assigns its first argument to the `hour` data member, its second argument to the `minutes` data member, and the third argument to the `ampm` data member.

   (c) Define the `ShowTime()` member function. The function displays the time in the following format: Hour:Minutes AM or PM. For example, 1:23 PM.

   (d) Define the function `Tick()`. The function adds 1 to the `minute` data member, unless the `minute` member is 59. In that case, set the `minute` data member to 0, and increase the `hour` member by 1 (if the `hour` member is 11, appropriately change the `ampm` member), unless the `hour` member is 12. In that case, set the `hour` member to 1.

8. Identify and correct any syntax errors in the following declaration of `Account` and its member functions.

```
class Account
{
    int     id_no;
    double balance,
    double rate;

public;
    void    Open(int, double, double);
    Calc_Interest();
    double Get_Balance();
    void Deposit(double);
    int Withdraw(double);
};
```

```
void Account::Open(double id, double bal, int rt)
{
  id_no   = id;
  balance = bal;
  rate    = rt;
}


inline double Account:Get_Balance()
{
  return balance;
}

double Account::Calc_Interest()
{
  double interest;

  interest = balance * rate;
  balance += interest;

  return interest;

void Account;;Deposit(double amount)
{
  balance += amount;
}



int Account::Withdraw(double amount)
{
  int result;

  if amount <= balance
    {
      balance -= amount;
      result = 1;
    }
  else
    result = 0;

  return result;
}
```

EXPERIMENTS 10.1

1. In dem10-1.cpp, omit the semicolon after the closing brace in the declaration of `Account`. Compile the resulting program. What message does the compiler issue?

2. Place the statement `cout << acc1.rate;` in `main()` in dem10-1.cpp. Compile the program. Explain any error messages.

3. In dem10-1.cpp, remove `Account::` from the definition header of the `Open()` function. Compile the resulting program. Explain any error messages.

4. In dem10-1.cpp, we defined the function `Calc_Interest()` inside the class declaration. Recode the declaration of `Account` so that the definition of `Calc_Interest()` is outside the class declaration. Recompile and execute the resulting program.

5. In dem10-1.cpp, place the statement `acc1.id_no = id;` after the declaration `Account acc1;` Compile the resulting program. What message does the compiler issue?

6. In dem10-1.cpp, change the declaration of `Account` to include the `Open()` member function in the `private` section. Compile the resulting program. What message does the compiler issue?

7. In dem10-2.cpp, we did not take into account the possible error of trying to deposit or withdraw a negative amount from an account. Change the `Deposit()` function so that it tests the parameter `amount` to see if it is negative. If so, the function should not make the deposit and should return 0. If the amount is nonnegative, the function should make the deposit and return 1. Make the necessary changes in `main()` to reflect the change in `Deposit()`. Change the `Withdraw()` member function similarly: If the amount of the withdrawal is negative, do not change the balance and return -1; if the amount to withdraw is nonnegative, the function should behave as it does in dem10-2.cpp. Make the necessary changes to `main()` to reflect the change in `Withdraw()`. Note that there are now two reasons why a withdrawal might not be possible.

8. Recode dem10-1.cpp using a structure rather than a class. Compile, execute, and test the resulting program. Is there any difference in how the program executes?

PROGRAMMING PROBLEMS 10.1

1. Declare a `WebPage` class. The class includes the following integer data members: The number of hits on the Web page (that is, the number of times the page is visited), the number of messages posted on the page site, and the number of downloads from the Web page. The member functions include the following: a function `Init_Page()` that initializes all the data members to zero; an accessor function for each data member of the class (`Get_Hits()`, `Get_Messages()`, and `Get_Downloads()`) that returns the value of that data member; a function for each data member that increases that data member by 1 (`Inc_Hits()`, `Inc_Messages()`, and `Inc_Downloads()`); and a function `Activity()` that returns the total activity for the site (hits+messages+downloads).

   Write a `main()` that declares and initializes a `WebPage` object. Write statements that increase the number of hits by 2, messages by 3, and downloads by 1. Display the number of hits, messages, and downloads for the page as well as the total activity for the page.

2. Declare an `OilTank` class. The class has the following integer data members: tank ID number, tank capacity in gallons, and current number of gallons in the tank (that is the tank's contents). The member functions include the following:

A three-argument function Init_Tank() that assigns its arguments to the tank number, capacity, and contents; an accessor function for each data member of the class (Get_Number(), Get_Capacity(), and Get_Contents()) that returns the value of the data member; a one-argument function, Add_Oil(), that increases the number of gallons in a tank by the amount that is its argument; and a one-argument function Remove_Oil() that decreases the number of gallons in a tank by the amount that is its argument.

Write a main() that declares an OilTank object and that initializes it to represent an empty oil tank with ID number 1234 that has a capacity of 1000 gallons. The program should ask the user to enter the number of gallons to be added to the tank. Add this number of gallons to the tank and then display the tank number, capacity, and new contents of the tank. Next, ask the user to enter the number of gallons to remove from the tank. Remove this number of gallons from the tank and then display the tank number, capacity, and new contents of the tank.

3. Declare a VehicleService class. the class has the following data members: The vehicle's service number (an integer), the number of hours (a double) of labor used to service the vehicle, the cost of parts (a double) to perform the service, and the total cost (a double) of the service. The member functions include the following: a one-argument function Init_Service() that sets the vehicle's service number to its argument and that sets the other data members to zero; an accessor function for each data member of the class (Get_Number(), Get_Hours(), Get_Parts(), and Get_Cost()) that returns the value of the data member; and for each of hours and parts, a one-argument function (Set_Hours() and Set_Parts()) that sets the value of the corresponding data member to the value of its argument. In the case of Set_Hours(), the function should also calculate the labor cost of those hours by multiplying the number of hours by 70.00 and adding this amount to the total cost of service. In the case of Set_Parts(), the function should add the cost of the parts to the total cost of service.

Write a main() that declares a VehicleService object that represents a vehicle with a service number of 432. The program should ask the user to enter the number of hours of labor spent on the vehicle and for the cost of parts to repair the vehicle. The program should apply that number of hours and cost of parts to the vehicle. Finally, the program should display a report that lists the vehicle service number, the number of hours spent repairing the vehicle, the cost of labor, the cost of parts and the total cost of repair.

4. Declare a class HotelRoom. The class has the following private data members: the room number (an integer), the room capacity (an integer representing the maximum number of people the room can accommodate), the occupancy status (an integer, 0 if the room is not occupied, otherwise the number of occupants in the room), and the daily rate (a double). The member functions include the following: a three-argument function InitRoom() that sets the room number to its first argument, the room capacity to the second argument, the room rate to the third argument, and the room occupancy status to 0; an accessor function for each data member of the class (Get_Number(), Get_Capacity(), Get_Status(), and Get_Rate()); and a one-argument function Change_Status() that changes

the occupancy status of the room to the value of its argument. The function should verify that the argument value does not exceed the room capacity. If it does, the function should return –1; and a one-argument function `Change_Rate()` that sets the room rate to the value of its argument.

Write a `main()` that creates a hotel room with room number 123, with a capacity of 4, and a rate of 150.00. Suppose a person checks in. The program should ask the user to enter the number of guests to occupy the room. Change the status of the room to reflect the number of guests that just checked in. Display the information about the room in a nice format. Now assume that the guests check out. Change the status of the room appropriately and display the information about the room. Next, change the room rate to 175.00. Finally, assume that another person checks in. Ask the user to enter the number of guests to occupy the room. Change the room's status accordingly and display the new information about the room.

10.2 Constructors and Destructors

In the last section, we applied the `Open()` member function to initialize an `Account` object. We now discuss how to initialize the data members of an object when the object is declared.

Constructors

A **constructor** is a class member function that automatically executes when an object of that class is instantiated. The name of the constructor function must be the same as the name of the class and the constructor function cannot have a return type (because it always results in creating a class object). If a constructor is not explicitly declared in the class declaration, by default, C++ provides the **default constructor**. The default constructor only creates the object—it does not initialize the object's data members.

NOTE 10.6—THE NAME OF A CONSTRUCTOR

If a constructor is explicitly declared in a class declaration, the constructor must have the same name as the class. The constructor cannot have a return type and must be `public`.

We begin with a simple example. Consider the following class and test program.

```
//dem10-3.cpp
//This program demonstrates a simple constructor function

#include <iostream.h>

using namespace std:
```

```
class Test_Class
{
  private:
    int n;

  public:
    Test_Class();
};

Test_Class::Test_Class()
{
  n = 0;

  cout << "\nConstructor Executed: Data member initialized to " << n;
}

int main()
{
  Test_Class tc_object;

  cout << "\nEnd of program";

  return 0;
}
```

Program Output

```
Constructor Executed: Data member initialized to 0
End of program
```

The scope resolution operator must still be used in the definition of the constructor because the definition is outside the class declaration. The program begins by declaring the Test_Class object tc_object. As soon as the object is created, the class's constructor function executes for the object. The data member n is initialized to 0 and the function displays the message "Constructor Executed". Note that we do not explicitly execute the constructor—it automatically executes whenever an object is created.

A constructor function can have arguments. In the following program, we change Test_Class's constructor by providing it with an argument. The value of the argument is assigned to the data member n in the code of the constructor function.

```
//dem10-4.cpp
//This program demonstrates a simple constructor function

#include <iostream.h>

using namespace std;

class Test_Class
```

```
{
  private:
    int n;

  public:
    Test_Class(int);
};

Test_Class::Test_Class(int i)
{
  n = i;

  cout << "\nConstructor Executed: Data member initialized to " << n;
}

int main()
{
  int i;

  cout <<"\nEnter a value for the object: ";
  cin >> i;

  Test_Class tc_object(i);

  cout << "\nEnd of program";

  return 0;
}
```

Program Output

```
Enter a value for the object: 7

Constructor Executed: Data member initialized to 7
End of program
```

The program begins by asking the user to enter a value for the object, which the program will pass to the constructor. To pass the argument to the constructor, we include the argument in parentheses after the object name in the declaration of the object. Once again, we do not explicitly use the name of the constructor. When the object is declared, the constructor executes and the argument that is written in parentheses after the object name is passed to the one-argument constructor. The constructor then assigns the value of the argument to the data member n and displays its message. See Experiment 1.

Note also that if we declare a constructor that has one or more arguments, the default no-argument constructor is no longer available to the program. In this case, every object that is declared must be initialized. Therefore, the following declaration, if included in main() of dem10-4.cpp, would be illegal. See Experiment 2.

```
Test_Class tc_object2; //Illegal: no-argument constructor is not available
```

If there is need for the no-argument constructor, you can, of course, code your own.

> ### NOTE 10.7—INITIALIZING OBJECTS
>
> In a class, if you declare a constructor with one or more arguments, the default no-argument constructor is no longer available to the program. Therefore, in this case, you must initialize every object you declare by providing the proper number of arguments. If necessary, you can regain the no-argument constructor by coding it yourself.

A Constructor for Class `Account`

The declaration of the `Account` class did not contain a constructor function. Therefore, the only constructor available was the default constructor. When we declared an `Account` object, the default constructor was automatically invoked for that object. The default constructor did not initialize the object's data members so we had to define a function, `Open()`, which initialized the data members of the object.

We now change the definition of `Account` to include a constructor. We remove the declaration of `Open()` because the constructor will initialize an `Account` object.

```
class Account
{
  private:
    int     id_no;
    double balance;
    double rate;

  public:
    Account(int, double, double);     //Constructor
    double Calc_Interest();
    double Get_Balance();
    void Deposit(double);
    int Withdraw(double);
};
```

You must use the scope resolution operator in the constructor's definition header if you define the function outside the class declaration.

```
Account::Account(int id, double bal, double rt)
{
  id_no   = id;
  balance = bal;
  rate    = rt;
}
```

id_no	balance	rate
5678	200.00	0.07

acc1 as created by the Account constructor

FIGURE 10.3

We can now create an `Account` object, for example, `acc`, with ID number 5678, a balance of $200, and an interest rate of 0.07 as follows.

```
Account acc(5678, 200.00, 0.07);
```

The initial values given to the object are enclosed in parentheses after the object's name, just as in a function call. The constructor is not explicitly invoked—when the object is declared, the constructor is automatically applied to the object using the provided arguments. Therefore, the arguments 5678, 200.00, and 0.07 are passed to the `Account` constructor. The constructor then assigns the argument values to the class's data members according to the statements in its definition. Figure 10.3 shows the object as created by the constructor.

To use the constructor in `main()`, we proceed as follows.

```
int main()
{
  int id;
  double bal;
  double rt;

  cout << "\nEnter Account ID: ";
  cin >> id;

  cout << "\nEnter Balance: ";
  cin >> bal;

  cout << "\nEnter Interest Rate: ";
  cin >> rt;

  Account acc1(id, bal, rt);
  .
  .
  .
}
```

Following is a complete program that uses the `Account` constructor.

```
//dem10-5.cpp

//This program uses an expanded version of the Account class
//introduced in dem10-2.cpp.
```

```cpp
//The program uses a constructor function to initialize an object.

#include <iostream.h>
#include <iomanip.h>

using namespace std:

class Account
{
  private:
    int     id_no:
    double balance:
    double rate:

  public:
        Account(int, double, double):
        double Calc_Interest():
        double Get_Balance():
        void Deposit(double):
        int Withdraw(double):
};

Account::Account(int id, double bal, double rt)
{
  id_no = id:
  balance = bal:
  rate = rt:
}

inline double Account::Get_Balance()
{
  return balance:
}

double Account::Calc_Interest()
{
  double interest:

  interest = balance * rate:
  balance += interest:

  return interest:
}

void Account::Deposit(double amount)
{
  balance += amount:
}


int Account::Withdraw(double amount)
```

```
{
  int result;

  if (amount <= balance)
    {
      balance -= amount;
      result = 1;
    }
  else
    result = 0;

  return result;
}

int main()
{
  cout << setprecision(2)
       << setiosflags(ios::fixed)
       << setiosflags(ios::showpoint);

  int id;
  double bal;
  double rt;
  double amount;

  cout << "\nEnter Account ID: ";
  cin >> id;

  cout << "\nEnter Balance: ";
  cin >> bal;

  cout << "\nEnter Interest Rate: ";
  cin >> rt;

  Account acc1(id, bal, rt);

  cout << "\nThe balance in the account is now " << acc1.Get_Balance();

  cout << "\n\nEnter an amount to deposit: ";
  cin >> amount;

  acc1.Deposit(amount);

  cout << "\n\nA deposit of " << amount << " was made.";
  cout << "\nThe balance in the account is now " << acc1.Get_Balance();

  acc1.Calc_Interest();

  cout << "\n\nInterest was applied to the account.";
  cout << "\nThe balance in the account is now " << acc1.Get_Balance();
```

```
cout << "\n\nEnter an amount to withdraw: ";
cin >> amount;

if (acc1.Withdraw(amount))
    cout << "\n\nA withdrawal of " << amount << " was made.";
else
    cout << "\n\nWITHDRAWAL NOT MADE: Insufficient funds.";

cout << "\nThe balance in the account is now " << acc1.Get_Balance();

return 0;
}
```

Program Output

```
Enter Account ID: 1234

Enter Balance: 100.00

Enter Interest Rate: 0.06

The balance in the account is now 100.00

Enter an amount to deposit: 50.00


A deposit of 50.00 was made.
The balance in the account is now 150.00

Interest was applied to the account.
The balance in the account is now 159.00

Enter an amount to withdraw: 60.00


A withdrawal of 60.00 was made.
The balance in the account is now 99.00
```

Destructors

When an object goes out of scope, C++ destroys the object. For example, if we declare an object inside a function, it is a local object and its storage class is automatic. When the function ends, the object is destroyed. By default, a class is given a **default destructor**, which is a function that destroys the object. Like a constructor, the default destructor is not called explicitly—it is automatically executed when the object goes out of scope. As is the case for a constructor, we can write our own destructor function for a class. The name of a destructor is the same as the name of the class prefixed by the tilde character ~. A destructor cannot have arguments and cannot have a return type.

NOTE 10.8—THE NAME OF A DESTRUCTOR

If a destructor is explicitly declared in a class declaration, the destructor must have the same name as the class prefixed by ~. The destructor cannot have a return type or arguments and must be `public`.

Our first example will be a destructor for the simple `Test_Class` introduced earlier.

```cpp
//dem10-6.cpp
//This program demonstrates a simple destructor function

#include <iostream.h>

using namespace std:

class Test_Class
{
  private:
    int n;

  public:
    Test_Class(int);
    ~Test_Class();
};

Test_Class::Test_Class(int i)
{
  n = i;

  cout << "\nConstructor Executed: Data member initialized to " << n;
}

Test_Class::~Test_Class()
{
  cout << "\n\nDestructor Executed for object with data member " << n;
}

int main()
{
  int i;

  cout <<"\nEnter a value for the first object: ";
  cin >> i;

  Test_Class tc_object1(i);

  cout << "\n\nEnter a value for the second object: ";
```

```
cin >> i;

Test_Class tc_object2(i);

cout << "\n\n***** End of program *****";

return 0;
}
```

Program Output

```
Enter a value for the first object: 1

Constructor Executed: Data member initialized to 1

Enter a value for the second object: 2

Constructor Executed: Data member initialized to 2

***** End of program *****

Destructor Executed for object with data member 2

Destructor Executed for object with data member 1
```

The order of the displayed messages is important. When the first object is declared, the constructor is executed for that object. When the second object is declared, the constructor is executed for that object. Both objects remain in existence until main() ends. Therefore, main() displays the message that the program ends. The destructors then are executed in the reverse order of object creation. C++ executes the destructor for the second object and then executes the destructor for the first object.

Assigning One Object to Another

Programming
Pointers

It is possible to assign one object to another object as long as they belong to the same class. In this case, the assignment is done on a member by member basis. For example, consider the following.

```
Test_Class tc_object1(4);

Test_Class tc_object2(0);

tc_object2 = tc_object1;
```

The one-argument constructor initializes the n data member of tc_object1 to 4 and the n data member of tc_object2 to 0. When the assignment is executed, the n data member of tc_object1, namely 4, is copied to the n data member of tc_object2.

We illustrate these points in the following program. We have added to Test_Class an accessor function, Get_Value(), that returns the value of the data member of the object.

```cpp
//dem10-7.cpp

//This program illustrates assigning one object to another.
//Note that initializing an object does not use the
//one-argument constructor.

#include <iostream.h>

using namespace std:

class Test_Class
{
  private:
    int n;

public:
  Test_Class(int);
  ~Test_Class();
  int Get_Value();
};

Test_Class::Test_Class(int i)
{
  n = i;

  cout << "\nConstructor Executed: Data member initialized to " << n;
}

Test_Class::~Test_Class()
{
  cout << "\n\nDestructor Executed for object with data member " << n;
}

inline int Test_Class::Get_Value()
{
  return n;
}

int main()
{
  Test_Class tc_object1(4);
  Test_Class tc_object2(0);

  cout << "\n\nAfter object creation:";
  cout << "\n\nObject 1: " << tc_object1.Get_Value();
  cout << "\nObject 2: " << tc_object2.Get_Value();
```

```
    tc_object2 = tc_object1;

    cout << "\n\nAfter object assignment:";
    cout << "\n\nObject 1: " << tc_object1.Get_Value();
    cout << "\nObject 2: " << tc_object2.Get_Value();

    Test_Class tc_object3 = tc_object1;

    cout << "\n\nAfter initializing object 3:";
    cout << "\n\nObject 3: " << tc_object3.Get_Value();

    return 0;
}
```

Program Output

```
Constructor Executed: Data member initialized to 4
Constructor Executed: Data member initialized to 0

After object creation:

Object 1: 4
Object 2: 0

After object assignment:

Object 1: 4
Object 2: 4

After initializing object 3:

Object 3: 4

Destructor Executed for object with data member 4

Destructor Executed for object with data member 4

Destructor Executed for object with data member 4
```

Programming
Pitfalls

The Test_Class constructor executes twice—once for tc_object1 and once for tc_object2. After creating the objects, the program displays the values of the data members of the objects. The program then assigns the value of tc_object1 to tc_object2. The assignment is done on a member by member basis. Therefore, the n data member of tc_object1 is copied to the n data member of tc_object2. The program verifies the assignment when it displays the values of the data members of the objects. Note that the one-argument constructor does not execute when the program creates and initializes tc_object3 by executing the following statement.

```
Test_Class tc_object3 = tc_object1;
```

The constructor's message does not display at this point in the program! The value of `tc_object3` is displayed by `main()`, but not by the constructor. The reason why the one-argument constructor does not execute when the program initializes `tc_object3` will have to wait for our discussion of the copy constructor in Chapter 11. Finally, at the end of the program, the destructor executes three times—once for each of the objects created by the program.

Note that an object of one class can be assigned to an object of another class if you define (by overloading the assignment operator) how the assignment is to be carried out. We shall discuss how this can be done in Chapter 12.

EXERCISES 10.2

1. Using the class declaration of dem10-5.cpp, which of the following are incorrect declarations of an `Account` object? Correct any errors.

```
Account acc1(1234, 200.00);
Account acc2(0,0,0);
Account acc3(3333, 300.00, 0.03)
Account acc4(4444, 400, 0.04);
```

2. Assume the following declarations.

```
Account acc7(7777, 100.00, 0.07);
Account acc8(8888, 200.00, 0.08);
```

What are the values of the data members of `acc8` after executing the following.

```
acc8 = acc7;
```

3. In the `Rectangle` class of Exercise 6, Section 10.1, replace the `Create-Rectangle()` function by a two-argument constructor. The constructor assigns its first argument to the `length` class member and its second argument to the `width` class member. Contrast how the constructor and the `Create-Rectangle()` function would be used in a program to create a rectangle of length 3 and width 5.

4. In the `DigitalClock` class of Exercise 7, Section 10.1, add a three-argument constructor that sets the three data members `hours`, `minutes`, and `ampm`. The constructor assigns its first argument to the `hour` data member, its second argument to the `minutes` data member, and the third argument to the `ampm` data member. Is the `SetTime()` member function still needed in the class?

5. Make the `Test_Class` constructor of dem10-3.cpp a `private` function. Compile and execute the resulting program. Explain what happens.

EXPERIMENTS 10.2

1. In dem10-4.cpp, remove the first `cout` statement and the `cin` statement. Compile and execute the program. What does the program output, and why?
2. In dem10-4.cpp, change the declaration of `tc_object` to the following.

```
Test_Class tc_object;
```

Compile and execute the program. What happens and why?

PROGRAMMING PROBLEMS 10.2

1. In the `WebPage` class of Programming Problem 1, Section 10.1, replace the class's `InitPage()` function by a no-argument constructor that initializes the three data members of the object being created (hits, messages, and downloads) to zero. Recode the `main()` that you wrote to include use of the constructor. Compile, execute, and test the resulting program.

2. In the `OilTank` class of Programming Problem 2, Section 10.1, replace the class's `InitTank()` member function by a three-argument constructor that initializes the three data members of the object being created (tank number, capacity, and contents) to the constructor's arguments. Recode the `main()` that you wrote to include use of the constructor. Compile, execute, and test the resulting program.

3. In the `VehicleService` class of Programming Problem 3, Section 10.1, replace the `InitService()` function by a one-argument constructor that sets the service number member of the object being created to its argument and that sets the other data members to zero. Recode the `main()` that you wrote to include use of the constructor. Compile, execute, and test the resulting program.

4. In the `HotelRoom` class of Programming Problem 4 in Section 10.1, replace the class's member function `Init_Room()` by a four-argument constructor that initializes the four data members of the object being created (room number, room capacity, room rate, occupancy status) to the constructor's arguments. Recode the `main()` you wrote to include use of the constructor. Compile, execute, and test the resulting program.

10.3 Overloading, Default Arguments, and Function Templates

In C++, you are allowed to have several different functions all with the same name (function overloading). This allows you to use one function name in different circumstances. You can also give default values to function arguments. In fact, you can even code a function template in which you define a function that is independent of the types of its arguments.

Overloading Constructors

C++ allows you to define several constructors for a class. This is called **function overloading** and will be discussed in a more general context later in this section. Overloading allows us to have constructors for different sets of circumstances. For example, we can combine the no-argument constructor of dem10-3.cpp and the one-argument constructor of dem10-4.cpp into the same class as follows:

```
//dem10-8.cpp
//This program demonstrates a simple constructor function
//The constructor is overloaded. There is a no-argument
//and a one-argument constructor.

#include <iostream.h>

using namespace std;

class Test_Class
{
  private:
    int n;

  public:
    Test_Class();        //No-argument constructor
    Test_Class(int);     //One-argument constructor
};

Test_Class::Test_Class()
{
  n = 0;

  cout << "\nConstructor Executed: Data member initialized to " << n;
}

Test_Class::Test_Class(int i)
{
  n = i;

  cout << "\n\nConstructor Executed: Data member initialized to " << n;
}
int main()
{
  int i;

  cout <<"\nEnter a value for the first object: ";
  cin >> i;

  Test_Class tc_object1(i);

  Test_Class tc_object2;
```

```
      cout << "\n\nEnd of program";

  return 0;
  }
```

Program Output

```
Enter a value for the first object: 9

Constructor Executed: Data member initialized to 9

Constructor Executed: Data member initialized to 0

***** End of program *****
```

Programming
Pointers

The C++ compiler distinguishes between the two constructors by the number and type of arguments provided in the declaration of an object. The following declaration uses the one-argument constructor.

```
Test_Class tc_object1(i);
```

On the other hand, the following declaration uses the no-argument constructor.

```
Test_Class tc_object2;
```

In `Account`, we have a constructor that allows us to create an account by giving an account number, a balance, and an interest rate. We might also want a constructor that allows us to create an account by giving only the account number, with the balance and interest rate being assigned default values of 0.00 and 0.04. We might also want a constructor that allows us to create an account by giving the account number and the balance, with the interest rate being assigned a default value of 0.04. You must declare all three constructors in the class declaration as follows.

```
class Account
{
  .
  .
  .
  public:
    Account(int, double, double);
    Account(int, double);
    Account(int);
  .
  .
  .
};
```

The constructor is now overloaded because we have three different meanings for the constructor depending on the number of arguments given in an `Account` object declaration. The three constructor definitions follow.

```
Account::Account(int id, double bal, double rt)
{
  id_no = id;
  balance = bal;
  rate = rt;
}

Account::Account(int id, double bal)
{
  id_no = id;
  balance = bal;
  rate = 0.04;
}

Account::Account(int id)
{
  id_no = id;
  balance = 0.0;
  rate = 0.04;
}
```

In `main()`, we can now write the following declarations.

```
Account acc3(3333, 100.00, 0.06);

Account acc2(2222, 200.00);

Account acc1(1111);
```

The first declaration uses the three-argument constructor and creates the account 3333 with a balance of 100.00 and interest rate of 0.06. The second declaration creates the account 2222 with an opening balance of 200.00 and the default interest rate of 0.04. The third declaration uses the one-argument constructor and creates the account 1111 with a default balance of 0.00 and a default interest rate of 0.04. See Experiment 1.

Default Arguments

Programming
Pointers

In the previous section we overloaded the `Test_Class` constructor to allow us to declare a `Test_Class` object either with or without an initial value. Sometimes we can achieve the effect of overloading a constructor by using a single constructor with **default arguments**. You must specify the default arguments in the constructor's declaration, not in its definition. See Note 10.9 on page 495. In the class declaration you must code the following.

```
public:
    Test_Class(int i = 0);      //One-argument constructor with default value
                                //which serves as a no-argument constructor
```

This declaration means that if we omit the argument when declaring a Test_Class object, the default value of 0 will be used for that argument. The following declaration creates a Test_Class object with a data member value of 0.

```
Test_Class tc_object;
```

It follows, therefore, that Test_Class has the equivalent of two constructors—a no-argument constructor, in which the data member of the object being declared defaults to 0, and a one-argument constructor, in which the object's data member is initialized to the argument value.

Following is a complete program that uses a one-argument constructor that defaults to the value 0 when omitted.

```
//dem10-9.cpp
//This program demonstrates a simple constructor function
//The constructor has one argument, which defaults to 0.

#include <iostream.h>

using namespace std;

class Test_Class
{
  private:
    int n;

  public:
    Test_Class(int i = 0);      //One-argument constructor with default value
};

Test_Class::Test_Class(int i)
{
  n = i;

  cout << "\n\nConstructor Executed: Data member initialized to " << n;
}
int main()
{
  int i;

  cout <<"\nEnter a value for the first object: ";
  cin >> i;

  Test_Class tc_object1(i);  //one-argument constructor
```

```
    Test_Class tc_object2;       //one—argument constructor with default value

    cout << "\n\nEnd of program";

return 0;
}
```

Program Output

```
Enter a value for the first object: 9


Constructor Executed: Data member initialized to 9

Constructor Executed: Data member initialized to 0

***** End of program *****
```

In the previous section we overloaded the `Account` constructor to allow us to declare `Account` objects in three different ways. When a constructor has more than one argument, the trailing arguments can be given default initial values in the constructor's declaration. See Note 10.9, which follows. For example, in the declaration of `Account`, we can code the following.

```
class Account
{
    .
    .
    .
  public:
    Account(int id, double bal = 0.0, double rt = 0.04);
    .
    .
    .
};

Account::Account(int id, double bal, double rt)
{
  id_no = id;
  balance = bal;
  rate = rt;
}
```

This gives `Account` the equivalent of three constructors—with one argument, two arguments, and three arguments. (Remember, by Note 10.7, `Account` no longer has a no-argument constructor.) When we declare an `Account` object, we can omit the last argument or the last two arguments. If we do so, the omitted arguments have the default values specified in the constructor's declaration. For example, we can now make the same declarations that we made in the previous section.

```
Account acc3(3333, 100.00, 0.06);

Account acc2(2222, 200.00);

Account acc1(1111);

Account acc0;    //Illegal — the no-argument constructor not available
```

The declaration for acc3 uses the three-argument constructor. The declaration for acc2 omits one argument. When omitting arguments, only trailing arguments can be omitted. Therefore, the missing argument in the declaration of acc2 must be that of the third argument, namely the rate. Referring to the definition of the constructor, the parameter id takes the value 2222 and the parameter bal takes the value 200.00 from the arguments in the declaration of acc2. The third argument, rt takes the default value 0.04 from the declaration of the constructor. The constructor then executes and assigns these values to the object's data members.

The declaration for acc1 omits two arguments so the last two arguments default to the values given in the declaration of the constructor. Again referring to the definition of the constructor, the parameter id takes the value 1111 from the object declaration, bal takes the default value of 0.00, and rt takes the default value of 0.04 from the constructor declaration. The constructor then executes and assigns these values to the object's data members. See Experiment 2.

The last declaration is illegal because the no-argument constructor is not available—see Note 10.7 and Experiment 3.

Note 10.9 summarizes the two rules you must follow when using default arguments in a constructor.

NOTE 10.9—DEFAULT ARGUMENTS IN A CONSTRUCTOR

- Default arguments must be specified in the declaration of the function.
- Only trailing arguments can be omitted.

Programming
Pitfalls

According to Note 10.9, the following declaration is illegal because there is a non-default argument after a default argument.

```
Account(int id, double bal = 0.00, double rt); //Illegal declaration
```

The following, however, is a legal declaration.

```
Account(int id, double bal, double rt = 0.04); //Legal declaration
```

Note that any function, not just constructors, can have default arguments. See Experiment 4.

General Function Overloading

Programming
Pointers

Any function can be overloaded in C++. The overloaded versions of a function must have the same return type and must differ in the number and/or the types of arguments. The following function interchanges its two integer arguments. See dem08-3R.cpp in Chapter 8.

```
void Swap(int& i, int& j)
{
  int temp;

  temp = i;
  i = j;
  j = temp;
}
```

If we were not allowed to overload Swap() and we wanted to write a function that interchanges two doubles, we would have to code a separate function, say Swap_Double(). However, in C++ we can overload the integer version of Swap() with the following double version of Swap().

```
void Swap(double& x, double& y)
{
  double temp;

  temp = x;
  x = y;
  y = temp;
}
```

When used in a program, the C++ compiler distinguishes between the two versions of Swap() by the data types of its arguments. Following is dem10-10.cpp, which illustrates function overloading.

```
//dem10—10.cpp

//This program demonstrates function overloading.

#include <iostream.h>

using namespace std;

void Swap(int&, int&);
void Swap(double&, double&);

int main()
```

```
{
   int    n = 3,
          m = 9;
   double d = 5.7,
          e = 3.14 ;

   cout << "\nn = " << n << " m = " << m;
   cout << "\nd = " << d << " e = " << e;

   Swap(n, m);
   Swap(d, e);

   cout << "\n\nAfter swapping:\n";

   cout << "\nn = " << n << " m = " << m;
   cout << "\nd = " << d << " e = " << e;

   return 0;
}

void Swap(int& i, int& j)
{
   int temp;

   temp = i;
   i = j;
   j = temp;
}

void Swap(double& x, double& y)
{
   double temp;

   temp = x;
   x = y;
   y = temp;
}
```

Program Output

```
n = 3 m = 9
d = 5.7 e = 3.14

After swapping:

n = 9 m = 3
d = 3.14 e = 5.7
```

Two versions of Swap() are declared—one for integers and one for doubles. In main() the compiler decides which version of Swap() to use by the type of its arguments. Thus, the first execution of Swap() uses the integer version and the second uses the double version. We leave as an exercise which version of `Swap()` is used in the following statement. See Experiment 5.

```
Swap(n, d);    //Which version is used?
```

Function Templates

The overloaded `Swap()` function of the previous section can be overloaded further for arguments that are `floats`, `longs`, `shorts`, and so on. We would, of course, have to code a different function for each argument type. A **function template** allows the programmer to code a function whose definition is independent of the data type of its arguments and/or its return type. In essence, a function template makes the compiler automatically create overloaded functions as needed by the program. A function template for the `Swap()` function is as follows.

```
template <class Type>
void Swap(Type& x, Type& y)
{
  Type temp;
  temp = x;
  x = y;
  y = temp;
}
```

The definition begins with the keyword `template` followed by the keyword `class` and an identifier, both enclosed in angle brackets. The word `template` tells the compiler that a template definition is being made. The angle bracket part of the definition tells the compiler that the identifier, in our case `Type`, is being used as the name of an arbitrary class. `Type` acts as a variable whose value can be any class. Recall that all the built-in data types, such as `int` and `double`, are classes as well as user-defined classes, such as `Account`.

Following the template declaration is the definition of the function. The only rule to remember when writing the function is to use the identifier `Type` whenever we wish to refer to the data type of a parameter or when we declare a variable. See the program that follows. In the function header we have `Swap(Type& x, Type& y)` instead of declaring the parameters of any specific type. In the function body we declare the variable `temp` as follows.

```
Type temp;
```

If the compiler sees `Swap(n, m)`, where n and m are integer variables, it creates a `Swap()` function with two `int` arguments. If the compiler sees `Swap(d, e)`, where d and e are `double` variables, it creates a `Swap()` function with two `double` arguments.

Following is the program dem10-11.cpp, which contains several examples of function templates.

```
//dem10-11.cpp

//This program demonstrates function templates.

#include <iostream.h>

using namespace std;


template <class Type>
inline Type Max(Type x, Type y)
{
   return (x > y)? x: y;
}

template <class Type>
void Swap(Type& x, Type& y)
{
   Type temp;
   temp = x;
   x = y;
   y = temp;
}
template <class TypeA, class TypeB>
TypeA Sum(TypeA x, TypeB y)
{
   TypeA r;

   r = x + y;

   return r;
}

template <class Type>
Type Total(Type a[], int n)
{
   Type t = 0;

   for (int i = 0; i < n; ++i)
       t += a[i];

   return t;
}

int main()
{
   int    i = 3,
          j = 5;
   double d = 8.62,
          e = 4.14;
```

```
float f_arr[6] = {1.2, 2.3, 3.4, 4.5, 5.6, 6.7};
int   i_arr[4] = {4, 5, 6, 7};

cout << "\ni = " << i << " and j = " << j;
cout << "\nd = " << d << " and e = " << e;

cout << "\n\nThe larger of i and j is " << Max(i, j);
cout << "\nThe larger of d and e is " << Max(d, e);

Swap(i, j);
Swap(d, e);

cout << "\n\ni = " << i << " and j = " << j;
cout << "\nd = " << d << " and e = " << e;

cout << "\n\nSum() applied to i and d is " << Sum(i, d);
cout << "\nSum() applied to d and i is " << Sum(d, i);

cout << "\n\nThe sum of f_arr[] is " << Total(f_arr, 6);
cout << "\nThe sum of i_arr[] is " << Total(i_arr, 4);

return 0;
}
```

Program Output

```
i = 3 and j = 5
d = 8.62 and e = 4.14

The larger of i and j is 5
The larger of d and e is 8.62

i = 5 and j = 3
d = 4.14 and e = 8.62

Sum() applied to i and d is 9
Sum() applied to d and i is 9.14

The sum of f_arr[] is 23.7
The sum of i_arr[] is 22
```

Note the function templates are defined before `main()`, which is required by most compilers. Since the function `Max()` returns the value of the larger of its arguments, its template uses `Type` for the function return type as well as for the parameter type. This function also illustrates the fact that a template can be an inline function. The function `Max()` represents another alternative to using either a macro or an ordinary inline function. As with a macro (see Chapter 5), for example

```
#define MAX(x, y) ( ((x) > (y))? (x): (y) ) ,
```

the template function `Max()` is independent of the argument type. However, the template function `Max()` is not subject to the side effects that sometimes make macros dangerous to use. In addition, the template function `Max()` is more versatile than an ordinary inline function because it is type-independent.

The second template function, `Swap()`, is the function we discussed previously. In the program, we use `Swap()` to interchange the values of two integers and two doubles. If we were not using a template function, we would have needed two separate functions to do the same job as was done in the previous section.

The function template `Sum()` shows that two different generic data types can be used in a function template. In `main()`, we apply `Sum()` twice: first using an integer-double argument pair, `Sum(i, d)`, and second using a double-integer argument pair, `Sum(d, i)`. In each case we obtain a result that is compatible with the data type of the first argument because the function `Sum()` declares a local variable `r`, whose type is that of the first argument, and returns the value of `r`.

The function `Total()` illustrates the fact that a template can include an array argument. In fact, a template can include arguments of any type.

If you attempt to use a function template for which the compiler cannot match types, the program will not compile. See Experiment 6.

EXERCISES 10.3

1. In the `Rectangle` class of Exercise 2, Section 10.2, add a no-argument constructor that creates a default 1×1 rectangle in two ways: first by coding a separate no-argument constructor, and then by using default arguments.

2. In the `DigitalClock` class of Exercise 3, Section 10.2, add a no-argument constructor that initializes the time on the clock to the equivalent of 12:00 A.M. in two ways: first by coding a separate no-argument constructor, and then by using default arguments.

3. Write a function template `Square()` that returns the square of its only argument.

4. Write a function template `Power()` that takes two arguments. The first argument should be of arbitrary type. The second argument is an integer. The function should return the first argument raised to the power indicated by its second argument. The return type should be that of its first argument.

5. Write a function template `Find()` that takes two arguments and returns an integer. The first argument is an array of arbitrary type. The second argument is an ordinary variable of the same type as the first argument. The function should return the array subscript of the first array element that exceeds the second argument. If no such element is found, the function should return -1.

EXPERIMENTS 10.3

1. In dem10-5.cpp, add a two-argument and one-argument constructor to `Account` as described in this section. Declare three `Account` objects in `main()`—one with the three-argument constructor, one with the two-argument constructor and one with the one-argument constructor. Compile, execute, and test the resulting program.

2. Replace the three constructors in the program of Experiment 1 by a single three-argument constructor in which the last two arguments default to 0.0 and 0.04, as described in this section. Declare two `Account` objects in `main()`: one in which the third argument defaults and one in which the second and third arguments default. Compile, execute, and test the resulting program.

3. In the program of Experiment 2, add the following declaration to `main()`.

```
Account acc0;
```

Compile the resulting program. What message does the compiler issue?

4. Any function can have default arguments. Compile and execute the following program. What are the results and why?

```
#include <iostream.h>

using namespace std:

int Sum(int i = 1, int j = 2);

int main()
{
   cout << Sum(3, 4) << endl;

   cout << Sum(6) << endl;

   cout << Sum() << endl;

   return 0;
}

int Sum(int i, int j)
{
   return i + j;
}
```

5. In dem10-10.cpp, add the following line in `main()` before `return 0`.

```
Swap(n, d);
```

Compile the resulting program. What happens?

6. In dem10-11.cpp, add the following lines in `main()` before `return 0`.

```
Sum(i, d);
Swap(i, d);
```

Compile the resulting program. What happens? Which line causes an error and why?

PROGRAMMING PROBLEMS 10.3

1. In the `WebPage` class of Programming Problem 1, Section 10.2, in addition to the no-argument constructor, code a three-argument constructor that initializes the data members of the object being created (hits, messages, and downloads) to its arguments. Recode the `main()` that you wrote to include use of the constructors. Compile, execute, and test the resulting program.

2. In the `OilTank` class of Programming Problem 2, Section 10.2, recode the three-argument constructor so that the third argument (the contents) defaults to zero. Recode the `main()` that you wrote to include use of the constructors. Compile, execute, and test the resulting program.

3. In the `VehicleService` class of Programming Problem 3, Section 10.2, replace the one-argument constructor by a four-argument constructor in which the first argument is the service number and the last three (for hours, parts, and total cost) default to zero. Recode the `main()` that you wrote to include use of the constructors. Compile, execute, and test the resulting program.

4. In the `HotelRoom` class of Programming Problem 4, Section 10.2, recode the four-argument constructor so that the third argument (the room rate) defaults to 89.00, and the fourth argument (the occupancy state) defaults to zero. Recode the `main()` you wrote to include the use of the constructor. Compile, execute, and test the resulting program.

5. Write, compile, execute and test a program that uses the function templates `Square()`, `Power()`, and `Find()` of Exercises 3, 4, and 5.

Chapter Review

Terminology

Define the following terms.

object	instantiation
class	accessor function
istream	mutator function
ostream	constructor
class	default constructor
public	destructor
private	default destructor
class member	function overloading
encapsulation	default arguments
scope resolution operator, : :	function template

Summary

- An object is one or more data values that define the state of the object, and a set of functions that can be applied to the object.
- A class is a general category that defines the characteristics of the data members of objects of that class and that defines the functions that can be applied to objects in that class.
- Use the `class` keyword to define a class.
- Class members can be `public` or `private`. Private members are accessible only to class member functions. Public members are accessible to all functions.
- All class member functions must be declared inside the class definition even if they are defined outside the class (Note 10.1).
- All class data members are accessible without qualification or declaration inside all class member functions (Note 10.2).
- If you define a class member function outside the class definition, in the function definition header you must qualify the name by the class name followed by the scope resolution operator, `::`, followed by the function name (Note 10.3).
- When a class member function is applied to an object, all class data member references in the function definition are to the data members of the object to which the function is being applied (Note 10.4).
- In C++, the only difference between a structure and a class is that in a class the default access specifier is `private`, whereas in a structure the default access specifier is `public`.
- A class member function is an accessor function if it does not change the value of any class data member.
- A class member function is a mutator function if it changes one or more class data members.
- A constructor is a class member function that executes when an object of that class is instantiated. A constructor must have the same name as the class name, cannot have a return type, and must be public (Note 10.6).
- If no constructor is explicitly declared for a class, C++ automatically provides the default no-argument constructor.
- If you explicitly declare a constructor, the default no-argument constructor is no longer available (Note 10.7).
- The class destructor function executes automatically when an object goes out of scope. An explicitly declared destructor's name is the same as the class name prefixed by the ~, cannot have a return type, and cannot have arguments. If no destructor is explicitly declared, C++ provides a default destructor (Note 10.8).
- An object can be assigned to another object provided the objects are of the same class. In this case, the assignment proceeds on a member by member basis.
- Several constructors can be provided for a class by using function overloading—functions that have the same name and return type but a different number and/or types of arguments.

- A constructor (indeed any function) can have default arguments, which must be specified in the function declaration. Only trailing arguments can be omitted (Note 10.9).
- Any function in C++ can be overloaded. The overloaded versions must have the same name and return type, and must differ in the number and/or types of arguments.
- Generic, or type-independent, functions can be defined using function templates.

Review Exercises

1. What is the difference between an object and a class?
2. What do the data members of a class and the function members of a class represent?
3. Give two places in a program where you can define a class member function. Are there any differences in the way a class member function is defined depending on where it is defined?
4. How do you use a class member function?
5. How do you refer to the data members of the object to which a member function is applied?
6. What is the difference between an accessor function and a mutator function? Which member functions should be made accessor functions?
7. What is a constructor function? What is a constructor function used for in a program? How must a constructor function be named? Why can't a constructor function have a return type? When is a constructor function executed? Must you explicitly code a constructor function for a class? What is the default constructor?
8. What is a destructor function? How must a destructor function be named? When is a destructor function executed? Must you explicitly code a destructor function for a class? What is the default destructor?
9. Under what circumstances can you assign one object to another? How is the assignment made?
10. What is function overloading? How does the compiler distinguish between uses of an overloaded function?
11. Which arguments in a constructor can be defaulted? Where do you specify the default values—in the prototype or in the definition?
12. What is a function template? How do you code a template function?

Chapter

11

Manipulating Objects

Objectives

- To use arrays and character pointers as class data members.

- To code a constructor that uses dynamic memory allocation.

- To code a destructor that de-allocates space that was allocated by a constructor.

- To code a copy constructor.

- To use `const` to code an accessor function so it can be applied to a constant object.

- To use `const` in a pointer declaration.

- To use `const` arguments in a function.

- To code an accessor function that returns a `const` pointer.

- To code a function that returns an object.

- To code a function that passes an object by value.

- To know when the copy constructor is used.

- To use the $->$ operator to access an object's members through a pointer.

- To code a function that passes an object by pointer.

- To code a function that passes an object by reference.

- To dynamically allocate space for objects.

- To code and use static data and function members.

This chapter discusses several techniques that allow you to manipulate objects in your programs. Section 11.1 shows you how to include array and pointer data members in a class. Section 11.2 covers the important topic of the copy constructor. Several uses of the keyword `const` are discussed in Section 11.3. Some of the this material can be omitted at first reading. You should *not* omit the sections on "Constant Arguments in Functions" and "Constant Arguments and the Copy Constructor." Section 11.4 shows how to write functions that use objects and how to pass objects by value, by pointer, and by reference. Section 11.5 shows how to dynamically allocate objects. This section is important to the material in Chapter 13, and therefore can be postponed until then. Finally, Section 11.6 discusses static data members and functions, which allow you to define instance-independent class data members and functions. This entire section may be omitted without loss of continuity.

11.1 Using Arrays, Pointers, and Dynamic Memory Allocation

To make the `Account` class of Chapter 10 more realistic, we now change the data type of `id_no`, the data member that stores the account number. We also include a pointer data member to store the account owner's name.

Array and Pointer Class Members

So far, we have assumed that the account number member of class `Account`, `id_no`, is an integer. The account number could be 4, or 73, or 12324, or 34567. In most applications, however, an account number or ID has a specific number of characters. We shall require our account ID to be four characters. The account ID number should be stored in a character array of size five (remember that we must have a position for the null character, `'\0'`.) Suppose we declare the following in the `private` section of the definition of `Account`.

```
char id_no[5];
```

As we shall see, redefining `id_no` in this way will cause us to change how we assign a value to `id_no` in the constructor for `Account`. We will also add to the definition of `Account` a data member that represents the name of the person holding the account. We could store the account holder's name in an array as we do for the ID number. However, we do not know how many characters will be in a person's name. If we use an array to store the name, the array size would have to be large enough to store the longest name. We would have to use a very large array, which would waste space for most names we encounter. Instead we shall make the `name` data member a character pointer and dynamically allocate exactly enough space for the account owner's name when we create the account.

```
char* name;
```

Following is the new declaration of `Account`, which includes the declaration of a new four-argument constructor with two default arguments, and the declaration of a destructor. We also add member functions to display the `id_no` and `name` members. We will see later why these functions do not return the `id_no` and `name` members and we will discuss a better way to handle the output of string data members of a class.

```
class Account
{
  private:
    char    id_no[5];
    char*   name;
    double balance;
    double rate;

  public:
    Account(char id[], char* n_p, double bal = 0.00, double rt = 0.04);
    ~Account();
    double Calc_Interest();
    double Get_Balance();
    void Deposit(double);
    int Withdraw(double);
    void Display_ID();
    void Display_Name();
};
```

The new constructor assumes that the first and second arguments are character strings. (Recall that an array name, without the brackets, is a pointer to the first element in the array.) We shall treat the first of these strings as a fixed size character array, and the second as a character pointer. To create an account with ID number 1111 belonging to Jane Doe with an opening balance of 200.00 and the default rate of 0.04, we would declare the following.

```
Account acc("1111", "Jane Doe", 200.00);
```

The constructor must copy the first argument "1111" into the member array `id_no[]`, and make the pointer member, `name`, point to the character string "Jane Doe". Accomplishing these tasks requires using string manipulation functions and the use of dynamic memory allocation. Following is the code for the constructor.

```
Account::Account(char id[], char* n_p, double bal, double rt)
{
  strcpy(id_no, id);  //copy first argument into id_no[]

  name = new char[strlen(n_p) + 1]; //create space for the name

  strcpy(name, n_p);  //copy second argument into new space
```

```
   balance = bal;
   rate    = rt;
}
```

The first statement in the constructor uses the library function `strcpy()` to copy the first argument into the five-character member array `id_no[]`. To make the member `name` point to the string that is the second argument requires two statements. The first statement uses the `new` operator to allocate enough space for a character array that will hold the second argument and assigns to `name` the pointer returned by `new`. (Note the use of the string function `strlen()`, which returns the number of characters in the second argument. We add one to the number returned by `strlen()` to have room for the null character.) After executing the assignment, `name` points to a character array that is exactly large enough to hold the string that is the second argument of the constructor. See Figure 11.1a. The second statement copies the second argument, which is pointed to by n_p, into the space pointed to by `name`. See Figure 11.1b.

The definition of the destructor function follows.

```
Account::~Account()
{
  cout << "\nAccount " << id_no << " terminated.";
  delete [] name;
}
```

When a program creates an `Account` object, the constructor allocates space on the heap for the account holder's name. When an object goes out of scope, that is when the object is destroyed, we must de-allocate that heap space by executing the `delete` statement in the class's destructor function. The process of de-allocating heap space when

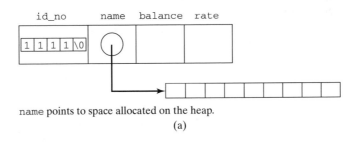

name points to space allocated on the heap.

(a)

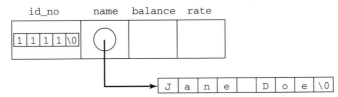

After the second argument is copied into the space pointed to by name.

(b)

FIGURE 11.1

it is no longer needed is sometimes called "**garbage collection**." Failure to de-allocate heap space causes the space to remain allocated but unusable because the pointer to that space, name, will no longer exist. If this happens for many Account objects, there will be a great deal of unusable space in main memory. Taken to the extreme, this could cause a program to run out of usable heap space memory. See Experiment 1.

We now incorporate the changed class into a program.

```
//dem11-1.cpp

//This program uses an expanded version of Account.
//The program uses a constructor with default arguments.
//The ID number is stored as an array and the name of the
//account holder is a character pointer. The constructor uses
//dynamic memory allocation.

#include <iostream.h>
#include <iomanip.h>
#include <string.h>

using namespace std;

class Account
{
  private:
    char   id_no[5];
    char*  name;
    double balance;
    double rate;

  public:
    Account(char id[], char* n_p, double bal = 0.00, double rt = 0.04);
    ~Account();
    double Calc_Interest();
    double Get_Balance();
    void Deposit(double);
    int Withdraw(double);
    void Display_ID();
    void Display_Name();
};

Account::Account(char id[], char* n_p, double bal, double rt)
{
  strcpy(id_no, id);  //copy first argument into id_no[]

  name = new char[strlen(n_p) + 1]; //create space for the name

  strcpy(name, n_p);  //copy second argument into new space

  balance = bal;
```

```
    rate    = rt;
  }


Account::~Account()
{
  cout << "\n\nAccount " << id_no << " terminated.";
  delete [] name;
}



inline double Account::Get_Balance()
{
  return balance;
}


double Account::Calc_Interest()
{
  double interest;

  interest = balance * rate;
  balance += interest;

  return interest;
}


void Account::Deposit(double amount)
{
  balance += amount;
}



int Account::Withdraw(double amount)
{
  int result;

  if (amount <= balance)
    {
      balance -= amount;
      result = 1;
    }
  else
    result = 0;

  return result;
}


void Account::Display_ID()
{
  cout << id_no;
}
```

```
void Account::Display_Name()
{
  cout << name;
}
int main()
{
  cout << setprecision(2)
       << setiosflags(ios::fixed)
       << setiosflags(ios::showpoint);

  char id[5];
  char buffer[81];  //Temporarily stores the name
  double bal;
  double rt;
  double amount;

  cout << "\nEnter Account ID: ";
  cin.getline(id, 5);

  cin.get();    //Clear the input buffer of newline character

  cout << "\nEnter Account Holder's Name: ";
  cin.getline(buffer, 81);

  cout << "\nEnter Balance: ";
  cin >> bal;

  cout << "\nEnter Interest Rate: ";
  cin >> rt;


  Account acc1(id, buffer, bal, rt);

  cout << "\nThe account number is ";
  acc1.Display_ID();
  cout << "\nThe owner of the account is ";
  acc1.Display_Name();


  cout << "\n\nThe balance in the account is now " << acc1.Get_Balance();

  cout << "\n\nEnter an amount to deposit: ";
  cin >> amount;

  acc1.Deposit(amount);

  cout << "\n\nA deposit of " << amount << " was made.";
  cout << "\nThe balance in the account is now " << acc1.Get_Balance();

  acc1.Calc_Interest();
```

```cpp
    cout << "\n\nInterest was applied to the account.";
    cout << "\nThe balance in the account is now " << acc1.Get_Balance();

    cout << "\n\nEnter an amount to withdraw: ";
    cin >> amount;

    if (acc1.Withdraw(amount))
        cout << "\n\nA withdrawal of " << amount << " was made.";
    else
        cout << "\n\nWITHDRAWAL NOT MADE: Insufficient funds.";

    cout << "\nThe balance in the account is now " << acc1.Get_Balance();

    return 0;
}
```

Program Output

```
Enter Account ID: 1234

Enter Account Holder's Name: Larrabee Maxwell

Enter Balance: 100.00

Enter Interest Rate: 0.06

The account number is 1234
The owner of the account is Larrabee Maxwell

The balance in the account is now 100.00

Enter an amount to deposit: 200.00


A deposit of 200.00 was made.
The balance in the account is now 300.00

Interest was applied to the account.
The balance in the account is now 318.00

Enter an amount to withdraw: 175.00


A withdrawal of 175.00 was made.
The balance in the account is now 143.00

Account 1234 terminated.
```

The program is fairly straightforward. Note that the destructor displays a message when the program ends.

EXPERIMENTS 11.1

1. Remove the destructor from `Account` in dem11-1.cpp. Use the following `main()`.

```
int main()
{
  for (long i = 1; i <= 10000; ++i)
    {
      Account acc("1111", "John Doe", 100.00, 0.05);
    }
  return 0;
}
```

Compile and execute the resulting program. Does the program run out of heap space? If not, replace the 10000 by 100000 and try again. Note: The program may take a while to execute. Why does this program waste heap space?

PROGRAMMING PROBLEMS 11.1

1. In the `WebPage` class of Programming Problem 1, Section 10.3, add the character pointer data member `page_url`, which represents the URL of the Web page (for example, www.cpp.edu). Replace the three-argument constructor by a four-argument constructor. The first argument should be a character pointer representing the URL of the Web page. The second, third, and fourth arguments represent the hits, messages, and downloads of the page. These last three arguments should all default to zero. Use dynamic memory allocation to reserve space for the URL. Code a destructor for the class that de-allocates space for the URL that was allocated in the constructor. The destructor should also display a message that indicates that it executed. Add a member function `Display_URL()` that displays the URL member. Recode the `main()` that you wrote to include use of the constructor, destructor, and new display functions. Compile, execute, and test the resulting program.

2. Recode the `OilTank` class of Programming Problem 2, Section 10.3 as follows. Replace the integer tank number member by a five-character array that represents the tank number. Add the character pointer member `company_name`, which represents the name of the company that owns the tank. Replace the three-argument constructor by a four-argument constructor. The first argument should be a string that represents the name of the company that owns the tank. The second argument should be a character string that represents the five-digit tank number. The third argument should be the capacity of the tank, and the fourth argument should represent the contents of the tank (which should default to zero.) Use dynamic memory allocation to reserve space for the company name. Code a destructor that de-allocates the space for the company name that was allocated in the constructor. The destructor should also display a message that indicates that it executed. Replace the `Get_Number()` member function

by the member function `Display_Number()` that displays the `id-no` member, and add the member function `Display_Company()` that displays the `company_name` member. Recode the `main()` that you wrote to include use of the constructor, destructor, and new display functions. Compile, execute, and test the resulting program.

3. Recode the `VehicleService` class of Programming Problem 3, Section 10.3, as follows. Replace the integer service number by a six-character array. Add a character pointer, `owner`, that represents the name of the owner of the vehicle. Replace the four-argument constructor by a five-argument constructor. The first argument should be a string that represents the service number. The second argument should be a string that represents the owner of the vehicle. The last three arguments (hours, parts, and total) default to zero. Add a destructor that de-allocates the space for the owner member that was allocated in the constructor. The destructor should also display a message that indicates that it executed. Replace the `Get_Number()` member function by the member function `Display_Number()` that displays the service number, and add the member function `Display_Owner()` that displays the owner name. Recode the `main()` that you wrote to include use of the constructor, destructor, and new display functions. Compile, execute, and test the resulting program.

4. Recode the `HotelRoom` class of Programming Problem 4, Section 10.3 as follows. Replace the integer room number by a character array that stores a three-character room number. Add the character pointer member `guest`, which stores the name of the guest occupying the room. Replace the `Get_Number()` member function by the member function `Display_Number()`, which displays the room number, and add the member function `Display_Guest()`, which displays the guest member. Replace the four-argument constructor by a five-argument constructor in which the first argument is the room number, the second argument is the room capacity, the third argument is the room rate (defaulting to 89.00), the fourth argument is the guest name (defaulting to the `NULL` pointer), and the fifth argument is the occupancy status (defaulting to zero). Use dynamic memory allocation to reserve space for the guest name. Code a destructor that de-allocates the space allocated by the constructor. The destructor should also display a message that it executed. Recode the `main()` that you wrote to include use of the constructor, destructor, and new display functions. Compile, execute, and test the resulting program.

11.2 The Copy Constructor

We mentioned in Chapter 10 that an object can be assigned to another object. The program dem10-7.cpp showed that when an object is initialized to another object, the constructor for the class is not executed. We now discuss the function that is executed during initialization, namely the copy constructor, and the circumstances under which you need to code a copy constructor for a class. Section 11.4 discusses two more uses of the copy constructor.

The Copy Constructor—A Simple Example

Programming
Pointers

In C++, there is a difference between assignment and initialization. In the operation of assignment, the receiving object must exist prior to the assignment. In initialization, the object is initialized during the process of creation. For example, consider the following.

```
int i = 7,
    j;


j = i;
```

The integer i is declared and initialized to 7. When i is created, it is created with the value 7. i never exists without a valid value. On the other hand, when j is declared, it does not receive a value. Therefore, it has a garbage value until a valid value is assigned to it. The assignment operation copies the value of i into the already existing object j, giving j a valid value.

This difference between assignment and initialization is also true of objects. Consider dem10-7.cpp, whose function main() and output we reproduce here.

```
void main()
{
  Test_Class tc_object1(4);
  Test_Class tc_object2(0);

  cout << "\n\nAfter object creation:";
  cout << "\n\nObject 1: " << tc_object1.Get_Value();
  cout << "\nObject 2: " << tc_object2.Get_Value();

  tc_object2 = tc_object1;

  cout << "\n\nAfter object assignment:";
  cout << "\n\nObject 1: " << tc_object1.Get_Value();
  cout << "\nObject 2: " << tc_object2.Get_Value();

  Test_Class tc_object3 = tc_object1;

  cout << "\n\nAfter initializing object 3:";
  cout << "\n\nObject 3: " << tc_object3.Get_Value();
}
```

Program Output

```
Constructor Executed: Data member initialized to 4
Constructor Executed: Data member initialized to 0

After object creation:

Object 1: 4
Object 2: 0
```

```
After object assignment:

Object 1: 4
Object 2: 4                          The constructor is not
                                     executed here.
After initializing object 3:


Object 3: 4

Destructor executed for object with data member 4

Destructor executed for object with data member 4

Destructor executed for object with data member 4
```

The class constructor executes only twice—once for `tc_object1` and once for `tc_object2`. The constructor is not executed for the object `tc_object3`, which is created by initialization and initialized to the object `tc_object1`. Therefore, `tc_object3` is created with the same data member values as `tc_object1`. `tc_object3`'s data member n always has a valid value.

Programming Pointers

Because the operation of initialization is different than that of assignment, a special constructor is used by C++ for initialization, namely the **copy constructor**. Just as for the ordinary constructor, if you do not explicitly code a copy constructor, your class is given the **default copy constructor**. The initialization of `tc_object3` in dem10-7.cpp is successful because the default copy constructor is used in the initialization. The default copy constructor copies the data members from `tc_object1` and initializes them, on a member by member basis, to the corresponding data members of `tc_object3`.

To code your own copy constructor, use Note 11.1.

NOTE 11.1—CODING THE COPY CONSTRUCTOR

- The copy constructor must, like other constructors, have the same name as the class.
- The copy constructor is distinguished from other constructors by the form of its argument, which is a reference to an object of the class for which it is the copy constructor.
- The syntax of the copy constructor declaration is as follows:

```
Class_Name (Class_Name& r_object);
```

- When coding a copy constructor, think of the constructor's argument as the object on the right side of the = in an initialization. In the copy constructor's code, to refer to the members of this object, use the parameter name `r_object`, followed by the dot operator, followed by the data member name.
- The copy constructor is applied to the object being created. Therefore, it is applied to the object on the left of the = in an initialization. Use unqualified member names to refer to the members of this object in the copy constructor's code.

For example, we can declare and code a copy constructor for `Test_Class` as follows.

```
class Test_Class
{
    .
    .
    .

  public:
    Test_Class(Test_Class&);        //Copy Constructor declaration
    .
    .
    .

};

Test_Class::Test_Class(Test_Class& tc_r)
{
  n = tc_r.n; //Copies the n data member of the object to the right
              //of the = in an initialization to the n data member
              //of the object being created.

  cout << "\n\nCopy Constructor executed: "
       << "Data member initialized to " << n;
}
```

The copy constructor is invoked when an object is initialized in a declaration. Therefore, the second declaration that follows causes the copy constructor to execute.

```
Test_Class tc1(3);        //the regular constructor executes
Test_Class tc2 = tc1;     //the copy constructor executes
```

Using Note 11.1, think of the parameter `tc_r` in the copy constructor definition as representing the right side of the = in an initialization. (In the second declaration `tc1`.) Thus, the copy constructor assigns to the n data member of the new object being created (the object `tc2` in the previous initialization) the corresponding data member of the object on the right side of the =, namely `tc_r.n` (which represents the n data member of `tc1`).

In Section 11.4 we will explain why the argument of the copy constructor must be a reference. The following program illustrates the use of the copy constructor.

```
//dem11-2.cpp

//This program illustrates the use of a copy constructor

#include <iostream.h>

using namespace std;
```

```
class Test_Class
{
  private:
    int n;

  public:
    Test_Class(int);  //One-argument constructor
    Test_Class(Test_Class&);  //Copy constructor
    ~Test_Class();
    int Get_Value();
};

Test_Class::Test_Class(int i)
{
  n = i;

  cout << "\nConstructor Executed: Data member initialized to " << n;
}

Test_Class::Test_Class(Test_Class& tc_r)
{
  n = tc_r.n;

  cout << "\n\nCopy constructor executed: "
       << "Data member initialized to " << n;
}

Test_Class::~Test_Class()
{
  cout << "\n\nDestructor Executed for object with data member " << n;
}

inline int Test_Class::Get_Value()
{
  return n;
}

int main()
{
  Test_Class tc_object1(4);
  Test_Class tc_object2(0);

  cout << "\n\nAfter object creation:";
  cout << "\n\nObject 1: " << tc_object1.Get_Value();
  cout << "\nObject 2: " << tc_object2.Get_Value();

  tc_object2 = tc_object1;

  cout << "\n\nAfter object assignment:";
  cout << "\n\nObject 1: " << tc_object1.Get_Value();
```

```
       cout << "\nObject 2: " << tc_object2.Get_Value();

       Test_Class tc_object3 = tc_object1;

       cout << "\n\nAfter initializing object 3:";
       cout << "\n\nObject 3: " << tc_object3.Get_Value();

       return 0;
   }
```

Program Output

```
Constructor Executed: Data member initialized to 0

After object creation:

Object 1: 4
Object 2: 0

After object assignment:

Object 1: 4
Object 2: 4

Copy constructor executed: Data member initialized to 4

After initializing object 3:

Object 3: 4

Destructor executed for object with data member 4

Destructor executed for object with data member 4

Destructor executed for object with data member 4
```

Note that the copy constructor executes when the program creates and initializes `tc_object3`.

A Copy Constructor for `Account`

Although it is not necessary to code a copy constructor for `Test_Class` in dem11-2.cpp (the default copy constructor works just as well), it is important to code your own copy constructor whenever the class contains a pointer as a data member. To see why, consider `Account`, which has a character pointer, `name`, as a data member. Since the class does not have an explicitly coded copy constructor, the class's default copy constructor will be used in any object initialization. Suppose that we make the following declarations in a program that uses `Account`. (We might make such an assignment to experiment with a copy of `acc1` without changing the original.)

```
Account acc1("1111", "Maxwell Larrabee");
Account acc2 = acc1;
```

Programming
Pitfalls

Because the default copy constructor is used in the initialization, `acc2` is a member by member copy of `acc1`. Therefore, the pointer `acc1.name` that points to the string "Maxwell Larrabee" gets copied into the pointer `acc2.name`. Note that the pointer, or the address, is copied, not the string that the pointer points to. Thus, we have the `name` pointer in two different objects pointing to the same area of the heap. See Figure 11.2. It follows that a change to the target of either of these pointers results in a change for both of them! If we change the string that the `name` member of `acc2` points to, we also change the string that the `name` member of `acc1` points to. This is exactly what we did not want to happen!

To correct this problem, we write a copy constructor for `Account` that copies the target of the `name` pointer.

```
Account::Account(Account& acc_r)
{
  strcpy(id_no, acc_r.id_no); //copy first argument into id_no[]

  name = new char[strlen(acc_r.name) + 1]; //create space for the name

  strcpy(name, acc_r.name); //copy second argument into new space

  balance = acc_r.balance;
  rate    = acc_r.rate;
}
```

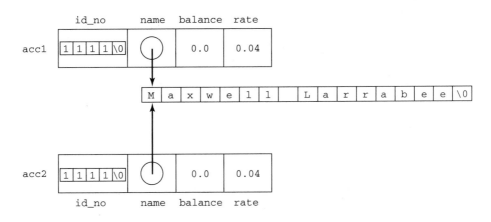

The pointer gets copied, so the name members point to the same heap space

FIGURE 11.2

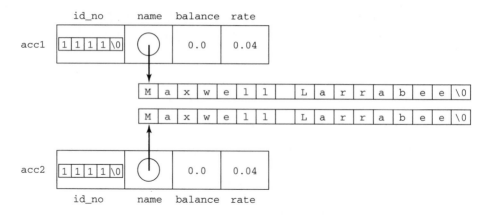

The initialization uses the copy constructor, so the name member in each object points to a different area of heap space.

FIGURE 11.3

Remember (see Note 11.1) that the argument in the copy constructor is the object on the right side of the = in an initialization and that the copy constructor is applied to the object being created. Within the copy constructor code, unqualified names refer to the object being created. Note the similarity between the code of the four-argument constructor and the copy constructor. First, the id_no member of the object being copied is copied into the id_no member of the object being created. Then space is allocated on the heap for a string exactly large enough to hold a copy of the name member of the object being copied. After copying the name into the new heap space, the balance and rate members of the object being copied are copied to the corresponding members of the object being created. If we make this copy constructor a member of Account, the following declarations result in the situation depicted in Figure 11.3.

```
Account acc1("1111", "Maxwell Larrabee");
Account acc2 = acc1;
```

Following is a program that illustrates the use of the copy constructor.

```
//dem11-3.cpp

//This program illustrates the use of the copy constructor
//in a class that has a pointer as a data member.

#include <iostream.h>
#include <iomanip.h>
#include <string.h>

using namespace std;
```

```
class Account
{
  private:
        char    id_no[5];
        char*   name;
        double balance;
        double rate;

  public:
        Account(char id[], char* n_p, double bal = 0.00, double rt = 0.04);
        Account(Account&);
        ~Account();
        double Calc_Interest();
        double Get_Balance();
        void Deposit(double);
        int Withdraw(double);
        void Display_ID();
        void Display_Name();
};


Account::Account(char id[], char* n_p, double bal, double rt)
{
  strcpy(id_no, id);  //copy first argument into id_no[]

  name = new char[strlen(n_p) + 1]; //create space for the name

  strcpy(name, n_p);  //copy second argument into new space

  balance = bal;
  rate    = rt;

  cout << "\n\nConstructor executed.";
}

Account::Account(Account& acc_r)
{
  strcpy(id_no, acc_r.id_no);  //copy first argument into id_no[]

  name = new char[strlen(acc_r.name) + 1]; //create space for the name

  strcpy(name, acc_r.name);  //copy second argument into new space

  balance = acc_r.balance;
  rate    = acc_r.rate;

  cout << "\n\nCopy constructor executed.";
}

Account::~Account()
```

```
{
  cout << "\n\nAccount " << id_no << " terminated.";
  delete [] name;
}


inline double Account::Get_Balance()
{
  return balance;
}

double Account::Calc_Interest()
{
  double interest;

  interest = balance * rate;
  balance += interest;

  return interest;
}

void Account::Deposit(double amount)
{
  balance += amount;
}


int Account::Withdraw(double amount)
{
  int result;

  if (amount <= balance)
    {
      balance -= amount;
            result = 1;
    }
  else
    result = 0;

  return result;
}

void Account::Display_ID()
{
  cout << id_no;
}


void Account::Display_Name()
{
  cout << name;
}
```

```cpp
int main()
{
  cout << setprecision(2)
       << setiosflags(ios::fixed)
       << setiosflags(ios::showpoint);

  char id[5];
  char buffer[81];  //Temporarily stores the name
  double bal;
  double rt;

  cout << "\nEnter Account ID: ";
  cin.getline(id, 5);

  cin.get();     //Clear the input buffer of new-line character

  cout << "\nEnter Account Holder's Name: ";
  cin.getline(buffer, 81);

  cout << "\nEnter Balance: ";
  cin >> bal;

  cout << "\nEnter Interest Rate: ";
  cin >> rt;

  Account acc1(id, buffer, bal, rt);

  cout << "\n\nAccount created with account number ";
  acc1.Display_ID();
  cout << "\n and owner name ";
  acc1.Display_Name();

  cout << "\n\nAccount now being created by initialization.";

  Account acc2 = acc1;

  cout << "\n\nInitialized account created with account number ";
  acc2.Display_ID();
  cout << "\n and owner name ";
  acc2.Display_Name();

  return 0;
}
```

Program Output

```
Enter Account ID: 1234

Enter Account Holder's Name: Maxwell Larrabee
```

```
Enter Balance: 100.00

Enter Interest Rate: 0.06


Constructor executed.

Account created with account number 1234
 and owner name Maxwell Larrabee

Account now being created by initialization.

Copy constructor executed.

Initialized account created with account number 1234
 and owner name Maxwell Larrabee

Account 1234 terminated.

Account 1234 terminated.
```

EXERCISES 11.2

1. How would the default copy constructor handle copying of the `id_no` data member in `Account`?
2. Add a copy constructor to the `Rectangle` class of Exercise 1, Section 10.3.
3. Add a copy constructor to the `DigitalClock` class of Exercise 2, Section 10.3

EXPERIMENTS 11.2

1. Remove the copy constructor from the declaration of `Account`. Use the following `main()`

```cpp
int main()
{
  Account acc1("1111", "Maxwell Larrabee");

  cout << "\nOwner of account is ";
  acc1.Display_Name();
  cout << endl;

  {
    Account acc2 = acc1;
  }

  Account acc3("3333", "Jane Doe");

  cout << "\nOwner of account is ";
```

```
        acc1.Display_Name();
        cout << endl;
        return 0;
    }
```

What is the output of the resulting program? Explain what happened.

PROGRAMMING PROBLEMS 11.2

1. Add a copy constructor to the `WebPage` class of Programming Problem 1, Section 11.1. The copy constructor should display a message that it executed. Test the copy constructor by initializing a `WebPage` object in `main()`.

2. Add a copy constructor to the `OilTank` class of Programming Problem 2, Section 11.1. The copy constructor should display a message that it executed. Test the copy constructor by initializing an `OilTank` object in `main()`.

3. Add a copy constructor to the `VehicleService` class of Programming Problem 3, Section 11.1. The copy constructor should display a message that it executed. Test the copy constructor by initializing a `VehicleService` object in `main()`.

4. Add a copy constructor to the `HotelRoom` class of Programming Problem 4, Section 11.1. The copy constructor should display a message that it executed. Test the copy constructor by initializing a `HotelRoom` object in `main()`.

11.3 Using `const` With Classes

The keyword `const` has several important uses relative to objects and class member functions.

Constant Objects and Functions

Programming
Pointers

It is possible to declare constant objects, just as it is possible to declare constant integers, doubles, and so on. A constant object is one whose data members cannot be changed. For example, consider `Test_Class` defined in the previous chapter with the additional member functions `Get_Value()` and `Change_Value()`.

```
#include <iostream.h>

using namespace std;

class Test_Class
{
    private:
        int n;
```

```
    public:
      Test_Class(int i = 0);      //One-argument constructor with default value
      int Get_Value();
      void Change_Value(int);
};

Test_Class::Test_Class(int i)
{
  n = i;

  cout << "\n\nConstructor Executed: Data member initialized to " << n;
}

inline int Test_Class::Get_Value()
{
  return n;
}

void Test_Class::Change_Value(int i)
{
  n = i;
}
```

Suppose we declare the following in main().

```
const Test_Class tc_object1(4);
Test_Class tc_object2(7);
```

The following assignment statement is illegal because tc_object1 is constant and we cannot modify a constant object in main().

```
tc_object1 = tc_object2; //Illegal—cannot modify a const object
```

Programming
Pitfalls

Because the object is constant, we cannot change the value of its data member, n. There is no way for the compiler to know the difference between an accessor member function (one that does not change a data member value) and a mutator function (one that changes a data member value). Therefore, the compiler will complain (with a warning or an error message) if you apply any of Test_Class's member functions to tc_object1. See Experiment 1.

```
tc_object1.Get_Value();      //Compiler complains
tc_object1.Change_Value();   //Compiler complains
```

Not allowing any member function to operate on a constant object is too severe a restriction. We want to be able to apply an accessor function to a constant object because such a function does not attempt to change the data members of the class. To tell the compiler that a member function is an accessor function and should be allowed to operate on constant objects, the function should be declared constant. This is done by adding the keyword `const` after the parentheses that follow the accessor function's name in both the declaration and definition of the function.

NOTE 11.2—CONSTANT MEMBER FUNCTIONS

Any class member function that is an accessor function (that is, does not change the value of any data member) should be declared as constant. This is done by adding the keyword `const` after the parentheses that follow the function's name in both the declaration and definition of the function. This allows such a member function to be applied to a constant object.

Following is a corrected version of the declaration of `Test_Class`.

```
#include <iostream.h>

using namespace std;

class Test_Class
{
  private:
    int n;

  public:
    Test_Class(int i = 0);    //One-argument constructor with default value
    int Get_Value() const;    //Accessor function declared as const
    void Change_Value(int);
};


Test_Class::Test_Class(int i)
{
  n = i;

  cout << "\n\nConstructor Executed: Data member initialized to " << n;
}

inline int Test_Class::Get_Value() const     //const required
{
  return n;
}

void Test_Class::Change_Value(int i)
{
  n = i;
}
```

The following program illustrates the use of constant member functions.

```cpp
//dem11-4.cpp

//This program illustrates constant member functions

#include <iostream.h>

using namespace std;

class Test_Class
{
  private:
    int n;

  public:
    Test_Class(int i = 0);    //One-argument constructor with default value
    int Get_Value() const;    //Accessor function
    void Change_Value(int);
};


Test_Class::Test_Class(int i)
{
  n = i;

  cout << "\n\nConstructor Executed: Data member initialized to " << n;
}

inline int Test_Class::Get_Value() const
{
  return n;
}

void Test_Class::Change_Value(int i)
{
  n = i;
}

int main()
{
  const Test_Class tc_object1(4);

  cout << "\nThe value of the object is " << tc_object1.Get_Value();

  tc_object1.Change_Value(7); //Causes Compiler Warning Message

  cout << "\nThe value of the object is " << tc_object1.Get_Value();

  return 0;
}
```

Program Output

```
Constructor Executed: Data member initialized to 4
The value of the object is 4
The value of the object is 7
```

`const` in Pointer Declarations

The keyword `const` can be used in two ways in a pointer declaration—one way declares the pointer itself to be a constant; the other way declares the target of the pointer to be a constant. If `const` immediately precedes the name of the pointer variable, the pointer variable is a constant. Therefore, once initialized, its value cannot be changed. Consider, for example, the following declarations.

```
int i = 4,
    j = 7;

int* const i_p = &i;    //i_p is constant. Therefore, its value, &i, cannot
                        //be changed. It must always point to i.
```

The declaration of `i_p` declares the pointer variable to be a constant. Thus, once initialized in the declaration, the pointer value cannot be changed. The following assignment is therefore illegal.

```
i_p = &j;    //Illegal because i_p is a constant
```

However, it is legal to change the value of the target of `i_p`.

```
*i_p = 5;    //Legal--the target of i_p is NOT constant.
```

If the keyword `const` appears before the data type in a pointer declaration, the target of the pointer is a constant. This means that the target of the pointer cannot be changed through the pointer. Consider the following declarations.

```
int n = 3,
    m = 5;

const int* n_p = &n;    //The target of n_p, namely n, cannot be
                        //changed through n_p.
```

The declaration of `n_p` declares the target of the pointer to be a constant, that is, `n_p` is a pointer to a constant data object. Because the target of `n_p` is a constant, you can think of `n_p` as a "read only" pointer. The following assignment is illegal.

```
*n_p = m;    //Illegal--the target of n_p is a constant
```

On the other hand, `n_p` is not itself a constant. We can make the following assignment.

```
n_p = &m;    //Legal--the pointer itself is not constant
```

Although we have changed what the pointer is pointing to, `n_p` is still a pointer to a constant object. It is illegal to change the target of `n_p`.

```
*n_p = 6;  //Illegal:cannot change target of pointer to a constant object.
```

However, we can still change the value of `m` as follows.

```
m = 6;
```

NOTE 11.3—READING CONSTANT POINTER DECLARATIONS

- If `const` immediately precedes the pointer variable name in a declaration, the pointer is a constant.
- If `const` precedes the data type in a pointer declaration, the target of the pointer is constant.

Mixing Constant and Non-Constant Pointers

An important principle to remember is the following.

NOTE 11.4—MIXING POINTERS

A declaration can impose a constant restriction, but cannot remove one.

Consider the following declarations.

```
int i = 9;
int* i_p = &i;
const int* j_p = i_p;     //Legal
```

Programming
Pitfalls

The pointer `i_p` is not a constant and neither is its target. However, the declaration of `j_p`, which initializes `j_p` to `i_p`, states that the target of `j_p` is a constant. The restriction that is imposed on `j_p` is that its target is a constant, a restriction that is not true for `i_p`. Therefore, it is valid to change `i`, the target if `i_p`, through `i_p` but not through `j_p`.

```
*i_p = 2;    //Legal: the target of i_p, namely i, is not constant
*j_p = 1;    //Illegal: the target of j_p, namely i, is a constant
             //when referenced through j_p
```

On the other hand, consider the following declarations.

```
int n = 8;
const int* n_p = &n;
int* m_p = n_p;    //Illegal—cannot remove a constant restriction
```

Programming
Pitfalls

The last declaration is illegal. The pointer n_p was declared as a pointer to a constant data object. The declaration of m_p is as an ordinary pointer. Therefore, initializing m_p, a non-constant pointer, to n_p, a constant pointer, is illegal.

Constant Arguments in Functions

The keyword const can also appear with pointer and reference arguments in a function. For example, consider the following function declaration.

```
void Func(char* p, const char* q);
```

In this case, the const in the second argument means that the target of q is a constant. The data pointed to by the argument q cannot be changed through the pointer.

NOTE 11.5—A CONST POINTER FUNCTION ARGUMENT

The keyword const appearing before a data type of a pointer argument in a function declaration means that the pointer's target is a constant. Therefore, the pointer's target cannot be changed in the body of the function.

For example, consider the following program, dem11-5.cpp, which is a version of dem08-4.cpp. The only way the programs differ is that in this version we declare the array argument of the function Avg() to be const. This assures that the function cannot change the elements in the array. See Experiment 2.

```
// dem11-5.cpp

// This program shows how find the average of the elements
// in an array. It finds the average by passing the array
// to a function that computes the average.
```

```cpp
#include <iostream.h>
#include <iomanip.h>

using namespace std;

#define NUM_QUIZZES 10

double Avg(const int [], int);

int main()
{
  int    grade[NUM_QUIZZES]; // The array to store the quiz grades
  int    quiz;               // The array subscript
  double grade_avg;

  cout << setiosflags(ios::fixed)
       << setiosflags(ios::showpoint)
       << setprecision(1);


  cout << "\nPlease enter " << NUM_QUIZZES << " integer quiz grades.\n\n";

  for (quiz = 0; quiz < NUM_QUIZZES; ++quiz)
    {
      cout << "\nEnter grade for quiz " << quiz + 1 << ": ";
      cin >> grade[quiz];
    }

  grade_avg = Avg(grade, NUM_QUIZZES);

  cout << "\nThe average quiz grade is " << grade_avg;

  return 0;

} // End of main()

double Avg(const int arr[], int size)
{
  int    i,               // The array subscript
         sum = 0;         // The accumulator
  double avg;             // The array average

  for (i = 0; i < size; ++i)
    sum += arr[i];

  avg = double(sum) / size;

  return avg;
}    // End of Avg()
```

Program Output

```
Please enter 10 integer quiz grades.


Enter grade for quiz 1: 67

Enter grade for quiz 2: 55

Enter grade for quiz 3: 83

Enter grade for quiz 4: 75

Enter grade for quiz 5: 57

Enter grade for quiz 6: 86

Enter grade for quiz 7: 58

Enter grade for quiz 8: 100

Enter grade for quiz 9: 86

Enter grade for quiz 10: 96

The average quiz grade is 76.3
```

Constant Arguments and the Copy Constructor

Programming
Pointers

If you include a copy constructor in a class definition, the argument should be declared `const` to ensure that the copy constructor code does not change anything in the argument. This is desirable because the copy constructor should copy and do nothing else. The declaration and definition of the copy constructor for `Account` are more safely coded as follows.

Declaration: `Account(const Account&);`

Definition Header: `Account::Account(const Account& acc_r)`

Accessor Functions That Return Constant Pointers

In `Account`, we do not have accessor functions that return the `id_no` or the `name` members of the class. Instead we use the functions `Display_ID()` and `Display_Name()`, which simply display the corresponding data member. If we code an accessor function for the `name` as follows,

```
char* Account::Get_Name()
{
  return name;
}
```

Programming
Pitfalls

when `main()` applies this to an `Account` object, `main()` will have access to the name member of the object through the pointer returned by `Get_Name()`. This would violate the principle of data hiding and subvert the fact that name is declared as `private` in the class declaration. For example, in the program dem11-6.cpp, `main()` uses the pointer returned by `Get_Name()` to change the name of the object to the string "XXX".

```
//dem11-6.cpp

//This program illustrates the use of the copy constructor
//in a class that has a pointer as a data member.
//The class contains accessor functions that return a const pointer.

#include <iostream.h>
#include <iomanip.h>
#include <string.h>

using namespace std;

class Account
{
  private:
    char    id_no[5];
    char*   name;
    double balance;
    double rate;

  public:
    Account(char id[], char* n_p, double bal = 0.00, double rt = 0.04);
    Account(const Account&);
    ~Account();
    double Calc_Interest();
    double Get_Balance();
    char * Get_Name();
    void Deposit(double);
    int Withdraw(double);
};


Account::Account(char id[], char* n_p, double bal, double rt)
{
  strcpy(id_no, id);  //copy first argument into id_no[]

  name = new char[strlen(n_p) + 1];  //create space for the name

  strcpy(name, n_p); //copy second argument into new space

  balance = bal;
  rate    = rt;
```

```
      cout << "\n\nConstructor executed.";
   }

Account::Account(const Account& acc_r)
{
   strcpy(id_no, acc_r.id_no);  //copy first argument into id_no[]

   name = new char[strlen(acc_r.name) + 1]; //create space for the name

   strcpy(name, acc_r.name);  //copy second argument into new space

   balance = acc_r.balance;
   rate    = acc_r.rate;

   cout << "\n\nCopy constructor executed.";
}

Account::~Account()
{
   cout << "\n\nAccount " << id_no << " terminated.";
   delete [] name;
}

inline double Account::Get_Balance()
{
   return balance;
}

inline char* Account::Get_Name()
{
   return name;
}

double Account::Calc_Interest()
{
   double interest;

   interest = balance * rate;
   balance += interest;

   return interest;
}

void Account::Deposit(double amount)
{
   balance += amount;
}


int Account::Withdraw(double amount)
{
```

```
      int result;

      if (amount <= balance)
        {
          balance -= amount;
              result = 1;
        }
      else
        result = 0;

      return result;
    }

int main()
{
  cout << setprecision(2)
       << setiosflags(ios::fixed)
       << setiosflags(ios::showpoint);

  char id[5];
  char buffer[81];   //Temporarily stores the name
  double bal;
  double rt;

  cout << "\nEnter Account ID: ";
  cin.getline(id, 5);

  cin.get();     //Clear the input buffer of new-line character

  cout << "\nEnter Account Holder's Name: ";
  cin.getline(buffer, 81);

  cout << "\nEnter Balance: ";
  cin >> bal;

  cout << "\nEnter Interest Rate: ";
  cin >> rt;

  cout << "\n\nAccount now being created.";

  Account acc1(id, buffer, bal, rt);

  cout << "\n\nAccount Owner: " << acc1.Get_Name();

  char* name = acc1.Get_Name();
  strcpy(name, "XXX");

  cout << "\n\nAccount Owner: " << acc1.Get_Name();

  return 0;
}
```

Program Output

```
Enter Account ID: 1234

Enter Account Holder's Name: Maxwell Larrabee

Enter Balance: 1000.00

Enter Interest Rate: 0.06


Account now being created.

Constructor executed.

Account Owner: Maxwell Larrabee

Account Owner: XXX

Account 1234 terminated.
```

To code a safe accessor function that returns a pointer, we make the function return a constant pointer. This assures that the object being pointed to cannot be changed through the pointer by the calling function.

NOTE 11.6—CODING AN ACCESSOR FUNCTION THAT RETURNS A POINTER

If an accessor member function returns a pointer to a private data member of the class, declare the function so that it returns a const pointer.

For example, in `Account`, a safe member function that returns the value of the name is the following.

```
const char* Get_Name()
{
  return name;
}
```

In `main()`, we could code the following, but we would then not be allowed to change the name of `acc1` through the pointer. See Experiment 2.

```
const char* name_p = acc1.Get_Name();
```

Programming
Pitfalls

Note that the following statement is illegal because it would remove a constant restriction. The pointer returned by `Get_Name()` is a pointer to a constant, whereas `name_p` is a non-constant pointer.

```
char* name_p = acc1.Get_Name(); //Illegal - removes constant restriction
```

The following program, dem11-7.cpp, illustrates this idea. We also code a similar accessor function for the ID number.

```
//dem11-7.cpp

//This program illustrates the use of the copy constructor
//in a class that has a pointer as a data member.
//The class contains accessor functions that return a const pointer.

#include <iostream.h>
#include <iomanip.h>
#include <string.h>

using namespace std;

class Account
{
  private:
    char   id_no[5];
    char* name;
    double balance;
    double rate;

  public:
    Account(char id[], char* n_p, double bal = 0.00, double rt = 0.04);
    Account(const Account&);
    ~Account();
    double Calc_Interest();
    double Get_Balance();
    const char* Get_Id();
    const char* Get_Name();
    void Deposit(double);
    int Withdraw(double);
};


Account::Account(char id[], char* n_p, double bal, double rt)
{
  strcpy(id_no, id);   //copy first argument into id_no[]

  name = new char[strlen(n_p) + 1]; //create space for the name

  strcpy(name, n_p);   //copy second argument into new space

  balance = bal;
  rate    = rt;

  cout << "\n\nConstructor executed.";
}


Account::Account(const Account& acc_r)
{
```

```
    strcpy(id_no, acc_r.id_no);   //copy first argument into id_no[]

    name = new char[strlen(acc_r.name) + 1]; //create space for the name

    strcpy(name, acc_r.name);   //copy second argument into new space

  balance = acc_r.balance;
  rate    = acc_r.rate;

  cout << "\n\nCopy constructor executed.";
}

Account::~Account()
{
  cout << "\n\nAccount " << id_no << " terminated.";
  delete [] name;
}


inline double Account::Get_Balance()
{
  return balance;
}

inline const char* Account::Get_Id()
{
  return id_no;
}

inline const char* Account::Get_Name()
{
  return name;
}

double Account::Calc_Interest()
{
  double interest;

  interest = balance * rate;
  balance += interest;

  return interest;
}

void Account::Deposit(double amount)
{
  balance += amount;
}
int Account::Withdraw(double amount)
{
  int result;
```

```cpp
    if (amount <= balance)
      {
        balance -= amount;
        result = 1;
      }
    else
      result = 0;

    return result;
}


int main()
{
  cout << setprecision(2)
       << setiosflags(ios::fixed)
       << setiosflags(ios::showpoint);

  char id[5];
  char buffer[81];  //Temporarily stores the name
  double bal;
  double rt;

  cout << "\nEnter Account ID: ";
  cin.getline(id, 5);

  cin.get();    //Clear the input buffer of new-line character

  cout << "\nEnter Account Holder's Name: ";
  cin.getline(buffer, 81);

  cout << "\nEnter Balance: ";
  cin >> bal;

  cout << "\nEnter Interest Rate: ";
  cin >> rt;

  cout << "\n\nAccount now being created.";

  Account acc1(id, buffer, bal, rt);

  cout << "\n\nAccount ID: " << acc1.Get_Id();
  cout << "\n\nAccount Owner: " << acc1.Get_Name();

  cout << "\n\nAccount now being created by initialization.";

  Account acc2 = acc1;

  return 0;
}
```

Program Output

```
Enter Account ID: 1234

Enter Account Holder's Name: Maxwell Larrabee

Enter Balance: 1000.00

Enter Interest Rate: 0.06


Account now being created.

Constructor executed.

Account ID: 1234

Account Owner: Maxwell Larrabee

Account now being created by initialization.

Copy constructor executed.

Account 1234 terminated.

Account 1234 terminated.
```

The accessor functions `Get_Id()` and `Get_Name()` return `const char*`. This guarantees that the calling function, `main()` in this case, cannot alter the target of the pointer that is returned by each function. Therefore, the `id_no` and `name` members of the class cannot be changed through these pointers.

EXERCISES 11.3

1. Write a statement that declares `c_p` as a constant character pointer and that initializes the pointer to the address of the character variable `ch`.

2. Write a statement that declares `d_p` as a pointer whose target , the double `db`, is a constant.

Suppose the following declarations in Exercises 3–9.

```
long r = 6;
long s = 19;
long* k_p = &s;
long* const l_p = &r;
const long* m_p = &r;
```

Which of the following statements is legal?

3. `r = 9;`

4. `*l_p = 4;`

5. `l_p = &s;`

6. `m_p = &s;`

7. `*m_p = 27;`

8. `long* n_p = m_p;`

9. `const long* q_p = k_p;`

EXPERIMENTS 11.3

1. Remove the keyword `const` in the declaration and definition of `Get_Value()` in dem11_4.cpp. Compile the resulting program. What messages does the compiler issue?

2. In dem11-5.cpp, place the following statement before the `return` statement in function `Avg()`.

```
arr[0] = 0;
```

Compile the resulting program. What happens and why?

3. In dem11-7.cpp, place the following statements at the end of `main()`.

```
const char* name_p = acc1.Get_Name();
*name_p = 'X';
```

Compile the resulting program. What happens and why?

PROGRAMMING PROBLEMS 11.3

1. Make the following changes to the `WebPage` class of Programming Problem 1, Section 11.2. Recode the copy constructor using `const` as described in this section. Replace the `Display_URL()` member function with a `Get_URL()` member function that returns a pointer to the URL. Recode `main()` as necessary. Compile, execute, and test the resulting program.

2. Make the following changes to the `OilTank` class of Programming Problem 2, Section 11.2. Recode the copy constructor using `const` as described in this section. Replace the `Display_Number()` member function and the `Display_Company()` member function by the member functions `Get_Number()` and `Get_Company()`, respectively, so that each returns a pointer to the corresponding data member. Recode `main()` as necessary. Compile, execute, and test the resulting program.

3. Make the following changes to the `VehicleService` class of Programming Problem 3, Section 11.2. Recode the copy constructor using `const` as described in this section. Replace the `Display_Number()` and `Display_Owner()` member functions by the member functions `Get_Number()` and `Get_Owner()`, respectively, so that each returns a pointer to the corresponding data member. Recode `main()` as necessary. Compile, execute, and test the resulting program.

4. Make the following changes to the `HotelRoom` class of Programming Problem 4, Section 11.2. Recode the copy constructor using `const` as described in this section. Replace the `Display_Number()` and `Display_Guest()` member functions by the member functions `Get_Number()` and `Get_Guest()`, respectively, so that each returns a pointer to the corresponding data member. Recode `main()` as necessary. Compile, execute, and test the resulting program.

11.4 Objects, Functions, and Pointers

An object, like a structure, is a data type. Therefore, a function can return an object and we can pass an object to a function as an argument. For example, we might want to write a function `Get_Account()` that prompts for all the data necessary to create an `Account` object and then returns a copy of the created object to the calling program. As another example, we might want a function `Display_Account()` that displays the account information of an `Account` object, which we pass to the function as an argument.

There are three ways to pass an object to a function—by value, by pointer, or by reference. In this section we discuss functions that return objects and the three methods of passing an object to a function.

Functions That Return an Object

In most of the programs that used `Account`, we prompted for the data to create an account by coding the necessary statements in `main()`. We now code a function `Get_Account()` that does the prompting for us and returns an `Account` object to `main()`.

In the definition header of `Get_Account()`, there is no need to use the class name and the scope resolution operator, `::`, because the function is not a member of `Account`. The function returns an `Account` object, which is the reason the identifier `Account` appears before the function name.

```
Account Get_Account()
{
  char id[5];
  char buffer[81];
  double bal;
  double rt;

  cout << "\nEnter Account ID: ";
  cin.getline(id, 5);
```

```
    cin.get();     //Clear the input buffer of new-line character

    cout << "\nEnter Account Holder's Name: ";
    cin.getline(buffer, 81);

    cout << "\nEnter Balance: ";
    cin >> bal;

    cout << "\nEnter Interest Rate: ";
    cin >> rt;

    cin.get();     //Clear the input buffer of new-line character

    Account acc(id, buffer, bal, rt);

    return acc;
}
```

This function contains most of the prompting code that appeared in `main()` in the programs that used `Account`. Note that we clear the input buffer by issuing `cin.get()` in two places. Remember that `cin.getline()` obtains characters up to and including the first new-line character. Therefore, we must remove the new-line character that remains in the buffer prior to executing the next `cin.getline()`. Failure to do so would cause `cin.getline()` to retrieve the null string. This explains the first use of `cin.get()`, which appears immediately prior to executing `cin.getline(buffer, 81)`. The reason for the second `cin.get()` is for the case where the function is executed again by `main()`. If `main()` executes `Get_Account()` a second time, the first input statement in the function, `cin.getline(id, 5)`, will retrieve the null string because there would be a new-line character still in the input buffer from the previous execution of `Get_Account()`. Therefore, the `cin.getline()` statement should be preceded by a `cin.get()`. If `cin.get()` is the last statement executed in the function, it will precede the next execution of `cin.getline()`.

Programming
Pitfalls

`Get_Account()` creates a local `Account` object, `acc`, using the data input by the user. The name member of `acc` points to space that is allocated on the heap by the `Account` constructor. The `return` statement sends a temporary copy of `acc` to the calling function. We shall say more about this momentarily. When the function ends, the local object `acc` goes out of scope and is destroyed. This causes the `Account` destructor to be executed, which deallocates the space that the name member of `acc` was pointing to. Now, if the `return` statement had sent a member by member copy of `acc` back to the calling function, the name member of that copy would be pointing to unallocated space. See Figure 11.4a. This corrupted pointer could cause the program to crash. To ensure that this does not happen, C++ uses the `Account` copy constructor to make a temporary copy of `acc`. Therefore, the name member of the temporary copy is pointing to a different place on the heap than was the name member of `acc`. See Figure 11.4b.

Following is a complete program that uses the new function. Before reading the paragraph that follows the output, take a careful look at the program output.

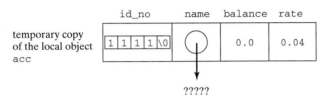

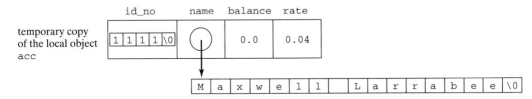

The temporary copy of the local variable acc would have a name
member that points to unallocated heap space.

(a)

Because the copy constructor is used to make the temporary copy of the local variable acc, the copy's
name points to a valid location on the heap that contains a copy of the name input by the user

(b)

FIGURE 11.4

```
//dem11-8.cpp

//This program illustrates the use of the copy constructor
//in a class that has a pointer as a data member

#include <iostream.h>
#include <iomanip.h>
#include <string.h>

using namespace std;

class Account
{
  private:
    char   id_no[5];
    char* name;
    double balance;
    double rate;

  public:
    Account(char id[], char* n_p, double bal = 0.00, double rt = 0.04);
    Account(const Account&);
    ~Account();
    double Calc_Interest();
    double Get_Balance();
```

```
    void Deposit(double);
    int Withdraw(double);
};


Account::Account(char id[], char* n_p, double bal, double rt)
{
  strcpy(id_no, id);  //copy first argument into id_no[]

  name = new char[strlen(n_p) + 1]; //create space for the name

  strcpy(name, n_p);  //copy second argument into new space

  balance = bal;
  rate    = rt;

  cout << "\n\nConstructor executed.";
}

Account::Account(const Account& acc_r)
{
  strcpy(id_no, acc_r.id_no);  //copy first argument into id_no[]

  name = new char[strlen(acc_r.name) + 1]; //create space for the name

  strcpy(name, acc_r.name);  //copy second argument into new space

  balance = acc_r.balance;
  rate    = acc_r.rate;

  cout << "\n\nCopy constructor executed.";
}

Account::~Account()
{
  cout << "\n\nAccount " << id_no << " terminated.";
  delete [] name;
}

inline double Account::Get_Balance()
{
  return balance;
}

double Account::Calc_Interest()
{
  double interest;

  interest = balance * rate;
  balance += interest;
```

```
    return interest;
}

void Account::Deposit(double amount)
{
  balance += amount;
}

int Account::Withdraw(double amount)
{
  int result;

  if (amount <= balance)
    {
      balance -= amount;
      result = 1;
    }
  else
    result = 0;

  return result;
}

Account Get_Account();

int main()
{
  cout << setprecision(2)
       << setiosflags(ios::fixed)
       << setiosflags(ios::showpoint);

  cout << "\n\nAccount now being created.";

  Account acc1 = Get_Account();

  cout << "\n\nAccount now being created by initialization.";

  Account acc2 = acc1;

  return 0;
}

Account Get_Account()
{
  char  id[5];
  char  buffer[81];
  double bal;
  double rt;

  cout << "\nEnter Account ID: ";
```

```
cin.getline(id, 5);

cin.get();      //Clear the input buffer of new-line character

cout << "\nEnter Account Holder's Name: ";
cin.getline(buffer, 81);

cout << "\nEnter Balance: ";
cin >> bal;

cout << "\nEnter Interest Rate: ";
cin >> rt;

cin.get();      //Clear the input buffer of new-line character

Account acc(id, buffer, bal, rt);

return acc;
}
```

Program Output

```
Account now being created.
Enter Account ID: 1111

Enter Account Holder's Name: John Molluzzo

Enter Balance: 100.00

Enter Interest Rate: 0.06


Constructor executed.

Copy constructor executed.

Account 1111 terminated.

Account now being created by initialization.

Copy constructor executed.

Account 1111 terminated.

Account 1111 terminated.
```

The message "Constructor executed" is produced by the constructor when the local object acc is created in the function Get_Account(). When the return statement executes, it makes a temporary copy of acc, which executes the copy constructor.

Programming
Pitfalls

The first "Account 1111 terminated" message executes as the local object `acc` is destroyed when the function ends. Back in `main()`, the temporary copy of `acc` that was created in the function, is assigned to the object `acc1`. *Note that this does not cause the copy constructor to execute.* Think of `acc1` becoming the temporary copy that was returned by the function. The next step in `main()` is the creation by initialization of `acc2`. This causes the copy constructor to execute. Finally, when `main()` ends, `acc1` and `acc2` are destroyed, which causes the destructor to execute for each of them.

NOTE 11.7—THE COPY CONSTRUCTOR AND FUNCTIONS THAT RETURN AN OBJECT

If you define a function that returns an object of a user-defined class, provide the class with a copy constructor.

Passing an Object by Value

Suppose we want to pass an object by value to the function `Display_Account()` in such a way that executing `Display_Account(acc1)` will display the account information. Assume the function definition header for `Display_Account()` is the following. We will supply the function code later.

```
Display_Account(Account acc)
```

Programming
Pointers

When the program executes `Display_Account(acc1)`, the function's parameter `acc` is *initialized* to the value of `acc1`. Therefore, the copy constructor for `Account`, which performs initializations, is used in passing the argument to the function. Recall that you should code your own copy constructor whenever the class has a data member that is a pointer. Because we are passing an object by value, we must make sure that our class contains a copy constructor.

NOTE 11.8—THE COPY CONSTRUCTOR AND PASSING AN OBJECT BY VALUE

If you pass an object by value to a function, make sure that you code a copy constructor for the class.

Following is program dem11-9.cpp, which illustrates the use of a copy constructor when passing an object by value.

```
//dem11-9.cpp

//This program illustrates passing an object by value.

//A copy constructor is required to ensure that a correct
//copy of the object is passed to the function.
```

```
#include <iostream.h>
#include <iomanip.h>
#include <string.h>

using namespace std;

class Account
{
  private:
    char   id_no[5];
    char*  name;
    double balance;
    double rate;

  public:
    Account(char id[], char* n_p, double bal = 0.00, double rt = 0.04);
    ~Account();
    Account(const Account&);
    const char* Get_Id() const;
    const char* Get_Name() const;
    double Calc_Interest();
    double Get_Balance();
    void Deposit(double);
    int Withdraw(double);
};


Account::Account(char id[], char* n_p, double bal, double rt)
{
  strcpy(id_no, id);  //copy first argument into id_no[]

  name = new char[strlen(n_p) + 1]; //create space for the name

  strcpy(name, n_p);  //copy second argument into new space

  balance = bal;
  rate    = rt;
}

Account::Account(const Account& acc_r)
{
  strcpy(id_no, acc_r.id_no);  //copy first argument into id_no[]

  name = new char[strlen(acc_r.name) + 1]; //create space for the name

  strcpy(name, acc_r.name);  //copy second argument into new space

  balance = acc_r.balance;
  rate    = acc_r.rate;
```

```
   cout << "\n\nCopy constructor executed.";
}

Account::~Account()
{
   cout << "\n\nAccount " << id_no << " terminated.";
   delete [] name;
}

inline const char* Account::Get_Id() const
{
   return id_no;
}

inline const char* Account::Get_Name() const
{
   return name;
}


inline double Account::Get_Balance()
{
   return balance;
}

double Account::Calc_Interest()
{
   double interest;

   interest = balance * rate;
   balance += interest;

   return interest;
}

void Account::Deposit(double amount)
{
   balance += amount;
}


int Account::Withdraw(double amount)
{
   int result;

   if (amount <= balance)
      {
         balance -= amount;
         result = 1;
```

```
    }
  else
    result = 0;

  return result;
}


void Display_Account(Account);     //Function prototype

int main()
{
  cout << setprecision(2)
       << setiosflags(ios::fixed)
       << setiosflags(ios::showpoint);

  char id[5];
  char buffer[81];  //Temporarily stores the name
  double bal;
  double rt;
  double amount;

  cout << "\nEnter Account ID: ";
  cin.getline(id, 5);

  cin.get();     //Clear the input buffer of new-line character

  cout << "\nEnter Account Holder's Name: ";
  cin.getline(buffer, 81);

  cout << "\nEnter Balance: ";
  cin >> bal;

  cout << "\nEnter Interest Rate: ";
  cin >> rt;


  Account acc1(id, buffer, bal, rt);

  Display_Account(acc1);

  cout << "\n\nEnter an amount to deposit: ";
  cin >> amount;

  acc1.Deposit(amount);

  cout << "\n\nA deposit of " << amount << " was made.";

  Display_Account(acc1);

  acc1.Calc_Interest();
```

```
    cout << "\n\nInterest was applied to the account.";

    Display_Account(acc1);

    cout << "\n\nName: " << acc1.Get_Name();

    cout << "\n\nEnter an amount to withdraw: ";
    cin >> amount   ;


    if (acc1.Withdraw(amount))
        cout << "\n\nA withdrawal of " << amount << " was made.";
    else
        cout << "\n\nWITHDRAWAL NOT MADE: Insufficient funds.";

    cout << "\n\nName: " << acc1.Get_Name();

    Display_Account(acc1);

    return 0;
}

void Display_Account(Account acc)
{
    cout << "\n\nData for Account# " << acc.Get_Id();

    cout << "\n\nOwner's Name: " << acc.Get_Name();

    cout << "\n\nAccount Balance: " << acc.Get_Balance();
}
```

Program Output

```
Enter Account ID: 1234

Enter Account Holder's Name: Maxwell Larrabee

Enter Balance: 100.00

Enter Interest Rate: 0.06


Copy constructor executed.

Data for Account# 1234

Owner's Name: Maxwell Larrabee

Account Balance: 100.00
```

```
Account 1234 terminated.

Enter an amount to deposit: 50.00


A deposit of 50.00 was made.

Copy constructor executed.

Data for Account# 1234

Owner's Name: Maxwell Larrabee

Account Balance: 150.00

Account 1234 terminated.

Interest was applied to the account.

Copy constructor executed.

Data for Account# 1234

Owner's Name: Maxwell Larrabee

Account Balance: 159.00

Account 1234 terminated.

Name: Maxwell Larrabee

Enter an amount to withdraw: 60.00


A withdrawal of 60.00 was made.

Name: Maxwell Larrabee

Copy constructor executed.

Data for Account# 1234

Owner's Name: Maxwell Larrabee

Account Balance: 99.00

Account 1234 terminated.

Account 1234 terminated.
```

Note that immediately before the lines displayed by `Display_Account()` the program displays the message from the copy constructor. The copy constructor executes when the parameter in `Display_Account()` is initialized to the value of the account being passed to the function. When the function ends, the function's parameter, which is an `Account` object, goes out of scope. The parameter is destroyed and the class's destructor executes, which is the cause of the destructor's message displays.

Programming
Pitfalls

What would happen if the programmer did not provide a copy constructor and instead relied on the default copy constructor? When the function `Display_Account()` is called for the first time, the default constructor would make a member by member copy of the argument and place it into the function's parameter. The `name` member of the parameter would be pointing to the same heap space as the argument. The problem arises when the function ends because `Account`'s destructor is executed. This causes the space pointed to by the parameter's `name` member to be de-allocated. But this is exactly the same space pointed to by the argument's `name` member. See Figure 11.5. The result is that the argument's `name` member is pointing to non-protected heap space. See Experiment 1.

We have now identified several ways in which the copy constructor is used in C++.

NOTE 11.9—WHEN THE COPY CONSTRUCTOR IS AND IS NOT USED

The copy constructor is used when:

- An object is created from an existing object of that class through initialization.
- An object is passed by value to a function.
- A temporary copy of an object is created to hold the return value of an object in a function that returns an object of that class.

The copy constructor is not used when:

- An object is assigned to another object of the same class.

The last point of Note 11.9 is important to keep in mind. If `acc1` and `acc2` are `Account` objects, the assignment `acc1 = acc2` does not execute the copy constructor because an object is not being created by the assignment. The assignment results in a member by member copy of `acc2` into `acc1`. We shall see how to code a safe assignment of an object that contains a pointer when we discuss how to overload the assignment operator in Chapter 12.

Pointers to Objects

You can declare a pointer to an object in the same way that you declare any other type of pointer. For example, consider `Test_Class` class.

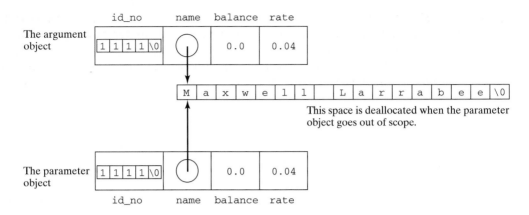

When the parameter object goes out of scope, the destructor deallocates the space it points to. Therefore, the argument's name member will then point to deallocated heap space.

FIGURE 11.5

```
class Test_Class
{
  private:
    int n;

  public:
    Test_Class(int i = 0);   //One-argument constructor with default value
    int Get_Value() const;
    void Change_Value(int);
};
```

In main(), we can make the following declarations, which are illustrated in Figure 11.6.

```
Test_Class tc_object(5);
Test_Class* tc_p = &tc_object;
```

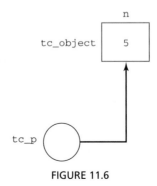

FIGURE 11.6

Programming
Pitfalls

Member functions can be applied to the target of an object pointer by using the **indirect member operator** $\rightarrow$ that we used for pointers to structures. Therefore, `tc_p` $\rightarrow$ `Get_Value()` applies the `Get_Value()` function to the target of `tc_p`. Recall that `tc_p` $\rightarrow$ `Get_Value()` is equivalent to `(*tc_p).Get_Value()`. The following will display the value of the target of `tc_p`, change the value of the target to 7, and display the new value.

```
cout << "\nThe value of the object is " << tc_p -> Get_Value();
tc_p -> Change_Value(7);
cout << "\nThe new value of the object is " << tc_p -> Get_Value();
```

In the program dem11-10.cpp, we use an object pointer to display the value of the object, to change its value, and then to display the new value.

```
//dem11—10.cpp

//This program illustrates the use of pointers to objects
//and the use of —> to apply member functions

#include <iostream.h>

using namespace std;

class Test_Class
{
   private:
     int n;

   public:
     Test_Class(int i = 0);      //One—argument constructor with default value
     int Get_Value() const;
     void Change_Value(int);
};


Test_Class::Test_Class(int i)
{
   n = i;

   cout << "\n\nConstructor Executed: Data member initialized to " << n;
}

inline int Test_Class::Get_Value() const
{
   return n;
}

void Test_Class::Change_Value(int i)
```

```
{
  n = i;
}

int main()
{
  Test_Class tc_object(5);
  Test_Class* tc_p = &tc_object;

  cout << "\nThe value of the object is " << tc_p -> Get_Value();

  tc_p -> Change_Value(7);    //Change the value of the pointer's target

  cout << "\nThe new value of the object is " << tc_p -> Get_Value();

  return 0;
}
```

Program Output

```
Constructor Executed: Data member initialized to 5
The value of the object is 5
The new value of the object is 7
```

Passing an Object by Pointer

Programming
Pointers

In the previous section we used the function `Display_Account()` to display the data in an `Account` object in a nice format. The object whose data we wanted to display was passed to the function using call by value. When we call the function, a copy of the object is passed to the function. Call by value can be very inefficient because an `Account` object is fairly large. It is more efficient to pass a pointer to the object to the function. Following is program dem11-11.cpp, which is a new version of dem11-10.cpp, that uses pointers in the definition of `Display_Account()`.

```
//dem11-11.cpp

//This program uses an expanded version of the Account class.
//The program uses a constructor with default arguments.
//The ID number is stored as an array and the name of the
//account holder is a character pointer. The constructor uses
//dynamic memory allocation.

#include <iostream.h>
#include <iomanip.h>
#include <string.h>

using namespace std;

class Account
```

```
{
  private:
    char   id_no[5];
    char*  name;
    double balance;
    double rate;

  public:
    Account(char id[], char* n_p, double bal = 0.00, double rt = 0.04);
    ~Account();
    const char* Get_Id() const;
    const char* Get_Name() const;
    double Calc_Interest();
    double Get_Balance();
    void Deposit(double);
    int Withdraw(double);
};


Account::Account(char id[], char* n_p, double bal, double rt)
{
  strcpy(id_no, id);  //copy first argument into id_no[]

  name = new char[strlen(n_p) + 1]; //create space for the name

  strcpy(name, n_p);  //copy second argument into new space

  balance = bal;
  rate    = rt;
}

Account::~Account()
{
  cout << "\n\nAccount " << id_no << " terminated.";
  delete [] name;
}

inline const char* Account::Get_Id() const
{
  return id_no;
}

inline const char* Account::Get_Name() const
{
  return name;
}


inline double Account::Get_Balance()
{
  return balance;
```

```
  }

double Account::Calc_Interest()
{
  double interest;

  interest = balance * rate;
  balance += interest;

  return interest;
}



void Account::Deposit(double amount)
{
  balance += amount;
}

int Account::Withdraw(double amount)
{
  int result;

  if (amount <= balance)
    {
      balance -= amount;
      result = 1;
    }
  else
    result = 0;

  return result;
}



void Display_Account(Account*);      //Function prototype

int main()
{
  cout << setprecision(2)
       << setiosflags(ios::fixed)
       << setiosflags(ios::showpoint);

  char id[5];
  char buffer[81];  //Temporarily stores the name
  double bal;
  double rt;
  double amount;

  cout << "\nEnter Account ID: ";
```

```
          cin.getline(id, 5);

          cin.get();       //Clear the input buffer of new—line character

          cout << "\nEnter Account Holder's Name: ";
          cin.getline(buffer, 81);

          cout << "\nEnter Balance: ";
          cin >> bal;

          cout << "\nEnter Interest Rate: ";
          cin >> rt;


          Account acc1(id, buffer, bal, rt);

          Display_Account(&acc1);

          cout << "\n\nEnter an amount to deposit: ";
          cin >> amount;

          acc1.Deposit(amount);

          cout << "\n\nA deposit of " << amount << " was made.";

          Display_Account(&acc1);

          acc1.Calc_Interest();

          cout << "\n\nInterest was applied to the account.";

          Display_Account(&acc1);

          cout << "\n\nName: " << acc1.Get_Name();

          cout << "\n\nEnter an amount to withdraw: ";
          cin >> amount;


      if (acc1.Withdraw(amount))
           cout << "\n\nA withdrawal of " << amount << " was made.";
      else
           cout << "\n\nWITHDRAWAL NOT MADE: Insufficient funds.";

      cout << "\n\nName: " << acc1.Get_Name();

      Display_Account(&acc1);

      return 0;
  }
```

```
void Display_Account(Account* acc_p)
{
    cout << "\nData for Account# " << acc_p -> Get_Id();

    cout << "\n\nOwner's Name: " << acc_p -> Get_Name();

    cout << "\n\nAccount Balance: " << acc_p -> Get_Balance();
}
```

Program Output

```
Enter Account ID: 1234

Enter Account Holder's Name: Maxwell Larrabee

Enter Balance: 100.00

Enter Interest Rate: 0.06

Data for Account# 1234

Owner's Name: Maxwell Larrabee

Account Balance: 100.00

Enter an amount to deposit: 50.00


A deposit of 50.00 was made.

Data for Account# 1234

Owner's Name: Maxwell Larrabee

Account Balance: 150.00

Interest was applied to the account.

Data for Account# 1234

Owner's Name: Maxwell Larrabee

Account Balance: 159.00

Name: Maxwell Larrabee

Enter an amount to withdraw: 90

A withdrawal of 90.00 was made.
```

```
Name: Maxwell Larrabee

Data for Account# 1234

Owner's Name: Maxwell Larrabee

Account Balance: 69.00

Account 1234 terminated.
```

References to Objects

You can define reference variables for objects in the same way that you define reference variables for the native data types. Consider the following declaration.

```
Account acc1("1111", "Maxwell Larrabee", 100.00, 0.06);
Account& acc_r = acc1;
```

The variable `acc_r` is a reference, that is an alias, to the variable `acc1`. Manipulating `acc_r` is equivalent to manipulating `acc1`. Therefore,

```
acc_r.Deposit(50.00);
```

deposits $50 into `acc1`.

Passing an Object by Reference

Programming
Pointers

We can also pass an object to a function by reference. References have all the advantages with objects that they have with other data types. Following is the program dem11-12.cpp, which is a version of dem11-11.cpp, that uses a reference rather than a pointer in the function `Display_Account()`.

```
//dem11—12.cpp

//This program uses an expanded version of the Account class.
//The program uses a constructor with default arguments.
//The ID number is stored as an array and the name of the
//account holder is a character pointer. The constructor uses
//dynamic memory allocation.

#include <iostream.h>
#include <iomanip.h>
#include <string.h>

using namespace std;

class Account
```

```
{
  private:
    char    id_no[5];
    char*   name;
    double  balance;
    double  rate;

  public:
    Account(char id[], char* n_p, double bal = 0.00, double rt = 0.04);
    ~Account();
    const char* Get_Id() const;
    const char* Get_Name() const;
    double Calc_Interest();
    double Get_Balance();
    void Deposit(double);
    int Withdraw(double);
};


Account::Account(char id[], char* n_p, double bal, double rt)
{
  strcpy(id_no, id);  //copy first argument into id_no[]

  name = new char[strlen(n_p) + 1]; //create space for the name

  strcpy(name, n_p);  //copy second argument into new space

  balance = bal;
  rate    = rt;
}

Account::~Account()
{
  cout << "\n\nAccount " << id_no << " terminated.";
  delete [] name;
}

inline const char* Account::Get_Id() const
{
  return id_no;
}

inline const char* Account::Get_Name() const
{
  return name;
}


inline double Account::Get_Balance()
{
```

```
    return balance;
  }

double Account::Calc_Interest()
{
  double interest;

  interest = balance * rate;
  balance += interest;

  return interest;
}

void Account::Deposit(double amount)
{
  balance += amount;
}


int Account::Withdraw(double amount)
{
  int result;

  if (amount <= balance)
    {
      balance -= amount;
      result = 1;
    }
  else
    result = 0;

  return result;
}


void Display_Account(const Account&); //Function prototype

int main()
{
  cout << setprecision(2)
       << setiosflags(ios::fixed)
       << setiosflags(ios::showpoint);

  char id[5];
  char buffer[81];  //Temporarily stores the name
  double bal;
  double rt;
  double amount;

  cout << "\nEnter Account ID: ";
```

```cpp
    cin.getline(id, 5);

    cin.get();    //Clear the input buffer of new-line character

    cout << "\nEnter Account Holder's Name: ";
    cin.getline(buffer, 81);

    cout << "\nEnter Balance: ";
    cin >> bal;

    cout << "\nEnter Interest Rate: ";
    cin >> rt;


    Account acc1(id, buffer, bal, rt);

    Display_Account(acc1);

    cout << "\n\nEnter an amount to deposit: ";
    cin >> amount;

    acc1.Deposit(amount);

    cout << "\n\nA deposit of " << amount << " was made.";

    Display_Account(acc1);

    acc1.Calc_Interest();

    cout << "\n\nInterest was applied to the account.";

    Display_Account(acc1);

    cout << "\n\nName: " << acc1.Get_Name();

    cout << "\n\nEnter an amount to withdraw: ";
    cin >> amount;

    if (acc1.Withdraw(amount))
        cout << "\n\nA withdrawal of " << amount << " was made.";
    else
        cout << "\n\nWITHDRAWAL NOT MADE: Insufficient funds.";

    cout << "\n\nName: " << acc1.Get_Name();

    Display_Account(acc1);

    return 0;
}


void Display_Account(const Account& acc)
```

```
{
    cout << "\nData for Account# " << acc.Get_Id();

    cout << "\n\nOwner's Name: " << acc.Get_Name();

    cout << "\n\nAccount Balance: " << acc.Get_Balance();
}
```

Program Output

```
Enter Account ID: 1234

Enter Account Holder's Name: Maxwell Larrabee

Enter Balance: 100.00

Enter Interest Rate: 0.06

Data for Account# 1234

Owner's Name: Maxwell Larrabee

Account Balance: 100.00

Enter an amount to deposit: 50.00


A deposit of 50.00 was made.
Data for Account# 1234

Owner's Name: Maxwell Larrabee

Account Balance: 150.00

Interest was applied to the account.

Data for Account# 1234

Owner's Name: Maxwell Larrabee

Account Balance: 159.00

Name: Maxwell Larrabee

Enter an amount to withdraw: 90.00


A withdrawal of 90.00 was made.
```

```
Name: Maxwell Larrabee
Data for Account# 1234

Owner's Name: Maxwell Larrabee

Account Balance: 69.00

Account 1234 terminated.
```

EXERCISES 11.4

Consider the following class declaration and object declaration in `main()`

```cpp
class ExerClass
{
  private:
    int p1;
    int p2;

  public:
    ExerClass (int a, int b) {p1 = a; p2 = b;}
    int Get_P1() {return p1;}
    int Get_P2() {return p2;}
    void Combine(int a) {p1 = p1 + p2 + a;}
};

void main()
{
  ExerClass ex1(3, 4);
  ExerClass* ex_p = &ex1;
  ExerClass ex2(7, 8);
  ExerClass& ex_r = ex2;
    .
    .
    .
}
```

What is output in each of Exercises 1–4? Work each independently of the others.

1. `cout << ex_p -> Get_P1();`

2. `ex_p -> Combine(6);`
   `cout << ex_p -> Get_P1();`

3. `cout << ex_r.Get_P2();`

4. `ex_p = &ex_r;`
   `ex_p -> Combine(5);`
   `cout -> ex2.Get_P1();`

5. Write a void function `Display_Exer()` that displays the data members of an `ExerClass` object in a nicely formatted way. Pass the object to the function by value.

6. Write a void function `Display_Exer()` that displays the data members of an `ExerClass` object in a nicely formatted way. Pass the object to the function by pointer.

7. Write a void function `Display_Exer()` that displays the data members of an `ExerClass` object in a nicely formatted way. Pass the object to the function by reference.

8. Code a `Display_Rectangle()` function for the `Rectangle` class. The function should display the length and the width of the rectangle in a nicely formatted way. Pass a `Rectangle` object to the function by pointer.

9. Code a `Display_Time()` function for the `DigitalClock` class. The function should display the time in the format hh:mm AM or PM. Pass a `DigitalClock` object to the function by reference.

EXPERIMENTS 11.4

1. Remove the copy constructor from dem11-9.cpp. Compile and execute the resulting program, if necessary several times, noting the name that is displayed by `Display_Account()`. When prompted for a name for the account, enter a name of at least eight characters. Does the program execute correctly? If not, explain why.

PROGRAMMING PROBLEMS 11.4

1. Code a display function that displays the data members of the `WebPage` class in a nicely formatted way. Use the function in a program to display the information about a Web page. Pass a `WebPage` object to the function by either
   a. value
   b. pointer
   c. reference
   Compile, execute, and test the resulting program.

2. Code a display function that displays the data members of the `OilTank` class in a nicely formatted way. Use the function in a program to display the information about an `OilTank` object. Pass an `OilTank` object to the function by either
   a. value
   b. pointer
   c. reference
   Compile, execute, and test the resulting program.

3. Code a display function that displays the data members of the `VehicleService` class in a nicely formatted way. Use the function in a program to display the

information about a vehicle. Pass a `VehicleService` object to the function by
either

   a. value

   b. pointer

   c. reference

Compile, execute, and test the resulting program.

4. Code a display function that displays the data members of the `HotelRoom` class
in a nicely formatted way. Use the function in a program to display the information about a hotel room. Pass a `HotelRoom` object to the function by either

   a. value

   b. pointer

   c. reference

Compile, execute, and test the resulting program.

11.5 Dynamic Allocation of Objects

Recall that integers, doubles, and other built-in data obejcts can be created and
destroyed dynamically by using the `new` and `delete` operators. We can also use these
operators to dynamically create and destroy objects.

Using `new` and `delete` With Objects

Programming
Pointers

Objects can be dynamically allocated by using the `new` operator. For example, the following dynamically allocates a `Test_Class` object and an `Account` object. Recall
from Note 8.6 that to code a `new` statement, you code a declaration for the object and
then remove the name of the object.

```
Test_Class* t_p = new Test_Class(5);
Account* acc_p = new Account(3456, "Smith", 250.00, 0.062);
```

The first statement declares a `Test_Class` pointer and sets it equal to the
address of a `Test_Class` object with an n data member value of 5. The one-argument
constructor is called when the object is created on the heap by the `new` operator. The
second statement declares an `Account` pointer and sets it equal to the address of an
`Account` object with an ID number of 3456, a name of Smith, a balance of $250 and a
rate of 0.062. The four-argument constructor is called when the object is created on the
heap by the `new` operator.

Suppose we want to write a program that prompts the user to create up to 10
`Account` objects. One way to handle the problem is to declare an array of 10
`Account` objects, each of which is not initialized with meaningful data. When the user
decides to create an account, the program fills the next available account object with
data. See Figure 11.7. This approach works but wastes space. Each of the `Account`
objects requires at least 25 bytes of main storage, not including the heap space needed

An array of ten `Account` object.

FIGURE 11.7

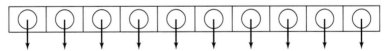

An array of ten `Account` pointers.

FIGURE 11.8

to store the names of the owners of the accounts. If the user decides to create only three accounts, the other seven `Account` objects will occupy 175 bytes, which will remain unused. While this does not seem to be a large amount of space, in a "real world" problem, an array of accounts might have to be of size 10,000 or greater. If such an array is only one-quarter filled, there would be a great deal of wasted space.

Instead of using an array of 10 `Account` objects, we can use an array of 10 `Account` object pointers. Such an array requires only about 40 bytes of storage. When the user creates an account, the program can dynamically allocate an `Account` object. See Figure 11.8. This approach uses only as many `Account` objects as are needed, thereby avoiding the wasted space of the first approach.

Following is program dem11-13.cpp, which illustrates using an array of object pointers. See Experiment 1 for an alternative solution that uses an array of objects.

```
//dem11-13.cpp

//This program illustrates the use of dynamically allocated
//objects

#include <iostream.h>
#include <iomanip.h>
#include <string.h>
#include <ctype.h>

using namespace std;

class Account
{
  private:
    char    id_no[5];
    char*   name;
    double  balance;
    double  rate;

  public:
    Account(char id[], char* n_p, double bal = 0.00, double rt = 0.04);
    ~Account();
```

```
      const char* Get_Id() const;
      const char* Get_Name() const;
      double Calc_Interest();
      double Get_Balance();
      void Deposit(double);
      int Withdraw(double);
};


Account::Account(char id[], char* n_p, double bal, double rt)
{
   strcpy(id_no, id);  //copy first argument into id_no[]

   name = new char[strlen(n_p) + 1]; //create space for the name

   strcpy(name, n_p);  //copy second argument into new space

   balance = bal;
   rate    = rt;
}

Account::~Account()
{
   cout << "\n\nAccount " << id_no << " terminated.";
   delete [] name;
}

inline const char* Account::Get_Id() const
{
   return id_no;
}

inline const char* Account::Get_Name() const
{
   return name;
}



inline double Account::Get_Balance()
{
   return balance;
}

double Account::Calc_Interest()
{
   double interest;

   interest = balance * rate;
   balance += interest;

   return interest;
}
```

```cpp
void Account::Deposit(double amount)
{
  balance += amount;
}




int Account::Withdraw(double amount)
{
  int result;

  if (amount <= balance)
    {
      balance -= amount;
      result = 1;
    }
  else
    result = 0;

  return result;
}



void Display_Account(Account&);     //Function prototypes
Account* Create_Account();

int main()
{
  cout << setprecision(2)
       << setiosflags(ios::fixed)
       << setiosflags(ios::showpoint);

  Account* account_table[10];

  int count = 0;
  char response;

  cout << "\nDo you want to create an account?(Y/N): ";
  response = cin.get();
  cin.get();               //Clear the input buffer

  while (toupper(response) == 'Y' && count < 10)
    {
      account_table[count] = Create_Account();
      ++count;
      cout << "\nDo you want to create an account?(Y/N): ";
      response = cin.get();
      cin.get();          //Clear the input buffer
    }
```

```
  //Display the accounts

  for (int i = 0; i < count; ++i)
    Display_Account(*account_table[i]);

  //Clean up

  for (i = 0; i < count; ++i)
      delete account_table[i];

  return 0;
}

void Display_Account(Account& acc)
{
  cout << "\nData for Account# " << acc.Get_Id();

  cout << "\n\nOwner's Name: " << acc.Get_Name();

  cout << "\n\nAccount Balance: " << acc.Get_Balance();
}

Account* Create_Account()
{
  char id[5];
  char buffer[81];
  double bal;
  double rt;

  Account* acc_ptr;

  cout << "\nEnter Account ID: ";
  cin.getline(id, 5);

  cin.get();    //Clear the input buffer of new-line character

  cout << "\nEnter Account Holder's Name: ";
  cin.getline(buffer, 81);

  cout << "\nEnter Balance: ";
  cin >> bal;

  cout << "\nEnter Interest Rate: ";
  cin >> rt;

  cin.get();    //Clear the input buffer of new-line character

  acc_ptr = new Account (id, buffer, bal, rt);

  return acc_ptr;
}
```

Program Output

```
Do you want to create an account?(Y/N): y

Enter Account ID: 1111

Enter Account Holder's Name: Maxwell Larrabee

Enter Balance: 1000.00

Enter Interest Rate: 0.06

Do you want to create an account?(Y/N): y

Enter Account ID: 2222

Enter Account Holder's Name: Adam Zapple

Enter Balance: 2000.00

Enter Interest Rate: 0.07

Do you want to create an account?(Y/N): y

Enter Account ID: 3333

Enter Account Holder's Name: Poly Ester

Enter Balance: 4444

Enter Interest Rate: 0.07

Do you want to create an account?(Y/N): n


Data for Account# 1111

Owner's Name: Maxwell Larrabee

Account Balance: 1000.00


Data for Account# 2222

Owner's Name: Adam Zapple

Account Balance: 2000.00


Data for Account# 3333
```

```
Owner's Name: Poly Ester

Account Balance: 4444.00

Account 4444 terminated.

Account 3333 terminated.

Account 2222 terminated.

Account 1111 terminated.
```

The program begins in `main()` with the declaration of the array `account_table[]` of 10 Account pointers. The variable `count` is used as a subscript for the array and is initialized to 0. After prompting the user, the program enters the `while` loop to create an account. The first statement in the loop body assigns the Account pointer returned by the function `Create_Account()` to the next available `account_table` pointer. Then `count` is incremented by 1 and the user is prompted again. The `while` loop continues creating accounts until either the user responds no or until 10 accounts are created. See Figure 11.9. When the program exits the `while` loop, a `for` loop displays the information for the created accounts by executing the function `Display_Account()` for each account created by the program. Note the argument in the function call. The identifier `account_table[i]` is a pointer to an Account object. Therefore, `*account_table[i]`, the target of that pointer, is an Account object. The function `Display_Account()` requires the name of an Account object as its argument because its argument is an Account reference. Finally, the last `for` loop deletes the dynamically allocated accounts.

EXERCISES 11.5

1. Declare a `Rectangle` class pointer that points to a dynamically allocated `Rectangle` object that has length 5 and width 8.

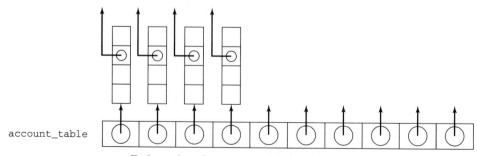

account_table

Each member of `account_table` is a pointer to an Account object.

FIGURE 11.9

2. Declare a `DigitalClock` class pointer that points to a dynamically allocated `DigitalClock` object that is initialized to 8:47 p.m.

3. Declare an array of 20 `Rectangle` objects.

4. Declare an array of 15 `DigitalClock` pointers.

EXPERIMENTS 11.5

1. Suppose you declare an array of objects such as the following.

```
Account account_objects[10];
```

This declaration is equivalent to declaring 10 `Account` objects, each with a no-argument constructor. Define a no-argument constructor for `Account`. The `id_no` member should contain the NULL string and the `name` member should be the NULL pointer. Initialize the values of `balance` and `rate` to 0.00. Now, with the no-argument constructor added to the class, recode dem11-13.cpp so it uses the `account_objects[]` array instead of an array of `Account` pointers.

PROGRAMMING PROBLEMS 11.5

1. Using the `WebPage` class of Programming Problem 1, Section 11.4, write a program that uses an array `web_site[]` of 20 `WebPage` pointers to store information about a set of Web pages. The program should ask the user to enter information about a Web page. The program should dynamically allocate space for a `WebPage` object and set an element of `web_site[]` to point to the `WebPage` object. After the user decides not to enter any more `WebPage` objects, the program should display all data in all the objects created by the program.

2. Using the `OilTank` class of Programming Problem 2, Section 11.4, write a program that uses an array `tank_farm[]` of 100 `OilTank` pointers to store information about a set of oil tanks. The program should ask the user to enter information about an oil tank. The program should dynamically allocate space for an `OilTank` object and set an element of `tank_farm[]` to point to the `OilTank` object. After the user decides not to enter any more `OilTank` objects, the program should display all data in all the objects created by the program.

3. Using the `VehicleService` class of Programming Problem 3, Section 11.4, write a program that uses an array `customer[]` of 10 `VehicleService` pointers to store information about a set of vehicles. The program should ask the user to enter information about a vehicle. The program should dynamically allocate space for a `VehicleService` object and set an element of `customer[]` to point to the `VehicleService` object. After the user decides not to enter any more `VehicleService` objects, the program should display all data in all the objects created by the program.

4. Using the `HotelRoom` class of Programming Problem 1, Section 11.4, write a program that uses an array `Hotel[]` of 200 `HotelRoom` pointers to store information

about a set of hotel rooms. The program should ask the user to enter information about a room. The program should dynamically allocate space for a `HotelRoom` object and set an element of `hotel[]` to point to the `HotelRoom` object. After the user decides not to enter any more `HotelRoom` objects, the program should display all data in all the objects created by the program.

11.6 Static Data Members and Functions

Sometimes it is necessary to have a class data member whose existence is independent of any object in that class. To manipulate such a class member requires a class member function that can be executed independently of any object in the class. In this section we show how to define such data and function members.

Static Data Members

Suppose that in the `Account` class we want all accounts to have the same interest rate. We could assign each `Account` object's `rate` member the same value, say 0.04. However, this is not advisable for two reasons. First, if each object has its own `rate` member, it might be possible for a function to change an individual account's rate. Then not all accounts would have the same rate. In addition, if we want to change the rate, we would have to change the `rate` member of every `Account` object that exists to the new value. Finally, it is not very efficient for each `Account` object to have its own `rate` member if the rate is to be the same for all accounts. All objects should share the same memory location for the rate.

A possible solution would be to declare a variable in `main()`, or perhaps to declare a global variable that holds the common value for the rate. This solution, however, is not acceptable because the rate for `Account` objects should be part of the class—it is a property of an `Account` object. The rate should also be a `private` member to assure that only an `Account` class member function can change its value.

Programming
Pointers

The solution that C++ offers is to declare the `rate` class member as a static data member. A `static` data member of a class is instance independent. That is, no matter how many class objects are created in the program, there is only one copy of the static data member. Therefore, its value is independent of the existence of any object. If we declare the `rate` member of class `Account` to be static, all `Account` objects will share this one value. If we change the value of `rate`, all `Account` objects will use this new value automatically.

Programming
Pointers

Since a static data member exists independently of any object, when does it get created and how does it get a value? Like all static variables (class members or not), a static class data member is created at compile time, prior to the execution of `main()`, and receives an initial value of 0. When we declare a data member as static in a class declaration, it is only a declaration, not a definition. (Remember that a class declaration is simply a blueprint for the structure of a class object. You cannot give a class data member a value in the class declaration.) Therefore, we must define a static member, and if necessary give it an initial value outside the class definition. Following is the declaration of the class `Account` with the rate data member declared as static.

```
class Account
{
  private:
    char   id_no[5];
    char*  name;
    double balance;
    static double rate;

  public:
    Account(char id[], char* n_p, double bal = 0.00);
    ~Account();
    const char* Get_Id() const;
    const char* Get_Name() const;
    double Calc_Interest();
    double Get_Balance();
    void Deposit(double);
    int Withdraw(double);

};

//Static data member definition

double Account::rate = 0.040;
```

Note that `rate` still remains private. Also, when we define `rate` outside the class definition, we do not use the keyword `static` again and we must qualify its name by the name of the class using the scope resolution operator. Finally, we have also changed the declaration of the constructor. You no longer need to include the rate in the constructor because all objects will now use the common static `rate` member.

> **NOTE 11.10—STATIC CLASS DATA MEMBERS**
>
> • Declare a class data member static by beginning its declaration with the keyword `static`.
> • A static data member is instance independent. All objects of the class share a static data member.
> • Define a static data member outside the class definition. In the definition, you must qualify the name of the data member by the name of the class.

Static Member Functions

Programming
Pointers

Another common use for a static class data member is to count the number of objects that are created by a program. For example, in the class `Account` we can declare a static integer variable `number_accounts` and initialize the variable to zero in its definition. When an `Account` object is created we increment `number_accounts`, and when an `Account` object is destroyed we decrement `number_accounts`. Therefore, we include the statement `++number_accounts;` in the `Account` class constructor and include the statement `−−number_accounts;` in the `Account` class destructor.

If we keep count of the number of objects by using the static data member number_accounts, we would want to access this variable at certain times to see how many accounts exist. As usual, we would want to define a member accessor function that returns the value of number_accounts. However, how would we use this function? We apply a member function through an object. But if number_accounts is static, it exists independently of any object. We should be able to access its value even if no Account objects exist. To access a static data member, you should use a **static member function**. Following is another declaration of class Account that includes the static data member number_accounts. We also show the new definitions of the constructor, the destructor, and the definition of the static accessor function, Total_Accounts(). Note that in the definition of the function Total_Accounts(), you do not use the keyword static.

```
class Account
{
  private:
    char id_no[5];
    char*  name;
    double balance;
    static double rate;
    static int number_accounts;

  public:
    Account(char id[], char* n_p, double bal = 0.00);
    ~Account();
    const char* Get_Id() const;
    const char* Get_Name() const;
    double Calc_Interest();
    double Get_Balance();
    void Deposit(double);
    int Withdraw(double);

    static int Total_Accounts();
};


//Static data member definitions

double Account::rate = 0.040;
int Account::number_accounts = 0;


Account::Account(char id[], char* n_p, double bal)
{
  strcpy(id_no, id);   //copy first argument into id_no[]

  name = new char[strlen(n_p) + 1]; //create space for the name

  strcpy(name, n_p);   //copy second argument into new space
```

```
    balance = bal;

    ++number_accounts;
}

Account::~Account()
{
    cout << "\n\nAccount " << id_no << " terminated.";
    delete [] name;

    --number_accounts;

    cout << "\nNumber Accounts Remaining: " << number_accounts;
}

int Account::Total_Accounts()
{
    return number_accounts;
}
```

A static member function, like a static data member, is instance independent. Thus, it can be executed independently of any object in the class. To execute such a function, you must qualify the function name with the class name and the scope resolution operator. Thus, to display the number of existing accounts, we can code the following statement.

```
cout << "\n\nNumber Existing Accounts: "
     << Account_Class::Total_Accounts() << endl;
```

NOTE 11.11—STATIC CLASS MEMBER FUNCTIONS

- Use a static member function to access a static data member.
- Declare a static class member function in the class declaration by preceding the function declaration by the keyword `static`.
- A static member function is instance independent.
- To execute a static member function, qualify the function name by the name of the class followed by the scope resolution operator.

Following is the program dem11-14.cpp, which illustrates the use of static data members and static functions.

```
//dem11—14.cpp

//This program illustrates the use of static data members
//and functions
```

```cpp
#include <iostream.h>
#include <iomanip.h>
#include <string.h>
#include <ctype.h>

class Account
{
  private:
    char    id_no[5];
    char*   name;
    double  balance;
    static double rate;
    static int number_accounts;

  public:
    Account(char id[], char* n_p, double bal = 0.00);
    ~Account();
    const char* Get_Id() const;
    const char* Get_Name() const;
    double Calc_Interest();
    double Get_Balance();
    void Deposit(double);
    int Withdraw(double);

    static int Total_Accounts();
};


//Static data member definitions

double Account::rate = 0.040;
int Account::number_accounts = 0;


Account::Account(char id[], char* n_p, double bal)
{
  strcpy(id_no, id);  //copy first argument into id_no[]

  name = new char[strlen(n_p) + 1]; //create space for the name

  strcpy(name, n_p);  //copy second argument into new space

  balance = bal;

  ++number_accounts;
}

Account::~Account()
{
  cout << "\n\nAccount " << id_no << " terminated.";
```

```cpp
      delete [] name;

  --number_accounts;

  cout << "\nNumber Accounts Remaining: " << number_accounts;
}

inline const char* Account::Get_Id() const
{
  return id_no;
}

inline const char* Account::Get_Name() const
{
  return name;
}


inline double Account::Get_Balance()
{
  return balance;
}

double Account::Calc_Interest()
{
  double interest;

  interest = balance * rate;
  balance += interest;

  return interest;
}

void Account::Deposit(double amount)
{
  balance += amount;
}



int Account::Withdraw(double amount)
{
  int result;

  if (amount <= balance)
    {
      balance -= amount;
      result = 1;
    }
  else
```

```
    result = 0;

  return result;
}

int Account::Total_Accounts()
{
  return number_accounts;

}


void Display_Account(Account&);      //Function prototypes
Account* Create_Account();

void main()
{
  cout << setprecision(2)
       << setiosflags(ios::fixed)
       << setiosflags(ios::showpoint);

  Account* account_table[10];

  int count = 0;
  char response;

  cout << "\nDo you want to create an account?(Y/N): ";
  response = cin.get();
  cin.get();               //Clear the input buffer

  while (toupper(response) == 'Y' && count < 10)
    {
      account_table[count] = Create_Account();
      account_table[count] -> Calc_Interest();

      ++count;

      cout << "\nDo you want to create an account?(Y/N): ";
      response = cin.get();
      cin.get();           //Clear the input buffer
    }

  //Display the accounts

  for (int i = 0; i < count; ++i)
    Display_Account(*account_table[i]);

  //Clean up

  for (i = 0; i < count; ++i)
    delete account_table[i];
}
```

```
void Display_Account(Account& acc)
{
  cout << "\n\n\nData for Account# " << acc.Get_Id();

  cout << "\n\nOwner's Name: " << acc.Get_Name();

  cout << "\n\nCurrent Account Balance: " << acc.Get_Balance();
}


Account* Create_Account()
{
  char id[5];
  char buffer[81];
  double bal;

  Account* acc_ptr;

  cout << "\nEnter Account ID: ";
  cin.getline(id, 5);

  cin.get();     //Clear the input buffer of new-line character

  cout << "\nEnter Account Holder's Name: ";
  cin.getline(buffer, 81);

  cout << "\nEnter Balance: ";
  cin >> bal;

  cin.get(); //Clear the input buffer of new-line character

  acc_ptr = new Account (id, buffer, bal);

  cout << "\n\nNumber Existing Accounts: "
       << Account::Total_Accounts() << endl;

  return acc_ptr;
}
```

Program Output

```
Do you want to create an account?(Y/N): y

Enter Account ID: 1111

Enter Account Holder's Name: Addam Zapple

Enter Balance: 100.00
```

```
Number Existing Accounts: 1

Do you want to create an account?(Y/N): y

Enter Account ID: 2222

Enter Account Holder's Name: Sal Monella

Enter Balance: 200.00


Number Existing Accounts: 2

Do you want to create an account?(Y/N): y

Enter Account ID: 3333

Enter Account Holder's Name: Polly Ester

Enter Balance: 300.00


Number Existing Accounts: 3

Do you want to create an account?(Y/N): n


Data for Account# 1111

Owner's Name: Addam Zapple

Current Account Balance: 104.00


Data for Account# 2222

Owner's Name: Sal Monella

Current Account Balance: 208.00


Data for Account# 3333

Owner's Name: Polly Ester

Current Account Balance: 312.00

Account 1111 terminated.
```

```
Number Accounts Remaining: 2

Account 2222 terminated.
Number Accounts Remaining: 1

Account 3333 terminated.
Number Accounts Remaining: 0
```

Programming
Pointers

Class `Account` has two static data members, `rate` and `number_accounts`, and one static member function, `Total_Accounts()`. As described previously, the definitions of the two static data members must be made outside the class declaration. The `rate` member is given the initial value 0.040 and the member `number_accounts` is given the initial value 0. The counter `number_accounts` is incremented in the class constructor and is decremented in the class destructor. We also display the value of `number_accounts` in the destructor after decrementing the counter. The definition of `Total_Accounts()` is similar to the definitions of the other member functions. It simply returns the value of `number_accounts`. Note that although `rate` is a static data member, any class member function can use `rate`. Thus, the member function `Calc_Interest()` uses `rate` in its calculation of the interest.

In `main()`, after soliciting a response from the user to create an account, the `while` loop body first executes the function `Create_Account()` to create an account. In addition to obtaining the data and dynamically creating an account object, `Create_Account()` also displays the value of `number_accounts` by using the static function `Total_Accounts()`. Note that to call the function, we must qualify the function name by the class name and the scope resolution operator. The program's output shows that each time we create an account, the `Create_Account()` function displays the number of accounts currently in existence. After creating the accounts, the first `for` statement displays the data for all the accounts. Finally, the second `for` statement deletes all the account objects that the program created. The program's output shows that the destructor displays the ID number of the account that is destroyed and the number of remaining accounts.

EXPERIMENTS 11.6

1. In dem11-14.cpp, remove the definitions (not the declarations) of the static variables `rate` and `number_accounts`. Compile the resulting program. What happens?

2. In dem11-14.cpp, remove the class name and scope resolution operator in the call to function `Total_Account()` that occurs in the function `Create_Account()`. Compile the resulting program. What happens?

3. Add the static public function `Change_Rate()` to class `Account` in dem11-14.cpp. The function should assign its only argument to the static data member `rate`. The function should return `void`. Test the function by including in

        `main()` statements that change the `rate` data member to a new value that is input by the user. Compile, execute, and test the resulting program.

4. Add a copy constructor to class `Account` in dem11-14.cpp. In addition to the assignment statements, the copy constructor should increment the static variable `number_accounts`. Test the constructor by creating an `Account` object in `main()` by initialization. Compile, execute, and test the resulting program.

5. A static data member can be a constant. For example, suppose we want the bank ID number to be a class data member. Because each account will have this bank ID number, it makes sense to declare it static so that all accounts can share the same memory location. However, the bank ID will not change, so it also makes sense to declare it a constant. Add the constant static data member `BANK_ID` to the `Account` class. To declare it constant, start the declaration of `BANK_ID` with the keyword `const`, but do not give it a value in the declaration. Also, begin the definition of `BANK_ID` with the keyword `const` and assign the constant its value, say 342. In addition to the data member `BANK_ID`, add a static accessor function, `Get_Bank_Id()`, that returns the value of `BANK_ID`. Write a `main()` to test the data member and the function `Get_Bank_Id()`. Compile, execute, and test the resulting program.

PROGRAMMING PROBLEMS 11.6

1. In Programming Problem 1, Section 11.5, add a static variable `number_pages` to the `WebPage` class to count the number of pages created by the program. Increment the counter in the class constructor and decrement it in the class destructor. Also, add a static accessor function that returns the value of `number _pages`. Make sure the resulting program displays the value of `number_pages` as each page is created and destroyed.

2. In Programming Problem 2, Section 11.5, add the static data member `number_ tanks` to class `OilTank`. Increment `number_tanks` in the class constructor and decrement it in the class destructor. Also, add a static accessor function that returns the value of `number_tanks`. The resulting program should display the number of tanks in the tank farm as they are created and destroyed.

3. In Programming Problem 3, Section 11.5, add the static data member `number_ vehicles` to the `VehicleService` class. Increment `number_vehicles` in the class constructor and decrement it in the class destructor. Also, add a static accessor function that returns the value of `number_vehicles`. The resulting program should display the number of vehicles being serviced as `VehicleClass` objects are being created and destroyed.

4. In Programming Problem 4, Section 11.5, add the static data member `number_ rooms` to the `HotelRoom` class. Increment `number_rooms` in the class constructor and decrement it in the class destructor. Also, add a static accessor member function to the class that returns the value of `number_rooms`. The resulting program should display the number of rooms occupied as guests check in and check out.

Chapter Review

．．

Terminology

Define the following terms.

garbage collection   `const` pointer
copy constructor   `const` argument
default copy constructor   indirect member operator, $\rightarrow$
`const` member function   `static`

Summary

- Arrays and pointers can be class data members.
- If a character pointer is a class data member, the class constructor should dynamically allocate space for the target of the pointer.
- If space is allocated for a pointer's target in a constructor, the space must be deallocated in the class destructor.
- A class's copy constructor executes when an object is created by initialization.
- A copy constructor must have the same name as the class, must have no return type, and its only argument must be a reference to an object of that class. The copy constructor's argument refers to the object on the right side of an initialization. The copy constructor is applied to the object being created (Note 11.1).
- If a class has a character pointer data member, its copy constructor should dynamically allocate space for the target of the pointer.
- You can create `const` objects. The only member functions that can be applied to such objects are accessor functions declared as `const` (Note 11.2).
- If `const` precedes a pointer name in a declaration, the pointer is constant (Note 11.3).
- If `const` precedes the data type in a pointer declaration, the target of the pointer is constant (Note 11.3).
- A declaration can impose a constant restriction, but cannot remove one (Note 11.4).
- The keyword `const` preceding the data type of a pointer in a function's argument means that the target of the pointer is a constant. Thus, the function cannot change the target of the pointer.
- The argument in a copy constructor should be `const`.
- An accessor function that returns a pointer data member should return a `const` pointer (Note 11.6).
- A function can return an object. If you define such a function, provide a copy constructor for the class (Note 11.7).
- You can pass an object to a function by value. If you define such a function, provide a copy constructor for the class (Note 11.8).

- The copy constructor is used in object initialization, when an object is passed to a function by value, and when a temporary is created on return of an object by a function that returns an object (Note 11.9).
- The copy constructor is not used when one object is assigned to another (Note 11.9).
- You can access a member of an object through a pointer by using the $\rightarrow$ operator.
- An object can be passed to a function by pointer.
- An object can be passed to a function by reference.
- Objects can be allocated dynamically by using `new`.
- A static data member is instance independent. Use the keyword `static` in its declaration in the class. A static data member must be defined outside the class declaration using the class name and the scope resolution operator (Note 11.10).
- Use a static member function to access a static data member. Such a function is instance independent. Declare the function inside the class declaration using the keyword `static`. Define the function as you would a normal member function. To execute the function independently of any class object, qualify the function name by the class name and scope resolution operator (Note 11.11).

Review Exercises

1. If a class contains a pointer member, explain why it is necessary to have an explicitly defined destructor.
2. What is the syntax of a copy constructor? When does C++ use the copy constructor? Why must a reference to the class be the argument of a copy constructor?
3. Which member functions are allowed to operate on a `const` object? How do you declare and define such functions?
4. Explain the difference between the following declarations:

```
double* const d_p1 = &d1;
const double* d_p1 = &d2;
```

5. Explain when it is advisable to have a `const` argument in a function.
6. Explain when it is advisable to have a member function return a constant pointer.
7. Why should you provide a class with a copy constructor if you define a function that returns an object of that class?
8. Why should you provide a class with a copy constructor if you pass an object of that class to a function by value?
9. If you pass an object `obj` to a function `Func()` by pointer, what operator must you use to apply the class member functions to `obj` within the body of `Func()`?
10. What are the differences between passing an object to a function by pointer and by reference?
11. What function is automatically executed when an object is created dynamically by the `new` operator? How do you use the `new` operator to create an object?

12. Explain why a static data member is sometimes needed in a class. What is meant by saying that a static data member is instance independent? Why must such a data member be defined outside the class declaration?

13. Explain why a static member function is sometimes needed in a class. Describe how to declare and define a static member function. How do you execute a static member function?

Chapter

12

Friends and Operator Overloading

Objectives

- To declare and code a `friend` function for a class.

- To decide when an overloaded operator should be a class member function or a `friend`.

- To know which operators cannot be overloaded.

- To know which overloaded operators must be class members.

- To overload the basic arithmetic operators.

- To know the meaning of the `this` pointer.

- To overload the assignment operator.

- To overload the insertion and extraction operators.

- To overload the compound assignment operators.

- To overload the relational operators.

- To overload the unary operators ++ and −−.

12.1 friend Functions

So far we have learned that the member functions of a class are the only functions that have access to the private data members of that class. However, there are times when it is desirable for a function that is not a member function to have access to the private data members of a class.

Defining a friend Function

Suppose that in a system that uses the Account class, we want to implement a function that transfers money from one account into another. A possible solution would be to write a function, Mem_Transfer(), as a member function of Account. The function would have two arguments: the first is the account we are transferring funds from, and the second is the amount of money to transfer. The account to which we apply the function would be the account to which we are transferring funds. For example, if acc1 and acc2 are accounts, the following statement would transfer $100 from acc2 to acc1.

```
acc1.Mem_Transfer(acc2, 100.00);
```

Although this approach works, the way in which we use the function is a bit awkward. Another approach would be to define a non-member function, Transfer1(), that takes three arguments: the first is the account receiving the funds, the second is the account giving the funds, and the third is the amount of the transfer. Thus, to transfer $100 from acc2 to acc1, we would code the following statement.

```
Transfer1(acc1, acc2, 100);
```

We can use the member functions of Account to code such a function. The function returns 1 if the transfer is successfully made and 0 otherwise.

```
int Transfer1(Account& acc1, Account& acc2, double amount)
{
  if (!acc2.Withdraw(amount))
    return 0;

  acc1.Deposit(amount);
  return 1;
}
```

Recall that Withdraw() returns 1 if the withdrawal is made and 0 otherwise. The if statement in Transfer1() returns 0 if the withdrawal is not made. An objection to this implementation of a transfer function is that the function requires executing two other functions, namely Withdraw() and Deposit(). The function would be much more efficient if it could directly access the data members of the parameters acc1 and acc2.

The solution is to create a `friend` **function**. A friend function of a class has the same access privileges as the function members of the class, but is not a member function. Therefore, a friend function of a class has access to all the private members of the class, just as though it were a member function. It is important to note that a class must declare a function to be a friend, not the other way around. It would violate the principle of data hiding if any function could declare itself a friend of a class! Follow the procedure in Note 12.1 to create a friend function.

NOTE 12.1—HOW TO WRITE A `friend` **FUNCTION**

To declare a function a friend function of a class,

- Declare the function inside the class declaration and precede the return type of the function with the keyword `friend`. It does not matter in which access category you define the function (`public` or `private`).

- When you define the function outside the class *do not* repeat the keyword `friend`. The keyword `friend` can appear only in a class declaration.

In the declaration of `Account`, we would code the following.

```
class Account
{
   friend int Transfer(Account&, Account&, double);

   private:
      .
      .
      .
   public:
      .
      .
      .
};
```

Note that we place the declaration of the friend function before either access specifier. We pass the two accounts to the function by reference because the function must change both `Account` objects that are passed as arguments. If we pass the `Account` objects by value, then the changes made by the function would be made to the function's parameters (which are copies of the arguments) and not to the arguments themselves. See Experiment 1. The code for the function follows.

```
int Transfer(Account& acc_r1, Account& acc_r2, double amount)
{
   //If amount exceeds acc_r2's balance, do nothing and return 0
```

```
    if (amount > acc_r2.balance)
      return 0;

    //Otherwise, make the transfer and return 1

    acc_r2.balance -= amount;   //decrease acc_r2's balance by amount
    acc_r1.balance += amount;   //increase acc_r1's balance by amount

    return 1;
}
```

This function is somewhat longer than Transfer1(), but it is more efficient because it does not have to execute functions to perform its task. Note that we can directly access the private data members of both accounts because Transfer() is a friend of Account. We must use the dot operator to access the data members of both parameters because Transfer() is not a class member function.

Following is a complete program that uses the Transfer() function.

```
//dem12-1.cpp

//This program illustrates the use of a friend function

#include <iostream.h>
#include <iomanip.h>
#include <string.h>

using namespace std;

class Account
{
    friend int Transfer(Account&, Account&, double);

  private:
    char id_no[5];
    char* name;
    double balance;
    double rate;

  public:
    Account(char id[], char* n_p, double bal = 0.00, double rt = 0.04);
    ~Account();
    const char* Get_Id() const;
    const char* Get_Name() const;
    double Calc_Interest();
    double Get_Balance() const;
    void Deposit(double);
    int Withdraw(double);
};
```

```
Account::Account(char id[], char* n_p, double bal, double rt)
{
  strcpy(id_no, id);  //copy first argument into id_no[]

  name = new char[strlen(n_p) + 1]; //create space for the name

  strcpy(name, n_p);  //copy second argument into new space

  balance = bal;
  rate    = rt;
}

Account::~Account()
{
  cout << "\n\nAccount " << id_no << " terminated.";
  delete [] name;
}

inline const char* Account::Get_Id() const
{
  return id_no;
}

inline const char* Account::Get_Name() const
{
  return name;
}

inline double Account::Get_Balance() const
{
  return balance;
}

double Account::Calc_Interest()
{
  double interest;

  interest = balance * rate;
  balance += interest;

  return interest;
}

void Account::Deposit(double amount)
{
  balance += amount;
}


int Account::Withdraw(double amount)
{
```

```
      int result;

      if (amount <= balance)
        {
          balance -= amount;
          result = 1;
        }
      else
        result = 0;

      return result;
    }

int Transfer(Account& acc_r1, Account& acc_r2, double amount)
{
    //If amount exceeds acc_r2's balance, do nothing and return 0

    if (amount > acc_r2.balance)
      return 0;

    //Otherwise, make the transfer and return 1

    acc_r2.balance -= amount; //decrease acc_r2's balance by amount
    acc_r1.balance += amount; //increase acc_r1's balance by amount

    return 1;
}



void Display_Account(Account&);     //Function prototype
Account Get_Account();              //Function prototype

int main()
{
    cout << setprecision(2)
         << setiosflags(ios::fixed)
         << setiosflags(ios::showpoint);

    double amount;

    Account acc1 = Get_Account();

    Display_Account(acc1);

    Account acc2 = Get_Account();

    Display_Account(acc2);

    cout << "\n\nEnter an amount to transfer from "
         << "the second account to the first: ";
```

```
   cin >> amount;

   if (Transfer(acc1, acc2, amount))
     {
        cout << "\nTransfer made. Updated Account Information:" << endl;
        Display_Account(acc1);
        Display_Account(acc2);
     }
   else
     cout << "\nTransfer could not be made.";

   return 0;
}

void Display_Account(Account& acc_r)
{
   cout << "\nData for Account# " << acc_r.Get_Id();

   cout << "\n\nOwner's Name: " << acc_r.Get_Name();

   cout << "\n\nAccount Balance: " << acc_r.Get_Balance() << endl;
}

Account Get_Account()
{
   char id[5];
   char buffer[81];
   double bal;
   double rt;

   cout << "\nEnter Account ID: ";
   cin.getline(id, 5);

   cin.get();    //Clear the input buffer of new-line character

   cout << "\nEnter Account Holder's Name: ";
   cin.getline(buffer, 81);

   cout << "\nEnter Balance: ";
   cin >> bal;

   cout << "\nEnter Interest Rate: ";
   cin >> rt;

   cin.get();    //Clear the input buffer of new-line character

   Account acc(id, buffer, bal, rt);

   return acc;
}
```

Program Output

```
Enter Account ID: 1111

Enter Account Holder's Name: Adam Zapple

Enter Balance: 100.00

Enter Interest Rate: 0.06

Data for Account# 1111

Owner's Name: Adam Zapple

Account Balance: 100.00

Enter Account ID: 2222

Enter Account Holder's Name: Poly Ester

Enter Balance: 200.00

Enter Interest Rate: 0.08

Data for Account# 2222

Owner's Name: Poly Ester

Account Balance: 200.00


Enter an amount to transfer from the second account to the first: 40.50

Transfer made. Updated Account Information:

Data for Account# 1111

Owner's Name: Adam Zapple

Account Balance: 140.50

Data for Account# 2222

Owner's Name: Poly Ester

Account Balance: 159.50


Account 2222 terminated.

Account 1111 terminated.
```

You should note two things about `main()`. First, it is necessary to clear the input buffer after the statement `cin >> rt;` because the next input statement executed by `main()` is a `cin.getline()`. If we did not clear the input buffer, `cin.getline()` would retrieve the new-line character from the buffer and would not allow entry of the second account ID. Second, it is necessary to place the `endl` manipulator at the end of the last `cout` statement in `Display_Account()` to clear the output buffer.

Finally, note how `main()` uses the function `Transfer()`. The `if` statement tests to see if the transfer was successful. If so, the program displays a message and the new account information. If the transfer was not successful, the program displays an appropriate message.

EXERCISES 12.1

1. Code the `Account` member function `Mem_Transfer()` that was discussed at the beginning of this section, which can be used to transfer money between accounts.

2. Code a friend function `Switch()` for the `Rectangle` class. The function should have two `Rectangle` reference arguments. The function should interchange the dimensions of its arguments. Why must the arguments be passed by reference?

3. Code a friend function `Synchronize()` for the `DigitalClock` class. The function should have two `DigitalClock` reference arguments. The function should reset the time of its first argument to that of its second argument. Must both of the arguments be passed by reference?

4. Code a friend function `Merge()` for the `Rectangle` class. The function should have two `Rectangle` arguments passed by value. The function should dynamically create a `Rectangle` object whose length is the sum of the lengths of its arguments, and whose width is the sum of the widths of its arguments. The function should return a `Rectangle` pointer, which points to the new object. Why is it safe to pass the arguments to `Merge()` by value rather than by reference?

EXPERIMENTS 12.1

1. Change the `Transfer()` function of dem12-1.cpp so that it passes its arguments by value rather than by reference. Recompile and execute the resulting program. Does the new `Transfer()` function work? Explain.

2. Rewrite dem12-1.cpp using the member function `Mem_Transfer()` discussed earlier. Recompile and execute the resulting program. Does the program work as it did using the `Transfer()` function?

3. Rewrite dem12-1.cpp using the function `Transfer1()` that was discussed in this section instead of the friend function `Transfer()`. Recompile and execute the resulting program. Does the program work as it did using the `Transfer()` function?

4. Omit the keyword `friend` in the declaration of `Account`. Recompile the program. Explain what happens.

5. Recode the `Transfer()` friend function of dem12-1.cpp by passing the arguments by pointer rather than by reference.

PROGRAMMING PROBLEMS 12.1

1. In the `OilTank` class of Chapters 10 and 11, add the friend function `Transfer()` that transfers oil from one tank to another. The function should have three arguments. The first is the ID number of the tank you are transferring oil from, the second is the ID number of the tank you are transferring oil to and the third argument is the amount of oil being transferred. Be sure that the function checks to see if there is enough oil in the transfer tank and that there is enough room in the other tank to hold the oil that is being transferred. Code a `main()` that tests the new friend function.

2. Sometimes a hotel guest wants to be transferred from one room to another. In the `HotelRoom` class of Chapters 10 and 11, add the friend function `Transfer()` that transfers a guest from one room to another. The function should have two arguments. The first should be the room number you are transferring guests from and the second should be the room number you are transferring guests to. The function should make appropriate changes to occupancy status of both rooms. Code a `main()` to test the new friend function.

12.2 Overloading Basic Arithmetic Operators

We have already noted that C++ allows constructor functions to be overloaded. C++ also allows the programmer to overload operators. We can therefore extend the meaning of the sum operator +, the insertion operator <<, and most other C++ operators. In this section we discuss how to overload the basic arithmetic operators. In the following sections we discuss overloading the other arithmetic operators, assignment, the insertion and extraction operators, and the relation operators.

Adding Two Objects

Consider `Test_Class`, which we have used in previous chapters.

```
#include <iostream.h>

using namespace std;

class Test_Class
{
  private:
    int n;

  public:
    Test_Class(int i = 0);  //One-argument constructor
```

```
    Test_Class(Test_Class&);   //Copy constructor
    ~Test_Class();
    int Get_Value();
};

Test_Class::Test_Class(int i)
{
  n = i;

  cout << "\nConstructor Executed: Data member initialized to " << n;
}

Test_Class::Test_Class(Test_Class& tc_r)
{
  n = tc_r.n;

  cout << "\n\nCopy constructor executed: "
       << "Data member initialized to " << n;
}

Test_Class::~Test_Class()
{
  cout << "\n\nDestructor Executed for object with data member " << n;
}

inline int Test_Class::Get_Value()
{
  return n;
}
```

Suppose we make the following declarations in `main()`.

```
Test_Class tc_object1(4);
Test_Class tc_object2(7);
Test_Class tc_object3;
```

Since a `Test_Class` object has only one data member, we might want to make the following assignment.

```
tc_object3 = tc_object1 + tc_object2;
```

For this statement to have meaning, the operation of addition would have to be extended to include adding two objects of type `Test_Class` to yield another object of type `Test_Class`. It would be appropriate for the assignment to assign the value 11 (the sum of the data members of `tc_object1` and `tc_object2`) to the data member of `tc_object3`. We can extend the meaning of addition in exactly this way by overloading the + operator.

With the few exceptions listed in Note 12.2, an operator can be overloaded as a member function or as a friend function. Some overloaded operators should be defined as class members, while others are better defined as friend functions. Although there are no iron-clad rules for deciding which overloaded operators should be member functions and which should be friends, we shall use the convention of Note 12.2. See Exercise 12.3.

NOTE 12.2—FRIEND AND MEMBER OPERATOR OVERLOADS

An overloaded operator that changes one of its operands should be defined as a member function of the class. All other overloaded operators should be defined as friend functions. However, the following operators *must* be overloaded as member functions. See Section 12.3.

assignment (=), function call (( )), subscript ([]), and indirect member operator (−>)

According to Note 12.2, therefore, operators such as addition, subtraction, multiplication, and division, as well as the insertion and deletion operators should be declared as friend functions. Operators such as the compound assignment operators (+=, − =, and so on) should be declared as class member functions.

We shall begin with the case of operators that are defined as friend functions. Such operators include the arithmetic operators and the insertion and extraction operators. Use the following syntax to declare an overloaded friend operator.

```
friend return-type operator operator-symbol (argument-list);
```

The keyword `operator` is mandatory and must immediately precede the symbol for the operator. For example, following is the declaration for an overload of addition for `Test_Class`, which must appear in the class declaration.

```
friend Test_Class operator + (const Test_Class&, const Test_Class&);
```

The two arguments in the function represent the two operands in the binary operation of addition. The first argument always represents the operand to the left of the operator and the second argument always represents the operand to the right of the operator.

NOTE 12.3—ARGUMENTS IN AN OVERLOADED FRIEND OPERATOR

In an overload of a binary operator as a friend function, the first argument of the overload always represents the left operand and the second argument of the overload always represents the right operand.

Here is the code of the overloaded addition operator.

```
Test_Class operator + (const Test_Class& left_op, const Test_Class& right_op)
{
  Test_Class temp_obj;    //Uses the default value of 0 for n

  temp_obj.n = left_op.n + right_op.n;

  return temp_obj;
}
```

We use the names `left_op` and `right_op` for the first and second arguments because they represent the left and right operands of the operator. If we code the expression `tc_object1 + tc_object2`, `tc_object1` is the value of `left_op` because it is to the left of the operator, and `tc_object2` is the value of `right_op` because it is to the right of the operator.

The overloaded addition operator returns a `Test_Class` object. Therefore, the first statement in the function declares a temporary `Test_Class` object `temp_obj`, whose value the function will return to the calling program. The next statement in the function assigns the sum of the n data members of `left_op` and `right_op` to `temp_obj`'s n data member. Finally, the function returns a copy of `temp_obj` to the calling program.

Adding an Object and an Integer

We might also want to be able to add an ordinary integer constant or integer variable to a `Test_Class` object. For example, consider the following declarations and assignment.

```
Test_Class tc_object1(4);
Test_Class tc_object2;

tc_object2 = tc_object1 + 15;
```

It would be reasonable for the assignment to assign 19 (the sum of the n data member of `tc_object1` and the integer constant 15) to the n data member of `tc_object2`. Note that in the assignment, the left operand to the addition is a `Test_Class` object and the right operand is an integer. Therefore, we want to overload the addition operator with the left operand, a `Test_Class` object, and the right operand, an integer. Following is the declaration and code of the overloaded addition operator.

```
friend Test_Class operator + (const Test_Class& left_op, const int right_op);
```

```
Test_Class operator + (const Test_Class& left_op, const int right_op)
```

```
{
  Test_Class temp_obj;

  temp_obj.n = left_op.n + right_op;

  return temp_obj;
}
```

With the preceding overload of addition, the following statement would not be allowed because the left operand is an integer and the right operand is a `Test_Class` object.

```
tc_object2 = 7 + tc_object1;
```

In the exercises you will code the overloaded addition operator with the left operand an integer and the right operand a `Test_Class` object. See Exercise 1.

Following is a complete program that uses the two overloads of addition. Note that we have commented out the `cout` statements in the constructor, copy constructor, and destructor to make the output simpler. See Experiment 1, which asks you to run the program with the `cout` statements put back into the program and to explain the resulting output.

```
//dem12-2.cpp

//This program illustrates the overloading of the addition operator

#include <iostream.h>

using namespace std;

class Test_Class
{
  friend Test_Class operator + (const Test_Class&, const Test_Class&);
  friend Test_Class operator + (const Test_Class&, const int);

  private:
    int n;

  public:
    Test_Class(int i = 0);  //One-argument constructor
    Test_Class(Test_Class&);  //Copy constructor
    ~Test_Class();
    int Get_Value();
};

Test_Class::Test_Class(int i)
```

```
  {
    n = i;

    //cout << "\nConstructor Executed: Data member initialized to " << n;
  }

  Test_Class::Test_Class(Test_Class& tc_r)
  {
    n = tc_r.n;

    //cout << "\n\nCopy constructor executed: "
    //          << "Data member initialized to " << n;
  }

  Test_Class::~Test_Class()
  {
    //cout << "\n\nDestructor Executed for object with data member " << n;
  }

  inline int Test_Class::Get_Value()
  {
    return n;
  }


  Test_Class operator + (const Test_Class& left_op, const Test_Class& right_op)
  {
    Test_Class temp_obj;

    temp_obj.n = left_op.n + right_op.n;

    return temp_obj;
  }

  Test_Class operator + (const Test_Class& left_op, const int right_op)
  {
    Test_Class temp_obj;

    temp_obj.n = left_op.n + right_op;

    return temp_obj;
  }


  int main()
  {
    Test_Class tc_object1(4);
    Test_Class tc_object2(7);
    Test_Class tc_object;
```

```
    cout << "\n\nPrior to adding the objects, the value of tc_object is "
         << tc_object.Get_Value();

    tc_object = tc_object1 + tc_object2;

    cout << "\n\nAfter adding the objects, the value of tc_object is "
         << tc_object.Get_Value();

    tc_object = tc_object1 + 15;

    cout << "\n\nAfter adding 15 to tc_object1, the value of tc_object is "
         << tc_object.Get_Value();

    return 0;
}
```

Program Output

```
Prior to adding the objects, the value of tc_object is 0

After adding the objects, the value of tc_object is 11

After adding 15 to tc_object1, the value of tc_object is 19
```

The object `tc_object` begins with the n data member having the default value of 0. After adding the objects `tc_object1` (with data member value 4) and `tc_object2` (with data member value 7) and assigning the result to `tc_object`, the value of the data member of `tc_object` is 11. Finally, after adding the integer 15 to `tc_object1` (with data member value 4) and assigning the result to `tc_object`, the data member of `tc_object` has the value 19.

Note that making the overloaded addition operator return a `Test_Class` object makes statements such as the following possible.

```
tc_object = tc_object1 + tc_object2 + tc_object3 + 6;
```

The first addition results in a temporary `Test_Class` object, which is then added to `tc_object3`, resulting in another `Test_Class` object. The third addition then adds this temporary object and the integer 6, resulting in still another temporary object. This last temporary object is assigned to `tc_object`.

Operator Overloading Rules

The following rules must be observed when overloading operators.

NOTE 12.4—RULES FOR OPERATOR OVERLOADING

- All operators can be overloaded except the following:

.	direct member (dot)
: :	scope resolution
? :	conditional
`sizeof`	size operator
`new`	allocation
`delete`	de-allocation
.*	direct pointer-to-member (we shall cover this operator at a later time)

- The following operators *must* be class member functions

=	assignment
( )	function call
[ ]	subscript
—>	indirect member

- You cannot change the unary/binary nature of an operator. Thus, division must remain a binary operator. If an operator is both unary and binary (for example, +), it can be overloaded either or both ways.

- You cannot override the predefined operator precedence rules.

EXERCISES 12.2

1. Code the prototype and the definition of an overload of addition for `Test_Class` in which the first argument is an integer and the second argument is an object of type `Test_Class`. The overloaded operator should return a `Test_Class` object whose n data member is the sum of the first argument and the n data member of the second.

2. Code the prototype and the definition of an overload of subtraction for `Test_Class` in which both arguments are of type `Test_Class`. The overloaded operator should return a `Test_Class` object whose n data member is the n data member of the first argument minus the n data member of the second.

3. Code prototypes and definitions of overloaded subtraction operators for `Test_Class` that allow the subtraction of an integer from a `Test_Class` object and that allow the subtraction of a `Test_Class` object from an integer.

4. Do Exercise 2 with multiplication replacing subtraction.

5. Do Exercise 3 with multiplication replacing subtraction.

6. Do Exercise 2 with division replacing subtraction. Be sure to check for division by zero and take appropriate action if such an attempt is made.

7. Do Exercise 3 with division replacing subtraction. Be sure to check for division by zero and take appropriate action if such an attempt is made.

8. Replace the `Merge()` friend function for the `Rectangle` class of Exercise 4, Section 12.1, by an overload of addition.

EXPERIMENTS 12.2

1. Remove the commented-out statements in the constructor, the copy constructor, and the destructor of program dem12-2.cpp. Compile and execute the program. Explain the resulting output.

2. Place the following statement at the end of `main()` in dem12-2.cpp.

```
tc_object = 7 + tc_object1;
```

What is the error message and explain why it is issued.

PROGRAMMING PROBLEMS 12.2

1. Write a program that uses `Test_Class` and all the operator overloads that you coded in Exercises 2–7. Compile, execute, and test the resulting program.

2. Write a program that uses the `Rectangle` class and the overload of addition from Exercise 8. Compile, execute, and test the resulting program.

12.3 Overloading Assignment and the `this` Pointer

In this section we discuss how to overload the assignment operator. To make the overloaded assignment work in the same way as assignment of the built-in types, we must use a special pointer, called `this`, that is available to every class member function.

Overloading Assignment

Programming
Pitfalls

We mentioned several times in the last few chapters that we can assign an object to another object of the same class. In doing so, the assignment is made on a member by member basis. This type of assignment is appropriate for `Test_Class` objects, which have a single integer data member. However, member by member copying is not appropriate for a class that has one or more pointers as data members. For example, if `acc1` and `acc2` are members of `Account`, they each have a `name` data member that points to the name of the person holding the account. Suppose we make the assignment `acc1 = acc2`. Since the copy is made on a member by member basis, the `name` members of both objects are now pointing to the name associated with `acc2`. See Figure 12.1. Thus, both are pointing to the same physical space on the heap. A change to the `name` member of either account would cause that change to occur in both. To avoid this, we must overload the assignment operator.

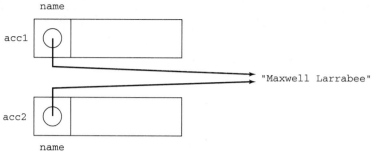

FIGURE 12.1

Programming
Pointers

You should code the overload of an operator in such a way that the overloaded operator behaves as much as possible like the operator behaves for the corresponding native C++ data types. For an overload of the assignment operator, the following should make sense for Account objects.

```
acc1 = acc2 = acc3;
```

Recall that in C++ every expression has a value. The value of an assignment is the left side of the assignment operator. Therefore, since assignment associates from right to left, the value of the first assignment, acc2 = acc3, is the object acc2. Then the second assignment assigns acc2 to acc1. To make the overloaded assignment operator behave like the usual assignment operator, we even want the following to work correctly.

```
(acc1 = acc2) = acc3;
```

In this case, the left assignment is executed first. The result is the object acc1, which is then assigned the value of acc3. See Experiment 1.

To make these multiple assignments work the way we want them to, our overload of assignment must return the object to which the operator is being applied. Therefore, the operator must return a reference to the first argument and not a copy of the first argument.

Assignment is a binary operator—it has a left and a right operand. Unlike when we overloaded addition, the assignment operation changes the left operand. It is best to think of assignment as operating on the left operand. Using Note 12.2, it follows that we should make the overloaded assignment operator a member function of Account and not a friend function.

The declaration of the operator follows. The one argument of the overloaded operator is the right side of the assignment operator. The left side of the assignment operator is the object to which the assignment is applied.

```
Account& operator = (const Account&);
```

> **NOTE 12.5—ARGUMENTS IN AN OVERLOADED MEMBER OPERATOR**
>
> When overloading a binary operator as a class member function, the object to which the function is applied represents the left operand and the one argument of the operator represents the right operand.

The `this` Pointer

Remember that each object has its own copies of the class data members, but there is only one copy of each class member function for all the objects a program might create. A member function knows on which object it is working by means of a special pointer that the system automatically provides and that you can use as you see fit. Within the code of any class member function, the pointer `this`, which is a keyword, always refers to the object to which the function is applied. When the C++ compiler translates the code of a member function, it precedes each reference to a data member by `this ->`. Although it is not necessary, if you wish, you can place the expression `this ->` before each data member name in a member function and the program will compile and execute correctly. For example, here is the original code for the constructor of `Test_Class`.

```
Test_Class::Test_Class(int i)
{
  n = i;

  //cout << "\nConstructor Executed: Data member initialized to " << n;
}
```

We can replace the preceding code by the following equivalent code. See Experiment 2.

```
Test_Class::Test_Class(int i)
{
  this -> n = i;

  //cout << "\nConstructor Executed: Data member initialized to " << n;
}
```

Since the `this` pointer points to the object on which the function is operating, `*this` refers to the object itself. We therefore make the overloaded assignment operator return `*this`, namely the left side of the equals sign.

> **NOTE 12.6—THE MEANING OF THE `this` POINTER**
>
> Within the code of a class member function, the pointer `this` points to the object to which the function is applied. Within the code of a class member function, `*this` represents the object to which the function is applied.

This is the code for the overloaded assignment operator.

```
Account& Account::operator = (const Account& right_op)
{
  if (&right_op == this)
     ;                        //Self assignment—do nothing
  else
     {
       strcpy(id_no, right_op.id_no);  //copy id of right_op into id_no[]

       delete [] name;

       name = new char[strlen(right_op.name) + 1]; //create space for the name

       strcpy(name, right_op.name);  //copy second argument into new space

       balance = right_op.balance;
       rate    = right_op.rate;
     }

  return *this;
}
```

Programming
Pointers

Since the overloaded assignment operator is a member function, within the member function an unqualified member name refers to the member of the object on which the function is operating, namely the operand to the left of the assignment operator. The object to the right of the assignment operator is represented by the parameter in the function definition, `right_op` in the preceding function. The data members of this object must be referenced using the dot operator.

Most of the function's code consists of an `if` statement. The condition in the `if` tests whether the right operand in the assignment equals the first operand. Thus, we are checking for a so-called self assignment, such as `acc1 = acc1`. If this condition is true, there is nothing to do so the null statement is executed. Otherwise, the members of the right operand are copied to the left operand in much the same way as is done in the code of the constructor and copy constructor.

Programming
Pitfalls

Note that it is necessary to de-allocate the space pointed to by the `name` member of the left operand. Failure to do so will leave that space allocated but unusable by the program. The following program tests the overloaded assignment operator.

```
//dem12—3.cpp

//This program illustrates overloading the assignment operator

#include <iostream.h>
#include <iomanip.h>
#include <string.h>

using namespace std;
```

```
class Account
{
   friend int Transfer(Account&, Account&, double);

   private:
      char    id_no[5];
      char*   name;
      double balance;
      double rate;

   public:
      Account(char id[], char* n_p, double bal = 0.00, double rt = 0.04);
      ~Account();
      const char* Get_Id() const;
      const char* Get_Name() const;
      double Calc_Interest();
      double Get_Balance() const;
      void Deposit(double);
      int Withdraw(double);

      Account& operator = (const Account&);
};


Account::Account(char id[], char* n_p, double bal, double rt)
{
   strcpy(id_no, id);   //copy first argument into id_no[]

   name = new char[strlen(n_p) + 1]; //create space for the name

   strcpy(name, n_p);   //copy second argument into new space

   balance = bal;
   rate    = rt;
}

Account::~Account()
{
   delete [] name;
}

inline const char* Account::Get_Id() const
{
   return id_no;
}

inline const char* Account::Get_Name() const
{
   return name;
}
```

```cpp
inline double Account::Get_Balance() const
{
  return balance;
}

double Account::Calc_Interest()
{
  double interest;

  interest = balance * rate;
  balance += interest;

  return interest;
}

void Account::Deposit(double amount)
{
  balance += amount;
}




int Account::Withdraw(double amount)
{
  int result;

  if (amount <= balance)
    {
      balance -= amount;
      result = 1;
    }
  else
    result = 0;

  return result;
}

int Transfer(Account& acc_r1, Account& acc_r2, double amount)
{
  //If amount exceeds acc_r2's balance, do nothing and return 0

  if (amount > acc_r2.balance)
    return 0;

  //Otherwise, make the transfer and return 1

  acc_r2.balance -= amount; //decrease acc_r2's balance by amount
  acc_r1.balance += amount; //increase acc_r1's balance by amount
```

```
     return 1;
}

Account& Account::operator = (const Account& right_op)
{
  if (&right_op == this)
     ;                     //Self assignment - do nothing
  else
    {
       strcpy(id_no, right_op.id_no);  //copy id of right_op into id_no[]

       delete [] name;

       name = new char[strlen(right_op.name) + 1]; //create space for the name

       strcpy(name, right_op.name);  //copy second argument into new space

       balance = right_op.balance;
       rate    = right_op.rate;
    }

  return *this;
}




void Display_Account(Account&);      //Function prototype
Account Get_Account();               //Function prototype

int main()
{
  cout << setprecision(2)
       << setiosflags(ios::fixed)
       << setiosflags(ios::showpoint);

  Account acc1 = Get_Account();

  Display_Account(acc1);

  Account acc2 = Get_Account();

  Display_Account(acc2);

  cout << "\n\nAssigning acc2 to acc1.\n";

  acc1 = acc2;

  Display_Account(acc1);
  Display_Account(acc2);
```

```
    return 0;
}

void Display_Account(Account& acc_r)
{
  cout << "\nData for Account# " << acc_r.Get_Id();

  cout << "\n\nOwner's Name: " << acc_r.Get_Name();

  cout << "\n\nAccount Balance: " << acc_r.Get_Balance() << endl;
}

Account Get_Account()
{
  char id[5];
  char buffer[81];
  double bal;
  double rt;

  cout << "\nEnter Account ID: ";
  cin.getline(id, 5);

  cin.get();     //Clear the input buffer of new-line character

  cout << "\nEnter Account Holder's Name: ";
  cin.getline(buffer, 81);

  cout << "\nEnter Balance: ";
  cin >> bal;

  cout << "\nEnter Interest Rate: ";
  cin >> rt;

  cin.get();     //Clear the input buffer of new-line character

  Account acc(id, buffer, bal, rt);

  return acc;
}
```

Program Output

```
Enter Account ID: 1111

Enter Account Holder's Name: Adam Zapple

Enter Balance: 100.00

Enter Interest Rate: 0.06
```

```
Data for Account# 1111

Owner's Name: Adam Zapple

Account Balance: 100.00

Enter Account ID: 2222

Enter Account Holder's Name: Poly Ester

Enter Balance: 200.00

Enter Interest Rate: 0.08

Data for Account# 2222

Owner's Name: Poly Ester

Account Balance: 200.00


Assigning acc2 to acc1.

Data for Account# 2222

Owner's Name: Poly Ester

Account Balance: 200.00

Data for Account# 2222

Owner's Name: Poly Ester

Account Balance: 200.00
```

The program creates two accounts by using the `Get_Account()` function and displays the contents of both accounts by using `Display_Account()`. Then the program assigns `acc2` to `acc1` and displays the contents of both accounts to show that the accounts are indeed the same.

EXERCISES 12.3

1. Recode the declaration of `Test_Class` in dem12-2.cpp by making the overload of the addition operator a member function rather than a friend function.

2. Code an overloaded subtraction operator for `Test_Class` that is a member function of the class. See Exercise 2 of Section 12.2.

3. Code an overloaded multiplication operator for `Test_Class` that is a member function of the class. See Exercise 4 of Section 12.3.

4. Code an overloaded division operator for `Test_Class` that is a member function of the class. See Exercise 6 of Section 12.3.

5. Code an overload of assignment for the `Rectangle` class.

6. Code an overload of assignment for the `DigitalClock` class.

EXPERIMENTS 12.3

1. Write a small program using the `Account` class to verify that the assignment

```
(acc1 = acc2) = acc3;
```

   assigns the object `acc3` to the object `acc1`.

2. In dem12-2.cpp, recode the constructor for `Test_Class` replacing the assignment n = i by the assignment `this -> n = i`. Does the program behave any differently?

PROGRAMMING PROBLEMS 12.3

1. Write a program using `Test_Class` that tests the overloaded subtraction, multiplication, and division operators of Exercises 2–4.

2. Overload the assignment operator for the `WebPage` class. Compile, execute, and test the class in a program.

3. Overload the assignment operator for the `OilTank` class. Compile, execute, and test the class in a program.

4. Overload the assignment operator for the `VehicleService` class. Compile, execute, and test the class in a program.

5. Overload the assignment operator for the `HotelRoom` class. Compile, execute, and test the class in a program.

12.4 Overloading the Insertion and Extraction Operators

The insertion and extraction operators can also be overloaded. In this section we discuss how to overload the insertion operator for `Account` and how to overload the extraction operator for `Test_Class`.

Overloading the Insertion Operator

In previous programs using `Account`, we used the function `Display_Account()` to display account information. Displaying data associated with an object can be simplified by overloading the insertion operator `<<`. The insertion operator is already overloaded. You can send integers, doubles, strings, and so on to the output stream by using `<<`. The operator behaves differently depending on the type of data that is sent to `cout`.

The insertion operator is a binary operator. The left operand, as we have used the operator, is cout, which is an object in the class ostream. The right operand is the data that we send to the output stream. As is the case with all C++ operators, the insertion operator has a value, which is the operator's left operand. Therefore, the value of the expression

```
cout << "\nHello";
```

is the object cout. This is why it is possible to "cascade" the insertion operator. For example, the statement

```
cout << "\nThe value of i is " << i;
```

works because the insertion operator associates from left to right. The first insertion sends the string "\nThe value of i is " to cout. The result of this operation is the first operand, namely cout. The second insertion sends the value of i to cout.

Programming
Pointers

We must take into account the fact that insertion returns its left operand if we want to be able to cascade insertion with Account objects. In addition, since insertion does not change the value of any object, it is better to code the overloaded insertion as a friend function. Following is the declaration of an overloaded insertion operator for Account.

```
friend ostream& operator << (ostream& , const Account&);
```

The return type of the operator is ostream& because, as noted, the value of the insertion operator should be the first argument, which is of type ostream. The first argument, as in overloading addition, is the left operand, which is an ostream object (cout in most cases). See Note 12.3. The second argument is the right operand, which is an Account object. Following is the code for the operator.

```
ostream& operator << (ostream& os, const Account& right_op)
{
  os << "\nData for Account# " << right_op.id_no;

  os << "\n\nOwner's Name: " << right_op.name;

  os << "\n\nAccount Balance: " << right_op.balance << endl;

  return os;
}
```

Make sure you understand how this function works. If acc1 is an Account object, we would code

```
cout << acc1;
```

This statement would call the version of $<<$ that is overloaded for `Account`. When the function is called, the parameter `os` becomes an alias for `cout` and the parameter `right_op` becomes an alias for `acc1`. The uses of $<<$ in the function send output to `cout`. The data member references are to the data members of `acc1`. Finally, the function returns `os`, the first operand, namely `cout`.

The following program illustrates the overloaded insertion operator.

```
//dem12-4.cpp

//This program illustrates overloading the insertion operator

#include <iostream.h>
#include <iomanip.h>
#include <string.h>

using namespace std;

class Account
{
   friend int Transfer(Account&, Account&, double);
   friend ostream& operator << (ostream&, const Account&);

   private:
      char   id_no[5];
      char*  name;
      double balance;
      double rate;

   public:
      Account(char id[], char* n_p, double bal = 0.00, double rt = 0.04);
      ~Account();
      const char* Get_Id() const;
      const char* Get_Name() const;
      double Calc_Interest();
      double Get_Balance() const;
      void Deposit(double);
      int Withdraw(double);

      Account& operator = (const Account&);
};

Account::Account(char id[], char* n_p, double bal, double rt)
{
   strcpy(id_no, id);  //copy first argument into id_no[]

   name = new char[strlen(n_p) + 1]; //create space for the name

   strcpy(name, n_p);  //copy second argument into new space

   balance = bal;
```

```
  rate    = rt;
}

Account::~Account()
{
  delete [] name;
}

inline const char* Account::Get_Id() const
{
  return id_no;
}

inline const char* Account::Get_Name() const
{
  return name;
}


inline double Account::Get_Balance() const
{
  return balance;
}

double Account::Calc_Interest()
{
  double interest;

  interest = balance * rate;
  balance += interest;

  return interest;
}

void Account::Deposit(double amount)
{
  balance += amount;
}


int Account::Withdraw(double amount)
{
  int result;

  if (amount <= balance)
    {
      balance -= amount;
      result = 1;
    }
  else
```

```
      result = 0;

  return result;
}

int Transfer(Account& acc_r1, Account& acc_r2, double amount)
{
  //If amount exceeds acc_r2's balance, do nothing and return 0

  if (amount > acc_r2.balance)
    return 0;

  //Otherwise, make the transfer and return 1

  acc_r2.balance -= amount; //decrease acc_r2's balance by amount
  acc_r1.balance += amount; //increase acc_r1's balance by amount

  return 1;
}

ostream& operator << (ostream& os, const Account& right_op)
{
  os << "\nData for Account# " << right_op.id_no;

  os << "\n\nOwner's Name: " << right_op.name;

  os << "\n\nAccount Balance: " << right_op.balance << endl;

  return os;
}



Account& Account::operator = (const Account& right_op)
{
  if (&right_op == this)
    ;                    //Self assignment - do nothing
  else
    {
      strcpy(id_no, right_op.id_no);  //copy id of right_op into id_no[]

      delete [] name;

      name = new char[strlen(right_op.name) + 1]; //create space for the name

      strcpy(name, right_op.name);  //copy second argument into new space

      balance = right_op.balance;
      rate    = right_op.rate;
    }
```

```
        return *this;
    }




Account Get_Account();                    //Function prototype

int main()
{
    cout << setprecision(2)
         << setiosflags(ios::fixed)
         << setiosflags(ios::showpoint);

    Account acc1 = Get_Account();

    cout << acc1;

    Account acc2 = Get_Account();

    cout << acc2;

    cout << "\n\nAssigning acc2 to acc1.\n";

    acc1 = acc2;

    cout << acc1 << acc2;

    return 0;
}



Account Get_Account()
{
    char id[5];
    char buffer[81];
    double bal;
    double rt;

    cout << "\nEnter Account ID: ";
    cin.getline(id, 5);

    cin.get();     //Clear the input buffer of new-line character

    cout << "\nEnter Account Holder's Name: ";
    cin.getline(buffer, 81);

    cout << "\nEnter Balance: ";
    cin >> bal;

    cout << "\nEnter Interest Rate: ";
    cin >> rt;
```

```
    cin.get();    //Clear the input buffer of new-line character

    Account acc(id, buffer, bal, rt);

    return acc;
}
```

Program Output

```
Enter Account ID: 1111

Enter Account Holder's Name: Adam Zapple

Enter Balance: 100.00

Enter Interest Rate: 0.06

Data for Account# 1111

Owner's Name: Adam Zapple

Account Balance: 100.00

Enter Account ID: 2222

Enter Account Holder's Name: Poly Ester

Enter Balance: 200.00

Enter Interest Rate: 0.08

Data for Account# 2222

Owner's Name: Poly Ester

Account Balance: 200.00


Assigning acc2 to acc1.

Data for Account# 2222

Owner's Name: Poly Ester

Account Balance: 200.00

Data for Account# 2222

Owner's Name: Poly Ester

Account Balance: 200.00
```

We have one instance of cascading in the program.

```
cout << acc1 << acc2;
```

Since the overload of << returns the left operand, the result of the first insertion is cout. Therefore, the second insertion sends acc2 to cout by using the overload of << again.

Overloading the Extraction Operator

Programming Pointers

The extraction operator can be overloaded in much the same way as we overloaded the insertion operator with a few important differences. The prototype for an extraction operator for Test_Class follows. Note that the function returns an istream object and the first operand is a reference to an istream object because we are doing input. Also, we do not declare the second operand as const because the operator will change the value of the data member of the object. Although the extraction operator changes one of its operands, we choose to declare it as a friend because the insertion operator is usually declared as a friend. See Exercises 1 and 2.

```
friend istream& operator >> (istream& , Test_Class&);
```

The code for the overloaded extraction operator is also similar to that of the code for the overload of the insertion operator. In fact, the function is simpler because we have only one data member to assign a value to. Note also that we use the parameter is as the name of the first operand because it represents the input stream.

```
istream& operator >> (istream& is, Test_Class& right_op)
{
  is >> right_op.n;

  return is;
}
```

The first argument is the left operand of the extraction operator, which will be the istream object cin. The function returns this operand so we can cascade the operator. Following is the program dem12-5.cpp that uses the overloaded insertion operator. In the exercises we will overload the insertion operator for Test_Class.

```
//dem12-5.cpp

//This program illustrates the overloading of the extraction operator

#include <iostream.h>

using namespace std;
```

```cpp
class Test_Class
{
  friend Test_Class operator + (const Test_Class&, const Test_Class&);
  friend Test_Class operator + (const Test_Class&, const int);
  friend istream& operator >> (istream&, Test_Class&);

  private:
      int n;

  public:
      Test_Class(int i = 0); //One-argument constructor
      Test_Class(Test_Class&); //Copy constructor
      ~Test_Class();
      int Get_Value();
};

Test_Class::Test_Class(int i)
{
  n = i;

  //cout << "\nConstructor Executed: Data member initialized to " << n;
}

Test_Class::Test_Class(Test_Class& tc_r)
{
  n = tc_r.n;

  //cout << "\n\nCopy constructor executed: "
  //        << "Data member initialized to " << n;
}

Test_Class::~Test_Class()
{
  //cout << "\n\nDestructor Executed for object with data member " << n;
}

inline int Test_Class::Get_Value()
{
  return n;
}


Test_Class operator + (const Test_Class& left_op, const Test_Class& right_op)
{
  Test_Class temp_obj;

  temp_obj.n = left_op.n + right_op.n;

  return temp_obj;
}
```

```
Test_Class operator + (const Test_Class& left_op, const int right_op)
{
  Test_Class temp_obj;

  temp_obj.n = left_op.n + right_op;

  return temp_obj;
}

istream& operator >> (istream& is, Test_Class& right_op)
{
  is >> right_op.n;

  return is;
}



int main()
{
  Test_Class tc_object1;
  Test_Class tc_object2;
  Test_Class tc_object3;

  cout << "\nEnter a value for the first object: ";
  cin >> tc_object1;

  cout << "\nEnter two values for the next two objects: ";
  cin >> tc_object2 >> tc_object3;

  cout << "\nThe data values for the three objects are: " << endl;
  cout << tc_object1.Get_Value() << endl;
  cout << tc_object2.Get_Value() << endl;
  cout << tc_object3.Get_Value() << endl;

  return 0;
}
```

Program Output

```
Enter a value for the first object: 1

Enter two values for the next two objects: 2 3

The data values for the three objects are:
1
2
3
```

Note that we cascade the insertion operator in the program. The result of `cin >> tc_object2` is the object `cin`. Therefore, the second extraction is equivalent to `cin >> tc_object3`.

EXERCISES 12.4

1. Code an overload of the insertion operator for `Test_Class`.
2. Code the overload of the extraction operator as a friend function of `Test_Class`.
3. Code an overload of the insertion operator for the `Rectangle` class. The output should be nicely formatted.
4. Code an overload of the extraction operator for the `Rectangle` class. Executing `cin >> rec;` allows the user to enter two numbers separated by a space; the first for the length and the second for the width.
5. Code an overload of the insertion operator for the `DigitalClock` class. The output should be nicely formatted.
6. Code an overload of the extraction operator for the `DigitalClock` class. Executing `cin >> clock;` should allow the user to enter three numbers separated by spaces; the first for the hour, the second for the minutes, and the third for AM(0) or PM(1).

EXPERIMENTS 12.4

1. Recode dem12-5.cpp using the overload of the insertion operator of Exercise 1. The program should not use the `Get_Value()` function.
2. Recode dem12-5.cpp using the overload of the extraction operator as a member function. Does the program behave differently?

PROGRAMMING PROBLEMS 12.4

1. Overload the insertion operator for the `WebSite` class so it displays the data members of the class in a nicely formatted way. Write a program that tests the operator. Compile, execute, and test the resulting program.
2. Overload the insertion operator for the `OilTank` class so it displays the data members of the class in a nicely formatted way. Overload the extraction operator for the class. The overload should prompt the user for the required information. Write a program that tests the operators. Compile, execute, and test the resulting program.
3. Overload the insertion operator for the `VehicleService` class so it displays the data members of the class in a nicely formatted way. Write a program that tests the operator. Compile, execute, and test the resulting program.
4. Overload the insertion operator for the `HotelRoom` class so it displays the data members of the class in a nicely formatted way. Overload the extraction operator for the class. The overload should prompt the user for the required information.

Write a program that tests the operators. Compile, execute, and test the resulting program.

12.5 Overloading Compound Assignment Operators

The compound assignment operators can also be overloaded.

Overloading += and −=

You can think of withdrawing money from an account as decreasing the account and of making a deposit as increasing an account. In Account, it would be reasonable to replace the Deposit() member function by an overload of += and to replace the Withdraw() member function by an overload of −=. Since either making a deposit or withdrawal to an account changes the object to which it is applied, we code the overloads of these operators as member functions.

Programming Pointers

Both the += and −= operators are considered assignment operators. As we did for our overload of assignment, the value of each of these operators will be the object to which the operator is applied. Each overload will return a reference to the object to which the operator is applied, namely the left operand. Therefore, each operator returns *this.

```
Account& Account::operator += (const double right_op)
{
  balance += right_op;

  return *this;
}

Account& Account::operator -= (const double right_op)
{
  balance -= right_op;

  return *this;
}
```

Following is dem12-6.cpp, which uses overloads of += and −=.

```
//dem12-6.cpp

//This program illustrates overloading the += and -= operators

#include <iostream.h>
#include <iomanip.h>
#include <string.h>

using namespace std;
```

```cpp
class Account
{
  friend int Transfer(Account&, Account&, double);
  friend ostream& operator << (ostream&, const Account&);

  private:
    char    id_no[5];
    char*   name;
    double balance;
    double rate;

  public:
    Account(char id[], char* n_p, double bal = 0.00, double rt = 0.04);
    ~Account();
    const char* Get_Id() const;
    const char* Get_Name() const;
    double Calc_Interest();
    double Get_Balance() const;

    Account& operator += (const double);
    Account& operator -= (const double);
    Account& operator = (const Account&);
};

Account::Account(char id[], char* n_p, double bal, double rt)
{
  strcpy(id_no, id);  //copy first argument into id_no[]

  name = new char[strlen(n_p) + 1]; //create space for the name

  strcpy(name, n_p);  //copy second argument into new space

  balance = bal;
  rate    = rt;
}

Account::~Account()
{
  delete [] name;
}

inline const char* Account::Get_Id() const
{
  return id_no;
}

inline const char* Account::Get_Name() const
{
  return name;
}
```

```
inline double Account::Get_Balance() const
{
  return balance;
}

double Account::Calc_Interest()
{
  double interest;

  interest = balance * rate;
  balance += interest;

  return interest;
}

Account& Account::operator += (const double right_op)
{
  balance += right_op;

  return *this;
}

Account& Account::operator -= (const double right_op)
{
  balance -= right_op;

  return *this;
}

ostream& operator << (ostream& os, const Account& right_op)
{
  os << "\nData for Account# " << right_op.id_no;

  os << "\n\nOwner's Name: " << right_op.name;

  os << "\n\nAccount Balance: " << right_op.balance << endl;

  return os;
}


Account& Account::operator = (const Account& right_op)
{
  if (&right_op == this)
    ;                        //Self assignment - do nothing
  else
    {
      strcpy(id_no, right_op.id_no);  //copy id of right_op into id_no[]

      delete [] name;
```

```
        name = new char[strlen(right_op.name) + 1]; //create space for the name

        strcpy(name, right_op.name);  //copy second argument into new space

        balance = right_op.balance;
        rate    = right_op.rate;
      }

   return *this;
}

int Transfer(Account& acc_r1, Account& acc_r2, double amount)
{
   //If amount exceeds acc_r2's balance, do nothing and return 0

   if (amount > acc_r2.balance)
     return 0;

   //Otherwise, make the transfer and return 1

   acc_r2.balance -= amount; //decrease acc_r2's balance by amount
   acc_r1.balance += amount; //increase acc_r1's balance by amount

   return 1;
}

Account Get_Account();            //Function prototype

int main()
{
   cout << setprecision(2)
        << setiosflags(ios::fixed)
        << setiosflags(ios::showpoint);

   double amount;

   Account acc1 = Get_Account();

   cout << acc1;

   cout << "\nEnter an amount to deposit: ";
   cin >> amount;

   acc1 += amount;

   cout << "\nAfter the deposit:\n\n" << acc1;

   cout << "\nEnter an amount to withdraw: ";
   cin >> amount;

   acc1 -= amount;
```

```
    cout << "\nAfter the withdrawal:\n\n" << acc1;

    return 0;
}


Account Get_Account()
{
    char id[5];
    char buffer[81];
    double bal;
    double rt;

    cout << "\nEnter Account ID: ";
    cin.getline(id, 5);

    cin.get();    //Clear the input buffer of new-line character

    cout << "\nEnter Account Holder's Name: ";
    cin.getline(buffer, 81);

    cout << "\nEnter Balance: ";
    cin >> bal;

    cout << "\nEnter Interest Rate: ";
    cin >> rt;

    cin.get();    //Clear the input buffer of new-line character

    Account acc(id, buffer, bal, rt);

    return acc;
}
```

Program Output

```
Enter Account ID: 1111

Enter Account Holder's Name: Maxwell Larrabee

Enter Balance: 200.00

Enter Interest Rate: 0.08

Data for Account# 1111

Owner's Name: Maxwell Larrabee

Account Balance: 200.00
```

```
Enter an amount to deposit: 50.00

After the deposit:


Data for Account# 1111

Owner's Name: Maxwell Larrabee

Account Balance: 250.00

Enter an amount to withdraw: 100.00

After the withdrawal:


Data for Account# 1111

Owner's Name: Maxwell Larrabee

Account Balance: 150.00
```

EXERCISES 12.5

1. Code the prototype and definition of an overload of += for `Test_Class`. The operator should increase the value of the n data member of the object to which it is applied by the value of the integer that is the right operand.

2. Code the prototype and definition of an overload of − = for `Test_Class`. The operator should decrease the value of the n data member of the object to which it is applied by the value of the integer that is the right operand.

3. Code the prototype and definition of an overload of *= for `Test_Class`. The operator should multiply the value of the n data member of the object to which it is applied by the value of the integer that is the right operand.

4. Code the prototype and definition of an overload of /= for `Test_Class`. The operator should divide the value of the n data member of the object to which it is applied by the value of the integer that is the right operand. Be sure to test for division by zero.

5. Recode the overload of += given in this section for `Account` as a friend function rather than as a class member function.

6. Recode the overload of − = given in this section for `Account` as a friend function rather than as a class member function.

PROGRAMMING PROBLEMS 12.5

1. In the `WebPage` class, add an overload of += that increases the number of hits on the page. Write a program to test the new operator. Compile, execute, and test the resulting program.

2. In the `OilTank` class, replace the member function `Add_Oil()` by an overload of the `+=` operator and the function `Remove_Oil()` by an overload of the `-=` operator. Write a program to test the new operators. Compile, execute, and test the resulting program.

3. In the `VehicleService` class, code an overload of `+=` that increases the number of hours of labor done on the vehicle. Write a program to test the new operator. Compile, execute, and test the resulting program.

4. In the `HotelRoom` class, add an overload of `+=` to add guests to a room and an overload of `-=` to remove guests from a room. Write a program to test the new operators. Compile, execute, and test the resulting program.

12.6 Overloading Relational Operators

The relational operators, `==`, `>`, `<`, and so on can sometimes be overloaded in a meaningful way.

Overloading `==`

What if we want to see if two account objects, say `acc1` and `acc2`, contain the same information? We could make such a test by using the accessor functions to get the values of the data members and then test them for equality. If the data members are equal, on a member by member basis, then the accounts contain the same information. This approach works (see Exercise 1), but it would be nice if we could simply code an `if` statement as follows.

```
if (acc1 == acc2)
...
else
...
```

Programming
Pitfalls

The problem with the solution is that the expression `acc1 == acc2` is illegal. See Experiment 1. There is no default test for equality that extends to objects in the same way as there is a default assignment that extends to objects. If we want to use a relation operator to test a relation between two objects, we must overload the operator. Since a relation operator does not change the objects involved, we shall code the overload of the equals operator as a friend function. Here is the prototype and code of the overloaded equals operator.

```
friend int operator == (Account&, Account&);
```

```
int operator == (Account& acc_left, Account& acc_right)
{
    if (strcmp(acc_left.id_no, acc_right.id_no))
```

```
              return 0;

   if (strcmp(acc_left.name, acc_right.name))
              return 0;

   if (acc_left.balance != acc_right.balance)
              return 0;

   if (acc_left.rate != acc_right.rate)
              return 0;

   return 1;
}
```

Programming
Pointers

To make the overloaded equals operator behave as the equals operator does
when comparing the native data types, we code the overload so that the operator
returns one if the operands are equal, and zero otherwise. Recall that the function
strcmp() returns a non-zero, that is true, value if the strings it compares are not
equal. Thus, the first if statement causes the function to return zero if the id_no
members of the objects being compared are not equal. Likewise, the second if statement causes the function to return zero if the name members of the objects being compared are not equal. The next two if statements cause the function to return zero if
the balance or the rate members of the objects being compared are not equal. If the
two objects differ in any of their members, the operator returns zero. Otherwise, the
operator returns one.

Following is program dem12-7.cpp, which illustrates the use of the overloaded ==
operator.

```
//dem12-7.cpp

//This program illustrates overloading the == operator

#include <iostream.h>
#include <iomanip.h>
#include <string.h>

using namespace std;

class Account
{
   friend int Transfer(Account&, Account&, double);
   friend ostream& operator << (ostream&, const Account&);
   friend int operator == (Account&, Account&);

   private:
     char   id_no[5];
     char*  name;
     double balance;
```

```
      double rate;

  public:
    Account(char id[], char* n_p, double bal = 0.00, double rt = 0.04);
    ~Account();
    const char* Get_Id() const;
    const char* Get_Name() const;
    double Calc_Interest();
    double Get_Balance() const;
    Account& operator += (const double);
    Account& operator -= (const double);
    Account& operator = (const Account&);
};


Account::Account(char id[], char* n_p, double bal, double rt)
{
  strcpy(id_no, id);  //copy first argument into id_no[]

  name = new char[strlen(n_p) + 1]; //create space for the name

  strcpy(name, n_p);  //copy second argument into new space

  balance = bal;
  rate    = rt;
}

Account::~Account()
{
  delete [] name;
}

inline const char* Account::Get_Id() const
{
  return id_no;
}

inline const char* Account::Get_Name() const
{
  return name;
}


inline double Account::Get_Balance() const
{
  return balance;
}

double Account::Calc_Interest()
{
```

```
      double interest;

      interest = balance * rate;
      balance += interest;

      return interest;
}

Account& Account::operator += (const double right_op)
{
   balance += right_op;

   return *this;
}

Account& Account::operator -= (const double right_op)
{
   balance -= right_op;

   return *this;
}

ostream& operator << (ostream& os, const Account& right_op)
{
   os << "\nData for Account# " << right_op.id_no;

   os << "\n\nOwner's Name: " << right_op.name;

   os << "\n\nAccount Balance: " << right_op.balance << endl;

   return os;
}


Account& Account::operator = (const Account& right_op)
{
   if (&right_op == this)
      ;                    //Self assignment - do nothing
   else
      {
         strcpy(id_no, right_op.id_no);  //copy id of right_op into id_no[]

         delete [] name;

         name = new char[strlen(right_op.name) + 1]; //create space for the name

         strcpy(name, right_op.name);  //copy second argument into new space

         balance = right_op.balance;
         rate    = right_op.rate;
      }
```

```
      return *this;
}

int Transfer(Account& acc_r1, Account& acc_r2, double amount)
{
   //If amount exceeds acc_r2's balance, do nothing and return 0

   if (amount > acc_r2.balance)
      return 0;

   //Otherwise, make the transfer and return 1

   acc_r2.balance -= amount;   //decrease acc_r2's balance by amount
   acc_r1.balance += amount;   //increase acc_r1's balance by amount

   return 1;
}

int operator == (Account& acc_left, Account& acc_right)
{
   if (strcmp(acc_left.id_no, acc_right.id_no))
      return 0;

   if (strcmp(acc_left.name, acc_right.name))
      return 0;

   if (acc_left.balance != acc_right.balance)
      return 0;

   if (acc_left.rate != acc_right.rate)
      return 0;

   return 1;
}

Account Get_Account();              //Function prototype

int main()
{
   cout << setprecision(2)
        << setiosflags(ios::fixed)
        << setiosflags(ios::showpoint);

   double amount;

   Account acc1 = Get_Account();

   cout << acc1;
```

```cpp
    Account acc2 = acc1;

    cout << "\nInitializing acc2 to the value of acc1.";

    if (acc1 == acc2)
      cout << "\n\nThe accounts are equal";
    else
      cout << "\n\nThe accounts are not equal";

    cout << "\n\nAdding $50.00 to Account 2" << endl;

    acc2 += 50.00;

    cout << acc2;

    if (acc1 == acc2)
      cout << "\nThe accounts are equal";
    else
      cout << "\nThe accounts are not equal";

    return 0;
}


Account Get_Account()
{
  char id[5];
  char buffer[81];
  double bal;
  double rt;

  cout << "\nEnter Account ID: ";
  cin.getline(id, 5);

  cin.get();    //Clear the input buffer of new-line character

  cout << "\nEnter Account Holder's Name: ";
  cin.getline(buffer, 81);

  cout << "\nEnter Balance: ";
  cin >> bal;

  cout << "\nEnter Interest Rate: ";
  cin >> rt;

  cin.get();    //Clear the input buffer of new-line character

  Account acc(id, buffer, bal, rt);

  return acc;
}
```

Program Output

```
Enter Account ID: 1234

Enter Account Holder's Name: John Smith

Enter Balance: 200.00

Enter Interest Rate: 0.07

Data for Account# 1234

Owner's Name: John Smith

Account Balance: 200.00

Initializing acc2 to the value of acc1.

The accounts are equal

Adding $50.00 to Account 2

Data for Account# 1234

Owner's Name: John Smith

Account Balance: 250.00

The accounts are not equal
```

The program asks the user to enter data for an account. Then the program initializes a second account to the first account. Therefore, the accounts are identical. This is verified by the program using the overloaded == operator in an if statement. The program then deposits $50 into the second account using the overloaded += operator and then again uses an if statement and the overloaded == operator to test the two accounts for equality. Of course, the accounts are no longer equal because their balances differ.

EXERCISES 12.6

1. Recode dem12-7.cpp without using the overloaded == operator. Instead, when the program needs to test for equality, test each of the data members for equality by using the corresponding accessor functions. You will need to code accessor functions to get the balance and the rate for an Account object.
2. Code an overload of the == operator for Test_Class. Two objects are equal if their n data members are equal.
3. Code an overload of the > operator for Test_Class. The object tc_object1 is greater than tc_object2 if its n data member is greater than the n data member of tc_object2.

4. Code an overload of the < operator for `Test_Class`. The object `tc_object1` is less than `tc_object2` if its n data member is less than the n data member of `tc_object2`.

5. Code an overload of the != operator for `Account` that uses the overload of the == operator that was developed in this section.

6. Code overloads of the <= operator and the >= operator for `Test_Class` that use the == operator from Exercise 2 and the overloads of > and < from Exercises 3 and 4.

PROGRAMMING PROBLEMS 12.6

1. Code an overload of the == operator for the `WebPage` class. Write a program that tests the new operator. Compile, execute, and test the resulting program.

2. Code an overload of the == operator for the `OilTank` class. Also overload the > operator. The operator should return one if the oil in the tank that is its left operand exceeds the oil in the tank that is its right operand. Write a program that tests the new operators. Compile, execute, and test the resulting program.

3. Code an overload of the == operator for the `VehicleService` class. Write a program that tests the new operator. Compile, execute, and test the resulting program.

4. Code an overload of the == operator for the `HotelRoom` class. Write a program that tests the new operator. Compile, execute, and test the resulting program.

12.7 Overloading Unary Operators

Unary operators, such as ++, − − , +, and − can also be overloaded. In the case of ++ and − −, however, you must take care to overload the pre-and post-versions of the operators properly.

Overloading ++

In some cases, it makes sense to overload the unary operators. For example, to overload the ++ operator for `Test_Class`, we might code the following prototype and function code.

```
Test_Class& operator ++ ();
```

```
Test_Class& Test_Class::operator ++ ()
{
  ++n;

  return *this;
}
```

Programming
Pointers

Note that the operator has no argument. The operator operates on the object to which it is applied. Thus, the data member n in the operator definition refers to the data member of the object to which the function is applied. The function returns a reference to that object. Thus we can code the following in main().

```
Test_Class tc_object(5);
++tc_object;
```

Overloading the Post-increment ++

The statement ++tc_object increments the data member of tc_object. However, what if we code the following statement?

```
tc_object++;
```

Programming
Pointers

This statement uses ++ as a post-increment operator. The compiler will not use the overload that we just coded. See Experiment 1. The post-increment operator requires a separate overload. To distinguish between the two, the compiler requires a "dummy" integer argument in the prototype and definition of the post-increment operator. There is no need to specify a parameter in the definition because the parameter is never used.

```
Test_Class& operator ++ (int);              //postincrement

Test_Class& Test_Class::operator ++ (int)
{
   n++;

   return *this;
}
```

When you use the post-increment operator in a program, the compiler uses the version with the dummy integer argument. Here is a program that uses both versions of the ++ operator.

```
//dem12-8.cpp

//This program illustrates overloading the ++ operator

#include <iostream.h>

using namespace std;

class Test_Class
{
   friend Test_Class operator + (const Test_Class&, const Test_Class&);
```

```
    friend Test_Class operator + (const Test_Class&, const int);
    friend istream& operator >> (istream&, Test_Class&);
    friend ostream& operator << (ostream&, Test_Class&);

  private:
    int n;

  public:
    Test_Class(int i = 0);  //One-argument constructor
    Test_Class(Test_Class&);  //Copy constructor
    ~Test_Class();
    Test_Class& operator ++();  //Prefix overload
    Test_Class& operator ++(int);     //Postfix overload
};

Test_Class::Test_Class(int i)
{
  n = i;

  //cout << "\nConstructor Executed: Data member initialized to " << n;
}

Test_Class::Test_Class(Test_Class& tc_r)
{
  n = tc_r.n;

  //cout << "\n\nCopy constructor executed: "
  //        << "Data member initialized to " << n;
}

Test_Class::~Test_Class()
{
  //cout << "\n\nDestructor Executed for object with data member " << n;
}

Test_Class operator + (const Test_Class& left_op, const Test_Class& right_op)
{
  Test_Class temp_obj;

  temp_obj.n = left_op.n + right_op.n;

  return temp_obj;
}

Test_Class operator + (const Test_Class& left_op, const int right_op)
{
  Test_Class temp_obj;

  temp_obj.n = left_op.n + right_op;
```

```
      return temp_obj;
}

istream& operator >> (istream& is, Test_Class& right_op)
{
  is >> right_op.n;

  return is;
}

ostream& operator << (ostream& os, Test_Class& right_op)
{
  os << right_op.n;

  return os;
}

Test_Class& Test_Class::operator ++ ()         //Preincrement overload
{
  ++n;

  return *this;
}

Test_Class& Test_Class::operator ++ (int)     //Postincrement overload
{
  n++;

  return *this;
}


int main()
{
  Test_Class tc_object(5);

  cout << "\nThe current value of the object is " << tc_object;

  ++tc_object;

  cout << "\n\nAfter a pre-increment the value of the object is "
          << tc_object;

  tc_object++;

  cout << "\n\nAfter a post-increment the value of the object is "
      << tc_object;

  return 0;
}
```

Program Output

```
The current value of the object is 5

After a pre-increment the value of the object is 6

After a post-increment the value of the object is 7
```

Note in the definition of Test_Class that we replace the Get_Value() member function by an overload of the << operator, which sends the value of the data member of the object to the output stream. We also commented out the cout statements in the constructor, the copy constructor and the destructor to make the program output simpler.

The program creates a Test_Class object with a data member value of 5. Then a pre-increment increases the data member to 6 and then a post-increment increases the data member to 7.

EXERCISES 12.7

1. Code a prototype and definition for an overload of the − − operator for Test_Class.

2. Code a prototype and definition for overloads of the unary + and − operators for Test_Class. The overload of unary + should place a + in front of the data member of the object and return a reference to the object. The overload of unary − should negate the data member of the object and return a reference to the object.

3. Code a prototype and definition for an overload of the ++ and − − operators for the Rectangle class. Applying ++ to a Rectangle object should increment the length and width by one. Applying − − to a Rectangle object should decrement the length and width by one. If either the length or the width are thereby decreased to zero or less, the default value of one should be assigned to that member.

4. Code a prototype and definition for an overload of the ++ operator for the DigitalClock class. Applying ++ to a DigitalClock object should increase the minutes member by one. Remember that increasing the minutes member by one can result in an increase in the hour member and a change to the ampm member.

EXPERIMENTS 12.7

1. Remove the prototype and the definition of the post-increment operator in dem12-8.cpp and keep main() as it is in the program. Compile the resulting program. What message does the compiler issue?

2. Add to the definition of Test_Class the overloads for − −, unary +, and unary − that you coded in Exercises 1 and 2. Write a program that tests the overloaded operators. Compile, execute, and test the resulting program.

3. Add to the `Rectangle` class the overloads of `++` and `−−` that you coded in Exercise 3. Write a program that tests the overloaded operators. Compile, execute, and test the resulting program.

4. Add to the `DigitalClock` class the overload of `++` that you coded in Exercise 4. Write a program that tests the overloaded operator. Compile, execute, and test the resulting program.

PROGRAMMING PROBLEMS 12.7

1. Overload the `++` operator for the `WebPage` class. Applying the operator to a `WebPage` object should increment the number of hits on the page. Code both a pre-increment and a post-increment. Write a program that tests the overloaded operator. Compile, execute, and test the resulting program.

2. Overload the `++` and `−−` operators for the `HotelRoom` class. Applying the `++` operator to a `HotelRoom` object increments the number of guests in the room. Applying the `−−` operator decrements the number of guests in the room. Code pre- and post- versions of both operators. Write a program that tests the overloaded operators. Compile, execute, and test the resulting program.

Chapter Review

Terminology

Define the following terms.

friend function	operator
friend	operator overload
function overload	this

Summary

- A friend function of a class has the same access privileges as member functions of the class, but is not itself a member function. Thus a friend function has access to a class's private members. Declare a friend function within a class with the keyword `friend` (Note 12.1).

- An overloaded operator that changes one of its operands should be defined as a member function of the class. All other overloaded operators should be friend functions (Note 12.2).

- To overload an operator that is a friend, use the following syntax for the prototype and function definition header.

```
friend return-type operator operator-symbol (argument-list)
```

- In an overload of a binary operator as a friend function, the first argument of the overload represents the left operand and the second argument represents the right operand (Note 12.3).
- Some operators cannot be overloaded. Some operators must be class member functions. You cannot change the unary/binary nature of an operator or override the operator precedence rules (Note 12.4).
- When overloading an operator that is a class member, use the following syntax in the prototype and function definition header.

return-type `operator` *operator-symbol (argument-list)*

- When overloading a binary operator as a class member, the object to which the function is applied represents the left operand and the one argument of the operator represents the right operand (Note 12.5).
- Within the code of a class member function, the `this` pointer points to the object to which the function is being applied. Therefore, within such a function, `*this` represents the object to which the function is applied (Note 12.6).
- The assignment operator can be overloaded as a class member function as follows.

class-name& `operator` `=` `(const` *class-name& right-operand* `)`

In this case, the function should return `*this`.

- The insertion operator can be overloaded as follows.

`friend ostream& operator << (ostream& os, const` *class-name& right-operand* `)`

In this case, the function should return `os`.

- The extraction operator can be overloaded as follows.

`friend istream& operator >> (istream& is,` *class-name& right-operand* `)`

In this case, the function should return `is`.

- The compound assignment operators should be overloaded as class member functions. For example, the `+=` operator can be overloaded as follows.

class-name& `operator` `+=` `(const` *data-type right-operand* `)`

In this case, the function should return `*this`.

- The relational operators, for example `==`, can be overloaded as follows.

`friend int operator == (`*class-name&, class-name&*`)`

In this case the function should return one if the objects are equal, and zero otherwise.

- The unary operators can be overloaded as class member functions. For example, the following is the prototype for an overload of the pre-increment ++ operator.

  class-name& `operator ++ ()`

  In this case, the function should return `*this`.

- To overload the post-increment ++ operator, you must use a dummy integer argument as follows.

  class-name& `operator ++ (int)`

  In this case, the function should return `*this`.

Review Exercises

1. What is a friend function and how is it declared?
2. Generally speaking, which overloaded operators should be declared as friend functions and which should be defined as class members? Which overloaded operators must be declared as member functions?
3. Explain the syntax for overloading a binary operator.
4. Explain the syntax for overloading a unary operator.
5. In an overloaded binary operator that is declared as a friend function, what does the first operand of the operator represent? What does the second operand of the operator represent?
6. In an overloaded binary operator that is declared as a member function, what is the left operand and what does the operand of the operator represent?
7. Can an overloaded unary operator have an argument? Explain.
8. Which operators cannot be overloaded?
9. What is the `this` pointer? When should you use it?
10. Give the syntax for the prototype and function definition header of an overload of the insertion operator. Why should the overload return a reference?
11. Is there a default equals operator available for a user-defined class?
12. Explain how to overload the pre- and post-decrement operators.

Chapter

13

Inheritance

Objectives

- To be familiar with the terminology of inheritance—object, class, base class, derived class, indirect and direct derivation, and the "is a" relation.

- To use direct derivation to derive a class from a base class.

- To use the `protected` access specifier.

- To know the accessibility of `public`, `private`, and `protected` class members of a base class in both publicly derived and privately derived classes.

- To know which functions are and are not inherited.

- To code a constructor for a derived class.

- To code a destructor for a derived class.

- To code a copy constructor for a derived class.

- To understand function overriding and when it takes place.

- To use the scope resolution operator to use an overridden base class function on a derived class object.

- To understand and use polymorphism.

- To correctly use pointers in a class hierarchy.

- To declare a virtual function.
- To apply a function polymorphicly through a pointer.
- To declare virtual destructors.
- To use pure virtual functions to create an abstract base class.

Introduction

If I tell you that I am in the market to buy a Sheltie, you will probably not know what I am talking about. You might think that a Sheltie is a bird or maybe a car. Suppose that now I tell you that a Sheltie is a dog. Immediately, you know some properties of the object that I want to buy—it has four legs, it is furry, and it has a tail and a wet nose. You make these deductions because you know that being a dog, a Sheltie inherits the properties that all dogs possess. In this chapter we will apply the ideas of inheritance to classes that we define in our programs.

A program may have more than one class. For example, in Chapter 10 we discussed a set of classes in an example ATM system that contained the `Customer` class, the `ATM` class and the `Account` class. When a system contains several classes, it is necessary to consider how the various classes are related and to include those relationships in your program solution. The most important way in which classes can be related is through what is called inheritance. For example, we can define an `Account` class from which we can derive, through inheritance, a `SavingsAccount` class and a `CheckingAccount` class. Each `SavingsAccount` object and `CheckingAccount` object inherits all the data members and all the function members of the `SavingsAccount` class. Classes related this way embody the "is a" relation. Thus, a `SavingsAccount` object "is an" `Account` object and a `CheckingAccount` object "is an" `Account` object. In this chapter we discuss how to derive one class from another and the implications of inheritance on class data members and functions.

13.1 Inheritance

One of the most important concepts in object-oriented programming is that of inheritance. Inheritance allows us to define a class in terms of another class, which makes it easier to create and maintain an application. We begin by discussing several examples.

Examples of Inheritance and Basic Terminology

So far we have considered problems in which there is only one class. Generally speaking, real world problems involve many classes. It is possible that some classes in a problem are not directly related in the sense that they do not share any member data or functions. For example, if we were designing a drawing program, we might define the classes `Rectangle` and `Circle` in such a way that they do not have any common data members or any common member functions. A rectangle would be described in terms of its length and width, and a circle in terms of its radius. Each class would have its own `Area()` and `Perimeter()` functions.

However, there are times when classes are related in a hierarchy that moves from the general to the specific. Such a hierarchy implements the "is a" relation in the sense that an object in a class that is below another class in the hierarchy "is an" object of the type in the class above. For example, in a banking application there might be three types of interest-bearing accounts: savings accounts, money market accounts, and certificates of deposit (CD). Each type of account "is an" interest-bearing account. The three account types have some common attributes (that is, data). For example, all three types of accounts have an ID number, owner's name, balance, and interest rate. The three account types also have some common member functions. For example, all three would have a `Calc_Interest()` function. Although all would have a `Withdraw()` function, each class's version of that function would behave differently. For example, a premature withdrawal from a CD requires that the bank impose a penalty on the interest earned.

The three types of accounts could be defined as separate classes, each with its own ID number, name, balance, and interest rate. However, this would not embody the fact that the three account types are specialized versions of a general type of account, the interest-bearing account. It would be better program design to arrange the classes in a hierarchy as shown in Figure 13.1. The relationship of classes in such a hierarchy, in which classes go from the general to the specific, is known as **inheritance**. The `Interest_Bearing_Account` class is known as the **base class** (sometimes also called the **parent class** or **super class**). The classes below the base class in the hierarchy are the **derived classes** (sometimes called **child classes** or **subclasses**).

When we declare such a class hierarchy in a program, `Interest_Bearing_Account` will include the ID number, name, balance, and rate members (shown to the right of the class in the figure). The derived classes **inherit** these members from the base class. In a derived class we declare only those members that are specific to that class. For example, the `CD` class would contain the data member `term` that stores the term of the CD (A CD is purchased for a specific number of months, the term of the account, at which time the owner has the option of withdrawing all or part of the balance. If the CD is renewed, a new interest rate would be in effect for the new term.) We shall see later that member functions can also be inherited.

As another example, suppose a video store requires us to write an inventory program that stores data about the items stocked by the store. The store sells several types of items—movies, specialized videos (exercise, sports, and so on), and video games for

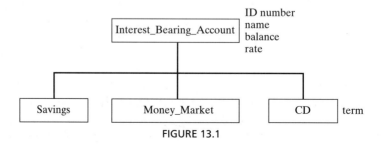

FIGURE 13.1

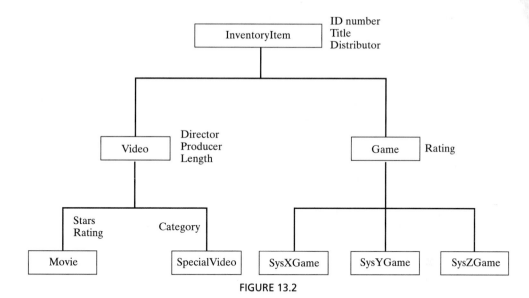

FIGURE 13.2

three types of game systems (System X, System Y, and System Z). We could design a program that uses five different, unrelated classes (Movie, SpecialVideo, SysXGame, SysYGame, and SysZGame). However, such a design would not reflect the fact that all are inventory items of some type, that some are movies and some are games, that the three types of game items are all game disks and not movies, and so on. If we arrange the classes in an inheritance hierarchy (Figure 13.2), we can more clearly see the relationships among the different inventory types. Again we show the data members of the class to the right of each class.

As mentioned previously, the idea of inheritance implements the "is a" relationship. For example, a movie is a video, a System X game is a video game, and so on. Therefore, it makes sense that derived classes inherit data from their base class. Since a movie is a video, it should have all the characteristics of a video. Likewise, since a System X game is a video game it should have all the characteristics of a video game. In the same manner, since a movie is a video, which in turn is an inventory item, a movie should also have all the characteristics of an inventory item.

The Video class, therefore, inherits all the data from the InventoryItem class. This means that all the members (ID_number, Title, Distributor) of the base class InventoryItem are also members of the derived Video class. It can happen, as it does in the hierarchy of Figure 13.2, that a class, which is derived from a base class, can itself serve as the base class of another class. This is the case for Video class, which is derived from InventoryItem, but is itself the base class for Movie and SpecialVideo. Both Movie and SpecialVideo inherit all the members of Video class including the members that Video inherits from InventoryItem class. We say that Video and Game are **directly derived** from InventoryItem; Movie and Special Video are directly derived from Video, but are **indirectly derived** from InventoryItem (through the Video class). See Exercises 2 and 3. Movie class has the following data members: ID_Number, Title, Distributor (indirectly derived from `InventoryItem`), `Director`, `Producer`, `Length` (directly derived from `Video`), and `Stars` and `Rating`.

Most member functions are also inherited in the hierarchy. (We mention the exceptions later in the chapter.) Once again, this should make sense because inheritance implements the "is a" relation. Suppose we have a function `Get_Title()` that is a member of the `InventoryItem` class. This function is inherited by all the classes derived from `InventoryItem`. Therefore, all the classes in the hierarchy have this same `Get_Title()` function as a member function. For example, because a `Movie` object is an `InventoryItem` object, by means of inheritance we can apply the `Get_Title()` member function to the `Movie` object.

Note that the classes `SysXGame`, `SysYGame`, and `SysZGame` do not have any data members that are specific to those classes. Why, then, are they separate classes? The reason is that these classes may behave differently when they are acted upon by the same member function. For example, if a `SysXGame` class object receives the message to display itself, it may behave differently than when a `SysYGame` class object receives the same message. We will discuss this further later in the chapter.

Defining Derived Classes

For simplicity, we shall first work with `Test_Class`, which we used in the previous three chapters. We want `Test_Class` to serve as a base class for `Derived_Test_Class`, which will also have a single data member, m. See Figure 13.3.

Here is the definition of `Test_Class` from the previous chapter. We have removed the overloaded addition operators and the `Get_Value()` function to keep the class as simple as possible.

```
class Test_Class
{
  private:
    int n;

  public:
```

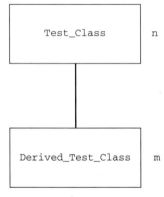

FIGURE 13.3

```
    Test_Class(int i = 0);     //One-argument constructor
    Test_Class(Test_Class&);  //Copy constructor
    ~Test_Class();            //Destructor
};
```

Programming
Pitfalls

As we mentioned in the previous section, any class that we derive from
`Test_Class` inherits all the data members of `Test_Class`, including the `private`
members and most of the member functions. Therefore, a `Derived_Test_Class`
object will have an n data member. However, since n is a `private` member of
`Test_Class`, it is not accessible to any function outside `Test_Class`. It follows that
although a `Derived_Test_Class` object has an n data member by means of inheritance, the object does not have access to that data member. A member function of
`Derived_Test_Class` does not have access to the n data member, even though n is
a data member of `Derived_Test_Class`. This is a bit awkward—the object does not
have access to one of its own data members. We could remedy this situation by declaring the access category of the n data member of `Test_Class` to be `public`. However
this would violate the principle of data hiding because every function would then have
access to the n data member of every `Test_Class` object. The answer that C++ provides to this dilemma is a third access category, `protected`. An item in a base class,
whether a data member or a function, that has access category `protected` behaves as
though it is a `private` item to all functions except member functions in classes
derived from the base class. Member functions in a derived class have access to all
`protected` items in the base class.

NOTE 13.1— THE `protected` ACCESS SPECIFIER

- A `protected` item in a base class behaves as though it is `private` to all functions
  except to member functions in classes derived from the base class.
- Member functions in a derived class have access to all `protected` members in the base
  class.

If we want the member functions of `Derived_Test_Class` to have access
to the n data member of `Test_Class`, we must change the access category of n to
`protected`.

```
class Test_Class
{
  protected:      //Data accessible to derived classes
    int n;

  public:
    Test_Class(int i = 0);  //One-argument constructor
    Test_Class(Test_Class&);  //Copy constructor
    ~Test_Class();
};
```

Now, how do we encode the fact that `Derived_Test_Class` is derived from `Test_Class`? To define `Derived_Test_Class` as derived from `Test_Class`, follow the name of the derived class with a colon followed by the keyword `public` and the name of the base class.

```
class Derived_Test_Class : public Test_Class
{
  protected:
      int m;

  public:
      Derived_Test_Class(int j = 0);
      Derived_Test_Class(Derived_Test_Class&);
      ~Derived_Test_Class();
};
```

Programming
Pointers

In this use, the keyword `public` means that we are publicly deriving this class from the base class. **Public derivation** means that the `protected` and `public` members of the base class are considered `protected` and `public` members of the derived class. The default type of deriving is `private` rather than `public`. If we omit the keyword `public`, the derived class will be privately derived from the base class. (We could also use the keyword `private` to indicate `private` derivation.) This would mean that the `protected` and `public` members of the base class would be considered `private` members of the derived class. No member function in a class derived from such a privately derived class would have access to the data members of the base class. It is common practice to include the word `public` or `private` and not use the default.

Programming
Pointers

We use `public` derivation if we want users of the derived class to have access to the `public` member functions of the base class. We use `private` derivation if we want to block users of the derived class from using the `public` member functions of the base class. Since private derivation is very unusual, we will not use it in this book.

NOTE 13.2—DERIVING A CLASS AND ACCESSIBILITY IN PUBLIC AND PRIVATE DERIVATION

To derive a class from a base class in the declaration of the derived class, follow the derived class's name by a colon, the keyword `public` or the keyword `private`, and the name of the base class. Table 13.1 summarizes accessibility in `public` and `private` derivation.

Consider the third row where we see the words `public`, `public`, `private` going from left to right. This means that a variable that is `public` in the base class (the word `public` in the first column) is considered `public` (the word `public` in the second column) in a class that is publicly derived from it. Likewise, a variable that is `public` in the base class is considered `private` (the word in the third column) in a class that is privately derived from the base class.

TABLE 13.1

Base Class Member Access Category	Derived Class Public Base Class	Derived Class Private Base Class
`private`	`private`	`private`
`protected`	`protected`	`private`
`public`	`public`	`private`

In a publicly derived class (the middle column), a variable or function has the same access category that it has in the base class. In a privately derived class (the rightmost column), all variables and functions are `private` no matter what their access category in the base class.

For example, consider the class hierarchy in Figure 13.4. The variable `a1` is a public data member of the base class `Class_A`. By inheritance, variable `a1` is also a data member of `Class_B`. What is the access category of variable `a1` as a data member of `Class_B`? According to the third row of Table 13.1, since `Class_B` is publicly derived from `Class_A`, the variable `a1` is also a public variable of `Class_B`. On the other hand, by inheritance, variable `a1` is also a data member of `Class_C`. However, from the third row of Table 13.1, `a1` is a private member of `Class_C` because `Class_C` is privately derived from `Class_A`. The two data members of `Class_C`, `c1` (which is public in `Class_C`) and the derived `a1` (which is private in `Class_C`) are inherited by `Class_D`. Therefore, from Table 13.1, `c1` is a public member and `a1` is a private member of `Class_D` because `Class_D` is publicly derived from `Class_C`. Note also that since `a1` is a private member of `Class_C`, it is not accessible to the member functions of `Class_D`.

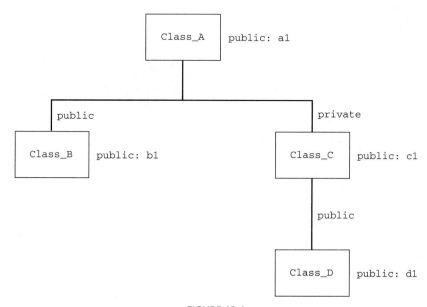

FIGURE 13.4

Note that we make the `m` data member of `Derived_Test_Class` `protected`. This ensures that if we derive a class from `Derived_Test_Class`, the `m` data member will be accessible as a `protected` member of all publicly derived classes.

Constructors in a Derived Class

Note 13.3 states which functions are inherited.

NOTE 13.3—FUNCTIONS THAT ARE NOT INHERITED

A derived class inherits all base class member functions with the following exceptions:

- constructors and copy constructors
- destructors
- overloaded operators
- `friend` functions

We must provide the derived class's constructors, copy constructors, and destructor. They are not inherited. If a function is a friend of the base class, it is not a friend of any derived class by means of inheritance. If you want such a function to be a friend of the derived class, you must declare it as such in the derived class. Likewise, if you overload an operator in a base class, you must overload it again in any derived class.

When we create a `Derived_Test_Class` object `dtc_object`, the object has two data members. It has an `n` data member inherited from `Test_Class` and it has an `m` data member from `Derived_Test_Class`. See Figure 13.5.

Suppose we want the following declaration to create a `Derived_Test_Class` object with an `m` data member value of 7 and an `n` data member value of 8.

```
Derived_Test_Class dtc_object1(7);
```

Programming Pointers

When we create an object of the class `Derived_Test_Class`, we also create an object of the class `Test_Class`. This is so because a `Derived_Test_Class` object "is a" `Test_Class` object. Therefore, when the constructor for `Derived_Test_Class` executes, the constructor for `Test_Class` also executes. In fact, the constructor for `Test_Class` executes before the constructor for `Derived_Test_Class`

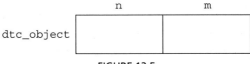

FIGURE 13.5

because the object must obtain its identity as a `Test_Class` object before it obtains its identity as a `Derived_Test_Class` object. The definition of the constructor for `Derived_Test_Class` reflects this.

```
Derived_Test_Class::Derived_Test_Class(int j) : Test_Class(j+1)
{
  m = j;

  cout << "\nDerived_ Test_Class Constructor Executed: "
      << "Data member initialized to "
      << m;
}
```

After the closing parenthesis in the function definition header is a colon followed by an explicit call to the one-argument constructor of the base class. This is called an **initialization list**. Items in the initialization list of a constructor are executed as the object is being created. For example, the act of creating a `Derived_Test_Class` object with an initial value of j causes the one-argument constructor for the base class to execute with an initial value of j+1. That causes the creation of a `Test_Class` object with an n data member having a value of j+1.

NOTE 13.4—DERIVED CLASS CONSTRUCTORS

- The constructor for a derived class should explicitly call the constructor of the base class.
- Call the base class constructor in an initialization list.

Programming
Pointers

The initialization list is not limited to calling the constructor of a base class. We can use it in any constructor to initialize data members. For example, following is the definition of the `Test_Class` constructor that we used in Chapter 12.

```
Test_Class::Test_Class(int i)
{
  n = i;

  cout << "\nTest_Class Constructor Executed: Data member initialized to "
      << n;
}
```

When we declare a `Test_Class` object, the object is created with an n data member that has a garbage value. When the constructor executes, the assignment statement in the constructor places the value of i (or the default value of 0) into n. There is, therefore, an instant of time when the n data member does not have a valid value.

The following definition of the `Test_Class` constructor uses an **initialization list** to place the value of i into n.

```
Test_Class::Test_Class(int i) : n(i)
{
  cout << "\nTest_Class Constructor Executed: Data member initialized to "
       << n;
}
```

Note that the assignment operator is not used in the initialization list. The expression n(i) says to initialize the value of n to i. With the previous initialization list, when a `Test_Class` object is created, the n data member is actually created with the value of i. Therefore, the n data member always has a valid value. There is no time during which n has a garbage value. Since this is a safer and more efficient way to initialize a data member in a constructor, we shall do so in the following programs.

If we apply this technique to the `Derived_Test_Class` constructor, we have the following.

```
Derived_Test_Class::Derived_Test_Class(int j) : Test_Class(j+1), m(j)
{
  cout << "\nDerived_ Test_Class Constructor Executed: "
       << "Data member initialized to "
       << m;
}
```

The initialization list for the constructor contains two statements separated by a comma. The first statement in the initialization list, which executes first, is the explicit call to the base class constructor. The second statement initializes the m data member to the value of j.

The Destructor in a Derived Class

Programming
Pointers

When an object in a derived class (`Derived_Test_Class`) is destroyed, we also destroy an object in the base class (`Test_Class`) because by inheritance, the object is also a base class (`Test_Class`) object. When the destructor for the derived class executes, the destructor for the base class should also execute. However, the destructor for the derived class should execute before the destructor for the base class. Unlike what we must do for constructors, we do not need to do anything special in the destructor's code for the system to call the destructor of the base class. The C++ system does this automatically. Following is dem13-1.cpp, which demonstrates how the constructors and destructors execute in a class hierarchy.

```
//dem13-1.cpp

//This program illustrates how constructors and destructors
//execute in a base class
```

```
#include <iostream.h>

using namespace std;

class Test_Class
{
  protected:
    int n;

  public:
    Test_Class(int i = 0); //One-argument constructor
    ~Test_Class();
};

Test_Class::Test_Class(int i) : n(i)
{
  cout << "\nTest_Class Constructor Executed: Data member initialized to "
       << n << endl << endl;
}



Test_Class::~Test_Class()
{
  cout << "\n\nTest_Class Destructor Executed for object with data member "
       << n;
}



class Derived_Test_Class : public Test_Class
{
  protected:
    int m;

  public:
    Derived_Test_Class(int j = 0);
    ~Derived_Test_Class();
};

Derived_Test_Class::Derived_Test_Class(int j) : Test_Class(j+1), m(j)
{
  cout << "\n\nDerived_Test_Class Constructor Executed: "
       << "Data member initialized to "
       << m;
}



Derived_Test_Class::~Derived_Test_Class()
{
  cout << "\n\n\nDerived_Test_Class Destructor Executed "
       << "for object with data member "
```

```
                   << m;
     }


     int main()
     {
       cout << "\nTest_Class object being created:\n\n";

       Test_Class tc_object1(4);

       cout << "\nDerived Test_Class object being created:\n\n";

       Derived_Test_Class dtc_object1(7);

       return 0;
     }
```

Program Output

```
Test_Class object being created:


Test_Class Constructor Executed: Data member initialized to 4


Derived Test_Class object being created:


Test_Class Constructor Executed: Data member initialized to 8



Derived_Test_Class Constructor Executed: Data member initialized to 7


Derived_Test_Class Destructor Executed for object with data member 7

Test_Class Destructor Executed for object with data member 8

Test_Class Destructor Executed for object with data member 4
```

Note the order of execution of the constructors. When the Test_Class object tc_object1 is created, the constructor for Test_Class executes. When the Derived_Test_Class object dtc_object1 is created, the Derived_Test_Class constructor is invoked. However, before any of its statements execute, a call is made to the base class constructor, Test_Class(). After executing and displaying its message, the Test_Class constructor ends. At that point, the body of the constructor for Derived_Test_Class executes and displays its message. When the program ends, the objects are destroyed in the reverse order of creation. Therefore, `dtc_object1` is destroyed first. The destructor for `Derived_Test_Class` executes and then the destructor for `Test_Class` executes. Finally, the `Test_Class` object `tc_object1` is destroyed. Therefore, the `Test_Class` destructor executes for this object.

The Copy Constructor in a Derived Class

If a derived class has a copy constructor, it should be treated in the same manner as an ordinary constructor. Therefore, the derived class's copy constructor definition should call the base class's copy constructor in an initialization list. Following is dem13-2.cpp, which illustrates how to code a copy constructor.

NOTE 13.5—THE COPY CONSTRUCTOR IN A DERIVED CLASS

- The copy constructor of a derived class should explicitly call the copy constructor of its base class.
- Call the base class's copy constructor in an initialization list.

```
//dem13-2.cpp

//This program illustrates the copy constructor in a derived class

#include <iostream.h>

using namespace std;

class Test_Class
{
  protected:
    int n;

  public:
    Test_Class(int i = 0); //One-argument constructor
    Test_Class(const Test_Class&); //Copy constructor
    ~Test_Class();
};

Test_Class::Test_Class(int i) : n(i)
{
  cout << "\nTest_Class Constructor Executed: Data member initialized to "
       << n << endl;
}

Test_Class::Test_Class(const Test_Class& tc_r) : n(tc_r.n)
```

```
{
   cout << "\n\nTest_Class Copy Constructor Executed: "
        << "Data member initialized to " << n;
}

Test_Class::~Test_Class()
{
   cout << "\n\nTest_Class Destructor Executed for object with data member "
        << n;
}

class Derived_Test_Class : public Test_Class
{
   protected:
     int m;

   public:
     Derived_Test_Class(int j = 0);
     Derived_Test_Class(const Derived_Test_Class&);
     ~Derived_Test_Class();
};

Derived_Test_Class::Derived_Test_Class(int j) : Test_Class(j+1), m(j)
{
   cout << "\nDerived_Test_Class Constructor Executed: "
        << "Data member initialized to "
        << m;
}

Derived_Test_Class::Derived_Test_Class(const Derived_Test_Class& dtc_r)
                         : Test_Class(dtc_r), m(dtc_r.m)
{
   cout << "\n\nDerived_Test_Class Copy Constructor Executed: "
        << "Data member initialized to " << m;
}

Derived_Test_Class::~Derived_Test_Class()
{
   cout << "\n\nDerived_Test_Class Destructor Executed "
        << "for object with data member "
        << m;
}

int main()
{
   Derived_Test_Class dtc_object1(7);
   Derived_Test_Class dtc_object2 = dtc_object1;

   return 0;
}
```

Program Output

```
Test_Class Constructor Executed: Data member initialized to 8

Derived_Test_Class Constructor Executed: Data member initialized to 7.

Test_Class Copy Constructor Executed: Data member initialized to 8

Derived_Test_Class Copy Constructor Executed: Data member initialized to 7

Derived_Test_Class Destructor Executed for object with data member 7

Test_Class Destructor Executed for object with data member 8

Derived_Test_Class Destructor Executed for object with data member 7

Test_Class Destructor Executed for object with data member 8
```

The code for the copy constructors is similar to the code for the constructors. Note that in the definition of the copy constructor for `Test_Class` we use the expression `n(tc_r.n)` in the initialization list. This initializes the `n` data member of the object being initialized to the value of the `n` data member of the object that is on the right side of the initialization. The definition of the copy constructor for `Derived_Test_Class` calls the copy constructor, `Test_Class(dtc_r)`, in its initialization list, and initializes the `m` data member of the object being initialized to the value of the `m` data member of the right side of the initialization, `m(dtc_r.m)`.

Once again note the order of execution of the constructors and destructors. The program first declares the `Derived_Test_Class` object `dtc_object1`. Therefore, the constructor for `Test_Class` executes first, followed by the execution of the constructor for `Derived_Test_Class`. Next, the program declares and initializes the `Derived_Test_Class` object `dtc_object2`. Since the object is initialized, the copy constructor is used. Just as in the case for the ordinary constructor, the copy constructor for the base class executes first. We see that the copy constructor for `Test_Class` executes first, followed by the execution of the copy constructor for `Derived_Test_Class`.

When the program ends, the destructors are invoked for the objects in the reverse order of object creation. First the destructor for `dtc_object2` executes, which in turn automatically executes the destructor for the base class `Test_Class`. The destructors for `dtc_object1` execute in a similar manner.

EXERCISES 13.1

Use the following class declarations to answer Exercises 1–16.

```
class Class_A
{
  private:
```

```cpp
    int A_private;
  protected:
    int A_protected;
  public:
    Class_A(int, int);
    void A_Pub_Func();
};

class Class_B : public Class_A
{
  private:
    int B_private;
  protected:
    int B_protected;
  public:
    Class_B(int, int);
    void B_Pub_Func();
};

class Class_C : private Class_A
{
  private:
    int C_private;
  protected:
    int C_protected;
  public:
    Class_C(int, int);
    void C_Pub_Func();
};

class Class_D : public Class_B
{
  private:
    int D_private;
  protected:
    int D_protected;
  public:
    Class_D(int, int);
    void D_Pub_Func();
};

class Class_E : public Class_C
{
  private:
    int E_private;
  protected:
    int E_protected;
  public:
    Class_E(int, int);
    void E_Pub_Func();
};
```

1. Draw the class hierarchy diagram for the classes.
2. Which classes are directly derived from Class_A?
3. Which classes are indirectly derived from Class_A?
4. Which classes can you call base classes?
5. Using Table 13.1 on page 659, list all the private, protected, and public members of Class_B, including those inherited from the base class.
6. Using Table 13.1, list all the private, protected, and public members of Class_C, including those inherited from the base class.
7. Using Table 13.3, list all the private, protected, and public members of Class_D, including those inherited from the base class.
8. Using Table 13.1, list all the private, protected, and public members of Class_E, including those inherited from the base class.
9. Write the code for the two-argument constructor for Class_A. The constructor should assign its first argument to the class's private data member and the second argument to its protected data member.
10. Write the code for the two-argument constructor for Class_B. The constructor should assign its first argument to the class's private data member and the second argument to its protected data member. Pass the same two arguments to the base class constructor using an initialization list.
11. Write the code for the two-argument constructor for Class_C. The constructor should assign its first argument to the class's private data member and the second argument to its protected data member. Pass the same two arguments to the base class constructor using an initialization list.
12. Write the code for the two-argument constructor for Class_D. The constructor should assign its first argument to the class's private data member and the second argument to its protected data member. Pass the same two arguments to the base class constructor using an initialization list.
13. Write the code for the two-argument constructor for Class_E. The constructor should assign its first argument to the class's private data member and the second argument to its protected data member. Pass the same two arguments to the base class constructor using an initialization list.

Assume the constructors of Exercises 9–13 and the following declarations, which are made in main().

```
Class_A a_object(1,1);
Class_B b_object(2,2);
Class_C c_object(3,3);
Class_D d_object(4,4);
Class_E e_object(5,5);
```

14. List the values of all the data members of a_object, b_object, c_object, d_object, and e_object.
15. Code a destructor for each of Class_A, Class_B, Class_C, Class_D, and Class_E.

16. Code a copy constructor for each of `Class_A`, `Class_B`, `Class_C`, `Class_D`, and `Class_E`

17. Write class declarations for the classes depicted in Figure 13.2. Choose how each class should be derived from its base class (`public` or `private`) based on how you think that the class data members should be accessible. Code only the data members of each class.

EXPERIMENTS 13.1

1. In dem13-1.cpp, remove the call `Test_Class(j+1)` from the initialization list of the constructor of Derived_Test_Class. Compile, execute, and test the resulting program. What are the results?

2. In dem13-2.cpp., remove the call `Test_Class(dtc_r)` from the initialization list of the copy constructor of Derived_Test_Class. Compile, execute, and test the resulting program. What are the results?

PROGRAMMING PROBLEMS 13.1

1. A Web page is one of several types of document that can constitute a Web site. Code a class `Document` from which you should derive the `WebPage` class of previous programming problems. The `Document` class should have a `url` member, which is a character pointer that represents the URL of the document, and the integer member `downloads`. Since `url` and `downloads` are members of `Document`, they and all associated functions should be removed from the `WebPage` class and placed into the `Document` class. In addition to `WebPage`, derive from `Document` the classes `DataFile` and `MultimediaFile`. The class `DataFile` should contain the integer member `num_records`, which represents the number of data records in the file, and the integer data member `record_size`, which represents the size in bytes of each record in the file. The class `MultimediaFile` should contain the integer member `file_type`, which represents the type of multimedia file, and the integer member `size`, which represents the size in KB of the file. Code all appropriate constructors, copy constructors, and destructors for the classes. Code a function `main()` to test the classes. Make sure to create objects of all types.

2. An `OilTank` is just one of several types of storage tanks that can be maintained at a storage facility. Code a class `StorageTank` from which you should derive the class `OilTank` of previous programming problems. `StorageTank` should have two data members: a character pointer `company_name`, which represents the name of the company that owns the tank, and a five-character array `id_no[]`, which represents the tank number. `OilTank` will inherit these data members, so you should remove the `company_name` and `id_no` from the class declaration of `OilTank`. The functions `Get_Name()` and `Get_ID()` should now be members of `StorageTank`. Also derive the class `GasTank` from `StorageTank`. A `GasTank` object represents a tank that stores natural gas. `GasTank` should contain the double data member `volume`, which represents the volume of the tank in cubic feet, and the double data member `contents`, which

represents the current volume of gas in the tank. GasTank should also have an Add() and a Remove() function. Code all appropriate constructors, copy constructors, and destructors for the classes. Code a function main() to test the classes. Make sure to create objects of all types.

3. The VehicleService class of previous programming problems was not very specific as to the type of vehicle being serviced. Different types of vehicles might be serviced according to different rate schedules. Change each of Set_Parts() and Set_Hours() member functions so that it only sets the value of the corresponding data member to the argument of the function. Neither function should change the value of the total cost of service. Derive from the classes PrivateVehicle and Truck from VehicleService. PrivateVehicle should have no additional data members. Truck should have an integer data member, num_axles, which represents the number of axles on the truck. Code all appropriate constructors, copy constructors, and destructors for the classes. Code a function main() to test the classes. Make sure to create objects of all types.

4. There are several types of rooms in a hotel. The HotelRoom class of previous programming problems was not specific as to the type of room. Assume that a hotel has guest rooms and meeting rooms. Modify the HotelRoom class as follows: Remove the capacity and status data members and associated member functions. Change the class's constructor, copy constructor, and destructor accordingly. Derive from the classes GuestRoom and MeetingRoom from HotelRoom. GuestRoom contains the following data members: the integer data member capacity, which represents the maximum number of guests that can occupy the room; the integer data member status, which represents the number of guests in the room (0 if unoccupied); and the integer data member days, which represents the number of days the guest occupies the room. MeetingRoom has the integer data member seats, which represents the number of seats in the room, and the integer data member status (1 if the room is booked for a meeting, 0 otherwise). Code all appropriate constructors, copy constructors, and destructors for the classes. Code a function main() to test the classes. Make sure to create objects of all types.

13.2 Functions in Class Hierarchies

According to Note 13.3, all functions are inherited except constructors, copy constructors, destructors, overloaded operators, and friend functions. This section discusses inherited functions.

Inheriting a Function

Suppose Test_Class contains the following member function Get_Value().

```
int Test_Class::Get_Value()
{
    return n;
}
```

Get_Value() is inherited by the derived class Derived_Test_Class. Therefore, we can apply Get_Value() to any Derived_Test_Class object as follows.

```
Derived_Test_Class dtc_object(7);

cout << "\n\nThe value returned by Get_Value() is "

        << dtc_object.Get_Value();
```

Programming Pointers

When a function is applied to an object of a certain class, the compiler checks to see if the function is a member function of that class. If the function is a class member, the compiler applies that function to the object. If the function is not a class member, the compiler checks to see if the function is a member of a base class (if there is one) of the class. If the function is a member of the class's base class, it applies that function to the object, and so on. In our case, the compiler sees that the function is not a member of Derived_Test_Class and so looks in the base class Test_Class. Since Get_Value() is a member function of Test_Class, the compiler applies the base class's Get_Value() function to dtc_object. It makes sense to do this because by means of inheritance, dtc_object is also a Test_Class object. The object dtc_object has an m data member of 7 and an n data member of 8. The previous cout statement will display.

```
The value returned by Get_Value() is 8
```

The program dem13-3.cpp verifies this.

```
//dem13-3.cpp

//This program illustrates how a function is inherited

#include <iostream.h>

using namespace std;

class Test_Class
{
  protected:
    int n;

  public:
      Test_Class(int i = 0); //One-argument constructor
      ~Test_Class();
      int Get_Value();
};
```

```
Test_Class::Test_Class(int i) : n(i)
{
     cout << "\nTest_Class Constructor Executed: Data member initialized to "
          << n << endl << endl;
}

Test_Class::~Test_Class()
{
   cout << "\n\nTest_Class Destructor Executed for object with data member "
          << n;
}

int Test_Class::Get_Value()
{
   return n;
}

class Derived_Test_Class : public Test_Class
{
   protected:
        int m;

   public:
        Derived_Test_Class(int j = 0);
        ~Derived_Test_Class();
};

Derived_Test_Class::Derived_Test_Class(int j) : Test_Class(j+1), m(j)
{
     cout << "\n\nDerived_Test_Class Constructor Executed: "
          << "Data member initialized to "
          << m;
}

Derived_Test_Class::~Derived_Test_Class()
{
   cout << "\n\n\nDerived_Test_Class Destructor Executed "
          << "for object with data member "
          << m;
}

int main()
{
   Derived_Test_Class dtc_object(7);
   cout << "\n\nThe value returned by Get_Value() is "
          << dtc_object.Get_Value();

   return 0;
}
```

Program Output

```
Test_Class Constructor Executed: Data member initialized to 8


Derived_Test_Class Constructor Executed: Data member initialized to 7

The value returned by Get_Value() is 8


Derived_Test_Class Destructor Executed for object with data member 7

Test_Class Destructor Executed for object with data member 8
```

Function Overriding

What happens if `Derived_Test_Class` and `Test_Class` have their own `Get_Value()` function? Consider the following program in which we have added a `Get_Value()` function to *both* `Test_Class` and `Derived_Test_Class`.

```cpp
//dem13-4.cpp

//This program illustrates the function overriding

#include <iostream.h>

using namespace std;

class Test_Class
{
  protected:
    int n;

  public:
    Test_Class(int i = 0); //One-argument constructor
    Test_Class(Test_Class&); //Copy constructor
    ~Test_Class();
    int Get_Value();
};

Test_Class::Test_Class(int i) : n(i)
{
  cout << "\nTest_Class Constructor Executed: Data member initialized to "
       << n << endl;
}

Test_Class::Test_Class(Test_Class& tc_r) : n(tc_r.n)
{
  cout << "\n\nTest_Class Copy constructor executed: "
```

```
            << "Data member initialized to " << n;
}

Test_Class::~Test_Class()
{
  cout << "\n\nTest_Class Destructor Executed for object with data member "
       << n;
}

inline int Test_Class::Get_Value()
{
  return n;
}

class Derived_Test_Class : public Test_Class
{
  protected:
    int m;

  public:
    Derived_Test_Class(int j = 0);
    Derived_Test_Class(Derived_Test_Class&);
    ~Derived_Test_Class();
    int Get_Value();
};

Derived_Test_Class::Derived_Test_Class(int j) : Test_Class(j+1), m(j)
{
  cout << "\nDerived_Test_Class Constructor Executed: "
       << "Data member initialized to "
       << m;
}

Derived_Test_Class::Derived_Test_Class(Derived_Test_Class& dtc_r)
                      : Test_Class(dtc_r), m(dtc_r.m)
{
  cout << "\n\nDerived_Test_Class Copy constructor executed: "
       << "Data member initialized to " << m;
}

Derived_Test_Class::~Derived_Test_Class()
{
  cout << "\n\nDerived_Test_Class Destructor Executed "
       << "for object with data member "
       << m;
}

inline int Derived_Test_Class::Get_Value()
{
  return m;
}
```

```
int main()
{
  Test_Class tc_object(3);
  Derived_Test_Class dtc_object(7);

  cout << "\n\nThe n value of the Test_Class object is "
       << tc_object.Get_Value();

  cout << "\n\nThe m value of the Derived_Test_Class object is "
       << dtc_object.Get_Value();

  return 0;
}
```

Program Output

```
Test_Class Constructor Executed: Data member initialized to 3

Test_Class Constructor Executed: Data member initialized to 8

Derived_Test_Class Constructor Executed: Data member initialized to 7

The n value of the Test_Class object is 3

The m value of the Derived_Test_Class object is 7

Derived_Test_Class Destructor Executed for object with data member 7

Test_Class Destructor Executed for object with data member 8

Test_Class Destructor Executed for object with data member 3
```

Programming
Pointers

In `main()`, we apply `Get_Value()` to two objects in different classes. The C++ compiler knows which `Get_Value()` function to use by the object to which the function is applied. In the first case, `Get_Value()` is applied to a `Test_Class` object. Therefore, the `Get_Value()` function from `Test_Class` is used. In the second case, `Get_Value()` is applied to a `Derived_Test_Class` object. Therefore, the `Get_Value()` function from `Derived_Test_Class` is used. This is known as **function overriding**—when a member function is applied to an object in a derived class, the function in the derived class overrides the function of the same name and signature (i.e. same number and types of arguments) in the base class.

If the function names are the same and the signatures are different, overriding does not take place. For example, suppose `Derive_Test_Class`'s `Get_Value()` function is defined as follows.

```
int Get_Value(int i)
{
  return m + i;
}
```

The function call `dtc_object.Get_Value()` uses the `Get_Value()` function of `Test_Class` and the function call `dtc_object.Get_Value(4)` uses the `Get_Value()` function of `Derived_Test_Class`. See Experiment 1.

Using the Scope Resolution Operator

Suppose again that `Test_Class` and `Derived_Test_Class` have their own `Get_Value()` function and that we want to apply the `Get_Value()` function of the base class to a `Derived_Test_Class` object in order to access its n data member.

To apply the base class's `Get_Value()` function to an object in the derived class, you must qualify the name of the function with the name of the class followed by the scope resolution operator `::`. Thus, the expression `dtc_object.Test_Class::Get_Value()` applies `Test_Class`'s `Get_Value()` function to `dtc_object`. The scope resolution operator can also be used to access a global variable when there is a local variable of the same name. See Experiment 2.

The following program, dem13-5.cpp, illustrates this use of the scope resolution operator.

```
//dem13-5.cpp

//This program illustrates the scope resolution operator

#include <iostream.h>

using namespace std;

class Test_Class
{
  protected:
    int n;

  public:
    Test_Class(int i = 0); //One-argument constructor
    Test_Class(const Test_Class&); //Copy constructor
    ~Test_Class();
    int Get_Value();
};

Test_Class::Test_Class(int i) : n(i)
{
  cout << "\nTest_Class Constructor Executed: Data member initialized to "
      << n << endl;
}

Test_Class::Test_Class(const Test_Class& tc_r) : n(tc_r.n)
{
  cout << "\n\nTest_Class Copy constructor executed: "
      << "Data member initialized to " << n;
}
```

```
Test_Class::~Test_Class()
{
  cout << "\n\nTest_Class Destructor Executed for object with data member "
       << n;
}


inline int Test_Class::Get_Value()
{
  return n;
}


class Derived_Test_Class : public Test_Class
{
  protected:
    int m;

  public:
    Derived_Test_Class(int j = 0);
    Derived_Test_Class(const Derived_Test_Class&);
    ~Derived_Test_Class();
    int Get_Value();
};

Derived_Test_Class::Derived_Test_Class(int j) : Test_Class(j+1), m(j)
{
  cout << "\nDerived_Test_Class Constructor Executed: "
       << "Data member initialized to "
       << m;
}


Derived_Test_Class::Derived_Test_Class(const Derived_Test_Class& dtc_r)
                                 : Test_Class(dtc_r), m(dtc_r.m)
{
  cout << "\n\nDerived_Test_Class Copy Constructor Executed: "
       << "Data member initialized to " << m;
}


Derived_Test_Class::~Derived_Test_Class()
{
  cout << "\n\nDerived_Test_Class Destructor Executed "
       << "for object with data member "
       << m;
}


inline int Derived_Test_Class::Get_Value()
{
  return m;
}


int main()
```

```
{
  Test_Class tc_object(3);
  Derived_Test_Class dtc_object(7);

  cout << "\n\nThe n value of the Test_Class object is "
       << tc_object.Get_Value();

  cout << "\n\nThe m value of the Derived_Test_Class object is "
       << dtc_object.Get_Value();

  cout << "\n\nThe n value of the Derived_Test_Class object is "
       << dtc_object.Test_Class::Get_Value();

  return 0;
}
```

Program Output

```
Test_Class Constructor Executed: Data member initialized to 3

Test_Class Constructor Executed: Data member initialized to 8

Derived_Test_Class Constructor Executed: Data member initialized to 7

The n value of the Test_Class object is 3

The m value of the Derived_Test_Class object is 7

The n value of the Derived_Test_Class object is 8

Derived_Test_Class Destructor Executed for object with data member 7

Test_Class Destructor Executed for object with data member 8

Test_Class Destructor Executed for object with data member 3
```

Note 13.6 summarizes the results of this section.

NOTE 13.6—FUNCTIONS IN A CLASS HIERARCHY

- A base class member function is inherited by all classes derived from it either directly or indirectly.
- If a derived class contains a function of the same name and signature as a function of the base class, the derived class's version of the function overrides the base class's version.
- To apply an overridden base class member function to a derived class object, qualify the function name with the base class name followed by the scope resolution operator : :.

EXERCISES 13.2

Use the following declarations to answer Exercises 1–7. They are the same classes used in Exercises 13.1 with the code provided for the `public` functions.

```
class Class_A
{
  private:
    int A_private;
  protected:
    int A_protected;
  public:
    Class_A(int, int);
    void A_Pub_Func() {cout << "\nClass_A's function";}
};

class Class_B : public Class_A
{
  private:
    int B_private;
  protected:
    int B_protected;
  public:
    Class_B(int, int);
    void B_Pub_Func(){cout << "\nClass_B's function";}
    void A_Pub_Func(){cout << "\nClass_B' A function";}
};

class Class_C : private Class_A
{
  private:
    int C_private;
  protected:
    int C_protected;
  public:
    Class_C(int, int);
    void C_Pub_Func(){cout << "\nClass_C's function";}
};

class Class_D : public Class_B
{
  private:
    int D_private;
  protected:
    int D_protected;
  public:
    Class_D(int, int);
    void D_Pub_Func(){cout << "\nClass_D's function";}
    void A_Pub_Func(){cout << "\nClass_D's A fucntion";}
};
```

```
class Class_E : public Class_C
{
  private:
    int E_private;
  protected:
    int E_protected;
  public:
    Class_E(int, int);
    void E_Pub_Func(){cout << "\nClass_E's function";}
};
```

Now assume that the following declarations have been made in `main()`.

```
Class_A a_object(1,1);
Class_B b_object(2,2);
Class_C c_object(3,3);
Class_D d_object(4,4);
Class_E e_object(5,5);
```

Which of the statements in Exercises 1–6 are legal? For those that are legal, state what each will display.

1. `a_object.A_Pub_Func();`
2. `b_object.A_Pub_Func();`
3. `d_object.A_Pub_Func();`
4. `b_object.C_pub_Func();`
5. `e_object.C_Pub_Func();`
6. `e_object.A_Pub_Func();`
7. How would you apply `Class_A`'s `A_Pub_Func()` to `b_object`? to `d_object`?

EXPERIMENTS 13.2

1. In dem13-4.cpp, redefine `Derived_test_Class`'s `Get_Value()` as follows.

   ```
   int Get_Value(int i){return m + i;}
   ```

   Include in `main()` the following statements:

   ```
   Derived_Test_Class dtc_object(5);

   cout << dtc_object.Get_Value() << endl;

   cout << dtc_object.Get_Value(4) << endl;
   ```

   What do the two `cout` statements display?

2. The scope resolution operator can be used to access a global variable when there is a local variable of the same name. For example, consider the following declarations. In the function `Func()`, `::n` refers to the global variable n.

```
int n = 6;

void Func()
{
  int n = 17;

  cout << "The local n = " << n << endl;
  cout << "The global n = " << ::n << endl;
}
```

Write a program that uses these declarations and tests the member function `Func()`.

PROGRAMMING PROBLEMS 13.2

1. In the `Document` class hierarchy of Programming Problem 1 in Section 13.1, do the following: Code an `Activity()` function for class `DataFile` that returns the number of bytes downloaded (`downloads` multiplied by `num_records` multiplied by `record_size`.) Code an `Activity()` function for class `Multimedia-File` that returns the number of bytes downloaded (`downloads` multiplied by the `size`). For each of `WebPage`, `DataFile`, and `MultimediaFile`, code an appropriate `Display()` function, which displays the data members (even the inherited ones) in a nicely formatted way. Write a `main()` in which you create objects from each of the three classes and apply the `Activity()` and `Display()` functions.

2. In the `StorageTank` class hierarchy of Programming Problem 2, Section 13.1, do the following: Code a `Display()` function for each of the classes `OilTank` and `GasTank` that displays the data members of the class (including the inherited ones) in an appropriately formatted way. Code a `Remainder()` function for `OilTank`, which returns the `capacity` minus the `contents` of a tank. Code a `Remainder()` function for `GasTank` that returns the `volume` minus the `contents` of a tank. Write a `main()` in which you create objects from each class and apply the `Display()` and `Remainder()` functions.

3. Using the `VehicleService` class hierarchy of Programming Problem 3, Section 13.1, do the following: `PrivateVehicle` should have a member function, `CalculateBill()`, that returns a `double` and has no arguments. The function should calculate the bill as follows: the number of hours multiplied by 70.00, plus the cost of parts. `Truck` should also have a `CalculateBill()` function that computes the bill as follows: the number of hours multiplied by 85.00, plus the cost of parts, plus the number of axles multiplied by 100.00. Code a `Display()` function for each of `PrivateVehicle` and `Truck`, which displays the data members of the class (including the inherited ones) in an appropriately formatted way. Code a `main()` in which you create objects of each type. Compute the bill for each object and display each object's information.

4. Using the `HotelRoom` class hierarchy of Programming Problem 4, Section 13.1, do the following: `GuestRoom` contains the function `CalculateBill()`, which returns the amount of the guest's bill. The bill is calculated as follows: the room rate

(this is inherited from `HotelRoom`) multiplied by the number of days of the stay, multiplied by the status (which represents the number of guests and is also inherited from `HotelRoom`). `MeetingRoom` also contains the function `CalculateBill()`, which returns the amount of the bill for renting the room for one day. The function calculates the bill as follows: the number of seats multiplied by 10.00, plus 500.00. Code a `Display()` function for each of `GuestRoom` and `MeetingRoom`, which displays the data members of the class (including the inherited ones) in an appropriately formatted way. Code a `main()` in which you create objects of each type. Compute the bill for each object and display each object's information.

13.3 Polymorphism

In a class hierarchy, several classes may contain their own version of a function. When using pointers to access objects, polymorphism allows the data type of the object to determine which of these functions is applied.

The Class Hierarchy

To focus on the important concepts in this section, we shall use a very simple class hierarchy based on familiar geometric figures and their areas. Suppose we are developing a drawing application that needs to define and manipulate simple geometric figures and compute their areas. The figures are rectangles, circles, and trapezoids. Since these are geometric shapes, we decide to derive them from the class `Shape`. Figure 13.6 shows the class hierarchy. The private data members of the class are to the right of each class in the figure. Each class will have a constructor, a destructor, and a function, `Area()`, that computes the area of the figure using the appropriate formula.

Problem: Suppose we want to enable the user to create a series of shapes of his or her own choosing. The user can first decide to create a rectangle of a certain size, then a circle with a certain radius, and so on. After the user has created the shapes, we want the program to display the areas of all the figures. How can we do this? The way you might think of approaching the problem is to create an array of shapes. However, all the elements in an array must be of the same type. We cannot place a rectangle object and a circle object into the same array because they are of different data types. The answer, as we shall see, is to use an array of `Shape` pointers and to employ the concept of polymorphism.

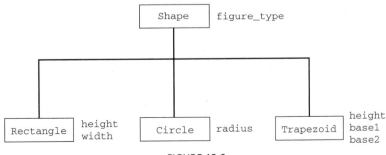

FIGURE 13.6

Defining the Classes

Here are the class declarations for the classes `Shape`, `Rectangle`, `Circle`, and `Trapezoid`. We define all functions in the class declarations for simplicity.

```
class Shape
{
  protected:
        const char* figure_type;
  public:
        Shape(const char* ft = "Default Figure") : figure_type(ft)
              {cout << "\n\nShape Constructor";}
        const char* Get_Type() {return figure_type;}
        ~Shape() {cout << "\n\nShape Destructor";}
        double Area() {return 0.0;}
};


class Rectangle : public Shape
{
  protected:
        double height, width;
  public:
        Rectangle(double h, double w): Shape("Rectangle"), height(h),width(w)
              {cout << "\nRectangle Constructor";}
        ~Rectangle() {cout << "\nRectangle Destructor";}
        double Area() {return height * width;}
};


class Circle : public Shape
{
  protected:
        double radius;
  public:
        Circle(double r) : Shape("Circle"), radius(r)
              {cout << "\n\nCircle Constructor";}
        ~Circle() {cout << "\n\nCircle Destructor";}
        double Area() {return 3.1416 * radius * radius;}
};


class Trapezoid : public Shape
{
  protected:
        double base1, base2, height;
  public:
        Trapezoid(double b1, double b2, double h)
                : Shape("Trapezoid"), base1(b1), base2(b2), height(h)
              {cout << "\n\nTrapezoid Constructor";}
        ~Trapezoid() {cout << "Trapezoid Destructor";}
        double Area() {return 0.5 * height * (base1 + base2);}
};
```

The base class `Shape` has one data member, `figure_type`, which points to the name of the type of figure (`Rectangle`, `Circle`, or `Trapezoid`). Since that name is a string constant, the data type of `figure_type` is `const char*`. We also include an accessor function `Get_Type()` that returns a pointer to the figure name. Both `figure_type` and `Get_Type()` are inherited by the `Rectangle`, `Circle`, and `Trapezoid` classes. The constructors perform initialization in their initialization lists. The body of each constructor and destructor displays an identification message.

Note that in the initialization list for the `Shape` constructor is `figure_type(ft)`. An entry in an initialization list is equivalent to an initialization. Therefore, `figure_type(ft)` is equivalent to the following where *a quoted string* represents a string constant such as the default value "Default Figure".

```
const char* figure_type = a quoted string;
```

We define a dummy `Area()` function in the `Shape` class that returns the value zero. Each of the other classes is derived publicly from class `Shape`. The constructors for `Rectangle`, `Circle`, and `Trapezoid` call the constructor for the base class `Shape` and pass to that constructor the name of the object being created. The `Area()` function for each class returns the area based on the formula for the area of that shape.

Pointers in a Class Hierarchy

We can declare a `Rectangle` pointer, a `Circle` pointer, or a `Trapezoid` pointer and have each point to an object of the appropriate type. For example, we could make the following declarations.

```
Rectangle r1(3, 5);
Circle c1(7);
Trapezoid t1(4, 2, 6);

Rectangle* r_p = &r1;
Circle* c_p = &c1;
Trapezoid* t_p = &t1;
```

A `Shape` pointer can point to a `Rectangle` object, a `Circle` object, or a `Trapezoid` object because by inheritance, each of these is a `Shape` object. Thus, continuing from the previous declarations, the following are legal.

```
Shape* s_p1;
Shape* s_p2;
Shape* s_p3;

s_p1 = &r1;
s_p2 = &c1;
s_p3 = &t1;
```

Although s_p1, s_p2, and s_p3 are Shape pointers, they are allowed to point to objects in any derived class. Note, however, that the converse is not true. That is, a Rectangle pointer (or a Circle pointer or Trapezoid pointer) cannot point to a Shape object.

NOTE 13.7—BASE CLASS POINTERS

- In a class hierarchy, a base class pointer can point to an object of any class derived (either directly or indirectly) from the base class.
- The converse is not true: A derived class pointer cannot point to a base class object.

The fact that a base class pointer can point to an object from a derived class brings up an interesting question. Using the previous declarations and assignments, suppose we now code the following.

```
cout    << "\nThe area of the rectangle is " << s_p1 -> Area();
```

The pointer s_p1 is a Shape pointer, but it points to a Rectangle object. Whose Area() function will the previous statement execute: that of the Rectangle class or that of the base class Shape? The output of the following program answers the question.

```
//dem13-6.cpp

//This program demonstrates the use of pointers and functions
//in a class hierarchy.

#include <iostream.h>
#include <iomanip.h>

using namespace std;

class Shape
{
  protected:
      const char* figure_type;
  public:
      Shape(const char* ft = "Default Figure") : figure_type(ft)
          {cout << "\n\nShape Constructor";}
      const char* Get_Type() {return figure_type;}
      ~Shape() {cout << "\n\nShape Destructor";}
      double Area() {return 0.0;}
};

class Rectangle : public Shape
{
  protected:
      double height, width;
```

```
    public:
        Rectangle(double h, double w): Shape("Rectangle"), height(h),width(w)
             {cout << "\nRectangle Constructor";}
        ~Rectangle() {cout << "\nRectangle Destructor";}
        double Area() {return height * width;}
};

class Circle : public Shape
{
  protected:
        double radius;
  public:
        Circle(double r) : Shape("Circle"), radius(r)
             {cout << "\n\nCircle Constructor";}
        ~Circle() {cout << "\n\nCircle Destructor";}
        double Area() {return 3.1416 * radius * radius;}
};

class Trapezoid : public Shape
{
  protected:
        double base1, base2, height;
  public:
        Trapezoid(double b1, double b2, double h)
              : Shape("Trapezoid"), base1(b1), base2(b2), height(h)
             {cout << "\n\nTrapezoid Constructor";}
        ~Trapezoid() {cout << "Trapezoid Destructor";}
        double Area() {return 0.5 * height * (base1 + base2);}
};

int main()
{
  cout << setprecision(4)
       << setiosflags(ios::fixed)
       << setiosflags(ios::showpoint);

  Shape* s_p1;
  Circle* c_p1;

  Circle c1(5);

  s_p1 = &c1;  //Shape pointer points to a Circle object

  c_p1 = &c1;  //Circle pointer points to a Circle object

  cout << "\n\nArea() applied through Circle pointer: " << c_p1 -> Area();

  cout << "\n\nArea() applied through Shape pointer: " << s_p1 -> Area();

  return 0;
}
```

Program Output

```
Shape Constructor.

Circle Constructor.

Area() applied through Circle pointer: 78.5400

Area() applied through Shape pointer: 0.0000

Circle Destructor.

Shape Destructor.
```

From the two lines displayed by `cout` in `main()`, we see that the `Area()` function applied to the `Circle` object through the `Circle` pointer yields the correct area of 78.5400. However, the `Area()` function that is applied to the `Circle` object through the `Shape` pointer is the `Area()` function from the `Shape` class. Although `s_p1` points to a `Circle` object, the base class function is invoked when it is applied to the object through a base class pointer. Function overriding does not work in this case.

Virtual Functions and Polymorphism

Programming
Pointers

The concept of **polymorphism** (literally, "many forms") extends function overriding to the case of objects in a derived class accessed through a base class pointer. To implement polymorphism, the function that is to be overridden must be declared to be `virtual`. The keyword `virtual` must appear in the declaration of the function in the base class. The following program demonstrates the difference that declaring `Area()` as a `virtual` function makes to the output of the previous program.

```cpp
//dem13-7.cpp

//This program demonstrates the use of a virtual function
//in a class hierarchy.

#include <iostream.h>
#include <iomanip.h>

using namespace std;

class Shape
{
  protected:
      const char* figure_type;
  public:
      Shape(const char* ft = "Default Figure") : figure_type(ft)
          {cout << "\n\nShape Constructor";}
```

```
        const char* Get_Type() {return figure_type;}
        ~Shape() {cout << "\n\nShape Destructor";}
        virtual double Area() {return 0.0;}          //virtual function
};

class Rectangle : public Shape
{
  protected:
    double height, width;
  public:
    Rectangle(double h, double w): Shape("Rectangle"), height(h),width(w)
        {cout << "\nRectangle Constructor";}
    ~Rectangle() {cout << "\nRectangle Destructor";}
    double Area() {return height * width;}
};

class Circle : public Shape
{
  protected:
      double radius;
  public:
      Circle(double r) : Shape("Circle"), radius(r)
          {cout << "\n\nCircle Constructor";}
      ~Circle() {cout << "\n\nCircle Destructor";}
      double Area() {return 3.1416 * radius * radius;}
};

class Trapezoid : public Shape
{
  protected:
      double base1, base2, height;
  public:
      Trapezoid(double b1, double b2, double h)
          : Shape("Trapezoid"), base1(b1), base2(b2), height(h)
            {cout << "\n\nTrapezoid Constructor";}
      ~Trapezoid() {cout << "Trapezoid Destructor";}
      double Area() {return 0.5 * height * (base1 + base2);}
};

int main()
{
  cout << setprecision(4)
       << setiosflags(ios::fixed)
       << setiosflags(ios::showpoint);

  Shape* s_p1;
  Circle* c_p1;

  Circle c1(5);

  s_p1 = &c1; //Legal pointer assignment
```

```
    c_p1 = &c1;

    cout << "\n\nArea() applied through Circle pointer: " << c_p1 -> Area();

    cout << "\n\nArea() applied through Shape pointer: " << s_p1 -> Area();

    return 0;
}
```

Program Output

```
Shape Constructor.

Circle Constructor.

Area() applied through Circle pointer: 78.5400

Area() applied through Shape pointer: 78.5400

Circle Destructor.

Shape Destructor.
```

This time, the second `cout` statement executes the `Area()` function of the target of the `Shape` pointer `s_p1`. It does so because we declared the `Area()` function in the base class `Shape` as a `virtual` function.

Polymorphism allows the choice of function to depend on the data type of the target of the pointer rather than the data type of the pointer. For polymorphism to work, follow the guidelines of Note 13.8.

NOTE 13.8—POLYMORPHISM

Polymorphism allows the choice of function to depend on the data type of the target of the pointer rather than on the data type of the pointer.

- For polymorphism to work, objects in the class hierarchy must be accessed through pointers.
- Only class member functions can be `virtual`.
- For a function in the derived class to override a `virtual` function in the base class, the function in the derived class must have the same name and signature (number and type of arguments) as the base class function.
- A function in a derived class with the same name and signature as a `virtual` function in a base class is also `virtual`, whether or not the `virtual` keyword appears in its declaration. (Thus, the `Area()` functions in the derived classes in the previous program are also `virtual`.)

`virtual` Destructors

Now consider the following program, dem13-8.cpp, in which we have replaced the statically declared object `c1` of the previous program by a dynamically allocated object pointed to by `s_p1`.

```
//dem13-8.cpp

//This program demonstrates the incorrect use of destructors
//in a class hierarchy.

#include <iostream.h>
#include <iomanip.h>

using namespace std;

class Shape
{
  protected:
      const char* figure_type;
  public:
      Shape(const char* ft = "Default Figure") : figure_type(ft)
          {cout << "\n\nShape Constructor";}
      const char* Get_Type() {return figure_type;}
      ~Shape() {cout << "\n\nShape Destructor";}
      virtual double Area() {return 0.0;}
};

class Rectangle : public Shape
{
  protected:
      double height, width;
  public:
      Rectangle(double h, double w): Shape("Rectangle"), height(h),width(w)
          {cout << "\nRectangle Constructor";}
      ~Rectangle() {cout << "\nRectangle Destructor";}
      double Area() {return height * width;}
};

class Circle : public Shape
{
  protected:
      double radius;
  public:
      Circle(double r) : Shape("Circle"), radius(r)
          {cout << "\n\nCircle Constructor";}
      ~Circle() {cout << "\n\nCircle Destructor";}
      double Area() {return 3.1416 * radius * radius;}
};

class Trapezoid : public Shape
```

```
{
  protected:
      double base1, base2, height;
  public:
    Trapezoid(double b1, double b2, double h)
         : Shape("Trapezoid"), base1(b1), base2(b2), height(h)
           {cout << "\n\nTrapezoid Constructor";}
    ~Trapezoid() {cout << "Trapezoid Destructor";}
    double Area() {return 0.5 * height * (base1 + base2);}
};

int main()
{
  cout << setprecision(4)
       << setiosflags(ios::fixed)
       << setiosflags(ios::showpoint);

  Shape* s_p1 = new Circle (5);

  cout << "\n\nArea() applied through Shape pointer: " << s_p1 -> Area();

  delete s_p1;

  return 0;
}
```

Program Output

```
Shape Constructor.

Circle Constructor.

Area() applied through Shape pointer: 78.5400

Shape Destructor.
```

When the `delete` statement is executed for `s_p1`, which points to a `Circle` object, only the destructor for the base class executes. This is because the destructor is applied to the object through the pointer. Since the base class destructor is not declared as `virtual`, applying the destructor to the target of `s_p1` executes the base class destructor and not the destructor of the derived class.

To properly execute the destructors, that is, to execute the destructor for the derived class and then execute the destructor for the base class, make the destructor of the base class a `virtual` function.

NOTE 13.9—VIRTUAL DESTRUCTORS

To ensure the proper execution sequence of destructors for dynamically allocated objects in a class hierarchy, declare the base class destructor as a `virtual` function.

The following program, dem13-9.cpp uses `virtual` destructors.

```cpp
//dem13-9.cpp

//This program demonstrates the correct use of destructors
//in a class hierarchy.

#include <iostream.h>
#include <iomanip.h>

using namespace std;

class Shape
{
  protected:
      const char* figure_type;
  public:
      Shape(const char* ft = "Default Figure") : figure_type(ft)
          {cout << "\n\nShape Constructor".}
      const char* Get_Type() {return figure_type;}
      virtual ~Shape() {cout << "\n\nShape Destructor".}
      virtual double Area() {return 0.0;}
};

class Rectangle : public Shape
{
  protected:
      double height, width;
  public:
      Rectangle(double h, double w): Shape("Rectangle"), height(h),width(w)
          {cout << "\nRectangle Constructor".}
      virtual ~Rectangle() {cout << "\nRectangle Destructor".}
      double Area() {return height * width;}
};

class Circle : public Shape
{
  protected:
      double radius;
  public:
      Circle(double r) : Shape("Circle"), radius(r)
          {cout << "\n\nCircle Constructor".}
      virtual ~Circle() {cout << "\n\nCircle Destructor".}
      double Area() {return 3.1416 * radius * radius;}
};

class Trapezoid : public Shape
{
  protected:
      double base1, base2, height;
  public:
```

```
        Trapezoid(double b1, double b2, double h)
              : Shape("Trapezoid"), base1(b1), base2(b2), height(h)
              {cout << "\n\nTrapezoid Constructor".}
        virtual ~Trapezoid() {cout << "Trapezoid Destructor".}
        double Area() {return 0.5 * height * (base1 + base2);}
};

int main()
{
  cout << setprecision(4)
       << setiosflags(ios::fixed)
       << setiosflags(ios::showpoint);

  Shape* s_p1 = new Circle (5);

  cout << "\n\nArea() for the " << s_p1 -> Get_Type()
       << " applied through Shape pointer: " << s_p1 -> Area();

  delete s_p1;

  return 0;
}
```

Program Output

```
Shape Constructor.

Circle Constructor.

Area() for the Circle applied through Shape pointer: 78.5400.

Circle Destructor.

Shape Destructor.
```

Now the destructors for the target of s_p1 are executed correctly. The destructor for the derived class is executed first, and then the destructor for the base class is executed. Note that we have also used the accessor function Get_Type(), which is also applied through the pointer.

Putting Polymorphism to Work

The following program solves the problem that we posed at the beginning of this section and which we repeat here. Suppose we want to enable the user to create a series of shapes of his or her own choosing. The user can first choose to create a rectangle of a certain size, then a circle with a certain radius, and so on. After the user has created the shapes, we want the program to display the areas of all the figures. How can we do this? The answer lies in creating an array of Shape pointers and using polymorphism with the Area() function. The following program solves our problem.

```cpp
//dem13—10.cpp

//This program demonstrates the use of polymorphism

#include <iostream.h>
#include <iomanip.h>

using namespace std;

class Shape
{
  protected:
      const char* figure_type;
  public:
      Shape(const char* ft = "Default Figure") : figure_type(ft) {}
      const char* Get_Type() {return figure_type;}
      virtual ~Shape() {}
      virtual double Area() {return 0.0;}
};

class Rectangle : public Shape
{
  protected:
      double height, width;
  public:
      Rectangle(double h, double w)
                : Shape("Rectangle"), height(h), width(w){}
      virtual ~Rectangle() {}
      double Area() {return height * width;}
};

class Circle : public Shape
{
  protected:
      double radius;
  public:
      Circle(double r) : Shape("Circle"), radius(r){}
      virtual ~Circle() {}
      double Area() {return 3.1416 * radius * radius;}
};

class Trapezoid : public Shape
{
  protected:
      double base1, base2, height;
  public:
      Trapezoid(double b1, double b2, double h)
            : Shape("Trapezoid"), base1(b1), base2(b2), height(h){}
      virtual ~Trapezoid() {}
      double Area() {return 0.5 * height * (base1 + base2);}
};
```

```
Shape* Get_Shape();

int main()
{
  cout << setprecision(4)
       << setiosflags(ios::fixed)
       << setiosflags(ios::showpoint);

  const int num_shapes = 5;

  Shape* shapes[num_shapes];

  for (int i = 0; i < num_shapes; ++i)
      shapes[i] = Get_Shape();

  cout << endl;

  for (i = 0; i < num_shapes; ++i)
      cout << "\nThe area of the " << shapes[i] -> Get_Type() << " is "
           << shapes[i] -> Area();

  for (i = 0; i < num_shapes; ++i)
      delete shapes[i];

  return 0;
}

Shape* Get_Shape()
{
  Shape* s_p; //To be returned by the function

  double height,
         width,
         radius,
         base1,
         base2;

  cout << "\n\nEnter the number of the shape you want to create:";
  cout << "\n\nFor a Rectangle, enter 1";
  cout << "\n\nFor a Circle, enter 2";
  cout << "\n\nFor a Trapezoid, enter 3";

  cout << "\n\nPlease make your selection: ";

  int response;

  cin >> response;

  switch (response)
```

```
    {
        case 1:
            cout << "\n\nEnter the height of the rectangle: ";
            cin >> height;
            cout << "\n\nEnter the width of the rectangle: ";
            cin >> width;

            s_p = new Rectangle(height, width);

            break;

        case 2:
            cout << "\n\nEnter the radius of the circle: ";
            cin >> radius;

            s_p = new Circle(radius);

            break;

        case 3:
            cout << "\n\nEnter the first base of the trapezoid: ";
            cin >> base1;
            cout << "\n\nEnter the second base of the trapezoid: ";
            cin >> base2;
            cout << "\n\nEnter the height of the trapezoid: ";
            cin >> height;

            s_p = new Trapezoid(base1, base2, height);

            break;

        default:
            cout << "\n\nInvalid selection. Creating default object.";

            s_p = new Shape();

            break;
    }

    return s_p;
}
```

Program Output

```
Enter the number of the shape you want to create:

For a Rectangle, enter 1
For a Circle, enter 2
For a Trapezoid, enter 3

Please make your selection: 1
```

```
Enter the height of the rectangle: 3


Enter the width of the rectangle: 5


Enter the number of the shape you want to create:

For a Rectangle, enter 1
For a Circle, enter 2
For a Trapezoid, enter 3

Please make your selection: 2


Enter the radius of the circle: 5.6


Enter the number of the shape you want to create:


For a Rectangle, enter 1
For a Circle, enter 2
For a Trapezoid, enter 3

Please make your selection: 3


Enter the first base of the trapezoid: 7


Enter the second base of the trapezoid: 8


Enter the height of the trapezoid: 9


Enter the number of the shape you want to create:

For a Rectangle, enter 1
For a Circle, enter 2
For a Trapezoid, enter 3

Please make your selection: 5


Invalid selection. Creating default object.
```

```
Enter the number of the shape you want to create:

For a Rectangle, enter 1
For a Circle, enter 2
For a Trapezoid, enter 3

Please make your selection: 1


Enter the height of the rectangle: 1


Enter the width of the rectangle: 1


The area of the Rectangle is 15.0000
The area of the Circle is 98.5206
The area of the Trapezoid is 67.5000
The area of the Default Figure is 0.0000
The area of the Rectangle is 1.0000
```

Note that we deleted the `cout` statements in the constructors and destructors to make the program's output shorter. All destructors are declared as `virtual` functions to allow the proper sequence of execution of the class destructors. Also, the `Area()` function in class `Shape` is declared to be `virtual`. This allows the appropriate `Area()` function to be applied through a `Shape` pointer. In `main()`, we declare an array `shapes[]` of `Shape` pointers. The first `for` loop assigns a `Shape` pointer returned by the function `Get_Shape()` to each element of `shape[]`.

When `Get_Shape()` executes, it presents the user with a menu of choices to create either a `Rectangle`, a `Circle`, or a `Trapezoid`. The `switch` statement determines the action taken based on the user's response. If, for example, the user wants to create a `Rectangle`, the function asks for the height and width of the rectangle. A new `Rectangle` object is created dynamically by using the `new` operator. Although this returns a `Rectangle` pointer, it is legal to assign it to `s_p`, which is a `Shape` pointer. If the user enters a number other than 1, 2, or 3, the default case in the `switch` statement creates a default `Shape` object.

Programming
Pointers

The first `for` loop initializes the `Shape` pointers in `shapes[]` to point to some combination of `Rectangle`, `Circle`, `Trapezoid`, and default objects. The elements of an array must all be of the same type, as are the elements of `shapes[]`—they are all `Shape` pointers. However, the elements of the array `shapes[]` *point* to objects of different types. For this reason, such an array is sometimes called a **heterogeneous array**.

The second `for` loop uses polymorphism. The `Area()` function is applied through the `shapes[i]` pointer on each iteration of this `for` loop. The `Area()` function that the loop uses depends entirely on the type of shape the pointer is pointing to (polymorphism). By contrast, the function Get_Type() is not polymorphically applied. There is only one Get_Type() function, which is a member of the Shape class, and which the other classes inherit.

Programming
Pointers

It is important to realize that when the program is compiled, the compiler has no idea which Area() function the loop will use when the program executes. In fact, a different Area() function can be applied on each iteration. C++ decides which function to use when the loop executes, not when the program compiles. This behavior is called **late** (or **dynamic**) **binding**, that is, which function to use in the call shapes[i] -> Area() is not decided until the code executes. This is in contrast to how the compiler handles the call to the Get_Shape() function in the first for loop. There the compiler knows which function will be executed at compile time (known as **early**, or **static, binding**.)

Finally, the third for loop in main() cleans up by deleting the objects that were created in the first for loop.

EXERCISES 13.3

Use the following class declarations to answer Exercises 1–11. *Note that some of the declarations are incomplete.*

```
class Class_A
{
  protected:
    int a;
  public:
    Class_A(int i)      //See Exercise 2
    int Func()          //See Exercise 6
};

class Class_B : public Class_A
{
  protected:
    int b;
  public:
    Class_B(int i)      //See Exercise 3
    int Func()          //See Exercise 7
};

class Class_C : public Class_B
{
  protected:
    int c;
  public:
    Class_C(int i)      //See Exercise 4
    int Func()          //See Exercise 8
};
```

```
class Class_D : public Class_A
{
  protected:
    int d;
  public:
    Class_D(int i)        //See Exercise 5
    int Func()            //See Exercise 9
};
```

1. Draw the hierarchy diagram for the classes.
2. Define the one-argument constructor for Class_A. The constructor should initialize the data member a to the value of the constructor's argument.
3. Define the one-argument constructor for Class_B. The constructor should initialize the data member b to the value of the constructor's argument and call the base class constructor with the same argument.
4. Define the one-argument constructor for Class_C. The constructor should initialize the data member c to the value of the constructor's argument and call the base class constructor with the same argument.
5. Define the one-argument constructor for Class_D. The constructor should initialize the data member d to the value of the constructor's argument and call the base class constructor with the same argument.
6. Declare the function Func() in Class_A so that it is a virtual function. The function should return the value of its protected data member.
7. Declare the function Func() in Class_B so that it returns the sum of its protected data members.
8. Define the function Func() of Class_C so that it returns the sum of all its protected data members.
9. Define the function Func() of Class_D so that it returns the product of its protected data members.
10. Define destructors for all the classes.
11. Declare a class, Class_E, that is derived publicly from Class_D and that has one protected integer data member e. Define an appropriate one-argument constructor for the class that is similar to the constructor of the other derived classes. Define a function Func() that returns the product of all the class's protected data members.

Assume the classes from Exercises 1–10. Now consider the following declarations that are made in main().

```
Class_C c_object(3);
Class_D d_object(4);

Class_A* a_p;
Class_B* b_p;
```

Use these declarations to answer Exercises 12–16.

12. What does the following display?

```
a_p = &c_object;

cout << a_p -> Func();
```

13. What does the following display?

```
a_p = &d_object;

cout << a_p -> Func();
```

14. What does the following display?

```
a_p = &b_object;

cout << a_p -> Func();
```

15. What does the following display?

```
b_p = &c_object;

cout << b_p -> Func();
```

16. What does the following display?

```
cout << d_object.Func() << endl;

cout << c_object.Func() << endl;
```

EXPERIMENTS 13.3

1. The output of dem13-10.cpp displays the area of each figure but does not give the dimensions of the figure. Use a `virtual Show_Dimension()` function in each class to display the dimension of each figure. Compile, execute, and test the resulting program.

PROGRAMMING PROBLEMS 13.3

1. Add the class `Square` to the hierarchy of Figure 13.6 by deriving it publicly from class `Rectangle`. Class `Square` should have a one-argument constructor that represents the side of the square. The `Area()` function for class `Square` should return the square of its side. Also add the class `RightTriangle` by deriving it publicly from `Shape`. `RightTriangle` should have two data members—`base` and `height`. The `Area()` function for `RightTriangle` should return `0.5 * base * height`. Now extend the program dem13-10.cpp by adding these classes. The `Get_Shape()` function should have a `switch` statement to accommodate the five classes in the hierarchy.

2. In the `Document` class hierarchy of Programming Problem 1, Section 13.2, do the following: Add the `virtual` functions `Activity()` and `Display()` to the `Document` class. `Activity()` should return 0 and `Display()` should display the word "Document." Declare all destructors as `virtual` functions. Code a *non-member* function `Get_Document()` that asks the user to choose a document type. Depending on the user's choice, the function should create an appropriate object and return a `Document` pointer. Code a `main()` in which you declare an array of 20 `Document` pointers. Assign values to the pointers in the array by obtaining a set of documents from the user by using `Get_Document()`. Then print the activity of each document and display all the information of each document.

3. In the `StorageTank` class hierarchy of Programming Problem 2, Section 13.2, do the following: Add the `virtual` function `Display()` to the `StorageTank` class. The function should display the words "Storage Tank". Declare all destructors as `virtual` functions. Code a *non-member* function `Get_Tank()` that asks the user to choose a tank type. Depending on the user's choice, create an appropriate object and return a `StorageTank` pointer. Code a `main()` in which you declare an array of 20 `StorageTank` pointers. Assign values to the pointers in the array by obtaining a set of tanks from the user using `Get_Tank()`. Then display the data for all the storage tanks.

4. In the `VehicleService` class hierarchy of Programming Problem 3, Section 13.2, do the following: Add the `virtual` functions `CalculateBill()` and `Display()` to the `VehicleService` class. `CalculateBill()` should return 0.00 and `Display()` should display the word "Vehicle". Declare all destructors as `virtual` functions. Code a *non-member* function `Get_Vehicle()` that asks the user to choose a vehicle type. Depending on the user's choice, create an appropriate object and return a `VehicleService` pointer. Code a `main()` in which you declare an array of 20 `VehicleService` pointers. Assign values to the pointers in the array by obtaining a set of vehicles from the user by using `Get_Vehicle()`. Apply the `CalculateBill()` function to all the vehicles. Then display the data for all the vehicles.

5. In the `HotelRoom` class hierarchy of Programming Problem 4, Section 13.2, do the following: Add the `virtual` functions `CalculateBill()` and `Display()` to the `HotelRoom` class. `CalculateBill()` should return 0.00 and `Display()` should display the words "Hotel Room". Declare all destructors as `virtual` functions. Code a *non-member* function `Get_Room()` that asks the user to choose a room type. Depending on the user's choice, create an appropriate object and return a `HotelRoom` pointer. Code a `main()` in which you declare an array of 20 `HotelRoom` pointers. Assign values to the pointers in the array by obtaining a set of rooms from the user by using `Get_Room()`. Apply the `CalculateBill()` function to all the rooms. Then display the data for all the rooms.

13.4 Abstract Base Classes

The class hierarchy presented in the previous section has `Shape` as the base class for three other classes. The way in which we defined class `Shape` made it possible to declare a `Shape` object even though such an object has no data members. (This in fact could be done in dem13-10.cpp by entering a number other than 1,2, or 3 when the menu is displayed.) Although it does not quite make sense to declare a `Shape` object, it is possible and sometimes desirable to do so.

Pure `virtual` Functions and Abstract Base Classes

In C++, we can define a class in such a way as to make it impossible to declare an object of that type. We do so by making the class an **abstract base class**, or **ABC**. To make a class an ABC, declare *any one* of its member functions as a **pure** `virtual` **function**. You can make a `virtual` function a pure `virtual` function by following Note 13.10.

NOTE 13.10—ABSTRACT BASE CLASSES AND PURE VIRTUAL **FUNCTIONS**

To declare a `virtual` function as a pure `virtual` function, thereby making the class an abstract base class, do the following:

- Place `= 0` after the function's argument list in the function's declaration in the class.
- Do not define the function in the class.

Programming
Pointers

Since a pure `virtual` function has no definition, it does not make sense to declare an object that would make use of such a function. Therefore, it is reasonable to call such a class "abstract" because you cannot create any "concrete" objects of that type. An ABC provides a standard interface (i.e. pure `virtual` functions) for the derived classes. The derived classes must specify the implementation of the interface (i.e. the definition of the those functions). By providing the definitions of all pure `virtual` functions in a derived class, we specify the class's interface. It is possible to create objects in that derived class.

We can make the `Shape` class an abstract base class as follows.

```
class Shape
{
  protected:
      const char* figure_type;
  public:
      Shape(const char* ft = "Default Figure") : figure_type(ft) {}
      const char* Get_Type() {return figure_type;}
      virtual ~Shape() {}
      virtual double Area() = 0;
};
```

Note that the `= 0` is placed after the right parenthesis of the argument list of `Area()`. The function is not defined inside the class declaration. Making `Area()` a pure `virtual` function implies that we expect the derived classes to provide their own definitions of `Area()`. The following declarations in `main()` would now be illegal.

```
Shape s;                    //Illegal object

Shape Func();               //Illegal return value

double Func(Shape s);    //Illegal value parameter
```

Because `Shape` is an abstract base class, you cannot create an object of type `Shape`. Therefore, the first declaration is illegal. The second declaration is illegal because it implies that the function `Func()` returns a `Shape` object. The statement implies that a `Shape` object is created by the return mechanism, which is illegal. Likewise, the third declaration is illegal because use of the function requires passing a `Shape` object by value, again requiring that a `Shape` object be created.

However, because pointers and references do not require object creation, the following declarations are legal.

```
Rectangle r(3, 5);

Shape& s_ref = r;

Shape* s_ptr = &r;

double Func(Shape*);
```

Recall that a `Shape` reference is an alias for a `Shape` object. Since a `Rectangle` object is by inheritance a `Shape` object, we can use a `Shape` reference for it. We have already discussed why it is legal for a `Shape` pointer to point to a `Rectangle` object.

The presence of just one pure `virtual` function makes the class an abstract base class. The class can contain other pure `virtual` functions, ordinary `virtual` functions, or non-`virtual` functions. See Experiment 1. If you now try to declare a `Shape` object, the compiler will issue an error message. See Experiment 2.

The following Note is important.

NOTE 13.11— ABSTRACT BASE CLASSES

- In each class derived from an abstract base class (ABC), each pure `virtual` function *must* either be defined or redeclared as a pure `virtual` function. See Experiment 3.
- In the latter case, the derived class also becomes an ABC. See Experiment 4.
- In a class hierarchy that is based on an ABC, the only way for a derived class to yield objects is to define an overriding function for each pure `virtual` function that it would inherit.

The Loan Class

Suppose a banker wants to compute the monthly payment on loans. The bank grants two types of loans. A simple interest loan is one in which interest is computed using the following simple interest formula.

```
interest = principal * rate * term
```

The `principal` is the amount of money borrowed. The `rate` is the yearly rate as a decimal. The `term` is the number of years of the loan. The total amount of the loan is the `principal` plus the `interest`.

```
loan_amount = principal + interest
```

To pay off the loan in equal monthly installments, divide the `loan_amount` by the number of months (`term * 12`) of the loan.

```
payment = loan_amount / (term * 12)
```

The second type of loan is an amortized loan. In this type of loan, the interest is computed monthly on the basis of the unpaid loan balance. Suppose you borrow $1000 at a yearly rate of 12%. This means that each month you must pay 1% interest (12% divided by the number of months) on the unpaid balance. Suppose that your monthly payment is $100. In the first month, you must pay 1% interest ($10) on the full $1000. Of the $100 payment, $90 is paid toward the principal and $10 is paid in interest. At the end of the first month, you owe the bank $910. Of your second $100 payment, $9.10 (1% of 910.00) is for interest and the remainder ($90.90) is paid toward the principal. At the end of the second month you owe the bank $819.10. This continues until the loan is repaid. Deriving the formula for the payment amount for an amortized loan is beyond the scope of this book. The reader is referred to almost any text that covers the mathematics of finance. We can, however, use the formula for the payment of an amortized loan, which follows. In the formula, P represents the principal, R the rate as a decimal, and T the term.

$$payment = \frac{P*R*(1 + R)^T}{(1 + R)^T - 1}$$

All loans, both simple and amortized, have common data. For example, all loans have a principal, rate, term, and payment. What differs is the way in which the interest is computed. Therefore, we might decide to have a `Loan` class from which we can derive the classes `Simple_Loan` and `Amortized_Loan`. Figure 13.7 shows the class hierarchy. The `Loan` class contains all the data members mentioned previously and the data member `loan_type`, which is a string equal to either "`Simple  Loan`" or "`Amortized  Loan`". Since it is meaningless to create a `Loan` object (how would you calculate its payments?), we make `Loan` an abstract base class. We shall make the function `Payment()` a pure `virtual` function in class `Loan` and specify how the payment is to be computed in each derived class.

Following are the definitions for the classes `Loan`, `Simple_Loan`, and `Amortized_Loan`.

```
class Loan
{
  protected:
      double principal;
```

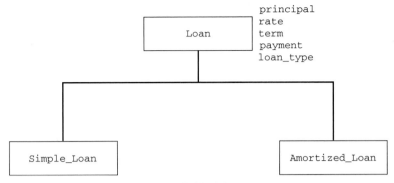

FIGURE 13.7

```
        double yearly_rate; //rate as a percent
        int    term_in_years;
        double payment;
        const char* loan_type;
    public:
        Loan (double prin, double rt, int term, const char* lt) :
                   principal(prin), yearly_rate(rt), term_in_years(term),
                   loan_type(lt), payment(0.0) {};
        virtual ~Loan() {}
        virtual void Payment() = 0; //pure virtual function
        void Display_Loan_Info();
};

void Loan::Display_Loan_Info()
{
   cout << "\n\nLoan Type: " << loan_type;
   cout << "\nPrincipal: " << principal;
   cout << "\nYearly Rate: " << yearly_rate;
   cout << "\nNumber of Years: " << term_in_years;
   cout << "\n\nMonthly Payment: " << payment;
}

//End of Class Loan    *******************************************

class Simple_Loan : public Loan
{
   public:
        Simple_Loan(double prin, double rt, int term)
             : Loan(prin, rt, term, "Simple Loan") {}
        ~Simple_Loan() {}
        void Payment();
};

void Simple_Loan::Payment()
{
   double interest = principal * term_in_years * (yearly_rate / 100);
```

```
    double loan_amount = principal + interest;

    payment = loan_amount / (term_in_years * 12);
}

//End of Class Simple_Loan *********************************************

class Amortized_Loan : public Loan
{
  public:
      Amortized_Loan(double prin, double rt, int term)
          : Loan(prin, rt, term, "Amortized Loan") {}
      ~Amortized_Loan() {}
      void Payment();

};

void Amortized_Loan::Payment()
{
  double monthly_rate = yearly_rate / 12 / 100;
  int term_in_months = term_in_years * 12;

  double power = pow(1 + monthly_rate, term_in_months);

  payment = (principal * monthly_rate * power) / (power - 1);
}

//End of Class Amortized_Loan *******************************************
```

The class `Loan` contains declarations of the `protected` data members mentioned previously. The member `loan_type` is declared `const char*` because, as we shall see shortly, it is initialized to a string constant. The `Loan` constructor has four arguments—the `principal`, `rate`, `term`, and `loan_type`. All the work of the constructor is done its initialization list. Note that the `payment` defaults to 0.0. The `Loan` destructor, declared as a `virtual` function, is an empty function included for completeness. The `Payment()` function is declared as a pure `virtual` function. This makes the `Loan` class an abstract base class. Each derived class has its own definition of `Payment()`. Finally, `Display_Loan_Info()` displays all the information about a loan. This function is inherited by the derived classes.

Class `Simple_Loan` is publicly derived from `Loan`. The `Simple_Loan` constructor has three arguments—the `principal`, `rate`, and `term`. However, the constructor's initialization list calls the `Loan` constructor with four arguments (recall from the previous paragraph that the fifth argument, the payment, defaults to 0.0). The fourth argument is the string constant "`Simple Loan`". The `Payment()` function for class `Simple_Loan` computes the payment using the simple interest formula as described previously.

The class `Amortized_Loan` is similar to `Simple_Loan`. The three-argument `Amortized_Loan` constructor calls the four-argument `Loan` constructor with the fourth argument equal to the string constant "Amortized Loan". The Payment() function of class Amortized_Loan computes the payment according to the formula described previously. To raise 1 + monthly_rate to a power, we use the standard math library function pow(). The function pow(), which returns a double, has two arguments that must both be doubles. The first is the base and the second the exponent. For example, pow(2.0, 5.0) returns 2^5, or 32.0. To use pow(), or any other function in the math library, you must include the header file math.h.

The following program, dem13-11.cpp, tests the classes by creating three loans.

```cpp
//dem13-11.cpp

#include <iostream.h>
#include <iomanip.h>
#include <math.h>

using namespace std;

class Loan
{
  protected:
        double principal;
        double yearly_rate; //rate as a percent
        int    term_in_years;
        double payment;
        const char* loan_type;
  public:
        Loan (double prin, double rt, int term, const char* lt) :
                   principal(prin), yearly_rate(rt),term_in_years(term),
                   loan_type(lt), payment(0.0) {};
        virtual ~Loan() {}
        virtual void Payment() = 0;      //pure virtual function
        void Display_Loan_Info();
};

void Loan::Display_Loan_Info()
{
  cout << "\n\nLoan Type: " << loan_type;
  cout << "\nPrincipal: " << principal;
  cout << "\nYearly Rate: " << yearly_rate;
  cout << "\nNumber of Years: " << term_in_years;
  cout << "\n\nMonthly Payment: " << payment;
}

//End of Class Loan     **********************************************

class Simple_Loan : public Loan
{
  public:
```

```cpp
        Simple_Loan(double prin, double rt, int term)
              : Loan(prin, rt, term, "Simple Loan") {}
        ~Simple_Loan() {}
        void Payment();
};

void Simple_Loan::Payment()
{
  double interest = principal * term_in_years * (yearly_rate / 100);
  double loan_amount = principal + interest;

  payment = loan_amount / (term_in_years * 12);
}

//End of Class Simple_Loan *******************************************

class Amortized_Loan : public Loan
{
  public:
        Amortized_Loan(double prin, double rt, int term)
              : Loan(prin, rt, term, "Amortized Loan") {}
        ~Amortized_Loan() {}
        void Payment();
};

void Amortized_Loan::Payment()
{
  double monthly_rate = yearly_rate / 12 / 100;
  int term_in_months = term_in_years * 12;

  double power = pow(1 + monthly_rate, term_in_months);

  payment = (principal * monthly_rate * power) / (power - 1);
}

//End of Class Amortized_Loan *******************************************


Loan* Get_Loan_Data();  //Prototype for function used by main()

int main()
{
  cout << setprecision(2)
       << setiosflags(ios::fixed)
       << setiosflags(ios::showpoint);

  const int num_loans = 3;

  Loan* loans[num_loans];
```

```
Number of Years: 3



Monthly Payment: 37.78

Loan Type: Amortized Loan
Principal: 1000.00
Yearly Rate: 12.00
Number of Years: 3

Monthly Payment: 33.21

Loan Type: Amortized Loan
Principal: 150000.00
Yearly Rate: 8.50
Number of Years: 30

Monthly Payment: 1153.37
```

The program uses the function `Get_Loan_Data()`, which returns a `Loan` pointer. The function asks the user to choose between a simple interest loan and an amortized loan. Then the function prompts for and obtains the principal, rate, and term of the loan. A `switch` statement then uses the `new` operator to create either a `Simple_Loan` object or an `Amortized_Loan` object depending on the user's response, and assigns the resulting pointer to a `Loan` pointer `l_p`. The function returns the value of `l_p`.

An array of `Loan` pointers is declared in `main()`. The processing in `main()` is accomplished in four `for` loops. The first executes `Get_Loan_Data()` for each pointer in the `loans[]` array. This assigns either a `Simple_Loan` object or an `Amortized_Loan` object to each pointer. The second `for` loop polymorphically applies the appropriate `Payment()` function through the `loans[]` pointers. Therefore, the correct payment formula will be applied to each loan depending on the loan type. In the third `for` loop, the inherited `Display_Loan_Info()` function is applied to each loan through the `loans[]` pointer. Finally, the fourth `for` loop deletes the space that was dynamically allocated in the first `for` loop.

EXERCISES 13.4

Use the following declarations to answer Exercises 1–5. Note that some of the declarations are incomplete.

```
class Class_A
{
  protected:
    int a;
```

```
  public:
    Class_A(int i) : a(i) {}
    int Func()              //See Exercise 1
};

class Class_B : public Class_A
{
  protected:
    int b;
  public:
    Class_B(int i) : b(i), Class_A(i) {}
    int Func()              //See Exercise 2
};

class Class_C : public Class_B
{
  protected:
    int c;
  public:
    Class_C(int i) : c(i), Class_B(i) {}
    int Func()              //See Exercise 3
};

class Class_D : public Class_A
{
  protected:
    int d;
  public:
    Class_D(int i) : d(i), Class_A(i) {}
    int Func()              //See Exercise 4
};
```

1. Declare `Func()` in `Class_A` so that `Class_A` becomes an abstract base class.
2. Declare `Func()` in `Class_B` so that `Class_B` becomes an abstract base class.
3. Define `Func()` in `Class_C` so that it returns the sum of the `protected` data members of the class.
4. Define `Func()` in `Class_D` so that it returns the product of the `protected` data members of the class.
5. Define destructors for the classes.

Based on the previous class declarations and the results of Exercies 1–5, which of the declarations in Exercises 6–10 are legal?

6. `Class_C Func6(int);`
7. `Class_B b_object;`
8. `Class_B * b_ptr;`
9. `int Func9(Class_A);`
10. `int Func10(Class_A &);`

11. In the `Shape` class hierarchy, add the class `Square`, which is derived from class `Rectangle`. The class should have one `double` data member, `s`, representing the side of the square. The class should also have an `Area()` member function that returns the value of `s*s`. The class should have a constructor that displays "Square Constructor" and calls the `Rectangle` constructor. The class should also have a destructor that displays "Square Destructor".

12. See Exercise 11. Write a program that declares a `Shape` pointer and sets it to a dynamically allocated `Square` object with a side of 6.5. Make the program display the area of the square by applying the `Area()` function through the pointer. In what sequence are the constructors and destructors executed? Which `Area()` function is executed?

EXPERIMENTS 13.4

1. Change the declaration of the `Shape` class of dem13-10.cpp in Section 13.3 to make `Shape` an abstract base class. Compile, execute, and test the resulting program.

2. See Experiment 1. Replace `main()` in dem13-10.cpp by one in which you declare a `Shape` object. Compile the resulting program. What message does the compiler issue?

3. See Experiment 1. Change the `Rectangle` class as follows: Do not define the `Area()` function and do not declare it as a pure `virtual` function. Compile the resulting program. What message does the compiler issue?

4. See Experiment 1. Change the `Rectangle` class as follows: Declare the `Area()` function so that it is a pure `virtual` function. Replace `main()` by one in which you declare a `Rectangle` object. Compile the resulting program. What message does the compiler issue?

PROGRAMMING PROBLEMS 13.4

1. Recode Programming Problem 1, Section 13.3, in such a way that `Shape` is an abstract base class by making `Area()` a pure `virtual` function.

2. Recode Programming Problem 2, Section 13.3, in such a way that `Document` is an abstract base class. Recode the `MultimediaFile` class so that it becomes an abstract base class by making the `Activity()` and `Display()` functions pure virtual functions. Derive from `MultimediaFile` two classes, `GraphicsFile` and `AudioFile`. `GraphicsFile` contains the integer data member `graphics_type` and `AudioFile` contains the integer data member `audio_type`. Code appropriate constructors, copy constructors, and destructors for the new classes. Code appropriate `Activity()` and `Display()` functions for the new classes. Code a `main()` that is similar to the one in Programming Problem 1, Section 13.3.

3. Recode Programming Problem 3, Section 13.3, in such a way that `StorageTank` is an abstract base class. Recode the `GasTank` class to make it an abstract base class by making the `Remainder()` and `Display()` functions pure `virtual` functions. Add the character pointer data member `tank_type` to the class.

Derive the two classes `PropaneTank` and `MethaneTank` from `GasTank`. Code appropriate constructors, copy constructors, and destructors for the new classes. Code appropriate `Remainder()` and `Display()` functions for the new classes. Code a `main()` that is similar to the one in Programming Problem 2, Section 13.3.

4. Recode Programming Problem 4, Section 13.3, in such a way that `Vehicle-Service` is an abstract base class. Recode the `PrivateVehicle` class to make it an abstract base class by making the `Display()` and `CalculateBill()` functions pure `virtual` functions. Add the character pointer data member `vehicle_type` to the class. Derive the two classes `FamilyVehicle` and `RecreationalVehicle` from `PrivateVehicle`. Code appropriate constructors, copy constructors, and destructors for the new classes. Also code `Display()` and `CalculateBill()` member functions for the new classes. To calculate the bill for a family vehicle, add to the cost of the parts the product of the hours and 70.00. To calculate the bill for a recreational vehicle, add to the cost of parts the product of the hours and 75.00. Code a `main()` that is similar to the one in Programming Problem 3, Section 13.3.

5. Recode Programming Problem 5, Section 13.3, in such a way that `HotelRoom` is an abstract base class. Make `GuestRoom` an abstract base class by making `Display()` and `CalculateBill()` pure `virtual` functions. Add the character pointer data member `room_type` to the class. Derive the two classes `SingleRoom` and `Suite` from `GuestRoom`. Code appropriate constructors, copy constructors, and destructors for the new classes. Also code `Display()` and `CalculateBill()` member functions for the new classes. Calculate the bill for a single room in the normal way. Calculate the bill for a suite by calculating the bill in the normal way and then adding a luxury tax of 6% of the regular bill. Code a `main()` that is similar to the one in Programming Problem 4, Section 13.3.

Chapter Review

Terminology

Define the following terms.

inheritance
base class
derived class
"is a" relation
direct dreivation
indirect derivation
protected
public derivation
private derivation

initialization list
function overriding
polymorphism
virtual function
heterogeneous array
late (or dynamic) binding
early (or static) binding
abstract base class
pure virtual function

Summary

- Classes can be related by means of inheritance. Inheritance embodies the "is a" relation.
- If a class inherits from another, the first class is derived from the other, which is in turn called the base class.
- A derived class inherits all the data members and member functions of the base class.
- Private members of a base class, although members of a derived class, are inaccessible to the member functions of the derived class. A `protected` member of a base class behaves as though it is `private` to all functions except member functions in a derived class. Thus, member functions in a derived class have access to all `protected` members in the base class (Note 13.1).
- To derive a class from a base class in the declaration of the derived class, follow the derived class's name by a colon, the keyword `public` or the keyword `private`, and the name of the base class (Note 13.2).
- All `private`, `protected`, and `public` base class members remain `private`, `protected`, and `public` as members of a publicly derived class. All base class members, regardless of their access category, are `private` members of a privately derived class (Table 13.1).
- With the following exceptions, a derived class inherits all base class member functions: constructors, copy constructors, destructors, overloaded operators, and `friend` functions (Note 13.3).
- The constructor of a derived class should explicitly call the base class constructor in an initialization list (Note 13.4). Properly coded, the base class constructor completes execution before the derived class constructor completes execution.
- Nothing special needs to be done to the code of derived class destructors. The derived class destructor completes execution before the base class destructor completes execution.
- The copy constructor of a derived class should explicitly call the copy constructor of its base class in an initialization list (Note 13.5).
- A function in a base class can be applied to a derived class object because the derived class inherits the base class function. However, if the derived class has a member function of the same name and signature (number and types of arguments) as a member function of the base class, when that function is applied to a derived class object, the function in the derived class overrides the function of the base class (Note 13.6).
- To apply an overridden base class member function to a derived class object, qualify the function name with the base class name followed by the scope resolution operator : : (Note 13.6).
- In a class hierarchy, a base class pointer can point to an object of any derived class. The converse is not true: A derived class pointer cannot point to a base class object (Note 13.7).
- The concept of polymorphism extends function overriding to the case of objects in a derived class accessed through base class pointers. Polymorphism allows the

choice of function to depend on the target of the pointer rather than the type of the pointer. C++ decides which function to use when the program executes. This is called late binding.

- For polymorphism to work, (a) objects must be accessed through pointers, (b) the function to be overridden must be declared `virtual` in the base class, and (c) the overriding function in the derived class must have the same name and signature as the base class function. Such a function is also `virtual` by default (Note 13.8).

- To ensure the proper execution sequence of destructors for dynamically allocated objects in a class hierarchy, declare the base destructor as a `virtual` function (Note 13.9).

- A heterogeneous array is an array of base class pointers. The pointers in such an array can point to any object in any class derived from the base class.

- An abstract base class is one for which it is impossible to instantiate an object. To make a class an abstract base class, declare one of its `virtual` functions a pure `virtual` function.

- To declare a `virtual` function a pure `virtual` function, place = 0 after the function's argument list in the function's declaration in the class, and do not define the function (Note 13.10).

- In each class derived from an abstract base class, each pure `virtual` function must either be defined or redeclared as a pure `virtual` function. In the latter case, the derived class becomes an abstract base class (Note 13.11).

- In a class hierarchy that is based on an abstract base class, the only way for a derived class to yield objects is to define an overriding function for each pure `virtual` function that it inherits (Note 13.11).

Review Exercises

1. Explain what it means to say that inheritance embodies the "is a" relation.
2. If class D is derived from class B, exactly what is and is not inherited by D from B? Include data members and function members?
3. Why is the `protected` access category needed?
4. Explain the difference between `public` and `private` class derivation.
5. Explain how a derived class's constructors must be coded relative to the base class constructors.
6. What is the difference between initializing a data member in the body of a constructor and initializing it in the constructor's initialization list?
7. In what order are the base class constructor and derived class constructor executed when a derived class object is instantiated?
8. In what order are the base class destructor and derived class destructor executed when a derived class object goes out of scope?
9. What is function overriding and how does it differ from function overloading?
10. How can you apply an overridden base class member to a derived class object?
11. Why does it make sense for a base class pointer to point to a derived class object?

12. What is polymorphism? What is a `virtual` function?
13. Why should class destructors in a class hierarchy be declared `virtual`?
14. What is a heterogeneous array and how is it useful?
15. Explain the difference between late and early binding.
16. What is an abstract base class and how do you declare one? What is the purpose of an abstract base class?

Chapter

14

Files

- To open a file in binary mode.
- To use the random access functions `seekg()`, `seekp()`, `tellg()`, and `tellp()` to process a file randomly.
- To create a binary sequential file of record structures.
- To use the `write()` member function to write a record structure to a binary file.
- To use the `read()` member function to read a record structure from a binary file.
- To code a random access file update program of a relative file of record structures.

14.1 Input/Output Streams

Files are handled differently in different programming languages. In C++, a file is treated as a stream of characters. See Figure 14.1. The characters in the file are made available to the program one at a time, in sequence. Input and output in C++ are known as **stream I/O**. The C++ language does not assume any organization to a file except its structure as a stream. To give a file an additional logical structure, the programmer must write program instructions to do so.

The Standard I/O Streams: Revisiting `cin` and `cout`

Since Chapter 1, you have been using the standard output stream `cout` and the standard input stream `cin`. By default, the standard input stream is "attached" to the keyboard. Therefore, `cin` receives its input from the keyboard. Likewise, the standard output stream, `cout`, is "attached" to the monitor display. Any data inserted into the `cout` output stream appears on the monitor. The standard input and output streams are automatically made available to every C++ program that contains the preprocessor directive `#include <iostream.h>`. We are now in a position to explain more fully the nature of `cin` and `cout`.

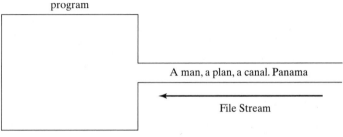

FIGURE 14.1

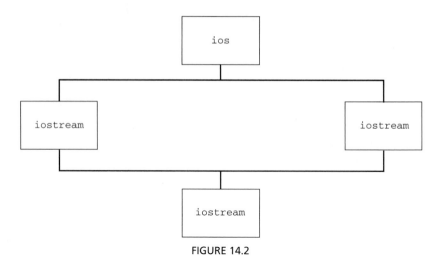

FIGURE 14.2

We have already mentioned that cin is an object of the class istream and that cout is an object of the class ostream. These two classes are actually part of a complex hierarchy of classes for doing input and output that are part of the C++ language. Figure 14.2 shows part of the hierarchy.

Programming
Pointers

The header file iostream.h contains the definition of the class iostream, which derives from both istream and ostream. A class like iostream, which is derived from two or more parent classes, is an example of **multiple inheritance**. In multiple inheritance, the derived class inherits all the members from all the classes from which it is derived. Thus, class iostream inherits all the members from istream, ostream, and also, indirectly, from the class ios, the class from which both istream and ostream are derived.

The istream class handles input and includes the definition of the extraction operator, >>. The object cin is a member of the class istream. The get() and getline() functions are members of the class istream. Therefore, they can be applied to an istream object such as cin. This is how we have been using these functions.

```
ch = cin.get();
cin.getline(buffer, 81);
```

Likewise, the ostream class handles output and includes the definition of the insertion operator, <<. The object cout is a member of the ostream class. The I/O manipulators that we have been using to control the form of the output to our programs are actually functions that use ostream and ios member functions to manipulate the output stream. For example, when the function setprecision() is sent to cout it determines the precision of the decimal numbers that are displayed by cout. Similarly, when the statement setiosflags(ios::showpoint) is sent to cout, it sets a one-bit flag in a data member of the class ios that determines that the output

stream will display the decimal point when a decimal number is output. (The scope resolution operator : : is necessary to ensure that the reference is to a data member of
the parent class.) See Experiment 1.

Text Files

For now, we shall assume that the files we are processing are text files. A **text file** consists of letters of the alphabet, digits, and special characters such as the comma,
hyphen, and period. At the end of each line of a text file is a new-line (' \n ') character.
Text files are produced using what is sometimes called an ASCII text editor, or simply
a text editor. Examples of such editors are Notepad in Windows 98 and the vi editor in
UNIX. Also, the editors that accompany C++ compilers, such as Turbo C++ and Visual
C++, are text editors. The text files used for input to the programs of this chapter can
be created by any of these editors. Note that files produced by a word processor such
as Microsoft Word are not text files. The .doc files produced by Word, for example, contain special formatting codes and other information about the document that are not
visible to the user. It is possible in most word processors, however, to choose to save a
file as a text file. See your word processor's documentation for details. We shall further
discuss text files and another type of file, binary files, in Section 14.3.

User-Declared Files

C++ allows the programmer to declare I/O streams, or files, other than the standard
ones. To perform input and output on named files requires that we create file objects in
classes that are designed for performing file operations. We must follow the steps of
Note 14.1 to work with a file in C++.

NOTE 14.1—TO WORK WITH A FILE IN C++

- Declare a file object of the appropriate mode (i.e. input or output or both).
- Open the file object and associate the object with a named file on your system.
- Perform operations on the file (i.e. read data from or write data to the file).
- Close the file.

Declaring the File Object

Programming
Pointers

To accomplish the first step of Note 14.1 (declare a file object), we must learn about
the three classes that support file I/O. Use the class ifstream to create input files. See
Figure 14.3. (Figure 14.3 contains a more complete picture of the classes in the C++ I/O
class hierarchy.) The class ifstream is derived from istream and a class called
fstreambase. The class fstreambase, which is derived from class ios, provides

#include <iostream.h>

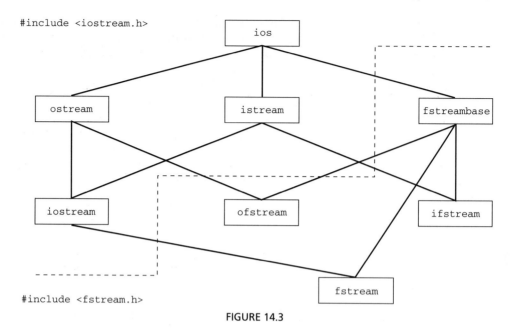

#include <fstream.h>

FIGURE 14.3

facilities for handling named files. Use the class `ofstream` to create output files. This class is derived from `ostream` and `fstreambase`. Finally, use the class `fstream` to create files that can be both input and output files. This class is derived from `iostream` and `fstreambase`. In Figure 14.3, the classes above the dotted line are declared in `iostream.h` and the classes below the dotted line are declared in `fstream.h`.

To use a file, first declare a file object of the appropriate type, as shown in the following declarations.

```
ofstream out_file;    //Declares an output file object called out_file

ifstream in_file;     //Declares an input file object called in_file

fstream io_file;  //Declares a file object io_file for either input or output
```

The first statement declares `out_file` as an `ofstream` object, that is, as an output file stream. This means that our program can place data into the `out_file` stream in much the same manner as we place data into the standard output stream, `cout`. The second statement declares `in_file` as an `ifstream` object. Therefore, our program can extract data from the `in_file` stream in much the same manner as we extract data from the standard input stream, `cin`. The third statement declares `io_file` as an object of the `fstream` class. Our program can use `io_file` as either an input stream or an output stream depending on the circumstances within the program and how we choose to open the file.

Opening the File

After declaring a file object, we must open the file and associate the file object with an actual physical file that resides on your computer system. The first of the previous file declarations, for example, declares `out_file` as an `ofstream` object. However, the output stream `out_file` has not yet been associated with, or attached to, an actual file. This situation is similar to declaring an integer variable and not assigning it a value. To use the variable meaningfully, you must assign it a value. Likewise, once we have declared a file object, we must associate that object with a file. We do this by opening the file using the `open()` member function. The following statement opens the `out_file` stream and attaches it to the file `outdata.dat`.

```
out_file.open("outdata.dat");
```

Programming
Pointers

From this point on in the program, all operations on the file object `out_file` will be performed on the file `outdata.dat`. Note that the argument of the `open()` member function must be a string. Therefore, the name of the file must be enclosed in quotes. In the absence of the directory path, the file will be opened in the folder in which the program is executed. The name of the file can include the path to the file on the computer system. In that case, the program will open the file in the appropriate folder. For example, the following statement opens the file `outdata.dat` in the root directory of the `a:` drive.

```
out_file.open("a:\outdata.dat");
```

A second way to create and open a file is by using the one-argument `ofstream` constructor. The following declaration creates in one step the `ofstream` object `out_file` and attaches it to the file `outdata.dat`.

```
ofstream out_file("outdata.dat");
```

The act of opening a file has several implications, which are mentioned in Note 14.2.

NOTE 14.2—OPENING A FILE

Opening a file (either by using the `open()` member function or by using the one-argument constructor when declaring the file object):

- Associates a real file on the computer system with the file object being opened.
- Opens the file in a mode appropriate to the type of file object.
- Creates a variable, which is part of the file object called the **file position indicator**, or **FPI**, that keeps track of the program's position in the file. The value of the FPI is the program's displacement into the file, that is the number of bytes from the first byte in the file.

Some explanation of the file position indicator is in order. The FPI helps your program keep track of where it is in the file. For example, when you open an `ofstream` file object, if the file that you are associating with the object does not exist, it is created automatically by the system. If the file does already exist, it is opened for output. In either case, the FPI is set to 0, the first byte position in the file. The first data your program writes to the file are placed beginning at that position. If the first write operation places seven characters in the file, the system automatically increases the FPI by seven. The next write operation will then cause data to be placed starting at displacement seven bytes from the beginning of the file. See Figure 14.4.

When you open an `ifstream` file object, that is an input file, the file that you are associating with the object must already exist. If it does not, an error occurs. We will address how to handle this error shortly. Assuming the file to be opened exists, the file's FPI is set to 0. The first data that we read from the file is extracted beginning at displacement 0. If we read five characters from the file, the FPI is increased by five. Therefore, the next reading of data from the file begins at displacement five. See Figure 14.5.

We shall discuss how the FPI works for `fstream` file objects when we cover them.

Processing the File

Programming
Pointers

We now know how to complete the first two steps of Note 14.1. For the third step, processing the file, the power of inheritance comes to the rescue! Once the `ofstream` object is created and opened, we can use any of the file output operations that we have used in this book, including the insertion operator ≪. Recall that the insertion opera-

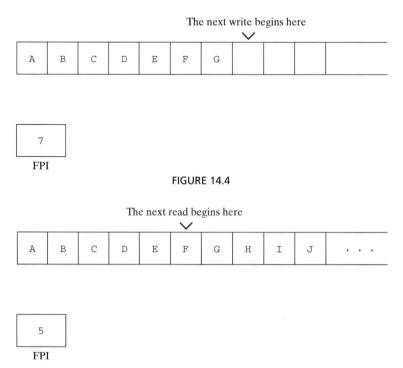

FIGURE 14.4

FIGURE 14.5

tor is declared in the class `ostream`, which is the class from which `ofstream` is derived. Reference Figure 14.3. Therefore, the class `ofstream` inherits the insertion operator. This allows us to do the following to write the string "Hello, World!" onto the file `outdata.dat` followed by a new-line character.

```
out_file << "Hello, World!" << endl;
```

Closing the File

After the program finishes processing the file, it should close the file. The C++ system automatically closes any open file when the program ends. However, it is good practice to close files using the `close()` member function. For example, the following statement closes `out_file`.

```
out_file.close();
```

The following program illustrates the simple use of an output file.

```
//dem14-1.cpp

//This program demonstrates simple file output

#include <fstream.h>
#include <iostream.h>

using namespace std;

int main()
{
  char buffer[81];

  ofstream out_file("outdata.dat");

  cout << "\nEnter your name: ";
  cin.getline(buffer, 81);

  out_file << buffer << endl;

  cout << "\nEnter the first line of your address: ";
  cin.getline(buffer, 81);

  out_file << buffer << endl;

  out_file.close();

  cout << "\nProgram Terminated";

  return 0;
}
```

Program Output

```
Enter your name: John Molluzzo

Enter the first line of your address: Pace University

Program Terminated
```

Other than the message `Program Terminated`, the program does not display any results on the monitor because the program places the user's name and address into the file `outdata.dat`. Following is a listing of the output file.

Listing of File outdata.dat

```
John Molluzzo
Pace University
```

Recall that the insertion operator is inherited by the `ofstream` class. It is meaningful, therefore, to apply the operator to an `ofstream` object such as `out_file`. We use the insertion operator `<<` to output our data to the file. We place data onto the `out_file` stream in the same way that we place data onto the standard output stream, `cout`.

Checking for Errors When Opening a File

The program dem14-1.cpp does not check for errors when the file is opened. Possible output file errors include disk errors and writing to a file on a nonexistent disk.

NOTE 14.3—ERRORS WHEN OPENING A FILE

If an error occurs when a file is opened, the value of the file object is zero.

The following program shows how to check for such an error. The first run of the program outputs to a file "outdata.dat", which is created in the folder in which the program executes. The second program run attempts to output to a file on disk M, which did not exist on the system on which the program was executed. (If you run this program on your system, you may have to change the drive letter. Choose a drive letter that is not in use on your system.)

```
//dem14-2.cpp

//This program demonstrates simple file output
//The program checks the file open for errors

#include <fstream.h>
#include <iostream.h>
#include <stdlib.h>

using namespace std;
```

```
int main()
{
  char buffer[81];
  char file_name[81];

  cout << "\nEnter the name of the file you want to write to: ";
  cin.getline(file_name, 81);

  ofstream out_file(file_name);

  if (!out_file)
    {
      cout << "\nERROR: File could not be opened.";
      exit(1);
    }

  cout << "\nEnter your name: ";
  cin.getline(buffer, 81);

  out_file << buffer << endl;

  cout << "\nEnter the first line of your address: ";
  cin.getline(buffer, 81);

  out_file << buffer << endl;

  out_file.close();

  cout << "\nProgram Terminated";

  return 0;
}
```

Program Output

Test Run 1

```
Enter the name of the file you want to write to: outdata.dat

Enter your name: John Molluzzo

Enter the first line of your address: Pace University

Program Terminated
```

Program Output

Test Run 2

```
Enter the name of the file you want to write to: m:outdata.dat

ERROR: File could not be opened.
```

In this program we allow the user to enter the name of the file to which the name and address will be written. The program obtains the file name from the user and places it into the array `file_name[]`. When the file object `out_file` is declared, we use the array name `file_name`, which is a character pointer, or string, as the argument to the constructor.

To check for errors when the file is opened, we test the file object as follows:

Programming
Pointers

```
if (!out_file)
  {
    cout << "\nERROR: File could not be opened.";
    exit(1);
  }
```

If the file is not opened properly, the value of `out_file` is zero. Testing `!out_file` is in effect saying "if `out_file` failed to open properly." In this case, an error message is sent to the standard output stream and the program is ended with the `exit(1)` statement. In the second program run, we entered the name of a file on disk M, which did not exist on the system on which the program was executed. Therefore, the second program run resulted in the error message.

Creating a Text File of Records

Although C++ treats all files as streams of characters, we can impose a logical structure on the file. A **record** is the set of data, or facts, concerning a particular entity. Each fact within a record is a **field**. For example, if we were to write a program to process the inventory for a small manufacturing company, we might design a part record. Each such record might consist of three fields: the ID number field, the quantity on hand field, and the price field. The entire set of part records is the inventory parts file.

There are several ways to construct records in C++. Since we are for now only considering text files, we shall construct records as follows: Each record in the file is a line of text. Therefore, in the stream of characters that constitutes the file, the new-line character separates records. The fields within each record are separated by one or more spaces. The fields in such a record are sometimes called **space separated**. The position within the record identifies the field. In the part record described in the previous paragraph, the ID number field would be first in the record, followed by the quantity on hand, followed by the price. Thus, a three-record parts inventory file, when viewed using a text editor, might look like the following.

```
23  145  24.95
15  46  67.99
65  230  11.95
```

The previous file is an example of a **sequential file**, which is a file whose records are stored in sequence one after the other. The program, prb14-1.cpp, creates a sequential parts inventory text file. It asks the user to enter data for a record in the file. Then the program writes the record to the parts file.

```cpp
//prb14-1.cpp

//This program demonstrates the creation of a simple text data
//parts inventory file in which the data items are space-separated.

#include <fstream.h>
#include <iostream.h>
#include <stdlib.h>
#include <iomanip.h>

using namespace std;

int main()
{
  char file_name[81];

  int    id_no;
  int    qoh;
  double price;

  int response;

  cout << "\nEnter the name of the new inventory file: ";
  cin.getline(file_name, 81);

  ofstream inventory_file(file_name);

  if (!inventory_file)
    {
      cout << "\nERROR: File could not be opened.";
      exit(1);
    }

  inventory_file << setprecision(2)
                 << setiosflags(ios::fixed)
                 << setiosflags(ios::showpoint);

  cout << "\nCreate an inventory record? (1 for Yes/0 for No): ";
  cin >> response;

  while (response)
  {
    // Get data for inventory record

    cout << "\nID Number: ";
    cin >> id_no;

    cout << "\nQuantity On Hand: ";
    cin >> qoh;

    cout << "\nPrice: ";
```

```
    cin >> price;

    //Write inventory record

    inventory_file << id_no << " " << qoh << " " << price << endl;

    cout << "\nCreate an inventory record? (1 for Yes/0 for No): ";
    cin >> response;
}

cout << "\n\nInventory File " << file_name << " created.";

inventory_file.close();

return 0;
}
```

Program Output

```
Enter the name of the new inventory file: invent.dat

Create an inventory record? (1 for Yes/0 for No): 1

ID Number: 10

Quantity On Hand: 100

Price: 10.00

Create an inventory record? (1 for Yes/0 for No): 1

ID Number: 20

Quantity On Hand: 200

Price: 20.00

Create an inventory record? (1 for Yes/0 for No): 1

ID Number: 30

Quantity On Hand: 300

Price: 30.00

Create an inventory record? (1 for Yes/0 for No): 1

ID Number: 40

Quantity On Hand: 4
```

```
Price: 400.00

Create an inventory record? (1 for Yes/0 for No): 1

ID Number: 50

Quantity On Hand: 500

Price: 500.00

Create an inventory record? (1 for Yes/0 for No): 0

Inventory File invent.dat created.
```

Listing of File invent.dat

```
10 100 10.00
20 200 20.00
30 300 30.00
40 4 400.00
50 500 500.00
```

The program first asks the user to enter the name for the inventory file. After obtaining the name from the user, the program opens the file as the `ofstream` file object `inventory_file` and tests to see if the file was opened properly. Next, the program sends the `setprecision()` and `setiosflags()` statements that we usually send to `cout` to `inventory_file`. This ensures that each value for the price field will retain the decimal point and have two digits to the right of the decimal when written to the output file. See Experiment 4.

The program then enters a `while` loop that creates the output file. In the loop body, the program asks for the ID number, quantity on hand, and price of an item. Then it writes an inventory record onto the file. Note that the program places a space between each field, and ends the record with a new-line character. Then the program asks the user if he or she wants to create another record. After exiting the loop, the program displays a message that it is finished and closes the file. See Experiment 5 for an extension to the program.

File Input

Now that we have created several files, how can we use these files for input to a program and read their contents? As mentioned previously, to create an input file, declare an `ifstream` file object and then open the file. For example, to open the file `outdata.dat` for input, we can execute the following statements.

```
ifstream in_file;
in_file.open("outdata.dat");
```

Alternatively, we can create and open the file at the same time using the one-argument constructor as follows.

```
ifstream in_file("outdata.dat");
```

Programming
Pointers

When we read data from a file, we must always check for the **end-of-file condition**. The end-of-file condition means that in processing the file the program has come to the end of the file. There is no more data to read from the file. The member function eof() returns 1 (that is, true) if the FPI is at the end of the file (what numeric value would the FPI have in this case?), and returns 0 otherwise. Assuming that in_file is an ifstream object that has been opened, if the value returned by in_file.eof() is 1, the end of file condition has been reached. Otherwise, it has not and the file contains more data that the program can process.

The following program illustrates how we can read and display the data that the program dem14-2.cpp placed into outdata.dat.

```
//dem14-3.cpp

//This program demonstrates simple file input

#include <fstream.h>
#include <iostream.h>
#include <stdlib.h>

using namespace std;

int main()
{
  char buffer[81];
  char file_name[81];

  cout << "\nEnter the name of the file you want to display: ";
  cin.getline(file_name, 81);

  ifstream in_file(file_name);

  if (!in_file)
    {
      cout << "\nERROR: File could not be opened.";
      exit(1);
    }

  cout << endl;

  while (!in_file.eof())
    {
      in_file.getline(buffer, 81);
      cout << buffer << endl;
    }
```

```
    in_file.close();

    cout << "\n\nProgram Terminated";

    return 0;
}
```

Program Output

```
Enter the name of the file you want to display: outdata.dat

John Molluzzo
Pace University


Program Terminated
```

We check for an error when opening the file in exactly the same way we did for an output file, by checking for a zero value for the `ifstream` object `in_file`. The copy and display of the file is done in the `while` loop. The loop condition checks for the end of file on the input file. If it is not the end of file (that is, `!in_file.eof()` is true), the program executes the loop body. In the loop body, the `getline()` member function reads a line from the input file in exactly the same way it reads lines entered at the keyboard using the standard input stream `cin`. (Recall that the `getline()` function is inherited from the class `istream`.) The `cout` statement then displays the line on the monitor.

Processing a Text File of Records

The following program, prb14-2.cpp, shows how to process the sequential text file of records that was created in prb14-1.cpp. The program reads through the inventory part file and displays only those part records for which the total value of that part (quantity on hand multiplied by the price) exceeds $3000.

```
//prb14-2.cpp

//This program demonstrates reading a text file of records
//whose data are space-separated.

#include <fstream.h>
#include <iostream.h>
#include <iomanip.h>
#include <stdlib.h>

using namespace std;

int main()
{
```

```
char file_name[81];

int    id_no;
int    qoh;
double price;
double total;

cout << setprecision(2)
     << setiosflags(ios::fixed)
     << setiosflags(ios::showpoint);

cout << "\nEnter the name of the inventory file: ";
cin.getline(file_name, 81);

ifstream inventory_file(file_name);

if (!inventory_file)
  {
    cout << "\nERROR: File could not be opened.";
    exit(1);
  }

cout << endl << endl;
cout << setw(8) << "ID No." << setw(10) << "Quantity"
     << setw(10) << "Price" << setw(12) << "Total"
     << endl << endl;

//Obtain the first inventory record

inventory_file >> id_no >> qoh >> price;

while (!inventory_file.eof())
{
  total = qoh * price;

  if (total > 3000.00)
    {
      cout << setw(8) << id_no << setw(10) << qoh
           << setw(10) << price << setw(12)<< total
           << endl;
    }

//obtain the next inventory record

inventory_file >> id_no >> qoh >> price;
}

inventory_file.close();

return 0;
}
```

Program Output

```
Enter the name of the inventory file: invent.dat


   ID No.     Quantity      Price         Total

      20         200        20.00        4000.00
      30         300        30.00        9000.00
      50         500       500.00      250000.00
```

The program begins by obtaining the name of the inventory file from the user and opening the file as the `ifstream` file object `inventory_file`. The program then displays a line of column headings.

Programming Pitfalls

When reading a file of records sequentially, that is one at a time, you must take care that your program processes the last record in the file and that it processes the record only once. Note 14.4 explains how to read a sequential input file of records.

NOTE 14.4—THE READ AHEAD RULE

To properly read all the records in a sequential input file:

1. Read the first record of the file immediately after opening the file.

2. Read the input file again as soon as the program completes processing the input data.

A typical program that processes such a file and uses `eof()` to detect the end of the file should have the following format, which is written in pseudocode.

```
open the input_file
read the first record
while (!input_file.eof())
  process the record
  read the next record
endwhile
```

The program code for prb14-2.cpp follows this outline. After the inventory file is opened, the program reads the first record by executing

```
inventory_file >> id_no >> qoh >> price;
```

This statement reads the first three numbers in the file, which represent the ID number, quantity on hand, and price, and places them into three variables. The program then enters the processing loop. If the program has not reached the end of the file, the `while` loop body calculates the total and tests to see if it exceeds 3000.00. If so, the program displays the values of id_no, qoh and price. This finishes processing the record so, by the Read Ahead Rule of Note 14.4, the program obtains the next record. When the end of file is reached, the program exits the loop, closes the inventory file, and ends. See Experiment 6.

File Input/Output

Programming
Pointers

We can use a file for both input and output in the same program. To do this, we need a file object that can serve as both an output and an input stream. The class fstream, which inherits from iostream, which in turn inherits from both ostream and istream, see Figure 14.3, is just what we need. Because a member of the fstream class can be used for either input or output, when the file is opened you must specify an opening mode as the open() function's second argument. (The open function is overloaded—it can take either one or two arguments.) The opening modes are specified by **access mode constants**, which are defined in the ios class, and therefore available to fstream. Some common opening modes are the following.

NOTE 14.5—ACCESS MODE CONSTANTS

ios::in	Opens the file for input (or reading)
ios::out	Opens the file for output (or writing)
ios::app	Opens the file for output beginning at the end of the file (or appending)

To open a file "outdata.dat" for input, we can code the following.

```
fstream file("outdata.dat", ios::in);
```

Programming
Pointers

When opening a file in either the ios::in or ios::out modes, the FPI is set to 0. Extracting or inserting data into the stream begins at the first character position in the file. When a file is opened in the ios::app, or the **append mode**, the FPI is set to the number of bytes in the file. Therefore, if we insert data into the file, it begins inserting at the end of the file. The new data is added to the original file contents.

The following program allows the user to enter his or her name and address and stores them in a text file. The program then displays the contents of the file. Next, the program asks the user to add the city, state, and zip code to the address, and finally displays the contents of the file again.

```
//dem14-4.cpp

//This program demonstrates simple file input and output
//The file is opened in in/out and app modes
```

```cpp
#include <fstream.h>
#include <iostream.h>
#include <stdlib.h>

using namespace std;

int main()
{
  char buffer[81];
  char file_name[81];

  cout << "\nEnter the name of the file you want to write to: ";
  cin.getline(file_name, 81);

  fstream file(file_name, ios::out);

  if (!file)
    {
      cout << "\nERROR: File could not be opened.";
      exit(1);
    }

  cout << "\nEnter your name: ";
  cin.getline(buffer, 81);

  file << buffer << endl;

  cout << "\nEnter the first line of your address: ";
  cin.getline(buffer, 81);

  file << buffer << endl;

  file.close();

  cout << "\nThe file you created is the following:"
       << endl << endl;

  file.open(file_name, ios::in);

  if (!file)
    {
      cout << "\nERROR: File could not be opened.";
      exit(1);
    }

  while (!file.eof())
    {
      file.getline(buffer, 81);
      cout << buffer << endl;
    }
```

```
        file.close();

        cout << "\nEnter the city, state, and zip in which you live: ";
        cin.getline(buffer, 81);

        cout << "\nThe information will be appended to your file." << endl;

        file.open(file_name, ios::app);

        if (!file)
          {
            cout << "\nERROR: File could not be opened.";
            exit(1);
          }

        file << buffer << endl;

        file.close();

        cout << "\nYour complete name and address is the following:"
             << endl << endl;

        file.open(file_name, ios::in);

        if (!file)
          {
            cout << "\nERROR: File could not be opened.";
            exit(1);
          }

        while (!file.eof())
          {
            file.getline(buffer, 81);

            cout << buffer << endl;
          }

        file.close();

        cout << "\nProgram Terminated";

        return 0;
}
```

Program Output

```
Enter the name of the file you want to write to: outdata.dat

Enter your name: John Molluzzo
```

```
Enter the first line of your address: Pace University

The file you created is the following:

John Molluzzo
Pace University

Enter the city, state, and zip in which you live: New York, NY 10038

The information will be appended to your file.

Your complete name and address is the following:

John Molluzzo
Pace University
New York, NY 10038


Program Terminated
```

The first time we open the file, we create the file object in the declaration. The next three times we open the file, the file object already exists. Therefore, it is only necessary to open the file in the appropriate mode using the `open()` member function. Note that after each time the file is opened with the open member function, we check for an error condition.

EXERCISES 14.1

In Exercises 1–9 write appropriate C++ statements.

1. Declare and open an output file object and attach it to the file `a:\file1.txt`.
2. Write your name and address onto the file of Exercise 1 on three separate lines.
3. Close the file of Exercise 1.
4. Declare and open an input file object and attach it to the file `c:\data\file2.txt`.
5. Read the first line of the file in Exercise 4 into a character array called `buffer[]`.
6. Close the file of Exercise 4.
7. Declare and open the file in Exercise 1 in the append mode.
8. Write your age onto the end of the file.
9. Close the file of Exercise 7.
10. Explain the difference between opening a file in the output mode and opening a file in the append mode.

EXPERIMENTS 14.1

1. Take any program that you have written that includes the manipulator `setios-flags()` and remove the `ios::` qualifier from the argument. Compile the resulting program. What happens and why?

2. In dem14-3.cpp, enter the name of a nonexistent file. How does the program behave?

3. In dem14-3.cpp, remove the `if` statement that tests for an error when the file is opened. Recompile and execute the resulting program. When prompted for a file name, enter the name of a nonexistent file. How does the program behave?

4. In prb14-1.cpp, remove the statement that sends `setprecision()` and `setiosflags()` messages to `inventory_file`. Compile, execute, and test the resulting program with the same data used in testing prb14-1.cpp. Examine the file created by the program. Does the data for the price contain decimal points?

5. In prb14-1.cpp, add a record counter to the program that is incremented each time a record is written to the inventory part file. After the program closes the inventory part file, the program should display the value of the record counter.

6. Verify that the Read Ahead Rule of Note 14.4 is needed. Remove the first read of the inventory file that is outside the `while` loop in prb14-2.cpp. Then move the read of the inventory file from the end of the `while` loop body to the beginning of the `while` loop body. Compile, execute, and test the resulting program. Does the program process the file correctly?

7. In dem14-4.cpp, omit the `ios::out` opening mode in the declaration of the `fstream` object file. Attempt to compile and execute the program. Explain what happens.

PROGRAMMING PROBLEMS 14.1

1. Write a program that combines the processing of programs prb14-1.cpp and 14-2.cpp. The program should create the parts inventory file by obtaining the data from the user. After creating the file, the program should then search through the file and display those records whose quantity on hand multiplied by price exceeds 3000.00. Declare the file as an `fstream` object so you can perform both input and output on the file.

2. A small business wants to create a file to store its customer information. Each record in the file is to contain the following data: customer ID number (an integer 01–50), first name, last name, city, zip code, and account balance. Write a program to create such a customer file. Set up the file as a sequential text file with space-separated fields.

3. Write a program that displays the file in Programming Problem 2 in column form with appropriate column headings.

4. The National Bank credit card company wishes to issue a new type of card, the Platinum Card, to its preferred customers. Write a program that prints a report

that lists all customers who will or can receive a Platinum Card. The customer data is contained in a text file. Each line of the text file contains the following space-separated fields: the customer ID number (a four-digit integer), credit limit, and account balance. If a customer has a credit limit of at least $2000 and an account balance of $500 or less, the customer will receive a Platinum Card. If a customer's credit limit is at least $2000 and the account balance is greater than $500, the customer will be sent a letter. The letter will state that if the customer's balance becomes $500 or less, he or she will receive a Platinum Card.

Each line of the report should list the customer ID number, credit limit, account balance, and the word APPROVED, LETTER, or DISAPPROVED. The report should contain appropriate column headings. At the end of the report, print the number of customers in each category.

14.2 Processing a File One Character at a Time

In the previous section we used the insertion operator to place data onto a text file, and the extraction operator and the `getline()` member function to extract data from a text file. In some cases it is either necessary or more efficient to extract and/or insert one character at a time onto a text file. In this section we discuss how to do this.

The `get()` and `put()` Member Functions

Programming
Pointers

To read and write one character to a file you can use the `get()` and `put()` member functions. These functions are faster than using the insertion and extraction operator. The `get()` member function extracts and returns one character from an input file. (We have already used the `get()` member function with the standard input stream, `cin`.) If `in_file` is an open `ifstream` object, `in_file.get()` returns the next available character from the `in_file` stream. The `get()` function retrieves whichever character is indicated by the FPI. Thus, if the FPI is six, `in_file.get()` retrieves the character that is six characters from the beginning of the file (that is, the seventh character in the file). Then, the `get()` function increases the FPI by one (7). The next execution of the `get()` function for the stream will retrieve the next character. See Figure 14.6a.

Programming
Pointers

In addition, the `get()` member function always detects the end of file condition, whereas the extraction operator >> does not. (Recall that in dem14-3.cpp and dem14-4.cpp we used the `eof()` member function to detect the end-of-file condition.) The `get()` member function returns EOF (end of file, a constant defined in `iostream.h`) if the end of file is reached in the input file.

If `out_file` is an open output stream, `out_file.put(ch)` places a copy of the character stored in the variable `ch` at the position indicated by the FPI. Then the `put()` function increases the FPI by one. See Figure 14.6b. The following program copies one text file to another, one character at a time.

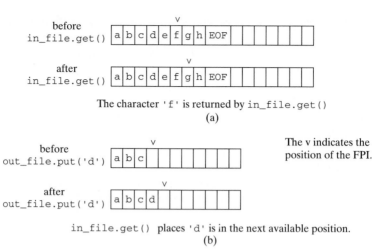

before
in_file.get() [a][b][c][d][e][f][g][h][EOF][ ][ ][ ][ ][ ]

after
in_file.get() [a][b][c][d][e][f][g][h][EOF][ ][ ][ ][ ][ ]

The character 'f' is returned by in_file.get()
(a)

before
out_file.put('d') [a][b][c][ ][ ][ ][ ][ ][ ][ ]

The v indicates the
position of the FPI.

after
out_file.put('d') [a][b][c][d][ ][ ][ ][ ][ ][ ]

in_file.get() places 'd' is in the next available position.
(b)

FIGURE 14.6

```cpp
//dem14-5.cpp

//This program copies one text file to another using get() and put()

#include <fstream.h>
#include <iostream.h>
#include <stdlib.h>

using namespace std;

int main()
{
  char file_name[81];
  char ch;

  cout << "\nEnter the name of the source file: ";
  cin.getline(file_name, 81);

  ifstream source_file(file_name);

  if (!source_file)
    {
      cout << "\nERROR: File cannot be opened.";
      exit(1);
    }

  cout << "\nEnter the name of the target file: ";
  cin.getline(file_name, 81);

  ofstream target_file(file_name);

  if (!target_file)
```

```
      {
        cout << "\nERROR: File cannot be opened.";
        exit(1);
      }

   while ((ch = source_file.get()) != EOF)
      target_file.put(ch);

   source_file.close();
   target_file.close();

   cout << "\n\nProgram Terminated.";

   return 0;
}
```

Program Output

```
Enter the name of the source file: outdata.dat

Enter the name of the target file: outdata.cpy



Program Terminated
```

Once again, the program does not display the resulting output file. Following is a listing of the file outdata.cpy.

Listing of outdata.cpy

```
John Molluzzo
Pace University
New York, NY 10038
```

Note how we test for the end of file in the `while` loop's condition. The expression `ch = source_file.get()` does not equal EOF if the `get()` did not reach the end of file. When it does reach the end of file, the expression equals EOF and the loop terminates.

Output to the Printer

Programming
Pointers

If you know the name assigned by your system to the printer (for example, "prn" in the DOS/Windows environment), you can treat the printer as an output stream. To open the printer for output, declare an `ofstream` object and attach the object to the printer. For example, the following statement declares the `ofstream` object `printer_file` and attaches it to the printer.

```
ofstream printer_file("prn");
```

All of the functions we have used for `ofstream` objects will work for `printer_file`, as will the insertion operator. The following statement will print the word "Hello" on the printer.

```
printer_file << "Hello" << endl;
```

Likewise, the following statement will display the character 'A' on the printer.

```
printer_file.put('A');
```

The following program, dem14-6.cpp, prints the contents of the file created by dem14-5.cpp double spaced on the printer.

```
//dem14-6.cpp

//This program prints the contents of a file, double spaced, on a printer

#include <fstream.h>
#include <iostream.h>
#include <stdlib.h>

using namespace std;

int main()
{
  char file_name[81];
  char ch;

  cout << "\nEnter the name of the source file: ";
  cin.getline(file_name, 81);

  ifstream source_file(file_name);

  if (!source_file)
    {
      cout << "\nERROR: File cannot be opened.";
      exit(1);
    }

  ofstream printer_file("prn");

  if (!printer_file)
    {
      cout << "\nERROR: Printer could not be opened.";
      exit(1);
    }

  printer_file << "Contents of the Source File - Double Spaced."
```

```
                        << endl << endl;

    while ((ch = source_file.get()) != EOF)
      {
        printer_file.put(ch);
        if (ch == '\n')
          printer_file.put(ch);
      }

    source_file.close();
    printer_file.close();

    cout << "\n\nProgram Terminated.";

    return 0;
}
```

Program Output—Displayed on the Monitor

```
Enter the name of the source file: outdata.cpy



Program Terminated
```

Program Output—Printed on the Printer

```
Contents of the Source File - Double Spaced.

John Molluzzo

Pace University

New York, NY 10038
```

After the program opens the source file and the printer file, it inserts a message (`Contents of the Source File - Double Spaced.`) into the `printer_file` stream using the insertion operator. Then a `while` loop successively reads characters from the source file and prints them on the printer. The `if` statement in the loop tests the character read by `get()` to see if it is a new-line character. If it is, the character is printed again, which achieves double spacing.

EXERCISES 14.2

1. Declare and open an output file object `test_file` and attach it to the file `testfile.dat`.
2. Write a `for` loop that places all the lowercase letters on this file, one character per line, using `put()`.

3. Close the file.

4. Open the file created in Exercises 1–3 as an input file.

5. Declare and open an output file object, `printer_file`, attached to the printer.

6. Write a `for` loop that uses `get()` and `put()` to read characters from the input file and places the uppercase version on the `printer_file`.

7. Close the files `test_file` and `printer_file`.

EXPERIMENTS 14.2

1. Recode dem14-2.cpp using `put()` instead of `cout`.

2. Recode dem14-3.cpp using `get()` instead of `cin`.

3. Recode dem14-5.cpp using `cin` and `cout`.

4. Recode prb14-2.cpp by making the program print its output on the printer rather than displaying it on the monitor.

PROGRAMMING PROBLEMS 14.2

1. Many grammar checking programs include a utility that computes statistics about a file. Write a program that asks the user for the name of a text file. The program should then count the number of characters, words, and sentences in the file. The program should display the number of characters, words, and sentences in the file, the average word length, and the average sentence length. Assume that white space (blanks, tabs, and new-line characters) separates words. Also assume that a period ends a sentence.

2. Write a program that compares the contents of two text files. If the files are identical, the program should display a message to that effect. If the files differ, the program should display an appropriate message and the number of bytes from the beginning of the files where they first differ.

3. When a compiler produces a source-code listing, it usually numbers the lines of the source code consecutively from one. Write a program that accepts the name of a text file and numbers its lines beginning at one. The output of the program should be a file with the same name as the source file and with the extension .lst. Remember to first remove any extension the file name has before adding the .lst.

4. The cloze procedure test is a quick way for a teacher to estimate the difficulty of a text book. The procedure consists of deleting every fifth word from a passage from the book. While reading the passage, the student is expected to replace the deleted words. Write a program that reads words from a text file and prepares a cloze test. For purposes of the test, a word is any sequence of alphabetic characters. Therefore, do not delete things such as hyphens and punctuation. Leave the first and last sentences intact. Begin at the second word in the second sentence and replace every fifth word by 15 underscores until 50 words are deleted.

The following table gives the suitability of the text.

Percent Correct	Suitability of Text
Below 40%	Too Hard
Between 40% and 60%	Appropriate for Instruction
Above 60%	Too Easy

Hittleman, Daniel R., *Developmental Reading*. Rand McNally College Publishing Co., Chicago: 1978.

14.3 Random Acess Files

In sections 14.1 and 14.2, we processed files **sequentially**, one character or record at a time. It is also possible to process the characters in a file **randomly**. A program can begin processing a file at any desired location within the file, then go to another location in the file, and so on at random.

Text and Binary Files

As we discussed in Section 14.1, all the files we have processed so far are **text files**. A text file, for example a C++ source-code program, is a sequence of characters that occasionally includes a new-line character. In some operating systems, most notably DOS/Windows, when a program places a new-line character into a file, the new-line character is physically stored as two characters: a carriage return and a line feed (CRLF). Similarly, when a program reads the CRLF pair from a text file, the system converts them into a single new-line character. Although the program "sees" only one character, the new-line character, the operating system is actually processing the CRLF pair.

When randomly processing a file, a program must know its exact position in the file. If we attempt to process a file that is opened as a text file (which is the default when using the opening modes previously discussed) randomly, the program can lose its place in the file. This can occur because of the conversion of the new-line character into the CRLF pair. Therefore, when we process a file randomly, we should not open the file as a text file.

When a program opens a file as a **binary file**, none of the characters is ever changed when read or written by the program. The program will process the new-line character, if it is stored as the CRLF pair, as a pair of characters instead of as a single character.

To open a file in binary mode, you must use the opening mode `ios::binary` together with one of the opening modes previously discussed. To do this requires use of `|`, the **bitwise OR** operator. Do not confuse the logical OR operator, `||`, with bitwise OR. Logical OR returns true, that is numeric 1, if either of its operands are true. Bitwise OR works at the bit level between its operands. If either of two bits is 1, the bitwise OR of them is 1. The only time bitwise OR results in a 0 bit is when the bits are both 0. Following is an example. Note that the only time we obtain a 0 is when both bits are 0.

```
  1010 1010          First operand
  0010 0111          Second operand
- - - - - - - - -
  1010 1111          Bitwise OR
```

Bitwise OR is used to set (that is, make 1) particular bits. Note in the example that if a bit in the first operand is 0, the result of the bitwise OR is to copy the corresponding bit of the second operand into the result. On the other hand, if a bit in the first operand is 1, the result of the bitwise OR is a 1 in the corresponding position of the result, no matter what the bit in the second operand. Thus, to set a bit to 1, bitwise OR it with 1. Bitwise ORing with 0 leaves the bit unchanged. For example, consider the following bitwise OR in which we do not know the second operand.

```
  0010 0000          First operand
  ???? ????          Second operand
- - - - - - - - -
  ??1? ????          Bitwise OR
```

No matter what the bit value of the second operand, the third bit from the left must be a 1 in the result.

The opening modes for files, for example `ios::in` and `ios::binary`, actually refer to specific bits in a status variable defined in the `ios` class. For illustrative purposes, suppose that opening a file in the `ios::in` mode results in setting the second bit of that variable to 1.

0100 0000

Also suppose that opening the file in `ios::binary` mode results in setting the fifth bit to 1.

0000 1000

Now if we open the file in `ios::in | ios::binary` mode, the resulting bitwise OR of the two modes would be as follows:

```
  0100 0000          ios::in
  0000 1000          ios::binary
- - - - - - - - -
  0100 1000          ios::in | ios::binary
```

The file would be opened in both the input and binary modes since both the input and binary bits are 1. The following statement would, therefore, open the file "bindata.dat" as a binary input file.

```
fstream in_file ("bindata.dat", ios::in | ios::binary);
```

It is also possible to open a file using three of the opening modes as follows.

```
fstream iofile("bindata.dat", ios::in | ios::out | ios::binary);
```

The file "bindata.dat" is open in the binary mode as both an input and an output file. The program can read and write data to the file without having to close and open the file between file operations.

Random Access Member Functions

The C++ I/O classes contain several member functions that enable a program to access a file randomly. Each of these functions manipulates the file's File Position Indicator, or FPI. Recall that the member functions `get()` and `put()` determine where to access the file by using the FPI. If we can manipulate the FPI, we can read or write characters to any desired location in the file.

The functions of Note 14.6 are available for stream objects.

NOTE 14.6—RANDOM ACCESS MEMBER FUNCTIONS

The following functions are available to perform random file access.

```
seekg(offset, mode)    // for input files - move to offset as indicated by mode.
seekp(offset, mode)    // for output files - move to offset as indicated by mode.
tellg() // for input files - returns the current value of the FPI (a long).
tellp() // for output files - returns the current value of the FPI (a long).
```

You can think of the suffix "p" in the function names as meaning "put" and the suffix "g" as meaning "get."

The *offset* must be a long integer (positive or negative). The *mode* can be any of the following:

```
ios::beg    //Places the FPI at the beginning of the file.
ios::cur    //Places the FPI at the current position in the file.
ios::end    //Places the FPI at the end of the file.
```

A few examples will illustrate the uses of these functions. Figure 14.7 shows the eight-character file `"fpitest.dat"`, which is opened as a binary file as follows.

```
fstream in_file("fpitest.dat", ios::in | ios::binary);
```

Opening the file in `ios::in` mode sets its FPI to zero, as Figure 14.7a shows. The caret shows the character that the FPI indicates. Figure 14.7b shows the FPI after executing `in_file.seekg(3L, ios::cur)`. (The suffix L causes the computer to

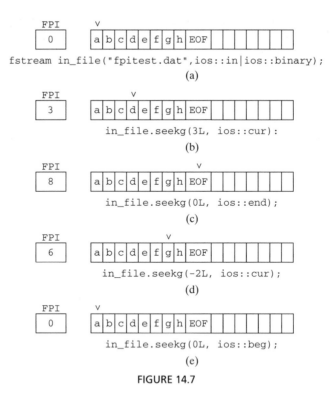

FIGURE 14.7

store the integer 3 as a `long` instead of the default type `int`. You can also use a type cast `(long)3` or `long(3)` in place of the suffix L.) Because the second argument of `seekg()` is `ios::cur`, the function initially does nothing to the value of the FPI. Because the first argument is 3L, `seekg()` adds three to the FPI. The value of the FPI is 3 and the character it indicates is `'d'`.

Figure 14.7c shows how to move the FPI to the end of the file by executing `in_file.seekg(0L, ios::end)`. Figure 14.7d shows that the first argument in `seekg()` can be negative. The statement `in_file.seekg(−2L, ios::cur)` subtracts two from the current value of the FPI. The statement "backs up" the FPI to the character `'g'`. Finally, as shown in Figure 14.7e, the statement `in_file.seekg(0L, ios::beg)` sets the FPI back to zero, which makes the FPI indicate the first character in the file.

You can use the function `tellg()` to find the value of the FPI at any point in your program. For example, the following statements calculate the size of a file in bytes.

```
long file_size;
in_file.seekg(0L, ios::end);
file_size = in_file.tellg();
```

The following program, dem14-7.cpp, illustrates these concepts. The program asks the user for the name of a file. The program then uppercases all the characters in the file. Note that the program does not make an uppercase version of the file while leaving the original intact. It opens the file, uppercases its characters, and closes the file.

```cpp
//dem14-7.cpp

//This program demonstrates the use of seekg() and tellg().
//The program uppercases a file that is provided by the user.

#include <iostream.h>
#include <fstream.h>
#include <stdlib.h>
#include <ctype.h>
#include <iomanip.h>

using namespace std;

int main()
{
  char file_name [51];
  char ch;

  cout << "\nEnter the file you want to uppercase: ";
  cin.getline(file_name, 51);

  fstream file(file_name, ios::in | ios::out | ios::binary);

  if (!file)
    {
      cout << "\nERROR: Could not open file.";
      exit(1);
    }

  while ( (ch = file.get()) != EOF)
    {
      ch = toupper(ch);
      file.seekg(-1L, ios::cur);
      file.put(ch);
      cout << setw(5) << file.tellg() << setw(6) << ch << endl;
    }

  cout << "\nCharacters processed: " << file.tellg();

  file.close();

  return 0;
}
```

Program Input File

```
abC De
fg
```

Program Output—Monitor

```
Enter the file you want to uppercase: test.txt
        1       A
        2       B
        3       C
        4
        5       D
        6       E
        7
        8

        9       F
       10       G
       11
       12


Characters processed: 12
```

Program Output—Output File

```
ABC DE
FG
```

The program begins by asking the user to enter the name of the file to be upper-cased. The program stores the name of the file in the array file_name[]. The program then creates an fstream object called file, which is opened as a binary file for both input and output. After checking that the file was opened correctly, the program enters the while loop. The while loop's condition gets a character from the file and tests for the end of file condition. If a character is read, the first statement in the loop body stores the uppercase version of the character in the variable ch. Since file.get() increased the FPI by one, the next statement in the loop body subtracts one from the FPI. This ensures that the next file operation, namely file.put(ch), places the character back into its original position in the file. Note that executing file.put(ch) again increases the FPI by one, so the next file.get() will retrieve the next character in the file. The last statement in the loop body displays the current value of the FPI using file.tellg() and the current value of ch. Finally, when the program exits the loop, it displays the number of characters processed, which is the number of characters in the file (remember that the new-line character is actually two characters). Can you explain why there is a blank line between the line that is numbered 8 and the line that is numbered 9?

EXERCISES 14.3

In Exercises 1–5, assume that the file `alpha.dat` contains only the 26 lowercase letters of the alphabet (abcd...wxyz). In each exercise, state the letter of the alphabet that the FPI indicates after executing the given instruction. Assume that the statements are executed in sequence.

1. `fstream input_file("alpha.dat", ios::in | ios::binary);`
2. `input_file.seekg(5L, ios::cur);`
3. `input_file.seekg(3L, ios::cur);`
4. `input_file.seekg(-3L, ios::end);`
5. `input_file.seekg(5L, ios::beg);`

In Exercises 6–15, assume that the file `alpha.dat` contains only the 26 lowercase letters of the alphabet (abcd...wxyz). In each exercise, either give the letter that the FPI indicates or state the change made to the file and the resulting value of the FPI. Assume that the statements are executed in sequence.

6. `fstream input_file("alpha.dat", ios::in | ios::out | ios::binary);`
7. `input_file.seekg(7L, ios::beg);`
8. `ch = input_file.get();`
9. `input_file.seekg(3L, ios::cur);`
10. `ch = input_file.get();`
11. `input_file.seekg(-5L, ios::end);`
12. `input_file.put('*');`
13. `ch = input_file.get();`
14. `input_file.seekg(-1L, ios::cur);`
15. `ch = input_file.get();`

In Exercises 16–19 , suppose that byte b contains the bits 1010 0101. Give the result of bitwise ORing b with the indicated byte.

16. `0000 0000`
17. `1111 1111`
18. `0101 1010`
19. `b`

EXPERIMENTS 14.3

1. Write a program that asks the user for the name of a file and then prints a capitalized version of the file on the printer.
2. Remove the `ios:binary` from the file opening mode in dem14-7.cpp. Compile and execute the resulting program. What happens? Carefully explain the resulting output.
3. A student writes the executable part of `main()` in dem14-7.cpp as follows. Does this version of the program work? If not, explain why.

```
cout << "\nEnter the file you want to uppercase: ";
cin.getline(file_name, 51);

fstream file(file_name, ios::in | ios::out | ios::binary);

while ( !file.eof() )
  {
    ch = input_file.get();

    input_file.seekg(-1L, ios::cur);
    input_file.put(toupper(ch));
    input_file.seekg(0L, ios::cur);
  }

input_file.close();
```

4. The bitwise AND operator, &, (not to be confused with the logical AND operator, &&) is defined as follows. If both of two bits are 1, then the bitwise AND of them is 1. Otherwise the bitwise AND of them is 0. Therefore, if either bit is 0, the bitwise AND of them is 0. Here is an example. Note that the only time we obtain a 1 is when both bits are 1.

1010 1010	First operand
0010 0111	Second operand
- - - - - - - - -	
0010 0010	Bitwise AND

Whereas the bitwise OR is used to turn on a bit, the bitwise AND is used to turn off a bit. Note that no matter what a bit is set to, ANDing it with a 0 will result in a 0. Anding a bit with a 1 leaves the bit unchanged. Now, suppose that byte b contains the bits 1010 0101. Give the result of bitwise ANDing b with the indicated byte.

  a. 0000 0000

  b. 1111 1111

  c. 0101 1010

  d. b

PROGRAMMING PROBLEMS 14.3

1. Write a program that asks the user to enter the name of a file. The program should display the number of characters in the file.

2. Write a program that asks the user to enter the name of a text file. The program should display on the monitor the contents of the file in reverse order, from the last character to the first.

3. Write a program that asks the user to enter the name of a text file. The program should display the middle character in the file on the monitor if there is an odd

number of characters in the file. If there is an even number of characters in the file, the program should display the middle two characters.

4. Write a program that asks the user to enter the name of a text file and a positive integer, *n*. The program should display on the monitor the *n*-th character in the file. If *n* exceeds the number of characters in the file, the program should display an error message.

14.4 Binary Sequential File Processing

In Section 14.1 we created and processed a text file of records in which each record was a line of text terminated by a new-line character. The fields in the file's records were text fields separated by one or more spaces. When processing such a file, each record is not read or written as a unit. To write a record to such a file requires writing each field separately. Likewise, to read a record from such a file requires reading each field separately. In C++, we can store and process all the data in a record as a unit by using a structure to implement the records in a file. For example, we could use the following structure for the part record of the inventory file of Section 14.1. Recall that each record in the part inventory file consists of three fields: the ID number field, the quantity on hand field, and the price field. The members of the structure are the fields of the record.

```
struct Part_Record
{
   char   id_no[3];
   int    qoh;
   double price;
};
```

The `Part_Record` structure is in binary form. Although the first member of the structure, `id_no`, is character data, it is of fixed size - three bytes. The `qoh` and `price` members are binary data, not text data. To illustrate the difference, suppose that the value of `qoh` for a specific record is 23450. If this is stored as text, it requires five bytes of memory. However, since 23450 is an integer, if stored as an integer (that is, in binary), it requires as little as two bytes on some systems. In fact, on a given computer system, all integers require the same amount of storage (two bytes on DOS/Windows systems; four bytes on UNIX systems) no matter what their values. The same is true of doubles (eight bytes on all systems.) Since each field in `Part_Record` is a fixed size (three bytes for `id_no`, two bytes for `qoh`, and eight bytes for `price`), there is no need to separate the fields by spaces. Also, when we write such records to a binary sequential file, the new-line character *will not* separate one record from the next. Instead, any program that processes this file distinguishes one record from the next by the length of the record. This is possible because all records in the file are the same size.

In this section we discuss how to create and process binary sequential files that consist of sequences of structures. That is, we discuss how to create and process a sequential binary file of records.

Creating a Binary Sequential File of Records

We first consider binary files that are created and accessed sequentially. Suppose that we have a data file of inventory records that was created using a text editor or by a program such as prb14-1.cpp in Section 14.1. Each record is a line in the file. Each line consists of a two-digit part number, an integer quantity on hand, and a decimal valued unit price. Spaces separate each of these fields from the others. The following is an example inventory file. The first field in each record is a two-character ID number. The second field is an integer representing the quantity on hand for the part. The third field is the price of the item.

```
23 145     24.95
15 46      67.99
65 230     11.95
56 37      73.95
59 1074     3.95
12 26     104.99
84 19      55.95
03 81      18.95
44 39      31.95
```

We wish to write a program that reads records from this file and writes them to a binary sequential file. We assume that the records of the binary sequential file are Part_Record structures, as described previously. One way to read records from the input text file is to use the extraction operator <<. Because we must obtain three fields from the file for each record, we use the function Read_Part_Record() to read a record from the file. The definition of the function is as follows.

```
void Read_Part_Record(ifstream& ifs, Part_Record& pr)
{
  ifs >> pr.id_no;
  ifs >> pr.qoh;
  ifs >> pr.price;
}
```

The function takes two arguments. The first argument is a reference to an ifstream object. Therefore, we shall pass the input file object name as the first argument. The second argument is a reference to a Part_Record structure. Therefore, we shall pass the name of a Part_Record structure as the second argument. The function reads three data items from the ifstream object, ifs, and places them into the three members of the part structure. The program can then manipulate the part structure.

Assume the following declarations in our program.

```
Part_Record part;
ifstream input_file(input_file_name);
```

To read a data from the input file, we could execute the following statement, which reads a record from `input_file` and places a copy of the record into the structure `part`.

```
Read_Part_Record(input_file, part);
```

Now that we can read data from the input file, we want to write it onto a binary file as a structure. To do this requires the member function `write()`, whose syntax is given in Note 14.7.

NOTE 14.7—THE SYNTAX OF THE MEMBER FUNCTION `write()`

The member function `write()`, which can be applied to any output file object opened in binary mode, has the following syntax.

```
write( (char*) ptr, item_size)
```

Here `ptr` is a pointer to the data that is to be written. The pointer must be cast as a character pointer because generally it will be pointing to some kind of structure. The second argument, `item_size`, is the number of bytes to be written, which is usually the size of the structure that is being written to the file. Use the operator `sizeof()`, which we will discuss, to have the system determine the number of bytes in the structure.

We cast the structure pointer as `(char*)` for the following reason. The people who coded the `write()` function could not know the data type of the first argument. The first argument could be a pointer to any structure that you choose. To allow `write()` to be used with any pointer, the function assumes its first argument to be a character pointer. Then, to use the function, the programmer simply casts the first argument as a character pointer.

Programming
Pointers

The operator `sizeof()` 1 is an operator, *not* a function. It returns the number of bytes required to store a variable of the type that is its argument. You use the `sizeof()` operator in much the same way you use a function. Place the name of a data type (one of C++'s built-in types or a user-defined type) in parentheses after `sizeof`. The value returned by the operator is the number of bytes required to store a variable of that type. Thus, `sizeof(int)` is the number of bytes required to store an integer in the system on which the function is evaluated. On a DOS/Windows system, `sizeof(int)` is two and on a UNIX system, `sizeof(int)` is four.

To write a copy of the structure variable `part` onto the file `input_file`, we execute the following statement.

```
input_file.write( (char*) &part, sizeof(Part_Record) );
```

In the first argument, &part is the address of (that is a pointer to) the area of storage that is to be copied onto the file. As required by the function, the (char*) casts the Part_Record pointer as a character pointer. The second argument is the number of bytes to copy.

Following is program dem14-8.cpp, which reads records from a text file and writes structures onto a binary sequential file of records.

```
//dem14-8.cpp

//This program creates a sequential file of structures from a text
//data file. It uses >> to obtain data from the text file
//and uses the write() member function to write structures
//onto the output file.

#include <iostream.h>
#include <fstream.h>
#include <stdlib.h>

using namespace std;

struct Part_Record
{
  char   id_no[3];
  int    qoh;
  double price;
};

void Read_Part_Record(ifstream&, Part_Record&);

int main()
{
  int record_count = 0;

  char input_file_name[51];
  char output_file_name[51];

  Part_Record part;

  cout << "\nEnter the name of the text file: ";
  cin.getline(input_file_name, 51);

  ifstream input_file(input_file_name);

  if (!input_file)
    {
      cout << "\nERROR: Could not open text file.";
      exit(1);
    }
```

```
   cout << "\nEnter the name of the sequential file: ";
   cin.getline(output_file_name, 51);

   ofstream output_file(output_file_name, ios::binary);

   if (!output_file)
     {
       cout << "\nERROR: Could not open sequential file: ";
       exit(1);
     }



   //Read the first record

   Read_Part_Record(input_file, part);

   while (!input_file.eof())
     {
       output_file.write( (char*)&part, sizeof(Part_Record) );

       ++record_count;

       Read_Part_Record(input_file, part);
     }

   cout << endl << endl << record_count << " records written.";

   input_file.close();
   output_file.close();

   return 0;
}

void Read_Part_Record(ifstream& ifs, Part_Record& pr)
{
  ifs >> pr.id_no;
  ifs >> pr.qoh;
  ifs >> pr.price;
}
```

Program Output—Monitor

```
Enter the name of the text file: dem14-8.in

Enter the name of the sequential file: dem14-8.out


9 records written.
```

Input File: dem14-8.in

```
23 145    24.95
15 46     67.99
65 230    11.95
56 37     73.95
59 1074    3.95
12 26    104.99
84 19     55.95
03 81     18.95
44 39     31.95
```

In the program, we first declare a counter, `record_count`, which counts the number of records the program processes. Two character arrays store the system names of the input and output files. The `Part_Record` structure `part` is where the program will place the data. The program then obtains the names of the input and output files and opens associated file objects. Note that the input file is opened, by default, as a text file, and the output file is opened as a binary file.

When reading a file sequentially, you must take care that your program processes the last input record, and that it processes it exactly once. Note 14.4, the Read Ahead Rule, applies here also: Read the first record after opening the file; Read the next record as soon as the program completes processing the input data.

The program code of dem14-8.cpp follows this outline. After the input file is opened, the program reads the first record using the function `Read_Part_Record()`. The program passes the name of the file and the `Part_Record` structure `part` as reference arguments to the function. In the body of the function, the extraction operator obtains the three fields and places each into the corresponding data member of the structure. The `while` loop then tests the end of file condition. If it is not the end of file, the loop body executes and processes the record. The processing is simply to write a copy of the record onto the sequential output file and to increment the record counter. Then the input file is read again. The program exits the loop when the end of file is reached. Then the program displays the number of records that were processed and closes the files.

Reading a Sequential File of Records

To read the records of the sequential file created by dem14-8.cpp, we need the member function `read()` whose syntax is given in Note 14.8.

NOTE 14.8—THE SYNTAX OF THE MEMBER FUNCTION `read()`

The member function `read()`, which can be applied to any input file object that is opened as a binary file, has the following syntax.

```
read( (char*) ptr, item_size)
```

Here `ptr` is a pointer to the location where the read data is to be stored. The pointer must be cast as a character pointer because it will generally be pointing to some kind of structure. The second argument, `item_size`, is the number of bytes to be read, which is usually the size of the structure that is being read from the file. Use the operator `sizeof()` to have the system determine the number of bytes in the structure.

Program dem14-9.cpp shows how to read the records from a sequential file of structures and to write them onto a file that is suitable for printing

```cpp
//dem14-9.cpp

//This program shows how to read a sequential file of structures.
//It uses the member function read() to read records from the file
//and uses << to print records to a disk text file in a form
//suitable for later printing. The program assumes that the input file
//has been previously created by the program dem14-8.cpp

#include <iostream.h>
#include <iomanip.h>
#include <fstream.h>
#include <stdlib.h>

using namespace std;

struct Part_Record
{
  char    id_no[3];
  int     qoh;
  double  price;
};

int main()
{
  Part_Record part;

  char input_file_name[51];
  char output_file_name[51];

  int record_count = 0;

  cout << "\nEnter the name of the printable file: ";
  cin.getline(output_file_name, 51);

  ofstream output_file(output_file_name);

  if (!output_file)
    {
      cout << "ERROR: Could not open printable file.";
      exit(1);
    }
```

```
output_file << setw(15) << "Part Number" << setw(15) << "Quan on Hand"
            << setw(15) << "Price" << endl << endl;

cout << "\nEnter the name of the sequential file: ";
cin.getline(input_file_name, 51);

ifstream input_file(input_file_name, ios::binary);

if (!input_file)
  {
    cout << "\nERROR: Could not open sequential file.";
    exit(1);
  }

input_file.read( (char*) &part, sizeof(Part_Record) );

while (!input_file.eof())
  {
    ++record_count;
    output_file << setw(15) << part.id_no << setw(15) << part.qoh
                << setw(15) << part.price << endl;

    input_file.read( (char *) &part, sizeof(Part_Record) );
  }

cout << endl << endl << record_count << " records read.";

input_file.close();
output_file.close();

return 0;
}
```

Program Output—Monitor

```
Enter the name of the printable file: dem14-9.out

Enter the name of the sequential file: dem14-8.out


9 records read.
```

Listing of dem14-8.out

Part Number	Quan on Hand	Price
23	145	24.95
15	46	67.99
65	230	11.95

56	37	73.95
59	1074	3.95
12	26	104.99
84	19	55.95
03	81	18.95
44	39	31.95

First, the program obtains the name of the printable file and opens it. Then it writes column headings onto the file using the insertion operator. Next, the program obtains the name of the sequential input file and opens it in binary mode. Using the Read Ahead Rule of Note 14.4 again, the program reads the first record from the input file using the `read()` member function. It then enters the `while` loop, where it increments `record_count` and writes the three structure members (the ID number, quantity on hand, and price) onto the output file. Since this completes processing the current record, the program then reads the next input record using `read()`. When the program reaches the end of file, the loop ends and the program displays the number of records processed. Finally, the program closes both files. A listing of the output file and the output that the program displays on the monitor is shown after the program code.

EXERCISES 14.4

Suppose a text file contains on each line, separated by spaces, a decimal number and an integer representing a price and a quantity.

1. Code a structure declaration `Item` for a structure to contain the price and quantity as members.
2. Code a function `Read_Item()` that reads a record from the file described into a structure variable of type `Item`.
3. Code a `write()` statement that writes an `Item` structure onto the binary file `item_file`, which is opened for output.
4. Code a `read()` statement that reads an `Item` structure from the binary file `item_file`, which is opened for input.

EXPERIMENTS 14.4

1. In dem14-08.cpp, omit the opening mode `ios::binary` in the declaration of `output_file`. Compile the resulting program. What happens and why?
2. In dem14-08.cpp, declare `output_file` as an `fstream` object. Make the appropriate changes to the program. Compile, execute, and test the resulting program. Do these changes make any difference?
3. In dem14-08.cpp, omit the first call to the function `Read_Part_Record()`. Compile, execute, and test the resulting program. What happens and why?
4. In dem14-08.cpp, omit the type cast `(char*)` in the `write()` function inside the `while` loop. Compile the resulting program. What happens and why? If the program compiles without error, execute the program. Do any run-time errors occur?

5. In dem14-09.cpp, omit the opening mode `ios::binary` from the declaration of `input_file`. Compile, execute, and test the resulting program. Explain the results.

PROGRAMMING PROBLEMS 14.4

1. (See Programming Problem 2, Section 14.1) A small business wants to create a file to store its customer information. Each record in the file is to contain the following data: customer ID number (a two-digit integer), first name, last name, city, zip code, and account balance. Design a record structure for the records of this file. Write a program to create a binary sequential customer file. The program should prompt the user for the information on each record and then create and store the record as a structure in the file.

2. Write a program that displays the file in Programming Problem 1 in column form with appropriate column headings on the printer and writes a copy of the report on a system file.

3. Write a program that creates a sequential binary file of account records. Each record in the file contains an ID number (a four-digit integer), a customer name, credit limit, and account balance. The program should ask the user to enter the data for each account. Then the program should write the data as a structure onto the account file.

4. (See Programming Problem 4, Section 14.1) The National Bank credit card company wishes to issue a new type of card, the Platinum Card, to its preferred customers. Write a program that prints a report that lists all customers who will or can receive a Platinum Card. The customer data is contained in the sequential file created in Programming Problem 3. Each record in the file contains the following fields: the customer ID number (a four-digit integer), the customer name, credit limit, and account balance. If a customer has a credit limit of at least $2000 and an account balance of $500 or less, the customer will receive a Platinum Card. If a customer's credit limit is at least $2000 and the account balance is greater than $500, the customer will be sent a letter. The letter will state that if the customer's balance becomes $500 or less, he or she will receive a Platinum Card.

   Each line of the report should list the customer ID number, customer name, credit limit, account balance, and either the word APPROVED, LETTER, or DISAPPROVED. The report should contain appropriate column headings. At the end of the report, print the number of customers in each category. Output the report to the printer and a system report file.

5. A retail store owner must submit a monthly report to the city government that lists each of the store's employees, together with each employee's gross pay for the month, city tax, and net pay. Write a program that prompts the user to enter each employee's name and gross pay for the month. If the employee's gross pay is $1000 or less, the city tax rate is 5% of the gross pay. If the gross pay exceeds $1000, the city tax is $50 plus 7.5% of the gross pay over $1000. The net pay is the gross pay less the city tax. The program should print the city tax report on a printer and create a binary sequential employee file. Each record in the file contains the employee's name, gross pay, city tax, and net pay.

6. Write a program that reads the binary sequential employee file created in Programming Problem 5 and displays a list of all employees whose gross pay exceeds $1000.

14.5 Random Record Input/Output

In this section we describe how to process a binary random access file of records. This requires using the techniques and functions of the previous sections. We begin by discussing a problem.

Random Access File Update

Problem: The accounts receivable department wants a program that will enable them to randomly access a file called `partfile.dat` that contains information on parts. Each record in the file contains a two-digit part number (01-99), the quantity on hand for the part, and the unit price of the part. The user must be able to do the following:

1. Add a record to the file.

2. Find a record in the file and change either the quantity on hand or the price, or both.

3. Delete a record from the file.

4. Display the contents of the file.

The program must be able to process the records in any order.

Programming
Pointers

We shall use a type of random file called a **relative file**. In a relative file, a program uses a record's position in the file to access the record. For our problem, we shall use the part number, which is an integer from 01 to 99, as the **relative record number**. Therefore, the record for part 01 is the first record in the file, the record for part 02 is the second record in the file, and so on. The 47th record in the file is the record for part number 47. Conceptually, the records in a relative file are stored sequentially. Therefore, a relative file is analogous to an array. See Figure 14.8.

Programming
Pointers

Before using a relative file, a program must create the file with enough space for the file's records. This empty file will contain records (structures) that are filled with null information. For example, all numeric fields will contain zero and any character string field will contain the null string. Our program must create a file of 99 structures of type `Part_Record` if the file does not already exist. The part number member of this structure, `id_no`, is a string. If the `id_no` member of a structure in this file contains the null string, we consider the record to be empty.

record 1	record 2		record 47	
01	02	• • •	47	• • •

A Relative File

FIGURE 14.8

Program Design

The logic of `main()` is simple. The program opens the file if it exists or creates it if it does not exist. The program then displays the main menu and takes the appropriate action depending on the user's menu choice. Following is the pseudocode for `main()`.

Pseudocode for main:

```
open partfile.dat or create it with null records
do
  get main menu choice
  switch (menu choice)
    case add:    add_record
    case delete: delete_record
    case change: change_record
    case display: display_file
    case quit:   quit program
    default:     display "Invalid Choice"
  endswitch
while( !quit )
close partfile.dat
```

The designs of the modules for adding, deleting, and changing a record and displaying the file are also straightforward. Following is the pseudocode for adding a record to the file.

Pseudocode for add_record:

```
get record number
validate record number
get rest of record data
find record position in file
if record does not already exist
  write record onto file
else
  display "Part already exists"
endif
```

The module begins by obtaining the record number from the user and validating the number (remember, the number must be between 01 and 99). If the record number is valid, the module obtains the rest of the record data from the user. Next, the module finds the position of the record in the file—that is, where to place the record in the file based on the record number. If there is no record currently occupying this position in the file, the record does not already exist and the module writes the record to the file. If there is a record occupying the position in the file, the record exists and the record cannot be added to the file. Therefore, the module displays an appropriate error message. Following is the pseudocode for the `delete_record` module.

Pseudocode for delete_record:

get record number
validate record number
find and read record from file
if record position is not occupied
  display "Record does not exist"
else
  delete record from file
endif

The `delete_record` module gets a record number from the user and then validates that the number is between 01 and 99. If the record number is in the valid range, the module finds that record position in the file and reads the contents of that position. If the record position is not occupied (remember, an "empty" record contains null information), the record does not exist and the module displays an appropriate error message. If the record position is occupied, the module deletes the record. Following is the pseudocode for `change_record`.

Pseudocode for change_record

get record number
validate record number
find and read record from file
if record position is not occupied
  display "Record does not exist"
else
  display current record contents
  do
    get change menu choice
    switch (change menu choice)
      case change q_o_h: get new q_o_h
      case change price: get price
      case quit and write: write changed record onto file
      default: display "Invalid Choice"
    endswitch
  while (!quit)

The module obtains and validates the number of the record to change. It then finds and reads that record from the file. If the record position is unoccupied, the record does not exist. The module displays an error message.

If the record position is occupied, the module makes the changes in a `do` loop. The module obtains a menu choice from the user. If the user chooses to change the quantity on hand field in the record, the module obtains the new quantity on hand from the user. If the user chooses to change the price field in the record, the module obtains the new price from the user. When satisfied with the changes to the record, the user can choose to write the record changes and quit the change module. The design of the `display_file` module follows.

Pseudocode for display_file:

move to start of the file
display column headings
for (rec_num = 1; rec_num <= 99; ++rec_num)
  read record
  if record is not empty
    print record
    increment record count
  endif
 endfor
print record count

The module begins by moving to the start of the file and displaying the column headings. The `for` loop then displays the file. For each record in the file, if the record is not empty, the module displays the record and increments the record count. After the module exits the `for` loop, it displays the record count.

To fully explain the rest of the program logic, we now discuss the program itself.

Program Code

Following is the code of prb14-3.cpp, our program solution to the random file update problem.

```
//prb14-3.cpp

#include <iostream.h>
#include <iomanip.h>
#include <fstream.h>
#include <stdlib.h>
#include <string.h>

using namespace std;

struct Part_Record
{
  char    id_no[3];
  int     qoh;
  double  price;
};

int Get_Menu_Choice();
void Add_Record(fstream&);
void Delete_Record(fstream&);
void Change_Record(fstream&);
int Get_Change();
void Display_File(fstream&);
int Valid_Rec_Num(long);
```

```
int main()
{
  int choice;
  int quit = 0;

  cout << setprecision(2)
       << setiosflags(ios::fixed)
       << setiosflags(ios::showpoint);

  fstream part_file;

  Part_Record null_part = { "", 0, 0.0};

  //Open the file for reading to see if file exists

  part_file.open("partfile.dat", ios::in | ios::binary);

  //If the file does not exist,
  //create a file of 99 dummy records.

  if (part_file.fail())
    {
      part_file.open("partfile.dat", ios::out | ios::binary);

      for (long rec_num = 1L; rec_num <= 99L; ++rec_num)
        part_file.write( (char *) &null_part, sizeof(Part_Record) );

      cout << "\nNull File Created.";
    }

  //Close the file

  part_file.close();

  //Open the file for both input and output

  part_file.open("partfile.dat", ios::in | ios::out | ios::binary);

  //Processing loop

  do
    {
      choice = Get_Menu_Choice();
      switch (choice)
        {
          case 1:
            Add_Record(part_file); break;
          case 2:
            Delete_Record(part_file); break;
```

```
              case 3:
                Change_Record(part_file); break;
              case 4:
                Display_File(part_file); break;
              case 5:
                quit = 1; break;
              default:
                cout << "\n\nInvalid Choice. Try Again.\n\n"; break;
          }
      }
    while (!quit);

    part_file.close();

    return 0;
} //End of main()

int Get_Menu_Choice()
{
    int choice;

    cout << "\n\nMain Menu";
    cout << "\n\n1 - Add a Record"
         << "\n2 - Delete a Record"
         << "\n3 - Change a Record"
         << "\n4 - Display the File"
         << "\n5 - Quit the Program";

    cout << "\n\nEnter your choice: ";
    cin >> choice;

    return choice;
} //End Get_Menu_Choice()

void Add_Record(fstream& file)
{
    Part_Record part;
    Part_Record temp_part;

    long rec_num;

    cin.get();

    cout << "\nEnter the data for a part:";
    cout << "\n\nPart Number (01-99): ";
    cin.getline(part.id_no, 3);

    rec_num = atol(part.id_no);
    if ( !Valid_Rec_Num(rec_num) )
        return;
```

```
      cout << "\nQuantity On Hand: ";
      cin >> part.qoh;

      cout << "\nPrice: ";
      cin >> part.price;

      file.seekg( (rec_num - 1) * sizeof(Part_Record), ios::beg);

      file.read( (char*)&temp_part, sizeof(Part_Record) );

      if ( strcmp(temp_part.id_no, "") == 0)
        {
          file.seekg( -(long)sizeof(Part_Record), ios::cur);
          file.write( (char*)&part, sizeof(Part_Record) );
          cout << "\nRecord " << part.id_no << " added to file.";
        }
      else
          cout << "\nPart already exists. Make another selection.";
   } //End of Add_Record

   void Delete_Record(fstream& file)
   {
     Part_Record part;
     Part_Record null_part = {"", 0, 0.0};

     long rec_num;

     cout << "\nEnter the number of the record to delete: ";
     cin >> rec_num;

     if (!Valid_Rec_Num(rec_num))
         return;

     file.seekg( (rec_num - 1) * sizeof(Part_Record), ios::beg);
     file.read( (char*) &part, sizeof(Part_Record) );

     if ( strcmp(part.id_no, "") == 0)
       cout << "\nThe record does not exist. Make another selection.";
     else
       {
          file.seekg(-(long)sizeof(Part_Record), ios::cur);
          file.write( (char*) &null_part, sizeof(Part_Record) );
          cout << "\nRecord " << rec_num << " deleted from file.";
       }

   } //End of Delete_Record

   void Change_Record(fstream& file)
   {
     Part_Record part;
     long rec_num;
```

```
int change;
int quit = 0;

cout << "\nEnter number of record to change: ";
cin >> rec_num;

if (!Valid_Rec_Num(rec_num))
    return;

file.seekg( (rec_num - 1) * sizeof(Part_Record), ios::beg);
file.read( (char*) &part, sizeof(Part_Record) );

if ( strcmp(part.id_no, "") == 0)
  {
    cout << "\nThe record does not exist. Make another selection.";
    return;
  }

cout << "\nThe current record contents are:\n\n";
cout << setw(20) << "Part Number"
     << setw(20) << "Quantity On Hand"
     << setw(20) << "Price" << endl << endl;
cout << setw(20) << part.id_no
     << setw(20) << part.qoh
     << setw(20) << part.price;

do
  {
    change = Get_Change();
    switch (change)
      {
        case 1:
          cout << "\nEnter Quantity On Hand: ";
          cin >> part.qoh;
          break;
        case 2:
          cout << "\nEnter Price: ";
          cin >> part.price;
          break;
        case 3:
          quit = 1;
          file.seekg(-(long)sizeof(Part_Record), ios::cur);
          file.write( (char*) &part, sizeof(Part_Record) );
          cout << "\nChanges made to record " << rec_num;
          break;
        default:
          cout << "\nInvalid Choice. Try Again.";
          break;
      }
  }
while (!quit);
```

```
  } //End of Change_Record()

int Get_Change()
{
  int change;

  cout << "\n\nChange Menu\n\n";
  cout << "1 - Change Quantity On Hand\n"
       << "2 - Change Price\n"
       << "3 - Write Changes and Return to Main Menu\n\n";
  cout << "Enter your choice: ";
  cin >> change;

  return change;
} //End Get_Change()

void Display_File(fstream& file)
{
  Part_Record part;
  long rec_num;
  long rec_count = 0L;

  file.seekg( 0L, ios::beg);

  cout << setw(20) << "\nPart Number"
       << setw(20) << "Quantity On Hand"
       << setw(20) << "Price" << endl << endl;

  for (rec_num = 1L; rec_num <= 99L; ++rec_num)
     {
       file.read( (char*) &part, sizeof(Part_Record) );
       if (strcmp(part.id_no, "") != 0)
         {
           cout << setw(20) << part.id_no
                << setw(20) << part.qoh
                << setw(20) << part.price << endl;
           ++rec_count;
         }
     }

  cout << "\n\nFile contains " << rec_count << " records.";

} //End of Display_File()

int Valid_Rec_Num(long rec_num)
{
  if ( rec_num < 1L || rec_num > 99L )
     {
       cout << "\n\nERROR: Invalid record number. Try again.";
       return 0;
     }
```

```
    else
        return 1;

} //End of Valid_Rec_Num()
```

Main() follows the logic of the pseudocode we developed in the last section. First, main() determines if the file exists by attempting to open the file for input. If the file does not exist, the open operation fails. The if statement uses the fail() member function. The fail() member function returns 1, that is true, if the attempted operation on the file fails. If you attempt to open a nonexistent file for input, the open fails. Therefore, the if statement tests true. In that case, the program opens the file for output (in this case the file is created), and 99 dummy records are written to the file. Whether the file does not exist and is created or if it already exists, the program then closes the file. To process the file randomly, the program now opens the file in both the input and output modes.

In the processing loop, main() obtains a menu choice from the user using the Get_Menu_Choice() function. Then a switch statement executes the function appropriate to the user's menu selection. The processing loop continues until the user selects the fifth menu choice.

Get_Menu_Choice() displays the menu of choices, one choice on a line, and obtains the choice using cin. Note that one cout displays the entire menu.

Add_Record() begins by using cin.get() to flush the stdin keyboard input buffer of the new-line character that was left in the buffer after the user made a menu choice. This is necessary because the first input function used by Add_Record() is cin.getline(). If we did not flush the keyboard input buffer, cin.getline() would retrieve the new-line character instead of the part number. The function obtains the part number and places it into the id_no member of the part structure variable. Then, the function uses atol() to convert the id_no string into the equivalent long int. Next, an if statement uses the function Valid_Rec_Num() to check that the record number is between 1 and 99. If rec_num is invalid, the function returns to main(). If rec_num is valid, the function obtains the quantity on hand and price from the user.

Add_Record() can now attempt to piace the record onto the file. First, seekg() adjusts the FPI to indicate the beginning of the record with record number rec_num. Each record in the file contains sizeof(Part_Record) bytes. The first byte of the record with record number rec_num is

```
(rec_num - 1) * sizeof(Part_Record)
```

bytes from the beginning of the file (Figure 14.9).

The read() then reads the record that it finds at this location into the structure variable temp_part. (Recall that this read() moves the FPI to the beginning of the next record.) If the id_no member of the record contains the null string, the record is empty. Therefore, we can add the new record. The seekg() backs up the FPI to the beginning of the record we just read. The write() then writes the new record onto

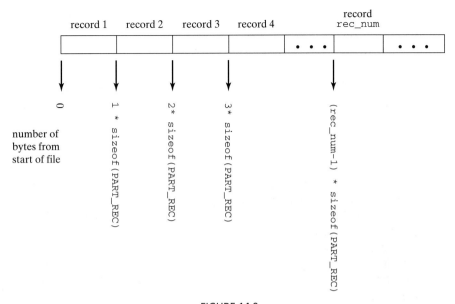

FIGURE 14.9

the file. If the `id_no` member of the record is not null, the record already exists. The function cannot add the record to the file and so it displays an error message.

`Delete_Record()` first asks for and obtains the record number of the record to delete. Then it uses `Valid_Rec_Num()` to verify that the record number is between 1 and 99. Next, `seekg()` adjusts the FPI to indicate the beginning of the record to delete and `read()` places a copy of the record into the structure variable `part`. Before deleting the record, `Delete_Record()` checks to see if the record is empty. If the record is empty, the `if` statement displays an error message. Otherwise `seekg()` backs up the FPI to the beginning of the record to delete and `write()` writes a null record in its place.

`Change_Record()` obtains and validates the record number in the same way as `Delete_Record()`. Next, it adjusts the FPI to indicate the beginning of the record to change and reads a copy of the record into the structure variable `part`. Since we cannot change a record that does not exist, the `if` statement checks to see if the record just read is empty. If it is empty, the function displays an error message and returns to `main()`. If the record is not empty, the function displays the contents of the record and executes a `do` statement to make the changes.

The first statement in the `do` loop body obtains the field to be changed from the user by executing `Get_Change()`, which is similar in form and content to `Get_Menu_Choice()`. The `switch` statement then acts on the value of `change`. If `change` is 1 or 2, the function obtains the appropriate data. If `change` is 3, the user wants to write the change onto the file. The `seekg()` backs up the FPI to the beginning of the record and the `write()` places a copy of the changed record onto the file.

The last function `main()` uses is `Display_File()`. After positioning the FPI to the beginning of the file, the function displays the column headings. Then, a `for` loop reads each record in the file. If the record is not empty, the `if` statement displays the record and increments `rec_count`. After the `for` loop ends, a `cout` displays the number of records in the file.

Following is a sample output for the program. See Experiment 2 for suggestions on testing the program.

Program Output

```
Null File Created.

Main Menu

1 - Add a Record
2 - Delete a Record
3 - Change a Record
4 - Display the File
5 - Quit the Program

Enter your choice: 1

Enter the data for a part:

Part Number (01-99): 11

Quantity On Hand: 123

Price: 45.99

Record 11 added to file.

Main Menu

1 - Add a Record
2 - Delete a Record
3 - Change a Record
4 - Display the File
5 - Quit the Program

Enter your choice: 1

Enter the data for a part:

Part Number (01-99): 22

Quantity On Hand: 234
```

```
Price: 67.95

Record 22 added to file.

Main Menu

1 - Add a Record
2 - Delete a Record
3 - Change a Record
4 - Display the File
5 - Quit the Program

Enter your choice: 1

Enter the data for a part:

Part Number (01-99): 33

Quantity On Hand: 345

Price: 67.89

Record 33 added to file.

Main Menu

1 - Add a Record
2 - Delete a Record
3 - Change a Record
4 - Display the File
5 - Quit the Program

Enter your choice: 4

        Part Number    Quantity On Hand              Price

                 11           123                    45.99
                 22           234                    67.95
                 33           345                    67.89


File contains 3 records.

Main Menu

1 - Add a Record
2 - Delete a Record
3 - Change a Record
4 - Display the File
5 - Quit the Program
```

```
Enter your choice: 3

Enter number of record to change: 22

The current record contents are:

            Part Number      Quantity On Hand            Price

                   22                  234               67.95

Change Menu

1 - Change Quantity On Hand
2 - Change Price
3 - Write Changes and Return to Main Menu

Enter your choice: 1

Enter Quantity On Hand: 203

Change Menu

1 - Change Quantity On Hand
2 - Change Price
3 - Write Changes and Return to Main Menu

Enter your choice: 3

Changes made to record 22

Main Menu

1 - Add a Record
2 - Delete a Record
3 - Change a Record
4 - Display the File
5 - Quit the Program

Enter your choice: 4
          Part Number      Quantity On Hand            Price

                   11            123               45.99
                   22            203               67.95
                   33            345               67.89

File contains 3 records.
```

```
Main Menu

1 - Add a Record
2 - Delete a Record
3 - Change a Record
4 - Display the File
5 - Quit the Program

Enter your choice: 3

Enter number of record to change: 33

The current record contents are:

          Part Number     Quantity On Hand              Price

                  33                   345              67.89

Change Menu

1 - Change Quantity On Hand
2 - Change Price
3 - Write Changes and Return to Main Menu

Enter your choice: 2

Enter Price: 70.89


Change Menu

1 - Change Quantity On Hand
2 - Change Price
3 - Write Changes and Return to Main Menu

Enter your choice: 3

Changes made to record 33

Main Menu

1 - Add a Record
2 - Delete a Record
3 - Change a Record
4 - Display the File
5 - Quit the Program

Enter your choice: 4
```

Part Number	Quantity On Hand	Price
11	123	45.99
22	203	67.95
33	345	70.89

File contains 3 records.

Main Menu

1 - Add a Record
2 - Delete a Record
3 - Change a Record
4 - Display the File
5 - Quit the Program

Enter your choice: 2

Enter the number of the record to delete: 11

Record 11 deleted from file.

Main Menu

1 - Add a Record
2 - Delete a Record
3 - Change a Record
4 - Display the File
5 - Quit the Program

Enter your choice: 4

Part Number	Quantity On Hand	Price
22	203	67.95
33	345	70.89

File contains 2 records.

Main Menu

1 - Add a Record
2 - Delete a Record
3 - Change a Record
4 - Display the File
5 - Quit the Program

Enter your choice: 5

1. Write a program that uses the operator `sizeof()` to find the number of bytes needed on your computer system to store a variable of the following types: `char`, `short`, `int`, `long`, `float`, and `double`.

2. Test prb14-3.cpp. First add at least five records to the file `partfile.dat`. This file will not exist before executing the program the first time, but the program should create it. Exit the program then execute the program again. The program should sense that the file `partfile.dat` already exists. Add at least two more records to the file. Display the current file. Now try the following to test the program. After each, display the file to verify the file's contents.

   a. Try to add a record that already exists.
   b. Change an existing record's quantity on hand field.
   c. Change an existing record's price field.
   d. Try to change a nonexistent record.
   e. Enter an invalid choice when asked which field to change.
   f. Delete an existing record.
   g. Try to delete a nonexistent record.
   h. Enter an invalid record number (say, 101) when asked for the record number of the record to delete.
   i. Make an invalid main menu choice.

3. Change prb14-3.cpp to allow the user to enter a record number and have that record displayed on the monitor. If the record does not exist, display an appropriate error message.

4. In the `Add_Record` module of prb14-3.cpp (see the pseudocode for `add_record`), it is probably more efficient to move "get rest of record data" into the `if` part of the module's `if` statement. Recode prb14-3.cpp appropriately.

5. In prb14-3.cpp, change the `Get_Menu_Choice()` function so that the user can enter A, D, C, L, or Q (also allow lowercase) instead of 1, 2, 3, 4, and 5. Also change the `Get_Change()` function to allow the user to enter Q, P, or W (also allow lowercase) instead of 1, 2, and 3.

6. What changes would you have to make to prb14-3.cpp if the `id_no` member of the `Part_Record` structure were stored as type `int` instead of a two-character string?

7. Change prb14-3.cpp as follows. Change the main menu that prb14-3.cpp displays so the user can choose to copy the file in one of several forms. This menu choice should lead to another menu. In the second menu, the user can choose to display the file on the terminal, print the file on the printer, or copy the file to a disk file.

8. Use enumerated types for the menu choices in prb14-3.cpp. For example, you might use the following `typedef` for the main menu choices.

```
typedef enum {add = 1, delete, change, display, quit} CHANGE;
CHANGE change;
```

Then, use the enumerated type values in the `switch` statement in `main()`. Define a similar `typedef` for the submenu choices in the function `Change_Record()`.

PROGRAMMING PROBLEMS 14.5

1. In the relative file that we created in prb14-3.cpp, a null string in the `id_no` member of the record identified an empty record. Another method of marking a record as empty is to place a one-character status field at the beginning of a record. If the field contains a blank, the record position in the file is empty. Otherwise, the record contains valid data. Change the `Part_Record` structure type to incorporate this idea and make all necessary changes to prb14-3.cpp. Add a one-character `status` member to the structure. When creating the file, place a blank into the `status` member of each record. When writing a record to the file, place a non-blank character, for example `'x'` in `status` to indicate the record is active.

2. A small business wants to create a file to store information on its customers. Each record in the file is to contain the following data: customer ID number (an integer 01–50), first name, last name, street address, city, zip code, and account balance. Write a program to create such a customer file. Set up the file as a relative file with the customer ID number as the relative record number.

3. Write a menu-driven program that allows the user to add, change, or delete a record from the customer file created in Programming Problem 2.

4. Write a program that asks the user for a specific zip code and then displays a list of all customers in the customer file created in Programming Problem 2 who have the given zip code. Be sure to format and appropriately label the output.

5. Write a program that asks the user for an account balance level and then displays a list of all customers in the customer file created in Programming Problem 2 who have an account balance greater than that entered. Be sure to format and appropriately label the output.

6. A small mutual fund company wants you to create a program to randomly access the data on stocks it holds. Presently, the data are stored in a text file, each line of which contains the following: a stock code, which is an integer between 100 and 999; the stock's current price; the change in the stock's price since the last trading day; the highest price for the stock during the last year; and the lowest price for the stock during the last year.

   Write a program that uses the text file to create a corresponding relative file. Translate the stock code to an appropriate relative record address.

7. Write a program that allows the user to randomly access the relative file created by Programming Problem 6. The program should allow the user to do the following:
   a. Enter a stock code and then display all the information about the stock, appropriately labeled.
   b. Add a new stock to the relative file.
   c. Delete a stock from the relative file.
   d. Change any of the data on a stock.

8. Periodically, usually at the end of a trading day, the mutual fund company of Programming Problem 6 wants to update the relative file of stock data. Assume that the new data on the stocks is in a transaction file (stored as a text file) each line of which has the following data: the stock code and the new closing price.

Write a program that updates the relative file. Do the following for each record in the transaction file:

    a. Make the current price of the corresponding record in the relative file equal to the new closing price.

    b. In the corresponding relative file record, make the price change equal to the difference between the old current value and the new current value.

    c. If the new current value is greater than the year's highest price, replace the year's highest price with the new current value.

    d. If the new current value is less than the year's lowest price, replace the year's lowest price with the new current value.

9. A personal computer manufacturing company keeps a relative file in which it stores data on the parts it uses to manufacture computers. Each record in the file contains the following data: part ID number (100–999), part name, quantity on hand, reorder quantity, and at most two ID numbers (01–99) of companies that supply the part. The manufacturing company also keeps a relative file of all suppliers of parts. Each record in that file contains the following data: supplier ID number (01–99), supplier name, street address, city, and zip code. Write a program that allows the user to enter a part number and then displays the suppliers of that part, including their addresses. Be sure to label the output appropriately.

10. As we mentioned in Chapter 9, you can load a table's values from a file. Recode dem09-3.cpp (specifically, recode the `Load_Part_Table()` function) so that the values for part table are loaded from a file. Assume the file containing the table data is a text file called `table.dat` stored in the same directory as the program. Each line of the text file contains the data for one table row: a seven-character part number, the quantity on hand, and the unit price.

Chapter Review

Terminology

Define the following terms.

stream I/O	end of file condition
`iostream` class	`eof()`
multiple inheritance	access mode constants
text file	`ios::in`
binary file	`ios::out`
`ifstream` class	`ios::app`
`fstreambase` class	`get()`
`ofstream` class	`put()`
`open()`	sequential file processing
File Position Indicator (FPI)	random file processing
`close()`	`ios::binary`

bitwise And `&`	`ios::end`
bitwise Or `|`	record
`seekg()`	field
`seekp()`	`write()`
`tellg()`	`sizeof()`
`tellp()`	`read()`
`ios::beg`	relative file
`ios::cur`	`fail()`

Summary

- All I/O in C++ is stream I/O. To give a file an additional structure, the programmer must write program instructions to do so.
- The class `iostream` is derived from classes `istream` and `ostream`.
- `cin` is a member of class `istream` and `cout` is a member of `ostream`.
- The functions `get()` and `getline()` are members of class `istream`, and therefore can be applied to `cin`.
- A text file consists of character data. At the end of each line in a text file is the new-line character.
- To declare an output file, declare an `ofstream` file object. The class `ofstream` derives from `ostream` and `fstreambase`.
- To open an `ofstream` object (an output file), and attach it to a system file, either use the `open()` member function or use the one-argument constructor of the `ofstream` class.
- Opening a file object attaches the object to a system file in an appropriate mode and creates the file's File Position Indicator (FPI) (Note 14.2).
- Every read and write operation changes the FPI.
- The insertion operator `<<` can be used to place data onto an `ofstream` file object.
- The `close()` member function can be used to close a file object.
- If an error occurs when opening a file, the value of the file object is zero (Note 14.3).
- A record is a set of data concerning a particular entity. Each fact within a record is a field.
- In a text file of records, spaces separate fields and the new-line character separates records.
- A sequential file is one whose records are stored in sequence.
- To declare an input file, declare an `ifstream` object. The class `ifstream` derives from `istream` and `fstreambase`.
- To open an `ifstream` object (input file), and attach it to a system file, either use the `open()` member function or use the one-argument constructor of the `ifstream` class.
- You can use the extraction operator `>>` as well as the `get()` and `getline()` functions to read data from an `ifstream` object.

- When reading an `ifstream` object, you must test for the end-of-file condition. The member function `eof()` returns one if the program reaches the end of file.
- Use the Read Ahead Rule to correctly process a sequential input file (Note 14.4). Read the first record after opening the file. Read the file again as soon as the program completes processing the input record.
- To declare a file that can be used for both input and output, declare an `fstream` file object. The `fstream` class derives from `iostream` (therefore, also from `istream` and `ostream`) and from `fstreambase`.
- When opening an `fstream` file object, specify its opening mode using either `ios::in`, `ios::out`, or `ios::app` (Note 14.5).
- The `get()` and `put()` member functions can be used to read and write one character to a file.
- You can output to the printer by attaching an output file object to your system's printer name (`"prn"` in DOS/Windows systems).
- In a text file on some systems (DOS/Windows), the new-line character is actually stored as a pair of characters—the carriage return/line feed pair. This pair is processed as though it were a single character. In a binary file, none of the characters is ever changed when read or written by the program.
- Use the access mode `ios::binary` to open a file in binary mode.
- The `seekg()` and `seekp()` member functions move the FPI to an indicated position in the file (Note 14.6).
- The `tellg()` and `tellp()` member functions return the value of the FPI. (Note 14.6).
- A structure can be used to store a record.
- A sequential binary file of records is a sequential file of structures.
- The `write()` member function can be used to write a structure onto a file (Note 14.7).
- The `read()` member function can be used to read a structure from a file (Note 14.8).
- A relative file is one in which a record's position in the file is used to access the record.
- A relative file can be processed randomly.

Review Exercises

1. How is input and output accomplished in C++?
2. Exactly what are `cin` and `cout` in terms of the classes `ostream` and `istream`?
3. Explain how to create and open a file object in C++.
4. What are the basic I/O classes and how are they related?
5. What is the File Position Indicator (FPI) and how is it affected by the various I/O functions?
6. If you do not explicitly close a file, what will C++ do when the program ends?
7. What is the end of file condition and how can your program detect it?

   8. How can you declare a file so that it can be used for both input and output?

   9. What are the three basic opening modes for a file and how do they affect the processing of the file?

   10. What member function can you use to read a single character from a file? To write a character to a file?

   11. How can you output to a printer?

   12. Explain the difference between sequential and random file access.

   13. Explain the difference between text and binary files. How do you declare a text file? A binary file?

   14. What is the bitwise OR and how is it used to set file opening modes?

   15. What are the two basic random access member functions and how are they used?

   16. What is a record? What is a field?

   17. Explain the differences in how the records and fields are stored in text files and binary files.

   18. What member function can place a record onto a file? Why should you use the `sizeof()` operator in this function?

   19. What member function can read a record from a file? Why should you use the `sizeof()` operator in this function?

   20. What is the Read Ahead Rule and why is it helpful?

   21. What is a relative file?

Appendix

A

Computers and Data

This appendix covers the ideas necessary to understand the first few chapters. First, we discuss a model computer system that will help you to understand many hardware-related ideas in the book. Next, we investigate how a computer stores characters, integers, and decimal numbers.

A.1 A Model Computer System

When discussing several concepts in this book, we use a simplified model of a computer consisting of the following. See Figure A.1.

1. Main memory—where programs are stored and data is manipulated.
2. Input and output ports—"gateways" through which data is passed to and from the computer.
3. Control unit—interprets and executes program instructions.

input port		output port
control unit		ALU
	operating system	
	Main Memory	

FIGURE A.1

4. Registers—special high-speed memory where the arithmetic/logic unit manipulates data.

5. Arithmetic/logic unit—carries out arithmetic and compare operations.

6. Operating System—a set of programs that help run the computer hardware and software.

Main Memory: The **main memory** of our model computer consists of cells of equal size called **bytes**. One byte is the amount of memory necessary to store one character, such as a letter of the alphabet, a digit, or a special character like a comma, a period, or a blank. We assume that these cells are arranged in a straight line, as Figure A.2 shows.

To keep track of the programs and data that reside in main memory, the computer identifies each byte by a numerical **address**. The first byte in main memory has address zero, the second byte address one, and so on to the last byte in the computer's main memory. See Figure A.2. Do not confuse the contents of a byte with the byte's address. The address of a byte specifies its location in main memory in much the same way as a house's address identifies its location in a city. Just as the contents of a house can change over time, the contents of a byte can change as a program executes. The address of the byte, however, is fixed and cannot change.

Main memory is important because of the following.

1. For a program to execute, it must reside in main memory.

2. For a program to manipulate data, the data must reside in main memory.

For example, suppose we want to execute a program that is stored on disk. Furthermore, suppose the program is to update data that is also stored on disk. To execute the program, you must first load it into main memory and begin its execution. When the program needs to update the data that is stored on disk, the program must transfer the data from the disk into main memory, operate on the data, and then transfer the updated data back onto the disk.

We assume that main memory has enough storage for our largest programs and for all our data.

The Control Unit: The **control unit** of our model computer interprets program instructions and carries them out. It can copy data from the main memory, place the data into the registers, pass the instruction that is to be executed to the arithmetic/logic unit, and copy the results from the registers back to main memory. It can accept data from outside the computer through one of the input ports and place that data into main memory. It can copy a portion of main memory and send it to an output device through one of the output ports. In short, the control unit interprets instructions and moves data from one part of the computer to another.

address	0	1	2	3	4	5	6	7	8	9	. . .
											. . .

FIGURE A.2

The Registers and the Arithmetic/Logic Unit: To do arithmetic on two numbers, the control unit must copy the numbers from main memory into special high speed memory locations called **registers**. We shall assume that our model computer has several registers—enough to enable it to carry out all necessary instructions. Once the control unit places the numbers into the registers, the **arithmetic/logic unit**, or **ALU**, can manipulate them. The ALU of our model computer contains electronic circuits that enable it to do the four basic arithmetic operations—addition, subtraction, multiplication, and division—on the contents of the registers. The ALU also does the logic operation of comparison. It can test the contents of two registers and decide how these data compare: are they equal, is one less than or greater than the other?

The following illustrates how the registers, ALU, and the control unit work together to execute an instruction. Suppose the computer is to carry out an instruction to add the numbers in locations A and B of main memory and place the sum in location C. The control unit makes copies of the numbers in A and B and transfers these values to two of the registers. Then, the control unit sends the ALU an instruction to add the two numbers. The ALU does the addition. The control unit then copies the result, which is in a register, into location C in main memory.

The Operating System: The **operating system** of a computer is a set of programs that helps control (or operate) the computer hardware and manage computer software (files and programs). Thus the operating system is the interface between the user and the computer system. The operating system keeps track of and maintains all input/output devices, main and auxiliary memory (such as floppy disks and hard disks), all current users of the system, and all files stored on the system. Large (or **mainframe**) IBM computers can use the OS, VS, MVS, or VM operating systems. Many medium size computers (or **minicomputers**) as well as some mainframes and PCs use the UNIX operating system. The most popular operating system for PCs (personal computers or **microcomputers**) is Windows.

Input and Output Ports: The computer communicates with its environment through the input and output ports.

An input port is connected to an **input device**, such as a keyboard or magnetic disk drive. The operating system supplies the data our programs process to the main memory of the computer through an input port via an input device. The operating system even gives our program to the computer through an input device so the computer can execute the program's instructions.

An output port is connected to an **output device** such as a printer, video monitor, or magnetic disk drive. The operating system outputs the data our programs produce through an output port and places that data on an output device.

Some devices, such as magnetic disk drives, serve as both input and output devices. Therefore it is possible for both an input and output port to be connected to the same device. For example, a program can obtain its data (input) from a disk drive and output its results (output) to the same disk.

We shall not be concerned with the characteristics of the different types of input and output devices. We assume that one input port is connected to the keyboard, one output port is connected to the video monitor, another output port is connected to a printer, and an input and an output port are connected to a magnetic disk drive. This reflects the usual setup for most computers.

A.2 Data Representation—Characters

Recall from Section A.1 that a **byte** is the amount of computer storage needed to store one character. But how is a character stored in a byte?

The ASCII Code: Typically, a byte is a set of eight miniature electronic switches, called **bits**, each of which is in either of two states—on or off. It is convenient to represent the two states by the digits 1 (for on) and 0 (for off). Thus a sequence of eight bits, that is eight 1s and 0s, represents the contents of a byte. We can then interpret a specific eight-bit pattern, such as 01000001, to mean a specific character, such as A. The bit patterns that represent particular letters, digits, and punctuation characters depend on the encoding scheme your computer uses. We will assume that your computer uses the **ASCII** code, which is the most widely used encoding scheme. (IBM mainframe computers use another encoding scheme, the EBCDIC code.)

Table A.1 shows the digits and the letters of the alphabet in the eight-bit ASCII code.

In ASCII code, the word Exam appears as follows in four consecutive bytes of main memory.

```
   E          x          a          m
01000101 01111000 01100001 01101101
```

TABLE A.1

0	00110000	M	01001101	i	01101001
1	00110001	N	01001110	j	01101010
2	00110010	O	01001111	k	01101011
3	00110011	P	01010000	l	01101100
4	00110100	Q	01010001	m	01101101
5	00110101	R	01010010	n	01101110
6	00110110	S	01010011	o	01101111
7	00110111	T	01010100	p	01110000
8	00111000	U	01010101	q	01110001
9	00111001	V	01010110	r	01110010
A	01000001	W	01010111	s	01110011
B	01000010	X	01011000	t	01110100
C	01000011	Y	01011001	u	01110101
D	01000100	Z	01011010	v	01110110
E	01000101	a	01100001	w	01110111
F	01000110	b	01100010	x	01111000
G	01000111	c	01100011	y	01111001
H	01001000	d	01100100	z	01100100
I	01001001	e	01100101		
J	01001010	f	01100110		
K	01101011	g	01100111		
L	01001100	h	01101000		

The Binary Number System and Characters: It is difficult to remember the ASCII codes in bit form because there are eight bits for each character. However, we can represent the codes in more compact form by taking advantage of the binary number system.

In the familiar decimal (or base 10) system, each digit position has a place value that is a power of 10. The units position is the rightmost position. As you go to the left in the number, each digit position has a place value that is the next power of 10.

$10^3 = 1000$	$10^2 = 100$	$10^1 = 100$	$10^0 = 1$
4	0	6	7

$$= 4(1000) + 0(100) + 6(10) + 7(1) = 4067$$

In the **binary (or base 2) number system**, we write numbers in terms of powers of two. Thus each bit position has a place value that is a power of two. The place values begin with units in the rightmost position, and continue with the successive powers of two as you go to the left. Since we are writing numbers as sums of powers of two, we need only two digits, 1 and 0, to represent numbers in the binary system.

We interpret the binary number 1001 as follows.

$2^3 = 8$	$2^2 = 4$	$2^1 = 2$	$2^0 = 1$
1	0	0	1

$$= 1(8) + 0(4) + 0(2) + 1(1)$$
$$= 1(8) + 0 + 0 + 1(1)$$
$$= 9 \text{ in decimal}$$

We can interpret each ASCII code in Table A.1 as an eight-bit binary number. For example, the letter A in the ASCII code is 01000001. As a binary number this code represents

$2^7 = 128$	$2^6 = 64$	$2^5 = 32$	$2^4 = 16$	$2^3 = 8$	$2^2 = 4$	$2^1 = 2$	1
0	1	0	0	0	0	0	1

$$= 1(64) + 0(1) = 65$$

Therefore the bit pattern that represents the letter A also can represent the decimal number 65. Similarly, the reader can verify that the ASCII bit pattern for the digit 4, 00110100, also can represent the decimal number 52 and the bit pattern for s, 01110011, can represent the decimal number 115.

It is important to realize that a bit pattern has no intrinsic meaning. Viewed as a character, the bit pattern 01000001 represents the letter A. Viewed as a binary number, the same bit pattern 01000001 represents the decimal number 65. It is up to you, the programmer, to decide how the program interprets the contents of a byte.

The Hexadecimal Number System and Characters: We can also use the **hexadecimal (or base 16) number system** to represent the bit patterns that make up the ASCII code. In the hexadecimal system, we write numbers in terms of powers of 16. Thus the place values are the successive powers of 16.

$16^3 = 4096$ $16^2 = 256$ $16^1 = 16$ $16^0 = 1$

Writing numbers in terms of powers of 16 requires the use of 16 hexadecimal digits. The decimal digits 0 through 9 represent the numbers zero through nine. The first six uppercase letters of the alphabet, A through F, represent the numbers 10 through 15. The first 16 hexadecimal numbers are

0, 1, 2, 3, 4, 5, 6, 7, 8, 9, A, B, C, D, E, F.

To find the decimal equivalent of the hexadecimal number 4BAD, proceed as follows.

$16^3 = 4096$ $16^2 = 256$ $16^1 = 16$ $16^0 = 1$

$= 4(4096) + 11(256) + 10(16) + 13(1)$

$= 19373$ in decimal

Table A.2 shows each hexadecimal digit as a four-bit binary number. Remember that leading zeros in a number have no effect on its value.

To represent the contents of an eight-bit byte in hexadecimal, group the eight bits into two sets of four. Then replace each set of four bits by its corresponding hexadecimal digit (see Table A.2). Thus,

TABLE A.2

Decimal	Hexadecimal	Binary
0	0	0000
1	1	0001
2	2	0010
3	3	0011
4	4	0100
5	5	0101
6	6	0110
7	7	0111
8	8	1000
9	9	1001
10	A	1010
11	B	1011
12	C	1100
13	D	1101
14	E	1110
15	F	1111

```
      (decimal)  (binary)
 A ---> 65 ---> 0100 0001
                                   (hexadecimal)
                  4 1 --->    41
```

To convert from hexadecimal to binary, reverse the process—expand each hexadecimal digit to its equivalent binary.

```
(hexadecimal)
    6D ---> 6 D
        0110 1101 ---> 109 ---> m
        (binary)    (decimal)
```

Since there are eight bits in a byte and each bit can have one of two possible values, there are $2^8 = 256$ characters in the ASCII code. Table A.3 lists only the printable character set and the corresponding ASCII decimal and hexadecimal codes.

Using Table A.3, my name in ASCII hexadecimal code is as follows.

```
J o h n   C .   M o l l u z z o
4A6F686E20432E204D6F6C6C757A7A6F
```

TABLE A.3

Decimal	Hex	Symbol	Decimal	Hex	Symbol	Decimal	Hex	Symbol
32	20	(blank)	64	40	@	96	60	`
33	21	!	65	41	A	97	61	a
34	22	"	66	42	B	98	62	b
35	23	#	67	43	C	99	63	c
36	24	$	68	44	D	100	64	d
37	25	%	69	45	E	101	65	e
38	26	&	70	46	F	102	66	f
39	27	'	71	47	G	103	67	g
40	28	(	72	48	H	104	68	h
41	29	)	73	49	I	105	69	i
42	2A	*	74	4A	J	106	6A	j
43	2B	+	75	4B	K	107	6B	k
44	2C	,	76	4C	L	108	6C	l
45	2D	–	77	4D	M	109	6D	m
46	2E	.	78	4E	N	110	6E	n
47	2F	/	79	4F	O	111	6F	o
48	30	0	80	50	P	112	70	p
49	31	1	81	51	Q	113	71	q
50	32	2	82	52	R	114	72	r
51	33	3	83	53	S	115	73	s
52	34	4	84	54	T	116	74	t
53	35	5	85	55	U	117	75	u
54	36	6	86	56	V	118	76	v
55	37	7	87	57	W	119	77	w
56	38	8	88	58	X	120	78	x
57	39	9	89	59	Y	121	79	y
58	3A	:	90	5A	Z	122	7A	z
59	3B	;	91	5B	[	123	7B	(
60	3C	<	92	5C	\	124	7C	|
61	3D	=	93	5D	]	125	7D	)
62	3E	>	94	5E	^	126	7E	~
63	3F	?	95	5F	_			

A.3 Data Representation—Integers

Integers (..., -3, -2, -1, 0, 1, 2, 3, ...) are the simplest type of number that you can use in a program. In mathematics, there are an infinite number of integers. However, a computer can represent only a finite number of integers because it has only a finite amount of main memory. The computer stores integers (positive, negative, and zero) in binary form. Depending on the computer and the computer language, an integer can occupy two or four bytes of main memory. The amount of storage required by an integer determines the range of integer values that the computer can represent.

For example, an IBM-PC stores an integer in two bytes, that is 16 bits. Since there are $2^{16} = 65536$ ways of arranging 16 zeros and ones, such a computer can represent 65536 integers (positive, negative, and zero) in two bytes. Half the integers in this range are negative (that is, less than zero) and half are nonnegative (that is, greater than or equal to zero). Therefore on an IBM-PC, a two-byte integer can have a value in the range -32768 (-2^{15}) to $+32767$ ($2^{15} - 1$).

Similarly, a Sun Workstation stores integers in four bytes and, consequently, can represent $2^{32} = 4294967296$ integers. Therefore a four-byte integer can have a value in the range $-2^{31} = -2147483648$ (about -2 billion) to $+2^{31} - 1 = +2147483647$ (about $+2$ billion).

All computers store nonnegative integers as binary numbers. The integer 14160 has the following representation as a two-byte binary number.

```
00110111 01010000
```

Most computers represent negative numbers in **2's complement** form, which allows the computer to do binary arithmetic efficiently. It is not important for our purposes to know how to derive the two's complement form of a negative number, so we shall not discuss how to do so. For us, it suffices to know that the first bit of a byte that represents a negative integer is one. For example, the two-byte integer 11111110 10011001 represents a negative number, namely -359.

A.4 Data Representation—Real Numbers

A **real number** is a number that has a decimal point, such as -73.456 and 0.029854. Most computers store real numbers in **floating point** form. To write a number in floating point form, move the decimal point to the right of the number's first significant digit (that is, its first nonzero digit) and multiply by an appropriate power of 10. For example,

```
-73.456 = -7.3456 × 10¹
```

The power of 10 is 1 because we moved the decimal point left one place to put it to the right of the digit 7. Also,

```
0.029854 = 2.9854 × 10⁻²
```

The power of 10 is -2 because we moved the decimal point right two places to put it to the right of the digit 2.

The decimal part of a number in floating point form is the number's **mantissa** and the power of 10 is the number's **exponent**.

When you place a real number in a computer's main memory, the computer stores only the mantissa and the exponent (it does not have to store the decimal point because it knows where the decimal point is). The number of bytes the computer uses to store a floating point number restricts the number of digits that can be in the mantissa and the range of possible exponents. The number of digits that can be in the mantissa is the **precision** of the number. Depending on the computer, a floating point number occupies either four or eight bytes of storage. A typical four-byte floating point number has a precision of seven digits and an exponent range of -38 to $+38$. A typical eight-byte floating point number has a precision of 15 digits and an exponent range of -308 to $+308$.

EXERCISES APPENDIX A

1. Define the following terms.

main memory	flowchart
byte	pseudocode
address	code
control unit	syntax error
ALU (arithmetic/logic unit)	program listing
operating system	source program
mainframe computer	source code
minicomputer	machine language
microcomputer	high-level language
CPU (central processing unit)	machine independent
input device	compiler
output device	object program
bit	external reference
ASCII	linker
binary system	resolving external references
hexadecimal system	executable code
2's complement	program development cycle
real number	warnings
floating point	run-time error
mantissa	logic error
exponent	faulty coding
precision	

Convert the binary numbers in Exercises 2–6 to the equivalent decimal numbers.

2. 1101001

3. 1000111

4. 111001001

5. 101010101

6. 100111010

Convert the hexadecimal numbers in Exercises 7–11 to the equivalent decimal numbers.

7. 3A1

8. 77

9. 10F

10. ABCD

11. 3E6F

12. Use Table A.3 to translate the title of this book into ASCII hexadecimal code.

13. Use Table A.3 to translate your name into ASCII hexadecimal code.

14. Translate the following hexadecimal ASCII message.

    4920686F706520796F752068617665207375636365737320696E20432E

In Exercises 15–19, write each decimal number in floating point form.

15. 528.9923

16. −9234.011

17. 3.677322

18. 0.00004520018

19. −0.00000004562155

In Exercises 20–22, write each floating point number in decimal form.

20. -6.342113×10^5

21. -6.342113×10^{-5}

22. 1.757822×10^0

23. Describe the five steps in the program development cycle.

24. What is the function of a compiler?

25. What is the function of a linker?

26. Describe the relationship between the source code, object code and the executable code.

27. Describe some errors that you can encounter during each step of the program development cycle.

Appendix

B

Program Control

This appendix discusses the standard ways of controlling the flow of control in a program through structured programming.

Structured programming is a technique for writing programs that uses only three logical control structures or patterns—sequence, selection, and iteration—and several derivatives of these three. You can code any proper program using combinations of these three control structures. By restricting the types of control structures, structured programming attempts to reduce program complexity, increase programmer productivity, produce more reliable code, and ease program maintenance.

B.1 Sequence

Sequence refers to doing things in order or sequence, one after the other. Figure B.1 shows a sequence structure in flowchart form and in pseudocode.

Figure B.1 shows that the program first executes statement 1, then statement 2, and finally statement 3.

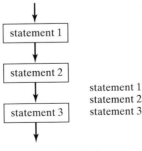

FIGURE B.1

Sequence is the natural way in which a computer executes instructions. To this point, all our sample programs have executed their instructions sequentially. A C++ program begins by executing the first executable statement of main(), followed by the second, and so on, until it encounters a statement that alters the sequential flow of execution. Statements that change the sequential execution of a program fall into two classes— selection statements and iteration statements.

B.2 Selection

Frequently a program must decide between two alternative paths based on the truth or falsity of a condition. This is the **selection** structure of structured programming. In this section we consider the basic selection structure, the if statement, and two structures derived from the if statement—nested if statements and the case structure.

The if Statement: Figure B.2 shows the flowchart and pseudocode forms of a typical if **statement**. An if statement flowchart tests the condition in the decision box (balance > 500.00). If the condition is true, the program executes the true part (add 1 to large_balance) and then executes the statement following the collector. If the condition is false, the program executes the false part (add 1 to small_balance) and then executes the statement following the collector.

The exits from the decision box are **branches**. Both branches from the decision box meet at a common point, which should be the only exit from the selection structure.

Read the pseudocode if statement of Figure B.2 as follows. If the condition (balance > 500.00) is true, execute the true part, which is everything between the condition and the pseudocode word else. Then, execute the statement that follows endif. The pseudocode word endif is a delimiter that indicates the end of the else part of the if statement and does not represent an executable statement. If the condition is false, execute the false part, which is everything between the pseudocode words else and endif. Then, execute the statement that follows endif.

Both exits from the condition box must lead to a common point. The branches of the flowchart in Figure B.2 meet in the collector. Whichever branch of the flowchart the program takes, control eventually leads to this collector.

The endif in the pseudocode of Figure B.2 acts as the collector in the flowchart. Whichever branch of the if the program takes, control eventually passes through the

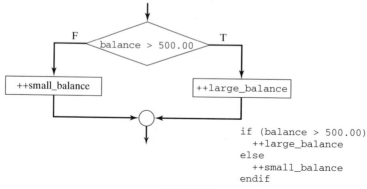

```
if (balance > 500.00)
    ++large_balance
else
    ++small_balance
endif
```

FIGURE B.2

endif and on to the next statement. We indent the true branch and the false branch, and align corresponding if-else-endif directly under each other.

An if statement need not have an else. For example, the flowchart and pseudocode of Figure B.3 have no else part.

The selection structure illustrates the **"straight-through" principle**, which we state in Note B.1.

NOTE B.1—THE STRAIGHT-THROUGH PRINCIPLE

Each control structure has exactly one entrance and one exit.

Therefore you should not code a condition as shown in Figure B.4

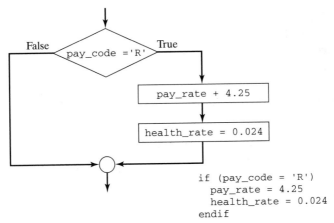

```
if (pay_code = 'R')
    pay_rate = 4.25
    health_rate = 0.024
endif
```

FIGURE B.3

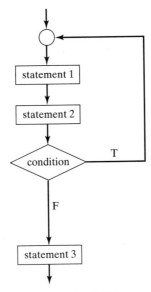

FIGURE B.4

Nested `if` **Statements:** Sometimes a program must test a condition only if a previously tested condition is true (or false). To code such a decision structure, you can **nest** `if` statements, that is, include an `if` statement in the true part or false part of another `if` statement.

Figure B.5 shows a nested `if` in which the program tests `state_code` only if `employee_code` equals `'A'`.

If `employee_code` equals `'A'`, then the program tests `state_code`. If `state_code` equals `'Y'`, then `tax` is assigned the value of `gross_pay` multiplied by 0.070. If `state_code` is unequal to `'Y'`, then `tax` is assigned the value of `gross_pay` multiplied by 0.045. Returning to the first decision, if `employee_code` is unequal to `'A'`, then the `tax` is assigned the value 0.00.

The Case Structure: The `if` statement provides only a two-way branch. If the condition in an `if` statement is true, the program takes one path. If the condition is false, the program takes another path. Sometimes a program requires a **multiway branch**. That is, depending on the value of a variable, the program can take one of several paths. For example, Table B.1 shows the commission rates that a real estate broker sets for selling properties according to the property code. A property code other than R, M, or C is invalid.

To select the proper commission rate, a program can test the property code using a nested `if` as in the following pseudocode.

```
if (property_code = 'R')
  commission_rate = 0.060
```

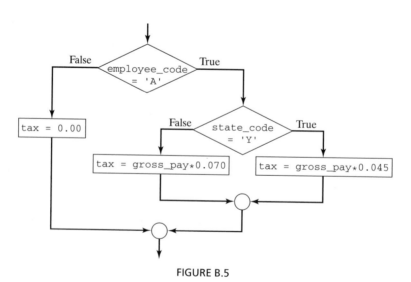

FIGURE B.5

TABLE B.1

Property Type	Code	Rate
Residential	R	0.060
Multi-Dwelling	M	0.050
Commercial	C	0.045

```
else
  if (property_code = 'M')
    commission_rate = 0.050
  else
    if (property_code = 'C')
      commission_rate = 0.045
    else
      print error message
    endif
  endif
endif
```

Another way of designing the code is as follows. Choosing the proper commission rate requires the program to select one of four possible alternatives depending on the value of `property_code`. This is a multi-way decision. Structured programming refers to a multi-way decision that is based on the value of a variable as a **case structure**. Figure B.6 shows the multi-way decision structure that our program requires flowcharted as a case structure.

In Figure B.6, the decision box contains the variable (`property_code`) that the program tests. There are as many exits from the decision box (four) as there are possible paths that the program can take. All exits from the decision box meet in a collector.

The case flowchart works as follows. The program first evaluates the variable (`property_code`) that appears in the decision box. Then the program takes the branch from the decision box that corresponds to the current value of the variable,

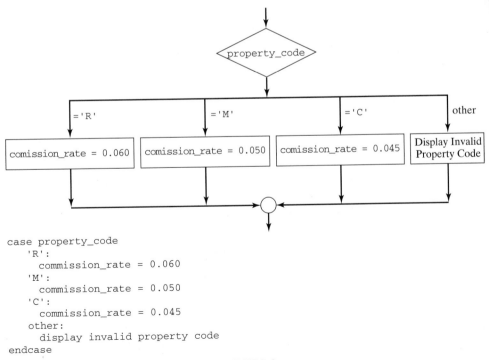

```
case property_code
    'R':
       commission_rate = 0.060
    'M':
       commission_rate = 0.050
    'C':
       commission_rate = 0.045
    other:
       display invalid property code
 endcase
```

FIGURE B.6

executes the statements in that branch, and exits the structure at the collector. If the variable does not equal any of the listed values, the program takes the branch labeled other, executes the appropriate statements, and exits the structure at the collector.

The corresponding `case` pseudocode statement works in the same way. The program evaluates the variable that appears after the pseudocode word `case`. Then, the program goes to the label that corresponds to the value of the variable, executes the appropriate statements, and exits the structure at the pseudocode word `endcase`. If the variable does not equal any of the `case` label values, the program goes to the label other, executes the statements located there, and exits the structure at the pseudocode word `endcase`.

For example, suppose that the user enters `'M'` for `property_code` when the program prompts for its value. When the program executes the case structure, it tests the value of `property_code`. Since the value of `property_code` is `'M'`, the program takes the `'M'` branch of the case structure, assigns the value 0.050 to the variable `commission_rate`, and then exits the case structure.

B.3 Iteration

Perhaps a computer's most powerful capability is its ability to quickly execute the same set of instructions repeatedly (possibly millions of times), without making a mistake. **Iteration** or **looping** is repeated execution of the same set of instructions.

Sometimes there is no way to tell in advance how often the same set of instructions is to execute. For example, suppose a program that you are writing for a stockbroker is to process a day's stock transactions. The program is to process each transaction in the same way. When you design the program, there is no way to know how many stock transactions will take place on a given day. Since we do not know how often the program is to repeat the transaction processing instructions, we refer to this type of iteration as **indefinite iteration**.

On the other hand, when designing a program, we sometimes know how often a set of instructions is to execute. For example, suppose a program must print a 10-row tax table. The set of instructions that calculates the tax for a given income and prints the corresponding row of the table must execute exactly 10 times. Since we know how often the set of instructions is to execute, we refer to this type of iteration as **definite iteration**.

In this section we consider three forms of iteration—indefinite iteration with a `while` loop, indefinite iteration with a `do` loop, and definite iteration with a `for` loop.

The `while` Loop: Figure B.7 shows the structure of a typical `while` **loop** in flowchart and pseudocode forms. The purpose of the loop is to count the number of times the user responds `'Y'` to a prompt. Since we do not know how often the user will respond `'Y'`, an indefinite iteration is appropriate.

Program execution enters the loop by first testing the **loop condition**, (`response = 'Y'`). If the loop condition is true (T), the **loop body** executes. In this example, the loop body consists of two statements. The loop body can generally consist of zero or more statements.

After executing the loop body, the program returns (or loops) to test the loop condition. Therefore the loop body repeatedly executes while the loop condition is true. This is why we call the loop of Figure B.7 a `while` loop. When (indeed, if) the loop condition tests false, control exits the loop. That is, program control proceeds to the statement following the `while` loop. At this point in the program, the variable `num_yeses` contains the number of times the user responded `'Y'` to the prompt.

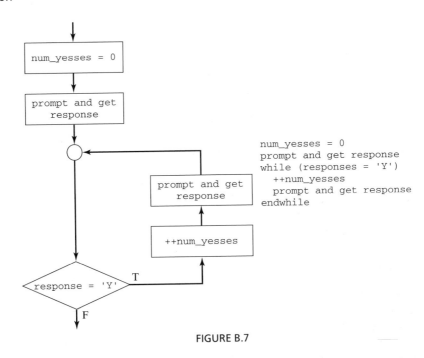

```
num_yesses = 0
prompt and get response
while (responses = 'Y')
    ++num_yesses
    prompt and get response
endwhile
```

FIGURE B.7

The structure of the pseudocode `while` loop is self-evident except, perhaps, for the word **endwhile**. `Endwhile` is a delimiter that indicates the end of the set of statements that make up the loop body and, as such, does not represent an executable statement.

Note B.2 lists two important facts to remember about `while` loops.

NOTE B.2—UNDERSTANDING `while` LOOPS

1. When the program encounters a `while` loop, it tests the loop condition first. If the loop condition is false the first time the program tests it, the loop body never executes.

2. Normally, when the program exits a `while` loop, the loop condition is false.

Again refer to the example `while` loop of Figure B.7. If the user enters `'N'` in response to the prompt that is immediately before the loop condition test, the loop body never executes. Then, the value of `num_yeses` is zero, which is correct. The user never responded `'Y'`.

Also, when the program exits the `while` loop, the loop condition must be false. When the program takes the false exit from the loop condition, the value of response must be something other than `'Y'`.

The do **Loop:** As Note B.2 states, the body of a `while` loop does not execute if the loop condition is false the first time a program executes the `while` statement. However, program logic sometimes requires the body of a loop to execute at least once, no matter what conditions prevail at the time the program encounters the loop.

For example, suppose we want to design a loop that counts the number of times the user answers a prompt. The `while` loop of Figure B.7 counts only the number of `'Y'` responses because the loop body executes only after the program tests the loop

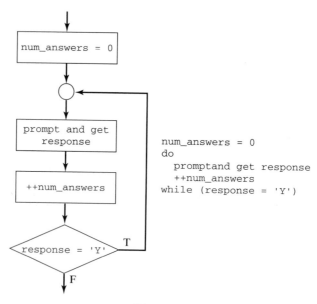

num_answers = 0
do
    promptand get response
    ++num_answers
while (response = 'Y')

FIGURE B.8

condition. The do **loop** of Figure B.8 is an indefinite iteration loop in which the loop body must execute at least once. This loop counts the total number of responses the user makes.

When the program encounters the do loop, the loop body executes first. (The loop counts every answer that the user enters.) Then the program tests the loop condition. If the condition is true, the program executes the loop body again, and so on. When the loop condition tests false, the program exits the loop.

Definite Iteration: When you know exactly how often the loop body must execute, it is appropriate to use a definite iteration loop. For example, you may require a program to display a tax table for yearly incomes ranging from $10,000.00 to $100,000.00 in intervals of $10,000.00. This table has exactly 10 rows. You could, therefore, design a loop that executes exactly 10 times, each time producing one row of the tax table. A variable, called a **counter**, usually controls the number of times that the body of a definite iteration loop executes. Consequently we also call an indefinite iteration loop a **counter-controlled loop**.

Figure B.9 shows a typical definite iteration flowchart box and the corresponding pseudocode.

When the program enters the definite iteration box of Figure B.9, it initializes the counter variable row to the value one. Next, the program tests the counter variable against its maximum value of 10. If the counter is less than or equal to this maximum value, the program executes the loop body once. Next, the program adjusts the loop counter. (In the flowchart of Figure B.9, the counter row is increased by one. However, a program can adjust the loop counter by any amount.) Again, the program tests the counter variable against its maximum value. The program stays in the loop until the counter variable exceeds its maximum value.

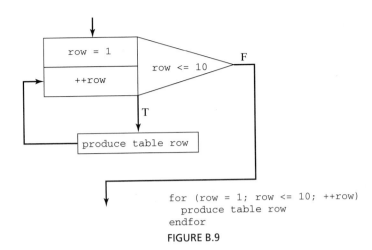

```
for (row = 1; row <= 10; ++row)
   produce table row
endfor
```
FIGURE B.9

A program must treat the loop counter in any definite iteration loop as the loop counter in Figure B.9. Note B.3 states these rules.

NOTE B.3—ITERATION LOOP COUNTERS

A program must do the following to a definite iteration loop counter.

1. *Initialize:* Before entering the loop body, the program must initialize the loop counter.
2. *Test:* The program must test the loop counter. If the counter satisfies the test, the program executes the loop body once. If the counter does not satisfy the test, the program exits the loop.
3. *Adjust:* After executing the loop body, the program must adjust the loop counter.

The pseudocode `for` statement of Figure B.9 works in essentially the same way as the definite iteration box. Semicolons separate the three things that the program must do to the loop counter. When the program encounters the `for` statement, it initializes the counter variable and then tests the value of the counter. If the counter is less than or equal to its maximum allowable value, the program executes the loop body. (The pseudocode word `endfor` delimits the body of the `for` loop.) Then the program adjusts the loop counter and tests the counter variable again.

Infinite Loops: The loop condition is the most important part of any iteration. Once in a loop, the program (theoretically, at least) can stay in the loop forever, unless there is some mechanism that tells the program to exit the loop. This mechanism is the loop condition. Each time the program executes the loop body, it should execute one or several instructions that *could* alter the truth or falsity of the loop condition.

For example, in Figure B.10, the integer variable i begins with a value of three. The loop condition is $i > 0$. The loop body consists of the statement "Decrease by 1". This is the statement that could affect the loop condition. Because i begins at 3,

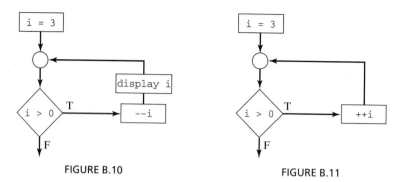

FIGURE B.10   FIGURE B.11

after three passes through the loop, the loop condition is false and the program exits the loop. The effect of the loop is to display the following:

```
2 1 0
```

Note B.4 is important to keep in mind when writing any program.

NOTE B.4—INFINITE LOOPS

When writing a loop, make sure the loop condition will eventually be false. If the loop condition is always true, the program will cycle the loop indefinitely, causing an **infinite loop**.

Figure B.11 shows an infinite loop. Since the integer variable i begins at three and is increased by one each time through the loop, i is always greater than 0.

Improper Loop Exits: The Straight-Through Principle (see Note B.1) applies to all three iteration control structures. Never allow a program to exit from a loop at any point other than the loop exit. The loop body should never contain a statement that would cause the program to transfer control outside the loop at a point other than the loop exit. For example, never allow the structure shown in Figure B.12. There are two exits from the iteration: one from condition 1 (which is the loop condition) and one from condition 2.

B.4 Combinations

You can build complicated control structures by "pasting" together the basic control structures. Use the Straight-Through Principle to ensure that you correctly paste the basic control structures. For example, consider Figure B.13 where C1, C2, and C3 represent conditions, and P1, P2, P3, P4, and P5 represent processing instructions.

The false branch of the C1 condition leads to another selection structure. The true branch of C1 leads to a sequence structure. The second part of this sequence is an iteration. Whichever branch the program takes out of C1, control eventually comes to the common exit.

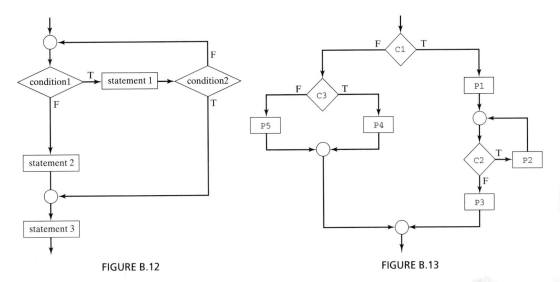

FIGURE B.12   FIGURE B.13

EXERCISES

1. Define the following terms.

structured programming
sequence
selection
if statement
branch
"straight-through" principle
nested if statement
multi-way branch
case structure
iteration
looping

indefinite iteration
definite iteration
while loop
loop condition
loop body
endwhile
do loop
counter
counter-controlled loop
infinite loop

2. Identify the basic control structures (sequence, selection, iteration) of which Figure B.14 is composed.

3. Identify the basic control structures (sequence, selection, iteration) of which Figure B.15 is composed.

4. In Figure B.16, find how often the loop body executes.

5. In Figure B.17, find how often the loop body executes.

6. In Figure B.18, find how often the loop body executes.

7. In Figure B.19, find how often the loop body executes.

8. What's wrong with the flowchart in Figure B.20? Can you correct it? (Adapted from *Techniques of Structured Programming and Design*, Yourdon, p. 164, Figure 4.16(a).)

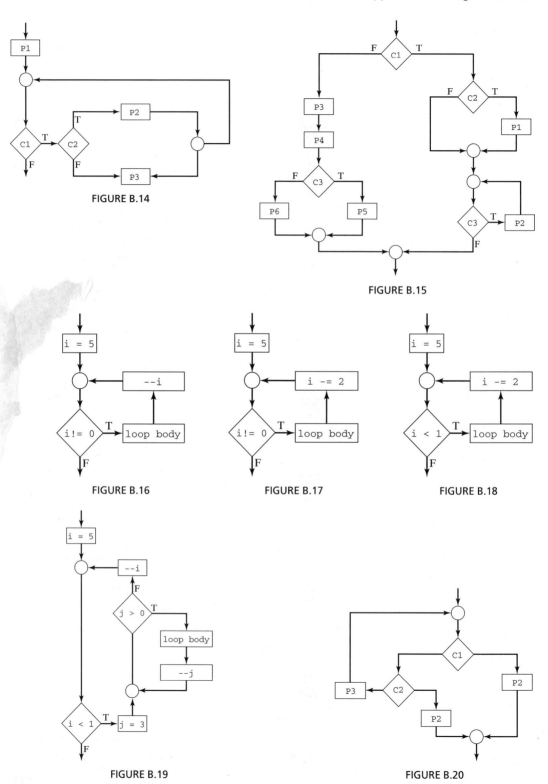

FIGURE B.14

FIGURE B.15

FIGURE B.16

FIGURE B.17

FIGURE B.18

FIGURE B.19

FIGURE B.20

Index

END-USER LICENSE AGREEMENT FOR MICROSOFT SOFTWARE

IMPORTANT-READ CAREFULLY: This Microsoft End-User License Agreement ("EULA") is a legal agreement between you (either an individual or a single entity) and Microsoft Corporation for the Microsoft software product identified above, which includes computer software and may include associated media, printed materials, and "online" or electronic documentation ("SOFTWARE PRODUCT"). The SOFTWARE PRODUCT also includes any updates and supplements to the original SOFTWARE PRODUCT provided to you by Microsoft. By installing, copying, downloading, accessing or otherwise using the SOFTWARE PRODUCT, you agree to be bound by the terms of this EULA. If you do not agree to the terms of this EULA, do not install , copy, or otherwise use the SOFTWARE PRODUCT.

SOFTWARE PRODUCT LICENSE

The SOFTWARE PRODUCT is protected by copyright laws and international copyright treaties, as well as other intellectual property laws and treaties. The SOFTWARE PRODUCT is licensed, not sold.

1. **GRANT OF LICENSE.** This EULA grants you the following rights:

   1.1 License Grant. Microsoft grants to you as an individual, a personal nonexclusive license to make and use copies of the SOFTWARE PRODUCT for the sole purposes of evaluating and learning how to use the SOFTWARE PRODUCT, as may be instructed in accompanying publications or documentation. You may install the software on an unlimited number of computers provided that you are the only individual using the SOFTWARE PRODUCT.

   1.2 Academic Use. You must be a "Qualified Educational User" to use the SOFTWARE PRODUCT in the manner described in this section. To determine whether you are a Qualified Educational User, please contact the Microsoft Sales Information Center/One Microsoft Way/Redmond, WA 98052-6399 or the Microsoft subsidiary serving your country. If you are a Qualified Educational User, you may either:

   (i) exercise the rights granted in Section 1.1, OR

   (ii) if you intend to use the SOFTWARE PRODUCT solely for instructional purposes in connection with a class or other educational program, this EULA grants you the following alternative license models:

   (A) Per Computer Model. For every valid license you have acquired for the SOFTWARE PRODUCT, you may install a single copy of the SOFTWARE PRODUCT on a single computer for access and use by an unlimited number of student end users at your educational institution, provided that all such end users comply with all other terms of this EULA, OR

   (B) Per License Model. If you have multiple licenses for the SOFTWARE PRODUCT, then at any time you may have as many copies of the SOFTWARE PRODUCT in use as you have licenses, provided that such use is limited to student or faculty end users at your educational institution and provided that all such end users comply with all other terms of this EULA. For purposes of this subsection, the SOFTWARE PRODUCT is "in use" on a computer when it is loaded into the temporary memory (i.e., RAM) or installed into the permanent memory (e.g., hard disk, CD ROM, or other storage device) of that computer, except that a copy installed on a network server for the sole purpose of distribution to other computers is not "in use". If the anticipated number of users of the SOFTWARE PRODUCT will exceed the number of applicable licenses, then you must have a reasonable mechanism or process in place to ensure that the number of persons using the SOFTWARE PRODUCT concurrently does not exceed the number of licenses.

2. **DESCRIPTION OF OTHER RIGHTS AND LIMITATIONS.**

   - **Limitations on Reverse Engineering, Decompilation, and Disassembly.** You may not reverse engineer, decompile, or disassemble the SOFTWARE PRODUCT, except and only to the extent that such activity is expressly permitted by applicable law notwithstanding this limitation.
   - **Separation of Components.** The SOFTWARE PRODUCT is licensed as a single product. Its component parts may not be separated for use on more than one computer.
   - **Rental.** You may not rent, lease or lend the SOFTWARE PRODUCT.
   - **Trademarks.** This EULA does not grant you any rights in connection with any trademarks or service marks of Microsoft.
   - **Software Transfer.** The initial user of the SOFTWARE PRODUCT may make a one-time permanent transfer of this EULA and SOFTWARE PRODUCT only directly to an end user. This transfer must include all of the SOFTWARE PRODUCT (including all component parts, the media and printed materials, any upgrades, this EULA, and, if applicable, the Certificate of Authenticity). Such transfer may not be by way of consignment or any other indirect transfer. The transferee of such one-time transfer must agree to comply with the terms of this EULA, including the obligation not to further transfer this EULA and SOFTWARE PRODUCT.
   - **No Support.** Microsoft shall have no obligation to provide any product support for the SOFTWARE PRODUCT.
   - **Termination.** Without prejudice to any other rights, Microsoft may terminate this EULA if you fail to comply with the terms and conditions of this EULA. In such event, you must destroy all copies of the SOFTWARE PRODUCT and all of its component parts.

3. **COPYRIGHT.** All title and intellectual property rights in and to the SOFTWARE PRODUCT (including but not limited to any images, photographs, animations, video, audio, music, text, and "applets" incorporated into the SOFTWARE PRODUCT), the accompanying printed materials, and any copies of the SOFTWARE PRODUCT are owned by Microsoft or its suppliers. All title and intellectual property rights in and to the content which may be accessed through use of the SOFTWARE PRODUCT is the property of the respective content owner and may be protected by applicable copyright or other intellectual property laws and treaties. This EULA grants you no rights to use such content. All rights not expressly granted are reserved by Microsoft.

4. **BACKUP COPY.** After installation of one copy of the SOFTWARE PRODUCT pursuant to this EULA, you may keep the original media on which the SOFTWARE PRODUCT was provided by Microsoft solely for backup or archival purposes. If the original media is required to use the SOFTWARE PRODUCT on the COMPUTER, you may make one copy of the SOFTWARE PRODUCT solely for backup or archival purposes. Except as expressly provided in this EULA, you may not otherwise make copies of the SOFTWARE PRODUCT or the printed materials accompanying the SOFTWARE PRODUCT.

5. **U.S. GOVERNMENT RESTRICTED RIGHTS.** The SOFTWARE PRODUCT and documentation are provided with RESTRICTED RIGHTS. Use, duplication, or disclosure by the Government is subject to restrictions as set forth in subparagraph (c)(1)(ii) of the Rights in Technical Data and Computer Software clause at DFARS 252.227-7013 or subparagraphs (c)(1) and (2) of the Commercial Computer Software-Restricted Rights at 48 CFR 52.227-19, as applicable. Manufacturer is Microsoft Corporation/One Microsoft Way/Redmond, WA 98052-6399.

6. **EXPORT RESTRICTIONS.** You agree that you will not export or re-export the SOFTWARE PRODUCT, any part thereof, or any process or service that is the direct product of the SOFTWARE PRODUCT (the foregoing collectively referred to as the "Restricted Components"), to any country, person, entity or end user subject to U.S. export restrictions. You specifically agree not to export or re-export any of the Restricted Components (i) to any country to which the U.S. has embargoed or restricted the export of goods or services, which currently include, but are not necessarily limited to Cuba, Iran, Iraq, Libya, North Korea, Sudan and Syria, or to any national of any such country, wherever located, who intends to transmit or transport the Restricted Components back to such country; (ii) to any end-user who you know or have reason to know will utilize the Restricted Components in the design, development or production of nuclear, chemical or biological weapons; or (iii) to any end-user who has been prohibited from participating in U.S. export transactions by any federal agency of the U.S. government. You warrant and represent that neither the BXA nor any other U.S. federal agency has suspended, revoked, or denied your export privileges.

7. **NOTE ON JAVA SUPPORT.** THE SOFTWARE PRODUCT MAY CONTAIN SUPPORT FOR PROGRAMS WRITTEN IN JAVA. JAVA TECHNOLOGY IS NOT FAULT TOLERANT AND IS NOT DESIGNED, MANUFACTURED, OR INTENDED FOR USE OR RESALE AS ON-LINE CONTROL EQUIPMENT IN HAZARDOUS ENVIRONMENTS REQUIRING FAIL-SAFE PERFORMANCE, SUCH AS IN THE OPERATION OF NUCLEAR FACILITIES, AIRCRAFT NAVIGATION OR COMMUNICATION SYSTEMS, AIR TRAFFIC CONTROL, DIRECT LIFE SUPPORT MACHINES, OR WEAPONS SYSTEMS, IN WHICH THE FAILURE OF JAVA TECHNOLOGY COULD LEAD DIRECTLY TO DEATH, PERSONAL INJURY, OR SEVERE PHYSICAL OR ENVIRONMENTAL DAMAGE.

MISCELLANEOUS

If you acquired this product in the United States, this EULA is governed by the laws of the State of Washington. If you acquired this product in Canada, this EULA is governed by the laws of the Province of Ontario, Canada. Each of the parties hereto irrevocably attorns to the jurisdiction of the courts of the Province of Ontario and further agrees to commence any litigation which may arise hereunder in the courts located in the Judicial District of York, Province of Ontario. If this product was acquired outside the United States, then local law may apply. Should you have any questions concerning this EULA, or if you desire to contact Microsoft for any reason, please contact Microsoft, or write: Microsoft Sales Information Center/One Microsoft Way/Redmond, WA 98052-6399.

LIMITED WARRANTY

LIMITED WARRANTY. Microsoft warrants that (a) the SOFTWARE PRODUCT will perform substantially in accordance with the accompanying written materials for a period of ninety (90) days from the date of receipt, and (b) any Support Services provided by Microsoft shall be substantially as described in applicable written materials provided to you by Microsoft, and Microsoft support engineers will make commercially reasonable efforts to solve any problem. To the extent allowed by applicable law, implied warranties on the SOFTWARE PRODUCT, if any, are limited to ninety (90) days. Some states/jurisdictions do not allow limitations on duration of an implied warranty, so the above limitation may not apply to you.

CUSTOMER REMEDIES. Microsoft's and its suppliers' entire liability and your exclusive remedy shall be, at Microsoft's option, either (a) return of the price paid, if any, or (b) repair or replacement of the SOFTWARE PRODUCT that does not meet Microsoft's Limited Warranty and that is returned to Microsoft with a copy of your receipt. This Limited Warranty is void if failure of the SOFTWARE PRODUCT has resulted from accident, abuse, or misapplication. Any replacement SOFTWARE PRODUCT will be warranted for the remainder of the original warranty period or thirty (30) days, whichever is longer. Outside the United States, neither these remedies nor any product support services offered by Microsoft are available without proof of purchase from an authorized international source.

NO OTHER WARRANTIES. TO THE MAXIMUM EXTENT PERMITTED BY APPLICABLE LAW, MICROSOFT AND ITS SUPPLIERS DISCLAIM ALL OTHER WARRANTIES AND CONDITIONS, EITHER EXPRESS OR IMPLIED, INCLUDING, BUT NOT LIMITED TO, IMPLIED WARRANTIES OR CONDITIONS OF MERCHANTABILITY, FITNESS FOR A PARTICULAR PURPOSE, TITLE AND NON-INFRINGEMENT, WITH REGARD TO THE SOFTWARE PRODUCT, AND THE PROVISION OF OR FAILURE TO PROVIDE SUPPORT SERVICES. THIS LIMITED WARRANTY GIVES YOU SPECIFIC LEGAL RIGHTS. YOU MAY HAVE OTHERS, WHICH VARY FROM STATE/JURISDICTION TO STATE/JURISDICTION.

LIMITATION OF LIABILITY. TO THE MAXIMUM EXTENT PERMITTED BY APPLICABLE LAW, IN NO EVENT SHALL MICROSOFT OR ITS SUPPLIERS BE LIABLE FOR ANY SPECIAL, INCIDENTAL, INDIRECT, OR CONSEQUENTIAL DAMAGES WHATSOEVER (INCLUDING, WITHOUT LIMITATION, DAMAGES FOR LOSS OF BUSINESS PROFITS, BUSINESS INTERRUPTION, LOSS OF BUSINESS INFORMATION, OR ANY OTHER PECUNIARY LOSS) ARISING OUT OF THE USE OF OR INABILITY TO USE THE SOFTWARE PRODUCT OR THE FAILURE TO PROVIDE SUPPORT SERVICES, EVEN IF MICROSOFT HAS BEEN ADVISED OF THE POSSIBILITY OF SUCH DAMAGES. IN ANY CASE, MICROSOFT'S ENTIRE LIABILITY UNDER ANY PROVISION OF THIS EULA SHALL BE LIMITED TO THE GREATER OF THE AMOUNT ACTUALLY PAID BY YOU FOR THE SOFTWARE PRODUCT OR U.S.$5.00; PROVIDED, HOWEVER, IF YOU HAVE ENTERED INTO A MICROSOFT SUPPORT SERVICES AGREEMENT, MICROSOFT'S ENTIRE LIABILITY REGARDING SUPPORT SERVICES SHALL BE GOVERNED BY THE TERMS OF THAT AGREEMENT. BECAUSE SOME STATES/JURISDICTIONS DO NOT ALLOW THE EXCLUSION OR LIMITATION OF LIABILITY, THE ABOVE LIMITATION MAY NOT APPLY TO YOU.

Si vous avez acquis votre produit Microsoft au CANADA, la garantie limitée suivante vous concerne :

GARANTIE LIMITÉE

GARANTIE LIMITÉE — Microsoft garantit que (a) la performance du LOGICIEL sera substantiellement en conformité avec la documentation qui accompagne le LOGICIEL, pour une période de quatre-vingt-dix (90) jours à compter de la date de réception; et (b) tout support technique fourni par Microsoft sera substantiellement en conformité avec toute documentation afférente fournie par Microsoft et que les membres du support technique de Microsoft feront des efforts raisonnables pour résoudre toute difficulté technique découlant de l'utilisation du LOGICIEL. Certaines juridictions ne permettent pas de limiter dans le temps l'application de la présente garantie. Aussi, la limite stipulée ci-haut pourrait ne pas s'appliquer dans votre cas. Dans la mesure permise par la loi, toute garantie implicite portant sur le LOGICIEL, le cas échéant, est limitée à une période de quatre-vingt-dix (90) jours.

RECOURS DU CLIENT — La seule obligation de Microsoft et de ses fournisseurs et votre recours exclusif seront, au choix de Microsoft, soit (a) le remboursement du prix payé, si applicable, ou (b) la réparation ou le remplacement du LOGICIEL qui n'est pas conforme à la Garantie Limitée de Microsoft et qui est retourné à Microsoft avec une copie de votre reçu. Cette Garantie Limitée est nulle si le défaut du LOGICIEL est causé par un accident, un traitement abusif ou une mauvaise application. Tout LOGICIEL de remplacement sera garanti pour le reste de la période de garantie initiale ou pour trente (30) jours, selon la plus longue de ces périodes. A l'extérieur des Etats-Unis, aucun de ces recours non plus que le support technique offert par Microsoft ne sont disponibles sans une preuve d'achat provenant d'une source authorisée.

AUCUNE AUTRE GARANTIE — DANS LA MESURE PRÉVUE PAR LA LOI, MICROSOFT ET SES FOURNISSEURS EXCLUENT TOUTE AUTRE GARANTIE OU CONDITION, EXPRESSE OU IMPLICITE, Y COMPRIS MAIS NE SE LIMITANT PAS AUX GARANTIES OU CONDITIONS IMPLICITES DU CARACTÈRE ADÉQUAT POUR LA COMMERCIALISATION OU UN USAGE PARTICULIER EN CE QUI CONCERNE LE LOGICIEL OU CONCERNANT LE TITRE, L'ABSENCE DE CONTREFAÇON DUDIT LOGICIEL, ET TOUTE DOCUMENTATION ÉCRITE QUI L'ACCOMPAGNE, AINSI QUE POUR TOUTE DISPOSITION CONCERNANT LE SUPORT TECHNIQUE OU LA FAÇON DONT CELUI-CI A ÉTÉ RENDU. CETTE GARANTIE LIMITÉE VOUS ACCORDE DES DROITS JURIDIQUES SPÉCIFIQUES.

PAS DE RESPONSABILITÉ POUR LES DOMMAGES INDIRECTS — MICROSOFT OU SES FOURNISSEURS NE SERONT PAS RESPONSABLES, EN AUCUNE CIRCONSTANCE, POUR TOUT DOMMAGE SPÉCIAL, INCIDENT, INDIRECT, OU CONSÉQUENT QUEL QU'IL SOIT (Y COMPRIS, SANS LIMITATION, LES DOMMAGES ENTRAINÉS PAR LA PERTE DE BÉNÉFICES, L'INTERRUPTION DES ACTIVITÉS, LA PERTE D'INFORMATION OU TOUTE AUTRE PERTE PÉCUNIAIRE) DÉCOULANT DE OU RELIE A LA LICENCE D'ACCES DU CLIENTET CE, MÊME SI MICROSOFT A ÉTÉ AVISÉE DE LA POSSIBILITÉ DE TELS DOMMAGES. LA RESPONSABILITÉ DE MICROSOFT EN VERTU DE TOUTE DISPOSITION DE CETTE CONVENTION NE POURRA EN AUCUN TEMPS EXCÉDER LE PLUS ÉLEVÉ ENTRE I) LE MONTANT EFFECTIVEMENT PAYÉ PAR VOUS POUR LA LICENCE D'ACCES DU CLIENT OU II) U.S.$5.00. ADVENANT QUE VOUS AYEZ CONTRACTÉ PAR ENTENTE DISTINCTE AVEC MICROSOFT POUR UN SUPPORT TECHNIQUE ÉTENDU, VOUS SEREZ LIÉ PAR LES TERMES D' UNE TELLE ENTENTE.

La présente Convention est régie par les lois en vigeur dans ela province d'Ontario, Canada. Chacune des parties à la présente reconnaît irrévocablement la compétence des tribunaux de la province d'Ontario et consent à instituer tout litige qui pourrait découler de la présente auprès des tribunaux situés dans le district judiciaire de York, province d'Ontario.

Au cas où vous auriez des questions concernant cette licence ou que vous désiriez vous mettre en rapport avec Microsoft pour quelque raison que ce soit, veuillez contacter la succursale Microsoft desservant votre pays, dont l'adresse est fournie dans ce produit, ou écrire à: Microsoft Sales Information Center, One Microsoft Way, Redmond, Washington 98052-6399

YOU SHOULD CAREFULLY READ THE FOLLOWING TERMS AND CONDITIONS BEFORE OPENING THIS CD-ROM PACKAGE. OPENING THIS CD-ROM PACKAGE INDICATES YOUR ACCEPTANCE OF THESE TERMS AND CONDITIONS. IF YOU DO NOT AGREE WITH THEM, YOU SHOULD PROMPTLY RETURN THE PACKAGE UNOPENED.

Prentice-Hall, Inc. provides this program and licenses its use. You assume responsibility for the selection of the program to achieve your intended results, and for the installation, use, and results obtained from the program. This license extends only to use of the program in the United States or countries in which the program is marketed by duly authorized distributors.

LICENSE

You may:

a. use the program;

b. copy the program into any machine-readable form without limit;

c. modify the program and/or merge it into another program in support of your use of the program.

LIMITED WARRANTY

THE PROGRAM IS PROVIDED "AS IS" WITHOUT WARRANTY OF ANY KIND, EITHER EXPRESSED OR IMPLIED, INCLUDING, BUT NOT LIMITED TO, THE IMPLIED WARRANTIES OF MERCHANTABILITY AND FITNESS FOR A PARTICULAR PURPOSE. THE ENTIRE RISK AS TO THE QUALITY AND PERFORMANCE OF THE PROGRAM IS WITH YOU. SHOULD THE PROGRAM PROVE DEFECTIVE, YOU (AND NOT PRENTICE-HALL, INC. OR ANY AUTHORIZED DISTRIBUTOR) ASSUME THE ENTIRE COST OF ALL NECESSARY SERVICING, REPAIR, OR CORRECTION.

SOME STATES DO NOT ALLOW THE EXCLUSION OF IMPLIED WARRANTIES, SO THE ABOVE EXCLUSION MAY NOT APPLY TO YOU. THIS WARRANTY GIVES YOU SPECIFIC LEGAL RIGHTS AND YOU MAY ALSO HAVE OTHER RIGHTS THAT VARY FROM STATE TO STATE.

Prentice-Hall, Inc. does not warrant that the functions contained in the program will meet your requirements or that the operation of the program will be uninterrupted or error free.

However, Prentice-Hall, Inc., warrants the CD-ROM(s) on which the program is furnished to be free from defects in materials and workmanship under normal use for a period of ninety (90) days from the date of delivery to you s evidenced by a copy of your receipt.

LIMITATIONS OF REMEDIES

Prentice-Hall's entire liability and your exclusive remedy shall be:

1. the replacement of any CD-ROM not meeting Prentice-Hall's "Limited Warranty" and that is returned to Prentice-Hall, or

2. if Prentice-Hall is unable to deliver a replacement CD-ROM or cassette that is free of defects in materials or workmanship, you may terminate this Agreement by returning the program.

IN NO EVENT WILL PRENTICE-HALL BE LIABLE TO YOU FOR ANY DAMAGES, INCLUDING ANY LOST PROFITS, LOST SAVINGS, OR OTHER INCIDENTAL OR CONSEQUENTIAL DAMAGES ARISING OUT OF THE USE OR INABILITY TO USE SUCH PROGRAM EVEN IF PRENTICE-HALL, OR AN AUTHORIZED DISTRIBUTOR HAS BEEN ADVISED OF THE POSSIBILITY OF SUCH DAMAGES, OR FOR ANY CLAIM BY ANY OTHER PARTY.

SOME STATES DO NOT ALLOW THE LIMITATION OR EXCLUSION OF LIABILITY FOR INCIDENTAL OR CONSEQUENTIAL DAMAGES, SO THE ABOVE LIMITATION OR EXCLUSION MAY NOT APPLY TO YOU.

GENERAL

You may not sublicense, assign, or transfer the license or the program except as expressly provided in this Agreement. Any attempt otherwise to sublicense, assign, or transfer any of the rights, duties, or obligations hereunder is void.

This Agreement will be governed by the laws of the State of New York.

Should you have any questions concerning this Agreement, you may contact Prentice-Hall, Inc., by writing to:

> Prentice Hall
> College Division
> Upper Saddle River, NJ 07458

YOU ACKNOWLEDGE THAT YOU HAVE READ THIS AGREEMENT, UNDERSTAND IT, AND AGREE TO BE BOUND BY ITS TERMS AND CONDITIONS. YOU FURTHER AGREE THAT IT IS THE COMPLETE AND EXCLUSIVE STATEMENT OF THE AGREEMENT BETWEEN US THAT SUPERSEDES ANY PROPOSAL OR PRIOR AGREEMENT, ORAL OR WRITTEN, AND ANY OTHER COMMUNICATIONS BETWEEN US RELATING TO THE SUBJECT MATTER OF THIS AGREEMENT.

ISBN: 0-13-577594-9